Learning Theories

An Educational Perspective

Fourth Edition

Dale H. Schunk
The University of North Carolina at Greensboro

PEARSON

Merrill
Prentice Hall

Upper Saddle River, New Jersey
Columbus, Ohio

To Caryl and Laura
For their love and support

Library of Congress Cataloging in Publication Data

Schunk, Dale H.
   Learning theories : an educational perspective / Dale H. Schunk.--4th ed.
      p.   cm.
   Includes bibliographical references and index.
   ISBN 0-13-038496-8
      1. Learning. 2. Cognition. 3. Learning, Psychology of. I. Title.

LB1060.S37 2004
370.15'23--dc21

2003054936

Vice President and Executive Publisher: Jeffery W. Johnston
Publisher: Kevin M. Davis
Editorial Assistant: Autumn Crisp
Production Editor: Mary Harlan
Production Coordinator: Tim Flem
Design Coordinator: Diane Lorenzo
Text Design and Illustrations: PublishWare
Cover Design: Rod Harris
Cover Image: Corbis
Production Manager: Laura Messerly
Director of Marketing: Ann Castel Davis
Marketing Manager: Amy June
Marketing Coordinator: Tyra Poole

This book was set in Garamond by PublishWare. It was printed and bound by R. R. Donnelley & Sons Company. The cover was printed by The Lehigh Press, Inc.

Pearson Education Ltd.
Pearson Education Singapore Pte. Ltd.
Pearson Education Canada, Ltd.
Pearson Education–Japan

Pearson Education Australia Pty. Limited
Pearson Education North Asia Ltd.
Pearson Educación de Mexico, S.A. de C.V.
Pearson Education Malaysia Pte. Ltd.

10 9 8 7 6 5 4 3 2

ISBN: 0-13-038496-8

Preface

Theory and research on human learning have expanded dramatically in recent years. This point is underscored by considering some of the topics addressed in this text that were not covered in the first edition published in 1991: constructivism, situated cognition, implicit theories, brain development, apprenticeships, peer collaboration, distance education, and E-learning. The relevance of each of these topics to human learning is now firmly established. Better integration with education of such disciplines as psychology, human development, and instructional technology has contributed to the expansion of the field of learning.

Despite all these changes, the primary objectives of this fourth edition remain the same as those of the previous three editions: (a) to inform students of learning theoretical principles, concepts, and research findings, especially as they relate to education, and (b) to provide applications of principles and concepts in settings where teaching and learning occur. Although different theories of learning are discussed, the text continues to focus on cognitive perspectives. This focus is consistent with the contemporary emphasis on learners as seekers and constructors of knowledge rather than as reactors to events.

STRUCTURE OF THIS TEXT

The text's 10 chapters are organized as follows. In the introductory chapter, I discuss learning theory, research, and issues, as well as historical foundations of the study of learning and the relation of learning to instruction. The end of this chapter includes three scenarios involving elementary, secondary, and college classes. Throughout the text these scenarios are used to demonstrate applications of principles of learning, motivation, self-regulation, and instruction. Chapter 2 presents behavioral theories of learning. Current cognitive and constructivist views of learning are covered in subsequent chapters: social cognitive theory (Chapter 3); information processing (Chapter 4); cognitive learning processes (Chapter 5); cognition and instruction (Chapter 6); and constructivism (Chapter 7). The final three chapters cover topics relevant to learning: motivation (Chapter 8); content-area learning (Chapter 9); and development and learning (Chapter 10).

NEW TO THIS EDITION

Readers familiar with prior editions will notice several content and organizational changes in this fourth edition, which reflect evolving theoretical and research emphases. Constructivism, which has become a major guiding framework in content learning and human development, is now covered in a separate chapter, although parts of this chapter—such as Vygotsky's theory—were included in prior editions.

To provide better integration of self-regulation and instruction with learning theories, these topics now are integrated within each of the theory chapters rather than appearing as stand-alone chapters. This change reflects the increasing tendency of researchers from different theoretical traditions to investigate how learning principles apply to instructional contexts and students' efforts to self-regulate their academic actions. One exception is Chapter 6, cognition and instruction. This chapter stands alone because of the sheer amount of material relevant to the topic. Separate chapters on motivation and development and learning remain for the same reason, although discussions of these topics are intermingled in other chapters. Chapter 10—development and learning—has been substantially revised and now includes sections on familial and sociocultural influences on learning and brain development. These additions, like the other changes in this volume, reflect the increased interest among educators in these topics and an expanding research base on their role in human learning. Rapid developments in technology necessitated further refocusing of the section on technology and instruction (now in Chapter 6), and the continued growth of research relevant to learning resulted in more than 175 new references added to this edition—most of which were published in the last 5 years.

This edition continues to provide many examples of learning concepts and principles applied to settings where learning occurs. Each chapter gives informal examples in text and detailed applications. Many of the latter are set in the scenarios described in Chapter 1. Most of the applications pertain to school-age learners, but applications to younger and older students and to nonschool settings also are included.

The text is intended for use by graduate students in education or related disciplines, as well as by upper-level undergraduates interested in education. I assume that most students have taken a prior course in education or psychology and work in an educational capacity or anticipate pursuing an educational career. In addition to courses on learning, the text is appropriate for any course that covers learning in more than a cursory fashion—for example, courses on motivation, educational psychology, human development, and instructional design.

ACKNOWLEDGMENTS

Several people deserve thanks for their assistance with this project. I remain indebted to many colleagues who over the years have enriched my thinking about learning processes and applications: Albert Bandura, Curt Bonk, James Chapman, Lyn Corno, Peg Ertmer, Marilyn Haring, Carolyn Jagacinski, Dave Lohman, Judith Meece, Sam Miller, the late John Nicholls, Frank Pajares, Paul Pintrich, Don Rice, Claire Ellen Weinstein, and Barry Zimmerman. They are wonderful mentors, friends, and colleagues. I continue to benefit from activities with members of professional organizations, especially the Motivation in Education Special Interest Group of the American Educational Research Association, and Division 15 (Educational Psychology) of the American Psychological Association. My learning also has been enhanced by many outstanding students, teachers, counselors, administrators, and superintendents with whom I have worked. Sincere thanks go to my graduate and undergraduate student collaborators for their assistance on research projects and for providing valuable feedback on this text.

I feel exceptionally fortunate that I have worked with Kevin Davis at Prentice Hall for 10 years. Kevin is intelligent, insightful, patient yet demanding, and ever cognizant of when and how to guide me. He is, unquestionably, the best editor I have ever known. Special thanks also are due to Autumn Crisp for her editorial assistance. I wish to thank the following reviewers of the previous editions: Joyce Alexander, Indiana University; Livingston Alexander, Troy State University, Montgomery; Scott W. Brown, University of Connecticut; Joanne B. Engel, Oregon State University; Daniel Fasko, Jr., Morehead State University; Victoria Fleming, Miami University; Verne C. Keenan, University of Colorado; Gary R. McKenzie, University of Texas, Austin; James E. O'Connor, North Carolina Center for the Advancement of Teaching; Carolyn Orange, University of Texas, San Antonio; Sarah Peterson, Northern Illinois University; Duane F. Shell, University of Texas, Austin; and Dennis A. Warner, Washington State University. In addition, I would like to thank the reviewers who critiqued the third edition and provided valuable suggestions for revisions: Joyce Alexander, Indiana University; John R. McClure, Northern Arizona University; Don Prickel, Oregon State University; and Christopher Wolters, University of Houston. At the University of North Carolina at Greensboro I am indebted to Suzanne Williams, Kathryn Kale, and Liz Meeks for assisting with many administrative tasks.

Finally, I am so thankful for Mil and Al Schunk—my late parents—for their unending love and encouragement. It was my dad who, at a time early in my career when I considered abandoning education, reminded me that education was one of the finest vocations one could pursue because an educator can make such a difference in countless lives and thereby improve the world's condition. Many friends outside of academia, such as Jim Tozer, Rob Eyman, Bill Gattis, and Doug Curyea, have helped me remember what are the truly important things in life. My deepest gratitude goes to my wife, Caryl, and my daughter, Laura, for their great understanding, support, and encouragement. Caryl provided much assistance with the examples and applications based on her experiences as a professional educator, and she helped me find writing time when I needed it the most. Laura, who was born in 1989 while I was writing the first edition of this text, is a charming and awesome daughter who has taught me so much about life, learning, and most important, love.

Educator Learning Center:
An Invaluable Online Resource

Merrill Education and the Association for Supervision and Curriculum Development (ASCD) invite you to take advantage of a new online resource, one that provides access to the top research and proven strategies associated with ASCD and Merrill—the Educator Learning Center. At **www.EducatorLearningCenter.com** you will find resources that will enhance your students' understanding of course topics and of current educational issues, in addition to being invaluable for further research.

How the Educator Learning Center will help your students become better teachers

With the combined resources of Merrill Education and ASCD, you and your students will find a wealth of tools and materials to better prepare them for the classroom.

Research

- More than 600 articles from the ASCD journal *Educational Leadership* discuss everyday issues faced by practicing teachers.
- A direct link on the site to Research Navigator™ gives students access to many of the leading education journals, as well as extensive content detailing the research process.
- Excerpts from Merrill Education texts give your students insights on important topics of instructional methods, diverse populations, assessment, classroom management, technology, and refining classroom practice.

Classroom Practice

- Hundreds of lesson plans and teaching strategies are categorized by content area and age range.
- Case studies and classroom video footage provide virtual field experience for student reflection.
- Computer simulations and other electronic tools keep your students abreast of today's classrooms and current technologies.

Look into the value of Educator Learning Center yourself

Preview the value of this educational environment by visiting **www.EducatorLearningCenter.com** and clicking on "Demo." For a free 4-month subscription to the Educator Learning Center in conjunction with this text, simply contact your Merrill/Prentice Hall sales representative.

Brief Contents

Contents

1

Learning: Introduction, Issues, Historical Perspectives

Learning involves the acquisition and modification of knowledge, skills, strategies, beliefs, attitudes, and behaviors. People learn cognitive, linguistic, motor, and social skills, and these can take many forms. At a simple level, children learn to solve 2 + 2 = ?, recognize *d* in the word *daddy*, tie their shoes, and play with other children. At a more complex level, students learn to solve long division problems, write term papers, ride a bicycle, and work cooperatively on a group project.

This book is about how human learning occurs, which factors influence it, and how learning principles apply in various educational contexts. Animal learning is de-emphasized, which is not intended to downgrade its importance because we have gained much knowledge about learning from animal research. But human learning is fundamentally different from animal learning because human learning is more complex, elaborate, rapid, and typically depends on the use of language. The power of human learning is especially evident in educational settings.

This chapter provides an overview of the study of learning. Initially, learning is defined and examined in settings where it occurs. The roles of learning theory and research are discussed, and methods commonly used to investigate learning are described. An overview is given of some important philosophical and psychological precursors of contemporary theory that helped to establish the groundwork for the application of learning theory to education. Critical issues in the study of learning are presented, followed by a discussion of the links between learning theory and instruction.

At the end of this chapter three scenarios are presented that involve learning with elementary, secondary, and college students. Background information is given about the learners, teachers, instruction, content, setting, and other critical features. In subsequent chapters, these scenarios will be used to exemplify the operation of learning principles. Readers will benefit from seeing how diverse learning principles are applied in a coherent fashion in the same settings.

This chapter should help to prepare you for an in-depth study of learning processes by providing a framework for understanding learning and some background material against which to view contemporary theories. When you finish studying this chapter, you should be able to do the following:

- Define learning and identify instances of learned and unlearned phenomena.

- Describe the major features of different research paradigms.

- Discuss the central features of different methods of assessing learning.

- Distinguish between rationalism and empiricism and explain the major tenets of each.

- Discuss how the work of Wundt, Ebbinghaus, the Structuralists, and the Functionalists helped to establish psychology as a science.

■ Explain differences between behavioral and cognitive theories with respect to various issues in the study of learning.

■ State some instructional principles common to many learning theories.

■ Explicate the ways that learning theory and educational practice complement and refine one another.

LEARNING DEFINED

People agree that learning is important, but they hold different views on the causes, processes, and consequences of learning. There is no one definition of learning that is universally accepted by theorists, researchers, and practitioners (Shuell, 1986).

This book emphasizes cognitive perspectives on learning that stress the influence of learners' thoughts and beliefs. Although people disagree about the precise nature of learning, here is a general definition of learning that is consistent with this cognitive focus and that captures the criteria most educational professionals consider central to learning.

Learning is an enduring change in behavior, or in the capacity to behave in a given fashion, which results from practice or other forms of experience.

Let us examine this definition in depth.

One criterion for defining learning is *behavioral change or change in the capacity for behavior*. People have learned when they become capable of doing something differently. Learning involves developing new actions or modifying existing ones. From a cognitive perspective we say that *learning is inferential*. We do not observe it directly but rather its products. Learning is assessed based on what people say, write, and do. Learning involves a changed capacity to behave in a given fashion because people often learn skills, knowledge, beliefs, or behaviors, without demonstrating them at the time learning occurs (see Chapter 3).

A second criterion inherent in this definition is that *behavioral change (or capacity for change) endures over time*. This excludes temporary behavioral changes (e.g., slurred speech) brought about by such factors as drugs, alcohol, and fatigue. Such changes are temporary because when the cause is removed, the behavior returns to its original state. At the same time, learning may not last forever; forgetting occurs. It is debatable how long changes must last to be classified as learned, but most people agree that changes of brief duration (e.g., a few seconds) are not learned.

A third criterion is that *learning occurs through practice or other forms of experience* (e.g., observing others). This criterion excludes behavioral changes that seem to be determined by heredity, such as maturational changes in children (e.g., crawling, standing). Nonetheless, the distinction between heredity and learning often is not clear-cut. People may be predisposed to act in given ways, but the actual development of the particular behaviors depends on the environment. Language offers a good example. As the human vocal apparatus matures, it becomes able to produce sounds, but the actual words produced are learned from interactions with others. Children raised by animals in the wilderness possess no human language and develop it slowly only with teaching (Lenneberg, 1967). In similar fashion, with normal development children crawl and stand, but the environment must be responsive and allow these behaviors to occur. Children whose movements are forcibly restrained will not develop normally.

LEARNING THEORY AND RESEARCH

Reviewing the roles of theory and research in the study of learning is useful. Some general functions of theory are discussed, along with important aspects of the research process. Readers familiar with these topics may wish to omit this section.

Functions of Theory

A *theory* is a scientifically acceptable set of principles offered to explain a phenomenon. Theories provide frameworks for interpreting environmental observations and serve as bridges between research and education (Suppes, 1974). Research findings can be organized and systematically linked to theories. Without theories, research findings would be disorganized collections of data, because researchers and practitioners would have no overarching frameworks to which the data could be linked. Even when researchers obtain findings that do not seem to be directly linked to theories, they still must attempt to make sense of data and determine whether any theories are applicable.

Theories reflect environmental phenomena and generate new research through the formation of *hypotheses*, or assumptions that can be empirically tested. Hypotheses often can be cast as if-then statements: "If I do X, then Y should occur," where X and Y might be such events as "praise students for their progress in learning" and "raise their self-confidence and achievement," respectively. Thus, we might test the hypothesis, "If we praise students when they make progress in learning, then they should display higher self-confidence and achievement than students who are not praised for their progress." A theory is strengthened when hypotheses are supported by data. Theories may require revision if data do not support hypotheses.

Researchers often explore areas where there is little theory to guide them. In that case they formulate research objectives or questions to be answered. Regardless of whether researchers are testing hypotheses or exploring questions, they need to specify the research conditions as precisely as possible. Because research forms the basis for theory development and has important implications for teaching, the next section examines types of research and the process of conducting research.

Conducting Research

To specify the research conditions, we need to answer such questions as: Who will participate? Where will the study be conducted? What procedures will be employed? What are the variables and outcomes to be assessed?

We must define precisely the phenomena we are studying. We provide conceptual definitions of phenomena and also define them *operationally*, or in terms of the operations, instruments, and procedures we use to measure the phenomena. For example, we might define *self-efficacy* (covered in Chapter 3) conceptually as one's perceived capabilities for learning or performing a task, and operationally by specifying how we assess self-efficacy in our study (e.g., one's score on a 30-item questionnaire). In addition to defining operationally the phenomena we study, we also must be precise about the procedure we follow. Ideally, we specify conditions so precisely that another researcher could replicate our study.

Research studies that explore learning employ various types of *paradigms* (models). The following paragraphs describe the correlational, experimental, and qualitative paradigms, followed by a discussion of laboratory and field studies (Table 1.1).

Correlational Research.   *Correlational research* deals with exploring relations that exist between variables. A researcher might hypothesize that self-efficacy is positively correlated with (related to) achievement such that the higher the students' self-efficacy the higher they achieve. To test this relation, the researcher might measure students' self-efficacy for solving mathematical problems and then assess how well they actually solve the problems. The researcher could statistically correlate the self-efficacy and achievement scores to determine the direction of the relation (positive, negative) and its strength (high, medium, low).

Correlational research helps to clarify relations among variables. Correlational findings often suggest directions for further research. If the researcher were to obtain a high positive correlation between self-efficacy and achievement, the next study might be an experiment that attempted to raise students' self-efficacy for learning and determine whether such an increase produced higher achievement.

A limitation of correlational research is that it cannot identify cause and effect. A positive correlation between self-efficacy and achievement could mean that (a) self-efficacy influences achievement, (b) achievement influences self-efficacy, (c) self-efficacy and achievement influence each other, or (d) self-efficacy and achievement are influenced by other, nonmeasured variables (e.g., parents, teachers). To determine cause and effect, an experimental study is necessary.

Table 1.1
Learning research paradigms.

Type	Qualities
Correlational	Examines relations between variables
Experimental	One or more variables are altered and effects on other variables are assessed
Qualitative	Concerned with description of events and interpretation of meanings
Laboratory	Project conducted in a controlled setting
Field	Project conducted in a natural setting (e.g., school, home, work)

Experimental Research.   In *experimental research* the researcher changes one or more (independent) variables and determines the effects on other (dependent) variables. The preceding researcher could form two groups of students, systematically raise perceptions of self-efficacy among students in one group and not among students in the other group, and assess achievement in the two groups. If the first group performs better, the researcher might conclude that self-efficacy influences achievement. While the researcher alters variables to determine their effects on outcomes, she or he must hold constant other variables that potentially can affect outcomes (e.g., learning conditions).

Experimental research can clarify cause-effect relations, which helps us understand the nature of learning. At the same time, experimental research often is narrow in scope. Researchers typically study only a few variables and try to minimize effects of others, which is difficult to do and somewhat unrealistic. Classrooms and other learning settings are complex places where many factors operate at once. To say that one or two variables cause outcomes may overemphasize their importance. It is necessary to replicate experiments and examine other variables to better understand effects.

Qualitative Research.   The *qualitative research* paradigm is characterized by intensive study, descriptions of events, and interpretation of meanings. The theories and methods used are referred to under various labels including qualitative, ethnographic, participant observation, phenomenological, constructivist, and interpretative (Erickson, 1986).

Qualitative research is especially useful when researchers are interested in the structure of events rather than their overall distributions, when the meanings and perspectives of individuals are important, when actual experiments are impractical or unethical, and when there is a desire to search for new potential causal linkages that have not been discovered by experimental methods (Erickson, 1986). Research is quite varied and can range from analyses of verbal and nonverbal interactions within single lessons to in-depth observations and interviews over longer periods. Methods may include observations, use of existing records, interviews, and think-aloud protocols (i.e., participants talk aloud while performing tasks). It is not the choice of method that characterizes this approach—all of the aforementioned methods could be used in correlational or experimental studies—but rather the depth and quality of data analysis and interpretation.

The preceding researcher might be curious about how self-efficacy contributes to the development of skills over time. She or he might work with a small group of students for several months. Through observations, interviews, and other forms of data collection, the researcher might examine how students' self-efficacy for learning relates to skill refinement in reading, writing, and mathematics.

Qualitative research yields rich sources of data, which are more intensive and thorough than those typically obtained in correlational or experimental research. This paradigm also can raise new questions and fresh perspectives on old questions that often are missed by traditional methods. A potential limitation is that because studies typically include only a few participants, they may not be representative of a larger population of students or teachers, which limits generalization of findings. Another limitation is that data collection, analysis, and interpretation can be very time consuming and therefore impractical for students wanting to graduate and professors wanting to build their publication records! Nonetheless, as a research model this paradigm offers a useful approach for obtaining data typically not collected with other methods.

Laboratory and Field Research.   *Laboratory research* is conducted in controlled settings, whereas *field research* is conducted where participants live, work, or attend school. During the first half of the twentieth century, most learning research was conducted on animals in laboratories. Today most learning research is conducted with people, and much is done in field settings. Any of the preceding research models (experimental, correlational, qualitative) can be applied in the laboratory or the field.

Laboratories offer a high degree of control over extraneous factors that can affect results, such as telephones ringing, people talking, windows to look out of, and other persons in the room who are not part of the study. Light, sound, and temperature can be regulated. Laboratories also allow researchers to leave their equipment set up over lengthy periods and have all materials at their immediate disposal.

Such control is not possible in the field. Schools are noisy and often it is difficult to find space to work. There are numerous distractions: Students and teachers walk by, bells ring, announcements are made over the public address system, fire drills are held. Rooms may be too bright or dark, cold or warm, and used for other purposes so researchers have to set up equipment each time they work. Interpreting results in light of these distractions can be a problem.

An advantage of field research is that results are highly generalizable to other similar settings because studies are conducted where people typically learn. In contrast, generalization of laboratory findings to the field is done with less confidence. Laboratory research has yielded many important insights on learning and researchers often attempt to replicate laboratory findings in the field.

Whether we choose the laboratory or the field depends on such factors as the purpose of the research, availability of participants, costs, and how we will use the results. If we choose the laboratory, we gain control but lose some generalizability, and vice-versa if we choose the field. In the field, researchers try to minimize extraneous influences so that they can be more confident that their results are due to the factors they are studying.

METHODS OF ASSESSING LEARNING

Assessing learning is difficult because we do not observe it directly but rather we observe its products or outcomes. There are several ways to assess these products or outcomes, including by direct observations, written responses, oral responses, ratings by others, and self-reports (Table 1.2).

Table 1.2
Methods of assessing learning.

Category	Definition
Direct observations	Instances of behavior that demonstrate learning
Written responses	Written performances on tests, quizzes, homework, papers, projects
Oral responses	Verbalized questions, comments, responses during learning
Ratings by others	Observers' judgments of learners on attributes indicative of learning
Self-reports	People's judgments of themselves
■ Questionnaires	Written ratings of items or answers to questions
■ Interviews	Oral responses to questions
■ Stimulated recalls	Recall of thoughts accompanying one's performances at given times
■ Think-alouds	Verbalizing aloud one's thoughts, actions, and feelings while performing a task
■ Dialogues	Conversations between two or more persons

Direct Observations

Direct observations are instances of student behavior that we observe to determine whether learning has occurred. Teachers employ direct observations frequently. A chemistry teacher wants students to learn laboratory procedures. The teacher observes students in the laboratory to determine whether they are implementing the proper procedures. A physical education instructor observes students dribble a basketball to determine how well they have learned the skill. An elementary teacher gauges how well students have learned the classroom rules based on their class behavior.

Direct observations are valid indexes of learning if they are straightforward and involve little inference by observers. They work best when the behaviors can be specified and then students observed to ascertain whether their behaviors match the standard.

A problem with direct observations is that they focus only on what can be observed and therefore bypass the cognitive and affective processes that underlie actions. Direct observations involve the products or outcomes of learning rather than the learning itself. Thus, the chemistry teacher knows that students have learned laboratory procedures but not what the students are thinking about while they are performing the procedures, how confident they are about performing well, and so forth.

A second problem is that although directly observing a behavior indicates that learning has occurred, the absence of appropriate behavior does not mean that learning has not occurred. *Learning is not the same as performance.* Many factors other than learning can affect performance. Students may not perform learned actions because they are unmotivated, ill, or busy doing other things. We have to rule out these other factors to conclude from the absence of performance that learning has not occurred. That requires making the assumption—which at times may be unwarranted—that since students usually try to do their best, if they do not perform, they have not learned.

Written Responses

Learning often is assessed based on students' *written responses*: tests, quizzes, homework, term papers, reports, and word-processing documents. Based on the level of mastery indicated in the responses, teachers decide whether adequate learning has taken place or whether additional instruction is needed because students do not fully comprehend the material. For example, assume that a teacher is planning a unit on the geography of Hawaii. Initially the teacher assumes that students know little about this topic. A pretest given prior to the start of instruction will support the teacher's belief if the students score poorly. The teacher retests students following the instructional unit. Gains in test scores lead the teacher to conclude that learners have acquired some knowledge.

Their relative ease of use and capacity for covering a wide variety of material makes written responses desirable indicators of learning. At the same time, there is the assumption that they reflect actual learning. As we saw earlier, there is a problem with that assumption because learning is inferential and many factors can affect performance of behavior even when students have learned. When we assume written responses are true indicators of learning, we believe that students are trying their best and that no extraneous factors (e.g., fatigue, illness, cheating) are operating such that their written work does not represent what they have learned. We must try to identify extraneous factors that can affect performance and cloud assessments of learning.

Oral Responses

Oral responses are an integral part of the school culture. Teachers call on students to answer questions during classroom recitations and gauge learning based on what they say. Students also ask questions during lessons. Questions indicating a lack of understanding signal that proper learning has not occurred.

Like written responses, we assume that oral responses are valid reflections of what students know. This assumption is not always warranted. Further, verbalization is itself a task, and there may be problems translating what one knows into its oral expression due to unfamiliar terminology, anxiety about speaking, or speech problems. Although teachers often try to rephrase what students say, such rephrasing may not accurately reflect the nature of students' thoughts.

Ratings by Others

Another way to assess learning is for individuals (e.g., teachers, parents, administrators, researchers, peers) to rate students on the quantity or quality of their learning. These *ratings by others* (e.g., "How well can Timmy solve problems of the type 52 × 36 = ?", "How much progress has Alicia made in her printing skills in the past six months?"), are useful data in addition to actual student responses. They also can help to identify students with exceptional needs (e.g., "How often does Matt need extra time to learn?", "How quickly does Jenny finish her work?").

An advantage of ratings by others is that observers may be more objective about students than students are about themselves (self-reports, discussed next). Ratings also can be made for learning processes that underlie actions (e.g., motivation, attitudes) and thereby provide data not attainable through direct observations. At the same time, ratings by others require more inference than do direct observations. It may be problematic to accurately rate students' ease of learning, depth of understanding, or attitudes. Further, ratings require observers to remember what students do and will be distorted when raters selectively remember only positive or negative behaviors.

Self-Reports

Self-reports are people's ratings of and statements about themselves. Self-reports take various forms: questionnaires, interviews, stimulated recalls, think-alouds, and dialogues.

Questionnaires present respondents with items or questions asking about their thoughts and actions. Respondents may record the types of activities they engage in, rate their perceived levels of competence, and judge how often or how long they engage in them (e.g., "How long have you been studying Spanish?", "How difficult is it for you to learn geometric theorems?"). Many self-report instruments ask respondents to record ratings on numerical scales ("On a 10-point scale where 1 = low and 10 = high, rate how good you are at reducing fractions.").

Interviews are a type of questionnaire in which an interviewer presents the questions or points to discuss and the respondent answers orally. Interviews typically are conducted individually, although groups can be interviewed. A researcher might describe a learning context and ask students how they typically learn in that setting (e.g., "When the teacher begins math instruction, what are your thoughts? How well do you think you will do?"). Interviewers may need to prompt respondents if replies are short or not forthcoming.

In the *stimulated recall* procedure, people work on a task and afterward recall their thoughts at various points during the task. Interviewers query them (e.g., "What were you thinking about when you got stuck here?"). If the performance was videotaped, respondents subsequently watch the tape and recollect, especially when interviewers stop the tape and ask questions. It is imperative that the recall procedure be accomplished soon after the performance so that participants do not forget their thoughts.

Think-alouds are procedures in which students verbalize aloud their thoughts, actions, and feelings while working on a task. Verbalizations may be recorded by observers and subsequently scored for level of understanding. Think-alouds require that respondents verbalize; many students are not used to talking aloud while working in school. Talking aloud may seem awkward to some and they may feel self-conscious or otherwise have difficulty verbalizing their thoughts. Investigators may have to prompt students if they do not verbalize.

Another type of self-report is the *dialogue,* which is a conversation between two or more persons while engaged in a learning task. Like think-alouds, dialogues can be recorded and analyzed for statements indicating learning and factors that seemed to affect learning in the setting. Although dialogues use actual interactions while students are working on a task, their analysis requires interpretation that may go beyond the actual elements in the situation.

The choice of self-report measure should match the purpose of the assessment. Questionnaires can cover a lot of material; interviews are better for exploring a few issues in depth. Stimulated recalls ask respondents to recall their thoughts at the time actions took place; think-alouds examine present thoughts. Dialogues allow for investigation of social interaction patterns.

Self-report instruments typically are easy to develop and administer; questionnaires are usually easy to complete and score. A problem can arise when inferences have to be drawn about students' responses. It is essential to have a reliable scoring system. Other concerns about self-reports are whether students are giving socially acceptable answers that do not match their beliefs, whether self-reported information corresponds to actual behavior, and whether young children are capable of self-reporting accurately. By guaranteeing that data are confidential researchers can help promote truthful answering. A good means of validating self-reports is to use multiple assessments (e.g., self-reports, direct observations, oral and written responses). There is evidence that beginning around the third grade self-reports are valid and reliable indicators of the beliefs and actions they are designed to assess (Assor & Connell, 1992), but researchers need to use self-reports carefully to minimize potential problems.

PRECURSORS OF MODERN LEARNING THEORIES

The roots of contemporary theories extend far into the past. Many of the problems addressed and questions asked by modern researchers are not new but rather reflect a universal desire for people to understand themselves, others, and the world about them.

This section traces the origins of contemporary learning theories, beginning with a discussion of philosophical positions on the origin of knowledge and its relation to the environment and concluding with some early psychological views on learning. Chapter 2 examines historical perspectives on learning by conditioning.

Historical information is beneficial because it provides groundwork for understanding current theories, many of whose ideas have their roots in historical views.

This review is selective and includes historical material relevant to learning in educational settings. Readers interested in a more comprehensive discussion should consult other sources (Bower & Hilgard, 1981; Heidbreder, 1933; Hunt, 1993).

Learning Theory and Philosophy

From a philosophical perspective learning can be discussed under the heading of *epistemology,* which refers to the study of the origin, nature, limits, and methods of knowledge. How can we know? How can we learn something new? What is the source of knowledge? The complexity of how humans learn is illustrated in the following excerpt from Plato's *Meno* (427?–347? B.C.):

> I know, Meno, what you mean . . . You argue that a man cannot enquire (*sic*) either about that which he knows, or about that which he does not know; for if he knows, he has no need to enquire (*sic*); and if not, he cannot; for he does not know the very subject about which he is to enquire (*sic*). (1965, p. 16)

Two positions on the origin of knowledge and its relationship to the environment are rationalism and empiricism. In varying degrees these positions are recognizable in current learning theories.

Rationalism.   *Rationalism* refers to the idea that knowledge derives from reason without aid of the senses. The distinction between mind and matter, which figures prominently in rationalist views of human knowledge, can be traced to Plato, who distinguished knowledge acquired via the senses from that gained by reason. Plato believed that things (e.g., houses, trees) are revealed to people via the senses, whereas individuals acquire ideas by reasoning or thinking about what they know. People have ideas about the world, and they learn (discover) these ideas by reflecting upon them. Reason is the highest mental faculty, because through reason people learn abstract ideas. The true nature of houses and trees can be known only by reflecting upon the ideas of houses and trees.

Plato escaped the dilemma in *Meno* by assuming that true knowledge, or the knowledge of ideas, is innate and is brought into awareness through reflection. Learning is recalling what exists in the mind. Information acquired with the senses by observing, listening, tasting, smelling, or touching constitutes raw materials rather than ideas. The mind is innately structured to reason and provide meaning to incoming sensory information.

The rationalist doctrine also is evident in the writings of René Descartes (1596–1650), a French philosopher and mathematician. Descartes employed doubt as a method of inquiry. By doubting, he arrived at conclusions that were absolute truths and not subject to doubt. The fact that he could doubt led him to believe that the mind (thought) exists, as reflected in his dictum, "I think, therefore I am." Through deductive reasoning from general premises to specific instances, he proved that God exists and concluded that ideas arrived at through reason must be true.

Like Plato, Descartes established a mind-matter dualism; however, for Descartes the external world was mechanical, as were the actions of animals. People are distinguished in their ability to reason. The human soul, or the capacity for thought, influences the body's mechanical actions, but the body acts on the mind by bringing in sensory experiences. Although Descartes postulated dualism, he also hypothesized mind-matter interaction.

The rationalist perspective was extended by the German philosopher Immanuel Kant (1724–1804). In his *Critique of Pure Reason* (1781), Kant addressed mind-matter dualism and noted that the external world is disordered but is perceived as orderly because order is imposed by the mind. The mind takes in the external world through the senses and alters it according to subjective, innate laws. The world never can be known as it exists but only as it is perceived. People's perceptions give the world its order. Kant reaffirmed the role of reason as a source of knowledge, but contended that reason operates within the realm of experience. Absolute knowledge untouched by the external world does not exist. Rather, knowledge is empirical in the sense that information is taken in from the world and interpreted by the mind.

In summary, rationalism is the doctrine that knowledge arises through the mind. Although there is an external world from which people acquire sensory information, ideas originate from the workings of the mind. Descartes and Kant believed that reason acts upon information acquired from the world; Plato thought that knowledge can be absolute and acquired by pure reason.

Empiricism.   *Empiricism* refers to the idea that experience is the only source of knowledge. This position derives from Aristotle (384–322 B.C.), who was Plato's student and successor. Aristotle drew no sharp distinction between mind and matter. The external world is the basis for human sense impressions, which in turn are interpreted as lawful (consistent, unchanging) by the mind. The laws of nature cannot be discovered through sensory impressions. Rather, they are discovered through reason as the mind takes in data from the environment. Unlike Plato, Aristotle believed that ideas do not exist independently of the external world. The latter is the source of all knowledge.

Aristotle contributed to psychology with his principles of association as applied to memory. The recall of an object or idea triggers recall of other objects or ideas similar to, different from, or experienced close in time or space to the original object or idea. The more often objects or ideas are associated, the more likely recall of one will trigger recall of the other. The notion of associative learning is prominent in many learning theories.

Another influential figure was British philosopher John Locke (1632–1704), who contributed to the movement away from Plato's belief that ideas could be discovered through reason alone. Locke developed a school of thought that was empirical but that stopped short of being truly experimental (Heidbreder, 1933). In his *Essay Concerning Human Understanding* (1690), Locke noted that there are no innate ideas; all knowledge derives from two types of experience: sensory impressions of the external world and personal awareness. At birth the mind is a *tabula rasa* (blank tablet). Ideas are acquired from sensory impressions and personal reflection on these impressions. Nothing can be in the mind that does not originate in the senses. The mind is composed of ideas that have been combined in different ways. The mind can be understood only by breaking down ideas into simple units. This atomistic notion of thought is associationist; complex ideas are collections of simple ones.

Locke made an important distinction between primary and secondary qualities of objects. *Primary qualities* are such characteristics as size, shape, weight, and number. They exist in the external world as part of the object or situation and are impressed on the mind. In contrast, perception of *secondary qualities* (e.g., color, sound, taste) depends on the person's sensory equipment and mind.

The issues Locke raised were debated by such profound thinkers as George Berkeley (1685–1753), David Hume (1711–1776), and John Stuart Mill (1806–1873). Berkeley believed that mind is the only reality. Only secondary qualities exist; there are no primary qualities. Berkeley was an empiricist because he believed that ideas derive from experiences; however, he also thought people impose qualities onto their sensory impressions. Hume agreed that people never can be certain about external reality, but he also believed that people cannot be certain about their own ideas. Individuals experience external reality through their ideas, which constitute the only reality. At the same time, Hume accepted the empiricist doctrine that ideas derive from experience and become associated with one another. Mill was an empiricist and associationist, but he rejected the idea that simple ideas combine in orderly ways to form complex ones. Mill argued that simple ideas generate complex ideas but that the latter need not be composed of the former. Simple ideas can produce a complex thought that might bear little obvious relation to the ideas of which it is composed. Mill's beliefs reflect the notion that the whole is greater than the sum of its parts, which is an integral assumption of Gestalt psychology (see Chapter 4).

In summary, empiricism holds that experience is the only form of knowledge. Beginning with Aristotle, empiricists have contended that the external world serves as the basis for people's impressions. Most accept the notion that objects or ideas associate to form complex stimuli or mental patterns. Locke, Berkeley, Hume, and Mill are among the better-known philosophers who espoused empiricist views.

Although philosophical positions and learning theories do not neatly map onto one another, behavioral theories typically are empiricist whereas cognitive theories are more rationalistic. Overlap often is evident; for example, most theories agree that much learning occurs through association. Cognitive theories stress association between cognitions and beliefs; behavioral theories emphasize the association of stimuli with responses and consequences.

Beginnings of the Psychological Study of Learning

The formal beginning of psychology as a science is difficult to pinpoint (Mueller, 1979), although systematic research of a psychological nature began to appear in the latter part of the nineteenth century. Two persons who had a significant impact on learning theory are Wundt and Ebbinghaus.

Wundt's Psychological Laboratory.   The first psychological laboratory was opened by Wilhelm Wundt (1832–1920) in Leipzig, Germany, in 1879, although William James had started a teaching laboratory at Harvard University four years earlier (Dewsbury, 2000).

Wundt wanted to establish psychology as a new science. His laboratory acquired an international reputation with an impressive group of visitors, and he founded a journal to report psychological research. The first research laboratory in the United States was opened in 1883 by G. Stanley Hall (Dewsbury, 2000; see Chapter 10).

Establishing a psychological laboratory was particularly significant because it marked the transition from the formal theorizing characteristic of philosophers to the emphasis on experimentation and instrumentation (Evans, 2000). The laboratory was a collection of scholars who conducted research aimed at providing scientific explanations of phenomena (Benjamin, 2000). In his book *Principles of Physiological Psychology* (1873), Wundt contended that psychology is the study of the mind. The psychological method should be patterned after the physiological method; that is, the process being studied should be experimentally investigated in terms of controlled stimuli and measured responses.

Wundt's laboratory attracted a new type of scientist who accepted the challenge to establish psychology as a science. The researchers investigated such phenomena as sensation, perception, reaction times, verbal associations, attention, feelings, and emotions. Wundt also was a mentor for many psychologists who subsequently opened laboratories in the United States (Benjamin, Durkin, Link, Vestal, & Acord, 1992). Although Wundt's laboratory produced no great discoveries or critical experiments in the history of psychology, it did establish psychology as a discipline and experimentation as the method of acquiring and refining knowledge.

Ebbinghaus's Verbal Learning. Hermann Ebbinghaus (1850–1909) was a German psychologist who was not connected with Wundt's laboratory but who nonetheless helped to validate the experimental method and thereby establish psychology as a science. Ebbinghaus investigated higher mental processes by conducting research on memory. He accepted the principles of association and believed that learning and the recall of learned information depend on the frequency of exposure to the material. Properly testing this hypothesis required using material with which participants were unfamiliar. Ebbinghaus invented *nonsense syllables,* which are three-letter consonant-vowel-consonant combinations (e.g., cew, tij).

Ebbinghaus was an avid researcher who often used himself as the subject of study. In a typical experiment, he would devise a list of nonsense syllables, look at each briefly, pause, and then look at the next syllable. In this manner, he determined how many times through the list (trials) it took to learn the entire list. He made fewer errors with repeated study of the list, needed more trials to learn more syllables, forgot rapidly at first but then more gradually, and required fewer trials to relearn syllables than to learn them the first time. He also studied a list of syllables some time after original learning and calculated a *savings score,* defined as the time or trials necessary for relearning as a percentage of the time or trials required for original learning. He also memorized some meaningful passages and found that meaningfulness made learning easier. Ebbinghaus compiled the results of his research in the book *Memory* (1885/1964).

Although important historically, there are concerns about this work. Ebbinghaus typically employed only one participant (himself) and it is unlikely he was unbiased or a typical learner. We also might question how well results for learning nonsense syllables generalize to meaningful learning (e.g., text passages). Nonetheless, he was a careful researcher and many of his findings were validated experimentally in later years. He was a pioneer in bringing higher mental processes into the experimental laboratory, and thus helped establish psychology as a science.

Structuralism and Functionalism

The work by Wundt and Ebbinghaus was systematic but confined to particular locations and of limited influence on psychological theory. The turn of the century marked the beginning of more widespread schools of psychological thought. Two perspectives that emerged were structuralism and functionalism. Although neither exists as a unified doctrine today, their early proponents were influential in the history of psychology as it relates to learning.

Structuralism.   Edward B. Titchener (1867–1927) was Wundt's student in Leipzig. In 1892 he became the director of the psychology laboratory at Cornell University. He imported Wundt's experimental methods into U.S. psychology.

Titchener's psychology eventually became known as *structuralism*. It represented a combination of associationism with the experimental method. Structuralists believed that human consciousness is a legitimate area of scientific investigation and they studied the structure or makeup of mental processes. They postulated that the mind is composed of associations of ideas and that to study the complexities of the mind one must break down these associations into single ideas (Titchener, 1909).

The experimental method used often by Wundt, Titchener, and other structuralists was *introspection,* which is a type of self-analysis. Titchener noted that scientists rely on observation of phenomena and that introspection is a form of observation. Participants in introspection studies verbally reported their immediate experiences following exposure to objects or events. For example, if shown a table they might report their perceptions of shape, size, color, and texture. They were told not to label, or report their knowledge about the object or the meanings of their perceptions. Thus, if they verbalized "table" while viewing a table, they were attending to the stimulus rather than to their conscious processes.

Introspection was uniquely psychological and helped to demarcate psychology from the other sciences. It was a professional method that required training in its use so that an introspectionist could determine when individuals were examining their own conscious processes rather than their interpretations of phenomena.

Unfortunately, introspection often was problematic and unreliable. It is difficult and unrealistic to expect people to ignore meanings and labels. When shown a table, it is natural that people say "table," think of uses, and draw on related knowledge. The mind is not structured to compartmentalize information so neatly, so by ignoring meanings introspectionists disregarded a central aspect of the mind. Watson (discussed in Chapter 2) decried the use of introspection, and its problems helped to rally support for an objective psychology that studied only observable behavior (Heidbreder, 1933). The ensuing emphasis on behavioral psychology dominated U.S. psychology for the first half of the twentieth century.

Another problem was that structuralists studied associations of ideas, but they had little to say about how these associations are acquired. Further, it was not clear that introspection was the appropriate method to study such higher mental processes as reasoning and problem solving, which are removed from immediate sensation and perception.

Functionalism.   While Titchener was at Cornell, developments in other locales challenged the validity of structuralism. Among these was work by the functionalists. *Functionalism* is the view that mental processes and behaviors of living organisms help them adapt to their environments (Heidbreder, 1933). This school of thought flourished at the University of Chicago with John Dewey (1867–1949) and James Angell (1869–1949). An especially prominent influence on functionalist thinking was the psychology of William James (1842–1910).

James's principal work was the two-volume series *The Principles of Psychology* (1890); an abridged version was published for classroom use (James, 1892). James was an empiricist who believed that experience is the starting point for examining thought, but he was not an associationist. He thought that simple ideas are not passive copies of environmental inputs but rather are the product of abstract thought and study.

James (1890) postulated that consciousness is a continuous process rather than a collection of discrete bits of information. One's "stream of thought" changes as experiences change. "Consciousness, from our natal day, is of a teeming multiplicity of objects and relations, and what we call simple sensations are results of discriminative attention, pushed often to a very high degree" (Vol. I, p. 224). James described the purpose of consciousness as helping organisms adapt to their environments.

Functionalists incorporated James's ideas into their doctrine. Dewey (1896) argued that psychological processes could not be broken into discrete parts and that consciousness must be viewed holistically. "Stimulus" and "response" describe the roles played by objects or events, but these roles could not be separated from the overall reality. Dewey cited an example from James (1890) about a baby who sees a candle burning, reaches out to grasp it, and experiences burned fingers. From a stimulus-response perspective, sight of the candle is a stimulus and reaching is a response; getting burned (pain) is a stimulus for the response of withdrawing the hand. Dewey argued that this sequence is better viewed as one large coordinated act in which seeing and reaching influence each other.

Functionalists were influenced by Darwin's writings on evolution and studied the utility of mental processes in helping organisms adapt to their environments and survive (Angell, 1907). Functional factors were bodily structures (because they allow organisms to survive), consciousness (because it has survived), and such cognitive processes as thinking, feeling, and judging. Functionalists were interested in how mental processes operate, what they accomplish, and how they vary with environmental conditions. They also saw the mind and body as interacting rather than existing separately.

Functionalists opposed the introspection method, not because it studied consciousness but rather because of how it studied consciousness. Introspection attempted to reduce consciousness to discrete elements, which functionalists believed was not possible. Studying a phenomenon in isolation does not reveal how it contributes to an organism's survival.

Dewey (1900) argued that the results of psychological experiments should be applicable to education and daily life. Although this goal was laudable, it also was problematic because the research agenda of functionalism was too broad to offer a clear focus. This weakness paved the way for the rise of behaviorism as the dominant force in U.S. psychology (Chapter 2). Behaviorism used experimental methods, and it was psychology's emphasis on experimentation and observable phenomena that helped to firmly secure its standing as a science (Tweney & Budzynski, 2000).

CRITICAL ISSUES IN THE STUDY OF LEARNING

Most professionals can accept in principle the definition of learning given at the outset of this chapter. When we move beyond the definition, we find less agreement on many learning issues. This section presents some of these issues and sources of controversy between theoretical perspectives (Table 1.3). Each of these issues is addressed in subsequent chapters covering various theories of learning.

How Does Learning Occur?

A basic issue in the study of learning concerns the process whereby learning occurs. We will distinguish between behavioral and cognitive theories of learning. (Constructivist theories, discussed in Chapter 7, have a cognitive focus.) Understanding some assumptions about these theories helps to provide a better grasp of the concepts underlying human learning principles.

Behavioral theories view learning as a change in the rate, frequency of occurrence, or form of behavior or response, which occurs primarily as a function of environmental factors. Behavioral theories contend that learning involves the formation of associations between stimuli and responses. In Skinner's (1953) view, for example, a response to a stimulus is more likely to occur in the future as a function

Table 1.3
Critical issues in the study of learning.

- How does learning occur?
- Which factors influence learning?
- What is the role of memory?
- What is the role of motivation?
- How does transfer occur?
- Which processes are involved in self-regulation?
- What are the implications for instruction?

of the consequences of prior responding: Reinforcing consequences make the response more likely to occur whereas punishing consequences make it less likely.

Behaviorism was a powerful force in psychology in the first half of the twentieth century, and most older theories of learning are behavioral. These theories explain learning in terms of observable phenomena. Behavioral theorists contend that explanations for learning need not include internal events (e.g., thoughts, beliefs, feelings), not because these processes do not exist (because they do) but rather because the causes of learning are observable environmental events.

In contrast, cognitive theories stress the acquisition of knowledge and skills, the formation of mental structures, and the processing of information and beliefs. From a cognitive perspective, learning is an internal mental phenomenon inferred from what people say and do. A central theme is the mental processing of information: its construction, acquisition, organization, coding, rehearsal, storage in and retrieval from memory, and forgetting. Although cognitive theorists stress the importance of mental processes in learning, they disagree over which processes are important. These differences are covered in subsequent chapters.

These conceptualizations of learning have important implications for educational practice. Behavioral theories imply that teachers should arrange the environment so that students can respond properly to stimuli. Cognitive theories emphasize making knowledge meaningful and taking into account learners' perceptions of themselves and their learning environments. Teachers need to consider how instruction affects students' thinking during learning.

Which Factors Influence Learning?

Behavioral and cognitive theories agree that differences among learners and in the environment can affect learning, but they diverge in the relative emphasis they give to these two factors. Behavioral theories stress the role of the environment—specifically, how stimuli are arranged and presented and how responses are reinforced. Behavioral theories assign less importance to learner differences than do cognitive theories. Two learner variables that behavioral theories do consider are *reinforcement history* (the extent to which the individual was reinforced in the past for performing the same or similar behavior) and *developmental status* (what the individual is capable of doing given his or her present level of development). Thus, cognitive handicaps will hinder learning of complex skills, and physical disabilities may preclude acquisition of motor behaviors.

Cognitive theories acknowledge the role of environmental conditions as influences on learning. Teachers' explanations and demonstrations of concepts serve as environmental inputs for students. Student practice of skills, combined with corrective feedback as needed, promotes learning. At the same time, cognitive theories contend that instructional factors alone do not fully account for students' learning (Pintrich, Cross, Kozma, & McKeachie, 1986). What students do with information—how they attend to, rehearse, transform, code, store, and retrieve it—is critically important. The ways that learners process information determine what, when, and how they learn, as well as what use they will make of the learning.

Cognitive theories emphasize the role of learners' thoughts, beliefs, attitudes, and values. For example, learners who doubt their capabilities to learn may not properly attend to the task or may work halfheartedly on it, which retards learning. Such learner thoughts as "Why is this important?" or "How well am I doing?" can affect learning. Teachers need to consider these thoughts in their lesson planning. Behavioral theories do not deny that these mental activities exist, but rather contend that they are not necessary to explain learning.

What Is the Role of Memory?

Learning theories differ in the role they assign to memory. Some behavioral theories conceive of memory in terms of neurological connections established as a function of behaviors being associated with external stimuli. More commonly, theorists discuss the formation of habitual ways of responding with little attention to how these behavioral patterns are retained in memory and activated by external events. Most behavioral theories view forgetting as caused by lack of responding over time.

Cognitive theories assign a prominent role to memory. Information processing theories equate learning with *encoding*, or storing knowledge in memory in an organized, meaningful fashion. Information is retrieved from memory in response to relevant cues that activate the appropriate memory structures. Forgetting is the inability to retrieve information from memory caused by interference, memory loss, or inadequate cues to access information. Memory is critical for learning, and how information is learned determines how it is stored in and retrieved from memory.

One's perspective on the role of memory has important implications for teaching. Behavioral theories posit that periodic, spaced reviews maintain responses' strength in learners' repertoires. Cognitive theories place greater emphasis on presenting material such that learners can organize it, relate it to what they know, and remember it in a meaningful fashion.

What Is the Role of Motivation?

Motivation is a major variable that affects all phases of learning and performance. Although a separate chapter is devoted to motivation (Chapter 8), its relevance to learning theories also is discussed in other chapters.

Theories of learning diverge in the role they assign to motivation. Behavioral theories define motivation as an increased rate or probability of occurrence of behavior, which results from repeating behaviors in response to stimuli or as a consequence of reinforcement. Skinner's (1968) operant conditioning theory contains no new principles to account for motivation: Motivated behavior is increased or continued responding produced by effective reinforcement. Students motivated to learn choose a task, persist at it, and expend effort to succeed, all of which are behaviors. Such internal processes as needs, goals, expectations, and emotions are not necessary to explain motivated behavior. Students display motivated behavior because they previously were reinforced for it and because effective reinforcers are present. Behavioral theories do not distinguish motivation from learning but rather use the same principles to explain all behavior.

In contrast, cognitive theories view motivation and learning as related but not identical (Schunk, 1991). Motivation and learning share some processes but also involve different functions. One can be motivated but not learn; one can learn without being motivated to do so. Although reinforcement can motivate students, its effects on behavior are not automatic but instead depend on how students interpret it. Students engage in activities they believe will be reinforced. When reinforcement history (what one has been reinforced for doing in the past) conflicts with present beliefs, people are more likely to act based on their beliefs (Bandura, 1986; Brewer, 1974). Research has identified many cognitive processes that motivate students; for example, goals, social comparisons, self-efficacy. By ignoring such processes behavioral theories cannot fully account for the complexity of human motivation.

Cognitive theories emphasize that motivation can help to direct attention and influence how information is processed. Social cognitive theory contends that motivation affects observational learning—a key form of human learning—and operates largely through such mechanisms as goal setting, self-efficacy, and outcome expectations (Bandura, 1986, 1997; see Chapter 3).

In older theories of learning, motivation is treated as a part of learning. Tolman's experiments on *latent learning* (see Chapter 3), which showed that learning could occur without reinforcement and that reinforcement affects performance rather than learning, helped to disentangle motivation from learning and establish the former as a topic in its own right (Weiner, 1990). Most educators believe that motivation can affect learning in many ways. Teachers need to consider the motivational effects of instructional practices and classroom factors to ensure that students remain motivated to learn.

How Does Transfer Occur?

Transfer refers to knowledge and skills being applied in new ways, with new content, or in situations different from where they were acquired (see Chapter 6). Transfer also explains the effect of prior learning on new learning—whether the former facilitates, hinders, or has no effect on the latter. Transfer is critical, for without it all learning would be situationally specific.

Behavioral theories stress that transfer depends on identical elements or similar features (stimuli) between situations. Behaviors transfer (or *generalize*) when the old and new situations share common elements. Thus, a student who learns that $6 \times 3 = 18$ should be able to perform this multiplication in different settings (school, home) and when the same numbers appear in a similar problem format (e.g., $36 \times 23 = ?$).

Cognitive theories postulate that transfer occurs when learners understand how to apply knowledge in different settings. How information is stored in memory is important. The uses of knowledge are stored along with the knowledge itself or can be easily accessed from another memory storage location. Situations need not share common elements.

Instructional implications of these views diverge. In the behavioral view, teachers should enhance the similarity between situations and point out common elements. Cognitive theories supplement these factórs by emphasizing that students' perceptions of the value of learning are critical. Teachers can address these perceptions by including in lessons information on how knowledge can be used in different settings, by teaching students rules and procedures to apply in situations to determine what knowledge will be needed, and by providing students with feedback on how skills and strategies can benefit them in different ways.

What Processes Are Involved in Self-Regulation?

Self-regulation (or *self-regulated learning*) refers to the process whereby learners systematically direct their thoughts, feelings, and actions toward the attainment of their goals (Zimmerman & Schunk, 2001). Research on self-regulation during learning began as an outgrowth of psychological investigations into self-control and the development of self-regulation in children (Zimmerman, 2001). Much early self-regulation research was conducted in therapeutic contexts, where researchers taught participants to alter such dysfunctional behaviors as aggression, addictions, sexual disorders, interpersonal conflicts, and behavioral problems in school (Mace & West, 1986). The topic has expanded to address academic studying and other forms of learning (e.g., social and motor skills) (Zimmerman & Schunk, 2001).

Researchers of different theoretical traditions postulate that self-regulation involves having a purpose or goal, employing goal-directed actions, monitoring strategies and actions, and adjusting them to ensure success. Theories differ in the mechanisms postulated to underlie students' use of cognitive and behavioral processes to regulate their activities.

Behavioral researchers posit that self-regulation involves setting up one's own contingencies of reinforcement: discriminative stimuli and consequences of responses. No new processes are needed to account for self-regulated behavior. Behavioral researchers focus on overt responses of learners: self-monitoring, self-instruction, self-reinforcement.

Cognitive researchers emphasize mental activities such as attention, rehearsal, use of learning strategies, and comprehension monitoring. These theorists also stress motivational beliefs about self-efficacy, outcomes, and perceived value of learning (Schunk, 2001). A key element is *choice*: For self-regulation to occur, learners must have some choice in their motives or methods for learning, time spent learning, criterion level of learning, the setting where learning occurs, and the social conditions in effect (Zimmerman, 1994, 1998). When learners have few if any choices, their behaviors are largely externally regulated rather than self-regulated.

What Are the Implications for Instruction?

Theories attempt to explain various types of learning but differ in their ability to do so (Bruner, 1985). Behavioral theories emphasize the forming of associations between stimuli and responses through selective reinforcement of correct responding. Behavioral theories seem best suited to explain simpler forms of learning that involve associations, such as multiplication facts, foreign language word meanings, and state capital cities.

Cognitive theories, on the other hand, explain learning in terms of such factors as information processing, memory networks, and student perceptions and interpretations of classroom factors (teachers, peers, materials, organization). Cognitive theories appear to be more appropriate for explaining complex forms of learning, such as solving mathematical word problems, drawing inferences from text, and writing essays.

It should be noted, however, that commonalities often exist among different forms of learning (Bruner, 1985). Learning to read is fundamentally different from learning to play the violin, but both benefit from attention, effort, and persistence. Learning to write term papers and learning to throw the javelin may not appear to be similar, but both are promoted by goal setting, self-monitoring of progress, corrective feedback from teachers and coaches, and feelings of intrinsic motivation.

Effective teaching requires that we determine the best theoretical perspectives for the types of learning we deal with and draw on the implications of those perspectives for teaching. When reinforced practice is important for learning, then teachers should schedule it. When learning problem-solving strategies is important, then we should study the implications of information processing theory. A continuing challenge for research is to specify similarities and differences among types of learning and identify effective instructional approaches for each.

RELATION OF LEARNING AND INSTRUCTION

Historical Perspective

Theories and research findings help to advance the field, but their ultimate contribution is their impact on teaching that improves learning. Although it may seem odd, historically there was little overlap between the fields of learning and instruction at the levels of theory, research, and application (Shuell, 1988). One reason for this lack of integration may have been that these fields traditionally have been dominated by persons with different interests. Most learning theorists and researchers were psychologists. A lot of learning research used nonhuman species. Animal research has certain benefits, but animals do not allow for proper exploration of instructional processes. In contrast, instruction was the domain of educators, many of who were primarily concerned with directly applying teaching methods to classrooms. This applied focus has not always lent itself well to exploring how learning processes are affected by instructional variations.

A second reason derives from the common belief that teaching is an art and not a science like psychology. As Highet (1950) wrote:

> [This book] is called *The Art of Teaching* because I believe that teaching is an art, not a science. It seems to me very dangerous to apply the aims and methods of science to human beings as individuals, although a statistical principle can often be used to explain their behavior in large groups and a scientific diagnosis of their physical structure is always valuable. But a "scientific" relationship between human beings is bound to be inadequate and perhaps distorted. (p. vii)

Highet does state, however, that teaching is inseparable from learning: Good teachers continue to learn about their subject areas and ways to encourage student learning.

Gage (1978) notes that the use of "art" in reference to teaching really is a metaphor. As a way to understand and improve teaching, critical study of the "art of teaching" has received little serious attention. Teaching as an art can become the object of the same type of scrutiny and scientific investigation as any other type of art, including drawing, painting, and musical composition. Thus, regardless of whether teaching is an art, it still can be improved through scientific study.

A third possible reason stems from the idea that different theoretical principles may govern the two domains. Sternberg (1986) contended that the link between cognition (or learning) and instruction requires separate theories for cognition and for instruction. In fact, although learning and instruction involve different principles, they interact in reciprocal fashion.

Shuell (1988) states: "Learning from instruction differs from traditional conceptions of learning and teaching considered separately" (p. 282). Learning from instruction involves an interaction between learners and contexts (e.g., teachers, materials, setting), whereas much learning studied in psychological research is less context-dependent. Sequencing of material, for example, affects learners' cognitive organizations and development of memory structures. In turn, how these structures develop affects what teachers do. Teachers who realize their instruction is not being comprehended will alter their approach; conversely, when students understand material that is being presented, teachers are apt to continue with their present approach.

Fourth, traditional research methods may have been inadequate to study both processes simultaneously. Research methods reflect the purpose of the investigation. *Process-product research* relates changes in teaching processes (such as number and type of questions asked, amount of warmth and enthusiasm displayed) to student products or outcomes (e.g., achievement, attitudes) (Dunkin & Biddle, 1974). Although this research paradigm has produced many useful results, it has neglected the important roles of teacher and student thoughts. Thus, we might know which type of questions produce higher student achievement but not why they do so (i.e., how questions change students' thinking). Process-product research also has focused primarily on student achievement and neglected many other outcomes relevant to learning (e.g., expectations, attributions, values). In short, a process-product model is not well designed to examine how students learn.

At the same time, much learning research has used experimental methods in which some conditions are varied and changes in outcomes are determined. Teaching methods often are held constant across changes in variables, which negates the potential effects of the former.

Fortunately, the situation has changed as researchers increasingly are examining learning processes during actual content instruction, especially in places where students typically learn (e.g., schools, workplaces). More attention is being devoted to how what is learned in school is related to what is needed outside of school (Anderson, Reder, & Simon, 1996). Researchers of different traditions accept the idea that instruction and learning interact and are best studied in concert. Indeed, instructional research can have a profound impact on learning theories and their applications (Glaser, 1990; Glaser & Bassok, 1989).

Instructional Commonalities

Regardless of perspective, theories share several instructional commonalities that enhance learning (Table 1.4). Most theories postulate that learners progress through stages or phases of learning that can be distinguished in various ways. One scheme classifies learners in terms of progressive skill levels: novice, advanced beginner, competent, proficient, expert (Shuell, 1990). Experts must determine how to classify learners according to such a scheme, but processes and behaviors often used in such classifications include speed and type of cognitive processing, ability to recognize problem formats, proficiency in dealing with problems that arise, organization and depth of knowledge structures, and ability to monitor performance and select strategies depending on personal and contextual factors.

Teaching and learning emphasize various factors as important in acquiring skills, strategies, and behaviors. These include organization of material to be taught, presentation of material in short steps (small units to be processed), opportunities for learner practice, provision of corrective feedback, and scheduling of review sessions (Rosenshine & Stevens, 1986; Shuell, 1988, 1990).

The role of practice is especially critical. Thorndike and other behaviorists believed that practice helps establish connections or associations between stimuli and responses. Cognitive views of learning stress practice as a means of building associations between concepts and propositions in memory (Anderson, 1990).

Ericsson, Krampe, and Tesch-Römer (1993) note that deliberate practice includes activities designed to improve current performance level. The development of skill requires time and energy by the individual as well as access to instructional materials, teachers, and facilities. Parents or other adults often invest financial resources and time and effort transporting their children to practices and competitions.

Research shows that a regimen of deliberate practice not only raises skillful performance but also reduces constraints of memory and cognitive processing limitations (Ericsson & Charness, 1994). Although abilities and natural talents are important, only extended intense training in a domain can result in expert performance.

Table 1.4 Instructional principles common to diverse learning theories.	■ Learners progress through stages/phases
	■ Material should be organized and presented in small steps
	■ Learners require practice, feedback, and review
	■ Social models facilitate learning and motivation
	■ Motivational and contextual factors influence learning

Many young children are not inclined to put in long hours improving skills. Parental support of periods in which children regularly practice is critical (Ericsson et al., 1993). Parents and other adults can serve as social models for practice of their own skills, provide children with feedback on their progress, and arrange for opportunities for children to practice and receive expert feedback (i.e., from teachers and coaches).

Most views of learning and instruction highlight the importance of learner motivational factors, including perceived value of learning, self-efficacy, positive outcome expectations, and attributions that emphasize ability, effort, and use of strategies (Stipek, 1996). In addition, research shows that learning environment factors affect what teachers do and how students learn (Ames, 1992a, 1992b; Shuell, 1996).

Integration of Theory and Practice

A goal of this book is to help you understand how learning theory and educational practice complement one another. Learning theory is no substitute for experience. Theory without experience can be misguided because it may underestimate the effects of situational factors. When properly used, theory provides a framework to use in making educational decisions.

Conversely, experience without theory may often be wasteful and potentially damaging. Experience without a guiding framework means that each situation is treated as unique, so decision making is based on trial and error until something works. Learning how to teach involves learning what to do in specific situations.

Theory and practice affect one another. Many theoretical developments eventually become implemented in classrooms. Contemporary educational practices—such as cooperative learning, reciprocal teaching, and adapting instruction to individual student differences—have strong theoretical underpinnings and research to support them.

Educational practice also influences theory. Experience can temper theory and either confirm theoretical predictions or suggest revisions. No learning theory is immutable. Theories are modified when research and experience present conflicting evidence or suggest additional factors to include. Early information processing theories were not directly applicable to school learning because they failed to consider factors other than those connected with the processing of knowledge. When cognitive psychologists began to study school content, theories were revised to incorporate personal and situational factors.

Educational professionals should strive to integrate theory, research, and practice. We must ask how learning principles and research findings might apply in and out of school. In turn, we should seek to advance our theoretical knowledge through results of informed teaching practice.

THREE LEARNING SCENARIOS

Following are three scenarios that are intended to be typical of contexts where school learning occurs. Throughout this text, these scenarios will serve to exemplify the application of a range of learning processes and demonstrate how learning can occur in a coherent fashion through systematic application of principles.

Kathy Stone's Third-Grade Class

Kathy Stone's class is one of five self-contained third-grade classes in a K–5 elementary school of 550 students. The school is located at the edge of a city next to a large suburban housing community. Kathy has been a teacher in this building for 8 years and previously taught second grade in another school for 4 years. She has been active in developing curriculum and has chaired several school and system-wide committees for implementing creative programs to expand the activities incorporated into the regular program.

There are 21 students in Kathy's class. Ethnic backgrounds are mixed; about 70% of the students are middle class and most of the rest are from families in government subsidized housing. There are 11 boys and 10 girls ranging in age from 8 to 10. Most students are eager to learn but some have difficulties due to learning disabilities, family, or emotional problems. Six students attend resource classes, two are in counseling for acting-out behaviors, and one is in counseling because her mother is battling cancer.

Students attend from 8:15 to 2:45 each day. They remain with Kathy for the major academic content areas: reading, writing, spelling, mathematics, science, social studies, health, computer applications. Students visit other teachers for art, music, physical education, and library. Students have an hour for lunch and recess, at which time they are supervised by special cafeteria and playground personnel. The wide range of abilities in the class presents challenges in implementing an effective curricular program.

Jim Marshall's Ninth-Grade American History Class

American History 1 is a core curriculum course that is required for graduation at a small-town high school. Usually two or more sections are offered each semester so that all high school students are able to enroll. Jim Marshall teaches this course as well as other courses in the history department. Jim has been teaching at this school for 14 years and has received several teaching awards and history grants.

There are 23 students in Jim's class; 19 are ninth-grade students and 4 are tenth-grade students who failed the class last year. Ethnic backgrounds are mixed; students primarily are middle class. Most students perform at an average or above-average level, although some are not motivated to participate in class or complete the assignments. In addition, 3 students have been identified as having a learning disability and receive help from a resource teacher.

The course meets daily for 50 minutes. The course objectives are for students to become more familiar with the major periods in American history beginning with the establishment of the 13 colonies through the U.S. space exploration program. Course objectives also include analyzing those time periods and examining the impact various events had on forming and shaping the United States. Units include lectures and demonstrations, small-group discussions, student research, history projects, and role playing.

Gina Brown's Undergraduate Educational Psychology Class

EDUC 107, Educational Psychology for Teachers, is a three-credit required course in the undergraduate teacher education program at a large university. Several sections of the course are offered each semester. Gina Brown, an associate professor in the College of Education, teaches one section. Gina has been on the faculty for 7 years. Prior to completing her doctorate, she taught mathematics for 10 years at the middle- and high-school levels.

There are 30 students in the class this semester: 12 elementary majors, 10 secondary majors, and 8 special education majors. Ethnic backgrounds are mixed; students primarily are middle class; ages range from 18 to 37 (mean = 20.7 years). The course meets 3 hours per week. There are lectures and discussions, and Gina incorporates videos of classrooms and Web-based applications. Students take a concurrent one-credit field experience class, which Gina supervises.

The course content is standard for an educational psychology course. Topics include development, individual differences, learning, motivation, classroom management, students with exceptional needs, assessment, and testing. Students complete projects (in conjunction with the field experience) and are tested on course content. There is a tremendous amount of material to cover, although student motivation generally is high because students believe that understanding these topics is important for their future success in teaching.

SUMMARY

The study of human learning focuses on how individuals acquire and modify their knowledge, skills, strategies, beliefs, and behaviors. Learning represents an enduring change in behavior or in the capacity to behave in a given fashion, which results from practice or other experiences. This definition excludes temporary changes in behavior due to illness, fatigue, or drugs, as well as behaviors reflecting genetic and maturational factors, although many of the latter require responsive environments to manifest themselves.

Theories provide frameworks for making sense of environmental observations. Theories serve as bridges between research and educational practices and as tools to organize and translate research findings into recommendations for educational practice. Types of research include correlational, experimental, and qualitative. Research may be conducted in laboratories or in field settings. Common ways to assess learning include direct observations, written and oral responses, ratings by others, and self-reports.

The scientific study of learning had its beginnings in writings of such early philosophers as Plato and Aristotle. Two prominent positions on how knowledge is acquired are rationalism and empiricism. The psychological study of learning began late in the nineteenth century. Structuralism and functionalism were active schools of thought at the beginning of the twentieth century with such proponents as Titchener,

Dewey, and James, but these positions suffered from problems that limited wide-spread applicability to psychology.

Theories of learning differ in how they address critical issues. Some of the more important issues concern how learning occurs, which factors influence learning, what the role of memory is, what the role of motivation is, how transfer occurs, which processes are involved in self-regulation, and what the theory's implications for instruction are.

Learning theory and educational practice often are viewed as distinct, but in fact they should complement one another. Neither is sufficient to ensure good teaching and learning. Theory alone may not fully capture the importance of situational factors. Practical experience without theory is situationally specific and lacks an overarching framework to organize knowledge of teaching and learning. Theory and practice help to refine one another.

Behavioral Theories

Psychology was an infant science at the beginning of the twentieth century, but exciting events were taking place in the United States and abroad. As we saw in the preceding chapter, two prominent schools of thought were structuralism and functionalism. Under Titchener's guidance, structuralism maintained its unique research focus despite problems with introspection, which placed it out of touch with important developments in science. Structuralists did not incorporate Darwin's work on adaptation and evolution into their views as did the functionalists. Whereas structuralism suffered from a highly restrictive agenda, functionalism had an overly broad focus because its proponents advocated too many research directions. Angell (1907) proposed that research address behavioral adaptation and the functions of various mental processes; Dewey (1900) encouraged research that applied to the real world (e.g., schools).

Against this background, behaviorism began its rise to become the leading psychological discipline (Rachlin, 1991). Its most strident advocate was John B. Watson, who contented that if psychology were to become an objective, experimental science, it must deal with observable, scientific subject matter (Watson, 1924). For psychologists, what was observable was behavior.

This chapter covers behavioral theories of learning. The hallmark of behavioral theories is not that they deal with behavior (all theories do that) but rather that they explain learning in terms of environmental events. While not denying the existence of mental phenomena, these theories contend that such phenomena are not necessary to explain learning.

The best-known behavioral theory is B. F. Skinner's *operant conditioning*. Before discussing this theory, we will present some historical work in the behavioral tradition to set the backdrop for Skinner's work. We will discuss Thorndike's connectionism, Pavlov's classical conditioning, Watson's behaviorism, and Guthrie's contiguous conditioning.

When you finish studying this chapter, you should be able to do the following:

- Explain how behaviors are learned according to connectionism theory.

- Discuss some of Thorndike's contributions to educational practice.

- Explain how responses become conditioned, extinguished, and generalized, according to classical conditioning theory.

- Describe a process whereby an emotional response might become conditioned to an initially neutral object.

- Explain, using contiguous conditioning principles, how movements are combined to become an act.

- Describe Skinner's three-term contingency model of operant conditioning and provide examples.

- Define and exemplify key operant conditioning concepts: reinforcement (positive, negative), punishment, generalization, discrimination, shaping, and Premack Principle.

- Discuss the operation of behavioral principles of self-regulation.

- Explain some key educational applications of operant principles to education: behavioral objectives, programmed instruction, contingency contracts, and Keller Plan.

CONNECTIONISM

Edward L. Thorndike (1874–1949) was a prominent U.S. psychologist whose theory of learning—*connectionism*—was dominant in the United States during the first half of the twentieth century. Unlike many early psychologists, he was interested in education and especially learning, transfer, individual differences, and intelligence (Hilgard, 1996; McKeachie, 1990). He applied an experimental approach by measuring achievement outcomes of school students. His impact on education is reflected in the Thorndike Award, the highest honor given by the Division of Educational Psychology of the American Psychological Association for distinguished contributions to educational psychology.

Trial-and-Error Learning

Thorndike's major work was the three-volume series *Educational Psychology* (1913a, 1913b, 1914). He postulated that the most fundamental type of learning involves the forming of associations (*connections*) between sensory experiences (perceptions of stimuli or events) and neural impulses (responses) that manifest themselves behaviorally. This is a behavioral theory because it emphasizes associations between stimuli and responses as the basis of learning.

Thorndike believed that learning often occurs by *trial and error* (selecting and connecting). Thorndike began studying learning with a series of experiments on animals (Thorndike, 1911). Animals in problem situations try to attain a goal (e.g., obtain food, reach a destination). From among the many responses they can perform, they select one, perform it, and experience the consequences. The more often they make a response to a stimulus, the more firmly that response becomes connected to that stimulus.

In a typical experimental situation, a cat was placed in a cage. The cat could open an escape hatch by pushing a stick or pulling a chain. After a series of random responses, the cat eventually escaped by making a response that opened the hatch. The cat then was put back into the cage. Over trials, the cat reached the goal (escaped) quicker and made fewer errors prior to responding correctly. A typical plot of results is shown in Figure 2.1.

Trial-and-error learning occurs gradually (incrementally) as successful responses are established and unsuccessful ones are abandoned. Connections are formed mechanically through repetition; conscious awareness is not necessary. Animals do not "catch on" or "have insight." Thorndike understood that human learning is more complex because people engage in other types of learning involving connecting

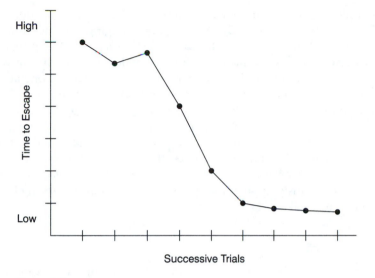

High

Time to Escape

Low

Successive Trials

Figure 2.1
Incremental performance over trials exemplifying Thorndike's trial-
and-error learning.

ideas, analyzing, and reasoning (Thorndike, 1913b). Nonetheless, the similarity in research results from animal and human studies led Thorndike to explain complex
learning with elementary learning principles. An educated adult possesses millions
of stimulus-response connections.

Laws of Exercise and Effect

Thorndike's basic ideas about learning are embodied in the Laws of Exercise and Effect. The *Law of Exercise* has two parts: The *Law of Use*—a response to a stimulus
strengthens their connection; the *Law of Disuse*—when a response is not made to a
stimulus the connection's strength is weakened (forgotten). The longer the time interval before a response is made, the greater is the decline in the connection's
strength.

The *Law of Effect* is central to Thorndike's theory (Thorndike, 1913b):

> When a modifiable connection between a situation and a response is made and is
> accompanied or followed by a satisfying state of affairs, that connection's strength is
> increased: When made and accompanied or followed by an annoying state of affairs,
> its strength is decreased. (p. 4)

The Law of Effect emphasizes the *consequences* of behavior: Responses resulting in satisfying (rewarding) consequences are learned; responses producing annoying (punishing) consequences are not learned. This is a functional account of
learning because satisfiers (responses that produce desirable outcomes) allow organisms to adapt better to their environments.

The following study illustrates application of the Law of Effect (Thorndike, 1927). Participants were shown 50 strips of paper, ranging in length from 3 to 27 centimeters (cm), one at a time. Next to each strip was a second strip that participants knew was 10 cm long. They initially estimated the length of each strip without feedback. Following this pretest, the 50 strips were presented again one at a time. After each estimate, they were told "right" or "wrong" by the experimenter. After the 50 strips were presented repeatedly over several days, they again were presented without feedback about accuracy of length judgments. Following training, participants' length estimates more closely approximated the actual lengths of the strips than had their prior estimates. Thorndike concluded that these results, which were similar to those from experiments in which animals were rewarded with food or freedom, support the idea that satisfying stimulus-response connections are strengthened and annoying ones are weakened.

Other Principles

Thorndike's (1913b) theory included many other principles relevant to education, two of which are the Law of Readiness and Associative Shifting. The *Law of Readiness* states that when one is prepared (ready) to act, to do so is rewarding and not to do so is punishing. If one is hungry, responses that lead to food are in a state of readiness, whereas other responses not leading to food are not in a state of readiness. If one is fatigued, it is punishing to be forced to exercise. Applying this idea to learning, we might say that when students are ready to learn a particular action (in terms of developmental level or prior skill acquisition), then behaviors that foster this learning will be rewarding. When students are not developmentally ready to learn or do not possess prerequisite skills, then attempting to learn is punishing and a waste of time.

Associative shifting refers to a situation in which responses made to a particular stimulus eventually are made to an entirely differently stimulus if, on repeated trials, there are small changes in the nature of the stimulus. These small changes involve adding some elements and removing others. Associative shifting is one means of facilitating *transfer*, or the use of knowledge in new settings (discussed later in this section and in Chapter 5).

Revisions to Thorndike's Theory

Thorndike revised the Laws of Exercise and Effect after being confronted with research evidence that did not support them (Thorndike, 1932). Thorndike discarded the Law of Exercise when he found that simple repetition of a situation does not necessarily "stamp in" responses. In one experiment, for example, participants closed their eyes and drew lines they thought were 2, 4, 6, and 8 inches long, hundreds of times over several days, without feedback on accuracy of the lengths (Thorndike, 1932). If the Law of Exercise were correct, then for any given length the response occurring most often during the first 100 or so drawings ought to become more frequent afterward, but Thorndike found no support for this idea. Rather, mean lengths changed over time; people apparently experimented with different lengths because they were unsure of the correct length. In sum, repetition of a situation does not enhance future likelihood of its occurrence.

With respect to the Law of Effect, Thorndike originally thought that the effects of satisfiers (rewards) and annoyers (punishments) were opposite but comparable, but research showed this was not the case. Rather, rewards strengthened connections but punishment did not necessarily weaken them (Thorndike, 1932). Instead, connections are weakened when alternative connections are strengthened. In one study (Thorndike, 1932), participants were presented with uncommon English words (e.g., *edacious, eidolon*). Each word was followed by five common English words, one of which was a correct synonym. On each trial, participants chose a synonym and underlined it, after which the experimenter said "right" (reward) or "wrong" (punishment). Reward improved learning, but punishment did not diminish the probability of that response occurring to that stimulus word.

Punishment suppresses responses, but they are not forgotten. Punishment is not an effective means of altering behavior because it does not teach students correct behaviors but rather simply informs them of what not to do. This is true even with cognitive skills. Brown and Burton (1978) have shown, for example, students sometimes learn "buggy algorithms" (incorrect rules) for solving problems (e.g., subtract the smaller number from the larger, column by column, 4371 − 2748 = 2437). When students are informed that this method is incorrect and are given corrective feedback and practice in solving problems correctly, they learn the correct method but they do not forget the old way.

Instructional Applications

As a professor of education at Teachers College, Columbia University, Thorndike wrote books that addressed such topics as educational goals, learning processes, teaching methods, curricular sequences, and techniques for assessing educational outcomes (Hilgard, 1996; Thorndike, 1906, 1912; Thorndike & Gates, 1929). Some of Thorndike's many contributions to education are the following.

Principles of Teaching. Schooling should help students form good habits. Thorndike (1912) noted:

- Form habits. Do not expect them to create themselves.
- Beware of forming a habit which must be broken later.
- Do not form two or more habits when one will do as well.
- Other things being equal, have a habit formed in the way in which it is to be used. (pp. 173–174)

The last principle cautions against teaching content that is removed from its applications: "Since the forms of adjectives in German or Latin are always to be used with nouns, they should be learned with nouns" (p. 174). Students need to understand how to apply knowledge and skills they acquire. Uses should be learned in conjunction with the content.

Sequence of Curricula.   A skill should be introduced (Thorndike & Gates, 1929):

- At the time or just before the time when it can be used in some serviceable way
- At the time when the learner is conscious of the need for it as a means of satisfying some useful purpose
- When it is most suited in difficulty to the ability of the learner
- When it will harmonize most fully with the level and type of emotions, tastes, instinctive and volitional dispositions most active at the time
- When it is most fully facilitated by immediately preceding learnings and when it will most fully facilitate learnings which are to follow shortly. (pp. 209–210)

Thorndike and Gates noted that these principles conflict with typical content placement in schools, where content is segregated by subject (e.g., social studies, mathematics, science). It is better to teach knowledge and skills and then show how they cut across different subjects. Thus, forms of government are appropriate topics not only in civics and history but also in English (how governments are reflected in literature) and foreign language (government structure in other countries). Some additional applications are shown in Application 2.1.

APPLICATION 2.1
Sequence of Curricula

Thorndike's views on the sequence of curricula closely parallel the current emphasis on integrated learning. His ideas suggest that as teachers plan units of study they not segregate related subject matter.

As Kathy Stone prepares a unit for her third-grade class in the fall, she might focus on using pumpkins. The students could study the significance of pumpkins to the American colonists (history) and where pumpkins currently are grown (geography), and they could look at data on the varieties of pumpkins grown (agriculture). They also could measure and chart the various sizes of pumpkins (mathematics), carve the pumpkins (art), plant pumpkin seeds and study their growth (science), and read and write stories about pumpkins (language arts). This approach provides a meaningful experience for children and "real life" learning of various skills.

In developing a history unit on the Civil War, Jim Marshall could go beyond just covering factual material and incorporate comparisons from other wars, attitudes and feelings of the populace during that time period, biographies and personalities of individuals involved in the war, the impact the war had on the United States, and the implications for the future. In addition, Mr. Marshall could work with other teachers in the building to expand the unit by examining the terrain of major battlefields (geography), weather conditions during major battles (science), and the emergence of literature (language arts) and creative works (art, music, drama) during that time period.

Transfer.   *Transfer* refers to the extent that strengthening/weakening of one connection produces a similar change in another connection (Hilgard, 1996; Thorndike, 1913b). Transfer occurs when situations have *identical elements* and call for similar responses. Thorndike and Woodworth (1901) found that practice or training in a skill in a specific context does not improve one's ability to execute that skill generally. Thus, training on estimating the area of rectangles does not advance learners' ability to estimate the areas of triangles, circles, and irregular figures. Skills should be taught with different types of educational content for students to understand how to apply them (Application 2.2).

Mental Discipline.   *Mental discipline* is the view that learning certain subjects (e.g., the classics, mathematics) enhances mental functioning better than other subjects. Thorndike (1924) tested this popular view with 8,500 students in grades 9 to 11. Students were given intelligence tests a year apart, and their programs of study that year were compared to determine whether certain courses were associated with greater intellectual gains. The results provided no support for mental discipline. Students who had greater ability to begin with made the best progress regardless of what they studied.

> If our inquiry had been carried out by a psychologist from Mars, who knew nothing of theories of mental discipline, and simply tried to answer the question, "What are the amounts of influence of sex, race, age, amounts of ability, and studies taken, upon the gain made during the year in power to think, or intellect, or whatever our stock intelligence tests measure," he might even dismiss "studies taken" with the comment,

---

APPLICATION 2.2
Facilitating Transfer

Thorndike suggested that drilling students on a specific skill does not help them master it nor does it teach them how to apply the skill in different contexts.

When teachers instruct secondary students how to use map scales, they must teach them to calculate miles from inches at the same time. Students become more proficient if they actually apply the skill on various maps and create maps of their own surroundings than if they are just given numerous problems to solve.

When elementary teachers begin working with students on liquid and dry measurement, having the students use a recipe to actually measure ingredients and create a food item is much more meaningful than using pictures, charts, or just filling cups with water or sand.

In medical school, having students actually observe and become involved in various procedures or surgeries is much more meaningful than just reading about the conditions in textbooks.

"The differences are so small and the unreliabilities are relatively so large that this factor seems unimportant." The one causal factor which he would be sure was at work would be the intellect already existent. Those who have the most to begin with gain the most during the year. Whatever studies they take will seem to produce large gains in intellect. (Thorndike, 1924, p. 95)

Thus, the intellectual value of studies resides not only in how much they improve students' ability to think but also in how they affect their interests and goals. Thorndike's research was influential and led educators to redesign curricula away from the mental discipline idea.

CLASSICAL CONDITIONING

In the early part of the twentieth century, many exciting events occurred in the United States that helped establish psychology as a science and learning as a legitimate field of study. At the same time, there were important developments in other countries. One of the most significant was the work of Ivan Pavlov (1849–1936), a Russian physiologist who won the Nobel Prize in 1904 for his work on digestion (Frolov, 1937).

Pavlov's legacy to learning theory was his work on classical conditioning (Cuny, 1965; Hunt, 1993; Windholz, 1997). While Pavlov was the director of the physiological laboratory at the Institute of Experimental Medicine in Petrograd, he noticed that dogs often would salivate at the sight of the attendant bringing them food or even at the sound of the attendant's footsteps. Pavlov realized that the attendant was not a natural stimulus for salivating (a reflexive action); rather, the attendant acquired this power by being associated with food.

Basic Processes

Classical conditioning is a multistep procedure that initially involves presenting an *unconditioned stimulus (UCS)*, which elicits an *unconditioned response (UCR)*. In his experiments, Pavlov placed a hungry dog in an apparatus and presented it with meat powder (UCS), which would cause the dog to salivate (UCR). To condition the animal requires repeatedly presenting an initially neutral stimulus for a brief period before presenting the UCS. Pavlov often used a ticking metronome as the neutral stimulus. In the early trials, the ticking of the metronome produced no salivation. Eventually, the dog salivated in response to the ticking metronome prior to the presentation of the food powder. The metronome had become a *conditioned stimulus (CS)* that elicited a *conditioned response (CR)* similar to the original UCR (Table 2.1). Repeated presentations of the CS without the UCS cause the CR to diminish in intensity and disappear, a phenomenon known as *extinction*.

Pavlov (1932b) explained conditioning and extinction in terms of neurological processes, although this explanation was speculative and not addressed by his research. He hypothesized that presentation of a CS neurally activates a portion of the cortex, which then associates with the portion activated by the UCS. Neural centers

Table 2.1
Classical conditioning
procedure.

Phase	Stimulus	Response
1	UCS (food powder)	UCR (salivation)
2	CS (metronome), then UCS (food powder)	UCR (salivation)
3	CS (metronome)	CR (salivation)

so activated thus become associated with one another. Inhibition diminishes the intensity of or extinguishes the CR, such as when an outside agent interferes with the CS (e.g., a dog is distracted by a noise at the moment the CS is presented).

Other Phenomena

Some other phenomena important in Pavlov's theory are spontaneous recovery, generalization, discrimination, and higher-order conditioning.

Spontaneous recovery occurs after a time lapse in which the CS is not presented and the CR presumably extinguishes. If the CS then is presented and the CR returns, we say that the CR spontaneously recovered from extinction. A CR that recovers will not endure unless the CS is presented again. Pairings of the CS with the UCS restore the CR to full strength.

Generalization means that the CR occurs to stimuli similar to the CS (Figure 2.2). Once a dog is conditioned to salivate in response to a metronome ticking at 70 beats per minute, it also may salivate in response to a metronome ticking faster or slower, as well as to ticking clocks or timers. The more dissimilar the new stimulus is to the CS, the less generalization occurs.

Discrimination is the complementary process and occurs when the dog learns to respond to the CS but not to other, similar stimuli. To train discrimination, an experimenter might pair the CS with the UCS and also present other, similar stimuli without the UCS. If the CS is a metronome ticking at 70 beats per minute, it is presented with the UCS, whereas other cadences (e.g., 50 and 90 beats per minute) are presented but not paired with the UCS.

Once a stimulus becomes conditioned, it can function as a UCS and *higher-order conditioning* can occur (Pavlov, 1927). If a dog has been conditioned to salivate at the sound of a metronome ticking at 70 beats per minute, the ticking metronome can function as a UCS for higher-order conditioning. A new neutral stimulus (such as a buzzer) can be sounded for a few seconds, followed by the ticking metronome. If, after a few trials, the dog begins to salivate at the sound of the buzzer, the buzzer has become a second-order CS. Conditioning of the third order involves the second-order CS serving as the UCS and a new neutral stimulus being paired with it. Pavlov (1927) reported that conditioning beyond the third order is difficult.

Higher-order conditioning is a complex process that is not well understood (Rescorla, 1972). The concept is theoretically interesting and might help to explain

Figure 2.2
Generalization curve showing decreased magnitude of conditioned response as a function of increased dissimilarity with the conditioned stimulus.

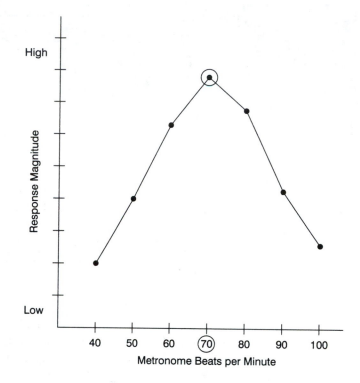

why some social phenomena (e.g., test failure) can cause conditioned emotional reactions such as stress and anxiety. Early in life, failure may be a neutral event. Often it becomes associated with disapproval from parents and teachers. Such disapproval may be an UCS that elicits anxiety. Through conditioning, failure can elicit anxiety. Cues associated with the situation also can become conditioned stimuli. Thus, students may feel anxious when they walk into a room where they will take a test or when a teacher passes out a test.

CSs capable of producing CRs are called *primary signals*. Unlike animals, people have the capacity for speech, which greatly expands the potential for conditioning (Windholz, 1997). Language constitutes the *second signal system*. Words or thoughts are labels denoting events or objects and can become CSs. Thus, thinking about a test or listening to the teacher discuss a forthcoming test may cause anxiety. It is not the test that makes students anxious but rather thoughts about the test; that is, its linguistic representation or meaning. The second signal system also provides information about conditioning variables, as discussed next.

Informational Variables

Pavlov believed that conditioning is an automatic process that occurs with repeated CS-UCS pairings and that repeated nonpairings extinguish the CR. In humans, however, conditioning can occur rapidly, sometimes after only a single CS-UCS pairing.

Repeated nonpairings of the CS and UCS may not extinguish the CR. Extinction seems highly context dependent (Bouton, Nelson, & Rosas, 1999). Reponses stay extinguished in the same context, but when the setting is changed CRs may recur. These findings call into question Pavlov's description of conditioning.

Research subsequent to Pavlov has shown that conditioning depends less on the CS-UCS pairing and more on the extent that the CS conveys information about the likelihood of the UCS occurring (Rescorla, 1972, 1976). As an illustration, assume there are two stimuli: One is always followed by a UCS and the other is sometimes followed by it. The first stimulus should result in conditioning, because it reliably predicts the onset of the UCS (Egger & Miller, 1963). It even may not be necessary to pair the CS and UCS; conditioning can occur by simply telling people that they are related (Brewer, 1974). Likewise, repeated CS-UCS nonpairings may not be necessary for extinction; telling people the contingency is no longer in effect can reduce or extinguish the CR.

An explanation for these results is that people form *expectations* concerning the probability of the UCS occurring (Rescorla, 1987). For a stimulus to become a CS, it must convey information to the individual about the time, place, quantity, and quality of the UCS. Even when a stimulus is predictive, it may not become conditioned if another stimulus is a better predictor. Rather than conditioning being automatic, it appears to be mediated by cognitive processes (Fuhrer & Baer, 1965). If people do not realize there is a CS-UCS link, conditioning does not occur. When no CS-UCS link exists, conditioning can occur if people believe it does. Although this contingency view of conditioning may not be entirely accurate (Papini & Bitterman, 1990), it provides a much different explanation for conditioning than Pavlov's and highlights its complexity.

Biological Influences

Pavlov (1927, 1928) believed that any perceived stimulus can be conditioned to any response that can be made. Subsequent research has shown that the generality of conditioning is limited. Within any species, responses can be conditioned to some stimuli but not to others. Conditioning depends on the compatibility of the stimulus and response with species-specific reactions (Hollis, 1997).

> Behavior is manifested at the juncture between the organism and its niche, and learning is an adjustive process that eases the misfits at that juncture. All organisms inherently possess the basic behavioral patterns that enable them to survive in their niches, but learning provides the fine tuning necessary for successful adaptation. (Garcia & Garcia y Robertson, 1985, p. 197)

An experiment by Garcia and Koelling (1966) with rats demonstrates the importance of biological factors. Some rats drank water accompanied by bright lights and noise (aversive stimulus—bright, noisy water). Rats either were shocked immediately or treated so that they became nauseous some time later. Other rats drank regular (saccharin) water and were either shocked or became nauseous later. Bright, noisy water plus shock led to a conditioned aversion to the water, but bright, noisy water plus nausea did not. Regular (saccharin) water plus nausea led to an aversion to the water, but regular water plus shock did not. The shock (an external event) was easily associated with the bright lights and noise (external cues) but not nausea (an internal event). Nausea became a CR to an internal stimulus (taste). Although the interval between drinking the water and nausea (an hour) was too long to satisfy a classical conditioning model, the results support the complexity of classical conditioning by suggesting that rats have developed an evolutionary mechanism to guard against taste aversions. In general, it appears that conditioning may occur only if stimuli somehow "belong" together and thus the process may serve to help animals adapt to their environments (Hollis, 1997).

Conditioned Emotional Reactions

Pavlov (1932a, 1934) applied classical conditioning principles to abnormal behavior and discussed how neuroses and other pathological states might develop. His views were speculative and unsubstantiated, but classical conditioning principles have been applied by others to dysfunctional behavior. A notable example is systematic desensitization, which is often used with individuals who possess debilitating fears (Wolpe, 1958) (Application 2.3).

Desensitization comprises three phases. In the first phase, therapist and client jointly develop an anxiety hierarchy of several situations graded from least-to-most anxiety-producing for the client. For a test-anxious student, low-anxiety situations might be hearing a test announcement in class and gathering together materials to study. Situations of moderate anxiety might be studying the night before the test and walking into class on the day of the test. High-anxiety situations could include receiving a copy of the test in class and not knowing the answer to a test question.

In the second phase, the client learns to relax by imagining pleasant scenes (e.g., lying on a beach) and cuing relaxation (saying "relax"). In the third phase, the client, while relaxed, imagines the lowest (least-anxious) scene on the hierarchy. This may be repeated several times, after which the client imagines the next scene. Treatment proceeds up the hierarchy until the client can imagine the most anxiety-producing scene without feeling anxious. If the client reports anxiety while imagining a scene, the client drops back down the hierarchy to a scene that does not produce anxiety. Treatment may need to span several sessions.

Desensitization involves counterconditioning. The relaxing scenes that one imagines (UCS) produce relaxation (UCR). Anxiety-producing cues (CS) are paired with the relaxing scenes. Relaxation is incompatible with anxiety. By initially pairing a weak anxiety cue with relaxation and by slowly working up the hierarchy, all of the anxiety-producing cues eventually should elicit relaxation (CR). Desensitization is an effective procedure that can be accomplished in a therapist's or counselor's office. It does not require the client to perform the activities on the hierarchy. A disadvantage is that the client must be able to imagine scenes. People differ in their ability to form mental images. Desensitization also requires the skill of a professional therapist or counselor and should not be attempted by anyone unskilled in its application.

APPLICATION 2.3
Emotional Conditioning

Principles of classical conditioning are relevant to some dysfunctional behaviors.

Children entering kindergarten or first grade may possess fears related to the new experiences. At the beginning of the school year, primary teachers might develop procedures to desensitize some of the children's initial fears. Teachers could plan preschool visitation sessions giving students the opportunity to meet their teacher and other students and to see their classroom and the seat with their name on it. On the first few days of school, the teacher might plan fun but relatively calm activities involving students getting to know their teacher, classmates, room, and school building. Students could tour the building, return to their room, and draw pictures. They might talk about what they saw. Students can be taken to offices to meet the principal, assistant principal, nurse, and counselor. They also could play name games in which they introduce themselves and then try to recall names of classmates.

These activities represent an informal desensitization procedure. For some children, cues associated with the school serve as stimuli eliciting anxiety. The fun activities elicit pleasurable feelings, which are incompatible with anxiety. Pairing fun activities with cues associated with school may cause the latter to become less anxiety producing.

Some education students may have anxieties about actually teaching complete lessons in front of an entire class. Anxieties should be lessened when students spend time in actual classrooms and gradually assume more responsibility for class instruction. Pairing these actual classroom and teaching experiences with formal study can desensitize fears related to being responsible for the learning of a classroom of children.

Some drama students have extreme problems with stage fright. Drama teachers may work with students to lessen these anxieties by practicing more on the actual stage and by opening up rehearsals to allow others to watch. Exposure to performing in front of others should help diminish some of the fears.

WATSON'S BEHAVIORISM

No historical account of learning would be complete without mention of John B. Watson (1878–1958), who generally is considered to be the founder and champion of modern behaviorism (Heidbreder, 1933; Hunt, 1993). Watson believed that schools of thought (e.g., functionalism) and research methods (e.g., introspection) that dealt with the mind were unscientific. If psychology were to become a science, it had to structure itself along the lines of the physical sciences, which examine observable and measurable phenomena. Behavior is the proper material for psychologists to study. Consciousness should not be studied through introspection because it is unreliable. Conscious experiences are not observable and people having such experiences could not be trusted to report them accurately (Murray, Kilgour, & Wasylkiw, 2000). As Watson contended:

> Psychology, as the behaviorist views it, is a purely objective, experimental branch of natural science which needs introspection as little as do the sciences of chemistry and physics. It is granted that the behavior of animals can be investigated without appeal to consciousness. . . . The position is taken here that the behavior of man and the behavior of animals must be considered on the same plane; as being equally essential to a general understanding of behavior. It can dispense with consciousness in a psychological sense. (Watson, 1914, p. 27)

Functionalism was similarly rejected because it dealt with consciousness. Thorndike's satisfiers and annoyers had no place in psychology because they were subjective mental concepts that were unobservable and unmeasurable (Watson, 1919). Watson considered thinking to be nothing more than talking to oneself (Watson, 1924; Watson & MacDougall, 1929). Thought without language was impossible (Murray et al., 2000).

Basic Processes

Watson (1916) thought that Pavlov's conditioning model was appropriate for building a science of human behavior. He was impressed with Pavlov's precise measurement of observable behaviors. Watson believed that Pavlov's model could be extended to account for diverse forms of learning and personality characteristics.

For example, newborns are capable of displaying three emotions: love, fear, and rage (Watson, 1926a). Through Pavlovian conditioning, these emotions become attached to stimuli to produce a complex adult emotional life. Fear in infants can arise from loud noises and loss of maternal support. Through pairing with UCSs, objects and places become CSs. Children who become separated from their parents in the woods might develop a conditioned fear of the woods. Higher-order conditioning can produce additional CRs. Watson (1926b) noted:

> Give me a dozen healthy infants, well-formed, and my own specified world to bring them up in and I'll guarantee to take any one at random and train him to become any type of specialist I might select—a doctor, lawyer, artist, merchant-chief and, yes, even into beggar-man and thief, regardless of his talents, penchants, tendencies, abilities, vocations and race of his ancestors. (p. 10)

Little Albert Experiment

Watson claimed to demonstrate the power of conditioning in the famous Little Albert experiment (Watson & Rayner, 1920). Albert was an 11-month-old infant who showed no fear of a white rat. During conditioning, a hammer was struck against a steel bar behind Albert as he reached out for the rat. "The infant jumped violently and fell forward, burying his face in the mattress" (p. 4). This sequence was immediately repeated. One week later when the rat was presented, Albert began to reach out but then withdrew his hand. The previous week's conditioning was apparent. During the second session, the rat and loud noise were paired several times, after which the rat was presented alone.

> The instant the rat was shown the baby began to cry. Almost instantly he turned sharply to the left, fell over on left side, raised himself on all fours and began to crawl away so rapidly that he was caught with difficulty before reaching the edge of the table. (Watson & Rayner, 1920, p. 5)

Tests over the next few days showed that Albert reacted emotionally to the rat's presence. There also was generalization of fear to a rabbit, dog, and fur coat. When Albert was retested a month later with the rat he showed a mild emotional reaction.

This study is widely cited as showing how conditioning can produce emotional reactions, but the influence of conditioning usually is not that powerful (Harris, 1979). As we saw in the preceding section, classical conditioning is a complex phenomenon; one cannot condition any response to any stimulus. Species have evolved mechanisms predisposing them to being conditioned in some ways and not in others (Hollis, 1997). Among humans, conditioning occurs when people are aware of the relation between the CS and the UCS, and information that the UCS may not follow the CS can produce extinction. Attempts to replicate Watson and Rayner's findings were not uniformly successful. Valentine (1930a), for example, found no evidence of conditioning when he used objects as the CS instead of animals.

Although Watson's research has little relevance for academic learning, he was an important figure. He spoke and wrote with conviction, and his adamant stance on behaviorism predominated psychology from around 1920 until the early 1960s (Hunt, 1993). His emphasis on the importance of the environment is readily seen in the ensuing work of Skinner (discussed later in this chapter) (Horowitz, 1992).

CONTIGUOUS CONDITIONING

Another individual who advanced a behavioral perspective on learning was Edwin R. Guthrie (1886–1959). Guthrie (1940) postulated learning principles that reflected associationism, and, like Watson, believed that a science of human behavior must be based on observable phenomena:

> The ability to learn . . . is what distinguishes those living creatures which common sense endows with minds. This is the practical descriptive use of the term "mind." Another use, the theological or mythological notion of mind as a substance, as a mysterious hidden cause of action, we may dismiss at once. Our interest is scientific, and we are dealing only with observable features of the world about us. (Guthrie, 1952, p. 3)

Acts and Movements

Guthrie's basic principle reflects the idea of *contiguity of stimuli and responses*:

> A combination of stimuli which has accomplished a movement will on its recurrence tend to be followed by that movement. (Guthrie, 1952, p. 23)

And alternatively,

> Stimulus patterns which are active at the time of a response tend, on being repeated, to elicit that response. (Guthrie, 1938, p. 37)

Movements are discrete behaviors that result from muscle contractions. Guthrie distinguished movements from *acts*, or large-scale classes of movements that produce an outcome. Playing the piano and writing with a pencil are acts that include many movements. A particular act may be accompanied by a variety of movements; the act may not specify the movements precisely. In basketball, for example, shooting a basket (an act) can be accomplished with a variety of movements.

Contiguity learning implies that performance of a behavior in a situation will be repeated when that situation recurs (Guthrie, 1959). Yet, contiguity learning is selective. At any given moment, a person is confronted with many stimuli, and associations cannot be made to all of them. Rather, only a small number of stimuli are selected, and associations are formed between them and responses. The contiguity principle also applies to memory. Verbal cues are associated with stimulus conditions or events at the time of learning (Guthrie, 1952). *Forgetting* involves new learning and is due to interference in which an alternative response is made to an old stimulus.

Associative Strength

Guthrie's basic principle was that learning occurs through pairing of stimulus and response. Guthrie (1942) postulated a second important principle, *associative strength*:

> A stimulus pattern gains its full associative strength on the occasion of its first pairing with a response. (p. 30)

He rejected the notion of associationism through frequency, as embodied in Thorndike's original Law of Exercise (Guthrie, 1930). Although Guthrie did not suggest that people learn complex behaviors by performing them once, he believed that on the first trial one or more movements become associated. Repetition of a situation adds movements, combines movements into acts, and establishes the act under different environmental conditions: "It appears that practice is necessary to the extent that the response must be elicitable from a variety of situations" (Guthrie, 1942, p. 32).

The Guthrie and Horton (1946) experiment with cats was interpreted as supporting this *all-or-none* principle of learning. Guthrie and Horton used a puzzle box similar to Thorndike's. Touching a post in the center triggered the mechanism that sprang open the door, allowing the cat to escape. When cats initially were placed in the box, they explored it and made a series of random movements. Eventually they made a response that released the mechanism and they escaped. Some cats hit the post with a paw; others brushed against it; others backed into it. The cat's last response (hitting the pole) was successful because it opened the door, and cats repeated their last response when put back into the box. The last movement became associated with the puzzle box, because it allowed the animal to escape.

Guthrie's position does not imply that once students successfully solve a long-division problem or balance a chemical equation they have mastered the requisite skills. Practice links the various movements involved in the acts of solving problems and balancing equations. The acts themselves may have many variations (types of problems and equations), and ideally should transfer—students should be able to solve problems and balance equations in different contexts. Guthrie accepted Thorndike's notion of identical elements. To produce transfer, behaviors should be practiced in the exact situations in which they will be called for, such as at the board, at desks, in small groups, and at home.

Rewards and Punishments

Guthrie believed that responses do not need to be rewarded to be learned. The key mechanism is *contiguity*, or close pairing in time between stimulus and response. The response does not have to be satisfying; a pairing without consequences could lead to learning.

> The future response to a situation can be best predicted in terms of what an animal has done in that situation in the past. Stimuli acting during a response tend on later occasions to evoke that response. (Guthrie, 1952, p. 127)

Guthrie (1952) disputed Thorndike's Law of Effect because satisfiers and annoyers are effects of actions; therefore, they cannot influence learning of previous connections but only subsequent ones. Rewards might help to prevent *unlearning* (forgetting) because they thwart new responses from being associated with stimulus cues. In the Guthrie and Horton (1946) experiment, the reward (escape from the box) took the animal out of the learning context and prevented acquisition of new associations to the box. Similarly, punishment will produce unlearning only if it causes the animal to learn something else.

Contiguity is a central feature of school learning. Flashcards help students learn arithmetic facts. Students learn to associate a stimulus (e.g., 4×4) with a response (16). Foreign-language words are associated with their English equivalents. In German, students study "das Buch" along with its English translation, "the book."

As an example of how rewards might prevent unlearning, consider a student who responds "16" to the flashcard "$4 \times 4 =$" and is rewarded (teacher says "Good"). The next time the student is presented with the same flashcard, the student is apt to reply "16"; the praise prevented formation of new associations to the flashcard.

Habit Formation and Change

Habits are simply behaviors established to many cues:

> The chief difficulty in the way of avoiding a bad habit is that the responsible cues are often hard to find, and that in many bad habit systems they are extremely numerous.

> Each rehearsal is responsible for a possible addition of one or more cues which tend to set off the undesired action. (Guthrie, 1952, p. 116)

Teachers who want students to behave well in school should link school rules with many cues. "Treat others with respect," needs to be linked with the classroom, computer lab, halls, cafeteria, gymnasium, auditorium, and playground. By applying this rule in each of these settings, students' respectful behaviors toward others become habitual. If students believe they only have to practice respect in the classroom, respecting others will not become a habit.

Guthrie (1952) wrote that the key to changing behavior is to "[f]ind the cues that initiate the action and to practice another response to these cues" (p. 115). Guthrie identified three methods for altering habits: the threshold, fatigue, and incompatible response methods (Table 2.2). Although these methods appear distinct on the surface, they all present cues for an habitual action but arrange for it not to be performed (Application 2.4).

In the *threshold* method, the cue (stimulus) for the habit to be changed (the undesired response) is introduced at such a weak level that it does not elicit the response; it is below the threshold level of the response. Gradually the stimulus is introduced at greater intensity until it is presented at full strength. Were the stimulus introduced at its greatest intensity, the response would be the behavior that is to be changed (the habit). For example, some children react to the taste of spinach by refusing to eat it. To alter this habit, parents might introduce spinach in small bites or mixed with a food that the child enjoys. Over time, the amount of spinach the child eats can be increased.

Table 2.2
Guthrie's methods for breaking habits.

Method	Explanation	Example
Threshold	Introduce weak stimulus. Increase stimulus, but keep it below threshold value that will produce unwanted response.	Introduce academic content in short blocks of time for children. Gradually increase session length, but not to a point where students become frustrated or bored.
Fatigue	Force child to make unwanted response repeatedly in presence of stimulus.	Give child who makes paper airplanes in class stack of paper and have child make each sheet into a plane.
Incompatible response	In presence of stimulus, have child make response incompatible with unwanted response.	Pair cues associated with media center with reading rather than talking.

APPLICATION 2.4
Breaking Habits

Guthrie's contiguity principle offers practical suggestions for how to break habits.

One application of the threshold method involves the time young children spend on academic activities. Young children have short atttention spans, so the length of time they can sustain work on one activity is limited. Most activities are scheduled to last no longer than 30–40 minutes. However, at the start of the school year, attention spans quickly wane and behavior problems often result. To apply Guthrie's theory, a teacher might, at the start of the year, limit activities to 15–20 minutes. Over the next few weeks the teacher could gradually increase the time students spend working on a single activity.

The threshold method also can be applied to teaching printing and handwriting. When children first learn to form letters, their movements are awkward and they lack fine motor coordination. The distances between lines on a page are purposely wide so children can fit the letters into the space. If paper with narrow lines is initially introduced, students' letters would spill over the borders and students might become frustrated. Once students can form letters within the larger borders, they can use paper with smaller borders to help them refine their skills.

The fatigue method can be applied when disciplining disruptive students who build paper airplanes and sail them across the room. The teacher can remove the students from the classroom, give them a large stack of paper, and tell them to start making paper airplanes. After the students have made several airplanes, the activity should lose its attraction and paper will become a cue for not building airplanes.

Some students continually race around the gym when they first enter their physical education class. To employ the fatigue method, the teacher might decide to have these students continue to run a few more laps after the class has begun.

The incompatible response method can be used with students who talk and misbehave in the media center. Reading is incompatible with talking. The media center teacher might ask the students to find interesting books and read them while in the center. Assuming that the students find the books enjoyable, the media center will, over time, become a cue for selecting and reading books rather than for talking with other students.

A social studies teacher has some students who regularly fall asleep in class. The teacher realized that using the board and overhead projector while lecturing was very boring. Soon the teacher began to incorporate other elements into each lesson, such as experiments, videotapes, and debates, in an attempt to involve students and raise their interest in the course.

In the *fatigue* method, the cue for engaging in the behavior is transformed into a cue for avoiding it. Here the stimulus is introduced at full strength and the individual performs the undesired response until he or she becomes exhausted. The stimulus becomes a cue for not performing the response. To alter a child's behavior of repeatedly throwing toys, parents might make the child throw toys until it is no longer fun.

In the *incompatible response* method, the cue for the undesired behavior is paired with a response incompatible with the undesired response; that is, the two responses cannot be performed simultaneously. The response to be paired with the cue must be more attractive to the individual than the undesired response. The stimulus becomes a cue for performing the alternate response. To stop snacking while watching TV, people should keep their hands busy (e.g., sew, paint, work crossword puzzles). Over time, watching TV becomes a cue for engaging in an activity other than snacking. Systematic desensitization (described earlier) also utilizes incompatible responses.

Guthrie (1952) believed that punishment is ineffective in altering habits. Punishment following a response cannot affect the stimulus-response association. Punishment given while a behavior is being performed may disrupt or suppress the habit but not change it. Punishment does not establish an alternate response to the stimulus. The threat of punishment even can prove to be exciting and bolster the habit. It is better to alter negative habits by replacing them with desirable ones (i.e., incompatible responses).

OPERANT CONDITIONING

Operant conditioning is a behavioristic theory formulated by B. F. (Burrhus Frederic) Skinner (1904–1990). Beginning in the 1930s, Skinner published a series of papers reporting results of laboratory studies with animals in which he identified the various components of operant conditioning. He summarized much of this early work in his influential book, *The Behavior of Organisms* (1938).

Skinner applied his ideas to many human problems. Early in his career he became interested in education and developed teaching machines and programmed instruction. *The Technology of Teaching* (Skinner, 1968) addresses such topics as instruction, motivation, discipline, and creativity. In 1948, after a difficult period in his life, he published *Walden Two*, which describes how behavioral principles can be applied to create a utopian society. Skinner (1971) addressed the problems of modern life and advocated applying a behavioral technology to the design of cultures in *Beyond Freedom and Dignity*. Skinner and others have applied operant conditioning principles to such domains as school learning and discipline, child development, social behaviors, mental illness, medical problems, substance abuse, and vocational training (DeGrandpre, 2000; Karoly & Harris, 1986).

As a young man, Skinner aspired to be a writer (Skinner, 1970):

> I built a small study in the attic and set to work. The results were disastrous. I frittered away my time. I read aimlessly, built model ships, played the piano, listened to the newly-invented radio, contributed to the humorous column of a local paper but wrote almost nothing else, and thought about seeing a psychiatrist. (p. 6)

He became interested in psychology after reading Pavlov's (1927) *Conditioned Reflexes* and Watson's (1924) *Behaviorism*. His subsequent career made a profound impact on the psychology of learning.

Despite his admission that "I had failed as a writer because I had had nothing important to say" (Skinner, 1970, p. 7), he was a prolific writer who channeled his literary aspirations into scientific writing that spanned six decades (Lattal, 1992). His dedication to his profession is evident in his giving an invited address at the American Psychological Association convention 8 days before his death (Holland, 1992; Skinner, 1990). The Association honored him with a special issue of its monthly journal *American Psychologist* (American Psychological Association, 1992). Although his theory largely has been disputed by current cognitive accounts of learning, his influence continues as behavioral principles are commonly applied to enhance student learning and behavior.

Conceptual Framework

This section discusses the assumptions underlying operant conditioning, how it reflects a functional analysis of behavior, and the implications of the theory for the prediction and control of behavior. The theory and principles of operant conditioning are complex (Dragoi & Staddon, 1999); those points most relevant to human learning are covered in this chapter.

Scientific Assumptions.   Pavlov traced the locus of learning to the nervous system and viewed behavior as a manifestation of neurological functioning. Skinner (1938) did not deny that neurological functioning accompanies behavior, but he believed a psychology of behavior can be understood in its own terms without reference to neurological or other internal events.

Skinner raised similar objections to modern cognitive views of learning that emphasize how people mentally process information. *Private events*, or responses made "within the organism's own skin," are accessible only to the individual and can be studied through people's verbal reports, which are forms of behavior (Skinner, 1953). Skinner did not deny the existence of attitudes, beliefs, opinions, desires, and other forms of self-knowledge, but rather qualified the role of these inner realities in a science of human behavior:

> A behavioristic analysis does not question the practical usefulness of reports of the inner world that is felt and introspectively observed. They are clues (1) to past behavior and the conditions affecting it, (2) to current behavior and the conditions affecting it, and (3) to conditions related to future behavior. Nevertheless, the private world within the skin is not clearly observed or known. (Skinner, 1974, p. 31)

Skinner (1987) contended that people do not experience consciousness or emotions but rather their own bodies and that internal reactions are responses to internal stimuli. A further problem with internal processes is that translating them into language is difficult, because language does not completely capture the dimensions of an internal experience (e.g., pain). Much of what is called *knowing* involves using language (verbal behavior). Thoughts are types of behavior that are brought about by other stimuli (environmental or private) and that give rise to responses (overt or covert). When private events are expressed as overt behaviors, behaviorists can determine their role in a functional analysis.

Functional Analysis of Behavior.   Skinner (1953) referred to his means of examining behavior as a functional analysis:

> The external variables of which behavior is a function provide for what may be called a causal or functional analysis. We undertake to predict and control the behavior of the individual organism. This is our "dependent variable"—the effect for which we are to find the cause. Our "independent variables"—the causes of behavior—are the external conditions of which behavior is a function. Relations between the two—the "cause-and-effect relationships" in behavior—are the laws of a science. A synthesis of these laws expressed in quantitative terms yields a comprehensive picture of the organism as a behaving system. (p. 35)

Learning is "the reassortment of responses in a complex situation"; *conditioning* refers to "the strengthening of behavior which results from reinforcement" (Skinner, 1953, p. 65). There are two types of conditioning: Type S and Type R. *Type S* is Pavlovian conditioning, characterized by the pairing of the reinforcing (unconditioned) stimulus with another (conditioned) stimulus. The S calls attention to the importance of the stimulus in eliciting a response from the organism. The response made to the eliciting stimulus is known as *respondent behavior.*

Although Type S conditioning explains conditioned emotional reactions, most human behaviors are emitted in the presence of stimuli rather than automatically elicited by them. Responses are controlled by their consequences, not by antecedent stimuli. This type of behavior, which Skinner termed *Type R* to emphasize the response aspect, is *operant behavior* because it operates on the environment to produce an effect.

> If the occurrence of an operant is followed by presentation of a reinforcing stimulus, the strength is increased. . . . If the occurrence of an operant already strengthened through conditioning is not followed by the reinforcing stimulus, the strength is decreased. (Skinner, 1938, p. 21)

Unlike respondent behavior, which prior to conditioning does not occur, the probability of occurrence of an operant is never zero because the response must be made for reinforcement to be provided. Reinforcement changes the likelihood or rate of occurrence of the response. Operants act upon their environment and become more or less likely to occur because of reinforcement.

Basic Processes

This section examines the basic processes in operant conditioning: reinforcement, extinction, primary and secondary reinforcers, the Premack Principle, punishment, schedules of reinforcement, generalization, and discrimination.

Reinforcement.   *Reinforcement* is responsible for response strengthening—increasing the rate of responding or making responses more likely to occur. A reinforcer (or *reinforcing stimulus*) is any stimulus or event following a response that leads to response strengthening. Reinforcers cannot be determined in advance but rather are defined by their effects (Skinner, 1953):

> The only way to tell whether or not a given event is reinforcing to a given organism under given conditions is to make a direct test. We observe the frequency of a selected response, then make an event contingent upon it and observe any change in frequency. If there is a change, we classify the event as reinforcing to the organism under the existing conditions. (pp. 72–73)

Reinforcers are situationally specific: They apply to individuals at given times under given conditions. What is reinforcing to a particular student during reading now may not be during mathematics now or during reading later. Despite this specificity, stimuli or events that reinforce behavior can, to some extent, be predicted (Skinner, 1953):

> We achieve a certain success in guessing at reinforcing powers only because we have in a sense made a crude survey; we have gauged the reinforcing effect of a stimulus upon ourselves and assume the same effect upon others. We are successful only when we resemble the organism under study and when we have correctly surveyed our own behavior. (p. 73)

Students typically find reinforcing such events as teacher praise, free time, privileges, stickers, and high grades. Nonetheless, one never can know for certain whether a consequence is reinforcing until it is presented after a response and we see whether behavior changes.

The basic operant model of conditioning is the *three-term contingency*:

$$S^D \rightarrow R \rightarrow S^R$$

A *discriminative stimulus* (S^D) sets the occasion for a response (R) to be emitted, which is followed by a *reinforcing stimulus* (S^R, or *reinforcement*). The reinforcing stimulus is any stimulus (event, consequence) that increases the probability the response will be emitted in the future when the discriminative stimulus is present. In more-familiar terms, we might label this the A-B-C model:

$$A \text{ (Antecedent)} \rightarrow B \text{ (Behavior)} \rightarrow C \text{ (Consequence)}$$

Positive reinforcement involves presenting a stimulus, or adding something to a situation, following a response, which increases the future likelihood of that response occurring in that situation. A *positive reinforcer* is a stimulus that, when presented following a response, increases the future likelihood of the response occurring in that situation.

Negative reinforcement involves removing a stimulus, or taking something away from a situation following a response, which increases the future likelihood that the response will occur in that situation. A *negative reinforcer* is a stimulus that, when removed by a response, increases the future likelihood of the response occurring in

Table 2.3
Reinforcement and punishment processes.

$S^D \rightarrow$	$R \rightarrow$	S^R
Discriminative Stimulus	Response	Reinforcing (Punishing) Stimulus
Positive Reinforcement (Present positive reinforcer)		
T gives independent study time	L studies*	T praises L for good work
Negative Reinforcement (Remove negative reinforcer)		
T gives independent study time	L studies	T says L does not have to do homework
Punishment (Present negative reinforcer)		
T gives independent study time	L wastes time	T gives homework
Punishment (Remove positive reinforcer)		
T gives independent study time	L wastes time	T says L will miss free time

*T refers to teacher and L to learner.

that situation. Some stimuli that often function as negative reinforcers are bright lights, loud noise, criticism, annoying people, and low grades. Positive and negative reinforcement have the same effect: They increase the future probability of the response (Table 2.3).

Assume that a teacher is holding a question-and-answer session with the class. The teacher asks a question (S^D), calls on a student volunteer who gives the correct answer (R), and praises the student (S^R). If student volunteering increases or remains at a high level, praise is a positive reinforcer and this is an example of positive reinforcement. Now assume that after a student gives the correct answer the teacher tells the student he or she does not need to do the homework assignment. If student volunteering increases or remains at a high level, the homework is a negative reinforcer and this is an example of negative reinforcement. Application 2.5 gives other examples of positive and negative reinforcement.

Extinction. *Extinction* involves the decline of response strength due to nonreinforcement. Students who raise their hands in class but never get called on may stop raising their hands. People who send many e-mail messages to the same individual but never receive a reply may eventually quit sending messages to that person.

How rapidly extinction occurs depends on the *reinforcement history* (Skinner, 1953). Extinction occurs quickly if few preceding responses have been reinforced. Responding is much more durable with a lengthier history of reinforcement. Extinction is not the same as *forgetting*. Responses that extinguish can be performed but

APPLICATION 2.5
Positive and Negative Reinforcement

Teachers can use positive and negative reinforcement as motivators to increase students' mastery of skills and time on task. For example, in teaching concepts in a science unit a teacher might ask students to complete questions at the end of the chapter. The teacher also might set up activity centers around the room that involve hands-on experiments related to the lesson. Students would circulate and complete the experiments contingent on their successfully answering the chapter questions (positive reinforcement). This contingency reflects the Premack Principle of providing the opportunity to engage in a more-valued activity (experiments) as a reinforcer for engaging in a less-valued one (completing chapter questions). Students who complete 80% of the questions correctly and who participate in a minimum of two experiments do not have to complete homework. This would function as negative reinforcement to the extent that students perceive homework as a negative reinforcer.

A middle school counselor working with a student on improving classroom behavior could have each of the student's teachers check "yes" or "no" as it relates to class behavior for that day (acceptable, unacceptable). For each "yes" the student receives 1 minute in the computer lab to play computer games (positive reinforcement for this student). At the end of the week the student can use the earned computer time following lunch. Further, if the student earns a minimum of 15 minutes in the lab, he or she does not have to take a behavior note home to be signed by parents (this assumes the student considers taking a behavior note home a negative reinforcer).

are not because of lack of reinforcement. In the preceding examples, the students still know how to raise their hands and the people still know how to send e-mail messages. Forgetting involves a true loss of conditioning over time in which the opportunities for responding have not been present.

Primary and Secondary Reinforcers.   Stimuli such as food, water, and shelter are called *primary reinforcers* because they are necessary for survival. *Secondary reinforcers* are stimuli that become conditioned through their association with primary reinforcers. A child's favorite milk glass becomes secondarily reinforcing through its association with milk (a primary reinforcer). A secondary reinforcer that becomes paired with more than one primary reinforcer is a generalized reinforcer. People work long hours to earn money (a generalized reinforcer), which they use to buy food and pay for housing and utilities.

Operant conditioning explains the development and maintenance of much social behavior with *generalized reinforcers*. Children may behave in ways to draw adults' attention. Attention is reinforcing because it is paired with primary reinforcers from adults (e.g., food, water, protection). Important educational generalized reinforcers are teachers' praise, high grades, privileges, honors, and degrees. These reinforcers often are paired with other generalized reinforcers, such as approval (from parents and friends) and money (a college degree leads to a good job).

Premack Principle.   Recall from earlier that we label a behavioral consequence as reinforcing only after we apply it and see how it affects future behavior. It is somewhat troubling that we must use common sense or trial and error in choosing reinforcers because we cannot know for certain in advance whether a consequence will function as a reinforcer.

Premack (1962, 1971) described a means for ordering reinforcers that allows one to predict reinforcers. The *Premack Principle* says that the opportunity to engage in a more-valued activity reinforces engaging in a less-valued activity, where "value" is defined in terms of the amount of responding or time spent on the activity in the absence of reinforcement. If a contingency is arranged such that the value of the second (contingent) event is higher than the value of the first (instrumental) event, an increase will be expected in the probability of occurrence of the first event (the reward assumption). If the value of the second event is lower than that of the first event, the likelihood of occurrence of the first event ought to decrease (the punishment assumption).

Suppose that a child is allowed to choose between working on an art project, going to the media center, reading a book in the classroom, or working at the computer. Over the course of 10 such choices the child goes to the media center 6 times, works at the computer 3 times, works on an art project 1 time, and never reads a book in the classroom. For this child, the opportunity to go to the media center is valued the most and should be an effective reinforcer for reading a book in the classroom. Considerable empirical evidence supports Premack's ideas, especially with respect to the reward assumption (Dunham, 1977).

The Premack Principle offers guidance for selecting effective reinforcers: Observe what people do when they have a choice, and order those behaviors in terms of likelihood. The order is not permanent, since the value of reinforcers can change. Any reinforcer, when applied often, can result in *satiation* and lead to decreased responding. Teachers who employ the Premack Principle need periodically to check students' preferences by observing them and asking what they like to do. Determining in advance which reinforcers are likely to be effective in a situation is critical in planning a program of behavioral change (Timberlake & Farmer-Dougan, 1991). The Premack Principle has proven to be most useful in this regard.

Punishment.   *Punishment* decreases the future likelihood of responding to a stimulus. Punishment may involve withdrawing a positive reinforcer or presenting a negative reinforcer following a response, as shown in Table 2.3. Assume that during a question-and-answer session a student repeatedly bothers another student when the teacher is not watching (teacher not watching = S^D; misbehavior = R). The teacher spots the misbehavior and says, "Stop bothering him" (S^R). If the student quits bothering the other student, the teacher's criticism operates as a negative re-inforcer. This is punishment for the student and negative reinforcement for the teacher (because the teacher's response stopped the misbehavior). Since the teacher's response was effective, the teacher is likely to repeat it in the future.

Instead of criticizing the student, assume that the teacher says, "You'll have to stay inside during recess today." If the student's misbehavior stops, recess operates as a positive reinforcer; its loss is punishing to the student and the cessation of student misbehavior is negatively reinforcing for the teacher.

Punishment *suppresses* a response but does not eliminate it; when the threat of punishment is removed, the punished response may return. The effects of punishment are complex. Punishment often brings about responses that are incompatible with the punished behavior and that are strong enough to suppress it (Skinner, 1953). Spanking a child for misbehaving may produce guilt and fear, which can suppress misbehavior. If the child misbehaves in the future, the conditioned guilt and fear may reappear and lead the child quickly to stop misbehaving. Punishment also conditions responses that lead one to escape or avoid punishment. Students whose teacher criticizes incorrect answers soon learn to avoid volunteering answers. Punishment can condition maladaptive behaviors, because punishment does not teach how to behave more productively. Punishment can further hinder learning by creating a conflict such that the individual vacillates between responding one way or another. If the teacher sometimes criticizes students for incorrect answers and sometimes does not, students never know when criticism is forthcoming. Such variable behavior can have emotional by-products—fear, anger, crying—that interfere with learning.

Punishment is used often in schools to deal with disruptions. Common punishments are loss of privileges, removals from the classroom, restitutions, in- and out-of-school suspensions, and expulsions (Maag, 2001). Yet there are several alternatives to punishment (Table 2.4). One is to *change the discriminative stimuli* for negative behavior. For example, a student seated in the back of the room may misbehave often. Teachers can change the discriminative stimuli by moving the disruptive student to the front of the class. Another alternative is to *allow the unwanted*

Table 2.4
Alternatives to punishment.

Alternative	Example
Change the discriminative stimuli	Move misbehaving student away from other misbehaving students.
Allow the unwanted behavior to continue	Have student who stands when he or she should be sitting continue to stand.
Extinguish the unwanted behavior	Ignore minor misbehavior so that it is not reinforced by teacher attention.
Condition an incompatible behavior	Reinforce learning progress, which occurs only when student is not misbehaving.

behavior to continue until the perpetrator becomes satiated, which is similar to Guthrie's fatigue method. A parent may allow a child throwing a tantrum to continue to throw it until he or she becomes fatigued. A third alternative is to *extinguish an unwanted behavior* by ignoring it. This may work well with minor misbehaviors (e.g., students whispering to one another), but when classrooms become disruptive, teachers need to act in other ways. A fourth alternative is to *condition incompatible behavior* with positive reinforcement. Teacher praise for productive work habits helps condition those habits. The primary advantage of this alternative over punishment is that it shows the student how to behave adaptively.

Schedules of Reinforcement.   Schedules refer to when reinforcement is applied (Ferster & Skinner, 1957; Skinner, 1938; Zeiler, 1977). A *continuous schedule* involves reinforcement for every correct response. This may be desirable while skills are being acquired: Students receive feedback after each response concerning the accuracy of their work. Continuous reinforcement helps to ensure that incorrect responses are not learned.

An *intermittent schedule* involves reinforcement for some but not all correct responses. This is common in classrooms, because it is impossible for teachers to reinforce each student for every correct or desirable response. Students are not called on every time they raise their hands, are not praised after working each problem, and are not constantly told they are behaving appropriately.

Intermittent schedules are defined in terms of time or number of responses. An *interval schedule* involves reinforcing the first correct response after a specific time period. In a *fixed-interval (FI) schedule*, the time interval is constant from one reinforcement to the next. An FI5 schedule means that reinforcement is delivered for the first response made after 5 minutes. Students who receive 30 minutes of free time every Friday (contingent on good behavior during the week) are operating under a fixed-interval schedule. In a *variable-interval (VI) schedule*, the time interval varies from occasion to occasion around some average value. A VI5 schedule means that on the average, the first correct response after 5 minutes is reinforced, but the time interval varies from trial to trial (e.g., 2, 3, 7, or 8 minutes). Students who receive 30 minutes of free time (contingent on good behavior) on an average of once a week, but not necessarily on the same day each week, are operating under a variable-interval schedule.

A *ratio schedule* depends on the number of correct responses or rate of responding. In a *fixed-ratio (FR) schedule*, every *n*th correct response is reinforced, where *n* is constant from trial to trial. An FR10 schedule means that every 10th correct response receives reinforcement. In a *variable-ratio (VR) schedule*, every *n*th correct response is reinforced, but the value varies from trial to trial around an average number *n*. A teacher may give free time after every fifth workbook assignment is completed (FR5) or periodically around an average of five completed assignments (VR5).

Reinforcement schedules produce characteristic patterns of responding, as shown in Figure 2.3. In general, ratio schedules produce higher rates than interval schedules. A limiting factor in ratio schedules is fatigue due to rapid responding. Fixed-interval schedules produce a scalloped pattern. Responding drops off immediately after reinforcement but picks up toward the end of the interval between re-

Figure 2.3
Patterns of responding under different reinforcement schedules.
Note: VR = variable ratio; FR = fixed ratio; FI = fixed interval; VI = variable interval.

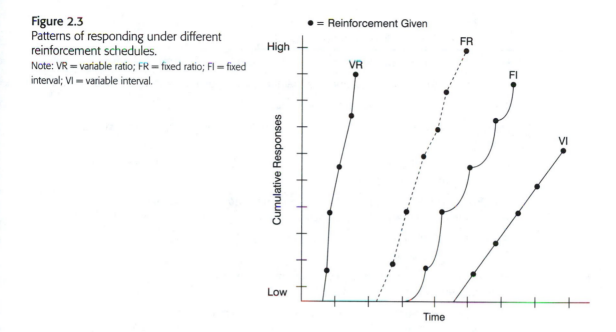

inforcements. The variable-interval schedule produces a steady rate of responding. Unannounced quizzes operate on variable-interval schedules and typically keep students studying regularly. Intermittent schedules are more resistant to extinction than continuous schedules: When reinforcement is discontinued, responding continues for a longer time if reinforcement has been intermittent rather than continuous. The durability of intermittent schedules can be seen in people's persistence at such events as playing slot machines, fishing, and bargain shopping.

Generalization. Once a certain response occurs regularly to a given stimulus, the response also may occur to other stimuli. This is called *generalization* (Skinner, 1953). Generalization seems troublesome for operant theory, because a response should not be made in a situation in which it never has been reinforced. Skinner explained generalization by noting that people perform many behaviors that lead to the final (reinforced) response. These component behaviors are often part of the chains of behavior of different tasks and therefore are reinforced in different contexts. When people are in a new situation, they are likely to perform the component behaviors, which produce an accurate response or rapid acquisition of the correct response.

To exemplify this process, consider that students with good academic habits come to class, attend to and participate in the activities, take notes, do the required reading, and keep up with the assignments. These component behaviors produce high achievement and grades. When such students begin a new class, it is not necessary that the content be similar to previous classes in which they have been enrolled. Rather, the component behaviors have received repeated reinforcement and thus are likely to generalize to the new setting.

Table 2.5
Suggestions for facilitating generalization.

Parental Involvement: Involve parents in behavioral change programs

High Expectations: Convey to students that they are capable of performing well

Self-Evaluation: Teach students to monitor and evaluate their behaviors

Contingencies: Withdraw artificial contingencies (e.g., tokens) and replace with natural ones (privileges)

Participation: Allow students to participate in specifying behaviors to be reinforced and reinforcement contingencies

Academics: Provide a good academic program because many students with behavior problems have academic deficiencies

Benefits: Show students how behavioral changes will benefit them by linking changes to activities of interest

Reinforcement: Reinforce students in different settings to reduce discrimination between reinforced and nonreinforced situations

Consistency: Prepare teachers in regular classes to continue to shape behaviors of students in special classes when they are mainstreamed into the regular program

---

This is not to suggest that generalization occurs automatically. O'Leary and Drabman (1971) noted that generalization "must be programmed like any other behavioral change" (p. 393). One problem with many behavior modification programs is that they change behaviors but the new behaviors do not generalize outside the training context. O'Leary and Drabman (1971) offer suggestions on ways to facilitate generalization (Table 2.5 and Application 2.6).

Discrimination.   *Discrimination*, the complementary process to generalization, involves responding differently (in intensity or rate) depending on the stimulus or features of a situation (Rilling, 1977). Although teachers want students to generalize what they learn to other situations, they also want them to respond discriminately. In solving mathematical word problems, teachers might want students to adopt a general problem-solving approach comprising such steps as determining the given and the needed information, drawing a picture, and generating useful formulas. Teachers also want students to learn to discriminate problem types (e.g., area, time-rate-distance, interest rate). Being able to identify quickly the type of problem enhances students' successes.

Spence (1936) proposed that to teach discrimination, desired responses should be reinforced and unwanted responses extinguished by nonreinforcement. In school, teachers point out similarities and differences among similar content and provide for periodic reviews to ensure that students discriminate properly and apply correct problem-solution methods. Terrace (1963) showed how to train animals to make

APPLICATION 2.6
Generalization

Generalization can advance skill development across subject areas. Finding main ideas is relevant to language arts, social studies, mathematics (word problems), and other content areas. For example, during a language arts class an instructor teaches students a strategy for finding main ideas. Once students master this strategy, the teacher explains how to modify its use for other academic subjects and asks students to think of uses. By teaching the strategy well in one domain and facilitating potential applications in other domains, teachers save much time and effort because they do not have to reteach the strategy in each content area.

Teaching expected behaviors (e.g., walking in the hall, raising a hand to speak) can also be generalized. For example, if all seventh-grade teachers decide to have students use the same format for the heading on all their papers, it could be explained in one class. Then students could be asked to use the same format (with minor alterations) in each of their other classes.

errorless discriminations by introducing the nonreinforced stimulus (pecking key) for short durations and at low intensities and gradually increasing the duration and intensity of the key.

Errors generally are thought to be disruptive and to produce learning of incorrect responses. Educators try to keep student errors to a minimum. Whether all errors need to be eliminated is debatable. Evidence from the motivational literature shows that students who learn to deal with errors in an adaptive manner subsequently persist longer on difficult tasks than do students who have experienced errorless learning (Dweck, 1975; see also Chapter 8 on Motivation).

Behavioral Change

Reinforcement can be given for making correct operant responses only when people know what to do. During learning, however, operant responses do not exist in final, polished form. If teachers wait to deliver reinforcement until learners emit the proper responses, many learners would never receive reinforcement because they never would acquire the responses. We now turn to a discussion of how behavioral change occurs in operant conditioning, which has important implications for learning.

Successive Approximations (Shaping). The basic operant conditioning method of behavioral change is *shaping*, or differential reinforcement of successive approximations to the desired form or rate of behavior (Morse & Kelleher, 1977). To shape behavior, one adheres to the following sequence:

- Identify what the student can do now (entry behavior)
- Identify the desired (terminal) behavior
- Identify potential reinforcers in the student's environment
- Break the terminal behavior (step 2) into small substeps to be mastered sequentially
- Move the student from the entry behavior to the terminal behavior by successively reinforcing each approximation to the terminal behavior

A natural instance of shaping can be seen in a student attempting to shoot a basketball from a point on the court. The first shot falls short of the basket. The student shoots harder the second time, and the ball hits the backboard. The student does not shoot quite as hard the third time, and the ball hits the right rim and bounces off. On the fourth attempt, the student shoots as hard as the third attempt but aims left. The ball hits the left rim and bounces off. Finally, the student shoots just as hard but aims slightly to the right, and the ball goes into the basket. Gradually the shot was honed to a more accurate form.

Shaping might be applied systematically with a hyperactive student who can work on a task for only 2 minutes before becoming distracted. The goal is to shape the student's behavior so she can work uninterrupted for 30 minutes. Initially the teacher delivers a reinforcer when the student works productively for 2 minutes. After several successful 2-minute intervals, the criterion for reinforcement is raised to 3 minutes. Assuming that she works uninterrupted for several 3-minute periods, the criterion is raised to 4 minutes. This process continues to the goal of 30 minutes as long as the student reliably performs at the criterion level. If the student encounters difficulty at any point, the criterion for reinforcement decreases to a level at which she can perform successfully.

An academic skill that might be shaped is teaching a student the multiplication facts for 6. Presently he only knows $6 \times 1 = 6$ and $6 \times 2 = 12$. To earn reinforcement, he must correctly recite these two plus $6 \times 3 = 18$. After he can do this reliably, the criterion for reinforcement is raised to include $6 \times 4 = 24$. This process continues until he accurately recites all the facts up to $6 \times 10 = 60$.

Chaining.   Most human actions are complex and include several three-term contingencies linked successively. For example, shooting a basketball requires dribbling, turning, getting set in position, and releasing the ball. Each response alters the environment, and this altered condition serves as the stimulus for the next response. *Chaining* is the process of producing or altering some of the variables that serve as stimuli for future responses (Skinner, 1953). A chain consists of a series of operants, each of which sets the occasion for further responses.

Consider a student balancing chemical equations. The first element of the first problem serves as the S^D, to which the student makes the appropriate response (R). This product (the S^R) is also the S^D for the next response necessary to balance the equation. This progression continues until the equation is balanced, which serves as the S^D to move to the next equation. Operations within each equation constitute a chain, and the entire problem set constitutes a chain.

Chains are similar to Guthrie's acts, whereas individual three-term contingencies resemble movements. Some chains acquire a functional unity; the chain is an integrated sequence such that successful implementation defines a skill. When skills are well honed, execution of the chain occurs automatically. Riding a bicycle consists of several discrete acts, yet an accomplished rider executes these with little or no conscious effort. Such automaticity is often present in cognitive skills (e.g., reading, solving math problems). Chaining is an especially important learning process and plays a critical role in the acquisition of skills (Gollub, 1977; Keller & Schoenfeld, 1950; Skinner, 1978).

Behavior Modification

Behavior modification (or *behavior therapy*) refers to the systematic application of behavioral learning principles to facilitate adaptive behaviors (Ullmann & Krasner, 1965). Behavior modification has been employed with adults and children in such diverse contexts as classrooms, counseling settings, prisons, and mental hospitals. It has been used to treat phobias, dysfunctional language, disruptive behaviors, negative social interactions, poor child rearing, and low self-control (Ayllon & Azrin, 1968; Becker, 1971; Keller & Ribes-Inesta, 1974; Ulrich, Stachnik, & Mabry, 1966). Lovaas (1977) successfully employed behavior modification to teach language to autistic children (Application 2.7).

Techniques. The basic techniques of behavior modification include reinforcement of desired behaviors and extinction of undesired ones. Punishment is rarely employed but, when used, more often involves removing a positive reinforcer than presenting a negative reinforcer.

In deciding on a program of change, behavior modifiers typically focus on the following three issues (Ullmann & Krasner, 1965):

- Which of the individual's behaviors are maladaptive, and which should be increased (decreased)?
- What environmental contingencies currently support the individual's behaviors (either to maintain undesirable behaviors or to reduce the likelihood of performing more adaptive responses)?
- What environmental features can be altered to change the individual's behavior?

Change is most likely when modifiers and clients agree that a change is needed and jointly decide on the desired goals. The first step in establishing a program is to define the problem in behavioral terms. For example, the statement, "Keith is out of his seat too often," refers to overt behavior that can be measured: One can keep a record of the amount of time that Keith is out of his seat. General expressions referring to unobservables ("Keith has a bad attitude") do not allow for objective problem definition.

The next step is to determine the reinforcers maintaining undesirable behavior. Perhaps Keith is getting teacher attention only when he gets out of his seat and not when he is seated. A simple plan is to have the teacher attend to Keith while he is

APPLICATION 2.7
Behavior Modification

Behavior modification for disruptive students is difficult because such students may display few appropriate responses to be positively reinforced. A teacher might use shaping to address a specific annoying behavior. Kathy Stone has been having problems with Erik, who continually pushes and shoves other students when the class gets in line to go somewhere in the building. When the class is going only a short distance, Mrs. Stone could inform Erik that if he stays in line without pushing and shoving, he will be the line leader on the way back to the class; however, if he pushes or shoves, he immediately will be removed from the line. If he is able to stay in the line appropriately, he is allowed to lead the line on the return walk. This procedure can be repeated until Erik can handle short distances. Mrs. Stone then can allow him to walk with the class for progressively longer distances until he can behave in line for any distance.

Another child in Kathy Stone's third-grade class, Susan, continually turns in messy work. Mrs. Stone might use generalized reinforcers such as special stickers (exchangeable for various privileges) to help Susan, whose work typically is dirty, torn, and barely readable. Susan is told if she turns in a paper that is clean, she can earn one sticker; if it is not torn, another sticker; and if the writing is neat, a third sticker. Once Susan begins to make improvements, Mrs. Stone gradually can move the rewards to other areas for improvement (e.g., correct work, finishing work on time).

seated and engaged in academic work and to ignore him when he gets out of his seat. If the amount of times that Keith is out of his seat decreases, teacher attention is a positive reinforcer.

A behavior modification program might employ such generalized reinforcers as points or tokens that students exchange for *backup reinforcers*, such as tangible rewards, free time, or privileges. Having more than one backup ensures that at least one will be effective for each student at all times. A behavioral criterion must be established to earn reinforcement. The five-step shaping procedure (discussed previously) can be employed. The criterion is initially defined as the level of entry behavior and progresses in small increments toward the goal. A point or token is given to the student each time the criterion is satisfied. To extinguish any undesirable behavior by Keith, the teacher should not give him too much attention if he gets out of his seat, but rather should inform him privately that because he does not satisfy the criterion, he does not earn a point or token.

Punishment is used infrequently but may be needed when behavior is illegal or becomes so disruptive that it cannot be ignored (e.g., students who fight or bring drugs to school). A common punishment is *time out* (from reinforcement). During time out, the student is removed from the class social context and placed in a corner or separate room. There the student continues to engage in academic work without peer social interaction or the opportunity to earn reinforcement. Another punishment is to remove positive reinforcers (free time, recess, privileges) for misbehavior.

Critics have argued that behavior modification shapes quiet and docile behaviors (Winett & Winkler, 1972). Although a reasonable amount of quiet is needed to ensure that learning occurs, some teachers seek a quiet classroom at all times, even when some noise from social interactions would facilitate learning. The use of behavior modification is neither inherently good nor bad. It can produce a quiet classroom or promote social initiations by withdrawn children (Strain, Kerr, & Ragland, 1981). Like the techniques themselves, the goals of behavior modification need to be thought out carefully by those implementing the procedures.

Cognitive Behavior Modification.   Researchers also have incorporated cognitive elements into behavior modification procedures. In *cognitive behavior modification*, learners' thoughts (when verbalized) function as discriminative and reinforcing stimuli. Thus, learners may verbally instruct themselves what to do and then perform the appropriate behavior. Cognitive behavior modification techniques often are applied with students with handicaps (Hallahan, Kneedler, & Lloyd, 1983), and used to reduce hyperactivity and aggression (Robinson, Smith, Miller, & Brownell, 1999). Meichenbaum's *self-instructional training* is an example of cognitive behavior modification (see Modeling Processes in Chapter 3).

Verbal Behavior

The first systematic attempt to extend operant conditioning principles to higher-order cognitive processes occurred when Skinner published *Verbal Behavior* (1957) to address language acquisition. He said verbal behavior is conditioned and shaped by the same stimuli and reinforcers that condition and shape nonverbal behavior. He acknowledged the unique biological endowment of human beings—the vocal apparatus and the predisposition to vocalize. Other than this endowment, there is nothing special about language; no new principles are needed to explain its acquisition or use.

Classification of Verbal Responses.   Skinner classified verbalizations in terms of their controlling variables. One type is the *mand*, which is a verbal response reinforced by a characteristic consequence and therefore under the functional control of relevant conditions. "Listen!" "Stop!" "More bread," and "Pass the salt," are mands that produce their unique consequences (the verbalized acts) when heard by another person. A listener's fulfillment of the mand is reinforcing and increases the likelihood the mand will be uttered in the future when a similar aversive state arises.

A second type of verbal response is the *tact*, which is a verbalization evoked by a particular object or event. Tacts name or describe discriminative stimuli. Young children's labeling responses (e.g., "mama," "doggie") are tacts that often are reinforced by adults with smiles, hugs, and verbal acknowledgments (e.g., "Yes, that's a dog-gie"). Because the same tact is often associated with many different reinforcements, it can become generalized and be uttered in different circumstances.

A third type is the *echoic.* One form is simple imitation. A father says to his infant, "Dada"; the infant responds, "Dada"; the father smiles and hugs the infant. A second type of echoic behavior is based on associations: ham: _____ (eggs), bread: _____ (butter). Echoics help one learn words, as when one reads a new word, looks it up in the dictionary, and repeats it several times.

Textual behaviors are verbal operants under the control of visual stimuli (tactual in Braille). An example is reading, which is reinforced by teachers and parents when children read well. Textual behaviors also are reinforced when they help establish other verbal responses. Reading books or looking up words in dictionaries establishes new word meanings, which one subsequently uses in speaking and writing. Students who study vocabulary words in preparation for the SAT or GRE are reinforced when some of these words appear on the test.

Autoclitic behaviors depend upon other verbal behaviors. Some autoclitics inform listeners of the types of verbal operants they accompany ("I see that," "I recall that"). Autoclitics can preface mands ("I ask you to pass the salt") and tacts ("I tell you that it's raining"). Other autoclitics convey strength of verbal response: "I suppose," "I guess," "I imagine." Autoclitics also describe the relation between a response and another response of a speaker or listener ("I agree," "I admit"); convey the emotional or motivational state of the speaker ("I hate to tell you this," "I know you'll be glad to hear"); and express negative verbal behavior ("I doubt that," "I don't remember"). Adverbs and adjectives are autoclitics, as are expressions modifying or indicating their relation to other verbalizations ("For example," "So to speak," "Just between you and me").

Verbal Behavior presents a theoretical analysis of how humans acquire and maintain language. Unfortunately, it contains only informal data and the theory has received little empirical testing. Behaviorists generally have been interested in issues other than language; linguists and psycholinguists typically subscribe to cognitive theories of language acquisition and use (Clark & Clark, 1977; Ehri, 1996; Juel, 1996; Segal, 1977; Stanovich, 1996). The issue is not whether people acquire any language via reinforcement; undoubtedly they do. Rather, the issue is whether reinforcement is the primary mechanism responsible for language acquisition.

Chomsky's Critique.   Linguist Noam Chomsky (1959) addressed this issue by arguing that a conditioning model is inappropriate for explaining language acquisition and comprehension:

> Careful study of this book (and of the research on which it draws) reveals . . . that the insights that have been achieved in the laboratories of the reinforcement theorist, though quite genuine, can be applied to complex human behavior only in the most gross and superficial way, and that speculative attempts to discuss linguistic behavior in these terms alone omit from consideration factors of fundamental importance that are, no doubt, amenable to scientific study. (p. 28)

Chomsky raised issues he thought an operant analysis could not adequately address. One issue concerns the nature of the stimulus to which one verbally responds. In operant conditioning, the stimulus must be specified or else it loses its objectivity and meaning as a scientific concept. Skinner (1957) gave the following example of stimulus control:

> The student who is learning to "spot" the composer of unfamiliar music or to name the artist or school of an unfamiliar picture is subjected to the same contingencies of differential reinforcement. Responses such as Mozart or Dutch are brought under the control of extremely subtle properties of stimuli when they are reinforced with "right" or punished with "wrong" by the community. (p. 108)

Chomsky (1959) disputed this point:

> Suppose instead of saying Dutch we had said *Clashes with the wall-paper, I thought you liked abstract work, Never saw it before, Tilted, Hanging too low, Beautiful, Hideous, Remember our camping trip last summer?*, or whatever else might come into our minds when looking at a picture. . . . Skinner could only say that each of these responses is under the control of some other stimulus property of the physical object. (p. 31)

Another issue concerns the process of language acquisition. Because an operant analysis deals only with surface features of language, it cannot explain how people acquire the *grammar* of a language—its underlying, abstract set of rules. The following sentences have different surface structures but identical "deep" structures and thus people understand them to mean the same thing:

The snake bit the boy.
The boy was bitten by the snake.

Neither can an operant analysis explain how people can acquire and comprehend more than one meaning of the utterance, "She is a pretty young girl." Once people understand grammar, they will comprehend utterances that they never have heard before ("Lucretia wore a smashingly awesome evening number").

At best, reinforcement can account for a small part of language acquisition. Children learn much sentence structure and vocabulary from television, reading, and social interactions. Children often initiate utterances they hear even when not reinforced for doing so. The exact mechanism underlying language acquisition is unknown, but it apparently involves developing an implicit understanding of grammatical structure that does not depend on teaching and reinforcement. The latter may assist language learning but are not necessary for it.

Skinner's *Verbal Behavior* was a failure, a portent of the general inadequacy of operant conditioning to explain higher-order mental processes (Bargh & Ferguson, 2000). Such phenomena as language, memory, reasoning, and problem solving cannot be addressed adequately without considering thinking. Researchers who currently study these phenomena use a cognitive perspective. MacCorquodale (1970) attempted to address Chomsky's language criticisms, but the consensus within the scientific community is that Chomsky's points are sound.

SELF-REGULATION

The reinforcement theory view of self-regulation derives primarily from the work of Skinner (Mace, Belfiore, & Hutchinson, 2001; Mace, Belfiore, & Shea, 1989). Operant behavior is emitted in the presence of discriminative stimuli. Whether behavior becomes more or less likely to occur in the future depends on its consequences: Behaviors that are reinforced are more likely to occur; those punished become less likely. Thus, teacher praise given to a student contingent on a high test score may encourage the student to continue studying hard for exams; teacher criticism given following a student's disruptive behavior may decrease the likelihood of disruptive behavior.

Reinforcement theorists have studied how individuals establish discriminative stimuli and reinforcement contingencies (Brigham, 1982). Self-regulated behavior involves choosing among alternative courses of action (Mace et al., 2001), typically by deferring an immediate reinforcer in favor of a different, and usually greater, future reinforcer (Rachlin, 1974). For example, Trisha who stays home on Friday night to study for an exam instead of going out with friends and Kyle who keeps working on an academic task despite taunting peers nearby are deferring immediate reinforcement, as is John in the next example.

John is having difficulty studying. Despite good intentions, he spends insufficient time studying and is easily distracted. A key to changing his behavior is to establish discriminative stimuli (cues) for studying. With the assistance of his high-school counselor, John establishes a definite time and place for studying (7 P.M. to 9 P.M. in his room with one 10-minute break). To eliminate distracting cues, John agrees not to use the phone, CD player, or TV during this period. For reinforcement, John will award himself one point for each night he successfully accomplishes his routine. When he receives 10 points, he can take a night off.

From a reinforcement theory perspective, one decides which behaviors to regulate, establishes discriminative stimuli for their occurrence, evaluates performance in terms of whether it matches the standard, and administers reinforcement. The three key subprocesses are self-monitoring, self-instruction, and self-reinforcement.

Self-Monitoring

Self-monitoring refers to deliberate attention to some aspect of one's behavior and often is accompanied by recording its frequency or intensity (Mace & Kratochwill, 1988). People cannot regulate their actions if they are not aware of what they do. Behaviors can be assessed on such dimensions as quality, rate, quantity, and originality. While writing a term paper, students may periodically assess their work to determine whether it states important ideas, whether they will finish it by the due date, whether it will be long enough, and whether it integrates their ideas in unusual fashion. One can engage in self-monitoring in such diverse areas as motor skills (how fast one runs the 100-meter dash), art (how original one's pen-and-ink drawings are), and social behavior (how much one talks at social functions).

Often students must be taught one or more self-monitoring methods (Belfiore & Hornyak, 1998; Lan, 1998; Ollendick & Hersen, 1984; Shapiro, 1987; see Application 2.8). Methods include narrations, frequency counts, duration measures, time-sampling measures, behavior ratings, and behavioral traces and archival records (Mace et al., 1989). *Narrations* are written accounts of behavior and the context in which it occurs. Narrations can range from very detailed to open-ended (Bell & Low, 1977). *Frequency counts* are used to self-record instances of specific behaviors during a given period (e.g., number of times a student turns around in his or her seat during a 30-minute seatwork exercise). *Duration measures* record the amount of time a behavior occurs during a given period (e.g., number of minutes a student studies during 30 minutes). *Time-sampling measures* divide a period into shorter intervals and record how often a behavior occurs during each interval. A 30-minute study period might be divided into six 5-minute periods; for each 5-minute period, students record whether they studied the entire time. *Behavior ratings* require estimates of how often a behavior occurs during a given time (e.g., always, sometimes, never). *Behavioral traces* and *archival records* are permanent records that exist independently of other assessments (e.g., number of worksheets completed, number of problems solved correctly).

In the absence of self-recording, selective memory of successes and failures can come into play. Our beliefs about outcomes often do not faithfully reflect our actual outcomes. Self-recording can yield surprising results. Students having difficulties studying who keep a written record of their activities may learn they are wasting more than half of their study time on nonacademic tasks.

There are two important criteria for self-monitoring: regularity and proximity (Bandura, 1986). *Regularity* means observing behavior on a continual basis instead of intermittently; for example, keep a daily record rather than recording behavior one day per week. Nonregular observation often yields misleading results. *Proximity* means that behavior is observed close in time to its occurrence rather than long afterward. It is better to write down what we do at the time it occurs rather than wait until the end of the day to reconstruct events.

Self-monitoring methods place responsibility for behavioral assessment on the student (Belfiore & Hornyak, 1998). These methods often lead to significant behavioral improvements or reactive effects. Self-monitored responses are consequences of behaviors, and like other consequences, they affect future responding. Self-recordings are immediate responses that serve to mediate the relationship between preceding behavior and longer-term consequences (Mace & West, 1986; Nelson & Hayes, 1981). Students who monitor their completion of workbook pages provide themselves with immediate reinforcers that mediate the link between seatwork and such distant consequences as teacher praise and good grades.

Research supports the benefits of self-monitoring on achievement outcomes. Sagotsky, Patterson, and Lepper (1978) had children periodically monitor their performances during mathematics sessions and record whether they were working on the appropriate instructional material. Other students set daily performance goals, and students in a third condition received self-monitoring and goal setting. Self-monitoring increased time on task and mathematical achievement; goal setting had

APPLICATION 2.8
Self-Monitoring

Self-monitoring makes students aware of existing behaviors and assists them in evaluating and improving those behaviors. In a special education self-contained or resource room, self-monitoring could help students improve on-task behavior, particularly if it is coupled with goal setting. The teacher could create individual charts divided into small blocks representing a short time period (e.g., 10 minutes). Once students are working independently at their seats or work stations, a soft bell could be sounded every 10 minutes. When the bell sounds, students could record on their charts what they are doing—writing, reading, daydreaming, or doodling. The teacher could help each student set individual goals related to the number of on-task behaviors expected in a day, which would be increased as the student's behavior improves.

In regular classrooms, teachers need to be careful about how they indicate time periods to self-monitoring students. Using a bell might disrupt other students and draw embarrassing attention to the students having difficulty. Mrs. Stone seats her third-grade self-monitoring students close to her so that she can gently tap the students' desks at the end of each time period or otherwise quietly indicate its end to these students.

Teachers also might work with high school and college students who are having difficulty using study time effectively. Jim Marshall has a couple of students who have difficulty completing assignments and reading all the material required for his history class. Mr. Marshall meets with these students after school each Monday and Friday to help them establish realistic goals for developing productive study habits. He also works with the students to set a time and record how much reading (by pages), note studying, writing, and so forth, they accomplish in a set time period. Using the goals and a timer, students can monitor their progress toward achieving the goals.

Gina Brown has some students who had difficulty completing their first paper for the educational psychology course. Dr. Brown had provided considerable guidance, but it was clear that these students were not working in sequential steps to complete the paper by the deadline. For the next paper, Dr. Brown met individually with each student and created a checklist of items and timetable necessary for completing the paper. She met with the students weekly and had them share their progress on the checklist and completion of the assignment. This helped the students in developing a tool that could be used for self-monitoring progress toward completing assignments made in any course.

minimal effects. For goal setting to affect performance, students initially may need to learn how to set challenging but attainable goals.

Schunk (1983d) provided subtraction instruction and practice to children who failed to master subtraction operations in their classrooms. One group (self-monitoring) reviewed their work at the end of each instructional session and recorded the number of workbook pages they completed. A second group (external monitoring) had their work reviewed at the end of each session by an adult who recorded the number of pages completed. No-monitoring children received the instructional program but were not monitored or told to monitor their work.

Self- and external-monitoring conditions in teaching subtraction led to higher self-efficacy, skill, and persistence, compared with no monitoring. The effects of the two monitoring conditions were comparable. The benefits of monitoring did not depend on children's performances during the instructional sessions, because the three treatment conditions did not result in different amounts of work completed. Monitoring progress, rather than who evaluated it, enhanced children's perceptions of their learning progress and self-efficacy.

Self-Instruction

Self-instruction refers to discriminative stimuli that set the occasion for self-regulatory responses leading to reinforcement (Mace et al., 1989). (Self-instruction should not be confused with Meichenbaum's [1977] self-instructional training procedure, as discussed in Chapter 3.) One type of self-instruction involves arranging the environment to produce discriminative stimuli. Students who realize they need to review class notes the next day might write themselves a reminder before going to bed. The written reminder serves as a cue to review, which makes reinforcement (i.e., a good grade on a quiz) more likely. Another type of self-instruction takes the form of statements (rules) that serve as discriminative stimuli to guide behavior. This type of self-instruction is included in the self-instructional training procedure.

Strategy instruction is an effective means of enhancing comprehension and self-efficacy among poor readers. Schunk and Rice (1986, 1987) taught remedial readers to use the following self-instruction strategy for working on reading comprehension passages:

> What do I have to do? (1) Read the questions. (2) Read the passage to find out what it is mostly about. (3) Think about what the details have in common. (4) Think about what would make a good title. (5) Reread the story if I don't know the answer to a question. (Schunk & Rice, 1987, pp. 290–291)

Children verbalize the individual steps prior to applying them to passages.

Self-instructional statements have been used to teach a variety of academic, social, and motor skills. These statements are especially helpful for students with learning disabilities who may also have attention disorders. Verbalizing statements keeps learners focused on a task. For example, a self-instruction procedure used to improve the handwriting of a student with learning disabilities is as follows (Kosiewicz, Hallahan, Lloyd, & Graves, 1982):

(1) Say aloud the word to be written. (2) Say the first syllable. (3) Name each of the letters in that syllable three times. (4) Repeat each letter as it is written down. (5) Repeat steps 2 through 4 for each succeeding syllable.

This sequence appeared on a card on the student's desk. During training, the student was praised for completing the steps. Once the student learned the procedure, praise was discontinued and the sequence was maintained by the consequence of better handwriting.

Self-Reinforcement

Self-reinforcement refers to the process whereby individuals provide themselves with a reinforcement contingent on their performing a response and that increases the likelihood of future responding (Mace et al., 1989). As discussed earlier, a reinforcer is defined on the basis of its effects. To illustrate, assume that Mitch is on a point system: He awards himself one point for each page he reads in his geography book. He keeps a record each week, and if his week's points exceed his previous week's points by 5%, he earns 30 minutes of free time on Friday. Whether this arrangement functions as self-reinforcement cannot be determined until it is known whether he regularly earns the free time. If he does (i.e., his average performance increases as the semester proceeds), then the reinforcement contingencies are regulating his academic behaviors.

Much research shows that reinforcement contingencies improve academic performance (Bandura, 1986), but it is unclear whether self-reinforcement is more effective than externally administered reinforcement (such as given by the teacher). Studies investigating self-reinforcement often contain problems (Brigham, 1982; Martin, 1980). In academic settings, the reinforcement contingency too often is set in a context that includes instruction and classroom rules. Students typically do not work on materials when they choose but rather when told to do so by the teacher. Students may stay on task primarily because of the teacher's classroom control and fear of punishment rather than because of reinforcement.

Self-reinforcement is hypothesized to be an effective component of self-regulated behavior (O'Leary & Dubey, 1979), but the reinforcement may be more important than the agent of reinforcement. Although self-reinforcement may enhance behavioral maintenance over time, during the acquisition of self-regulatory skills explicitly providing reinforcement may be more important. By failing to consider cognitive and affective factors, the reinforcement position offers an incomplete account for the scope and complexity of self-regulated learning.

INSTRUCTIONAL APPLICATIONS

Skinner (1954, 1961, 1968, 1984) wrote extensively on how his ideas can be applied to solve educational problems. He believed that there is too much aversive control. Although students rarely receive corporal punishment, they often work on assignments not because they want to learn or because they enjoy them but rather to avoid such negative outcomes as teacher criticism, loss of privileges, and a trip to the principal.

A second concern is that reinforcement occurs infrequently and often not at the proper time. Teachers attend to each student for only a few minutes each day. While students are engaged in seatwork, several minutes elapse between when they finish an assignment and when they receive teacher feedback. Consequently, students may perform operations incorrectly, and teachers must spend additional time giving corrective feedback.

A third point is that the scope and sequence of curricula do not ensure that all students acquire skills. Students do not learn at the same pace. To cover all the material, teachers usually move to the next lesson before all students have mastered the previous one.

Skinner contended that these and other problems cannot be solved by paying teachers more money, lengthening the school day and year, raising standards, or toughening teacher certification requirements. Rather, he recommended better use of instructional time. Since it is unrealistic to expect students to move through the curriculum at the same rate, individualizing instruction would improve efficiency.

Skinner believed that teaching required properly arranging reinforcement contingencies. No new principles were needed in applying operant conditioning to education. Instruction is more effective when (1) teachers present the material in small steps, (2) learners actively respond rather than passively listen, (3) teachers give feedback immediately following learners' responses, and (4) learners move through the material at their own pace.

The basic process of instruction involves shaping. The goal of instruction (terminal behavior) and the students' entry behaviors are identified. Substeps (behaviors) leading from the entry behavior to the terminal behavior are formulated. Each substep represents a small modification of the preceding one. Students are moved through the sequence using various approaches including demonstrations, small-group work, and individual seatwork. Students actively respond to the material and receive immediate feedback.

This instructional approach involves specifying learners' present knowledge and desired objectives in terms of what learners do. Terminal behaviors often are specified as behavioral objectives, to be discussed shortly. Individual differences are taken into account by beginning instruction at learners' present performance levels and allowing them to progress at their own rates. Given the prevailing teaching methods in our educational system, these goals seem impractical: Teachers would have to begin instruction at different points and cover material at different rates for individual students. Programmed instruction circumvents these problems: Learners begin at the point in the material corresponding to their performance levels, and they progress at their own rates.

Behavioral Objectives

Behavioral objectives are clear statements of the intended student outcomes of instruction. Objectives can range from general to specific. General or vague objectives such as "improve student awareness" can be fulfilled by almost any kind of instruction. At the opposite extreme, objectives that are overly specific and document every minute change in student behavior are time consuming to write and can cause teachers to lose sight of the most important learning outcomes. Optimal objectives fall somewhere between these extremes (Application 2.9).

A behavioral objective describes "what the student will be doing when demonstrating his achievement and how you will know he is doing it" (Mager, 1962, p. 53). Four parts of a good objective are:

- The specific group of students
- The actual behaviors students are to perform as a consequence of instructional activities
- The conditions or contexts in which the students are to perform the behaviors
- The criteria for assessing student behaviors to determine whether objectives have been met

A sample objective with the parts identified is:

Given eight addition problems with fractions of unlike denominators (3), the fourth-grade math student (1) will write the correct sums (2) for at least seven of them (4).

Behavioral objectives can help determine the important learning outcomes, which aid in lesson planning and testing to assess learning. Formulating objectives also helps teachers decide what content students can master. Given unit-teaching objectives and a fixed amount of time to cover them, teachers can decide which objectives are more important and focus on them. Although objectives for lower-level learning outcomes (e.g., knowledge and comprehension) are generally easier to specify, good behavioral objectives can be written to assess higher-order outcomes (application, analysis, synthesis, evaluation) as well.

APPLICATION 2.9
Behavioral Objectives

As teachers prepare lessons and complete lesson plans, it is important that they decide on specific behavioral objectives and plan activities to assist students in mastering these objectives. Instead of an art teacher planning a lesson with the objective, "Have students complete a pen-and-ink drawing of the front of the building," the teacher should decide on the major objective for the students to master. Is it to use pen and ink or to draw the front of the school building? The objective may be better stated as follows: "Have the students draw the major lines of the front of the building in correct perspective (materials/medium: drawing paper, pens, ink)."

A kindergarten teacher writes that she wants "Students to go to art, music, and physical education in an orderly fashion." For that age child, it would be better if the teacher would spell out the objective in more specific terms; for example, "Students should move to other classrooms by walking in a line without talking and by keeping their hands to themselves."

Research shows that students who are provided with behavioral objectives have better verbatim recall of verbal information compared with students not provided with objectives (Faw & Waller, 1976; Hamilton, 1985). Objectives may cue students to process the information at the appropriate level; thus, when students are given objectives requiring recall, they engage in rehearsal and other strategies that facilitate that type of recall. Research also shows that providing students with objectives does not enhance learning of material unrelated to the objectives (Duchastel & Brown, 1974), which suggests that students may concentrate on learning material relevant to the objectives and disregard other material.

The effect of objectives on learning depends on students' prior experience with them and on how important they perceive the information to be. Training in using objectives or familiarity with criterion-based instruction leads to better learning compared to the absence of such training or familiarity. When students can determine on their own what material is important to learn, providing objectives does not facilitate learning. Telling students the objectives is more important when they do not know what material is important.

Text structure can moderate the effect of objectives on learning. Information made salient by being in a prominent position is recalled well even when objectives are not provided (Muth, Glynn, Britton, & Graves, 1988). Duchastel (1979) cites the example of text entitled, "Fast Breeder Reactors," which covers future electrical needs, rational utilization of fossil fuels, nuclear reactors, nuclear breeding, and doubling time. "Nuclear reactors" is high in the content structure of the text because it precedes more detailed nuclear fission content. A passage entitled "Future Energy Sources" covers emerging alternative energy sources, solar energy, nuclear reactors, geothermal resources, and laser fusion. "Nuclear reactors" is in the same (third) position in both passages, but in the second it is one of many alternatives, so its importance is diminished. Duchastel found that providing objectives enhances recall when target information is low in the content structure, although Muth et al. (1988) found benefits of objectives on recall regardless of whether content was high or low in text. These authors suggest that rehearsal prompted by objectives produces better memory storage.

Programmed Instruction

Programmed instruction (PI) refers to instructional materials developed in accordance with behavioral principles of learning (O'Day, Kulhavy, Anderson, & Malczynski, 1971). In the 1920s, Sidney Pressey designed machines to use primarily for testing. Students were presented with multiple-choice questions, and they pressed a button corresponding to their choice. If students responded correctly, the machine presented the next choice; if they responded incorrectly, the error was recorded and they continued to respond to the item.

Skinner revived Pressey's machines in the 1950s and modified them to incorporate instruction (Skinner, 1958). These teaching machines presented students with material in small steps (frames). Each frame required learners to make an overt response. Material was carefully sequenced and broken into small units to minimize errors. Students received immediate feedback on the accuracy of each response. They moved to the next frame when their answer was correct. When it was incorrect, supplementary material was provided. Although errors occurred, the programs were designed to minimize errors and ensure that learners typically succeeded (Benjamin, 1988).

There are many benefits when students generally perform well, but research suggests that preventing errors may not be desirable. Dweck (1975), for example, found that an occasional failure increased persistence on difficult tasks more than did constant success. Further, constant success is not as informative of one's capabilities as is occasionally having difficulty because the latter highlights what one can and cannot do. This is not to suggest that teachers should let students fail, but rather that under the proper circumstances students can benefit from tasks structured so that they occasionally encounter difficulty.

PI does not require the use of a machine. A book by Holland and Skinner (1961) is a program teaching behavioral principles. Many computer software programs are forms of PI incorporating principles of behavioral instruction (Application 2.10).

PI incorporates several learning principles (O'Day et al., 1971). First, behavioral objectives specify what students should perform on completion of the instruction. Second, the unit is subdivided into sequenced frames, each of which presents a small bit of information and a test item to which learners respond. Although a lot of material may be included in the program, the frame-to-frame increments are small. Third, learners work at their own pace. Fourth, learners respond to questions as they work through the program. Responses can include supplying words in blanks, providing numerical answers, and choosing which of several statements best describes the idea being presented. Fifth, feedback depends on the learner's response. If the learner is correct, the next item is given. If the learner answers incorrectly, additional remedial information is presented and the idea is tested in slightly different form.

Because PI reflects the shaping process, performance increments are small and learners almost always respond correctly. Linear and branching programs are distinguished according to how they treat learner errors. *Linear programs* are structured in such a way that all students proceed through them in the same sequence (but not necessarily at the same rate). Regardless of whether students respond correctly or incorrectly to a frame, they move to the next frame where they receive feedback on the accuracy of their answer. Linear programs are based on the notion that answering incorrectly increases the likelihood of future incorrect responses. Programs minimize errors by covering the same material in more than one frame and by prompting student responses (Figure 2.4).

Branching programs are set up so that students' movement through them depends on how they answer the questions (Figure 2.5). Each frame asks a question and follows with two or more alternative answers. The student's next frame depends on the answer. In a book, each alternative may list a page to turn to; at a computer a new frame will appear after the student responds. Branching programs take into account individual differences: Students who learn quickly skip frames and bypass much of the repetition of linear programs, whereas slower learners receive additional

APPLICATION 2.10
Instructional Planning

Instructional programs involve designing instruction to move students systematically in small steps through material. This notion is especially useful with students who have encountered learning problems. Assume that Jim Marshall is teaching his American history students to learn all the U.S. presidents and the dates for each term of office. Most students are able to handle all the memorization of the names and dates in sequence with no problem, but students with learning problems are having difficulty mastering all the information. Mr. Marshall decides to modify the method of instruction for the latter students by dividing the unit into a series of short lessons. Each lesson addresses a certain time period and focuses on the presidents in office at that time, providing students smaller groups of names to memorize in one sitting. At the end of each lesson, the students are expected to know the content as well as the names of the presidents, building on each previous lessons.

A physical education teacher realizes that elementary students may not be able to immediately play basketball even though they know the rules of the game. Therefore, he begins by playing games and doing fun drills and activities that will help the students develop skills in dribbling, passing the ball, and shooting baskets from different locations. Once the children develop some mastery with the skills needed, then the actual game of basketball can be introduced.

Gina Brown knows that many of her students have never had any exposure to psychology. Although the majority of her undergraduate students are very capable and highly motivated she knows that looking through the abundance of material covered in the textbook and course packet could be overwhelming to even the best of students. Therefore, on the first day of class Professor Brown provides the students with a syllabus that breaks the course content into several major units. Within each unit are specific objectives, reading assignments, and study questions.

instruction. A disadvantage is that working through a branching program in book form can be very confusing. Should students lose their place, it may be time consuming to find it. Branching programs also may not provide sufficient repetition to ensure that all students learn concepts well.

Research suggests that linear and branching programs promote student learning equally well and that PI is as effective as conventional classroom teaching (Bangert, Kulik, & Kulik, 1983; Lange, 1972; Silberman, Melaragno, Coulson, & Estavan, 1961). Whether PI is used instead of traditional instruction depends in part on how well existing programs cover the required scope and sequence of instruction. PI seems especially useful with students who demonstrate skill deficiencies; working through

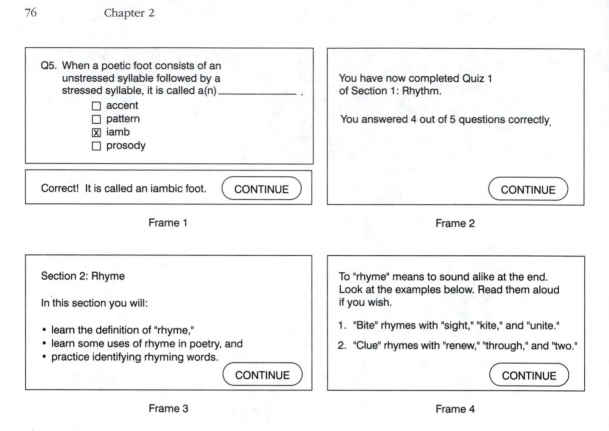

Figure 2.4
Frames from a linear program.

programs provides remedial instruction and practice. PI also is useful for independent study on a topic because students work through programs on their own.

Programmed instruction in computer format is a type of *computer-based instruction (CBI)*. Until recently CBI was the most common application of computer learning in schools (Jonassen, 1996). CBI often is used for drills and tutorials. Whereas drills review information, tutorials are interactive: They present information and feedback to students and respond based on students' answers (e.g., branching programs).

Studies investigating CBI in college courses yield beneficial effects on students' achievement and attitudes (Kulik, Kulik, & Cohen, 1980). Several CBI features are firmly grounded in learning theory and research. Computers command students' attention and provide immediate feedback, which can be of a type typically not given in class (e.g., how present performances compare with prior performances to highlight progress). Computers individualize content and rate of presentation.

Although drills and tutorials place strict limitations on how students interact with material, one advantage of CBI is that many programs allow personalization; students

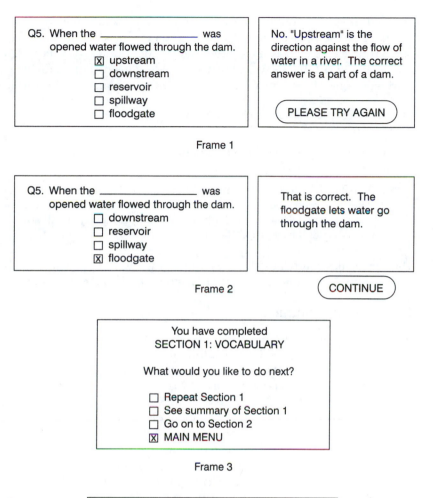

Frame 1

Frame 2

Frame 3

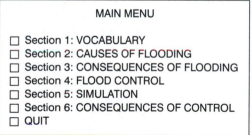

Frame 4

Figure 2.5
Frames from a branching program.

enter information about themselves, parents, and friends, which is then included in the instructional presentation. Personalization can produce higher achievement than other formats (Anand & Ross, 1987; Ross, McCormick, Krisak, & Anand, 1985). Anand and Ross (1987) gave elementary children instruction in dividing fractions according to one of three problem formats (abstract, concrete, personalized):

(Abstract) There are three objects. Each is cut in half. In all, how many pieces would there be?

(Concrete) Billy had three candy bars. He cut each of them in half. In all, how many pieces of candy did Billy have?

(Personalized for Joseph) Joseph's teacher, Mrs. Williams, surprised him on December 15 when she presented Joseph with three candy bars. Joseph cut each one of them in half so that he could share the birthday gift with his friends. In all, how many pieces of candy did Joseph have? (pp. 73–74)

The personalized format led to better learning and transfer than the abstract format and to more positive attitudes toward instruction than the concrete format.

Contingency Contracts

A *contingency contract* is an agreement between teacher and student specifying what work the student will accomplish and the expected outcome (reinforcement) for successful performance (Homme, Csanyi, Gonzales, & Rechs, 1970). A contract can be made verbally, although it usually is written. Teachers can devise the contract and ask if the student agrees with it, but it is customary for teacher and student to formulate it jointly. An advantage of joint participation is that students may feel more committed to fulfilling the contract's terms. When people participate in goal selection, they often are more committed to attaining the goal than when they are excluded from the selection process (Locke & Latham, 1990).

Contracts specify goals or expected outcomes in terms of particular behaviors to be displayed. The "contingency" is the expected outcome, which often can be reduced to, "If you do this, then you will receive that." The behaviors should be specific—for example, "I will complete pages 1–30 in my math book with at least 90% accuracy," or "I will stay in my seat during reading period." Such general behaviors as, "I will work on my math," or "I will behave appropriately," are unacceptable. With young children, time frames should be brief; however, objectives can cover more than one time, such as successive 30-minute periods or during each social studies period for one week. Contracts may include academic and nonacademic behaviors (Application 2.11).

Developing contracts with students and monitoring progress is time consuming. Fortunately, most learners do not require contracts to behave appropriately or accomplish work. Contracts seem especially helpful as a means of assisting students to work on assignments more productively. A lengthy, long-term assignment can be subdivided into a series of short-term goals with due dates. This type of plan helps students keep up with the work and turn in material on time.

APPLICATION 2.11
Contingency Contracting

A contingency contract represents a systematic application of reinforcement principles to change behavior. It can be used to change any type of behavior, such as completing work, not disrupting the class, and participating in discussions. When developing a contract, a teacher should make sure that the reward is something that really interests and motivates the students.

Assume that Mrs. Stone has tried unsuccessfully to apply several motivational techniques to encourage James, a student in her class, to complete work in language arts. Mrs. Stone and James might jointly develop a contract to address the inappropriate behaviors. They should discuss the problem, identify the desired behavior, and list the consequences and time frame for fulfilling the terms of the contract. A sample contract might be as follows:

Contract for the Week of January 9–13

I will complete my language arts seatwork with 80% accuracy in the time allotted during class.

If I complete my seatwork, I will be allowed to participate in a learning center activity.

If I do not complete my seatwork, I will miss recess and complete my work at that time.

Monday:	_____ Completed	_____ Not completed
Tuesday:	_____ Completed	_____ Not completed
Wednesday:	_____ Completed	_____ Not completed
Thursday:	_____ Completed	_____ Not completed
Friday:	_____ Completed	_____ Not completed

Bonus: If I complete my work 3 out of 5 days, I will be able to work in the computer lab for 30 minutes on Friday afternoon.

_____   _____
Student signature/Date   Teacher signature/Date

Contracts are based on the principle that goals that are specific, temporally close at hand, and difficult but attainable will maximize performance (Schunk, 1990, 1991). Contracts also convey information to students about their progress in completing the task. Such progress information raises student motivation and achievement (Locke & Latham, 1990; Schunk, 1994). Contracts should promote achievement if they reinforce student progress in learning or in accomplishing more on-task behavior.

Keller Plan

The *Keller Plan*, or *Personalized System of Instruction (PSI)*, reflects many operant conditioning principles (Keller, 1966, 1968; Keller & Sherman, 1974). The central features are student self-pacing, mastery learning, and extensive self-study of the course material (Keller, 1977). The course is divided into units, and students must pass each unit exam with a minimum score (e.g., 80%) before they can begin the next unit. There often are fewer whole-class meetings compared with conventionally taught courses. Students study the course material on their own or in small groups, frequently consult with teaching assistants, and decide how quickly or slowly they want to complete the material. Grades reflect the number of units completed, with a certain percentage of the grade based on a final exam. The Keller Plan has been used widely in college undergraduate courses in diverse fields including psychology, engineering, and biology.

Evaluations of the effectiveness of Keller Plan courses in fostering learning have been positive (Callahan & Smith, 1990; Robin, 1976; Ryan, 1974). Kulik, Kulik, and Cohen (1979) reviewed 75 studies comparing Keller Plan courses with courses taught in conventional fashion. Outcome measures included instructors' course grades, course ratings, course completions, and student study time. PSI generally led to higher student achievement, less variability in achievement, and higher student ratings; no differences were obtained for course withdrawal or student study time.

The finding about study time is interesting because students who do not adequately pace themselves will fall behind and may drop the course. Robin (1976) found higher withdrawal rates in PSI courses than in conventionally taught courses and more study time in PSI courses; however, when the number of hours students spent in lectures was added to the time for conventional courses, there was no difference in study time. Kulik et al. (1979) found different effects for PSI depending on the subject area. PSI was particularly effective in mathematics, engineering, and psychology. Differences in the outcomes of PSI and conventional courses were smaller when some PSI features (e.g., unit tests) were incorporated into conventional courses.

A follow-up evaluation of mastery-learning programs (which included PSI) yielded conflicting results (Kulik, Kulik, & Bangert-Drowns, 1990). Interestingly, programs were more effective in the social sciences than in mathematics, natural sciences, and the humanities. Studies showing strongest effects also tended to use locally developed rather than standardized measures of student achievement, required students to move through the material at the teacher's (rather than the student's) pace, and required high scores on unit quizzes. These authors also found greater benefits for low-aptitude students and fewer benefits for high-aptitude students.

Future research should resolve conflicting results on the effectiveness of PSI. For now, we can say that PSI seems to be most useful in courses whose content easily subdivides into units and in which extensive self-study is possible. It may be less appropriate in courses where greater discussion and student interaction are desired or where material is approached in more holistic (less analytical) fashion.

SUMMARY

Behavioral theories dominated the psychology of learning for the first half of the twentieth century. Such theories explain learning in terms of environmental events. Mental processes are not necessary to explain the acquisition, maintenance, and generalization of behavior.

The learning theories of Thorndike, Pavlov, Watson, and Guthrie are of historical importance. Although these theories differ, each views learning as a process of forming associations between stimuli and responses. Thorndike believed that responses to stimuli are strengthened when followed by satisfying consequences. Pavlov experimentally demonstrated how stimuli could be conditioned to elicit responses by being paired with other stimuli. Watson proposed that Pavlov's model could be extended to cover diverse forms of learning and personality development. Guthrie hypothesized that a contiguous relation between stimulus and response established their pairing. Although these theories are no longer viable in their original form, many of their principles are evident in current theoretical perspectives. These theories and the research they generated helped to establish the psychology of learning as a legitimate area of study.

Operant conditioning—the learning theory formulated by B. F. Skinner—is based on the assumption that features of the environment (stimuli, situations, events) serve as cues for responding. Reinforcement strengthens responses and increases their future likelihood of occurring when the stimuli are present. It is not necessary to refer to underlying physiological or mental states to explain behavior.

The basic operant conditioning model is a three-term contingency involving a discriminative stimulus (antecedent), response (behavior), and reinforcing stimulus (consequence). The consequences of behaviors determine the likelihood that people will respond to environmental cues. Reinforcing consequences increase behavior; punishing consequences decrease behavior. Some other important operant conditioning concepts are extinction, generalization, discrimination, primary and secondary reinforcers, and reinforcement schedules.

Shaping is the process used to alter behavior. Shaping involves differential reinforcement of successive approximations of the desired behavior toward its terminal form or frequency of occurrence. Complex behaviors are formed by chaining together simple behaviors in successive three-term contingencies. Behavior modification programs have been commonly applied in diverse contexts to promote adaptive behaviors.

The generality of operant conditioning principles has been challenged by cognitive theorists who contend that by ignoring mental processes operant conditioning offers an incomplete account of human learning. This limitation is especially apparent in Skinner's explanation of language learning, which has been criticized by linguists and psycholinguists who view language as governed by underlying mental structures. Stimuli and reinforcement may explain some human learning, but much research shows that to explain learning we must take into account people's thoughts, beliefs, and feelings.

Operant principles have been applied to many aspects of teaching and learning. Foremost is their use in behavioral objectives, programmed instruction, contingency contracts, and the Keller Plan. Research evidence generally shows positive effects of these applications on student achievement. Problems persist, however, with operant conditioning's position on the role of understanding in behavior, the learning-performance distinction, the influence of reinforcement, and the effects of success-only learning. Regardless of theoretical orientation, one can apply behavioral methods to facilitate student learning and achievement.

3 Social Cognitive Theory

The preceding chapter focused on behavioral theories of learning, which held sway for the first half of the twentieth century. Beginning in the late 1950s and early 1960s, behavioral theories were challenged on many fronts. Their influence waned to the point where today the major theoretical perspectives are cognitive.

One of the challenges to behavioral theories came from studies on observational learning conducted by Albert Bandura and his colleagues. A central finding of this research was that people could learn new actions merely by observing others perform them. Observers did not have to perform the actions at the time of learning. Reinforcement was not necessary for learning to occur. These findings disputed central assumptions of behavioral theories.

This chapter covers *social cognitive theory*, which stresses the idea that much human learning occurs in a social environment. By observing others, people acquire knowledge, rules, skills, strategies, beliefs, and attitudes. Individuals also learn from models the usefulness and appropriateness of behaviors and the consequences of modeled behaviors, and they act in accordance with beliefs about their capabilities and the expected outcomes of their actions.

The focus of this chapter is on Bandura's (1986, 1997, 2001) social cognitive theory. Bandura was born in Alberta, Canada, in 1925. He received his doctorate in clinical psychology from the University of Iowa, where he was influenced by Miller and Dollard's (1941) *Social Learning and Imitation* (discussed later in this chapter). After arriving at Stanford University in

the 1950s, Bandura began a research program exploring the influences on social behavior. He believed that learning theories in vogue at that time offered incomplete explanations of the acquisition and performance of prosocial and deviant behaviors:

> Indeed, most prior applications of learning theory to issues concerning prosocial and deviant behavior . . . have suffered from the fact that they have relied heavily on a limited range of principles established on the basis of, and mainly supported by, studies of animal learning or human learning in one-person situations. (Bandura & Walters, 1963, p. 1)

Bandura formulated a comprehensive theory of observational learning that he has gradually expanded to encompass acquisition and performance of diverse skills, strategies, and behaviors. Social cognitive principles have been applied to the learning of cognitive, motor, social, and self-regulatory skills, as well as to the topics of violence (live, televised), moral development, and societal values.

Bandura is a prolific writer. Beginning with the book *Social Learning and Personality Development*, written in 1963 with Richard Walters, he has authored several other books, including *Principles of Behavior Modification* (1969), *Aggression: A Social Learning Analysis* (1973), *Social Learning Theory* (1977b), and *Social Foundations of Thought and Action: A Social Cognitive Theory* (1986). With the publication of *Self-Efficacy: The Exercise of Control* (1997), Bandura extended his theory to address ways

83

people seek control over important events of their lives through self-regulation of their thoughts and actions. The basic processes involve setting goals, judging anticipated outcomes of actions, evaluating progress toward goals, and self-regulating thoughts, emotions, and actions.

> Another distinctive feature of social cognitive theory is the central role it assigns to self-regulatory functions. People do not behave just to suit the preferences of others. Much of their behavior is motivated and regulated by internal standards and self-evaluative reactions to their own actions. After personal standards have been adopted, discrepancies between a performance and the standard against which it is measured activate evaluative self-reactions, which serve to influence subsequent behavior. An act, therefore, includes among its determinants self-produced influences. (Bandura, 1986, p. 20)

We begin by discussing the conceptual framework of social cognitive theory, along with its underlying assumptions about the nature of human learning and behavior. A significant portion of the chapter is devoted to modeling processes. The various influences on learning and performance are described with special emphasis on the critical influences of goals and self-efficacy, which are key processes. Self-regulation is discussed from a social cognitive perspective, and some implications of the theory for instruction are provided.

When you finish studying this chapter, you should be able to do the following:

- Describe and exemplify the process of triadic reciprocal causality.

- Distinguish between enactive and vicarious learning and between learning and performance.

- Define and exemplify three functions of modeling.

- Discuss the subprocesses of observational learning.

- Explain the various factors that affect observational learning and performance.

- Discuss the roles of goal properties and other goal aspects on learning.

- Distinguish between outcome expectations and self-efficacy and give examples of each.

- Discuss how features of models (e.g., peers, multiple, coping) affect self-efficacy and learning.

- Explain a social cognitive perspective of self-regulation.

- Understand some key implications of the theory for educational practice.

CONCEPTUAL FRAMEWORK FOR LEARNING

Social cognitive theory makes several assumptions about learning and the performance of behaviors. These assumptions address the reciprocal interactions among persons, behaviors, and environments; enactive and vicarious learning (i.e., the ways learning occurs); and the distinction between learning and performance.

Reciprocal Interactions

Bandura (1982a, 1986, 2001) discusses human behavior within a framework of *triadic reciprocality*, or reciprocal interactions among behaviors, environmental variables, and personal factors such as cognitions (Figure 3.1):

Figure 3.1
Triadic reciprocality model of causality.
Source: *Social Foundations of Thought and Action* by Bandura, ©
Reprinted by permission of Pearson Education, Inc. Upper Saddle
River, NJ.

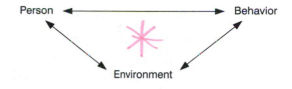

In the social cognitive view people are neither driven by inner forces nor automatically shaped and controlled by external stimuli. Rather, human functioning is explained in terms of a model of triadic reciprocality in which behavior, cognitive and other personal factors, and environmental events all operate as interacting determinants of each other. (Bandura, 1986, p. 18)

Triadic reciprocality is evident in an important construct in Bandura's (1982b, 1997) theory: *perceived self-efficacy,* or beliefs concerning one's capabilities to organize and implement actions necessary to learn or perform behaviors at designated levels. With respect to the interaction of self-efficacy (personal factor) and behavior, research shows that self-efficacy beliefs influence such achievement behaviors as choice of tasks, persistence, effort expenditure, and skill acquisition (person → behavior; Schunk, 1991, 2001). In turn, how students act modifies their self-efficacy. As students work on tasks, they note their progress toward their learning goals (e.g., completing workbook pages, finishing sections of a term paper). Such progress indicators convey to students that they are capable of performing well and enhance their self-efficacy for continued learning (behavior → person).

Research on students with learning disabilities has demonstrated the interaction between self-efficacy and environmental factors. Many such students hold a low sense of self-efficacy for performing well (Licht & Kistner, 1986). Individuals in students' social environments may react to students based on attributes typically associated with students with learning disabilities (e.g., low self-efficacy) rather than on the individuals' actual abilities (person → environment). Some teachers, for example, judge such students less capable than students without disabilities and hold lower academic expectations for them, even in content areas where students with learning disabilities are performing adequately (Bryan & Bryan, 1983). In turn, teacher feedback can affect self-efficacy (environment → person). When a teacher tells a student, "I know you can do this," the student likely will feel more confident about succeeding.

Students' behaviors and classroom environments influence one another in many ways. Consider a typical instructional sequence in which the teacher presents information and asks students to direct their attention to the board. Environmental influence on behavior occurs when students look at the board without much conscious deliberation (environment → behavior). Students' behaviors often alter the instructional environment. If the teacher asks questions and students give the wrong answers, the teacher may reteach some points rather than continue the lesson (behavior → environment).

Enactive and Vicarious Learning

In social cognitive theory:

> Learning is largely an information processing activity in which information about the structure of behavior and about environmental events is transformed into symbolic representations that serve as guides for action. (Bandura, 1986, p. 51)

Learning occurs either *enactively* through actual doing or *vicariously* by observing models perform (e.g., live, symbolic, portrayed electronically).

Enactive learning involves learning from the consequences of one's actions. Behaviors that result in successful consequences are retained; those that lead to failures are refined or discarded. Operant conditioning theory also says that people learn by doing, but social cognitive theory provides a different explanation. Skinner (1953) noted that cognitions may accompany behavioral change but do not influence it (see Chapter 2). Social cognitive theory contends that behavioral consequences, rather than strengthening behaviors as postulated in operant theory, serve as sources of *information* and *motivation*. Consequences inform people of the accuracy or appropriateness of behavior. People who succeed at a task or are rewarded understand that they are performing well. When people fail or are punished, they know that they are doing something wrong and may try to correct the problem. Consequences also motivate people. People strive to learn behaviors they value and believe will have desirable consequences, whereas they avoid learning behaviors that are punished or otherwise not satisfying. People's cognitions, rather than consequences, affect learning.

Much human learning occurs *vicariously*, or without overt performance, by the learner at the time of learning. Common sources of vicarious learning are observing or listening to models who are live (appear in person), symbolic or nonhuman (e.g., televised talking animals, cartoon characters), on electronic sources (e.g., television, computer, videotape), or in printed materials (books, magazines). Vicarious sources accelerate learning over what would be possible if people had to perform every behavior for learning to occur. Vicarious sources also save people from personally experiencing negative consequences. We learn that poisonous snakes are dangerous through teaching by others, reading books, watching films, and so forth, rather than by experiencing the unpleasant consequences of their bites.

Learning complex skills typically occurs through action and observation. Students first observe models explain and demonstrate skills, then practice them. Aspiring golfers, for example, do not simply watch professionals play golf; rather, they engage in much practice and receive corrective feedback from instructors. Students observe teachers explain and demonstrate skills. Through observation, students often learn some components of a complex skill and not others. Practice gives teachers opportunities to provide corrective feedback to help students perfect their skills. As with enactive learning, response consequences from vicarious sources inform and motivate observers. Observers are more apt to learn modeled behaviors leading to successes than those resulting in failures. When people believe that modeled behaviors are useful, they attend carefully to models and mentally rehearse the behaviors.

Learning and Performance

Social cognitive theory distinguishes between new learning and performance of previously learned behaviors. Unlike behavioral theories, which contend that learning involves connecting responses to stimuli or following responses with consequences, social cognitive theory asserts that learning and performance are distinct processes. Although much learning does, in fact, occur by doing, we learn a great deal by observing rather than by doing. Whether we ever perform what we learn by observing depends on factors such as our motivation, interest, incentives to perform, perceived need, physical state, social pressures, and type of competing activities. Reinforcement, or the belief that it will be forthcoming, affects performance rather than learning.

Tolman and Honzik (1930) conducted an early experimental demonstration of the learning-performance distinction. These researchers investigated *latent learning*, which is observational learning in the absence of a goal or reinforcement. Two groups of rats were allowed to wander through a maze for 10 trials. One group always was fed in the maze, whereas the other group was never fed. Rats fed in the maze quickly reduced their time and number of errors in running the maze, but time and errors for the other group remained high. Starting on the 11th trial, some rats from the nonreinforced group received food for running the maze. Both their time and number of errors quickly dropped to the levels of the group that always had been fed; the running times and error rates for rats that remained nonreinforced did not change. Rats in the nonreinforced group had learned features of the maze by wandering through it without reinforcement. When food was introduced, the latent learning quickly displayed itself.

By observing models, students acquire knowledge they may not demonstrate at the time of learning (Rosenthal & Zimmerman, 1978). Although some school activities (e.g., review sessions) involve performance of previously learned skills, much time is spent learning. Students acquire *declarative knowledge* in the form of facts, scripts (e.g., events of a story), and organized passages (words in a song or poem). Students also acquire *procedural knowledge* (concepts, rules, algorithms), as well as *conditional knowledge* (knowing when to employ forms of declarative and procedural knowledge and why it is important to do so; Miller, 1994; Paris, Cross, & Lipson, 1984; Paris, Lipson, & Wixson, 1983). Any of these forms of knowledge can be acquired but not demonstrated when learning occurs. For example, students might learn that skimming is a useful procedure for acquiring the gist of text but may not employ that knowledge until they are at home reading a magazine.

The model portrayed in Figure 3.1 does not imply that the directions of influence are always the same. At any given time, one factor may predominate: When environmental influences are weak, personal factors predominate. For instance, students allowed to write a report on a book of their choosing will select one they enjoy. However, a person caught in a burning house is apt to evacuate quickly; the environment dictates the behavior.

Much of the time the three factors interact. As a teacher presents a lesson to the class, students think about what the teacher is saying (environment influences cognition—a personal factor). Students who do not understand a point raise their hands to ask a question (cognition influences behavior). The teacher reviews the point (behavior influences environment). Eventually the teacher gives students work to accomplish (environment influences cognition, which influences behavior). As students work on the task, they believe they are performing it well (behavior influences cognition). They decide they like the task, ask the teacher if they can continue to work on it, and are allowed to do so (cognition influences behavior, which influences environment).

MODELING PROCESSES

Modeling is a critical component in social cognitive theory. *Modeling* is a general term that refers to behavioral, cognitive, and affective changes deriving from observing one or more models (Berger, 1977; Rosenthal & Bandura, 1978; Schunk, 1987, 1998; Zimmerman, 1977). Historically, modeling was discussed as *imitation*, but "modeling" is a far more inclusive concept. We will cover some historical work to provide a background against which the significance of modeling research by Bandura and others can be appreciated.

Theories of Imitation

Throughout history, people have viewed imitation as an important means of transmitting behaviors (Rosenthal & Zimmerman, 1978). The ancient Greeks used the term *mimesis* to refer to learning through observation of the actions of others and of abstract models exemplifying literary and moral styles. Other perspectives on imitation relate it to instincts, development, conditioning, and instrumental behavior (Table 3.1).

Imitation Is an Instinct.   At the beginning of the twentieth century, the dominant scientific view was that people possessed a natural instinct to imitate the actions of others (James, 1890; Tarde, 1903). James believed that imitation was largely responsible

Table 3.1
Theories of imitation.

View	Assumptions
Instinct	Observed actions elicit an instinctive drive to copy those actions.
Developmental	Children imitate actions that fit with existing cognitive structures.
Conditioned response	Behaviors are imitated and reinforced through shaping. Imitation becomes a generalized response class.
Instrumental behavior	Imitation becomes a secondary drive through repeated reinforcement of responses matching those of models. Imitation results in drive reduction.

for socialization, but he did not explain the process by which imitation occurs. McDougall (1926) restricted his definition of imitation to the instinctive overt copying by one person of the actions of another.

Behaviorists rejected the instinct notion because it assumed the existence of an internal drive, and possibly a mental image, intervening between a stimulus (action of another person) and response (copying of that action). Watson (1924) believed that the so-called instinctive behaviors of people resulted largely from training and therefore were learned.

Imitation Is Limited by Development. Piaget (1962) offered a different view of imitation. He believed that human development involves the acquisition of *schemes,* or cognitive structures that underlie and make possible organized thought and action (Flavell, 1985). Thoughts and actions are not synonymous with schemes; they are overt manifestations of schemes. Schemes available to individuals determine how they react to events. Schemes reflect prior experiences and comprise one's knowledge at any given time.

Schemes presumably develop through maturation and experiences slightly more advanced than one's existing cognitive structures. Imitation is restricted to activities corresponding to existing schemes. Children may imitate actions they understand, but they should not imitate actions incongruent with their cognitive structures. Development, therefore, must precede imitation. This view severely limits the potential of imitation to create and modify cognitive structures.

Little empirical support exists for this restricted developmental position (Rosenthal & Zimmerman, 1978). In an early study, Valentine (1930b) found that infants could imitate actions within their capabilities that they had not previously performed. Infants showed a strong tendency to imitate unusual actions commanding attention. The imitation was not always immediate, and actions often had to be repeated before infants would imitate them. The individual performing the original actions was important: Infants were most likely to imitate their mothers. These and other results (Rosenthal & Zimmerman, 1978) show that imitation is not a simple reflection of developmental level but rather may serve an important role in promoting development.

Imitation Is Conditioned. Behaviorists construed imitation in associationist terms. Humphrey (1921) wrote that imitation is a type of circular reaction in which each response serves as a stimulus for the next response. A baby may start crying (response) because of a pain (stimulus). The baby hears its own crying (auditory stimulus), which then serves as a stimulus for subsequent crying. Through conditioning, small reflex units form progressively more complex response chains.

Skinner's (1953) operant conditioning theory treats imitation as a generalized response class (see Chapter 2). In the three-term contingency ($S^D \rightarrow R \rightarrow S^R$), a modeled act serves as the S^D (discriminative stimulus). Imitation occurs when an observer performs the same response (R) and receives reinforcement (S^R). This contingency becomes established early in life. For example, a parent makes a sound ("Dada"), the child imitates, and the parent delivers reinforcement (smile, hug). Once an imitative response class is established, it can be maintained on an intermittent reinforcement schedule. Children imitate the behaviors of models (parents, friends) as long as the models remain discriminative stimuli for reinforcement.

A limitation of this view is that one can imitate only those responses one can perform. In fact, much research shows that diverse types of behaviors can be acquired through observation (Rosenthal & Zimmerman, 1978). Another limitation concerns the necessity of reinforcement to produce and sustain imitation. Research by Bandura and others shows that observers learn from models in the absence of reinforcement to models or observers (Bandura, 1986). Tolman found that reinforcement primarily affected learners' performance of previously learned responses rather than new learning (discussed later in this chapter).

Imitation Is Instrumental Behavior.   Miller and Dollard (1941) proposed an elaborate theory of imitation, or *matched-dependent behavior*, which contends that imitation is instrumental learned behavior because it leads to reinforcement. Matched-dependent behavior is matched to (is the same as) that of the model and depends on or is elicited by the model's action.

Miller and Dollard believed that initially the imitator responds to behavioral cues in trial-and-error fashion, but eventually the imitator performs the correct response and is reinforced. Responses performed by imitators previously were learned.

This conception of imitation as learned instrumental behavior was an important advance in its scientific study, but the view contains problems. Like other historical views, this theory postulates that new responses are not created through imitation; rather, imitation represents performance of learned behaviors. This view cannot account for learning through imitation, for delayed imitation (i.e., when imitators perform the matching responses some time after the actions are performed by the model), or for imitated behaviors that are not reinforced (Bandura & Walters, 1963). This narrow conception of imitation restricts its usefulness to imitative responses corresponding closely to those portrayed by models.

Functions of Modeling

We turn now to a discussion of the important functions served by modeling. Bandura (1986) distinguished three important functions: response facilitation, inhibition/disinhibition, and observational learning (Table 3.2).

Response Facilitation.   People learn many skills and behaviors that they do not perform because they lack motivation to do so. *Response facilitation* refers to modeled actions that serve as social prompts for observers to behave accordingly. Consider an elementary teacher who has set up an attractive display in a corner of the classroom. When the first students enter in the morning, they spot the display and immediately go to look at it. When other students enter the room, they see a group in the corner, so they, too, move to the corner to see what everyone is looking at. Several students together serve as a social prompt for others to join them, even though the latter may not know why the others are gathered.

Table 3.2
Functions of modeling.

Function	Underlying Process
Response facilitation	Social prompts create motivational inducements for observers to model the actions ("going along with the crowd").
Inhibition and disinhibition	Modeled behaviors create expectations in observers that similar consequences will occur should they model the actions.
Observational learning	Subprocesses include attention, retention, production, and motivation.

Response facilitation effects are common. Have you ever seen a group of people looking in one direction? This can serve as a cue for you to look in the same direction. Newcomers at meetings of volunteer groups may watch with interest as a basket is passed for donations. If most people put in a dollar, that serves as a signal that a dollar is an acceptable donation. Note that response facilitation does not reflect true learning because people already know how to perform the behaviors. Rather, the models serve as cues for observer's actions. Observers derive information about the appropriateness of behavior and may be motivated to perform the actions if models receive positive consequences.

Response facilitation modeling may occur without conscious awareness. Chartrand and Bargh (1999) found evidence for a *Chameleon effect,* whereby people nonconsciously mimic behaviors and mannerisms of those in their social environments. The simple perception of behavior may trigger a response to act accordingly.

Inhibition/Disinhibition.   Observing a model can strengthen or weaken inhibitions to perform behaviors previously learned. *Inhibition* occurs when models are punished for performing certain actions, which in turn stops or prevents observers from acting accordingly. *Disinhibition* occurs when models perform threatening or prohibited activities without experiencing negative consequences, which leads observers to perform the same behaviors. Inhibitory and disinhibitory effects on behavior occur because the modeled displays convey to observers that similar consequences are probable if they perform the modeled behaviors. Such information also may affect emotions (e.g., increase or decrease anxiety) and motivation.

Teachers' actions can inhibit or disinhibit classroom misbehavior. Unpunished student misbehavior may prove disinhibiting: Students who observe modeled misbehavior not punished might start misbehaving themselves. Conversely, misbehavior in other students may be inhibited when a teacher disciplines one student for misbehaving. Observers are more likely to believe that they, too, will be disciplined if they continue to misbehave and are spotted by the teacher.

Inhibition and disinhibition are similar to response facilitation in that behaviors reflect actions people already have learned. One difference is that response facilitation generally involves behaviors that are socially acceptable, whereas inhibited and disinhibited actions often have moral or legal overtones (i.e., involve breaking rules or laws) and have accompanying emotions (e.g., fears). Looting often gets out of hand during a riot because looters go unpunished, which disinhibits looting (an illegal act) in some observers.

Observational Learning. Observational learning through modeling occurs when observers display new patterns of behavior that, prior to exposure to the modeled behaviors, have a zero probability of occurrence even when motivation is high (Bandura, 1969). A key mechanism is the information conveyed by models to observers of ways to produce new behaviors (Rosenthal & Zimmerman, 1978). Observational learning comprises four subprocesses: attention, retention, production, and motivation (Bandura, 1986; see Table 3.3).

The first subprocess is observer *attention* to relevant events so that they are meaningfully perceived. At a given moment one can attend to many activities. As discussed later in this chapter, characteristics of the model and the observer influence one's attention to models. Task features also command attention, especially unusual size, shape, color, or sound. Teachers often make modeling more distinctive with bright colors and oversized features. Attention also is influenced by perceived functional value of modeled activities. Modeled activities that observers believe are important and more likely to lead to rewarding outcomes command greater attention. Students believe that most teacher activities are highly functional because they are intended to enhance student learning. Learners also are apt to believe that their teachers are highly competent, which enhances attention. Factors that promote the perception of model competence are modeled actions that lead to success and symbolic indicators of competence, such as one's title or position.

Table 3.3
Subprocesses of observational learning

Subprocess	Activities
Attention	Student attention is directed by physically accentuating relevant task features, subdividing complex activities into parts, using competent models, and demonstrating usefulness of modeled behaviors.
Retention	Retention is increased by rehearsing information to be learned, coding in visual and symbolic form, and relating new material to information previously stored in memory.
Production	Behaviors produced are compared to one's conceptual (mental) representation. Feedback helps to correct deficiencies.
Motivation	Consequences of modeled behaviors inform observers of functional value and appropriateness. Consequences motivate by creating outcome expectations and raising self-efficacy.

2.   The second subprocess is *retention,* which requires cognitively organizing, rehearsing, coding, and transforming modeled information for storage in memory. Observational learning postulates two modes of storing knowledge. A modeled display can be stored as an image, in verbal form, or both (Bandura, 1977b). Imaginal coding is especially important for activities not easily described in words; for example, motor skills performed so rapidly that individual movements merge into a larger organized sequence or act (e.g., golf swing). Much cognitive skill learning relies upon verbal coding of rules or procedures. (Storage of information in memory is discussed in Chapter 4.)

Rehearsal, or the mental review of information, serves a key role in the retention of knowledge. A study by Bandura and Jeffery (1973) demonstrated benefits of coding and rehearsal. Adults were presented with complex modeled movement configurations. Some participants coded these movements at the time of presentation by assigning to them numerical or verbal designators. Other participants were not given coding instructions but were told to subdivide the movements to remember them. In addition, participants either were or were not allowed to rehearse the codes or movements following presentation. Both coding and rehearsal enhanced retention of modeled events; individuals who coded and rehearsed showed the best recall. Rehearsal without coding and coding without rehearsal were less effective.

3.   The third observational learning subprocess is *production,* which involves translating visual and symbolic conceptions of modeled events into overt behaviors. Many simple actions may be learned by simply observing them; subsequent production by observers indicates learning. Rarely, however, are complex behaviors learned solely through observation. Most complex skills are learned through a combination of modeling, guided practice, and corrective feedback. Learners often will acquire a rough approximation of a complex skill by observing modeled demonstrations (Bandura, 1977b). They refine their skills with practice, corrective feedback, and reteaching.

Problems in producing modeled behaviors arise not only because information is inadequately coded but also because learners experience difficulty translating coded information in memory into overt action. For example, a child may have a basic understanding of how to tie shoelaces but not be able to translate that knowledge into behavior. Teachers who suspect that students are having trouble demonstrating what they have learned may need to test students in different ways.

4.   *Motivation,* the fourth subprocess, influences observational learning because people are more likely to attend to, retain, and produce those modeled actions that they feel are important. Individuals do not demonstrate all the skills, strategies, and behaviors they acquire through observation; rather, they perform those actions they believe will result in rewarding outcomes and avoid acting in ways they believe will be responded to negatively (Schunk, 1987). They form expectations about anticipated outcomes of actions based on consequences experienced by them and models (Bandura, 1997). Persons also act based on their values. They perform activities they value and avoid those they find unsatisfying, regardless of the consequences to themselves or others. People forego money, prestige, and power when they believe activities they must engage in to receive these rewards are unethical (e.g., questionable business practices).

Motivation is a critical subprocess of observational learning that teachers promote in various ways, including making learning interesting, relating material to student interests, having students set goals and monitor goal progress, providing feedback indicating increasing competence, and stressing the value of learning. These and other factors are considered in Chapter 8.

Cognitive Skill Learning

Observational learning expands the range and rate of learning over what could occur through shaping (see Chapter 2), where each response is performed and reinforced. Modeled portrayals of cognitive skills are standard features in classrooms. In a common instructional sequence, a teacher explains and demonstrates the skill to be acquired, after which the students receive guided practice while the teacher checks for student understanding. The skill is retaught if students experience difficulty. When the teacher is satisfied students have a basic understanding, they may engage in independent practice while the teacher periodically monitors their work. Examples of teacher modeling are given in Application 3.1.

Many features of instruction incorporate models. Two especially germane applications of modeling to instruction are cognitive modeling and self-instruction.

Cognitive Modeling.   *Cognitive modeling* incorporates modeled explanation and demonstration with verbalization of the model's thoughts and reasons for performing given actions (Meichenbaum, 1977). In teaching division skills, a teacher might verbalize the following in response to the problem $276 \div 4$:

> First I have to decide what number to divide 4 into. I take 276, start on the left and move toward the right until I have a number the same as or larger than 4. Is 2 larger than 4? No. Is 27 larger than 4? Yes. So my first division will be 4 into 27. Now I need to multiply 4 by a number that will give an answer the same as or slightly smaller than 27. How about 5? $5 \times 4 = 20$. No, too small. Let's try 6. $6 \times 4 = 24$. Maybe. Let's try 7. $7 \times 4 = 28$. No, too large. So 6 is correct.

Cognitive modeling can include other types of statements. Errors may be built into the modeled demonstration to show students how to recognize and cope with them. Self-reinforcing statements, such as "I'm doing well," also are useful, especially with students who encounter difficulties learning and doubt their capabilities to perform well.

Research substantiates the useful role of cognitive modeling and shows that modeling combined with explanation is more effective in teaching skills than explanation alone (Rosenthal & Zimmerman, 1978). Schunk (1981) compared the effects of cognitive modeling with those of didactic instruction on children's long-division self-efficacy and achievement. Children lacking division skills received instruction and practice. In the cognitive modeling condition, students observed an adult model explain and demonstrate division operations while applying them to sample problems. In the didactic instruction condition, students reviewed instructional material that explained and demonstrated the operations, but they were not exposed to models. Cognitive modeling enhanced children's division achievement better than did didactic instruction.

APPLICATION 3.1
Teacher Modeling

Teachers serve as models when they help students acquire skills. Modeled demonstrations typically are incorporated into lessons designed to teach students diverse skills such as solving mathematics problems, diagramming sentences, installing batteries in cars, and joining pieces of wood.

Modeled demonstrations can be used to teach elementary school children how to head their papers properly. For instance, Kathy Stone, in her third-grade class, might draw on a transparency or section of a chalkboard a sketch of the paper students are using. Mrs. Stone then can review the heading procedure step by step, explaining and demonstrating how to complete it.

In his ninth-grade American history class, Jim Marshall models how to study for a test. Working through several chapters, he explains and demonstrates how to locate and summarize the major points for each section.

In a middle school life skills class, students can learn how to insert a sleeve into a garment through modeled demonstrations. The teacher might begin by describing the process and then use visual aids to portray the procedure. The teacher could conclude the presentation by demonstrating the process at a sewing machine.

A large group of students in Gina Brown's undergraduate class has been coming to her office after class with questions about how to present their findings from their field projects. During the next class, Dr. Brown uses a recent research project she has completed to demonstrate how one might present findings to a group. She uses handouts, charts, overheads, and PowerPoint® to illustrate ways to present data.

Some other applications of teacher modeling are the following. In physical education students can learn how to perform volleyball shots (e.g., serve, set) by observing the teacher demonstrate the actions and then practicing the skills. In drama class the teacher can model various performance skills while working with students as they practice a play. The teacher can demonstrate desired voice inflections, mood, volume, and body movements for each character in the play. In a first-grade word decoding lesson using phonics the teacher can demonstrate sounding out each letter in a list of words.

Self-Instruction. Meichenbaum (1977) described a *self-instruction* procedure designed to teach students how to regulate their activities during learning. In an early study, Meichenbaum and Goodman (1971) incorporated cognitive modeling into this self-instructional training procedure with impulsive second graders in a special education class. The procedure included:

- **Cognitive modeling**: Adult tells child what to do while adult performs the task.
- **Overt guidance**: Child performs under direction of adult.
- **Overt self-guidance**: Child performs while instructing himself or herself aloud.
- **Faded overt self-guidance**: Child whispers instructions while performing task.
- **Covert self-instruction**: Child performs while guided by inner silent speech.

Self-instruction often is used to slow down children's rate of performing. An adult model used the following statements during a line-drawing task:

> Okay, what is it I have to do? You want me to copy the picture with the different lines. I have to go slow and be careful. Okay, draw the line down, down, good; then to the right, that's it; now down some more and to the left. Good, I'm doing fine so far. Remember go slow. Now back up again. No, I was supposed to go down. That's okay, just erase the line carefully. . . . Good. Even if I make an error I can go on slowly and carefully. Okay, I have to go down now. Finished. I did it. (Meichenbaum & Goodman, 1971, p. 117)

Note that the model made a mistake and showed how to deal with it. This is an important form of learning for students with hyperactivity and behavioral problems because they often become frustrated and quit easily following errors. Meichenbaum and Goodman found that cognitive modeling slowed down response times, but that the self-instructions decreased errors.

Self-instruction has been used with a variety of tasks and types of students (Fish & Pervan, 1985). It is especially useful for students with learning disabilities (Wood, Rosenberg, & Carran, 1993), and in teaching students to work strategically. In teaching reading comprehension, the preceding instructions might be modified as follows: "What is it I have to do? I have to find the topic sentence of the paragraph. The topic sentence is what the paragraph is about. I start by looking for a sentence that sums up the details or tells what the paragraph is about" (McNeil, 1987, p. 96). Statements for coping with difficulties ("I haven't found it yet, but that's all right") can be built into the modeled demonstration.

Rule Learning

Modeling is useful during the process of acquiring rules governing language use and concept attainment (Zimmerman & Rosenthal, 1974; see Chapter 5 for a discussion of concept learning). In contrast to Skinner's ideas about language acquisition (Chapter 2), social cognitive theory assumes very little language is acquired through shaping or mimicry of verbalizations by others. Social cognitive research has not explored the "deep" cognitive structures that are of concern to linguists and psycholinguists, but rather it has investigated whether rule-governed language use is facilitated through exposure to models (Rosenthal & Zimmerman, 1978).

The general procedure involved in language rule learning is to expose the observer to one or more models using a grammatical construction that reflects the rule. Over time the model holds the rule constant while varying nonrelevant task aspects (e.g., words used by the model). If the observer then can model the construction, it reflects rule learning rather than simple imitation of words or sound patterns.

In 1966 Bandura and Harris showed young children common nouns, and children constructed a sentence with each noun. They created different experimental conditions. Some children were exposed to models who demonstrated the desired construction (e.g., passive verbs) and who took turns with them in making up sentences. Reinforcement (stars exchangeable for gifts) was given to some children for making up passive constructions, as well as to the models for children assigned to a modeling condition. In another condition (problem-solving set), children were advised to determine what aspect of the construction earned them a star. This study also investigated the effects of these treatments on prepositional phrases, a second type of grammatical construction.

The use of passive constructions remained generally low after training; modeling combined with reinforcement and problem-solving set produced the greatest number. With prepositional phrases, reinforcement combined with a problem-solving set (with or without modeling) yielded significant increases following training. The children did not simply mimic the model's responses; they acquired the grammatical rule and generated their own sentences, some of which were quite novel. This study shows that social influences can modify grammatical constructions of young children.

A number of studies have demonstrated that exposure to models is effective in teaching children abstract nonlinguistic rules (Rosenthal & Zimmerman, 1978). An early study by Rosenthal, Moore, Dorfman, and Nelson (1971) studied the acquisition and transfer of a simple coordination rule. Children observed a model demonstrate the rule: Construct a three-marble triangle in the same color as the disk stimulus (e.g., construct two blue triangles if two blue disks are presented). For some children, the model also verbalized while responding. Prior to modeling, children showed no evidence of the modeled response. Modeling produced increases in the appropriate response; the addition of verbalized descriptive statements by the model facilitated children's transfer of the rule to disks of mixed colors. These results highlight the efficacy of using modeled demonstrations to teach concepts.

Motor Skill Learning

Social cognitive theory postulates that motor skill learning involves constructing a mental model that provides the conceptual representation of the skill for response production and serves as the standard for correcting responses subsequent to receiving feedback (Bandura, 1986; McCullagh, 1993; Weiss, Ebbeck, & Wiese-Bjornstal, 1993). The conceptual representation is formed by transforming observed sequences of behaviors into visual and symbolic codes to be cognitively rehearsed. Individuals usually have a mental model of a skill before they attempt to perform it. For example, by observing tennis players, individuals construct a mental model of such activities as the serve, volley, and backhand. These mental models are rudimentary in that they require feedback and correction to be perfected, but they allow learners to perform approximations of the skills at the outset of training. In the case of novel or complex behaviors, learners may have no prior mental model and need to observe modeled demonstrations before attempting the behaviors.

The social cognitive approach to motor skill learning differs from traditional explanations. Adams's (1971) *closed-loop theory* postulates that people develop perceptual (internal) traces of motor skill movements through practice and feedback. These traces serve as the reference for correct movements. As one performs a behavior, one receives internal (sensory) and external (knowledge of results) feedback and compares the feedback to the trace. The discrepancy serves to correct the trace. Learning is enhanced when feedback is accurate, and eventually the behavior can be performed without feedback. Adams distinguished two memory mechanisms, one that produces the response and one that evaluates its correctness.

A different view is based on *schema theory* (Schmidt, 1975). (This theory as it relates to information processing is covered in Chapter 4.) Schmidt postulated that people store in memory much information regarding motor skill movements including the initial conditions, the characteristics of the generalized motor sequence, the results of the movement, knowledge of results, and sensory feedback. Learners store this information in two general schemas, or organized memory networks comprising related information. The recall schema deals with response production; the recognition schema is used to evaluate responses. Social cognitive theory (Bandura, 1986) contends that by observing others, people form a cognitive representation that initiates subsequent responses and serves as a standard for evaluating the correctness of responses. Motor learning theories differ from social cognitive theory in that the former place greater emphasis on error correction after acting and postulate two memory mechanisms to store information and evaluate accuracy (McCullagh, 1993). Social cognitive theory also highlights the role of personal cognitions (goals and expectations) in the development of motor skills (Application 3.2).

A problem in motor skill learning is that learners cannot observe aspects of their performances that lie outside their field of vision. People who are swinging a golf club, kicking a football, throwing a baseball, high jumping, or pole vaulting cannot observe many aspects of these sequences. Not being able to see what one is doing requires one to rely on kinesthetic feedback and compare it with one's conceptual representation. The absence of visual feedback makes learning difficult.

Carroll and Bandura (1982) exposed learners to models performing a motor skill, and then asked them to reproduce the motor pattern. The experimenters gave some learners concurrent visual feedback of their performances by running a video camera and allowing them to observe their real-time performances on a monitor. Other learners did not receive visual feedback. When visual feedback was given before learners formed a mental model of the motor behavior, it had no effect on performance. Once learners had an adequate model in mind, visual feedback enhanced their accurate reproduction of the modeled behaviors. Visual feedback eliminated discrepancies between their conceptual models and their actions once the former were in place.

Research also has examined the efficacy of using models to teach motor skills. Weiss (1983) compared the effects of a silent model (visual demonstration) with those of a verbal model (visual demonstration plus verbal explanation) on the learning of a six-part motor skill obstacle course. Older children (ages 7 through 9 years) learned equally well with either model; younger children (ages 4 through 6 years)

APPLICATION 3.2
Motor Skill Learning

Observational learning is useful for learning motor skills. To teach students to dribble a basketball, physical education teachers begin with skill exercises, such as standing stationary and bouncing the ball and moving and bouncing the ball with each step. After introducing each skill leading to the final sequence, teachers can demonstrate slowly and precisely what the students are to model. The students then should practice that skill. If students have difficulty on a particular step, teachers can repeat the modeled demonstration before the students continue practicing.

For high school students to successfully learn a dance to perform in the spring musical, the teacher needs to demonstrate and slowly progress toward putting the dance to music. The teacher may break up the dance, working on each step separately, gradually combining steps and eventually putting all the various steps together with the music.

learned better with the verbal model. Perhaps the addition of the verbalizations created a cognitive model that helped to maintain children's attention and assisted with coding of information in memory. Weiss and Klint (1987) found that children in visual-model and no-model conditions who verbally rehearsed the sequence of actions learned the motor skills better than children who did not verbally rehearse. Collectively these results suggest that some form of verbalization may be critically important in acquisition of motor skills.

INFLUENCES ON LEARNING AND PERFORMANCE

Observing models does not guarantee that learning will occur or that learned behaviors will be performed later. Several factors influence vicarious learning and performance of learned behaviors (Table 3.4). These factors affect individuals' attention, information processing, perceptions of the usefulness of learning, and assessment of their competence and capabilities for learning. Developmental status, model prestige and competence, and vicarious consequences are discussed here; outcome expectations, goal setting, and self-efficacy are discussed in sections that follow.

Developmental Status of Learners

Students' abilities to learn from models depend on developmental factors (Bandura, 1986). Young children have difficulty attending to modeled events for long periods and distinguishing relevant from irrelevant cues. Information processing functions such as rehearsing, organizing, and elaborating (Chapters 4 and 5) improve with development.

Table 3.4
Factors affecting observational learning and performance.

Characteristic	Effects on Modeling
Developmental status	Improvements with development include longer attention and increased capacity to process information, use strategies, compare performances with memorial representations, and adopt intrinsic motivators.
Model prestige and competence	Observers pay greater attention to competent, high-status models. Consequences of modeled behaviors convey information about functional value. Observers attempt to learn actions they believe they will need to perform.
Vicarious consequences	Consequences to models convey information about behavioral appropriateness and probable outcomes of actions. Valued consequences motivate observers. Similarity in attributes or competence signals appropriateness and heightens motivation.
Outcome expectations	Observers are more likely to perform modeled actions they believe are appropriate and will result in rewarding outcomes.
Goal setting	Observers are more likely to attend to models who demonstrate behaviors that help observers attain goals.
Self-efficacy	Observers attend to models when they believe they are capable of learning or performing the modeled behavior. Observation of similar models affects self-efficacy ("If they can do it, I can too").

Older children acquire a more extensive knowledge base to help them comprehend new information, and they become more capable of using memory strategies. Young children may encode modeled events in terms of physical properties (e.g., a ball is round, it bounces, you throw it), whereas older children often represent information visually or symbolically.

With respect to the production process, information acquired through observation cannot be performed if children lack the requisite physical capabilities. Production also requires translating into action information stored in memory, comparing performance with memorial representation, and correcting performance as necessary. The ability to self-regulate one's actions for longer periods increases with development. Motivational inducements for action also vary depending on development. Young children are motivated by the immediate consequences of their actions. As children mature, they are more likely to perform modeled actions consistent with their goals and values.

Model Prestige and Competence

Modeled behaviors vary in usefulness. Behaviors that successfully deal with the environment command greater attention than those that do so less effectively. People attend to a model in part because they believe they might face the same situation themselves and they want to learn the necessary actions to succeed. Students attend to a teacher because the teacher prompts them but also because they believe they will have to demonstrate the same skills and behaviors. When models compete for attention, people are more likely to attend to *competent* models demonstrating actions that observers believe they will have to perform.

Model competence is inferred from the outcomes of modeled actions (success, failure) and from symbols that denote competence. An important attribute is *prestige*. Models who have gained distinction are more apt to command attention than those of lower prestige. Attendance usually is higher at a talk given by a well-known person than by one who is less known. In most instances, high-status models have ascended to their positions because they are competent and perform well. Their actions have greater functional value for observers, who are apt to believe that rewards will be forthcoming if they act accordingly.

Parents and teachers are high-status models for most children. The scope of adult influence on children's modeling can generalize to many domains. Although teachers are important models in the development of children's intellect, their influence typically spreads to such other areas as social behaviors, educational attainments, dress, and mannerisms (Rosenthal & Bandura, 1978). The effects of model prestige often generalize to areas in which models have no particular competence, such as when adolescents adopt the products touted by prominent athletes in commercials. Modeling becomes more prevalent with development, but young children are highly susceptible to adult influence (Application 3.3).

Vicarious Consequences to Models

As explained earlier, the functional value of modeled behavior—whether it results in success or failure, reward or punishment—influences modeling by observers. Vicarious consequences to models can affect observers' learning and performance of modeled actions. Observers who watch as models are rewarded for their actions are more likely to attend to the models and rehearse and code their actions for retention. Vicarious rewards motivate observers to perform the same actions themselves. Thus, vicarious consequences serve to *inform* and *motivate* (Bandura, 1986).

Information.   The consequences experienced by models convey information to observers about the types of actions most likely to be effective. Vicarious consequences affect observers when they believe that similar actions by them will produce comparable results. Observing competent models perform actions that result in success conveys information to observers about the sequence of actions one should use to succeed. By observing modeled behaviors and their consequences, people form beliefs concerning which behaviors will be rewarded and which punished.

APPLICATION 3.3
Model Attributes

People attend to models partly because they believe they will have to face the same situations themselves. Effective use of model prestige and competence can help motivate secondary students attend to lessons related to topics such as drug and alcohol use, suicide prevention, and sex education.

If the use of alcohol is a problem in a high school, school personnel might deliver a program on alcohol education and abuse (prevention, treatment) to include speakers from outside the school. Influential speakers would be recent high school and college graduates, persons who have successfully overcome problems with alcohol, and those who work with alcohol abusers. The relative similarity in age of the models to the students, coupled with the models' personal experiences, should make the models appear highly competent. Such individuals might have more impact on the students than literature or lessons taught by teachers and counselors.

At the elementary school level, using peers to help teach academic skills can promote learning and self-efficacy among the learners. Children may identify with other children who have had the same difficulties. Kathy Stone has four students in her class who are having trouble learning to divide. Mrs. Stone pairs these four students with students who have demonstrated that they understand the concept and the process of long division. A child explaining to a classmate how to solve a long-division problem will use terminology that is easy for the classmate to understand.

In a classic demonstration of the role of vicarious consequences on behavior, Bandura, Ross, and Ross (1963) exposed children to live aggressive models, filmed aggression, or aggression portrayed by cartoon characters. The models, who pummeled a Bobo doll by hitting, throwing, kicking, and sitting on it, were neither rewarded nor punished, which most likely conveyed to the observers that the modeled behaviors were acceptable. Children subsequently were allowed to play with a Bobo doll. Compared with youngsters not exposed to aggression, children who viewed aggressive models displayed significantly higher levels of aggression. The type of aggressive model (live, filmed, cartoon) made no difference in children's level of aggression.

Similarity to models is hypothesized to be an important factor in gauging behavioral appropriateness and forming beliefs (Schunk, 1987). The more observers are like models, the greater is the probability that observers will consider similar actions socially appropriate and will produce comparable results. Model attributes often are predictive of the functional value of behaviors. Most social situations are structured so that behavioral appropriateness depends on factors such as age, sex, or status. Similarity ought to be especially influential when observers have little information about functional value. Thus, modeled tasks with which observers are unfamiliar or those that are not immediately followed by consequences may be highly influenced by similarity in model attributes (Akamatsu & Thelen, 1974).

Some psychological theories postulate that children are more likely to attend to and learn from models of their own sex (Maccoby & Jacklin, 1974). Research evidence suggests, however, that the sex of a model affects performance rather than learning (Perry & Bussey, 1979; Spence, 1984). Children learn from models of both sexes and categorize behaviors as appropriate for both sexes or as more appropriate for members of one sex. Children who perform behaviors appropriate for members of either sex or for members of their sex may do so because they believe those behaviors have greater functional value than sex-inappropriate behaviors; that is, they believe the former behaviors are more likely to be rewarded (Schunk, 1987). Model sex, therefore, seems important as a conveyor of information about task appropriateness (Zimmerman & Koussa, 1975). When children are uncertain about the sex appropriateness of a modeled behavior, they may model same-sex peers because they are more likely to think that those actions are socially acceptable.

Model-observer similarity in age is important when children perceive the actions of same-age peers to be more appropriate for themselves than the actions of younger or older models (Schunk, 1987). Whether children are more likely to emulate peers or adults depends on their perceptions of which actions have greater functional value. Brody and Stoneman (1985) found that in the absence of competence information, children were more likely to model the actions of same-age peers. When children were provided with competence information, modeling was enhanced by similar competence regardless of model age.

Researchers have no evidence that children learn any better or worse from peers or adults; they have found evidence, however, that peers and adults use different teaching strategies. Child teachers often use nonverbal demonstrations and link instruction to specific items (e.g., how to do it); adults typically employ more verbal instruction stressing general principles and relate information to be learned to other material (Ellis & Rogoff, 1982). Peer instruction may be quite beneficial with students with learning disabilities and with those who do not process verbal material well.

The highest degree of model-observer similarity occurs when one is one's own model. Behavioral change resulting from observing one's own behaviors, or *self-modeling* (Dowrick, 1983), has been used to develop social, vocational, motor, cognitive, and instructional skills. In a typical procedure, one is videotaped while performing and subsequently views the tape. Observing a self-model tape is a form of review and is especially informative for skills one cannot watch while performing (e.g., gymnastics).

Performances that contain errors are problematic (Hosford, 1981). Commentary from a knowledgeable individual while the performer is viewing the tape helps to prevent the performer from becoming discouraged; the expert can explain how to execute the skills better the next time. Errorless performances are portrayed by videotaping a skillful performance or by editing errors out of the tape. Viewing a skillful performance conveys that one is capable of learning and can continue to make progress with further work, which raises self-efficacy.

Schunk and Hanson (1989b) found benefits of self-modeling during acquisition of arithmetic (fraction) skills. Children who showed low pretest achievement received instruction and problem-solving practice. Self-modeling students were video-taped while successfully solving problems and were shown their tapes, others were videotaped but not shown their tapes until after the study was completed (to control for potential effects of taping), and students in a third condition were not taped (to control for effects of participation). Self-modeling children scored higher on self-efficacy for learning, motivation, and posttest self-efficacy and achievement. Researchers found no differences between mastery self-model students who viewed tapes of their successful problem solving and self-model children whose tapes portrayed their gradual improvement as they acquired skills, which supports the point that the perception of progress or mastery can build efficacy (Schunk, 1989).

Motivation. Vicarious consequences serve a motivational function: Observers who see models rewarded become motivated to act accordingly. Perceived similarity enhances motivational effects. Observing similar others perform a behavior can lead observers to try it. These motivational effects depend in part on self-efficacy (Bandura, 1982b, 1997). Observing similar others succeed raises observers' self-efficacy and motivates them to try the task; they are apt to believe that if others can succeed, they can as well. Such motivational effects are common in classrooms. Students who observe other students performing a task well may be motivated to try their best.

Reinforcing models influences observers' behaviors (Rosenthal & Zimmerman, 1978). Of particular educational importance is the observation of effort that leads to success (Schunk, 1989). Seeing others succeed with effort and receiving praise from teachers may motivate observing peers to work harder. Often students become more motivated from watching similar others succeed than those who they believe are superior in competence.

This is not to suggest that vicarious success will sustain behavior over long periods. Actual performance successes eventually become necessary. Motivation is boosted when students observe teachers giving praise and high grades to others for hard work and good performances; motivation is sustained over time when students believe their own efforts are leading to better performances.

GOALS AND EXPECTATIONS

Among the important variables that affect observational learning and performance of learned behaviors are observers' goals and their expectations of success and of outcomes of actions. This section covers goals and outcome expectations; self-efficacy is addressed in the next section.

Goals

Much human behavior is sustained over long periods in the absence of immediate external incentives. Such persistence occurs as a result of goal setting and self-evaluation of progress. A *goal* reflects one's purpose and refers to quantity, quality, or rate of performance (Locke & Latham, 1990; Locke, Shaw, Saari, & Latham, 1981; Schunk, 1990). *Goal setting* involves establishing a standard or objective to serve as the aim of one's actions. People can set their own goals or goals can be established by others (parents, teachers, supervisors).

Goals were a central feature of Tolman's (1932, 1942, 1951, 1959) theory of *purposive behaviorism.* Like most psychologists of his time, Tolman was trained in behaviorism. From a methodological perspective, Tolman's experiments resembled those of such theorists as Thorndike and Skinner (Chapter 2) because they dealt with responses to stimuli under varying environmental conditions. At the same time, he disagreed with behaviorists on their molecular definition of behavior as a series of stimulus-response connections and on their focus on discrete actions. He contended that conditioning theories do not adequately explain learning because it is more than the strengthening of responses to stimuli. Rather, he recommended a focus on *molar behavior*—a large sequence of goal-directed behavior.

The "purposive" aspect of Tolman's (1932) theory refers to his belief that behavior is goal directed: "Behavior . . . always seems to have the character of getting-to or getting-from a specific goal-object, or goal situation" (p. 10). Stimuli in the environment (e.g., objects, paths) are means to goal attainment. They cannot be studied in isolation; rather, entire behavioral sequences must be studied to understand why people engage in particular actions. High school students whose goal is to attend a leading university study hard in their classes. By focusing only on the studying, researchers miss the purpose of the behavior. The students do not study because they have been reinforced for studying in the past. Rather, studying is a means to intermediate goals (learning, high grades), which, in turn, enhance the likelihood of acceptance to the university. "Because behavior is purposive it also is cognitive: And such purposes and such cognitions are just as evident . . . if this behavior be that of a rat as if it be that of a human being" (Tolman, 1932, p. 12).

Tolman's suggestion that rats and other lower animals pursue goals and act as if they have cognitions was not well received by behaviorists. Tolman qualified his use of "purpose" and "cognition" by noting that they are defined objectively. The behavior of people and animals is goal oriented. They act "as if" they are pursuing a goal and have chosen a means for attainment. Thus, Tolman went well beyond simple stimulus-response associations to discuss underlying cognitive mechanisms.

Contemporary social cognitive theory contends that an important source of goal information is modeled standards, such as when students strive to perform a task as well as or better than teachers or peers. Goals enhance learning and performance through their effects on perceptions of progress, self-efficacy, and self-evaluations (Bandura, 1988; Locke & Latham, 1990; Schunk, 1990). Initially, people must make a *commitment* to attempt to attain their goals; goals do not affect performance without commitment (Locke & Latham, 1990). As they work on the task, they compare their current performances with goals. Positive self-evaluations of progress raise self-efficacy and sustain motivation. A perceived discrepancy between present performance and the goal may create dissatisfaction, which can enhance effort. Goals also can be acquired through modeling. People are more likely to attend to models when they believe the modeled behaviors will help them attain their goals.

Goals motivate people to exert effort necessary to meet task demands and to persist at the task over time (Locke & Latham, 1990). Greater effort and persistence pay off with better performance. Goals also direct individuals' attention to relevant task features, behaviors to be performed, and potential outcomes and can affect how they process information. Goals give people "tunnel vision" to focus on the task, select task-appropriate strategies, and decide on the effectiveness of their approach, all of which are likely to raise performance.

Goals, by themselves, do not automatically enhance learning and motivation. Rather, the goal properties of specificity, proximity, and difficulty enhance self-perceptions, motivation, and learning (Table 3.5 and Application 3.4).

Specificity.   Goals that incorporate specific standards of performance are more likely to enhance learning and activate self-evaluations than are general goals (e.g., "Do your best;" Locke & Latham, 1990). Specific goals boost task performance by better describing the amount of effort success requires, and they promote self-efficacy because evaluating progress toward an explicit goal is straightforward.

Much research attests to the effectiveness of specific goals in raising performance (Bandura, 1988; Locke & Latham, 1990; Schunk, 1990). Schunk (1983b) provided children with instruction and practice solving long-division problems. During the sessions some children received a specific goal denoting the number of problems to complete; others had a general goal to work productively. Within each condition, half of the children received comparative information on the number of problems that peers completed (which matched the session goal) to convey that goals were attainable. Goals raised self-efficacy; goals plus comparative information led to the highest self-efficacy and achievement.

Schunk (1984a) compared the effects of goals with those of rewards. Children received long-division instruction and practice over sessions. Some were offered rewards based on the number of problems completed, others pursued goals (number of problems to complete), and children in a third condition received rewards and goals. The three conditions promoted motivation during the sessions; rewards plus goals resulted in the highest division self-efficacy and achievement. Combining re-

Table 3.5
Goal properties and their effects.

Goal Property	Effects on Behavior
1. Specificity	Goals with specific standards of performance increase motivation and raise self-efficacy because goal progress is easy to gauge.
2. Proximity	Proximal goals increase motivation and self-efficacy and are especially important for young children who may not divide a long-term goal into a series of short-term goals.
3. Difficulty	Challenging but attainable goals raise motivation and self-efficacy better than easy or hard goals.

APPLICATION 3.4
Goal Properties

Goal properties are easily incorporated into lessons. In her third-grade class, Kathy Stone introduced a new spelling unit to her class by stating the following goal:

> Of our 20 words this week, I know that all of you will be able to learn to spell the first 15. We are going to work very diligently in class on these words, and I expect you to do the same at home. With our work at school and at home, I know that all of you will be able to spell these words correctly by Friday. The last 5 words are more difficult. These will be our bonus words.

This goal is specific, but for some children it is distant and might be viewed as too difficult. To ensure that all students achieve the overall goal, Mrs. Stone sets short-term goals each day: "Today we are going to work on these 5 words. By the end of class time I know that you will be able to spell these 5 words." Children should view the daily goals as easier to attain than the weekly goal. To further ensure goal attainment, Mrs. Stone will make sure that the 15 words selected for mastery by Friday challenge the students but are not overly difficult.

A teacher working with students on keyboarding might establish a words-per-minute goal for students to reach by the end of the semester:

> Students, this semester I know that all of you will be able to learn to use the keyboard. Some of you because of other experiences or certain dexterity talent will be able to type faster, but I know that all of you will be able to enter at least 30 words per minute with no mistakes by the end of the semester.

To help students achieve this goal, the teacher might set weekly short-term goals. Thus, the first week the goal might be 10 words per minute with no mistakes, the second week 12 words per minute, and so forth, increasing the number each week.

wards with goals provided children with two sources of information to use in gauging learning progress.

Specific goals are especially effective with children (Bandura & Schunk, 1981). Elementary school lessons and activities tend to be structured as a series of specific and short-term goals, which keeps motivation and learning high.

Proximity.   Goals are distinguished by how far they project into the future. Proximal, short-term goals are closer at hand, are achieved more quickly, and result in greater motivation directed toward attainment than more temporally distant, long-term goals. Although benefits of proximal goals are found regardless of developmental status, short-term goals are needed with children because they have short time frames of reference and are not fully capable of representing distant outcomes in thought. Proximal goals fit well with normal lesson planning, as elementary teachers plan activities around blocks of time. Goals often are proximal and specific, such as when teachers ask children to finish three workbook pages in 20 minutes.

Bandura and Schunk (1981) gave children subtraction instruction with practice opportunities over seven sessions. Children received seven packets of material. Some pursued a proximal goal of completing one packet each session; a second group received a distant goal of completing all packets by the end of the last session; a third group was given a general goal of working productively. Proximal goals led to the highest motivation during the sessions, as well as the highest subtraction self-efficacy, achievement, and intrinsic interest (based on the number of problems solved during a free-choice period). The distant goal resulted in no benefits compared with the general goal.

Manderlink and Harackiewicz (1984) gave adults normative information on word puzzles and asked them to set a proximal goal (for this puzzle) or a distant goal (for all puzzles). Expectations for goal attainment were assessed on the pretest and twice during the trials; following the experiment, participants judged their perceived competence. Proximal and distant goals did not differentially affect performance, but proximal goal participants judged expectation of goal attainment and perceived competence as higher. Distant goals led to higher ratings of interest, possibly because participants felt extrinsic pressure to set proximal goals.

Difficulty. Goal difficulty refers to the level of task proficiency required as assessed against a standard. The amount of effort people expend to attain a goal depends on the proficiency level required. Individuals expend greater effort to attain a difficult goal than an easy one.

Difficulty level and performance do not bear an unlimited positive relationship to each other. Positive effects due to goal difficulty depend on students having sufficient ability to reach the goal. Difficult goals do not enhance performance in the absence of prerequisite skills. Also important are people's beliefs in their abilities. Learners who think they are not competent enough to reach a goal hold low expectations for success, do not commit themselves to attempting to attain the goal, and work halfheartedly. When students believe they cannot accomplish a task, teachers should encourage their students to work on the task and give them feedback concerning their progress.

Schunk (1983c) gave children a difficult (but attainable) or an easier goal of completing a given number of long-division problems during each instructional session. To prevent students from believing goals were too difficult, the teacher gave half of each group attainment information ("You can work 25 problems"); the other half received comparative information indicating that similar peers completed that many. Difficult goals enhanced motivation; children who received difficult goals and attainment information displayed the highest self-efficacy and achievement.

Locke, Frederick, Lee, and Bobko (1984) had college students give uses for common objects. Half of the students were assigned a difficult goal; others set their own goals. Subsequently all participants set individual goals. Students assigned difficult goals set higher goals and generated more uses than those initially allowed to set their own goals. When participants set their own goals, self-efficacy related positively to goal level and commitment.

Self-Set Goals.   Researchers have found that allowing students to set their goals enhances self-efficacy and learning, perhaps because self-set goals produce high goal commitment. Schunk (1985) provided subtraction instruction to sixth graders with learning disabilities. Some set daily performance goals, others had comparable goals assigned, and a third group worked without goals. Self-set goals led to the highest judgments of confidence for attaining goals, as well as the highest self-efficacy for solving problems and subtraction achievement. Children in the two groups with goals demonstrated greater motivation during the instructional sessions than did those without goals.

Hom and Murphy (1985) classified college students as high or low in achievement motivation to self-set or assigned-goal conditions. Self-set participants decided how many anagrams they could solve; assigned-goal participants were given comparable goals. All students judged confidence for goal attainment (a measure analogous to self-efficacy). Students high in achievement motivation performed equally well under the two goal conditions; self-set goals enhanced the performances of students low in achievement motivation.

Goal Progress Feedback.   Goal progress feedback provides information about progress toward goals. Such feedback is especially valuable when people cannot derive reliable information on their own and should raise self-efficacy, motivation, and achievement when it informs people that they are competent and can continue to improve by working diligently. Higher efficacy sustains motivation when people believe that continued effort will allow them to attain their goals. Once individuals attain goals, they are more likely to adopt new goals (Schunk, 1989).

Schunk and Rice (1991) taught students with reading problems a strategy to answer comprehension questions. Children were given a product goal of answering questions, a process goal of learning to use the strategy, or a process goal plus progress feedback that linked performance with strategy use and conveyed that they were making progress toward their goal of learning to use the strategy to answer questions. Following the instruction, goal-plus-feedback children demonstrated higher reading self-efficacy and achievement than did learners assigned to the process and product goal conditions. Schunk and Swartz (1993a, 1993b) obtained comparable results in writing achievement with average-achieving and academically gifted elementary school children. These authors also found that self-efficacy and achievement generalized across types of writing tasks and maintained themselves over time.

Contracts and Conferences.   Research supports the point that contracts and conferences help raise students' learning, no doubt in part because they incorporate goal-setting principles. Tollefson, Tracy, Johnsen, Farmer, and Buenning (1984) worked with junior high students with learning disabilities. Each week for 4 weeks the students selected spelling words or math problems from a list of moderately difficult words or problems. Following the study, students predicted how many they would answer correctly on a test. The goal and a study plan were stated in a written contract, which was intended to help students take personal responsibility for their actions and show that effort enhances achievement (see the discussion of attribution theory in Chapter 8). After each test, students charted their scores and made an attribution for the outcome. Compared with students assigned to a no-treatment control condition, goal-setting students placed greater emphasis on effort as a cause of outcomes and set more realistic goals as shown by a small discrepancy between goal and performance.

Gaa (1973, 1979) found that goal-setting conferences enhance students' learning and self-evaluations. First and second graders were assigned to one of three conditions: conferences with goal setting, conferences without goal setting, or no conferences (Gaa, 1973). All children received the same in-class reading instruction. Children in the goal-conference condition met with the researcher once a week for 4 weeks. They received a list of reading skills and selected those they would attempt to accomplish the following week. They also received feedback on their previous week's goal accomplishments. Children who participated in conferences without goals met with the experimenter for the same amount of time but received only general information about material covered previously and what would be covered the following week. Children who participated in goal-setting conferences attained the highest level of reading achievement. At the end of training, they showed the smallest discrepancy between goals set and mastered. Thus, proximal goal setting was shown to promote accurate perceptions of capabilities.

Outcome Expectations

Outcome expectations are personal beliefs about the anticipated outcomes of actions. Outcome expectations were among the earliest cognitive variables to be included in explanations of learning. Tolman (1949) discussed the *field expectancy*, defined as "an immanent cognitive determinant aroused by actually presented stimuli" (Tolman, 1932, p. 444). Expectancies involve relationships between stimuli (S_1–S_2) or among a stimulus, response, and stimulus (S_1–R–S_2). Relations between stimuli concern what stimulus is apt to follow what other stimulus; for example, the sound of thunder follows lightning. In three-term relations, people develop the belief that a certain response to a given stimulus produces a certain result. If one's goal is to get to a roof (S_2), the sight of the ladder (S_1) could lead one to the think, "If I place this ladder against the house (R), I can get to the roof." This is similar to Skinner's (1953; see Chapter 2) three-term contingency except that Tolman conceived of this type of relation as reflecting a cognitive expectancy.

Expectancies are important because they help people form *cognitive maps,* or internal plans comprising expectancies of which actions are needed to attain goals. People follow signs to a goal; they learn meanings rather than discrete responses. People use their cognitive maps to determine the best course of action to attain a goal.

Tolman tested his ideas in an ingenious series of experiments (Tolman, Ritchie, & Kalish, 1946a, 1946b). In one study, rats were trained to run an apparatus, shown in Figure 3.2 (Maze 1). Subsequently, the apparatus was replaced with one in which the original path was blocked. Conditioning theories predict that animals will choose

Figure 3.2
Experimental arrangement to study expectancy learning.
Source: Adapted from "Studies in Spatial Learning," by E. C. Tolman, B. F. Ritchie, and D. Kalish, 1946, *Journal of Experimental Psychology, 36*, pp. 13–24.

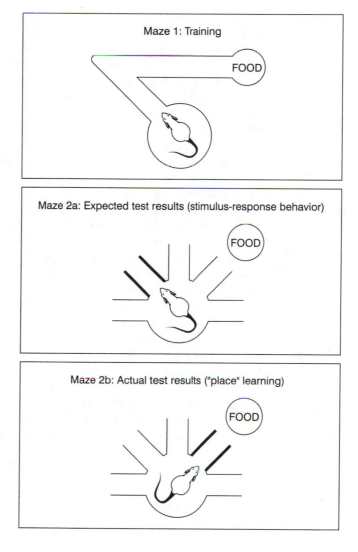

a path close to the original one, as shown in Figure 3.2 (Maze 2a). In fact, rats most frequently chose a path following the direction in which they originally found food (Maze 2b). These results support the idea that the animals formed a cognitive map of the location of the food and responded based on that map rather than on prior responses to stimuli.

According to social cognitive theory (Bandura, 1986, 1997), people form beliefs about what the consequences of given actions will be based on personal experiences and observations of models. Individuals act in ways they believe will be successful and attend to models who will teach them valued skills. Outcome expectations sustain behaviors over long periods when people believe their actions will eventually produce desired outcomes.

The expectations can refer to external outcomes ("If I try my best on this exam, I will make a good grade on it") or to internal ones ("If I try my best on this exam, I will feel good about myself"). An important type of outcome expectation relates to progress in skill learning ("If I try my best, I will become a better reader"). Students who believe they are making little or no progress in learning may become demoralized and lackadaisical. In many instances, progress occurs slowly and students notice little day-to-day change. Reading comprehension is a good example. Students improve their skills in reading longer and more difficult passages, in finding main ideas, in drawing inferences, and in reading for details, but progress is slow. Teachers need to inform students explicitly of their progress when it may not be immediately apparent.

The influential role of outcome expectations was demonstrated by Shell, Murphy, & Bruning (1989). College students completed measures of self-efficacy and outcome expectancies for reading and writing, and tests of reading and writing achievement were given. The self-efficacy assessments asked students to rate their competencies in performing various reading and writing tasks (e.g., letter from a friend, employment application, short fiction story). For the outcome expectancy measure, students judged the importance of reading and writing skills for achieving such life goals as getting a job, being financially secure, and being happy in life.

The results showed that both self-efficacy and outcome expectancies related positively to actual achievement in those domains. The relations were stronger in reading than in writing. Across both domains, self-efficacy was more strongly related to achievement than outcome expectancies, although results for the latter variable were significant and added to the prediction of achievement. This study also showed a generalized interrelation between beliefs and performance as the expectancy beliefs for each domain related significantly to achievement in the other domain, which suggests that teachers' attempts to improve students' self-efficacy and outcome expectations in one literacy area may generalize to other areas.

SELF-EFFICACY

Conceptual Overview

Self-efficacy refers to personal beliefs about one's capabilities to learn or perform actions at designated levels (Bandura, 1977a, 1977b, 1986, 1993, 1997). Self-efficacy is a belief about what one is capable of doing; it is not the same as knowing what to do. In gauging efficacy, individuals assess their skills and their capabilities to translate those skills into actions. Self-efficacy is a key to promoting a sense of *agency* in people that they can influence their lives (Bandura, 1997, 2001).

Self-efficacy and outcome expectations do not have the same meaning. Self-efficacy refers to perceptions of one's capabilities to produce actions; outcome expectations involve beliefs about the anticipated outcomes of those actions. Students may believe that a positive outcome will result from certain actions but also believe that they lack the competence to produce those actions. For example, Jeremy may believe that if he correctly answers the teacher's questions, the teacher will praise him (positive outcome expectation). He also may desire to receive praise from the teacher. He may, however, not attempt to answer the teacher's questions if he doubts his capabilities to answer them correctly (low self-efficacy).

Despite self-efficacy and outcome expectations being conceptually distinct, they often are related. Students who typically perform well have confidence in their learning capabilities and expect (and usually receive) positive outcomes for their efforts. At the same time, there is no necessary relation between self-efficacy and outcome expectations. Even students with high self-efficacy for learning may expect a low grade as an outcome if they think that the teacher does not like them.

Although some evidence indicates that perceptions of self-efficacy generalize to different tasks (Smith, 1989), theory and research suggest that self-efficacy is primarily a domain-specific construct (Pajares, 1996). Thus, it is meaningful to speak of self-efficacy for drawing inferences from text, balancing chemical equations, solving fractions, running certain times at track events, and so on. Efficacy is distinguished from *self-concept,* which refers to one's collective self-perceptions formed through experiences with and interpretations of the environment and which depends heavily on reinforcements and evaluations by significant others (Shavelson & Bolus, 1982; Wylie, 1979). Self-efficacy refers to perceptions of specific capabilities; self-concept is one's general self-perception that includes efficacy in different areas (see Chapter 8).

Self-efficacy depends in part on student abilities. In general, high-ability students feel more efficacious about learning compared with low-ability students; however, self-efficacy is not another name for ability. Collins (1982) identified high-, average-, and low-ability students in mathematics. Within each level, she found students of high and low efficacy. She gave students problems to solve and told them they could rework those they missed. Ability was positively related to achievement, but students with high self-efficacy solved more problems correctly and chose to rework more problems they missed (regardless of ability level) than those with low self-efficacy.

Researchers hypothesize that self-efficacy has diverse effects in achievement settings (Bandura, 1993; Pajares, 1996, 1997; Schunk, 1989, 1991). Efficacy can influence choice of activities. Students with low efficacy for learning may avoid attempting tasks; those who judge themselves efficacious should participate more eagerly. Efficacy also can affect effort expenditure, persistence, and learning. Students who feel efficacious about learning generally expend greater effort and persist longer than students who doubt their capabilities, especially when they encounter difficulties. In turn, these behaviors promote learning.

People acquire information about their efficacy in a given domain from their performances, observations of models (vicarious experiences), forms of social persuasion, and physiological indexes (e.g., heart rate, sweating). Actual performances offer the most valid information for assessing efficacy. Successes generally raise efficacy and failures lower it, although an occasional failure (success) after many successes (failures) should not have much effect.

Students acquire much information about their capabilities through knowledge of how others perform. *Similarity* to others is an important cue for gauging one's efficacy (Brown & Inouye, 1978; Rosenthal & Bandura, 1978; Schunk, 1987, 1998). Observing similar others succeed raises observers' self-efficacy and motivates them to try the task because they believe that if others can succeed, they can as well. At the same time, a vicarious increase in efficacy can be negated by subsequent personal failures. Students who observe peers fail may believe they lack the competence to succeed, which can dissuade them from attempting the task.

Students often receive persuasive information from teachers that they possess the capability to perform well ("You can do it"). Although positive feedback enhances efficacy, this increase will not endure for long if students subsequently perform poorly. Learners also acquire some efficacy information from physiological symptoms they experience. Emotional symptoms (sweating, trembling) might be interpreted to mean they are not capable of learning. When learners notice they are experiencing less stress to academic demands, they may feel more efficacious for mastering the task.

Information acquired from these sources does not influence efficacy automatically but is cognitively appraised (Bandura, 1982b, 1993, 1997). Efficacy appraisal is an inferential process in which persons weigh and combine the contributions of personal, behavioral, and environmental factors. In forming efficacy assessments, students consider factors such as ability, effort expended, task difficulty, teacher assistance, and number and pattern of successes and failures (Bandura, 1981, 1997).

Self-Efficacy in Achievement Situations

Self-efficacy is especially germane to school learning and other achievement situations. Social (environmental) factors can affect many self (personal) variables, such as learners' goals, self-efficacy, outcome expectations, attributions, self-evaluations of learning progress, and self-regulatory processes. In turn, self influences can affect social environments, as when learners decide they need more instruction on a skill and seek out a qualified teacher (Schunk, 1999).

Achievement outcomes such as goal progress, motivational indexes (choice of activities, effort, persistence), and learning are affected by social and self influences. In turn, learner actions affect these factors. As students work on tasks, they evaluate their learning progress. Perceptions of progress substantiate their self-efficacy for learning, which sustains motivation and learning. As teachers observe students' progress, they model corrective instruction based on students' demonstrated skills.

A key process here is the *internalization* of social variables to self influences. Learners transform information acquired from the social environment into mechanisms of self-regulatory control. Further, with increased skill acquisition this unidimensional social-to-self transformation process becomes a bi-directional interactive process as learners alter and adjust their social environments to further enhance their achievement (Schunk, 1999). Self-regulatory control is discussed in greater depth later in this chapter.

Models and Self-Efficacy

The models in one's environment provide an important source of information for gauging self-efficacy. Interestingly, Bandura, Barbaranelli, Caprara, and Pastorelli (1996) found that parents' academic aspirations for their children affected both children's academic achievements and their self-efficacy. Parents are key models in children's social environments.

Adult Models.   A wealth of research indicates that exposing students to adult models influences their self-efficacy for learning and performing well. Zimmerman and Ringle (1981) had children observe a model unsuccessfully attempt to solve a puzzle for a long or short time and verbalize statements of confidence or pessimism, after which children attempted to solve the puzzle themselves. Observing a confident but nonpersistent model raised self-efficacy; children who observed a pessimistic but persistent model lowered their self-efficacy. Relich, Debus, and Walker (1986) found that exposing low-achieving children to models explaining mathematical division and providing them with feedback stressing the importance of ability and effort had a positive effect on self-efficacy.

Schunk (1981) showed that both cognitive modeling and didactic instruction raised self-efficacy; however, cognitive modeling led to greater gains in division skill and to more accurate perceptions of capabilities as these children's efficacy judgments corresponded more closely to their actual performances. Students who received only didactic instruction overestimated what they could do. Regardless of treatment condition, self-efficacy related positively to persistence and achievement.

Peer Models.   Observing similar peer models performing a task well can raise observers' self-efficacy, which is validated when they work at the task successfully. Brown and Inouye (1978) investigated perceived similarity in competence to models. College students judged self-efficacy for solving anagrams and attempted to solve them, after which they were told they performed better than or the same as a model. They then observed a model fail, judged self-efficacy, and attempted the anagrams again. Telling students they were more competent than the model led to higher self-efficacy and persistence than telling them they were equal in competence.

One way to raise self-efficacy is to use *coping models*, who initially demonstrate the typical fears and deficiencies of observers but gradually improve their performance and gain confidence in their capabilities. Coping models illustrate how determined effort and positive self-thoughts overcome difficulties. In contrast, *mastery models* demonstrate faultless performance and high confidence from the outset (Thelen, Fry, Fehrenbach, & Frautschi, 1979). Coping models enhance perceived similarity and efficacy for learning among students who are more likely to view the initial difficulties and gradual progress of coping models as more similar to their typical performances than the rapid learning of mastery models.

Schunk and Hanson (1985) worked with elementary school children who had difficulties learning subtraction with regrouping. Children observed videotapes portraying a peer mastery model, a peer coping model, a teacher model, or no model. In the peer-model conditions, an adult teacher provided instruction, after which the peer solved problems. The peer mastery model easily grasped operations and verbalized positive achievement beliefs reflecting high self-efficacy and ability, low task difficulty, and positive attitudes. The peer coping model initially made errors and verbalized negative achievement beliefs but gradually performed better and verbalized coping statements (e.g., "I need to pay attention to what I'm doing"). Eventually, the coping model's problem-solving behaviors and verbalizations matched those of the mastery model. Teacher-model children observed videotapes portraying only the teacher providing instruction; no-model children did not view videotapes. All children judged self-efficacy for learning to subtract and received instruction and practice.

Self-efficacy and achievement were raised more by observing a peer model than by observing a teacher model or no model; the teacher-model condition promoted these outcomes better than no model. Researchers noted no differences between the mastery and coping conditions. Possibly children focused more on what the models had in common (task success) than on their differences. Although children's prior successes in subtraction were limited to problems without regrouping, they had these experiences to draw on and may have concluded that if the model could learn, they could as well.

Another important variable is *number of models*. Compared with a single model, multiple models increase the probability that observers will perceive themselves as similar to at least one of the models (Thelen et al., 1979). Students who might easily discount the successes of a single model may be especially swayed by observing several successful peers and think that if all these models can learn, they can as well.

Schunk, Hanson, and Cox (1987) investigated the effects of single and multiple coping and mastery models. These researchers used a task (fractions) on which children had experienced few prior successes. Viewing a single coping model or multiple coping or mastery models enhanced children's self-efficacy and achievement better than viewing a single mastery model. For these low achievers, the coping models were more effective, although observing several peers learn rapidly yielded comparable effects.

In a follow-up study, Schunk and Hanson (1989a) further explored variations in perceived similarity by exposing average-achieving children to one of three types of peer models. Mastery models easily grasped arithmetic operations and verbalized positive beliefs (e.g., "I know I can do this one"). Coping-emotive models initially experienced difficulties and verbalized negative statements (e.g., "I'm not very good at this"), after which they verbalized coping statements (e.g., "I'll have to work hard on this one") and displayed coping behaviors; eventually they performed as well as mastery models. Coping-alone models performed in identical fashion to coping-emotive models but never verbalized negative beliefs.

Coping-emotive models led to the highest self-efficacy for learning. Mastery and coping-alone children perceived themselves as equal in competence to the model; coping-emotive children viewed themselves as more competent than the model. The belief that one is more talented than an unsuccessful model can improve efficacy and motivation. Following an instructional program the three conditions did not differ in efficacy or achievement, which shows that actual task experience outweighed initial effects due to watching models.

Peer models have been used to promote prosocial behaviors. Strain et al. (1981) showed how peers can be taught to initiate social play with withdrawn children by using verbal signals (e.g., "Let's play blocks") and motor responses (handing child a toy). Such peer initiations typically increase target children's subsequent social initiations. Training peer initiators is time consuming but well worth the effort because methods of remedying social withdrawal (prompting, reinforcement) require nearly continuous teacher involvement. Application 3.5 discusses some additional uses of peer models.

Building Self-Efficacy with Peer Models

Observing similar peers performing a task increases students' self-efficacy for learning. This idea is applied when a teacher selects certain students to complete mathematics problems at the board. By demonstrating success, the peer models help raise observers' self-efficacy for performing well. If ability levels in a class vary considerably, the teacher might pick peer models at different levels of ability. Students in the class are more likely to perceive themselves as similar in competence to at least one of the models.

Peers who readily master skills may help teach skills to observing students but may not have much impact on the self-efficacy of those students who experience learning difficulties. For the latter, students with learning difficulties who have mastered the skills may be excellent models.

For example, in Jim Marshall's American history class the students have been working on learning the battles of the Civil War. Because so many battles occurred, learning all of them has been difficult for some of the students. Mr. Marshall places his students into three groups: Group 1 consists of students who mastered the material immediately; Group 2, students who have been working hard and are gradually developing mastery; and Group 3, students who still are having difficulty. Mr. Marshall pairs Groups 2 and 3 for peer tutoring. Using maps and charts the students work together color coding and learning the groups of battles together.

Teachers also can refer to peer models whom other students observe. Teachers can point out the concentration and hard work of the models. For instance, as Mrs. Stone moves about the room monitoring seatwork, she provides learners with social comparative information (e.g., "See how well Kevin is working? I'm sure that you can work just as well"). Teachers need to ensure that learners view the comparative performance as one they can attain; judicious selection of referent students is necessary.

Peers also can enhance students' efficacy during small-group work. Successful groups are those in which each member has some responsibility and members share rewards based on their collective performance. The use of such groups helps to reduce negative ability-related social comparisons by students experiencing learning difficulties. Teachers need to select tasks carefully because unsuccessful groups do not raise efficacy.

In selecting students for working on group projects, Gina Brown might assess students' abilities for skills needed (e.g., writing, analyzing, interpreting, researching, organizing) and then form groups by assigning students with different strengths to each group.

Motor Skills

Research shows that self-efficacy predicts the acquisition and performance of motor skills (Bandura, 1997; Poag-DuCharme & Brawley, 1993; Wurtele, 1986). For example, Gould and Weiss (1981) found benefits due to model similarity. College women viewed a similar model (female student with no athletic background) or dissimilar model (male physical education professor) perform a muscular endurance task. While performing, the model made either positive or negative self-efficacy statements; irrelevant- and no-statement conditions also were included. Students who viewed the similar model performed the task better and judged self-efficacy higher than those who observed dissimilar models. Regardless of treatment condition, self-efficacy related positively to performance.

George, Feltz, and Chase (1992) replicated these results using female college students and models performing a leg-extension endurance task. Students who observed nonathletic male or female models extended their legs longer and judged self-efficacy higher than those who observed an athletic model. Among these unskilled observers, model ability was a more important similarity cue than model gender.

Lirgg and Feltz (1991) exposed sixth-grade girls to a skilled or unskilled teacher or peer videotaped model demonstrating a ladder-climbing task; girls in a control group observed no model. Girls then judged self-efficacy for climbing successively higher levels on the ladder and performed the task over trials. Control students demonstrated poorer performance than those exposed to models; among the latter, children who viewed a skilled model (adult or peer) performed better than those who observed an unskilled model. Skilled-model girls also judged self-efficacy higher.

Bandura and Cervone (1983) showed the importance of feedback during motor skill acquisition. College students operated an ergometer by alternatively pushing and pulling arm levers that resisted their efforts. Some participants pursued a goal of increasing performance by 40% over the baseline, others were told they had increased their performance by 24%, those in a third condition received goals and feedback, and control-group participants received neither goals nor feedback. Goals combined with feedback improved performance most and instilled a sense of self-efficacy for goal attainment, which predicted subsequent effort.

In follow-up research (Bandura & Cervone, 1986), participants received a goal of 50% improvement over baseline. Following their performance, they received false feedback indicating they achieved an increase of 24%, 36%, 46%, or 54%. Self-efficacy was lowest for the 24% group and highest for the 54% condition. After students set goals for the next session and performed the task again, effort expenditure related positively to goals and self-efficacy across all conditions.

Poag-DuCharme and Brawley (1993) found that self-efficacy helped to predict involvement by individuals in community-based exercise programs. Self-efficacy was assessed for performing in-class activities and for overcoming barriers to exercising and scheduling problems. These measures related positively to the initiation and maintenance of regular exercise. These results suggest that promoting exercise requires attention to developing individuals' efficacy for coping with problems in scheduling and actual engagement.

Lee (1988) explored the relations among self-efficacy, individual and group goals, and team winning percentage. Goal factors assessed were: team goals; participation and planning; coach's support, feedback, and rewards; conflict and stress; and specific, difficult goals. Team goals and participation and planning were positively related to winning percentage; conflict and stress were negatively related. Self-efficacy correlated positively with winning percentage. Causal analyses showed that team goals and self-efficacy directly affected winning percentage.

Instructional Self-Efficacy

Self-efficacy is relevant to teachers as well as students (Pajares, 1996; Tschannen-Moran, Hoy, & Hoy, 1998). *Instructional efficacy* refers to personal beliefs about one's capabilities to help students learn. Instructional efficacy should influence teachers' activities, effort, and persistence with students (Ashton, 1985; Ashton & Webb, 1986). Teachers with low efficacy may avoid planning activities they believe exceed their capabilities, not persist with students having difficulties, expend little effort to find materials, and not reteach in ways students might understand better. Teachers with higher efficacy are more apt to develop challenging activities, help students succeed, and persevere with students who have problems. These motivational effects on teachers enhance student achievement. Ashton and Webb found that teachers with higher self-efficacy were likely to have a positive classroom environment, support students' ideas, and address students' needs. Teacher self-efficacy was a significant predictor of student achievement. Woolfolk and Hoy (1990) obtained comparable results among preservice teachers.

Much research has investigated the dimensions of instructional efficacy that relate best to student learning (Gibson & Dembo, 1984; Woolfolk & Hoy, 1990). Ashton and Webb (1986) distinguish *teaching efficacy*, or outcome expectations about the consequences of teaching in general, from *personal efficacy*, defined as self-efficacy to perform particular behaviors to bring about given outcomes. As mentioned earlier, self-efficacy and outcome expectations often are related but need not be. A teacher might have a high sense of personal efficacy but lower teaching efficacy if he or she believes that most student learning is due to home and environmental factors outside of the teacher's control. Other research suggests that instructional efficacy reflects an internal-external distinction; internal factors represent perceptions of personal influence and power; external factors relate to perceptions of influence and power of elements that lie outside the classroom (Guskey & Passaro, 1994).

An important challenge for pre- and in-service teacher education programs is to develop methods for increasing teachers' instructional efficacy by incorporating efficacy-building sources (actual performances, vicarious experiences, persuasion, physiological indexes). Internships where students work with teacher mentors provide actual performance success plus expert modeling. Teacher models not only teach observers skills but also build their self-efficacy for succeeding in the classroom (Application 3.6).

APPLICATION 3.6
Instructional Self-Efficacy

Self-efficacy among teachers is developed in the same ways as among students. An effective means of building efficacy is to observe someone else model specific teaching behaviors. A new elementary teacher might observe his or her mentor teacher implement the use of learning centers before the new teacher introduces the same activity. By observing the mentor, the new teacher acquires skill and self-efficacy for being able to implement the centers.

Self-efficacy in beginning teachers also may be aided by observing teachers with a few years of teaching experience successfully perform actions; new teachers may perceive greater similarity between themselves and other new teachers than with more experienced ones.

Practicing behaviors helps to develop skills and also builds self-efficacy. Music teachers will increase their self-efficacy for teaching pieces to the class by practicing those same pieces themselves on the piano after school until they know them well and feel confident about working with students. When teachers learn to use a new computer program before introducing it to their classes they will feel more self-efficacious about teaching their students to use the program.

Becoming more knowledgeable about a particular subject increases self-efficacy for discussing the subject more accurately and completely. Jim Marshall might read several books and articles about the Great Depression prior to developing the unit for class. The added knowledge should raise his self-efficacy for helping students learn about this significant period in American history. Gina Brown should review the work of significant researchers for each major topic area included in the course discussions. This provides students with information beyond what is in the text and builds her self-efficacy for effectively teaching the content.

Health and Therapeutic Activities

Self-efficacy has proven to be highly predictive of health and therapeutic behaviors (Bandura, 1997; Maddux, 1993). A model commonly applied to explain health behavior change is the Health Belief Model (Rosenstock, 1974). This model assigns a prominent role to four cognitive factors in affecting health behaviors: perceived susceptibility (personal assessment of risk for a given health threat), perceived severity of the health threat, perceived benefits of the behavior recommended to reduce the threat, and perceived barriers to action (personal belief of possible undesirable consequences that could result from performing the recommended preventive behavior). Perceived barriers is the component with the strongest empirical support;

it relates closely to self-efficacy (Maddux, 1993). A newer health behavior goal model (Maes & Gebhardt, 2000) includes perceived competence (analogous to self-efficacy) as a key process.

The important function of self-efficacy as a predictor of health behaviors is evident in many studies (DiClemente, 1986; Strecher, DeVellis, Becker, & Rosenstock, 1986). Self-efficacy correlates positively with controlled smoking (Godding & Glasgow, 1985), positively with longest period of smoking cessation (DiClemente, Prochaska, & Gilbertini, 1985), negatively with temptation to smoke (DiClemente et al., 1985), and positively with weight loss (Bernier & Avard, 1986). Love (1983) found that self-efficacy to resist bulimic behaviors correlated negatively with binging and purging. Bandura (1994) discusses the role of self-efficacy in the control of HIV infection.

In DiClemente's (1981) study, individuals who had recently quit smoking judged their efficacy to avoid smoking in situations of varying stress levels; they were surveyed months later to determine maintenance. Maintainers judged self-efficacy higher than relapsers. Also, self-efficacy was a better predictor of future smoking than was smoking history or demographic variables. Self-efficacy for avoiding smoking in various situations correlated positively with weeks of successful abstinence. People tended to relapse in situations where they had judged their self-efficacy low for avoiding smoking.

Bandura and others have investigated how well self-efficacy predicts therapeutic behavioral changes (Bandura, 1991). In one study (Bandura, Adams, & Beyer, 1977), adult snake phobics received a participant modeling treatment in which a therapist initially modeled a series of progressively more threatening encounters with a snake. After phobics jointly performed the various activities with the therapist, they were allowed to perform on their own to help enhance their self-efficacy. Compared with phobics who only observed the therapist model the activities and with those who received no training, participant-modeling clients demonstrated the greatest increases in self-efficacy and approach behaviors toward the snake. Regardless of treatment, self-efficacy for performing tasks was highly related to clients' actual behaviors. In a related study, Bandura and Adams (1977) found participant modeling superior to systematic desensitization. These results support Bandura's (1982b, 1997) contention that performance-based treatments combining modeling with practice offer the best basis for gauging self-efficacy and produce greater behavioral change.

Self-efficacy has generated much research. Evidence shows that self-efficacy predicts diverse outcomes such as smoking cessation, pain tolerance, athletic performance, assertiveness, coping with feared events, recovery from heart attack, and sales performance (Bandura, 1986, 1997). Self-efficacy is a key variable influencing career choices (Lent, Brown, & Hackett, 2000), and research shows that children's self-efficacy affects the types of occupations in which they believe they can succeed (Bandura, Barbaranelli, Caprara, & Pastorelli, 2001). Self-efficacy researchers have employed diverse settings, participants, measures, treatments, tasks, and time spans. The generality of the self-efficacy construct undoubtedly will be extended in future research.

SELF-REGULATION

Conceptual Framework

Social cognitive principles have been applied extensively to self-regulation (Bandura, 1997, 2001; B. Zimmerman, 2000). From a social cognitive perspective, self-regulation requires learner *choice* (Figure 3.3; Zimmerman, 1994, 1998). This does not mean that learners always take advantage of the available choices, especially when they are uncertain what to do and ask the teacher. When all task aspects are controlled, however, it is accurate to speak of achievement behavior being "externally controlled" or "controlled by others." This type of situation results when a teacher gives students no latitude in why, how, when, what, where, and with whom to complete a task. The potential for self-regulation varies depending on choices available to learners.

The left column in Figure 3.3 (Learning Issues) lists the questions of importance in learning: "Why should I learn?," "How should I learn?," "When shall I learn?,"

Learning Issues	Learning Dimensions	Learner Conditions	Self-regulation Attributes	Self-regulation Subprocesses
Why	Motive	Choose to participate	Self-motivated	Self-efficacy and self-goals
How	Method	Choose method	Planned or automatized	Strategy use or routinized performance
When	Time	Choose time limits	Timely and efficient	Time management
What	Behavior	Choose outcome behavior	Self-aware of performance	Self-observation, self-judgment, self-reaction
Where	Physical environment	Choose setting	Environmentally sensitive and resourceful	Environmental structuring
With whom	Social	Choose partner, model, or teacher	Socially sensitive and resourceful	Selective help seeking

Figure 3.3
Conceptual framework for studying self-regulation.

"What shall I learn?," "Where shall I learn?," and "With whom shall I learn?" The second column, Learning Dimensions, lists the personal and environmental characteristics involved in the aspect of self-regulation. For example, the question "Why should I learn?" involves learners' motives, whereas the question "What shall I learn?" refers to behavior.

The third column, Learner Conditions, shows the choices potentially available to learners and is critical for determining the extent of self-regulation possible in an achievement situation. We might ask whether learners can choose to participate in the task, the learning method to use, the time limits to spend, the level of outcome behavior, the learning setting, and their partners for participation.

In some classrooms little self-regulation is possible. Suppose a teacher told students they had to write a 10-page typewritten, double-spaced paper on an assigned topic, containing at least 10 references, completed in 3 weeks, and written individually in the library and at home. Assuming the teacher further specified the paper format, the teacher is directing most of this assignment.

In contrast, assume Jim wants to learn to play the guitar. He chooses to engage in this task. The method he chooses is to take lessons from a teacher. He takes one 45-minute lesson per week and practices 1 hour per day. His goal is to be proficient enough to play at social gatherings so others can sing along. He practices the guitar at home at night. Besides his teacher, he enlists the aid of a friend who plays the guitar and asks him technical questions about finger positions and tuning. Jim has almost complete control over the situation, so it allows for maximum self-regulation.

Many situations lie somewhere between these extremes. Teachers may give a term paper assignment but allow students to choose from several topics. Students also may be able to decide on the resources they use, where they write, and how long the paper will be. It therefore makes sense to speak of the degree of self-regulation rather than ask whether one is self-regulated.

The final two columns of the figure show the important attributes and subprocesses involved in each dimension of self-regulation. Interventions designed to enhance self-regulatory skills in students often focus on one or two areas and provide students with instruction and practice on those components. A wealth of evidence shows that self-regulatory competencies can be enhanced through educational interventions (Schunk & Ertmer, 2000; Schunk & Zimmerman, 1994, 1998).

Social Cognitive Processes

The classical social cognitive perspective viewed self-regulation as comprising three processes: self-observation (or self-monitoring), self-judgment, and self-reaction (Bandura, 1986; Kanfer & Gaelick, 1986; Schunk, 1994; Zimmerman, 1990) (Table 3.6). Students enter learning activities with such goals as acquiring knowledge and problem-solving strategies, finishing workbook pages, and completing experiments. With these goals in mind, students observe, judge, and react to their perceived progress. These processes are not mutually exclusive but rather interact with one another.

Table 3.6
Subprocesses of self-regulation.

Self-Observation	Self-Judgment	Self-Reaction
Regularity	Types of standards	Evaluative motivators
Proximity	Goal properties	Tangible motivators
Self-recording	Goal importance	
	Attributions	

Source: *Social Foundations of Thought and Action*, by Bandura, © Reprinted by permission of Pearson Education, Inc., Upper Saddle River, NJ.

Self-Observation.   *Self-observation* involves judging observed aspects of their behavior against standards and reacting positively or negatively. People's evaluations and reactions set the stage for additional observations of the same behavioral aspects or others. These processes also do not operate independently of the environment (Zimmerman, 1986, 1989, 1990). Students who judge their learning progress as inadequate may react by asking for teacher assistance, which alters their environment. In turn, teachers may instruct students in a more efficient strategy, which students then use to promote their learning. That environmental influences (e.g., teachers) can assist the development of self-regulation is important, because educators are increasingly advocating that students be taught self-regulatory skills (Schunk & Zimmerman, 1994, 1998).

Self-observation is conceptually similar to self-monitoring (Chapter 2) and is commonly taught as part of self-regulatory instruction (Lan, 1998; Zimmerman, Bonner, & Kovach, 1996); however, by itself it usually is insufficient to self-regulate behavior over time. Standards of goal attainment and criteria in assessing goal progress are necessary.

Self-Judgment.   *Self-judgment* refers to comparing present performance level with one's goal. Self-judgments depend on the type of self-evaluative standards employed, properties of the goal, importance of goal attainment, and attributions.

Self-evaluative standards may be absolute or normative. Absolute standards are fixed; normative standards are based on performances of others. Students whose goal is to complete six workbook pages in 30 minutes gauge their progress against this absolute standard. Grading systems often reflect absolute standards (e.g., A = 90–100, B = 80–89).

Normative standards frequently are acquired by observing models (Bandura, 1986). Socially comparing one's performances with those of others is an important way to determine the appropriateness of behaviors and self-evaluate performances (Veroff, 1969). When absolute standards are nonexistent or ambiguous, social comparisons become more probable (Festinger, 1954). Students have numerous opportunities to compare their work with that of their peers. Absolute and normative standards often are employed in concert, as when students have 30 minutes to complete six pages and compare their progress with peers to gauge who will be the first to finish.

Standards inform and motivate. Comparing performance with standards indicates goal progress. Students who complete three pages in 10 minutes realize they have finished half of the work in less than half of the time. The belief that they are making progress enhances their self-efficacy, which sustains their motivation to complete the task. Similar others, rather than those much higher or lower in ability, offer the best basis for comparison, because students are apt to believe that if others can succeed, they will too (Schunk, 1987).

Schunk (1983b) compared the effects of social comparative information with those of goal setting during a division training program. Half of the children were given performance goals during each instructional session; the other half were advised to work productively. Within each goal condition, half of the students were told the number of problems other similar children had completed (which matched the session goal) to convey that goals were attainable; the other half were not given comparative information. Goals enhanced self-efficacy; comparative information promoted motivation. Children who received both goals and comparative information demonstrated the highest skill acquisition.

An important means of acquiring self-evaluative standards is through observation of models. Bandura and Kupers (1964) exposed children to a peer or adult demonstrating stringent or lenient standards while playing a bowling game. Children exposed to high-standard models were more likely to reward themselves for high scores and less likely to reward themselves for lower scores compared with those assigned to the low-standard condition. Adult models produced stronger effects than peers. Davidson and Smith (1982) had children observe a superior adult, equal peer, or inferior younger child set stringent or lenient task standards. Children who observed a lenient model rewarded themselves more often for lower scores than those who observed a stringent model. Children's self-reward standards were lower than those of the adult, equal to those of the peer, and higher than those of the younger child. Model-observer similarity in age might have led children to believe that what was appropriate for the peer was appropriate for them.

Observation of models affects self-efficacy and achievement behaviors. Zimmerman and Ringle (1981) exposed children to an adult model who unsuccessfully attempted to solve a wire puzzle for a long or short period and who verbalized statements of confidence or pessimism. Children who observed a pessimistic model persist for a long time lowered their efficacy judgments. Perceived similarity to models is especially influential when observers experience difficulties and possess self-doubts about performing well (Schunk & Hanson, 1985; Schunk et al., 1987).

Goal properties—specificity, proximity, difficulty—were discussed earlier. They are especially influential with long-term tasks (Kanfer & Kanfer, 1991). Teachers can assist students who have doubts about writing a good term paper by breaking the task into short-term goals (e.g., selecting a topic, conducting background research, writing an outline). Learners are apt to believe they can accomplish the subtasks, and completing each subtask develops their self-efficacy for producing a good term paper. Other examples are given in Application 3.7.

APPLICATION 3.7
Goal Setting and Self-Regulation

Goal setting is a useful self-regulatory skill for completing long-term tasks. Many students have doubts about finishing a history project that includes a display and a research paper. Mr. Marshall assists his students by breaking the assignment into short-term goals. If students have a 6-week period to complete the project, their first task might be to choose a topic after researching various topics. Mr. Marshall allows 1 week for research, after which students submit their topics with a brief explanation of their selections. The second week is spent in more specific research and in developing an outline for the paper. After the outlines are submitted and feedback from Mr. Marshall is received, students have 2 weeks to work on the initial drafts of their papers and to draw a sketch of the items to be included in their displays. Mr. Marshall then reviews their progress and provides feedback. Students can revise papers and develop displays during the final 2 weeks.

A law student can become overwhelmed when trying to memorize and analyze numerous landmark cases in preparing for moot court. Law professors can help throughout the semester by having students set realistic goals and by helping students organize their studying. Students might begin by establishing goals to learn the cases for major categories (substantive, procedural, public, private, and international law) in a set time period. Within each major goal category subgoals can be created; for example, for the major goal category of private law, subgoals can be established for ownership and use of property, contracts between individuals, family relationships, and redress by way of compensation for harm inflicted on one person by another.

Allowing students to set goals for learning enhances goal commitment (Locke & Latham, 1990) and promotes self-efficacy (Schunk, 1990). Schunk (1985) found support for this in a study with children with learning disabilities. Some children set mathematical subtraction problem-solving goals for themselves each session, others were assigned comparable goals by a teacher, and others received instruction but no goals. Self-set goals led to higher expectancies of goal attainment compared with goals set by others. Relative to the other two conditions, self-set goals produced the highest self-efficacy and greatest skill acquisition.

Self-judgments reflect in part the *importance of goal attainment*. When individuals care little about how they perform, they may not assess their performance or expend effort to improve it (Bandura, 1986). People judge their progress in learning for goals they value. Sometimes goals that originally hold little value become more important when people receive feedback indicating they are becoming skillful. Thus, novice piano players initially may hold ill-defined goals for themselves (e.g., play better). As their skill develops, people begin to set specific goals (learn to play a particular piece) and judge progress relative to these goals.

Attributions (perceived causes of outcomes; see Chapter 8), along with goal progress judgments, can affect self-efficacy, motivation, achievement, and affective reactions (Schunk, 1994, 2001). Students who believe they are not making good progress toward their goals may attribute their performances to low ability, which negatively impacts expectancies and behaviors. Students who attribute poor progress to lackadaisical effort or an inadequate learning strategy may believe they will perform better if they work harder or switch to a different strategy (Schunk, 1989). With respect to affective reactions, people take more pride in their accomplishments when they attribute them to ability and effort than to external causes (Weiner, 1985). People are more self-critical when they believe that they failed due to personal reasons rather than to circumstances beyond their control.

Attributional feedback can enhance self-regulated learning (Schunk, 1989). Being told that one can achieve better results through harder work can motivate one to do so, because the feedback conveys that one is capable (Andrews & Debus, 1978; Dweck, 1975; Schunk, 1989). Providing effort feedback for prior successes supports students' perceptions of their progress, sustains their motivation, and increases their efficacy for further learning (Schunk, 1982a; Schunk & Cox, 1986).

The timing of attributional feedback may be important. Early task successes constitute a prominent cue for forming ability attributions. Feedback linking early successes with ability (e.g., "That's correct; you're good at this") should enhance learning efficacy. Many times, however, effort feedback for early successes is more credible, because when students lack skills they have to expend effort to succeed. As students develop skills, ability feedback better enhances self-efficacy (Schunk, 1983a).

Self-Reaction. Self-reactions to goal progress motivate behavior (Bandura, 1986). The belief that one is making acceptable progress, along with the anticipated satisfaction of accomplishing the goal, enhances self-efficacy and sustains motivation. Negative evaluations do not decrease motivation if individuals believe they are capable of improving (Schunk, 1989). If students believe they have been lackadaisical but can progress with enhanced effort, they are apt to feel efficacious and redouble their efforts. Motivation does not improve if students believe they lack the ability and will not succeed no matter how hard they try (Schunk, 1982a).

Instructions to people to respond evaluatively to their performances promote motivation; people who think they can perform better persist longer and expend greater effort (Kanfer & Gaelick, 1986). Perceived progress is relative to one's goals; the same level of performance can be evaluated differently. Some students are content with a B in a course, whereas others are satisfied only with an A. Assuming that people feel capable of improving, higher goals lead to greater effort and persistence than lower goals (Bandura & Cervone, 1983).

Contingent on their task progress of goal attainment, people routinely reward themselves tangibly with work breaks, new clothes, and evenings out with friends. Social cognitive theory postulates that the anticipated consequences of behavior, rather than the actual consequences, enhance motivation (Bandura, 1986). Grades are given at the end of courses, yet students typically set subgoals for accomplishing their work and reward and punish themselves accordingly.

Tangible consequences also affect self-efficacy. External rewards that are given based on actual accomplishments enhance efficacy. Telling students that they will earn rewards based on what they accomplish instills a sense of self-efficacy for learning (Schunk, 1989). Self-efficacy is validated as students work on a task and note their progress. Receipt of the reward further validates efficacy, because it symbolizes progress. Rewards not tied to performances (e.g., given for spending time on the task regardless of what one accomplishes) may convey negative efficacy information; students might infer they are not expected to learn much because they are not capable (Schunk, 1983e).

Cyclical Nature of Self-Regulation

Social cognitive theory emphasizes the interaction of personal, behavioral, and environmental factors (Bandura, 1986, 1997; Zimmerman, 2000, 2001). Self-regulation is a cyclical process because these factors typically change during learning and must be monitored. Such monitoring leads to changes in an individual's strategies, cognitions, affects, and behaviors.

This cyclical nature is captured in Zimmerman's (1998) three-phase self-regulation model (Figure 3.4). This model also expands the classical view, which covers task engagement, because it includes the key functions performed before and after engagement. The forethought phase precedes actual performance and refers to processes that set the stage for action. The performance (volitional) control phase involves processes that occur during learning and affect attention and action. During the self-reflection phase, which occurs after performance, people respond to their efforts.

Various self-regulatory processes come into play during the different phases. Thus, learners enter learning situations with varying goals and self-efficacy for attaining them. Performance control involves implementing learning strategies that affect motivation and learning. During periods of self-reflection learners engage in self-evaluation, which is addressed next.

Self-Evaluation and Self-Regulation   Effective self-regulation requires goals and motivation (Bandura, 1986; Kanfer & Kanfer, 1991; Zimmerman, 1989). Students must regulate their actions and underlying achievement cognitions, beliefs, intentions, and

Figure 3.4
Self-regulation cycle phases.
Source: From "Developing Self-Fulfilling Cycles of Academic Regulation: An Analysis of Exemplary Instructional Models," by B. J. Zimmerman, 1998, in D. H. Schunk and B. J. Zimmerman, (Eds.)., *Self-Regulated Learning: From Teaching to Self Reflective Practice* (pp. 3). New York: Guilford Press.

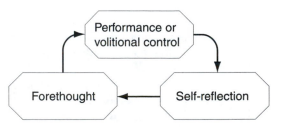

affects. Research increasingly substantiates the prediction that self-monitoring of achievement beliefs sustains learning efforts and promotes achievement (Schunk, 1989; Schunk & Zimmerman, 1994; Zimmerman et al., 1996; Zimmerman & Martinez-Pons, 1992).

Effective self-regulators develop self-efficacy for self-regulating their learning (Zimmerman, Bandura, & Martinez-Pons, 1992) and for performing well (Bouffard-Bouchard, Parent, & Larivee, 1991). Of critical importance is self-evaluation of capabilities and progress in skill acquisition. Self-evaluation comprises self-judgments of present performance by comparing it to one's goal and self-reactions to those judgments by deeming performance noteworthy, unacceptable, and so forth. Positive self-evaluations lead students to feel efficacious about learning and motivated to continue to work diligently because they believe they are capable of making further progress (Schunk, 1991). Low self-judgments of progress and negative self-reactions will not necessarily diminish self-efficacy and motivation if students believe they are capable of succeeding but that their present approach is ineffective (Bandura, 1986). Such students may alter their self-regulatory processes by working harder, persisting longer, adopting what they believe is a better strategy, or seeking help from teachers and peers (Schunk, 1990). These and other self-regulatory activities are likely to lead to success (Zimmerman & Martinez-Pons, 1992).

Research substantiates the hypothesis that self-evaluations of capabilities and progress in skill acquisition affect achievement outcomes (Schunk & Ertmer, 2000). Investigations with children during learning of mathematical skills (Schunk & Hanson, 1985; Schunk et al., 1987) and writing skills (Schunk & Swartz, 1993a, 1993b) show that self-efficacy for learning or improving skills assessed prior to instruction predict motivation and skill acquisition.

Bandura and Cervone (1983) obtained benefits of goals and self-evaluative feedback among college students on motor-skill performance. A similar study showed that the greater the students' dissatisfaction with their performances and the higher their self-efficacy for performing well, the stronger was their subsequent effort expenditure (Bandura & Cervone, 1986). Cervone, Jiwani, and Wood (1991) found that providing individuals with a specific goal enhanced the effects of self-efficacy and self-evaluation on performance.

Students may not spontaneously self-evaluate their capabilities. One means of highlighting progress is to have them periodically assess their progress. Explicit capability self-evaluations constitute a type of self-monitoring because students must attend to their present performance and compare it with their prior performance to note progress. By making performance improvements salient, such self-monitoring is apt to raise self-efficacy, sustain self-regulatory activities, and promote skills. White, Kjelgaard, and Harkins (1995) noted that self-evaluation augments the effects of goals on performance when goals are informative of one's capabilities.

Schunk (1996) conducted two studies that investigated how goals and self-evaluation affect achievement outcomes. Fourth graders received instruction and practice on fractions over several sessions. Students worked under conditions involving either a goal of learning how to solve problems (learning goal) or a goal of merely solving them (performance goal). In Study 1, half of the students in each goal condition evaluated their problem-solving capabilities. The learning goal (with or without self-evaluation) and the performance goal with self-evaluation led to higher self-efficacy, skill, self-directed performance, and task orientation than did the performance goal without self-evaluation. In Study 2, all students in each goal condition evaluated their progress in skill acquisition. The learning goal led to higher motivation and achievement outcomes than did the performance goal.

Schunk and Ertmer (1999) examined how goals and self-evaluation affected self-efficacy, achievement, and self-reported competence and use of self-regulatory strategies. College undergraduates worked on computer projects over three sessions. Students received a process goal of learning computer applications or a product goal of performing them. In the first study, half of the students in each goal condition evaluated their progress in learning after the second session. The process goal led to higher self-efficacy, self-judged learning progress, and self-regulatory competence and strategy use; the opportunity for self-evaluation promoted self-efficacy. In the second study, self-evaluation students assessed their progress after each session. Frequent self-evaluation produced comparable results when coupled with a process or product goal. Collectively, these results suggest that infrequent self-evaluation complements learning process goals but that multiple self-evaluations outweigh the benefits of process goals and raise achievement outcomes for all students.

Having students self-monitor their performance and evaluate their capabilities or progress in learning makes it clear that they have become more competent, and this perception strengthens self-efficacy and enhances self-regulated learning efforts. This research has implications for teaching. Students may not normally be in the habit of evaluating their skills or learning progress; thus, they may require instruction in self-evaluation and frequent opportunities to practice it. Suggestions for incorporating self-evaluation in learning settings are given in Application 3.8.

Learning Strategies.   Self-regulated learners believe acquisition of proficiency is a strategically controllable process and accept responsibility for their achievement outcomes (Zimmerman & Martinez-Pons, 1992). According to social cognitive theory, self-regulated strategy use is influenced by students' self-belief systems. As Zimmerman (1989, 1990, 2000, 2001) notes, self-regulated learners are metacognitively aware of strategic relations between self-regulatory processes and learning outcomes, feel self-efficacious about using strategies, have academic goals of learning, have control over debilitating thoughts and anxiety, and believe that strategy use will help them attain goals at higher levels.

The social cognitive perspective on self-regulation reflects Bandura's (1986) notion of triadic reciprocality. This system contrasts with noncognitive (behavioral) views (Chapter 2), which, although they employ some of the same methods (e.g., self-recording) are limited in that they do not include powerful cognitive learning strategies. This system also contrasts with closed negative feedback loops (Carver & Scheier, 1990, 2000). In this view, learners compare performance feedback continuously against learning goals. If feedback indicates substandard performance, they try to improve. Reductions in negative feedback are motivating, and once the goal is

APPLICATION 3.8
Incorporation of Self-Evaluation into Learning

Teaching students to evaluate their progress and learning can begin as early as preschool and kindergarten. Teachers initially might use simple self-checking. Children might be asked to assemble various shaped blocks to form a larger shape (rectangle, square, triangle, hexagon). Samples of various ways to combine the smaller blocks to make the shape can be drawn on cards and placed in an envelope at an activity center. Older elementary students might be given an activity sheet that accompanies a hands-on task with the answers for the sheet listed on the back so they can check their work.

With development, students' self-checking can be integrated into daily activities. Students can also be taught to evaluate their learning by utilizing pretests and practice tests; for example, with the learning of spelling words and math facts. More complicated and thorough practice tests can be used with middle school and high school students, allowing them to determine how much studying to do and what activities they need to complete to master the unit goals.

achieved, work on the task ceases. This closed feature is a significant impediment to students' continuing motivation (Anderman & Maehr, 1994).

Social cognitive theorists argue that self-regulatory systems are open: Goals and strategic activities change based on self-evaluations of feedback. Goal progress and attainment raises learners' self-efficacy and can lead to their adopting new, more-difficult goals (Schunk, 1990). Further, students who feel efficacious about learning select what they believe are useful learning strategies, monitor their performances, and alter their task approach when their present methods do not appear to function properly (Zimmerman, 1989, 1990). Research shows that self-efficacy relates positively to productive use of self-regulatory strategies (Zimmerman & Martinez-Pons, 1990; Zimmerman et al., 1992). Results from a series of studies support the notion that altering goals and strategies is adaptive during learning (Kitsantas & Zimmerman, 1998; Zimmerman & Kitsantas, 1996, 1997). In particular, self-regulation was enhanced by shifting from process to product goals as learning improved.

The dynamic nature of self-regulation is further highlighted in the interaction of social and self influences (Table 3.7; Schunk, 1999; Schunk & Zimmerman, 1997). Initial learning often proceeds best when learners observe social models, after which they become able to perform skills in rudimentary fashion with appropriate guidance and feedback. As learners develop competence, they enter a self-controlled phase where they can match their actions with internal representations of the skill. At the final level, learners develop self-regulatory processes that they employ to further refine skills and select new goals. Skills and self-efficacy beliefs are

Table 3.7
Social and self influences on self-regulation.

Level of Development	Social Influences	Self Influences
Observational	Modeling, verbal description	
Imitative	Social guidance and feedback	
Self-controlled		Internal standards, self-reinforcement
Self-regulated		Self-regulatory processes, self-efficacy beliefs

strengthened and internalized throughout this sequence. Although it is possible that learners could skip early phases if they enter with some skill, this sequence is useful in planning instruction to develop skills and self-regulatory competence.

INSTRUCTIONAL APPLICATIONS

Many ideas in social cognitive theory lend themselves well to instruction and student learning. Particularly important are applications involving models, self-efficacy, and self-regulation.

Models

Teacher models facilitate learning and provide self-efficacy information. Students who observe teachers explain and demonstrate concepts and skills are apt to learn and believe that they are capable of further learning. Teachers also provide persuasive self-efficacy information to students. Teachers who introduce lessons by stating that all students can learn and that by working diligently they will master the new skills instill in students self-efficacy for learning, which is substantiated when students successfully work on the task. In studies in which models act one way and tell observers to act differently, children are more influenced by actions than verbalizations (Bryan & Walbek, 1970). Teachers need to ensure that their instructions to students (e.g., "keep your desk tidy") are consistent with their own actions (teacher's desk is tidy).

In similar fashion, peer models can affect student motivation and learning. Relative to teachers, peers may be more focused on "how to do it," which improves learning in observers. Further, observing a similar peer succeed instills a vicarious sense of self-efficacy for learning in observers, which is validated when they perform well (Schunk, 1987). When using peers, it helps to choose models such that all students can relate to at least one. This may mean using multiple peer models, where the peers represent varying levels of skill.

Self-Efficacy

The role of self-efficacy in learning is well substantiated. In determining which in-structional methods to use, it is important that their effects on students' self-efficacy be determined along with their effects on learning. It may be that a method that pro-duces learning does not enhance self-efficacy. For example, providing students with extensive assistance is apt to aid their learning, but it will not do much for students' self-efficacy for being able to learn or perform well on their own. As Bandura (1986, 1997) recommends, periods of self-directed mastery, where students practice skills independently, are needed.

Similarly, although using models in teaching is helpful for learning, attention should be paid to the potential effects of the models on students' self-efficacy. Com-petent models teach skills, but similar models are best for self-efficacy. Having the best mathematics student in the class demonstrate operations may teach skills to the observers, but many of the latter may not feel efficacious because they may believe that they never will be as good as the model. Often top students serve as tutors for less-capable students, which may improve learning but should be accompanied by periods of independent practice to build self-efficacy.

Social cognitive theory makes it clear that teachers' self-efficacy is as important as that of students because teachers' self-efficacy can affect what they do prior to, during, and after instruction (Ashton & Webb, 1986; Tschannen-Moran, Hoy, & Hoy, 1998). Compared with teachers who have less confidence in their abilities, those with higher efficacy encourage student learning better through planning of activities and in their interactions with students (e.g., as they help students cope with academic demands). Teachers' self-efficacy rises when students show progress; teachers may not necessarily find little student progress discouraging if they believe different teaching strategies may produce better results.

Goddard, Hoy, and Hoy (2000) discuss *collective teacher efficacy*, or perceptions of teachers in a school that their efforts as a whole will positively affect students. Al-though research on collective teacher efficacy is scant (Bandura, 1993; Pajares, 1997), the notion is receiving increased attention in part because it seems critical to effec-tive school reform.

Collective teacher efficacy depends on having solid support from administrators who encourage improvement and who facilitate such efforts by creating an envi-ronment free of roadblocks. Collective efficacy also depends on reliable sources of self-efficacy information (Bandura, 1997). Teachers who work collaboratively to achieve common goals (performance mastery) and who benefit from mentors as role models (vicarious information) are apt to feel collectively self-efficacious.

Thorough teacher preparation that includes internships with master teachers and continuing professional development can help teachers learn strategies to use in challenging situations, such as how to foster learning in students with varying abili-ties, how to work with students with limited English proficiency, and how to involve parents in their children's learning. By removing impairments to teaching (e.g., ex-cess paperwork), administrators allow teachers to focus on curricular improvement and student learning.

Self-Regulation

Self-regulation, like other skills, can be learned (B. Zimmerman, 2000). Effective methods for teaching self-regulation often include social models, corrective feedback, strategy instruction and practice, goal setting, and self-evaluations of learning progress (Schunk & Ertmer, 2000). As discussed earlier in this chapter, the key is for students to internalize these social influences so they become part of their self-regulatory processes (Schunk, 1999).

Academic self-regulation improvement is aided when students receive opportunities for self-directed practice in diverse settings. Goal setting, for example, is a general strategy that can be applied to academic, social, and motor skills, to improve performance (Locke & Latham, 1990). Teachers who work together across disciplinary lines can foster goal setting and other self-regulatory skills (e.g., self-monitoring) by showing students how to apply them in the settings.

SUMMARY

Social cognitive learning theory contends that people learn from their social environments. In Bandura's theory, human functioning is viewed as a series of reciprocal interactions among personal factors, behaviors, and environmental events. Within this framework, learning is construed as an information processing activity in which knowledge is cognitively represented as symbolic representations serving as guides for action. Learning occurs enactively through actual performances and vicariously by observing models, by listening to instructions, and by engaging with print or electronic materials. The consequences of behavior are especially important. Behaviors that result in successful consequences are retained; those that lead to failures are discarded.

Much historical work exists on imitation, but these perspectives do not fully capture the range and influence of modeling processes. Bandura and colleagues have shown how modeling greatly expands the range and rate of learning. Various modeling effects are distinguished: inhibition and disinhibition, response facilitation, and observational learning. Observational learning through modeling expands the learning rate, as well as the amount of knowledge acquired. Subprocesses of observational learning are attention, retention, production, and motivation.

According to social cognitive theory, observing a model does not guarantee learning or later ability to perform the behaviors. Rather, models provide information about probable consequences of actions and motivate observers to act accordingly. Factors influencing learning and performance are developmental status of learners, prestige and competence of models, vicarious consequences to models, goals, outcome expectations, and perceived self-efficacy.

Researchers have tested Bandura's theory in a variety of contexts involving cognitive, social, motor, health, instructional, and self-regulatory skills. In the area of self-regulation, key processes are self-observation, self-judgment, and self-reaction.

Self-regulation also occurs prior to (forethought) and following (self-reflection) task engagement. Important instructional applications of social cognitive theory involve models, self-efficacy, and self-regulation. Much learning of complex skills occurs through a combination of enactive and vicarious learning. Observers acquire an approximation of the skill by observing models. Subsequent practice of the skill allows teachers to provide corrective feedback to learners. With additional practice, learners refine and internalize self-regulatory skills and strategies.

Information Processing

Information processing theories focus on how people attend to environmental events, encode information to be learned and relate it to knowledge in memory, store new knowledge in memory, and retrieve it as needed (Shuell, 1986). The tenets of information processing are as follows: "Humans are processors of information. The mind is an information-processing system. Cognition is a series of mental processes. Learning is the acquisition of mental representations" (Mayer, 1996, p. 154).

Information processing is not the name of a single theory; it is a generic name applied to theoretical perspectives dealing with the sequence and execution of cognitive events. As a scientific discipline, information processing focuses on cognitive processes and has been influenced by advances in communications and computer technology. Early information processing research was conducted in experimental laboratories and dealt with phenomena such as eye movements, recognition and recall times, attention to stimuli, and interference in perception and memory. Information processing approaches have been applied to learning, memory, problem solving, visual and auditory perception, cognitive development, and artificial intelligence.

Although researchers in a variety of disciplines have explored information processing, its principles have not always lent themselves readily to school learning, curricular structure, and instructional design. This situation does not imply that information processing has little educational relevance, only that many po-

tential applications are yet to be developed. Most information processing research has explored basic processes. Researchers increasingly are applying principles to educational settings involving such subjects as reading, mathematics, and science learning, and applications remain research priorities.

This chapter covers information processing perspectives on human learning. Initially we discuss the assumptions of information processing and give an overview of a prototypical two-store memory model. The bulk of the chapter is devoted to explicating the component processes of attention, perception, short-term (working) memory, and long-term memory (storage, retrieval, forgetting). Relevant historical material on verbal learning and Gestalt psychology is mentioned, along with alternative views involving levels of processing and of memory activation. The chapter concludes by addressing the related topic of mental imagery.

When you finish studying this chapter, you should be able to do the following:

- Describe the major components of a cognitive information processing system: attention, perception, short-term (working) memory, long-term memory.

- Distinguish different views of attention and explain how attention affects learning.

- Compare and contrast the Gestalt and information processing theories of perception.

- Discuss the major forms of verbal learning research.
- Differentiate short- and long-term memory on the basis of capacity, duration, and component processes.
- Define propositions and explain their role in encoding and retrieval of long-term memory information.

- Explain the major factors that influence encoding, retrieval, and forgetting.
- Explain the dual-code theory and apply it to mental imagery.

INFORMATION PROCESSING SYSTEM

Assumptions

Information processing theorists challenge the behavioristic idea that all learning involves forming associations between stimuli and responses. These theorists do not dismiss associationism; forming associations between bits of knowledge helps to facilitate their acquisition and storage in memory. Rather, information processing theorists are less concerned with external conditions and focus more on *internal (mental) processes* that intervene between stimuli and responses. Learners are active seekers and processors of information. They select and attend to features of the environment, transform and rehearse information, relate new information to previously acquired knowledge, and organize knowledge to make it meaningful (Mayer, 1996).

Information processing researchers differ in their views on how learners engage in cognitive processes, but they share some common assumptions. One is that information processing occurs in stages that intervene between receiving a stimulus and producing a response. A corollary is that the form of information, or how it is represented mentally, differs depending on the stage. The stages are qualitatively different from one another.

Another assumption is that human information processing is analogous to computer processing, at least metaphorically. The human system functions similar to a computer: It receives information, stores it in memory, and retrieves it as necessary. Researchers differ in how far they extend this analogy. For some, the computer analogy is nothing more than a metaphor. Others employ computers to simulate activities of humans. The field of *artificial intelligence* is concerned with programming computers to engage in human activities such as thinking, using language, and solving problems (see Chapter 6).

Information processing researchers also generally assume that information processing is involved in all cognitive activities: perceiving, rehearsing, thinking, problem solving, remembering, forgetting, and imaging (Farnham-Diggory, 1992; Mayer, 1996; Shuell, 1986). Information processing extends beyond the domain of human learning as traditionally delineated. This chapter is concerned primarily with those informational functions most germane to learning.

Figure 4.1
Information processing model of
learning and memory.

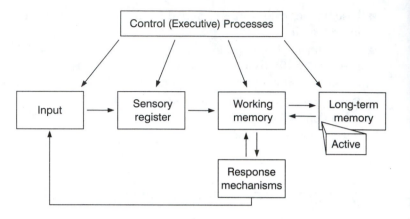

Two-Store (Dual-Memory) Model

Figure 4.1 shows a human information processing model. This model incorporates the idea of stages of processing. Although it is generic, it closely corresponds to the model originally proposed by Atkinson and Shiffrin (1968, 1971).

Information processing begins when a stimulus input (e.g., visual, auditory) impinges on one or more senses (e.g., hearing, sight, touch). The appropriate *sensory register* receives the input and holds it briefly in sensory form. It is here that *perception (pattern recognition)* occurs, which is the process of assigning meaning to a stimulus input. This typically does not involve naming; naming takes time, and information stays in the sensory register for only a fraction of a second. Rather, perception involves equating an input with known information.

The sensory register transfers information to *short-term memory (STM)*. STM is a *working memory (WM)* and corresponds roughly to awareness, or what one is conscious of at a given moment. WM is limited in capacity. Miller (1956) proposed that it holds seven plus or minus two units of information. A unit is a meaningful item: a letter, word, number, or common expression (e.g., "bread and butter"). WM also is limited in duration; for units to be retained in WM they must be rehearsed. Without rehearsal, information is lost after a few seconds.

While information is in WM, related knowledge in *long-term memory (LTM),* or permanent memory, is activated and placed in WM to be integrated with the new information. To name all the state capitals beginning with the letter *A*, students recall the names of states—perhaps by region of the country—and scan the names of their capital cities. When students who do not know the capital of Maryland learn "Annapolis," they can store it with "Maryland" in LTM.

Experts debate whether information ever is lost from LTM. Some researchers contend that it can be, whereas others say that failure to recall reflects a lack of good retrieval cues rather than forgetting. If Sarah cannot recall her third-grade teacher's name (Mapleton), she might be able to if given the hint, "Think of trees." Regardless of theoretical perspective, researchers agree that information remains in LTM for a long time.

Control (executive) processes regulate the flow of information throughout the information processing system. Rehearsal is an important control process that occurs in WM. For verbal material, rehearsal takes the form of repeating information aloud or subvocally. Other control processes include coding (putting information into a meaningful context), imaging (visually representing information), implementing decision rules, organizing information, monitoring level of understanding, and using retrieval strategies. We discuss control processes throughout the next two chapters.

Critique

The two-store model can account for many research results. One of the most consistent research findings is that when people have a list of items to learn, they tend to recall best the initial items (*primacy effect*) and the last items (*recency effect*), as portrayed in Figure 4.2. According to the two-store model, initial items receive the most rehearsal and are transferred to LTM, whereas last items are still in WM at the time of recall. Middle items are recalled the poorest because they are no longer in WM at the time of recall (having been pushed out by subsequent items), they receive fewer rehearsals than initial items, and they are not properly stored in LTM.

Research suggests, however, that learning may be more complex than the basic two-store model stipulates (Baddeley, 1998). One problem with this model is that it does not fully specify how information moves from one store to the other. The control processes notion is plausible but vague. We might ask: Why do some inputs proceed from the sensory registers into WM and others do not? Which mechanisms decide that information has been rehearsed long enough and transfer it into LTM? How is information in LTM selected to be activated? Another concern is that this model

Figure 4.2
Serial position curve showing errors in recall as a function of item position.

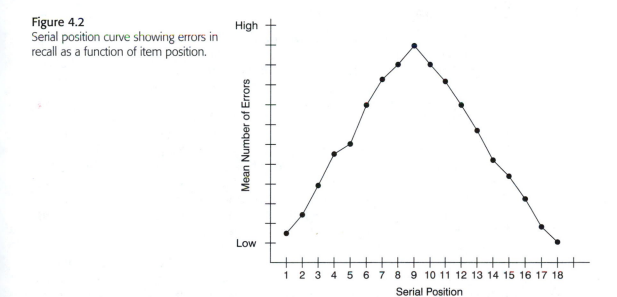

seems best suited to handle verbal material. How nonverbal representation occurs with material that may not be readily verbalizable, such as modern art and well-established skills, is not clear.

The model also is vague about what really is learned. Consider people learning word lists. With nonsense syllables, they have to learn the words themselves and the positions in which they appeared. When they already know the words, they must only learn the positions; for example, "cat" appeared in the fourth position, followed by "tree." People must take into account their purpose in learning and modify learning strategies accordingly. What mechanism underlies these processes (some of which are not cognitive)?

Whether all components of the system are used at all times is also an issue. Thus, WM is useful when people are acquiring knowledge and need to relate incoming information to knowledge in LTM. But we do many things automatically: get dressed, walk, ride a bicycle, respond to simple requests (e.g., "Do you have the time?"). For many adults, reading (decoding) and simple arithmetic computations are automatic processes that place little demand on cognitive processes. Such automatic processing may not require the operation of WM. How does automatic processing develop and what mechanisms govern it?

These and other issues not addressed well by the two-store model (e.g., the role of motivation in learning and the development of self-regulation) do not disprove the model; rather, they are issues to be addressed. Although most information processing researchers accept in principle some variation of this model, alternative conceptions of the information processing system exist. Before describing components of the system in greater detail, we will consider levels of processing and activation level theories.

Levels of Processing

Levels of processing conceptualizes memory according to the *type* rather than the location of processing that information receives (Craik, 1979; Craik & Lockhart, 1972; Craik & Tulving, 1975; Lockhart, Craik, & Jacoby, 1976). This view does not incorporate such stages or structural components as WM or LTM. Rather, different ways to process information exist (levels at which it is processed): physical (surface), acoustic (phonological, sound), semantic (meaning). These three levels are dimensional, with physical processing being the most superficial and semantic processing being the "deepest." For example, suppose you are reading and the next word is *wren*. This word can be processed on a surface level (e.g., it is not capitalized), a phonological level (rhymes with *den*), or a semantic level (small bird). Each level represents a more elaborate type of processing than the preceding level; processing the meaning of *wren* expands the information content of the item more than acoustic processing, which expands content more than surface-level processing.

These three levels seem conceptually similar to the sensory register, WM, and LTM of the two-store model. Both views contend that processing becomes more elaborate with succeeding stages or levels. The levels of processing model, however, does not assume that the three types of processing constitute stages. In levels of processing, one does not have to move to the next process to engage in more elaborate processing; depth of processing can vary within a level. *Wren* can receive low-level semantic processing (small bird) or more extensive semantic processing (its similarity to and difference from other birds).

Another difference between the two information processing models concerns the order of processing. The two-store model assumes that if information is processed, it is done so first by the sensory register, then by WM, and finally by LTM. Levels of processing does not make a sequential assumption. To be processed at the meaning level, information does not have to be first processed at the surface and sound levels (beyond what processing is required for information to be received) (Lockhart et al., 1976).

The two models also have different views of how type of processing affects memory. In levels of processing, the "deeper" the level at which an item is processed, the better the memory because the memory trace is more ingrained. Once an item is processed at a particular point within a level, additional processing at that point should not improve memory. In contrast, the two-store model contends that memory can be improved with additional processing of the same type. This model predicts that the more a list of items is rehearsed, the better it will be recalled.

Some research evidence supports levels of processing. Craik and Tulving (1975) presented individuals with words. As each word was presented, they were given a question to answer. The questions were designed to facilitate processing at a particular level. For surface processing, people were asked, "Is the word in capital letters?" For phonological processing they were asked, "Does the word rhyme with *train?* " For semantic processing, "Would the word fit in the sentence, 'He met a _____ in the street'?" The time people spent processing at the various levels was controlled. Subsequent recall was best when items were processed at a semantic level, next best at a phonological level, and worst at a surface level.

Levels of processing implies, therefore, that student understanding is better when material is processed at deeper levels. Glover, Plake, Roberts, Zimmer, and Palmere (1981) found that asking students to paraphrase ideas while they read essays significantly enhanced recall compared with activities that did not draw on previous knowledge (e.g., identifying key words in the essays). Simple instructions to read slowly and carefully did not assist students during recall.

Despite these positive findings, levels of processing theory has problems. One concern is whether semantic processing always is deeper than the other levels. The sounds of some words (*kaput*) are at least as distinctive as their meanings ("ruined"). In fact, recall depends not only on level of processing but also on type of recall task. Morris, Bransford, and Franks (1977) found that, given a standard recall task, semantic coding produces better results than rhyming coding; however, given a recall task emphasizing rhyming, asking rhyming questions during coding produces better recall than semantic questions. Moscovitch and Craik (1976) proposed that deeper processing during learning results in a higher potential memory performance, but whether that potential is realized depends on whether conditions at retrieval match those during learning.

Another concern with levels of processing theory involves the issue of whether additional processing at the same level produces better recall. Nelson (1977) gave participants one or two repetitions of each stimulus (word) processed at the same level. Two repetitions produced better recall, contrary to the levels of processing hypothesis. Other research shows that additional rehearsal of material facilitates retention and recall as well as automaticity of processing (Anderson, 1990; Jacoby, Bartz, & Evans, 1978).

A final issue concerns the nature of a level. Investigators have argued that because we have no objective measure of levels, we do not know how processing at different levels affects learning and memory (Baddeley, 1978; Nelson, 1977). Time is a poor criterion of level because some surface processing (e.g., "Does the word have the following letter pattern: consonant-vowel-consonant-consonant-vowel-consonant?") can take longer than semantic processing ("Is it a type of bird?"). Neither is processing time within a given level indicative of deeper processing (Baddeley, 1978, 1998). A lack of clear understanding of levels may limit the usefulness of this perspective.

Resolving these issues may require combining levels of processing with the two-store idea to produce a refined memory model. For example, information in WM might be related to knowledge in LTM superficially or more elaborately. Also, the two memory stores might include levels of processing within each store. Semantic coding in LTM may lead to a more extensive network of information and a more meaningful way to remember information than surface or phonological coding.

Activation Level

An alternative concept of memory, but one similar to the two-store and levels of processing models, contends that memory structures vary in their *activation level* (Anderson, 1990). In this view, we do not have separate memory structures but rather one memory with different activation states. Information may be in an active or inactive state. When active, the information can be accessed quickly. The active state is maintained as long as information is attended to. Without attention, the activation level will decay, in which case the information can be activated by the memory structure being reactivated (Collins & Loftus, 1975).

Active information can include information entering the information processing system and information that has been stored in memory (Baddeley, 1998). Regardless of the source, active information either is currently being processed or can be processed rapidly. Active material is roughly synonymous with WM but the former category is broader than the latter. WM includes information in immediate consciousness, whereas active memory includes that information plus material that can be accessed easily. For example, if I am visiting Aunt Frieda and we are admiring her flower garden, that information is in WM, but other information associated with Aunt Frieda's yard (trees, shrubs, dog) may be in an active state.

Rehearsal allows information to be maintained in an active state (Anderson, 1990). As with working memory, only a limited number of memory structures can be active at a given time. As one's attention shifts, activation level changes.

We encounter the activation level idea again later in this chapter because the concept is critical for storage of information and its retrieval from memory. The basic notion involves *spreading activation*, which means that one memory structure may activate another structure adjacent (related) to it (Anderson, 1990). Activation spreads from active to inactive portions of memory. The level of activation depends on the strength of the path along which the activation spreads and on the number of competing (interfering) paths. Activation spread becomes more likely with increased practice, which strengthens structures, and less likely with length of retention interval as strength weakens.

The activation level model has as a primary advantage a clear means for explaining retrieval of information from memory. By dispensing with the notion of separate memory stores, the model eliminates the potential problem of transferring information from one store to the other. At the same time, this model has not escaped the dual-store's problems because it too dichotomizes the information system (active-inactive). We also have the problem of the strength level needed for information to pass from one state to another. Thus, we intuitively know that information may be partially activated (e.g., a crossword item on the "tip of your tongue"—you know it but cannot recall it), so we might ask what level of activation is needed for material to be considered active. These concerns notwithstanding, the activation level model offers important insights into the processing of information.

ATTENTION

We now examine in greater depth the components of the two-store model. From an information processing perspective, human learning requires attention, perception, encoding, storage, and retrieval (Shuell, 1986). This section discusses attention; perception, encoding, storage, and retrieval are addressed in subsequent sections.

The word *attention* is heard often in educational settings. Students do not pay attention to instructions or directions; they have a short attention span or an attention deficit disorder. These expressions describe students who do not attend to the teacher or the instructional material. Even high-achieving students do not always attend to instructionally relevant events. At any time, sights, sounds, smells, tastes, and sensations bombard us; we cannot and should not attend to them all. Our attentional capabilities are limited; we can attend to a few things at once. Thus, attention can be construed as the process of selecting some of many potential inputs.

Alternatively, attention can refer to a limited human resource expended to accomplish one's goals and to mobilize and maintain cognitive processes (Grabe, 1986). Attention is not a bottleneck in the information processing system through which only so much information can pass. Rather, it describes a general limitation on the entire human information processing system.

Theories of Attention

Research has explored how people select inputs for attending. In *dichotic listening* tasks, people wear headphones and receive different messages in each ear. They are asked to "shadow" one message (report what they hear); most can do this quite well. Cherry (1953) wondered what happened to the unattended message. He found that listeners knew when it was present, whether it was a human voice or a noise, and when it changed from a male to a female voice. They typically did not know what the message was, what words were spoken, which language was being spoken, or whether words were repeated.

Broadbent (1958) proposed a model of attention known as *filter theory.* In this view, incoming information from the environment is held briefly in a sensory system. Based on their physical characteristics, pieces of information are selected for further processing by the perceptual system. Information not acted on by the perceptual system is filtered out—not processed beyond the sensory system. Attention is selective because it lets only some messages through for further processing. In dichotic listening studies, filter theory proposes that listeners select a channel based on instructions given to them. They know only some details about the other message because the physical examination of information occurs prior to filtering.

Subsequent work by Treisman (1960, 1964) identified problems with filter theory. Treisman found that during dichotic listening experiments, listeners routinely shift their attention between ears depending on the location of the message they are shadowing. If they are shadowing the message coming into their left ear, and if the message suddenly shifts to the right ear, they continue to shadow the original message and not the new message coming into the left ear. Selective attention depends not only on the physical location of the stimulus but also on its meaning. Treisman proposed that rather than blocking out messages, attention simply turns them down to make them less salient than those being attended to. Information inputs initially are subjected to different tests for physical characteristics and content. Following this preliminary analysis, one input is selected for attention.

Treisman's model is problematic in the sense that much analysis must precede attending to an input, which is puzzling because presumably the original analysis involves some attention. Norman (1976) proposed that all inputs are attended to in sufficient fashion to activate a portion of LTM. At that point, one input is selected for further attention based on the degree of activation, which depends on the context. An input is more likely to be attended to if it fits into the context established by prior inputs. While people read, for example, many outside stimuli impinge on their sensory system, yet they attend to the printed symbols.

In Norman's view, then, stimuli activate portions of LTM, but attention involves more complete activation. Neisser (1967) suggested that preattentive processes are involved in head and eye movements (e.g., refocusing attention) and in guided movements (walking, driving). Preattentive processes are automatic—people implement them without conscious mediation. In contrast, attentional processes are deliberate and require conscious activity. In support of this point, Logan (2002) postulates that attention and categorization occur together. As an object is attended to, it is categorized based on information in memory. Attention, categorization, and memory are three aspects of deliberate, conscious cognition.

Attention and Learning

Attention is a necessary prerequisite of learning. In learning to distinguish letters, a child learns the distinctive features: To distinguish *b* from *d*, students must attend to the position of the vertical line on the left or right side of the circle, not to the mere presence of a circle attached to a vertical line. To learn from the teacher, students must attend to the teacher's voice and ignore other sounds. To develop reading comprehension skills, students must attend to the printed words and ignore such irrelevancies as page size and color.

As skills become routinized, information processing requires less conscious attention. In learning to work multiplication problems, students must carefully attend to each step in the process and check their computations. Once students learn multiplication tables and the algorithm, working problems becomes automatic and is triggered by the input. Research shows that much cognitive skill processing becomes automatic (Phye, 1989).

Differences in the ability to control attention are associated with student age, hyperactivity, intelligence, and learning disabilities (Grabe, 1986). Attentional deficits are associated with learning problems. Hyperactive students, for example, are characterized by excessive motor activity, distractibility, and low academic achievement. They have difficulty focusing and sustaining attention on academic material. They may be unable to block out irrelevant stimuli effectively, which overloads their processing systems. The primary task may be lost among competing stimuli. Sustaining attention over time requires that students work in a strategic manner and monitor their level of understanding. Research shows that normal achievers and older children sustain attention better than do low achievers and younger learners on tasks requiring strategic processing (Short, Friebert, & Andrist, 1990).

Teachers can spot attentive students by noting their eye focus, their ability to begin working on cue (after directions are completed), and physical signs (e.g., handwriting) indicating they are engaged in work (Good & Brophy, 1984). Physical signs alone may not be sufficient; strict teachers can keep students sitting quietly even though students may not be engaged in class work.

Teachers can promote better student attention to relevant material through the design of classroom activities (Application 4.1). Eye-catching displays or actions at the start of lessons engage student attention. Teachers who move around the classroom—especially when students are engaged in seatwork—help sustain student attention on the task. Other suggestions for focusing and maintaining student attention are given in Table 4.1.

Attention and Reading

A consistent research finding is that students are more likely to recall important text elements than less important ones (R. Anderson, 1982; Grabe, 1986). Good and poor readers locate important material and attend to it for longer periods (Ramsel & Grabe, 1983; Reynolds & Anderson, 1982). What distinguishes these readers is not attention control but rather subsequent processing and comprehension. Perhaps poor readers, being more preoccupied with basic reading tasks (e.g., decoding), become distracted from important material and do not process it adequately for retention and retrieval. Research has not established what good and poor readers do while attending to important material, although good readers may relate the information to what they know, make it meaningful, and rehearse it, all of which improve comprehension (Resnick, 1981).

APPLICATION 4.1
Student Attention in the Classroom

Various practices help keep classrooms from becoming too predictable and repetitive, which decreases attention. Teachers can vary their presentations, materials used, student activities, and personal qualities such as dress and mannerisms. Lesson formats for young children should be kept short. Teachers can sustain a high level of activity through student involvement and by moving about to check on student progress.

Kathy Stone might include the following activities in a language arts lesson in her third-grade class. As students begin each section of a teacher-directed exercise, they can point to the location on their papers or in their book. The way sections are introduced can be varied: Students can read together in small groups, individual students can read and be called on to explain, or Mrs. Stone can introduce the section. The way students' answers are checked also can be varied: Students can use hand signals or respond in unison, or individual students can answer and explain their answers. As students independently complete the exercise, Mrs. Stone moves about the room, checks progress, and assists those having difficulty learning or maintaining task focus.

In music class the teacher might increase student attention by using varied activities such as vocal exercises, singing certain selections, using instruments to complement the music, and adding movement to instruments. The teacher might combine activities or vary their sequence to keep the classroom from being too predictable. Small tasks also can be varied to increase attention, such as the way a new music selection is introduced. The teacher might play the entire selection, then model by singing the selection, and then involve the students in the singing. Alternatively, for the last activity the teacher could divide the selection into parts, work on each of the small sections, and then combine these sections to complete the full selection.

Research suggests that the importance of text material affects subsequent recall through differential attention (R. Anderson, 1982). Text elements apparently are processed to some minimal level so importance can be assessed. Based on this evaluation, the text element either is dismissed in favor of the next element (unimportant information) or receives additional attention (important information). Comprehension suffers when students do not pay adequate attention. Assuming attention is sufficient, the actual types of processing students engage in must differ to account for subsequent comprehension differences. Better readers may engage in much automatic processing initially and attend to information deemed important, whereas poorer readers might engage in automatic processing less often.

Table 4.1
Suggestions for focusing and maintaining student attention.

Device	Implementation
Signals	Signal to students at the start of lessons or when they are to change activities.
Movement	Move while presenting material to the whole class. Move around the room while students are engaged in seatwork.
Variety	Use different materials and teaching aids. Use gestures. Do not speak in a monotone.
Interest	Introduce lessons with stimulating material. Appeal to students' interests at other times during the lesson.
Questions	Ask students to explain a point in their own words. Stress that they are responsible for their own learning.

Hidi (1995) notes that attention is required during many phases of reading: processing orthographic features, extracting meanings, judging information for importance, and focusing on important information. This suggests that attentional demands will vary considerably depending on the purpose of reading—for example, extracting details, comprehending, new learning. Future research—especially in the neurophysiological domain—should help to clarify these issues (see Chapter 10).

PERCEPTION

Perception (pattern recognition) refers to attaching meaning to environmental inputs received through the senses. For an input to be perceived, it must be held in a sensory register and compared with knowledge in LTM. These registers and the comparison process are discussed in the next section.

Gestalt theory was an early cognitive psychological view that challenged many of the assumptions of behaviorism. Although Gestalt theory no longer is viable, it offered many important principles that are found in current conceptions of perception and learning. We discuss this theory first and then describe perception from an information processing perspective.

Gestalt Theory

The Gestalt movement began with a small group of psychologists in early twentieth-century Germany. In 1912, Max Wertheimer wrote an article on apparent motion. The article was significant among German psychologists but had no influence in the

United States, where the Gestalt movement had not yet begun. The subsequent publication in English of Kurt Koffka's *The Growth of the Mind* (1924) and Wolfgang Köhler's *The Mentality of Apes* (1925) helped the Gestalt movement spread to the United States. Many Gestalt psychologists, including Wertheimer, Koffka, and Köhler, eventually emigrated to the United States, where they applied their ideas to psychological phenomena.

In a typical demonstration of the perceptual phenomenon of apparent motion, two lines close together are exposed successively for a fraction of a second with a short time interval between each exposure. An observer sees not two lines but rather a single line moving from the line exposed first toward the line exposed second. The timing of the demonstration is critical. If the time interval between exposure of the two lines is too long, the observer sees the first line and then the second but no motion. If the interval is too short, the observer sees two lines side by side but no motion.

This apparent motion is known as the *phi phenomenon* and demonstrates that subjective experiences cannot be explained by referring to the objective elements involved. Observers perceive movement even though none exists. Phenomenological experience (apparent motion) differs from sensory experience (exposure of lines). The attempt to explain this and related phenomena led Wertheimer to challenge psychological explanations of perception as the sum of one's sensory experiences, because these explanations did not take into account the unique wholeness of perception.

Meaningfulness of Perception.   Imagine a woman named Betty who is 5 feet tall. When we view Betty at a distance, our retinal image is much smaller than when we view Betty close up. Yet Betty is 5 feet tall and we know that regardless how far away she is. Although the perception (retinal image) varies, the meaning of the image remains constant.

The German word *Gestalt* has no literal English translation. Its approximate meaning is "form," "shape," or "configuration" (Köhler, 1947/1959). The essence of the Gestalt view is that objects or events are viewed as organized wholes. The basic organization involves a figure (what one focuses on) against a ground (the background). What is meaningful is the configuration, not the individual parts (Koffka, 1922). A tree is not a random collection of leaves, branches, roots, and trunk; it is a meaningful configuration of these elements. When viewing a tree, people typically do not focus on individual elements but rather on the organized whole. The human brain transforms objective reality into mental events organized as meaningful wholes. This capacity to view things as wholes is an inborn quality, although perception is modified by experience and training (Leeper, 1935). As Köhler (1947/1959) explained:

> There is, in the first place, what is now generally called the *organization* of sensory experience. The term refers to the fact that the sensory fields have in a way their own social psychology. Such fields appear neither as uniformly coherent continua nor as patterns of mutually indifferent elements. What we actually perceive are, first of all, specific entities such as things, figures, etc., and also groups of which these entities are members. This demonstrates the operation of processes in which the content of certain areas is unified, and at the same time relatively segregated from its environment. (p. 71)

Gestalt theory originally applied to perception, but when its European proponents emigrated to the United States, they confronted the U.S. emphasis on learning. Applying Gestalt ideas to learning was not difficult. In the Gestalt view, learning is a cognitive phenomenon involving perceptions of things, people, or events in a different way (Koffka, 1922, 1926). One reorganizes experiences into a different perception. Much human learning is *insightful,* which means that the transformation from ignorance to knowledge occurs rapidly. When confronted with a problem, individuals figure out what is known and what needs to be determined. They then think about possible solutions. Insight occurs when people suddenly "see" how to solve the problem.

Gestalt theorists disagreed with the behaviorists about the role of consciousness. In Gestalt theory, only through conscious awareness can meaningful perception and insight occur. They also disputed the idea that complex phenomena can be broken into elementary parts. Behaviorism stressed associationism—the whole is equal to the sum of the parts. Gestalt psychologists felt that the whole is meaningful and loses meaning when it is reduced to individual components. Instead, the whole is greater than the sum of its parts. Interestingly, Gestalt psychologists agreed with behaviorists in objecting to introspection, but for a different reason. Behaviorists viewed it as an attempt to study consciousness; Gestalt theorists felt it was inappropriate to attempt to modify perceptions to correspond to objective reality. People who used introspection tried to separate meaning from perception, whereas Gestalt psychologists believed that perception is meaningful.

Principles of Organization.   Gestalt theory postulates that people use principles to organize their perceptions. Some of the most important principles are figure-ground relation, proximity, similarity, common direction, simplicity, and closure (Figure 4.3; Koffka, 1922; Köhler, 1926, 1947/1959).

The principle of *figure-ground relation* postulates that any perceptual field may be subdivided into a figure against a background. Such salient features as size, shape, color, and pitch distinguish a figure from its background. When figure and ground are ambiguous, perceivers may alternatively organize the sensory experience one way and then another (Figure 4.3a).

The principle of *proximity* states that elements in a perceptual field are viewed as belonging together according to their closeness to one another in space or time. Most people will view the lines in Figure 4.3b as three groups of three lines each, although other ways of perceiving this configuration are possible. This principle of proximity also is involved in the perception of speech. People hear (organize) speech as a series of words or phrases separated with pauses. When people are unfamiliar with speech sounds (foreign languages), they have difficulty discerning pauses.

The principle of *similarity* means that elements that are similar in respects such as size or color are perceived as belonging together. Viewing Figure 4.3c, people tend to see a group of three short lines, followed by a group of three long lines, and so on. Proximity can outweigh similarity; when dissimilar stimuli are closer together than similar ones (Figure 4.3d), the perceptual field tends to be organized into four groups of two lines each.

Figure 4.3
Examples of Gestalt principles.

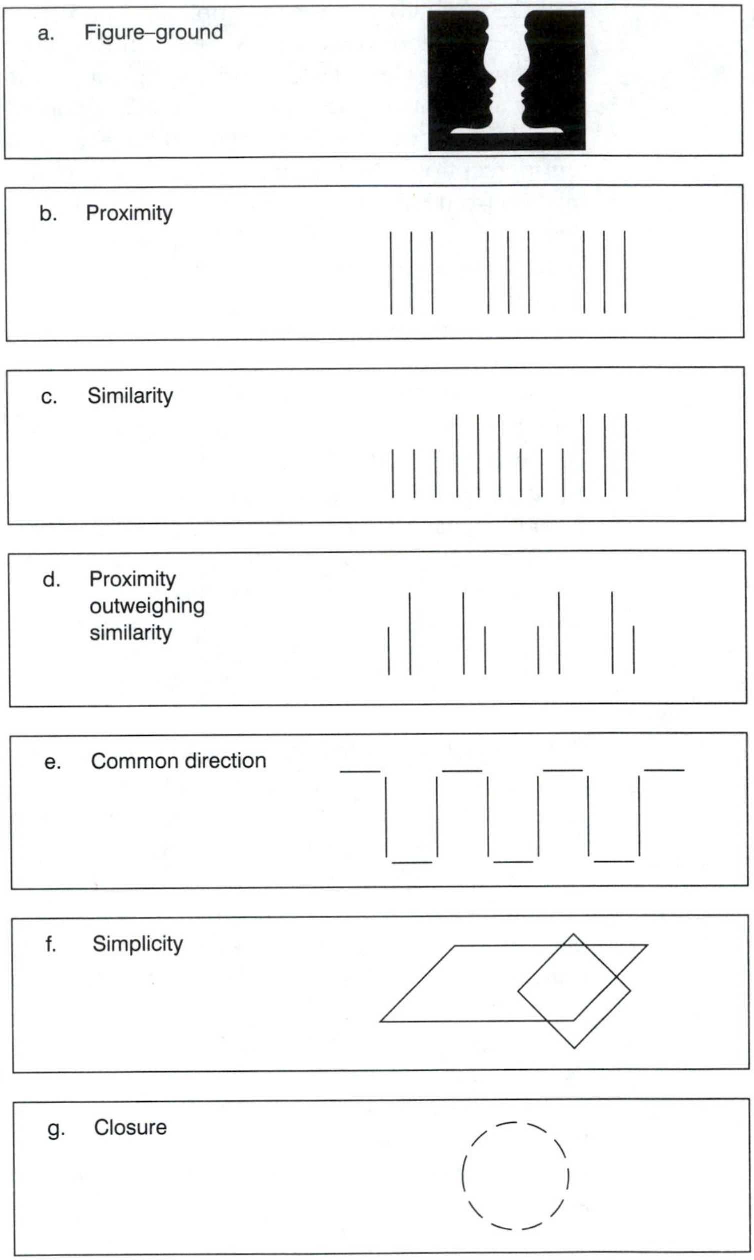

a. Figure–ground

b. Proximity

c. Similarity

d. Proximity outweighing similarity

e. Common direction

f. Simplicity

g. Closure

The principle of *common direction* implies that elements appearing to constitute a pattern or flow in the same direction are perceived as a figure. The lines in Figure 4.3e are most likely to be perceived as forming a distinct pattern. The principle of common direction also applies to an alphabetic or numeric series in which one or more rules define the order of items. Thus, the next letter in the series *abdeghjk* is *m*, as determined by the rule: Beginning with the letter *a* and moving through the alphabet sequentially, list two letters and omit one.

The principle of *simplicity* states that people organize their perceptual fields in simple, regular features and tend to form good Gestalts comprising symmetry and regularity. This idea is captured by the German word *Pragnanz*, which, roughly translated, means, "terseness or precision." Individuals are most likely to see the visual patterns in Figure 4.3f as one geometrical pattern overlapping another rather than as several irregularly shaped geometric patterns. The principle of *closure* means that people fill in incomplete patterns or experiences. Despite the missing lines in the pattern shown in Figure 4.3g, people tend to complete the pattern and see a meaningful picture.

Many of the concepts embodied in Gestalt theory are relevant to our perceptions; however, Gestalt principles are quite general and do not address the actual mechanisms of perception. To say that individuals perceive similar items as belonging together does not explain how they perceive items as similar in the first place. Gestalt principles are illuminating but not explanatory. For this we need information processing principles, which are discussed next.

Sensory Registers

In information processing theory, environmental inputs are received through the senses: vision, hearing, touch, smell, and taste. Each sense has its own register that holds information briefly in the same form in which it is received; that is, visual information is held in visual form, auditory information in auditory form, and so on. Information stays in the sensory register for only a fraction of a second. Some sensory input is transferred to WM for further processing. Other input is erased and replaced by new input. The sensory registers operate in parallel fashion because several senses can be engaged simultaneously and independently of one another. The two sensory memories that have been most extensively explored are the *icon* (vision) and the *echo* (hearing; Neisser, 1967).

In a typical experiment to investigate iconic memory, a researcher presents learners with rows of letters briefly (e.g., 50 milliseconds) and asks them to report as many as they remember. They commonly report only four to five letters from an array. Early work by Sperling (1960) provides insight into iconic storage. Sperling presented learners with rows of letters, then cued them to report letters from a particular row. Sperling estimated that, after exposure to the array, they could recall about nine letters. Sensory memory could hold more information than was previously believed, but while participants were recalling letters, the traces of other letters quickly faded. Sperling also found that recall varied inversely with length of time between the end of a presentation of the array and the beginning of recall: The longer the interval, the poorer the recall. This finding supports the idea that forgetting involves *trace decay,* or the loss of a stimulus from a sensory register over time.

Researchers debate whether the icon is actually a memory store or a persisting image. Sakitt argues that the icon is located in the rods of the eye's retina (Sakitt, 1976; Sakitt & Long, 1979). The active role of the icon in perception is diminished (but not eliminated) if the icon is a physical structure. Not all researchers agree with Sakitt's position, and further research is necessary.

Evidence of an auditory structure (*echoic memory*) similar in function to iconic memory exists. Studies by Darwin, Turvey, and Crowder (1972) and by Moray, Bates, and Barnett (1965) yielded results comparable to Sperling's (1960). Research participants heard three or four sets of recordings simultaneously and then were asked to report one. Findings showed that the echo is capable of holding more information than can be recalled. Similar to iconic information, traces of echoic information rapidly decay following removal of stimuli. The echoic decay does not seem to be quite as rapid as the iconic, but periods beyond 2 seconds between cessation of stimulus presentation and onset of recall produce poorer recall.

LTM Comparisons

Perception depends on objective characteristics and prior experiences. Environmental inputs have tangible physical properties. Assuming normal color vision, everyone who looks at an orange golf ball will recognize it as an orange object, but only those familiar with golf will recognize it as a golf ball. The types of information people have acquired accounts for the different meanings they assign to objects.

Perception also is affected by people's expectations. We perceive what we expect and fail to perceive what we do not expect. Have you ever thought you heard your name spoken, only to realize that another name was being called? For instance, while waiting to meet a friend at a public place or to pick up an order in a restaurant, you may hear your name because you expect to hear it. Also, people may not perceive things whose appearance has changed or that occur out of context. You may not recognize coworkers you meet at the beach because you do not expect to see them dressed in beach attire.

An information processing theory of perception is *template matching*, which holds that people store *templates*, or miniature copies of stimuli, in LTM. When they encounter a stimulus, they compare it with existing templates and identify the stimulus if a match is found. This view is appealing but problematic. People would have to carry around millions of templates in their heads to be able to recognize everyone and everything in their environment. Such a large stock would exceed the brain's capability. Template theory also does a poor job of accounting for stimulus variations. Chairs, for example, come in all sizes, shapes, colors, and designs; hundreds or thousands of templates would be needed just to perceive a chair.

The problems with templates can be solved by assuming that they can have some variation. Prototype theory addresses this. *Prototypes* are abstract forms that include the basic ingredients of stimuli (Klatzky, 1980). Prototypes are stored in LTM and are compared with encountered stimuli that are subsequently identified based on the prototype they match or resemble in form, smell, sound, and so on. Some research supports the existence of prototypes (Franks & Bransford, 1971; Posner & Keele, 1968).

A major advantage of prototypes over templates is that each stimulus has only one prototype instead of countless variations; thus, identification of a stimulus should be easier because comparing it with several templates is not necessary. One concern with prototypes deals with the amount of acceptable variability of the stimuli, or how closely a stimulus must match a prototype to be identified as an instance of that prototype.

A variation of the prototype model involves *feature analysis* (Klatzky, 1980). In this view, one learns the critical features of stimuli and stores them in LTM as images or verbal codes. When a stimulus enters the sensory register, its features are compared with memorial representations. If enough of the features match, the stimulus is identified. For a chair, the critical features may be legs, seat, and a back. Many other features (e.g., color, size) are irrelevant. Any exceptions to the basic features need to be learned (e.g., bleacher chairs that have no legs). Unlike the prototype analysis, information stored in memory is not an abstract representation of a chair but rather includes its critical features. One advantage of feature analysis is that each stimulus does not have just one prototype, which partially addresses the concern about the amount of acceptable variability. Klatzky (1980) provides some empirical support for feature analysis, and future research will most likely clarify this process.

Treisman (1992) proposed that perceiving an object establishes a temporary representation in an object file, which collects, integrates, and revises information about its current characteristics. The contents of the file may be stored as an object token. For newly perceived objects, we try to match the token to a memorial representation (dictionary) of object types, which may or may not succeed. The next time the object appears, we retrieve the object token, which specifies its features and structure. The token will facilitate reperception if all of the features match but may impair it if many do not match. Much research is addressing the process through which object tokens form.

Regardless of how LTM comparisons are made, research shows that pattern recognition proceeds in two fashions: bottom-up processing and top-down processing (Anderson, 1980; Bobrow & Norman, 1975; Lindsay & Norman, 1977; Resnick, 1985). *Bottom-up processing* analyzes features and builds a meaningful representation to identify stimuli. Beginning readers typically use bottom-up processing when they encounter letters and new words and attempt to sound them out. People also use bottom-up processing when experiencing unfamiliar stimuli (e.g., handwriting).

Perception would proceed very slowly if the memory always analyzed features in detail. In *top-down processing*, individuals develop expectations regarding perception based on the context. Once they become familiar with situations, they anticipate events and perceive in accordance with those. Skilled readers build a mental representation of the context while reading and expect certain words and phrases in the text (Resnick, 1985). The earlier example of erroneously hearing your name called (because you expected to hear it) and not recognizing coworkers (because you did not expect to see them) are instances of top-down processing. Effective top-down processing depends on extensive prior knowledge.

TWO-STORE MEMORY MODEL

The two-store memory model serves as our basic information processing perspective on learning and memory. Before discussing this in depth, we will provide some historical information that led to its development. For this we turn to research on verbal learning.

Verbal Learning

Stimulus-Response Associations.   The impetus for research on verbal learning derived from the work of Ebbinghaus (Chapter 1), who construed learning as gradual strengthening of associations between verbal stimuli (words, nonsense syllables). With repeated pairings, the response *dij* became more strongly connected with the stimulus *wek*. Other responses also could become connected with *wek* during learning of a list of paired nonsense syllables, but these associations became weaker over trials.

Ebbinghaus showed that various factors affect the ease or speed with which one typically learns a list of items. Three important factors are *meaningfulness* of items, *degree of similarity* between them, and *length of time* separating study trials (Klatzky, 1980). Words (meaningful items) are learned more readily than nonsense syllables. With respect to similarity, the more alike items are to one another, the harder they are to learn. Similarity in meaning or sound can cause confusion. An individual asked to learn several synonyms such as *gigantic, huge, mammoth*, and *enormous* may fail to recall some of these but instead may recall words similar in meaning but not on the list (*large, behemoth*). With nonsense syllables, confusion occurs when the same letters are used in different positions (*xqv, kbq, vxb, qvk*). The length of time separating study trials can vary from quite short (*massed practice*) to longer (*distributed practice*). When interference is probable (discussed later in this chapter), distributed practice yields better learning (Underwood, 1961).

Learning Tasks.   Verbal learning researchers commonly employed three types of learning tasks: serial, paired-associate, and free-recall. In *serial learning*, people recall verbal stimuli in the order in which they were presented. Serial learning is involved in such school tasks as memorizing a poem or the steps in a problem-solving strategy. Results of many serial learning studies typically yield a *serial position curve* (see Figure 4.2). Words at the beginning and end of the list are readily learned, whereas middle items require more trials for learning. The serial position effect may arise due to differences in distinctiveness of the various positions. People must remember not only the items themselves but also their positions in the list. The ends of a list appear to be more distinctive and are therefore "better" stimuli than the middle positions of a list.

In *paired-associate learning*, one stimulus is provided for one response item (e.g., *cat-tree, boat-roof, bench-dog*). Participants respond with the correct response upon presentation of the stimulus. Paired-associate learning has three aspects: discrimination among the stimuli, learning the responses, and learning which responses accompany which stimuli. Debate has centered on the process by which paired-associate learning occurs and the role of cognitive mediation. Researchers originally assumed learning is incremental and each stimulus-response association is gradually strengthened. This view is supported by the typical learning curve (Figure 4.4). The number of errors people make is high at the beginning, but errors decrease with repeated presentations of the list.

Work by Estes (1970) and others suggested a different perspective. Although list learning improves with repetition, learning of any given item has an *all-or-none* character: The learner either knows the correct association or does not know it. Over trials, the number of learned associations increases. A second issue involves *cognitive mediation.* Rather than simply memorizing responses, learners often impose their organization to make material meaningful. They may use cognitive mediators to link stimulus words with their responses. For the pair *cat-tree*, one might picture a cat running up a tree or think of the sentence, "The cat ran up the tree." When presented with *cat*, one recalls the image or sentence and responds with *tree*. Research shows that verbal learning processes are more complex than originally believed (Klatzky, 1980).

In *free-recall learning*, learners are presented with a list of items and recall them in any order. Free recall lends itself well to organization imposed to facilitate memory. Often during recall, learners group words presented far apart on the original list (Bower, 1970). Groupings often are based on similar meaning or membership in the same category (e.g., rocks, fruits, vegetables).

In a classic demonstration of the phenomenon of *categorical clustering,* learners were presented with a list of 60 nouns, 15 each drawn from the following categories: animals, names, professions, and vegetables (Bousfield, 1953). Words were presented in scrambled order; however, learners tended to recall members of the same category together. The tendency to cluster increases with the number of repetitions of the list (Bousfield & Cohen, 1953) and with longer presentation times for

Figure 4.4
Learning curve showing errors as a function of study trials.

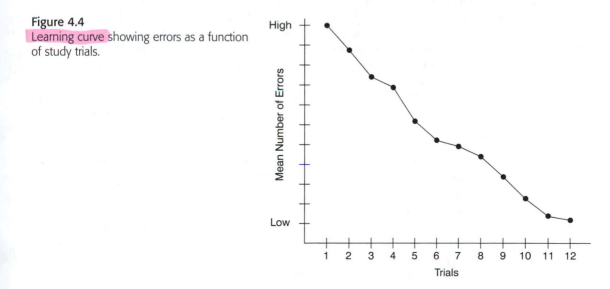

items (Cofer, Bruce, & Reicher, 1966). Clustering has been interpreted in associationist terms (Wood & Underwood, 1967); that is, words recalled together tend to be associated under normal conditions, either to one another directly (e.g., *pear-apple*) or to a third word (*fruit*). A cognitive explanation is that individuals learn both the words presented and the categories of which they are members (Cooper & Monk, 1976). The category names serve as mediational cues: When asked to recall, learners retrieve category names and then their members. Clustering provides insight into the structure of human memory and supports the Gestalt notion that individuals organize their experiences.

Verbal learning research identified the course of acquisition and forgetting of verbal material. At the same time, the idea that associations could explain learning of verbal material was too simplistic. This became apparent when researchers moved beyond simple list learning to more meaningful forms such as learning from text. From an educational perspective, one might question the relevance of learning lists of nonsense syllables or words paired in arbitrary fashion. In school, verbal learning occurs within meaningful contexts, for example, word pairs (e.g., state capitals, English translations of foreign words); ordered phrases and sentences (poems, songs); and meanings for vocabulary words. With the advent of information processing views of learning and memory, many of the ideas propounded by verbal learning theorists were discarded or substantially modified. Recent work by information processing researchers has addressed learning and memory of context dependent verbal material. We now turn to a key information processing topic—working memory.

Short-Term (Working) Memory

Once a stimulus is attended to and perceived, the input is transferred to *short-term (working) memory* (WM or STM; Baddeley, 1992, 1998, 2001). WM is our memory of immediate consciousness. Incoming information (verbal and visual/spatial) is stored for a short time and is worked on by being rehearsed or related to information activated in LTM. As students read a text, WM holds for a few seconds the last words or sentences they read. Students might try to remember a particular point by repeating it several times (rehearsal) or by asking how it relates to a topic discussed earlier in the book (relate to information in LTM). As another example, assume that a student is multiplying 45 by 7. WM holds these numbers (45 and 7), along with the product of 5 and 7 (35), the number carried (3), and the answer (315). The information in WM ($5 \times 7 =$?) is compared with activated knowledge in LTM ($5 \times 7 = 35$). Also activated in LTM is the multiplication algorithm, and these procedures direct the student's actions.

Research has provided a reasonably detailed picture of the operation of WM. *WM is limited in duration:* If not acted upon quickly, information in WM decays. In a classic study (Peterson & Peterson, 1959), participants were presented with a nonsense syllable (e.g., *khv*), after which they performed an arithmetic task before attempting to recall the syllable. The purpose of the arithmetic task was to prevent learners from rehearsing the syllable, but because the numbers did not have to be stored, they did not interfere with storage of the syllable in WM. The longer participants spent on the distracting activity, the poorer was their recall of the nonsense syllable. These findings imply a fragile WM; information is quickly lost if not learned well. If, for example, you are given a phone number to call but then are distracted before being able to dial it or write it down, you may not be able to recall it.

WM also is limited in capacity: It can hold only a small amount of information. Miller (1956) suggested that the capacity of WM is seven plus or minus two items, where items are such meaningful units as words, letters, numbers, and common expressions. One can increase the amount of information by *chunking*, or combining information in a meaningful fashion. The phone number 555–1960 consists of seven items, but it can easily be chunked to two as follows: "Triple 5 plus the year Kennedy was elected President."

Sternberg's (1969) research on *memory scanning* provides insight into how information is retrieved from WM. Participants were presented rapidly with a small number of digits that did not exceed the capacity of WM. They then were given a test digit and were asked whether it was in the original set. Because the learning was easy, participants rarely made errors; however, as the original set increased from two to six items, the time to respond increased about 40 milliseconds per additional item. Sternberg concluded that people retrieve information from active memory by successively scanning items.

Control (executive) processes direct the processing of information in WM, as well as the movement of knowledge into and out of WM (Baddeley, 2001). Control processes include rehearsal, predicting, checking, monitoring, and metacognitive activities (Chapter 5). Control processes are goal directed; they select information relevant to people's plans and intentions from the various sensory receptors. Information deemed important is rehearsed. *Rehearsal* (repeating information to oneself aloud or subvocally) can maintain information in WM and improve recall (Baddeley, 2001; Rundus, 1971; Rundus & Atkinson, 1970).

Environmental or self-generated cues activate a portion of LTM, which then is more accessible to WM. The working (active) memory holds a representation of events occurring recently, such as a description of the context and the content. Researchers debate whether active memory constitutes a separate memory store or merely an activated portion of LTM (Calfee, 1981).

Long-Term Memory

Research has shown that knowledge representation in LTM depends on *frequency* and *contiguity* (Baddeley, 1998). The more often an idea is encountered, the stronger its representation in memory. Furthermore, two experiences that occur closely in time are apt to be linked in memory, so that when one is remembered the other is activated. Thus, information in LTM is represented in *associative structures*.

Information processing models often use computers for analogies, but some important differences exist, which are highlighted by associative structures. *Human memory is content addressable*: Information on the same topic is stored together, so that knowing what is being looked for will most likely lead to recalling the information (Baddeley, 1998). In contrast, *computers are location addressable*: Computers have to be told where information is stored. The nearness of one program or data set on a disk to others on the same disk is purely arbitrary. Another difference is that information is stored precisely in computers. Human memory is less precise but often more colorful or informative. The name *Daryl Crancake* is stored in a computer's memory as "Daryl Crancake." In human memory it may be stored as "Daryl Crancake" or become distorted to "Darrell," "Darel," or "Derol," and "Cupcake," "Cranberry," or "Crabapple."

A useful analogy for the human mind is a library. Information in a library is content addressable in that books on similar content are stored under similar call numbers. Information in the mind (as in the library) is also cross-referenced (Calfee, 1981). Knowledge that cuts across different content areas can be accessed through either area. For example, Amy may have a memory slot devoted to her 21st birthday. The memory includes what she did, whom she was with, and what gifts she received. These topics can be cross-referenced as follows: The jazz CDs she received as gifts are cross-referenced in the memory slot dealing with music. The fact that her next-door neighbor attended is filed in the memory slot devoted to the neighbor and neighborhood.

Knowledge stored in LTM varies in its richness. Each person has vivid memories of pleasant and unpleasant experiences. These memories can be exact in their details covering who, what, where, and when. Other types of knowledge stored in memories are mundane and impersonal: word meanings, arithmetic operations, and excerpts from famous documents.

To account for the differences in memory, Tulving (1972, 1983) proposed a distinction between episodic and semantic memory. *Episodic memory* includes information associated with particular times and places that is personal and autobiographical. The fact that the word *cat* occurs in position three on a learned word list is an example of episodic information, as is information about what Anne did on her 21st birthday and which night this week Joe called. *Semantic memory* involves general information and concepts available in the environment and not tied to a particular context. Examples include the words to the "Star Spangled Banner" and the chemical formula for water (H_2O). The knowledge, skills, and concepts learned in school are semantic memories. The two types of memories often are combined, as when a child tells a parent, "Today in school I learned [episodic memory] that Columbus discovered America in 1492 [semantic memory]."

More recently, researchers have explored differences between declarative and procedural memories (Gupta & Cohen, 2002). *Declarative memory* involves remembering new events and experiences. Information typically is stored in declarative memory quickly, and it is the memory most impaired in patients with amnesia. *Procedural memory* is memory for skill, procedural, and language learning. Information in procedural memory is stored gradually—often with extensive practice—and may be difficult to describe (e.g., riding a bicycle). We return to this distinction shortly.

Another important issue concerns the *form* or *structure* in which LTM stores knowledge. Paivio (1971) proposed that knowledge is stored in *verbal* and *visual* forms, each of which is functionally independent but interconnected. Concrete objects—dog, tree, book—tend to be stored as images, whereas abstract concepts—love, truth, honesty—and linguistic structures are stored in verbal codes. Knowledge can be stored both visually and verbally: You may have a pictorial representation of your home and also be able to describe it verbally. Paivio postulated that for any piece of knowledge, an individual has a preferred storage mode activated more readily than the other. Dual-coded knowledge may be remembered better, which has important educational implications and confirms the general teaching principle of explaining (verbal) and demonstrating (visual) new material (Clark & Paivio, 1991).

Paivio's work is discussed further in the section on mental imagery later in this chapter. His views have been criticized on the grounds that a visual memory exceeds the brain's capacity and requires some brain mechanism to read and translate the pictures (Pylyshyn, 1973). Some theorists contend that knowledge is stored only in verbal codes (J. Anderson, 1976, 1980; Collins & Quillian, 1969; Newell & Simon, 1972; Norman & Rumelhart, 1975; Quillian, 1969). Verbal models do not deny that knowledge can be represented pictorially but postulate that the ultimate code is verbal and that pictures in memory are reconstructed from verbal codes. Table 4.2 shows some characteristics and distinctions of memory systems.

The associative structures of LTM are *propositional networks*, or interconnected sets comprising nodes or bits of information (Anderson, 1990; Calfee, 1981). A *proposition* is the smallest unit of information that can be judged true or false. The statement, "My 80-year-old uncle lit his awful cigar," consists of the following propositions:

- I have an uncle.
- He is 80 years old.
- He lit a cigar.
- The cigar is awful.

Various types of propositional knowledge are represented in LTM. *Declarative knowledge* refers to facts, subjective beliefs, scripts (e.g., events of a story), and organized passages (e.g., Declaration of Independence). *Procedural* knowledge consists of concepts, rules, and algorithms. Declarative and procedural knowledge are

Table 4.2
Characteristics and distinctions of memory systems.

Type of Memory	Characteristics
Short-term	Limited capacity (about seven items), short duration (in absence of rehearsal), immediate consciousness
Long-term	Theoretically unlimited capacity, permanent storage, information activated when cued
Episodic	Information in LTM associated with particular events, times, places
Semantic	Information in LTM involving general knowledge and concepts, not tied to specific contexts
Verbal	Propositions (units of information) and procedures coded as meanings
Visual (iconic)	Information coded as pictures, images, scenes

discussed in this chapter. *Conditional knowledge* is knowing when to employ forms of declarative and procedural knowledge and why it is beneficial to do so (see Chapter 5; Gagné, 1985; Paris et al., 1983).

Learning can occur in the absence of overt behavior because learning involves the formation or modification of propositional networks; however, overt performance typically is required from students to ensure they have acquired skills. Research on skilled actions shows that people typically execute behaviors according to a sequence of planned segments (Bilodeau, 1966; Ericsson et al., 1993; Fitts & Posner, 1967; VanLehn, 1996). Individuals select a performance routine they expect will produce the desired outcome, periodically monitor their performances, make corrections as necessary, and alter their performances following corrective feedback. Because performances often need to vary to fit contextual demands, people find that practicing adapting skills in different situations is helpful.

Transfer (see Chapter 5) refers to the links between propositions in memory and depends on information being cross-referenced or the uses of information being stored along with it. Students understand that skills and concepts are applicable in different domains if that knowledge is stored in the respective networks. Teaching students how information is applicable in different contexts ensures that appropriate transfer occurs.

Influences on Encoding

Encoding is the process of putting new (incoming) information into the information processing system and preparing it for storage in LTM. Encoding usually is accomplished by *making new information meaningful* and *integrating it with known information in LTM.* Although information need not be meaningful to be learned—one unfamiliar with geometry could memorize the Pythagorean theorem without understanding what it means—meaningfulness improves learning and retention.

Simply attending to and perceiving stimuli do not ensure that information processing will continue. Many things teachers say in class go unlearned (even though students attend to the teacher and the words are meaningful) because students do not continue to process the information. Important factors that influence encoding are organization, elaboration, and schema structures.

Organization. Gestalt theory and research showed that well-organized material is easier to learn and recall (Katona, 1940). Miller (1956) argued that learning is enhanced by classifying and grouping bits of information into organized chunks. Memory research demonstrates that even when items to be learned are not organized, people often impose organization on the material, which facilitates recall (Klatzky, 1980). Organized material improves memory because items are linked to one another systematically. Recall of one item prompts recall of items linked to it. Research supports the effectiveness of organization for encoding among children and adults (Basden, Basden, Devecchio, & Anders, 1991).

One way to organize material is to use a hierarchy into which pieces of information are integrated. Figure 4.5 shows a sample hierarchy for animals. The ani-

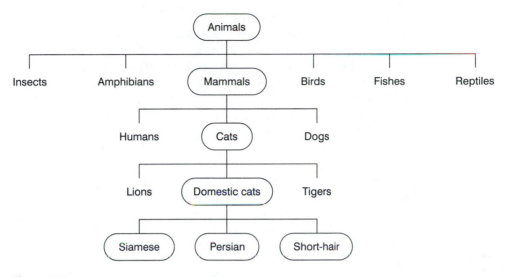

Figure 4.5
Memory network with hierarchical organization.

mal kingdom as a whole is on top, and underneath are the major categories (e.g., mammals, birds, reptiles). Individual species are found on the next level, followed by breeds.

Other ways of organizing information include the use of mnemonic techniques (see Chapter 5) and mental imagery (discussed later in this chapter). Mnemonics enable learners to enrich or elaborate material (e.g., by forming the first letters of words to be learned into an acronym, familiar phrase, or sentence). Some mnemonic techniques employ imagery; in remembering two words (e.g., *honey* and *bread*), one might imagine them interacting with each other (honey on bread). Using audiovisuals in instruction may help to improve students' imagery.

Elaboration.   *Elaboration* is the process of expanding upon new information by adding to it or linking it to what one knows. Elaborations assist encoding and retrieval because they link the to-be-remembered information with other knowledge. Recently learned information is easier to access in this expanded memory network. Even when the new information is forgotten, people often can recall the elaborations (Anderson, 1990).

Rehearsing information keeps it in WM but does not elaborate it. We will distinguish *maintenance rehearsal* (repeating information over and over) from *elaborative rehearsal* (relating the information to something already known). Students learning U.S. history can simply repeat "D-Day was June 6, 1944," or they can elaborate it by relating it to something they know (e.g., the same year that Roosevelt was elected president for the fourth time).

Mnemonic devices elaborate information in different ways. Once such device is to form the first letters into a meaningful sentence. For example, to remember the order of the planets you might learn the sentence, "*My very educated mother just served us nine pizzas,*" in which the first letters correspond to those of the planets (*M*ercury, *V*enus, *E*arth, *M*ars, *J*upiter, *S*aturn, *U*ranus, *N*eptune, *P*luto). You would first recall the sentence and then reconstruct planetary order based on the first letters.

Students may be able to devise elaborations, but if they cannot, they do not need to labor needlessly when teachers can provide effective elaborations. To assist storage in memory and retrieval, elaborations must make sense. Elaborations that are too unusual may not be remembered. Precise, sensible elaborations facilitate memory and recall (Bransford et al., 1982; Stein, Littlefield, Bransford, & Persampieri, 1984).

Schemata.   A *schema* (plural *schemata*) is a structure that organizes large amounts of information into a meaningful system. Larger units are needed to organize propositions representing bits of information into a coherent whole (Anderson, 1990). A schema is a stereotype specifying a standard pattern or sequence of steps associated with a particular concept, skill, or event (Rumelhart & Ortony, 1977). Schemata are types of plans we learn and use during our environmental interactions.

In an early study, Bartlett (1932) found that schemata aid in comprehending information. In this experiment, a participant read a story about an unfamiliar culture, after which she or he reproduced it for a second participant, who reproduced it for a third participant, and so on. By the time the story reached the 10th person, its unfamiliar context had been changed to one participants were familiar with (e.g., a fishing trip). Bartlett found that as stories were repeated, they changed in predictable ways. Unfamiliar information was dropped, a few details were retained, and the stories became more like participants' experiences. They altered incoming information to fit their preexisting schemata.

Any well-ordered sequence can be represented as a schema. One type of schema is "going to a restaurant." The steps consist of activities such as being seated at a table, looking over a menu, ordering food, being served, not cleaning up the dishes, receiving a bill, leaving a tip, and paying the bill. Schemata are important because they indicate what to expect in a situation. People recognize a problem when reality and schema do not match. Have you ever been in a restaurant where one of the expected steps did not occur (e.g., you receive a menu but no one returns to your table)?

Common educational schemata involve following laboratory procedures, studying, and comprehending stories. When given material to read, students activate the type of schema they believe is required. If students are to read a passage and answer questions about main ideas, they may periodically stop and quiz themselves on what they believe are the main points (Resnick, 1985).

Schemata assist encoding because they elaborate new material into a meaningful structure. Using a schema highlights important information. When learning material, students attempt to fit information into the schema's spaces. Less important or optional schema elements may or may not be learned. In reading works of literature, students who have formed the schema for a tragedy can easily fit the characters and actions of the story into the schema. They expect to find elements such as good versus evil, human frailties, and a dramatic denouement. When these events occur, they are fit into the schema students have activated for the story (Application 4.2).

APPLICATION 4.2
Schema Structures

Teachers can increase learning by helping students develop schemata. A schema is especially helpful when learning can occur by applying an ordered sequence of steps. Kathy Stone might teach the following schema to her children to assist their reading of unfamiliar words:

- Read the word in the sentence to see what might make sense.
- Look at the beginning and ending of the word—reading the beginning and the ending is easier than the whole word.
- Think of words that would make sense in the sentence and that would have the same beginning and ending.
- Sound out all the letters in the word.
- If these steps do not help identify the word, try looking it up in a dictionary.

(With some modifications, this schema for figuring out new words can be used by students of any age.)

In his American history class, Jim Marshall might teach his students to use a schema to locate factual answers to questions listed at the end of the chapter:

- Read through all of the questions.
- Read the chapter completely once.
- Reread the questions.
- Reread the chapter slowly and use paper markers if you find a section that seems to fit with one of the questions.
- Go back and match each question with an answer.
- When you find the answer, write it and the question on your paper.
- If you cannot find an answer, use your index to locate key words in the question.
- If you still cannot locate the answer, ask Mr. Marshall for help.

Schemata may facilitate recall independently of their benefits on encoding. Anderson and Pichert (1978) presented college students with a story about two boys skipping school. Students were advised to read it from the perspective of either a burglar or a home buyer; the story had elements relevant to both. Students recalled the story and later recalled it a second time. For the second recall, half of the students were advised to use their original perspective and the other half the other perspective. On the second recall, students recalled more information relevant to the second perspective but not to the first perspective and less information unimportant to the second perspective that was important to the first perspective. Kardash, Royer, and Greene (1988) also found that schemata exerted their primary benefits at the time of recall rather than at encoding. Collectively, these results suggest that at retrieval, people recall a schema and attempt to fit elements into it. This reconstruction may not be accurate but will include most schema elements. (*Production systems*, which we consider later, bear some similarity to schemata.)

LONG-TERM MEMORY: STORAGE

This section discusses how information is stored in long-term memory (LTM). Although our knowledge about LTM is limited because we do not have a window into the brain, research has painted a reasonably consistent picture of the storage process. The following sections cover the topics of information retrieval from LTM and forgetting.

Our characterization of LTM involves a structure with knowledge being represented as locations or nodes in networks, with networks connected (associated) with one another. When discussing networks, we deal primarily with declarative knowledge and procedural knowledge. We cover conditional knowledge in Chapter 5, along with metacognitive activities that monitor and direct cognitive processing. It is assumed that most knowledge is stored in LTM in verbal codes, but the role of imagery also is addressed at the end of this chapter.

Propositions

The Nature of Propositions.   A *proposition* is the smallest unit of information that can be judged true or false. Propositions are the basic units of knowledge and meaning in LTM (Anderson, 1990; Kosslyn, 1984; Norman & Rumelhart, 1975). Each of the following is a proposition:

- The Declaration of Independence was signed in 1776.
- 2 + 2 = 4.
- Aunt Frieda hates turnips.
- I'm good in math.
- The main characters are introduced early in a story.

These sample propositions can be judged true or false. Note, however, that people may disagree on their judgments. Carlos may believe that he is bad in math, but his teacher may believe that he is very good.

The exact nature of propositions is not well understood. Although they can be thought of as sentences, it is more likely that they are meanings of sentences (Anderson, 1990). Research supports the point that we store information in memory as propositions rather than as complete sentences. In a research study, Kintsch (1974) gave participants sentences to read that were of the same length but varied in the number of propositions they contained. The more propositions contained in a sentence, the longer it took participants to comprehend it. This implies that, although students can generate the sentence, "The Declaration of Independence was signed in 1776," what they most likely have stored in memory is a proposition containing only the essential information (Declaration of Independence—signed—1776). With certain exceptions (e.g., memorizing a poem), it seems that people usually store meanings rather than precise wordings.

Propositions form networks that are composed of individual nodes or locations. Nodes can be thought of as individual words, although their exact nature is unknown but very probably abstract. For example, students taking a history class very likely have a "history class" network comprising such nodes as "book," "teacher," "location," "name of student who sits on their left," and so forth.

Propositional Networks.   Propositions are formed according to a set of rules. Researchers disagree on which rules constitute the set, but they generally believe that rules combine nodes into propositions and, in turn, propositions into higher-order structures or *networks*, which are sets of interrelated propositions.

Anderson's *ACT theory* (J. Anderson, 1976, 1990, 1993, 1996; Anderson, Reder, & Lebiere, 1996) proposes an ACT-R network model of LTM with a propositional structure. A proposition is formed by combining two nodes with a *subject-predicate link* or association; one node constitutes the subject and another node the predicate. Examples are (implied information): "Fred (is) rich" and "Shopping (takes) time." A second type of association is the *relation-argument link*, where the relation is verb (in meaning) and the argument is the recipient of the relation or what is affected by the relation. Examples are "eat cake" and "solve puzzles." Relation arguments can serve as subjects or predicates to form complex propositions. Examples are "Fred eat(s) cake," and "solv(ing) puzzles (takes) time."

Propositions are interrelated when they share a common element. Common elements allow people to solve problems, cope with environmental demands, draw analogies, and so on. Without common elements transfer would not occur; all knowledge would be stored separately and information processing would be slow. One would not recognize that knowledge relevant to one domain is also relevant to other domains.

Figure 4.6 shows an example of a propositional network. The common element is "cat" because it is part of the propositions, "The cat walked across the front lawn," and "The cat caught a mouse." One can imagine that the former proposition is linked with other propositions relating to one's house, whereas the latter is linked with propositions about mice.

Evidence suggests that propositions are organized in hierarchical structures. Collins and Quillian (1969) showed that people store information at the highest level of generality. For example, the LTM network for "animal" would have stored at the highest level such facts as "moves" and "eats." Under this category would come such species as "birds" and "fish." Stored under "birds" are "has wings," "can fly," and "has feathers." The fact that birds eat and move is not stored at the level of "bird" because that information is stored at the higher level of animal. Collins and Quillian found that retrieval times increased the farther apart concepts were stored in memory.

The hierarchical organization idea has been modified somewhat by research showing that information is not always hierarchical. Thus, "collie" is closer to "mammal" than to "animal" in an animal hierarchy, but people are quicker to agree that a collie is an animal than a mammal (Rips, Shoben, & Smith, 1973).

Propositions:
"The cat walked across the front lawn."
"The cat caught a mouse."

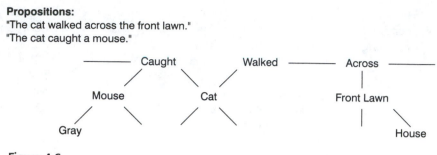

Figure 4.6
Sample propositional network.

Furthermore, familiar information may be stored both with its concept and at the highest level of generality (Anderson, 1990). If you have a bird feeder and you often watch birds eating, you might have "eat" stored with both "birds" and "animals." This finding does not detract from the central idea that propositions are organized and interconnected. Although some knowledge may be hierarchically organized, much information is probably organized in a less systematic fashion in propositional networks.

Storage of Declarative Knowledge

Basic Processes.   Declarative knowledge (knowing that something is the case) includes facts, beliefs, opinions, generalizations, theories, hypotheses, and attitudes about oneself, others, and world events (Gupta & Cohen, 2002; Paris et al., 1983). It is acquired when a new proposition is stored in LTM, usually in a related propositional network (J. Anderson, 1976, 1990). ACT theory postulates that declarative knowledge is represented in chunks comprising the basic information plus related categories (Anderson, 1996; Anderson, Reder, & Lebiere, 1996).

The storage process operates as follows. First, the learner receives new information, such as when the teacher makes a statement or the learner reads a sentence. Next, the new information is translated into one or more propositions in the learner's WM. At the same time, related propositions in LTM are cued. The new propositions are associated with the related propositions in WM through the process of spreading activation (discussed in the following section). As this point, learners might generate additional propositions. Finally, all the new propositions—those received and those generated by the learner—are stored together in LTM (Hayes-Roth & Thorndyke, 1979).

Figure 4.7 illustrates this process. Assume that a teacher is presenting a unit on the U.S. Constitution and says to the class, "The Vice President of the United States serves as President of the Senate but does not vote unless there is a tie." This statement may cue other propositional knowledge stored in students' memories relating to the Vice President (e.g., elected with the President, becomes President when the

Statement:
"The Vice President of the United States serves as President of the Senate but does
not vote unless there is a tie."

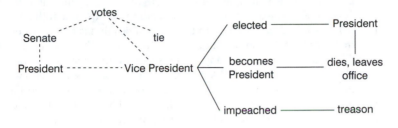

Figure 4.7
Storage of declarative knowledge.
Note: Dotted lines represent new knowledge; solid lines indicate knowledge in long-term
memory.

President dies or resigns, can be impeached for crimes of treason) and the Senate
(e.g., 100 members, two elected from each state, 6-year terms). Putting these propositions together, the students should infer that the Vice President would vote if 50
senators voted for a bill and 50 voted against it.

Storage problems can occur when students have no preexisting propositions
with which to link new information. Students who have never heard of the U.S. Constitution and do not know what a constitution is will draw a blank when they hear
the word for the first time. Conceptually meaningless information can be stored in
LTM, but students learn better when new information is related to something they
know. Showing students a facsimile of the U.S. Constitution or relating it to something they have studied (e.g., Declaration of Independence) gives them a referent to
link with the new information.

Even when students have studied related material, they may not automatically
link it with new information. Often the links need to be made explicit. When discussing the function of the Vice President in the Senate, teachers could remind students of the composition of the U.S. Senate and the other roles of the Vice President. Propositions sharing a common element are linked in LTM only if they are
active in WM simultaneously. This point helps to explain why students might fail
to see how new material relates to old material, even though the link is clear to
the teacher. Instruction that best establishes propositional networks in learners'
minds incorporates review, organization of material, and reminders of things they
know but are not thinking of now.

As with many memory processes, meaningfulness, organization, and elaboration
facilitate storing information in memory. Meaningfulness is important because meaningful information can be easily associated with preexisting information in memory.
Consequently, less rehearsal is necessary, which saves space and time of information in WM.

A study by Bransford and Johnson (1972) provides a dramatic illustration of the role of meaningfulness in storage and comprehension. Consider the following passage:

> The procedure is actually quite simple. First you arrange things into different groups. Of course, one pile may be sufficient depending on how much there is to do. If you have to go somewhere else due to lack of facilities that is the next step, otherwise you are pretty well set. It is important not to overdo things. That is, it is better to do too few things at once than too many. In the short run this may not seem important, but complications can easily arise. A mistake can be expensive as well. At first the whole procedure will seem complicated. Soon, however, it will become just another facet of life. It is difficult to foresee any end to the necessity for this task in the immediate future, but then one never can tell. After the procedure is completed one arranges the materials into different groups again. Then they can be put into their appropriate places. Eventually they will be used once more and the whole cycle will then have to be repeated. However, that is part of life. (p. 722)

Without prior knowledge this passage is difficult to comprehend and store in memory because relating it to existing knowledge in memory is hard to do. However, knowing that it is about "washing clothes" makes remembering and comprehension easier. In fact, Bransford and Johnson found that students who knew the topic re-called about twice as much as those who were unaware of it. The importance of meaningfulness in learning has been demonstrated in numerous other studies (Anderson, 1990; Chiesi, Spilich, & Voss, 1979; Spilich, Vesonder, Chiesi, & Voss, 1979).

Organization facilitates storage because well-organized material is easier to re-late to preexisting memory networks than is poorly organized material (Anderson, 1990). To the extent that material can be organized into a hierarchical arrangement, it provides a ready structure to be accepted into LTM. Without an existing LTM net-work, creating a new LTM network is easier with well-organized information than with poorly organized information.

Elaboration, or the process of adding information to material to be learned, im-proves storage because by elaborating information learners may be able to relate it to something they know. Through spreading activation the elaborated material may be quickly linked with information in memory. For example, a teacher might be dis-cussing the Mt. Etna volcano. Students who can elaborate that knowledge by relat-ing it to their personal knowledge of volcanoes (e.g., in Hawaii) will be able to as-sociate the new and old information in memory and better retain the new material.

Spreading Activation.   *Spreading activation* helps to explain how new information is linked to knowledge in LTM (Anderson, 1983, 1984, 1990; Collins & Loftus, 1975). The basic underlying principles are as follows (Anderson, 1984):

- Human knowledge can be represented as a network of nodes, where nodes corre-spond to concepts, and links to associations among these concepts.
- The nodes in this network can be in various states that correspond to their levels of activation. More active nodes are processed "better."
- Activation can spread along these network paths by a mechanism whereby nodes can cause their neighboring nodes to become active. (p. 61)

Anderson (1990) cites the example of an individual presented with the word *dog*. This word is associatively linked with such other concepts in the individual's LTM as *bone, cat,* and *meat*. In turn, each of these concepts is linked to other concepts. The activation of *dog* in LTM will spread beyond *dog* to linked concepts, with the spread lessening with concepts farther away from *dog*.

Experimental support for the existence of spreading activation was obtained by Meyer and Schvaneveldt (1971). These investigators used a reaction time task that presented participants with two strings of letters and asked them to decide whether both were words. Words associatively linked (*bread, butter*) were recognized faster than words not linked (*nurse, butter*).

Spreading activation results in a larger portion of LTM being activated than knowledge immediately associated with the content of WM. Activated information stays in LTM unless it is deliberately accessed, but this information is more readily accessible to WM. Spreading activation also facilitates transfer of knowledge to different domains. Transfer depends on propositional networks in LTM being activated by the same cue, so students recognize that knowledge is applicable in the domains.

Schemata.   Propositional networks represent small pieces of knowledge. *Schemata* are large networks that represent the structure of objects, persons, and events (Anderson, 1990). Structure is represented with a series of "slots," each of which corresponds to an attribute. In the schema or slot for "houses," some attributes (and their values) might be as follows: material (wood, brick), contains (rooms), function (human dwelling). Schemata are hierarchical; they are joined to superordinate ideas (building) and subordinate ones (roof).

Brewer and Treyens (1981) found research support for the underlying nature of schemata. Individuals were asked to wait in an office for a brief period, after which they were brought into a room where they wrote down everything they could recall about the office. Recall reflected the strong influence of a schema for "office." They correctly recalled the office having a desk and a chair (typical attributes) but not that the office contained a skull (nontypical attribute). Although the office had no books (typical attribute), many persons incorrectly recalled books.

Schemata are important during teaching and for transfer. Once students learn a schema, teachers can activate this knowledge when they teach any content to which the schema is applicable. Suppose an instructor teaches a general schema for describing geographical formations (e.g., mountain, volcano, glacier, river). The schema might contain the following attributes: height, material, and activity. Once students learn the schema, they can employ it to categorize new formations they study. In so doing, they would create new schemata for the various formations.

Storage of Procedural Knowledge

Procedural knowledge, or knowledge of how to perform cognitive activities (Anderson, 1990; Gupta & Cohen, 2002; Hunt, 1989; Paris et al., 1983), is central to much school learning. We use procedural knowledge to solve mathematical problems, summarize information, skim passages, and perform laboratory techniques.

Procedural knowledge may be stored as verbal codes and images, much the same way as declarative knowledge is stored. ACT theory posits that procedural knowledge is stored as a production system (Anderson, 1996; Anderson, Reder, & Lebiere, 1996). A *production system* (or *production*) is a network of condition-action sequences (rules), in which the condition is the set of circumstances that activates the system and the action is the set of activities that occurs (Anderson, 1990; Andre, 1986). A production consists of if-then statements: If statements (the condition) include the goal and test statements, and then statements are the actions. For example:

IF the goal is to drive a standard transmission and the car is in first gear and the car is going more than 10 miles an hour

THEN shift the car into second gear. (Anderson, 1990)

Productions are forms of procedural knowledge that include the conditions under which they are applicable. They typically are represented in LTM as propositions and acquired in the same fashion through the process of forming networks and spreading activation. Productions are extremely important during problem solving (see Chapter 5).

PRODUCTION SYSTEMS AND CONNECTIONIST MODELS

Production systems and connectionist models provide paradigms for examining the operation of cognitive learning processes (Anderson, 1996; Smith, 1996). This section explains the role of production systems in cognitive skill learning. Connectionist models represent a relatively new perspective on cognitive learning. To date there is little research on connectionist models that is relevant to education. Additional sources provide further information about connectionist models (Bourne, 1992; Farnham-Diggory, 1992; Siegler, 1989).

Production Systems

ACT theory specifies that a *production system* (or *production*) is a network of condition-action sequences (rules), in which the condition is a set of circumstances that activates the system and the action is the set of activities that occurs (Anderson, 1990, 1996; Anderson, Reder, & Lebiere, 1996; Andre, 1986). A production consists of *if-then statements:* If statements (the condition) include the goal and test statements and then statements are the actions. As an example:

IF I see two numbers and they must be added,

THEN decide which is larger and start with that number and count up to the next one. (Farnham-Diggory, 1992, p. 113)

Productions are forms of procedural knowledge that can have conditions (conditional knowledge) attached to them. They also include declarative knowledge. Learning involves a good deal of problem solving, and productions help one solve problems.

Skill Acquisition.   Learning procedures for performing skills often occurs slowly (J. Anderson, 1982). First, learners represent a sequence of actions in terms of declarative knowledge. Each step in the sequence is represented as a proposition. Gradually, learners drop out individual cues and integrate the separate steps into a continuous sequence of actions. For example, children learning to add a column of numbers are apt initially to perform each step slowly, possibly even verbalizing it aloud. As they become more skillful, adding becomes part of a smooth sequence that occurs rapidly and without deliberate, conscious attention.

A major constraint on skill learning is the size limitation of WM (Baddeley, 2001). Procedures would be learned quicker if WM could simultaneously hold all the declarative knowledge propositions. Because it cannot, students must combine propositions slowly and periodically stop and think (e.g., "What do I do next?"). WM contains insufficient space to create large procedures in the early stages of learning. As propositions are combined into small procedures, the latter are stored in WM simultaneously with other propositions. In this fashion, larger productions are gradually constructed.

These ideas explain why skill learning proceeds faster when students can perform the prerequisite skills. When the latter exist as well-established productions, they are in WM at the same time as new propositions to be integrated. In learning to solve long-division problems, students who know how to multiply simply recall the procedure when necessary; it does not have to be learned along with the other steps in long division. Children with reading disabilities seem to lack the capability to effectively process and store information at the same time (de Jong, 1998).

In some cases, specifying the steps in detail is difficult. For example, thinking creatively may not follow the same sequence for each student. Teachers can model creative thinking to include such self-questions as, "Are there any other possibilities?" Whenever steps can be specified, teacher demonstrations of the steps in a procedure, followed by student practice, are effective (Rosenthal & Zimmerman, 1978).

One problem with the learning of procedures is that students might view them as lockstep sequences to be followed regardless of whether they are appropriate. Gestalt psychologists showed how *functional fixedness,* or an inflexible approach to a problem, hinders problem solving (Duncker, 1945; discussed in Chapter 5). Adamantly following a sequence while learning may assist its acquisition, but learners also need to understand the circumstances under which other methods are more efficient.

Practice and Feedback.   Sometimes students overlearn skill procedures to the point that they avoid using alternative, easier procedures. At the same time, few, if any, alternatives exist for many of the procedures students learn (decoding words, adding numbers, determining subject-verb agreement). Overlearning these skills to the point of automatic production becomes an asset to students and makes easier learning new skills (e.g., drawing inferences, writing term papers) that require mastery of these basic skills.

One might argue that teaching problem-solving or inference skills to students deficient in basic mathematical facts and decoding, respectively, makes little sense. Research shows that poor grasp of basic number facts is related to low performance on complex arithmetic tasks (Romberg & Carpenter, 1986; Tait, Hartley, & Anderson,

1973), and slow decoding relates to poor comprehension (Calfee & Drum, 1986; Perfetti & Lesgold, 1979). Not only is skill learning affected, but self-efficacy (Chapter 3) suffers as well.

Practice is essential to instate basic procedural knowledge (Lesgold, 1984). In the early stages of learning, students require corrective feedback highlighting the portions of the procedure they implemented correctly and those requiring modification. Often students learn some parts of a procedure but not others. As students gain skill, teachers can point out their progress in solving problems quicker or more accurately.

As discussed in Chapter 5, transfer of procedural knowledge occurs when the knowledge is linked in LTM with different content. Transfer is aided by having students apply the procedures to the different forms of content and altering the procedures as necessary. General problem-solving strategies (also discussed in Chapter 5) are applicable to different academic content. Exercises calling for different skills can finely tune learners' applications of them. Review activities in arithmetic, for example, might contain addition, subtraction, multiplication, and division of whole numbers, mixed numbers, and fractions.

Critique.   Productions clearly are relevant to cognitive learning, but several issues about production systems need to be addressed. ACT theory posits a single set of learning processes to account for diverse phenomena. This view conflicts with other cognitive perspectives that delineate different learning processes (Shuell, 1986). Rumelhart and Norman (1978) identify three types of learning. *Accretion* involves encoding new information in terms of existing schemata; *restructuring* (schema creation) is the process of forming new schemata; *tuning* (schema evolution) refers to the slow modification and refinement of schemata that occurs when using them in various contexts. These involve different amounts of practice: much for tuning and less for accretion and restructuring.

ACT is essentially a computer program designed to simulate learning. As such, it may not address the range of factors involved in human learning. One issue concerns how people know which production to use in a given situation, especially if situations lend themselves to different productions being employed. Productions may be ordered in terms of likelihood, but a means for deciding what production is best given the circumstance must be available. Also of concern is the issue of how productions are altered. For example, if a production does not work effectively, do learners discard it, modify it, or retain it but seek more evidence? What is the mechanism for deciding when and how productions are changed?

Another concern relates to Anderson's (1983, 1990) claim that productions begin as declarative knowledge. This assumption is too strong because evidence indicates that this sequence is not always followed (Hunt, 1989). Because representing skill procedures as pieces of declarative knowledge is essentially a way station along the road to mastery, one might question whether students should learn the individual steps. The individual steps will eventually not be used, so time may be better spent allowing students to practice them. Providing students with a list of steps they can refer to as they gradually proceduralize the knowledge facilitates learning and enhances self-efficacy (Schunk, 1989).

Finally, one might question whether production systems, as generally described, are nothing more than glorified stimulus-response (S-R) associations (Mayer, 1992). Propositions (bits of procedural knowledge) become linked in memory so that when one piece is cued, others also are activated. Anderson (1983) acknowledges the associationist nature of productions but believes they are more advanced than simple S-R associations because they incorporate goals. Perhaps, as is the case with S-R theories, ACT can explain performance better than it can explain learning. These questions need to be addressed by research and related to learning of academic skills to establish the usefulness of productions in education better.

Connectionist Models

A second line of recent theorizing about complex cognitive processes involves *connectionist models* (or *connectionism,* but not to be confused with Thorndike's connectionism discussed in Chapter 2; Baddeley, 1998; Farnham-Diggory, 1992; Smith, 1996). Like productions, connectionist models represent computer simulations of learning processes. These models link learning to neural system processing where impulses fire across synapses to form connections. The assumption is that higher-order cognitive processes are formed by connecting a large number of basic elements (such as neurons; Anderson, 1990; Anderson, Reder, & Lebiere, 1996; Bourne, 1992). Connectionist models include distributed representations of knowledge (i.e., spread out over a wide network), parallel processing (many operations occur at once), and interactions among large numbers of simple processing units (Siegler, 1989). Connections may be at different stages of activation (Smith, 1996) and linked to input into the system, output, or one or more in-between layers.

Rumelhart and McClelland (1986) described a system of *parallel distributed processing (PDP).* This model is useful for making categorical judgments about information in memory. These authors provided an example involving two gangs and information about gang members including age, education, marital status, and occupation. In memory, the similar characteristics of each individual are linked. For example, Members 2 and 5 would be linked if they both were about the same age, married, and engaged in similar gang activities. To retrieve information about Member 2, we could activate the memory unit with the person's name, which in turn would activate other memory units. The pattern created through this spread of activation corresponds to the memory representation for the individual.

Connectionist units bear some similarity to productions in that both involve memory activation and linked ideas. At the same time, differences exist. In connectionist models all units are alike, whereas productions contain conditions and actions. Units are differentiated in terms of pattern and degree of activation. Another difference concerns rules. Productions are governed by rules. Connectionism has no set rules. Neurons "know" how to activate patterns; after the fact we may provide a rule as a label for the sequence (e.g., rules for naming patterns activated; Farnham-Diggory, 1992).

One problem with the connectionist approach is explaining how the system knows which of the many units in memory to activate and how these multiple activations become linked in integrated sequences. This process seems straightforward in the case of well-established patterns; for example, neurons know how to react to a ringing telephone, a cold wind, and a teacher announcing "Everyone pay attention!" With less-established patterns the activations may be problematic. We also might ask how neurons become self-activating in the first place. This question is important because it helps to explain the role of connections in learning and memory. Although the notion of connections seems plausible and grounded in what we know about neurological functioning, to date these models have been more useful in explaining perception rather than learning and problem solving (Mayer, 1992). The latter applications require considerable research.

LONG-TERM MEMORY: RETRIEVAL

Retrieval Strategies

What happens when a student is asked a question such as, "What does the Vice President of the United States do in the Senate?" The question enters the student's WM and is broken into propositions, which activate associated networks in LTM. The process by which this occurs is not well understood, but the available evidence indicates that information activates associated information in memory networks. Through *spreading activation*, related propositions are activated and examined to determine if they answer the question. If they do, that information is translated into a sentence and verbalized to the questioner or into motor patterns to be written. If the activated propositions do not answer the query, activation spreads until the answer is located. When insufficient time is available for spreading activation to locate the answer, students may make an educated guess (J. Anderson, 1976).

Much cognitive processing occurs automatically. We routinely remember our home address and phone number, Social Security number, and close friends' names. People are often unaware of all the steps taken to answer a question. However, when people must judge several activated propositions to determine whether the propositions properly answer the question, they are more aware of the process.

Because knowledge is encoded in propositional form, retrieval proceeds even though the information to be retrieved does not exist in exact form in memory. If a teacher asks whether the Vice President would vote on a bill when the initial vote was 51 for and 49 against, students could retrieve the proposition that the Vice President votes only in the event of a tie. Thus, by implication, the Vice President would not vote. Processing like this, which involves construction, takes longer than when a question requires information coded in memory in the same form, but students should respond correctly assuming they activate the relevant propositions in LTM. The same process is involved in rule learning and transfer (Chapter 5); students learn a rule (e.g., the Pythagorean theorem in mathematics) and recall and apply it to arrive at solutions of problems they have never seen before.

Encoding Specificity

Retrieval depends on the manner of encoding (process of putting new information into the information processing system). According to the *encoding specificity hypothesis* (Thomson & Tulving, 1970), the manner in which knowledge is encoded determines which retrieval cues will effectively activate that knowledge. In this view, the best retrieval occurs when retrieval cues match those present during learning (Baddeley, 1998).

Some experimental evidence supports encoding specificity. When people are given category names while they are encoding specific instances of the categories, they recall the instances better if they are given the category names at recall than if not given the names (Klatzky, 1980). A similar benefit is obtained if they learn words with associates and then are given the associate names at recall than if not given the associates. Brown (1968) gave students a partial list of U.S. states to read; others read no list. Subsequently all students recalled as many states as they could. Students who received the list recalled more of the states on the list and fewer states not on it.

Encoding specificity also includes context. In one study (Godden & Baddeley, 1975), scuba divers learned a word list either on shore or underwater. On a subsequent free recall task, learners recalled more words when they were in the same environment as the one in which they learned the words than when they were in the other environment.

Encoding specificity can be explained in terms of spreading activation among propositional networks. Cues associated with material to be learned are linked in LTM with the material at the time of encoding. During recall, presentation of these cues activates the relevant portions in LTM. In the absence of the same cues, recall depends on recalling individual propositions in memory. Because the cues lead to spreading activation (not the individual propositions or concepts), recall is facilitated by presenting the same cues at encoding and recall. Other evidence suggests that retrieval is guided in part by expectancies about what information is needed and that people may distort inconsistent information to make it coincide with their expectations (Hirt, Erickson, & McDonald, 1993).

Retrieval of Declarative Knowledge

Although declarative knowledge often is processed automatically, experts find no guarantee that it will be integrated with relevant information in LTM. Meaningfulness, elaboration, and organization enhance the potential for declarative information to be effectively processed and retrieved. Application 4.3 provides some classroom examples.

Meaningfulness.   Nonmeaningful information will not activate information in LTM and will be lost unless students rehearse it repeatedly until it becomes established in LTM, perhaps by forming a new propositional network. One also can connect the sounds of new information, which are devoid of meaning, to other similar sounds. The word *constitution*, for example, may be linked phonetically with other uses of the word stored in learners' memories (e.g., *Constitution Avenue*).

APPLICATION 4.3
Organizing Information by Networks

Teachers enhance learning when they develop lessons to assist students to link new information with knowledge in memory. Information that is meaningful, elaborated, and organized is more readily integrated into LTM networks.

A teacher planning a botany unit on the reproduction of different species of plants might start by reviewing common plant knowledge that students have stored in their memories (e.g., basic structure, conditions necessary for growth). As the teacher introduces new information, students examine familiar live plants that reproduce differently to make the experience more meaningful. Factual information to be learned can be elaborated by providing visual drawings and written details regarding the reproductive processes. For each live plant examined, students can organize the new information by creating outlines or charts to show the means of reproduction.

An art teacher planning a design unit might start by reviewing the various elements of color, shape, and texture. As the teacher introduces new techniques related to placement, combination of the various elements, and balance as it relates to the whole composition, manipulatives of various shapes, colors, and textures are provided for each student to use in creating different styles. The students can use the manipulatives to organize the elements and media they want to include in each of their own design compositions.

Meaningful information is more likely to be retained because it easily connects to propositional networks. Teachers assist by pointing out connections to students. Not only does meaningfulness promote learning, it also saves time. Propositions in WM take time to process; Simon (1974) estimates that each new piece of information takes 10 seconds to encode, which means that only six new pieces of information can be processed in a minute. Even when information is meaningful, much knowledge is lost before it can be encoded. Although every piece of incoming information is not crucially important and some loss usually does not significantly impair learning, students typically retain little information even under the best circumstances.

Elaboration. Elaboration is the process of adding to information being learned in the form of examples, details, inferences, or anything that serves to link new and old information. A learner might elaborate the role of the Vice President in the Senate by thinking through the roll call and, when there is a tie, having the Vice President vote.

Elaboration facilitates learning because it is a form of rehearsal: By keeping information active in WM, elaboration increases the likelihood that information will be permanently stored in LTM. This facilitates retrieval, as does the fact that elaboration establishes links between old and new information. Students who elaborate the role of the Vice President in the Senate link this new information with what they know about the Senate and the Vice President. Well-linked information in LTM is easier to recall than poorly linked information (Stein et al., 1984).

Although elaboration promotes storage and retrieval, it also takes time. Comprehending sentences requiring elaboration takes longer than sentences not requiring elaboration (Haviland & Clark, 1974). For example, the following sentences require drawing an inference that Marge took her checkbook to the grocery store: "Marge went to the grocery store," and "Marge wrote a check for her groceries." The link is clarified in the following sentences: "Marge took her checkbook with her when she went to the grocery store," and "Marge wrote a check for her groceries." Making explicit links between adjoining propositions assists their encoding and retention.

An important aspect of learning is deciding on the importance of information. Not all learned information needs to be elaborated. Comprehension is aided when students elaborate only the most important aspects of text (Reder, 1979). Elaboration aids retrieval by providing alternate paths along which activation can spread, so that if one path is blocked, others are available (J. Anderson, 1976). Elaboration also provides additional information from which answers can be constructed (Reder, 1982), such as when students must answer questions with information in a different form from that of the learned material.

In general, almost any type of elaboration is better than none for encoding and retrieving information; however, some elaborations are more effective than others. Activities such as taking notes or asking oneself how new information relates to what one knows build propositional networks. Effective elaborations link propositions and stimulate accurate recall. Elaborations not linked well to the content do not aid recall (Mayer, 1984).

Organization. *Organization* takes place by breaking information into parts and specifying relationships between parts. In studying U.S. government, organization might involve breaking government into three branches (executive, legislative, judicial), breaking each of these into subparts, and so on. Older students employ organization more often, but elementary children are capable of using organizational principles (Meece, 2002). For example, children studying leaf patterns often organize leaves by size, shape, and edge pattern.

Organization improves retrieval by linking relevant information; when retrieval is cued, spreading activation accesses the relevant propositions in LTM. Teachers routinely organize material, but student-generated organization is also effective for retrieval. Instruction on organizational principles assists learning. Consider a schema for understanding stories with four major attributes: setting, theme, plot, and resolution (Rumelhart, 1975, 1977). The setting ("Once upon a time . . .") places the action in a context. The theme is then introduced, which consists of characters who have certain experiences and goals. The plot traces the actions of the characters to attain their goals. The resolution describes how the goal is reached or how the characters adjust to not attaining the goal. By describing and exemplifying these phases of a story, teachers help students learn to identify them on their own.

Retrieval of Procedural Knowledge

Retrieval of procedural knowledge is similar to that of declarative knowledge. Retrieval cues trigger associations in memory, and the process of spreading activation activates and recalls relevant knowledge. Thus, if students are told to perform a given procedure in chemistry laboratory, they will cue that production in memory, recall it, and implement it.

In many tasks, declarative and procedural knowledge interact, so retrieval of both is necessary. While adding fractions, students use procedures (i.e., convert to lowest common denominator, add numerators) and declarative knowledge (addition facts). During reading comprehension, some processes operate as procedures (decoding, monitoring comprehension), whereas others involve only declarative knowledge (word meanings). People typically employ procedures to acquire declarative knowledge, such as mnemonic techniques to remember declarative knowledge (see Chapter 5). Having declarative information is typically a prerequisite for successfully implementing procedures. To solve for square roots, students must know multiplication facts.

Declarative and procedural knowledge are alike in that each varies tremendously in scope. Individuals possess declarative knowledge about the world, themselves, and others; they understand procedures for accomplishing diverse tasks. Procedural and declarative knowledge are different in that *procedures transform information.* Such declarative statements as "2 × 2 = 4" and "Uncle Fred smokes smelly cigars" change nothing, but applying the long-division algorithm to a problem changes an unsolved problem into a solved one.

Another difference is in speed of processing. Retrieval of declarative knowledge often is slow and conscious. Even assuming people know the answer to a question, they may have to think for some time to answer it. For example, consider the time needed to answer "Who was the U.S. President in 1867?" Once procedural knowledge is established in memory, it is retrieved quickly and often automatically. Skilled readers decode printed text automatically; they do not have to consciously reflect on what they are doing. Processing speed distinguishes skilled from poor readers (de Jong, 1998). Once we learn how to multiply, we do not have to think about what steps to follow to solve multiplication problems.

The differences in declarative and procedural knowledge have implications for teaching and learning. Students may have difficulty with a particular content area because they lack domain-specific declarative knowledge or because they do not understand the prerequisite procedures. Discovering which is deficient is a necessary first step for planning remedial instruction. Not only do deficiencies hinder learning, they also produce low self-efficacy (Chapter 3). Students who understand how to divide but do not know multiplication facts become demoralized when they consistently arrive at wrong answers.

LONG-TERM MEMORY: FORGETTING

We forget a lot, despite our best intentions. *Forgetting* refers to the loss of information from memory or to the inability to access information. Researchers disagree about whether information ever is truly lost from memory or whether it still is present but cannot be retrieved because it has been distorted, the retrieval cues are inadequate, or other information is interfering with its recall. Forgetting has been studied experimentally since the time of Ebbinghaus (see Chapter 1). Before presenting information processing perspectives on forgetting, which involve interference and decay, we will discuss historical work on interference.

Verbal Learning

Interference Theory. One of the contributions of the verbal learning tradition was the *interference theory of forgetting.* According to this theory, learned associations are never completely forgotten. Forgetting results from competing associations that lower the probability of the correct association being recalled; that is, other material becomes associated with the original stimulus (Postman, 1961; Underwood, 1957). The problem lies in retrieving information from memory, rather than in memory itself (Crouse, 1971).

Two types of interference were experimentally identified (see Table 4.3). *Retroactive interference* occurs when new verbal associations make remembering prior associations difficult. *Proactive interference* refers to older associations that make newer learning more difficult.

To demonstrate retroactive interference, an experimenter might ask two groups of individuals to learn Word List A. Group 1 then learns Word List B, while group 2 engages in a competing activity to prevent rehearsal of List A. Both groups then attempt to recall List A. Retroactive interference occurs if the recall of Group 2 is better than that of Group 1. For proactive interference, Group 1 learns List A while

Table 4.3
Interference and forgetting

	Retroactive Interference		Proactive Interference	
Task	Group 1	Group 2	Group 1	Group 2
Learn	A	A	A	—
Learn	B	—	B	B
Test	A	A	B	B

Note: Each group learns the task to some criterion of mastery. The "—" symbol indicates a period of time in which the group is engaged in another task that prevents rehearsal but does not interfere with the original learning. Interference is demonstrated if Group 2 outperforms Group 1 on the test.

Group 2 does nothing. Both groups then learn List B and attempt to recall List B. Proactive interference occurs if the recall of Group 2 surpasses that of Group 1.

Retroactive and proactive interference occur often in school. Retroactive interference is seen among students who learn words with regular spellings and then learn words that are exceptions to spelling rules. If, after some time, they are tested on the original words, they might alter the spellings to those of the exceptions. Proactive interference is evident among students taught first to multiply and then to divide fractions. When subsequently tested on division, they may simply multiply without first inverting the second fraction. Application 4.4 offers suggestions for dealing with interference.

Interference theory represented an important step in specifying memory processes. Early theories of learning postulated that learned connections leave a memory "trace" that weakens and decays with nonuse. Skinner did not postulate an internal memory trace but suggested that forgetting results from lack of opportunity to respond due to the stimulus being absent for some time. Each of these views has shortcomings. Although some decay may occur (discussed later), the memory trace notion is vague and difficult to verify experimentally. The nonuse position holds at times, but exceptions do exist; for example, being able to recall information after

---

APPLICATION 4.4
Interference in Teaching and Learning

Proactive and retroactive interference occur often in teaching and learning. Teachers may not be able to completely eliminate interference, but they can minimize its effects by recognizing areas in the curricula that easily lend themselves to interference. For example, students learn to subtract without regrouping and then to subtract with regrouping. In Kathy Stone's third-grade class she often finds that when she gives students review problems requiring regrouping, some students do not regroup. To minimize interference, she teaches students the underlying rules and principles and has them practice applying the skills in different contexts. Mrs. Stone makes an effort to point out similarities and differences between the two types of problems and to teach students how to decide whether regrouping is necessary. Frequent reviews help to minimize interference.

When spelling words are introduced at the primary level, words often are grouped by phonetic similarities (e.g., *crate, slate, date, state, mate, late*); however, when children learn certain spelling patterns, it may confuse them as they encounter other words (e.g., *weight* or *wait* rather than *wate*; *freight* rather than *frate*). Mrs. Stone provides additional instruction regarding other spellings for the same sounds and exceptions to phonetic rules along with periodic reviews over time. This reinforcement should help alleviate confusion and interference among students.

many years of nonuse (e.g., names of some elementary school teachers) is not unusual. Interference theory surmounts these problems by postulating how information in memory becomes confused with other information. It also specifies a research model for investigating these processes.

Other Views.   Postman and Stark (1969) suggested that *suppression*, rather than interference, causes forgetting. Participants in learning experiments hold in active memory material they believe they will need to recall later. Those who learn List A and then are given List B are apt to suppress their responses to the words on List A. Such suppressions would last while they are learning List B and for a while thereafter. In support of this point, the typical retroactive interference paradigm produces little forgetting when learners are given a recognition test on the original Word List A rather than asked to recall the words (Klatzky, 1980).

Tulving (1974) postulated that forgetting represents *inaccessibility of information* due to improper retrieval cues. Information in memory neither decays, is confused, nor is lost. Rather, the memory trace is intact but cannot be accessed. Memory of information depends on the trace being intact and on having adequate retrieval cues. Perhaps you cannot remember your home phone number from many years ago. Tulving's view says that you may not have forgotten it; rather, the memory is submerged because your current environment is different from that of years ago and the cues associated with your old home phone number—your house, street, neighborhood—are absent. This principle of *cue-dependent forgetting* also is compatible with the common finding that people perform better on recognition than on recall tests. In the cue-dependent view, they should perform better in recognition tests because more retrieval cues are provided; in recall tests, they supply their own cues.

Later research on interference suggests that interference occurs (e.g., people confuse elements) when the same cognitive schema or plan is used on multiple occasions (Thorndyke & Hayes-Roth, 1979; Underwood, 1983). Interference theory continues to provide a viable framework for investigating forgetting.

Information Processing

From an information processing perspective, *interference* refers to a blockage of the spread of activation across memory networks (Anderson, 1990). For various reasons, when people attempt to access information in memory the activation process is thwarted. Although the exact mechanism for blocking activation is not completely understood, theory and research suggest various causes of interference.

One factor that can affect whether structures are activated is the *strength of original encoding*. Information that originally is strongly encoded, such as by frequent rehearsal or extensive elaboration, is more likely to be accessed than information that originally is weakly encoded.

A second factor is the number of *alternative network paths* down which activation can spread (Anderson, 1990). Information that can be accessed via many routes is more likely to be remembered than information that is only accessible via fewer paths. For example, if I want to remember the name of Aunt Frieda's parakeet (Mr.

T), I should associate that with many cues, such as my friend Mr. Thomas, the fact that when Mr. T spreads his wings it makes the letter *T*, and the idea that his constant chirping taxes my tolerance. Then, when I attempt to recall the name of the parakeet I can access it via my memory networks for Aunt Frieda and for parakeets. If these fail, then I still have available the networks for my friends, the letter *T*, and things that tax my tolerance. In contrast, if I associate only the name "Mr. T" with the bird, then the number of alternative paths available for access is fewer and the likelihood of interference is greater.

A third factor is the *amount of distortion or merging of information.* Throughout this chapter we have discussed the memory benefits of organizing, elaborating, and making information meaningful by relating it to what we know. Whenever we engage in these practices, we change the nature of information, and in some cases we merge it with other information or subsume it under more general categories. We will see in Chapter 6 that such merging and subsumption facilitate *meaningful verbal learning* (Ausubel, 1963, 1968). Sometimes, however, such distortion and merging may cause interference and make recall more difficult than if information is remembered on its own.

Interference is an important cause of forgetting, but it is unlikely that it is the only one (Anderson, 1990). It appears that some information in LTM *decays* systematically with the passage of time and independently of any interference. Wickelgren (1979) has traced systematic decay of information in time intervals ranging from 1 minute to 2 weeks. The data decay rapidly at first with decay gradually tapering off. Researchers find little forgetting after 2 weeks.

The position that forgetting occurs because of decay is difficult to affirm or refute. Failure to recall even with extensive cuing does not unequivocally support a decay position because it still is possible that the appropriate memory networks were not activated. Similarly, the fact that the decay position posits no psychological processes responsible for forgetting (rather only the passage of time) does not refute the position. Memory traces include both perceptual features and reactions to the experiences (Estes, 1997). Decay or changes (perturbations) in one or both cause forgetting and memory distortions. Furthermore, the decay process may be physiological (Anderson, 1990). Research shows that synapses (junctions between neurons) can deteriorate with lack of use in the same way muscles do with nonuse.

Decay is commonly cited as a reason for forgetting. You may have learned French in high school but now some years later cannot recall many vocabulary words. You might explain that as, "I haven't used it for so long that I've forgotten it." Furthermore, forgetting is not always bad. Were we to remember everything we have ever learned, our memories would be so overcrowded that new learning would be very difficult. In some ways forgetting is facilitative because it rids us of information that we have not used and thus may not be important. Research also shows that forgetting leads people to act, think, judge, and feel differently than they would in the absence of forgetting (Riccio, Rabinowitz, & Axelrod, 1994). In the classroom, forgetting has profound effects for teaching and learning; Application 4.5 offers some suggestions for lessening the chances of forgetting.

Minimizing Forgetting of Academic Learning

Forgetting is a problem when learned knowledge is needed to move to new learning. To help children retain important information and skills, teachers might do the following:

- Periodically review important information and skills during classroom activities.
- Assign classwork and homework that reinforce previously learned material and skills.
- Send home fun learning packets during long vacation breaks that will reinforce various information and skills acquired.
- When introducing a new lesson or unit, review previously learned material that is needed for mastering the new material.

When Kathy Stone introduces long division, some third graders have forgotten how to regroup in subtraction, which can slow the new learning. Mrs. Stone spends a couple of days reviewing subtraction—especially problems requiring regrouping—as well as drilling the students on multiplication and simple division facts. She also gives homework that reinforces the same skills.

Assume that a physical education teacher is teaching a basketball unit over several days. At the start of each class, the teacher might review the skills taught in the previous class before he or she introduces the new skill that day. Periodically the teacher could spend an entire class period reviewing all the skills (e.g., dribbling, passing, shooting, playing defense) that the students have been working on up to that point. Some remedial instruction may be necessary if students have forgotten some of these skills so that they will be able to play well once the teacher begins to organize games.

In Gina Brown's educational psychology class the students have been assigned an application paper that focuses on motivation techniques. During the semester, Dr. Brown introduced various motivational theories. Many of the students have forgotten some of these. To help the students prepare for writing their papers, Dr. Brown spends one class period reviewing the major motivation theories. Then she divides students into small groups and has each group write a brief summary of one of the theories with some classroom applications. After working in small groups, each group shares its findings with the entire class.

MENTAL IMAGERY

Mental imagery is central to the study of LTM. This section discusses how information is represented in images and individual differences in the ability to use this source of representation.

Representation of Spatial Information

Mental imagery refers to mental representations of visual/spatial knowledge including physical properties of the objects or events represented. Visual stimuli that are attended to are held briefly in veridical form in the sensory register and then are transferred to WM. The WM representation appears to preserve some of the physical attributes of the stimulus it represents (Gagné, Yekovich, & Yekovich, 1993). Images are analog representations that are similar but not identical to their referents (Shepard, 1978).

Imagery has been valued as far back as the time of the ancient Greeks. Plato felt that thoughts and perceptions are impressed on the mind as a block of wax and are remembered as long as the images last (Paivio, 1970). Simonides, a Greek poet, believed that images are associative mediators. He devised the *method of loci* as a memory aid (Chapter 6). In this method, information to be remembered is paired with locations in a familiar setting.

Mental imagery also has been influential in discoveries. Shepard (1978) describes Einstein's *Gedanken experiment* that marked the beginning of the relativistic reformulation of electromagnetic theory. Einstein imagined himself traveling with a beam of light (186,000 miles per second), and what he saw corresponded neither to light nor to anything described by Maxwell's equations in classical electromagnetic theory. Einstein reported that he typically thought in terms of images and only reproduced his thoughts in words and mathematical equations once he conceptualized the situation visually. The German chemist Kekulé supposedly had a dream in which he visualized the structure of benzene, and Watson and Crick apparently used mental rotation to break the genetic code.

In contrast to images, propositions are discrete representations of meaning not resembling their referents in structure. The expression "New York City" no more resembles the actual city than virtually any three words picked at random from a dictionary. An image of New York City containing skyscrapers, stores, people, and traffic is more similar in structure to its referent. The same contrast is evident for events. Compare the sentence, "The black dog ran across the lawn," with an image of this scene.

Mental imagery is a controversial topic (Kosslyn, 1980). A central issue is how closely mental images resemble actual pictures: Do they contain the same details as pictures or are they fuzzy pictures portraying only highlights? The visual pattern of a stimulus is perceived when its features are linked to a LTM representation. This implies that images can only be as clear as the LTM representations (Pylyshyn, 1973). To the extent that mental images are the products of people's perceptions, images are likely to be incomplete representations of stimuli (Klatzky, 1980).

Support for the idea that people use imagery to represent spatial knowledge comes from studies where participants were shown pairs of two-dimensional pictures, each of which portrayed a three-dimensional object (Cooper & Shepard, 1973; Shepard & Cooper, 1983). The task was to determine if the two pictures in each pair portrayed the same object. The solution strategy involved mentally rotating one object in each pair until it matched the other object or until the individual decided that no amount of rotation would yield an identical object. Reaction times were a direct function of the number of mental rotations needed. Although these and other data suggest that people employ images to represent knowledge, they do not directly address the issue of how closely images correspond to actual objects.

To the extent that students use imagery to represent spatial and visual knowledge, imagery is germane to educational content involving concrete objects. When teaching a unit about different types of rock formations (mountains, plateaus, ridges), an instructor could show pictures of the various formations and ask students to imagine them. In geometry, imagery could be employed when dealing with mental rotations. Pictorial illustrations improve students' learning from texts (Carney & Levin, 2002; see Application 4.6 for more examples).

Evidence shows that people also use imagery to think about abstract dimensions. Kerst and Howard (1977) asked students to compare pairs of cars, countries, and animals on the concrete dimension of size and on an appropriate abstract dimension (e.g., cost, military power, ferocity). The abstract and concrete dimensions yielded similar results: As items became more similar, reaction times increased. For instance, in comparing size, comparing a bobcat and an elephant is easier than comparing a rhinoceros and a hippopotamus. How participants imagined abstract dimensions or whether they even used imagery is not clear. Perhaps they represented abstract dimensions in terms of propositions, for example, by comparing the United States and Jamaica on military power using the proposition, "(The) United States (has) more military power (than) Jamaica." Knowledge maps, which are pictorial representations of linked ideas, aid student learning (O'Donnell, Dansereau, & Hall, 2002).

Imagery in LTM

Most researchers agree that images are used in WM but disagree whether they are retained in LTM (Kosslyn & Pomerantz, 1977; Pylyshyn, 1973). Paivio's (1971, 1978, 1986; Clark & Paivio, 1991) *dual-code theory* directly addresses this issue. According to Paivio, LTM has two means of representing knowledge: A *verbal* system incorporating knowledge expressed in language and an *imaginal* system storing visual and spatial information. These systems are interrelated—a verbal code can be converted into an imaginal code and vice versa—but important differences exist. The verbal system is suited for abstract information, whereas the imaginal system is used to represent concrete objects or events. As Paivio (1971) notes:

> Which mode [visual, imaginal] will be functionally dominant in a given situation will depend on the nature and demands of the situation. One of the important determining characteristics, already considered, is the abstractness-concreteness of the situation or task: Imagery is particularly functional when the task is relatively concrete, and verbal processes become increasingly necessary for both the "flights" and the "perchings" of

APPLICATION 4.6
Using Imagery in the Classroom

Imagery can be used to increase student learning. One application involves instructing students on three-dimensional figures (e.g., cubes, spheres, cones) to include calculating their volumes. Verbal descriptors and two-dimensional diagrams are also used, but actual models of the figures greatly enhance teaching effectiveness. Allowing students to hold the shapes fosters their understanding of the concept of volume.

Imagery can be applied in physical education. When students are learning an exercise routine accompanied by music, the teacher can model in turn each portion of the routine initially without music, after which students close their eyes and think about what they saw. The students then perform each part of the routine. Later the teacher can add music to the individual portions.

Imagery can be used in language arts. For a unit involving writing a paragraph that gives directions for performing a task or making something, Mrs. Stone asks her third-grade students to close their eyes and think about the individual steps (e.g., of making a peanut butter and jelly sandwich). Once students finish imagining the task, they can visualize each step while writing it down.

Art teachers can use imagery to teach students to follow directions. The teacher might give the following directions orally and write them on the board: "Close your eyes and visualize on a piece of art paper a design including four circles, three triangles, and two squares, with some of the shapes overlapping one another." While students' eyes are closed, the teacher might ask the following questions to ensure that students are using imagery: How many circles do you see? How many triangles? How many squares? Are any of the shapes touching? Which ones?

Dance teachers might have their students close their eyes while listening to the music to which they will be performing. Then they might ask the students to imagine themselves dancing, visualizing every step and movement. The teacher also might ask students to visualize where they and their classmates are on the stage as they dance.

Jim Marshall took his American history classes to a Civil War battlefield and had them imagine what it must have been like to fight a battle at that site. Later in class he had students produce a map on the computer that duplicated the site and then create various scenarios for what could have happened as the Union and Confederate forces fought.

the stream of thought as the task is more abstract. These functional differences are presumably related to the differential availability of images and verbal processes in abstract task situations. (pp. 32–33)

Shepard's experiments support the utility of imagery and offer indirect support for the dual-code theory. Other supporting evidence comes from research showing that when recalling lists of concrete and abstract words, people recall concrete words better than abstract ones (Klatzky, 1980). The dual-code theory explanation of this finding is that concrete words can be coded verbally and imaginally, whereas abstract words usually are coded only verbally. At recall, people draw on both memory systems for the concrete words, but only the verbal system for the abstract words. Other research on imaginal mnemonic mediators supports the dual-code theory (Chapter 5).

In contrast, *unitary theory* postulates that all information is represented in LTM in verbal codes (propositions). Images in WM are reconstructed from verbal LTM codes. Indirect support for this notion comes from Mandler and Johnson (1976) and Mandler and Ritchey (1977). As with verbal material, people employ schemata while acquiring visual information. They remember scenes better when elements are in a typical pattern; memory is poorer when elements are disorganized. Meaningful organization and elaboration of information into schemata improve memory for scenes much as they do for verbal material. This finding suggests the operation of a common process regardless of the form of information presented.

This debate notwithstanding, using concrete materials and pictures enhances memory. Such instructional tools as manipulatives, audiovisual aids, and computer graphics facilitate learning. Although concrete devices are undoubtedly more important for young children because they lack the cognitive capability to think in abstract terms, students of all ages benefit from information presented in multiple modes.

Individual Differences

The extent to which people actually use imagery to remember information varies as a function of cognitive development. Kosslyn (1980) proposed that children are more likely to use imagery to remember and recall information than adults, who rely more on propositional representation. Kosslyn gave children and adults statements such as, "A cat has claws," and "A rat has fur." The task was to determine validity of the statements. Kosslyn reasoned that adults could respond quicker because they could access the propositional information from LTM, whereas children would have to recall the image of the animal and scan it. To control for adults' better information processing in general, some adults were asked to scan an image of the animal, whereas others were free to use any strategy.

Adults were slower to respond when given the imagery instructions than when free to choose a strategy, but no difference was found for children. These results show that imagery is the strategy children use even when they are free to do otherwise, but they do not address whether children cannot use propositional information (because of cognitive limitations) or whether they can but choose not to because they find scanning to be more effective.

Use of imagery also depends on effectiveness of performing the component processes. Apparently two types of processes are involved. One set of processes helps to activate stored memories of parts of images. Another set serves to arrange parts into the proper configuration. These processes may be localized in different parts of the brain. Individual differences in imagery can result because people differ in how effectively this dual processing occurs (Kosslyn, 1988).

The use of imagery by people of any age depends on what is to be imagined. Concrete objects are more easily imagined than abstractions. Another factor that influences use of imagery is one's ability to employ it. *Eidetic imagery*, or photographic memory (Leask, Haber, & Haber, 1969), actually is unlike a photograph; the latter is seen as a whole, whereas eidetic imagery occurs in pieces. People report that an image appears and disappears in segments rather than all at once.

Eidetic imagery is found more often in children than in adults (Gray & Gummerman, 1975), yet even among children it is uncommon (about 5%). Eidetic imagery may be lost with development, perhaps because propositional representation replaces imaginal thinking. It also is possible that adults retain the capacity to form clear images but do not routinely do so because their propositional systems can represent more information. Just as memory can be improved, the capacity to form images can most likely be developed, but most adults do not explicitly work to sharpen their imaginal systems.

SUMMARY

Information processing theories focus on attention, perception, encoding, storage, and retrieval of knowledge. Information processing involves cognitive processes and has been influenced by advances in communications and computer technology.

Important historical influences on contemporary information processing views are Gestalt psychology and verbal learning. Gestalt theorists stressed the role of organization in perception and learning. Verbal learning researchers used serial learning, free recall, and paired-associate tasks. A number of important findings were obtained from verbal learning research. Free-recall studies showed that organization improves recall and that people impose their own organization when none is present. One of the major contributions was work in interference and forgetting.

A common information processing paradigm involves a two-store (dual-memory) model. In this system, information enters through the sensory registers. Although there is a register for each system, most research has been conducted on the icon (visual) and echo (auditory) registers. At any one time, only a limited amount of information can be attended to. Attention may act as a filter or a general limitation on capacity of the human system. Inputs attended to are perceived by being compared with information in LTM.

Information enters WM or STM, where it is retained through rehearsal and linked with related information in LTM. Information may be encoded for storage in LTM. Encoding is facilitated through organization, elaboration, meaningfulness, and links with schema structures. LTM is organized by content, and information is cross referenced with related content. Control processes monitor and direct the flow of information through the system.

Alternative views of memory conceive of it in terms of levels of processing and activation. Each of these views has advantages and disadvantages, and some integration of views possibly may best characterize memory.

Research on attention and perception often focuses on the mechanism for representing information. Theories stress critical features, templates, and prototypes. Research shows that WM is limited in capacity and duration. LTM appears to be very large. The basic unit of knowledge is the proposition, and propositions are organized in networks. Types of knowledge include declarative, procedural, and conditional. Large bits of procedural knowledge may be organized in production systems. Networks further are linked in connectionist fashion through spreading activation to enhance cross-referencing and transfer. Retrieval of knowledge depends on its accessing in LTM. Failure to retrieve may result from decay of information or interference. Information may be best retrieved with cues present during encoding (encoding specificity).

Although much evidence exists for information being stored in memory in verbal form (meanings), evidence also exists for storage of images. Images are analog representations: They are similar but not identical to their referents. Dual-code theory postulates that the imaginal system primarily stores concrete objects and events and the verbal system stores more abstract information expressed in language. Conversely, images may be reconstructed in WM from verbal codes stored in LTM. Developmental evidence shows that children are more likely than adults to represent knowledge as images, but imaginal representation can be developed in persons of any age.

CHAPTER ■ ■ ■ ■ ■ ■ ■ ■ ■

5 Cognitive Learning Processes

In Chapter 4 we studied the basic elements of the human information processing system: attention, perception, short-term or working memory (STM, WM), and long-term memory (LTM; encoding, retrieval, forgetting). This chapter extends this analysis to the operation of cognitive processes during learning. We begin by discussing conditional knowledge and metacognition, which are central to cognitive learning. Subsequent sections cover concept learning, problem solving, transfer, and self-regulation.

There is debate among professionals on the extent that the processes discussed in this chapter are involved in most, if not all learning. Problem solving, for example, is thought by some to be the key process in learning (Anderson, 1993), whereas others limit its application to settings where specific conditions prevail (Chi & Glaser, 1985). From an educational perspective, teachers are apt to agree on the centrality across domains of such processes as concept learning, problem solving, transfer, and metacognition, and educators increasingly are urging that these topics be incorporated into content instruction (Pressley & McCormick, 1995). The processes discussed in this chapter are integral components of complex types of cognitive learning

that occur in school subjects such as science, mathematics, and writing (see Chapter 9). Many of them also figure prominently in theories of skill acquisition (Chapter 6).

When you finish studying this chapter you should be able to do the following:

- Understand why conditional knowledge is important for learning and discuss variables affecting metacognition.

- Distinguish properties of concepts and explain models of concept learning.

- Discuss historical views of problem solving and the role of general strategies (heuristics).

- Describe information processing methods for solving problems.

- Differentiate historical views of transfer and provide a cognitive explanation for transfer of knowledge, skills, and strategies.

- Explain self-regulation from an information processing perspective and give examples of self-regulatory strategies used by proficient learners.

- Devise a plan that students might use to improve their academic studying.

CONDITIONAL KNOWLEDGE AND METACOGNITION

Declarative and procedural knowledge were discussed in Chapter 4. A concern about information processing models is that they primarily describe learning rather than explain it. Thus, we know that inputs are received into WM, rehearsed, coded, linked with relevant information, and stored in LTM, but we might ask why any of these activities happen. Especially during learning—when processing is not automatic—we need an explanation for how the system processes information. For example, what determines how much rehearsal takes place? How is relevant information selected in LTM? How do people know what knowledge is required in different situations?

The topic of metacognition addresses these issues. *Metacognition* refers to higher-order cognition. To begin, we discuss the role of conditional knowledge and then show how metacognitive processes help to integrate information processing.

Conditional Knowledge

Conditional knowledge is understanding when and why to employ forms of declarative and procedural knowledge (Paris et al., 1983, 1984). Possessing the requisite declarative and procedural knowledge to perform a task does not guarantee students will perform it well. Students reading a social studies text may know what to do (read a chapter), understand the meanings of vocabulary words (declarative knowledge), and know how to decode, skim, find main ideas, and draw inferences (procedural knowledge). When they start reading, they might skim the chapter. As a consequence, they perform poorly on an end-of-chapter comprehension test.

This type of situation is not uncommon. Achievement depends on knowing facts and procedures and on knowing when and why to employ that knowledge. In the preceding example, conditional knowledge includes knowing when skimming is appropriate. One might skim a newspaper for the gist of the news, but skimming should not be used to comprehend textual content.

Conditional knowledge helps students select and employ declarative and procedural knowledge to fit task goals. To decide to read a chapter carefully and then do it, students should believe that careful reading is appropriate for the task at hand; that is, this strategy has functional value because it will allow them to comprehend the material.

Learners who do not possess conditional knowledge about when and why skimming is valuable will employ it at inappropriate times. If they believe it is valuable for all reading tasks, they may indiscriminately employ it unless otherwise directed. If they believe it has no value, they may never use it unless directed.

From an information processing perspective, conditional knowledge most likely is represented in LTM as propositions in networks and linked with the declarative and procedural knowledge to which it applies. Conditional knowledge actually is a form of declarative knowledge because it is "knowledge that"—for example, knowledge that skimming is valuable to get the gist of a passage and knowledge that summarizing text is valuable to derive greater understanding. Conditional knowledge also is included in procedures: Skimming is valuable as long as I can get the gist, but if I find that I am not getting the gist, I should abandon skimming and read more carefully. The three types of knowledge are summarized in Table 5.1.

Conditional knowledge is an integral part of self-regulated learning discussed later in this chapter (Schunk & Zimmerman, 1994, 1998). Self-regulated learning requires

Table 5.1
Comparison of types of knowledge.

Type	Knowing	Examples
Declarative	That	Historical dates, number facts, episodes (what happened when), task features (stories have a plot and setting), beliefs ("I am good in math").
Procedural	How	Math algorithms, reading strategies (skimming, scanning, summarizing), goals (breaking long-term goals into subgoals).
Conditional	When, Why	Skim the newspaper because it gives the gist but does not take much time; read texts carefully to gain understanding.

that students decide which learning strategy to use prior to engaging in a task (Zimmerman, 1989, 1990, 1994). While students are engaged in a task, they assess task progress (e.g., their level of comprehension) using metacognitive processes. When comprehension problems are detected, students alter their strategy based on conditional knowledge of what might prove more effective.

Metacognition and Learning

Metacognition refers to the deliberate conscious control of cognitive activity (Brown, 1980):

> What is metacognition? It has usually been broadly and rather loosely defined as any knowledge or cognitive activity that takes as its object, or regulates, any aspect of any cognitive enterprise. . . . It is called metacognition because its core meaning is "cognition about cognition." Metacognitive skills are believed to play an important role in many types of cognitive activity, including oral communication of information, oral persuasion, oral comprehension, reading comprehension, writing, language acquisition, perception, attention, memory, problem solving, social cognition, and various forms of self-instruction and self-control. (Flavell, 1985, p. 104)

Metacognition comprises two related sets of skills. First, one must understand what skills, strategies, and resources a task requires. Included in this cluster are finding main ideas, rehearsing information, forming associations or images, using memory techniques, organizing material, taking notes or underlining, and using test-taking techniques. Second, one must know how and when to use these skills and strategies to ensure the task is completed successfully. These monitoring activities include checking level of understanding, predicting outcomes, evaluating the effectiveness of efforts, planning activities, deciding how to budget time, and revising or switching to other activities to overcome difficulties (Baker & Brown, 1984). Collectively, metacognitive activities reflect the strategic application of declarative, procedural, and conditional knowledge to tasks (Schraw & Moshman, 1995).

Metacognitive skills develop slowly. Young children are not fully aware of which cognitive processes various tasks involve. For example, they typically are poor at recognizing that they have been thinking and recalling what they were thinking about (Flavell, Green, & Flavell, 1995). They may not understand that disorganized passages are harder to comprehend than organized ones or that passages containing unfamiliar material are more difficult than those composed of familiar material (Baker & Brown, 1984). Monitoring activities are employed more often by older children and adults than by young children; however, older children and adults do not always monitor their comprehension and often are poor judges of how well they have comprehended text (Baker, 1989).

Conversely, young children are cognitively capable of monitoring their activities on simple assignments. In general, learners are more likely to monitor their activities on tasks of intermediate difficulty as opposed to easy tasks (where monitoring may not be necessary) or on very difficult tasks (where one may not know what to do or may quit working).

Metacognitive abilities begin to develop around ages 5 to 7 and continue throughout the time children are in school, although within any age group there is much variability (Flavell, 1985; Flavell et al., 1995). Preschool children are capable of learning some strategic behaviors (Kail & Hagen, 1982), but as a result of schooling, children develop the awareness they can control what they learn by the strategies they use (Duell, 1986). Flavell and Wellman (1977) hypothesized that children form generalizations concerning how their actions influence the environment; for example, they learn "what works" for them to promote school achievement. This is especially true with memory strategies, perhaps because much school success depends on memorizing information (Application 5.1).

Variables Influencing Metacognition

Metacognitive awareness is influenced by variables associated with learners, tasks, and strategies (Duell, 1986; Flavell & Wellman, 1977).

Learner Variables. Learners' levels of development influence their metacognition (Alexander, Carr, & Schwanenflugel, 1995). Older children understand their own memory abilities and limitations better than younger children do (Flavell, Friedrichs, & Hoyt, 1970; Flavell et al., 1995). Flavell et al. (1970) presented children with study material and told them to study it until they thought they could accurately recall the information. Children aged 7 to 10 were more accurate in judging their readiness to recall than were the children aged 4 to 6. Older children were also more aware that their memory abilities differ from one context to another. Children of the same age showed variations in memory abilities.

Learners' abilities to monitor how well they have done on a memory task also vary. Older children are more accurate in judging whether they have recalled all items they were to recall and whether they can recall information. Wellman (1977) presented children with pictures of objects and asked them to name the objects. If

APPLICATION 5.1
Metacognition

Teachers can help students develop their metacognitive skills. A teacher working with students on listening comprehension might include situations such as listening to an enjoyable story, a set of explicit directions, and a social studies lecture. For each situation, the teacher could ask students why they would listen in that setting; for example, enjoyment and general theme (stories), specific elements (directions), facts and concepts (social studies). Then the teacher could work with students to develop listening skills such as retelling in their own words, visualizing, and taking notes. To foster conditional knowledge, the teacher can discuss with students the various listening techniques that seem most appropriate for each situation.

A teacher helping students with memory skills might give them a long list of items to memorize. The teacher could work with the students on recollection by teaching them various ways to reconstruct the list of items on the basis of partial cues. The students might be encouraged to explore various effective memorization techniques: putting the items into categories; visualizing a picture that contains the items; associating the items with a familiar setting or task; using acronyms that include the first letter of each item; creating a jingle, poem, or song that incorporates the items; or repeating the list several times. Then the teacher could work with the students in determining which technique works best for each individual and with which type of memorization task.

children could not name them, they were asked whether they would recognize the name. Compared with kindergartners, third graders were more accurate at predicting which object names they would be able to recognize.

Task Variables.   Knowing the relative difficulty of different forms of learning and retrieving from memory various types of information are parts of metacognitive awareness. Although kindergartners and first graders believe that familiar or easily named items are easier to remember, older children are better at predicting that categorized items are easier to recall than conceptually unrelated items (Duell, 1986). Older children are more likely to believe that organized stories are easier to remember than disorganized pieces of information. With respect to the goal of learning, sixth graders know better than second graders that students should use different reading strategies depending on whether the goal is to recall a story word for word or in their own words (Myers & Paris, 1978).

Strategy Variables.   Metacognition depends on the strategies learners employ. Children as young as ages 3 and 4 can use memory strategies to remember information, but their ability to use strategies improves with development. Older children are able to state more things they can do to help them remember. Regardless of age, children are more likely to think of external things (write a note) than internal ones (think about doing something). Students' use of such memory strategies as rehearsal and elaboration also improves with development (Duell, 1986).

Although many students are capable of using metacognitive strategies, they may not know which strategies aid learning and retrieval from LTM and they may not employ those that are helpful (Flavell, 1985; Zimmerman & Martinez-Pons, 1990). Salatas and Flavell (1976) asked kindergartners, third graders, and college students to recall all list items that exhibited a given property (e.g., were breakable). Even though the young children often reported that conducting a thorough search for information is important (Duell, 1986), only the college students spontaneously recalled each item and decided whether it exhibited the given property.

Simply generating a strategy does not guarantee its use. This *utilization deficiency* is more common in younger children (Justice, Baker-Ward, Gupta, & Jannings, 1997), and appears to stem from children's understanding of how a strategy works. Older learners understand that the intention to use a strategy leads to strategy use, which produces an outcome. Younger children typically have only partial understanding of the links between intentions, actions, and outcomes. Metamemorial understanding develops between the ages of 3 and 6 (Wellman, 1990).

Task, strategy, and learner variables typically interact when students engage in metacognitive activities. Learners consider the type and length of material to be learned (task), the potential strategies to be used (strategy), and their skill at using the various strategies (learner). If learners think that note taking and underlining are good strategies for identifying main points of a technical article and if they believe they are good at underlining but poor at taking notes, they likely will decide to underline. As Schraw and Moshman (1995) note, learners construct metacognitive theories that include knowledge and strategies that they believe will be effective in a given situation.

Metacognition and Behavior

Understanding which skills and strategies help us learn and remember information is necessary but not sufficient to enhance our achievement. Even students who are aware of what helps them learn do not consistently engage in metacognitive activities for a variety of reasons. In some cases, metacognition may be unnecessary because the material is easily learned or can be processed automatically. Learners also might be unwilling to invest the effort to employ metacognitive activities. The latter are tasks in their own right; they take time and effort. Learners may not understand fully that metacognitive strategies improve their performances, or they may believe they do but that other factors, such as time spent in learning or effort expended, are more important for learning (Borkowski & Cavanaugh, 1979; Flavell & Wellman, 1977; Schunk & Rice, 1993).

The facts that metacognitive activities improve achievement but that students may not automatically use them present a quandary for educators. Students need to be taught a menu of activities ranging from those applying to learning in general (e.g., determining the purpose in learning) to those applying to specific situations (e.g., underlining important points in text), and be encouraged to use them in various contexts (Belmont, 1989). Although the *what* component of learning is important, so are the *when, where,* and *why* of strategy use. Teaching the *what* without the latter will only confuse students and could prove demoralizing; students who know what to do but not when, where, or why to do it might hold low self-efficacy for performing well in school (see Chapter 3).

Learners often need to be taught basic declarative or procedural knowledge along with metacognitive skills (Duell, 1986). Students need to monitor their understanding of main ideas, but the monitoring is pointless if they do not understand what a main idea is or how to find one. Teachers need to encourage students to employ metacognitive strategies and provide opportunities for them to apply what they have learned outside of the instructional context. Students also need feedback on how well they are applying a strategy and how strategy use improves their performance (Schunk & Rice, 1993; Schunk & Swartz, 1993a). A danger of teaching a metacognitive strategy in conjunction with only a single task is that students will see the strategy as applying only to that task or to highly similar tasks, which does not foster transfer. Experts recommend using multiple tasks to teach strategies (Borkowski, 1985; Borkowski & Cavanaugh, 1979).

CONCEPT LEARNING

The Nature of Concepts

Much cognitive learning involves concepts. *Concepts* are labeled sets of objects, symbols, or events that share common characteristics (critical attributes). A concept is a mental construct or representation of a category that allows one to identify examples and nonexamples of the category (Howard, 1987). *Concept learning* refers to forming representations to identify attributes, generalize them to new examples, and discriminate examples from nonexamples. Concepts may involve concrete objects (e.g., "table," "chair," "cat") or abstract ideas (e.g., "love," "democracy," "wholeness"). In fact, there are many types of concepts (for a detailed review see Medin, Lynch, & Solomon, 2000).

Early studies by Bruner, Goodnow, and Austin (1956) explored the nature of concepts. Learners were presented with boxes portraying geometrical patterns. Each pattern could be classified using four different attributes: number of stimuli (one, two, three); shape (circle, square, cross); color (red, green, black); and number of borders on the box (one, two, three). The task was to identify the concept represented in different subsets of the boxes.

The configuration of features in a concept-learning task can be varied to yield different concepts. A *conjunctive concept* is represented by two or more features (e.g., two red circles). Other features (number of borders) are not relevant. A *disjunctive concept* is represented by one of two or more features; for example, two circles of any color or one red circle. A *relational concept* specifies a relationship between features that must be present. An example of a relational concept is that the number of objects in the figure must outnumber the number of borders; type of object and color are unimportant.

Bruner et al. (1956) found that concept learners tend to formulate a hypothesis about the rule underlying the concept. Rules can be expressed in if-then form. For example, a rule classifying a cat might be as follows: "If it is domesticated, has four legs, fur, whiskers, a tail, is relatively small, purrs, and vocalizes 'meow,' then it is a cat." Although exceptions exist, this rule will accurately classify cats most of the time. Generalization occurs when the rule is applied to a variety of cats.

The behavioral position on concept learning (Chapter 2) is that people learn associations gradually and that learning builds up slowly (Spence, 1937). In contrast to this *continuity* position, Bruner et al. (1956) found that people form rules quickly. For any given concept, they retain the rule as long as it correctly identifies instances and noninstances of the concept and they modify it when it fails to do so. Bruner's view represents a *noncontinuity* position.

Learners acquire concepts better when they are presented with *positive instances*, or examples of the concept. Learning is much slower with *negative (non-) instances* (e.g., nonexamples). When trying to confirm the rule underlying the concept, people prefer to receive positive rather than negative instances (Wason, 1960).

Since this early work, two distinct views have emerged concerning the nature of concepts. The *classical theory* approach derives from the work of Bruner and others and postulates that concepts involve rule formation that defines the critical features, or the intrinsic (necessary) attributes, of the concept (Gagné, 1985; Smith & Medin, 1981). Through experiences with the concept, one formulates a rule that satisfies the conditions and retains the rule as long as it functions effectively.

This view predicts that different instances of a concept should be recognized equally quickly because each instance is judged against critical features. This is not the case, however. Most people find some instances of a category (e.g., a dolphin is a mammal) more difficult to verify than others (e.g., a dog is a mammal). This highlights the problem that many concepts cannot be defined in terms of a set of critical attributes.

A second perspective is *prototype theory* (Rosch, 1973, 1975, 1978). A *prototype* is a generalized image of the concept, which may include only some of the concept's defining attributes. When confronted with an instance, one recalls the most likely prototype from LTM and compares it to the instance to see if they match. Prototypes may include some *nondefining (optional) attributes*. In cognitive psychology, prototypes often are thought of as *schemata* (Andre, 1986), or organized forms for the knowledge we have about a particular concept. (Schemata are discussed in Chapter 4 in conjunction with information processing.)

Research supports the prototype theory prediction that instances closer to the prototype (e.g., prototype = "bird"; instances = "robin," "sparrow") are recognized quicker than those less typical (e.g., "owl," "ostrich"; Rosch, 1973). One concern with prototype theory is that it implies that people would store in LTM thousands of prototypes, which will consume much more space than rules. A second concern is that learners easily could form incorrect prototypes if they are allowed to include some nondefining characteristics and not all necessary ones.

Combining the features-analysis and prototype positions is possible. Given that prototypes include critical features, we might employ prototypes to classify instances of concepts that are fairly typical (Andre, 1986). For instances that are ambiguous, we may employ critical feature analysis, which might modify the list of critical features to incorporate the new features. From a developmental perspective, children in transition about the meaning of a concept may simultaneously keep a prior hypothesis in mind as they are developing a revised one (Goldin-Meadow, Alibali, & Church, 1993).This interpretation is consistent with Klausmeier's position, which is discussed next.

Concept Attainment

One way to develop prototypes is to be exposed to a typical instance of the concept that reflects the classic attributes (Klausmeier, 1992). A second way is by abstracting features from two or more examples of objects in the class; for birds, this might mean "feathers," "two legs," "beak," "flies," although not every feature applies to every member of the class. Prototypes are refined and expanded when one is exposed to new examples of the concept; thus, "lives in the jungle" (parrot) and "lives by the ocean" (seagull).

Gagné (1985) formulated a view of learning and instruction (Chapter 6) that includes concepts as a central form of learning. Learners initially must have basic prerequisite capabilities to discriminate among stimulus features (i.e., distinguish relevant from irrelevant features).

In Gagné's (1985) view, concept learning involves a *multistage sequence.* First, the stimulus feature is presented as an instance of the concept along with a noninstance. The learner confirms the ability to make the discrimination. In the next (generalization) stage, the learner identifies instances and noninstances. Third, the stimulus feature—which is to become the concept—is varied and presented along with noninstances. Concept attainment is verified by asking for identification of several instances of the class using stimuli not previously employed in learning. Throughout the process, correct responses are reinforced and contiguity learning occurs (see Guthrie, Chapter 2) by presenting several instances of the concept in close association.

Klausmeier (1990, 1992) developed and tested a model of concept attainment. This model postulates a four-stage sequence: concrete, identity, classificatory, formal. Competence at each level is necessary for attainment at the next level. The process of concept attainment represents an interaction of development, informal experience, and formal education.

At the *concrete level,* learners can recognize an item as the same one previously encountered when the context or spatial orientation in which it was originally encountered remains the same. This level requires learners to attend to the item, discriminate it as different from its surroundings on the basis of one or more defining attributes, represent it in LTM as a visual image, and retrieve it from LTM to compare it with a new image and determine that it is the same item. Thus, a learner might learn to recognize an equilateral triangle and discriminate it from a right or isosceles triangle.

The *identity level* is characterized by recognizing an item as the same one previously encountered when the item is observed from a different perspective or in a different modality. This stage involves the same processes as at the concrete level as well as the process of generalization. Thus, the learner will be able to recognize equilateral triangles in different orientations or positions on a page.

The *classificatory level* requires that learners recognize at least two items as being equivalent. Additional generalization is involved; in the case of equilateral triangles, this involves recognizing a smaller and larger equilateral triangle as equivalent. The process continues until the learner can recognize examples and nonexamples; at this stage, however, the learner may not understand the basis for classification (e.g., equality of side length and angles). Being able to name the concept is not necessary at this level but, as in the preceding stages, it can facilitate concept acquisition.

Finally, the *formal level* requires the learner to identify instances and nonexamples of the concept, name the concept and its defining attributes, give a definition of the concept, and specify the attributes that distinguish the concept from other closely related ones (i.e., three equal sides and angles). Mastery of this stage requires the learner to implement classificatory-level cognitive processes and a set of higher-order thinking processes involving hypothesizing, evaluating, and inferring.

This stage model has instructional implications for learners at various points in development. Thus, instruction can be spread over several grades in which concepts are periodically revisited at higher levels of attainment. Young children initially are provided with concrete referents and, with development, become able to operate at more abstract cognitive levels. For example, young children may learn the concept of "honesty" by seeing specific examples (e.g., not stealing, giving back something that is not yours); as they grow older, they can understand the concept in more abstract and complex terms (e.g., discuss benefits of honesty).

Teaching of Concepts

As did Klausmeier, Tennyson and his colleagues developed a model of concept teaching based on empirical research (Tennyson, 1980, 1981; Tennyson, Steve, & Boutwell, 1975). This model includes the following steps (Tennyson & Park, 1980):

- Determine the structure of the concept to include superordinate, coordinate, and subordinate concepts and identify the critical and variable attributes (e.g., features that can legitimately vary and not affect the concept).
- Define the concept in terms of the critical attributes and prepare several examples with the critical and variable attributes.
- Arrange the examples in sets based on the attributes and ensure that the examples have similar variable attributes within any set containing examples from each coordinate concept.
- Order and present the sets in terms of the divergence and difficulty of the examples and order the examples within any set according to the learner's current knowledge.

Most concepts can be represented in a hierarchy with *superordinate* (higher) and *subordinate* (lower) concepts. For any given concept, similar concepts may be at roughly the same level in the hierarchy; these are known as *coordinate* concepts. For example, the concept "domestic cat" has "cat family" and "mammal" as superordinate concepts, the various breeds (short hair, Siamese) as subordinate concepts, and other members of the cat family (lion, jaguar) as coordinate concepts. The concept has critical attributes (e.g., paws, teeth) and variable attributes (hair length, eye color). A *set* comprises examples and nonexamples (dog, squirrel) of the concept.

Although the concept should be defined with its critical attributes before examples and nonexamples are given, presenting a definition does not ensure students will learn the concept. Examples should differ widely in variable attributes, and nonexamples should differ from examples in a small number of critical attributes at once. This mode of presentation prevents students from overgeneralizing (classifying nonexamples as examples) and undergeneralizing (classifying examples as nonexamples). Pointing out relationships among examples is an effective way to arrange sets to foster generalization. O'Donnell et al. (2002) showed that learning is facilitated with knowledge maps where ideas are interlinked. (Application 5.2 contains suggestions for teaching concepts.)

The optimal number of examples to present depends on such concept characteristics as number of attributes and degree of abstractness of the concept. Abstract concepts usually have fewer perceptible examples than concrete concepts, and examples of the former may be difficult for learners to grasp. Concept learning also depends on learner attributes such as age and prior knowledge (Tennyson & Park, 1980). Older students learn better than younger ones, and students with more relevant knowledge outperform those lacking such knowledge.

In teaching concepts, presenting examples that differ in optional attributes but have relevant attributes in common so that the latter can be clearly pointed out, along with the irrelevant dimensions, is often helpful. In teaching children the concept of "right triangle," for example, the size is irrelevant, as is the direction it faces. One might present right triangles of various sizes pointing in different directions. Using worked examples is an effective cognitive instructional strategy (Atkinson, Derry, Renkl, & Wortham, 2000).

Not only must students learn to generalize right triangles, they must also learn to distinguish them from other triangles. To foster concept discrimination, teachers should present negative instances that clearly differ from positive instances. As students' skills develop, they can be taught to make finer discriminations. The suggestions shown in Table 5.2 are helpful in teaching students to generalize and discriminate among concepts.

This model requires a careful analysis of the taxonomic structure of a concept. Structure is well specified for many concepts (e.g., the animal kingdom), but for many others—especially abstract concepts—the links with higher- and lower-order concepts, as well as with coordinate concepts, are problematic. Future research might attempt to integrate Tennyson's ideas with other perspectives on concept instruction and with recent research on novice and expert students to determine differences in their knowledge and strategies (Chapter 9).

APPLICATION 5.2
Teaching of Concepts

Concept learning involves identifying attributes, generalizing them to new examples, and discriminating examples from nonexamples. Using superordinate, coordinate, and subordinate concepts and critical and variable attributes to present the concept to be learned should help students clearly define its structure.

A kindergarten teacher presenting a unit to teach students to identify and distinguish shapes (circle, square, rectangle, oval, triangle, diamond) might initially have children group objects alike in shape and identify critical attributes (e.g., a square has four straight sides, the sides are the same length) and variable attributes (squares, rectangles, triangles, and diamonds have straight sides but a different number of sides of different lengths and arranged in different ways). The teacher might then focus on a particular shape by presenting different examples representing each shape so children can compare attributes with those of other shapes. As for content progression, the teacher might introduce shapes familiar to students (e.g., circle and square) before moving to less common ones (e.g., parallelogram).

Kathy Stone introduces a unit on mammals by having her third-grade students sort a list of various animals into the major animal groups. Then the students discuss the major differences between the various animal groups. After reviewing these facts, Mrs. Stone focuses on the amphibian group by expanding the knowledge about the physical characteristics and by moving into other attributes such as eating habits and the ideal environment and climate.

In American history, Jim Marshall listed on the board the various immigrant groups that settled in America. After reviewing the time periods when each group came to America, he and the students discussed the differences as to why each group came, where they predominantly located in the country, and what types of trades they practiced. Then they described the impact of each group separately and collectively on the growth and development of America.

Motivational Processes

In a seminal article, Pintrich, Marx, and Boyle (1993) contended that conceptual change also involves *motivational processes* (e.g., goals, expectations, needs), which information processing models have tended to neglect. These authors argue that four conditions are necessary for conceptual change to occur. First, dissatisfaction with one's current conceptions is needed; change is unlikely if people feel their conceptions are accurate or useful. Second, the new conception must be intelligible—people must understand a conception in order to adopt it. Third, the new conception must be

Table 5.2
Steps for generalizing and discriminating concepts.

Step	Examples
Name concept	Chair
Define concept	Seat with a back for one person
Give relevant attribute	Seat, back
Give irrelevant attributes	Legs, size, color, material
Give examples	Easy chair, high chair, beanbag chair
Give nonexamples	Bench, table, stool

plausible—learners must understand how it fits with other understandings of how it might be applied. Finally, they must perceive the new conception as fruitful—being able to explain phenomena and suggesting new areas of investigation or application.

Motivational processes enter at several places in this model. For example, research shows that students' goals direct their attention and effort and their self-efficacy relates positively to motivation, use of effective task strategies, and skill acquisition (Schunk, 1991). Furthermore, students who believe that learning is useful and that task strategies are effective display higher motivation and learning (Borkowski, 1985; Pressley, Woloshyn, Lysynchuk, Martin, Wood, & Willoughby, 1990; Schunk & Rice, 1993). Goals, self-efficacy, and self-evaluation of competence have been shown to promote learning and self-regulation in such domains as reading comprehension, writing, mathematics, and decision making (Pajares, 1996; Schunk & Swartz, 1993a; Wood & Bandura, 1989; Zimmerman & Bandura, 1994).

In short, the literature suggests that conceptual change involves an interaction of students' cognitions and motivational beliefs (Pintrich et al., 1993). We revisit conceptual change in Chapter 9 as it applies to scientific thinking. For now, we should note that this point has implications for teaching. Rather than simply provide knowledge, teachers must take students' preexisting ideas into account when planning instruction and ensure that instruction includes motivational factors.

PROBLEM SOLVING

One of the most important types of cognitive processing that occurs often during learning is problem solving. Problem solving has been a topic of study for many years—we review historical material in this section—but interest in the topic has burgeoned with the growth of cognitive psychology. Some theorists (e.g., Anderson, 1993) consider problem solving to be the key process in learning, especially in domains such as science and mathematics. Although "problem solving" and "learning" are not synonymous, the former often is involved in the latter and particularly when learners can exert some degree of self-regulation over learning and when the learning involves challenges and nonobvious solutions. These conditions often are found during content-area learning (Chapter 9).

Problem Solving Defined

A *problem* is a "situation in which you are trying to reach some goal, and must find a means for getting there" (Chi & Glaser, 1985, p. 229). The problem may be to answer a question, compute a solution, locate an object, secure a job, teach a student, and so on. *Problem solving* refers to people's efforts to achieve a goal for which they do not have an automatic solution.

Regardless of content area and complexity, all problems have certain things in common. Problems have an initial state—the problem solver's current status or level of knowledge. Problems have a goal—what the problem solver is attempting to attain. Most problems also require the solver to break the goal into subgoals that, when mastered (usually sequentially), result in goal attainment. Finally, problems require performing operations on the initial state and the subgoals, where operations are activities (behavioral, cognitive) that alter the nature of those states (Anderson, 1990; Chi & Glaser, 1985).

Based on this definition, not all learning activities include problem solving. Problem solving technically is not involved when students' skills become so well established that they automatically execute actions to attain goals, which happens with many skills in different content domains. It also may not be involved in low-level (possibly trivial) learning, where students know what to do to learn. At the same time, students learn new skills and new uses for previously learned skills, so many school activities might involve problem solving at some point during learning.

Historical Influences

As a backdrop to current cognitive views of problem solving, we will examine some historical perspectives: trial and error, insight, and heuristics.

Trial and Error.   Thorndike's (1913b) research with cats (Chapter 2) required problem solving; the problem was how to escape from the cage. Thorndike conceived of problem solving as *trial and error*. The animal was capable of performing certain behaviors in the cage. From this behavioral repertoire, the animal performed one behavior and experienced the consequences. After a series of random behaviors, the cat made the response that opened the hatch leading to escape. With repeated trials, the cat made fewer errors before performing the escape behavior and the time required to solve the problem diminished. The escape behavior (response) became connected to cues (stimuli) in the cage.

All of us occasionally use trial and error to solve problems; we simply perform actions until one works. However, trial and error is not reliable and often not effective. It can waste time, may never result in a solution, may lead to a less-than-ideal solution, and can have negative effects. In desperation, a teacher might use a trial-and-error approach by trying different reading materials with a student having difficulty reading until she begins to read better. This approach might be effective but also might expose her to materials that prove frustrating and thereby retard her reading progress.

Insight. Problem solving often is thought to involve *insight*, or the sudden awareness of a likely solution. Wallas (1921) studied great problem solvers and formulated a four-step model as follows:

- ***Preparation:*** A time to learn about the problem and gather information that might be relevant to its solution.
- ***Incubation:*** A period of thinking about the problem, which may also include putting the problem aside for a time.
- ***Illumination:*** A period of insight when a potential solution suddenly comes into awareness.
- ***Verification:*** A time to test the proposed solution to ascertain whether it is correct.

Wallas's stages were descriptive and not subjected to empirical verification. Gestalt psychologists (Chapter 4) also postulated that much human learning is insightful and involves a change in perception. Learners initially think about the ingredients necessary to solve a problem. They integrate these in various ways until the problem is solved. When learners arrive at a solution, they do so suddenly and with insight.

An important educational application of Gestalt theory is in the area of problem solving, or *productive thinking* (Duncker, 1945; Luchins, 1942; Wertheimer, 1945). The Gestalt view stresses the role of *understanding*—comprehending the meaning of some event or grasping the principle or rule underlying performance. In contrast, rote memorization—although used often by students—is inefficient and rarely used in life outside of school (Application 5.3).

Research by Katona (1940) demonstrated the utility of rule learning compared with memorization. In one study, participants were asked to learn number sequences (e.g., 816449362516941). Some learned the sequences by rote, whereas others were given clues to aid learning (e.g., "Think of squared numbers"). Learners who determined the rule for generating the sequences retained them better than those who rotely memorized.

Rules lead to better learning and retention than memorization because rules give a simpler description of the phenomenon so less information must be learned. In addition, rules help organize material. To recall information, one recalls the rule and then fills in the details. In contrast, memorization entails recalling more pieces of information. Memorization generally is inefficient because most situations have some organization (Wertheimer, 1945). Problems are solved by discovering the organization of the situation and the relationship of the individual elements to the problem solution. By arranging and rearranging these elements, learners eventually gain insight into the solution.

Köhler (1926) did well-known work on problem solving with apes on the island of Tenerife during World War I. In one experiment, Köhler put a banana just out of reach of an ape in a cage; the ape could fetch the banana by using a long stick or by putting two sticks together. Köhler concluded that problem solving is insightful: Animals survey the situation, suddenly "see" the means for attaining the goal, and test the solution. The apes' first problem-solving attempts failed as they

APPLICATION 5.3
Role of Understanding in Learning

Teachers want students to understand concepts rather than simply memorize how to complete tasks. Gestalt psychologists believed that an emphasis on drill and practice, memorization, and reinforcement resulted in trivial learning and that understanding was achieved by grasping rules and principles underlying concepts and skills.

Teachers often use hands-on experiences to help students understand the structure and principles involved in learning. In biology, students might memorize what a cross section of a bean stem looks like under a microscope, but they may have difficulty conceptualizing the structures in the living organism. Mock-ups assist student learning. A large, hands-on model of a bean stem that can be taken apart to illustrate the internal structures should enhance student understanding of the stem's composition and how the parts function.

Talking about child care in a high school family studies class is not nearly as beneficial as the 1 hour each week students spend helping children at a local daycare center and applying what they have been studying.

In discussing the applications of learning theories, it is preferable that students see firsthand the utilization of techniques that enhance student learning. Gina Brown has her educational psychology students observe in school classrooms. As they observe, she has them list examples of situations where various learning principles are evident.

tried different ineffective strategies (e.g., throwing a stick at the banana). Eventually they saw the stick as an extension of their arms and used it accordingly.

In another situation (Köhler, 1925), the animal could see the goal but not attain it without turning away and taking an indirect route. For example, the animal might be in a room with a window and see food outside. To reach the goal, the animal must exit the room via a door and proceed down a corridor that led outside. In going from the presolution to the solution phase, the animal might try a number of alternatives before settling on one and employing it. Insight occurred when the animal tested a likely solution.

A barrier to problem solving is *functional fixedness,* or the inability to perceive different uses for objects or new configurations of elements in a situation (Duncker, 1945). In a classic study, Luchins (1942) gave individuals problems that required them to obtain a given amount of water using three jars of different sizes. Persons from ages 9 to adult easily learned the formula that always produced the correct amount. Intermixed in the problem set were some problems that could be solved using a simpler formula. Persons generally continued to apply the original formula. Cuing them that there might be an easier solution led some to discover the simpler methods, although many persisted with the original formula. This research shows that when students do not understand a phenomenon, they may blindly apply a known algorithm and fail to understand that easier methods exist. This procedure-bound nature of problem solving can be overcome when different procedures are emphasized during instruction (Chen, 1999).

Gestalt theory had little to say about how problem-solving strategies are learned or how learners could be taught to be more insightful. Wertheimer (1945) believed that teachers could aid problem solving by arranging elements of a situation so that students would be more likely to perceive how the parts relate to the whole. Such general advice is not particularly helpful for classroom teachers.

Heuristics

Another way to solve problems is to use *heuristics*, which are general methods for solving problems that employ principles (rules of thumb) that usually lead to a solution (Anderson, 1990). Polya (1945/1957) described heuristics as follows:

> Modern heuristic endeavors to understand the process of solving problems, especially the mental operations typically useful in this process. It has various sources of information none of which should be neglected. A serious study of heuristic should take into account both the logical and psychological background, it should not neglect what . . . older writers . . . have to say about the subject, but it should least neglect unbiased experience. Experience in solving problems and experience in watching other people solving problems must be the basis on which heuristic is built. In this study, we should not neglect any sort of problem, and should find out common features in the way of handling all sorts of problems; we should aim at general features, independent of the subject matter of the problem. The study of heuristic has "practical" aims; a better understanding of the mental operations typically useful in solving problems could exert some good influence on teaching. (pp. 129–130)

Polya's list of mental operations involved in problem solving is as follows:

- Understand the problem.
- Devise a plan.
- Carry out the plan.
- Look back.

Understanding the problem involves asking such questions as "What is the unknown?" and "What are the data?" It often helps to draw a diagram representing the problem and the given information. In devising a plan, one tries to find a connection between the data and the unknown. Breaking the problem into subgoals is useful, as is thinking of a similar problem and how that was solved (i.e., use analogies). The problem may need to be restated. While carrying out the plan, checking each step to ensure it is being properly implemented is important. Looking back means examining the solution: Is it correct? Is there another means of attaining it?

Bransford and Stein (1984) formulated a similar heuristic known as IDEAL:

- *I*dentify the problem.
- *D*efine and represent the problem.

- *Ex*plore possible strategies.
- *Act* on the strategies.
- *L*ook back and evaluate the effects of your activities.

The Creative Problem Solving (CPS) model offers another example of a generic problem-solving framework (Treffinger, 1985). This model comprises three major components: understanding the problem, generating ideas, planning for action (Treffinger, 1995).

Understanding the problem begins with a general goal or direction for problem solving. After important data (e.g., facts, opinions, concerns) are obtained, a specific goal or question is formulated. The hallmark of generating ideas is divergent thinking to produce options for attaining the goal. Planning for action includes examining promising options and searching for sources of assistance and ways to overcome resistance.

General heuristics are most useful when one is working with unfamiliar content (Andre, 1986). They are less effective when one is working within a familiar domain, because as domain-specific skills develop, students increasingly use established procedural knowledge for that content. General heuristics have an instructional advantage: They can help students become systematic problem solvers. Although the heuristic approach may appear to be inflexible, there actually is flexibility in how steps are carried out. For many students, a heuristic will be more systematic than their current problem-solving approaches and will lead to better solutions. Polya's emphasis on watching others solve problems reminds us of the current emphasis on novice-expert paradigms of learning (Chapter 9).

Information Processing Model

In the early days of information processing theory and research, Newell and Simon (1972) proposed a model of problem solving that involves a problem space with a beginning state, a goal state, and possible solution paths leading through subgoals and requiring application of operations. The problem solver forms a mental representation of the problem and performs operations to reduce the discrepancy between the beginning and goal states. The process of operating on the representation to find a solution is known as *the search* (Andre, 1986).

The first step in problem solving is to form a mental representation. Similar to Polya's first step (understand the problem), representation requires translating known information into a model in memory. The internal representation consists of propositions, and possibly images, in WM. The problem also can be represented externally (e.g., on paper, computer screen, chalkboard). Information in WM activates related knowledge in LTM, and the solver eventually selects a problem-solving strategy. As people solve problems, they often alter their initial representation and activate new knowledge, especially if their problem solving does not succeed. Thus, problem solving includes evaluating goal progress.

The problem representation determines what knowledge is activated in memory and, consequently, how easy the problem is to solve (Holyoak, 1984). If solvers incorrectly represent the problem by not considering all aspects or by adding too many

APPLICATION 5.4
Problem Solving

Various ways exist to help students improve their problem-solving skills. When students solve mathematical word problems, Mrs. Stone encourages them to state each problem in their own words, draw a sketch, decide what information is relevant, and state the ways they might solve the problem. These and other similar questions help focus students' attention on important task aspects and guide their thinking:

- What information is important?
- What information is missing?
- Which formulas are necessary?
- What is the first thing to do?

Another way to assist students is to encourage them to view a problem from varying perspectives. During an exercise in which Jim Marshall's high school students categorize wartime figures who had a predominant impact on the United States (e.g., Churchill, Hitler), they discuss various ways these figures could be categorized, such as by personality type, political makeup of countries they ruled, goals of the war, and the effect their leadership and goals had on the United States. This exercise illustrates different ways to organize information, which aids problem solving.

Teachers also can teach strategies. In a geography lesson, students might be given the following problem: "Pick a state (not your own) that you

constraints, the search process is unlikely to identify a correct solution path (Chi & Glaser, 1985). No matter how clearly solvers subsequently reason, they will not reach a correct solution unless they form a new representation. Not surprisingly, problem-solving training programs typically devote a lot of time to the representation phase (Andre, 1986).

Problem-Solving Strategies

Problem-solving strategies are general or specific. *General strategies* can be applied to problems in several domains regardless of content; *specific strategies* are useful only in a particular domain. For example, breaking a complex problem into subproblems (subgoal analysis) is a general strategy applicable to problems such as writing a term paper, choosing an academic major, and deciding where to live. Conversely, tests that one might perform to classify laboratory specimens are task-specific.

General strategies are useful when one is working on problems where solutions are not immediately obvious. Useful general strategies are generate-and-test believe could attract new residents, and create a poster depicting the most important attributes of that state." A working backward strategy could be taught as follows:

Goal: Create a poster depicting the state's important attributes.

Subgoal: Decide how to portray the attributes in a poster.

Subgoal: Decide which attributes to portray.

Subgoal: Decide which state to pick.

Initial Subgoal: Decide which attributes attract new residents.

To attain the initial subgoal, students could brainstorm in small groups to determine which factors attract people to a state. They then could conduct library research to check on which states possess these attributes. Students could reconvene to discuss the attributes of different states and decide on one. They then would decide which attributes to portray in the poster and how to portray them, after which they would create their poster and present it to the class.

When students are developing problem-solving skills, teachers might want to give clues rather than answers. A teacher working with younger children on categorizing might give the children a word list of names of animals, colors, and places to live. Children are most likely to experience some difficulty categorizing the names. Rather than telling them the answers, the teacher could provide clues such as, "Think of how the words go together. How are *horse* and *lion* alike? How are *pink* and *house* different?

strategies, means-ends analysis, analogical reasoning, and brainstorming. General strategies are less useful than domain-specific strategies when working with highly familiar content. Some examples of problem solving in learning contexts are given in Application 5.4.

Generate-and-Test Strategy.   The generate-and-test strategy is useful when a limited number of problem solutions can be tested to see if they attain the goal (Resnick, 1985). This strategy works best with problems with multiple solutions that can be ordered in terms of likelihood and where at least one solution is apt to solve the problem.

As an example, assume that you walk into a room, flip the light switch, but the light does not come on. Possible causes include: the bulb is burned out; the electricity is turned off; the switch is faulty; the lamp socket is faulty; the circuit breaker is tripped; the fuse is blown; or the wiring has a short. You will probably generate and test the most likely solution (replace the bulb); if this does not solve the problem, you may generate and test other likely solutions. Although content does not need to be highly familiar, some knowledge is needed to use this method effectively.

Prior knowledge establishes the hierarchy of possible solutions; current knowledge influences solution selection. Thus, if you notice an electric utility truck in your neighborhood, you would determine if the power is shut off.

Means-Ends Analysis.   To use *means-ends analysis,* one compares the current situation with the goal and identifies the differences between them (Resnick, 1985). Subgoals are set to reduce the differences. One performs operations to accomplish the subgoal, at which point the process is repeated until the goal is attained.

Newell and Simon (1972), who studied means-ends analysis, formulated a computer simulation program called the General Problem Solver (GPS). GPS breaks a problem into subgoals, each representing a difference from the current state. GPS starts with the most important difference and uses operations to eliminate that difference. In some cases, the operations must first eliminate another difference prerequisite to the more important one.

Means-ends analysis is a powerful problem-solving heuristic. When subgoals are properly identified, means-ends analysis is most likely to solve the problem. One drawback is that with complex problems means-ends analysis taxes WM because one may have to keep track of several subgoals. Forgetting a subgoal thwarts problem solution.

Means-ends analysis can proceed from the goal to the initial state (*working backward*) or from the initial state to the goal (*working forward*). In working backward, one starts with the goal and asks what subgoals are necessary to accomplish it. One then asks what is necessary to attain these subgoals and so forth, until the initial state is reached. To work backward, therefore, one plans a series of moves, each designed to attain a subgoal. Successfully working backward requires a fair amount of knowledge in the problem domain to determine goal and subgoal prerequisites.

Working backward is frequently used to prove geometric theorems. One starts by assuming that the theorem is true and then works backward until the postulates are reached. A geometric example is shown in Figure 5.1. The problem is to solve for angle *m*. Working backward, students realize that they need to determine angle *n*, because angle *m* = 180° – angle *n* (straight line = 180°). Continuing to work

Figure 5.1
Means-ends analysis applied to a
geometry problem.

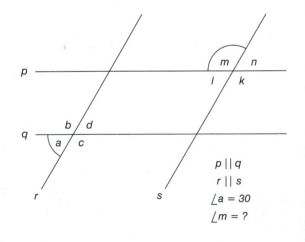

backward, students understand that because the parallel lines intersect, the corresponding angle d on line q equals angle n. Drawing on their geometric knowledge, students determine that angle d = angle a, which is 30°. Thus, angle n = 30°, and angle m = 180° − 30° = 150°.

As another example of working backward, suppose one has a term paper due in 3 weeks. The last step before turning it in is to proofread it (to do the day before the paper is due). The step before that is to type and print the final copy (allow 1 day). Before that, one makes final revisions (1 day), revises the paper (3 days), and types and prints the draft copy (1 day). Continuing to work backward, we might allow 5 days to write the draft, 1 day to outline, 3 days for library research, and 1 day to decide on a topic. We allow a total of 17 days to spend in part working on the paper. So we need to begin 4 days from today.

A second type of means-ends analysis is working forward, sometimes referred to as *hill climbing* (Mayer, 1992). The problem solver starts with the current situation and does something to alter it in the hope of moving closer to the goal. Several alterations usually are necessary to attain the goal. One danger is that working forward sometimes proceeds based on superficial problem analysis. Although each step represents an attempt to attain a necessary subgoal, one can easily veer off on a tangent or arrive at a dead end.

As an example of a working forward strategy, consider students in a laboratory who have various substances in jars. Their goal is to label the substances in their jars. To do so, they perform a series of tests on the substances which, if correctly done, will result in a solution. This represents a working forward strategy because each test moves students closer to their goal of classifying their substances. The tests are ordered and the results show what the substances are not, as well as what they might be. To prevent students from going off on the wrong track, the teacher sets up the procedure carefully and ensures that students understand how to perform the tests.

Analogical Reasoning.   Another general problem-solving strategy is to use *analogical reasoning*, which involves drawing an analogy between the problem situation (the target) and a situation with which one is familiar (the base or source; Anderson, 1990; Chen, 1999; Hunt, 1989). One works the problem through the familiar domain and then relates the solution to the problem situation (Holyoak & Thagard, 1997). From an information processing perspective, analogical reasoning involves accessing the familiar domain's network in LTM and mapping it onto (relating it to) the problem situation in WM (Halpern, Hansen, & Riefer, 1990). Successful application requires that the familiar situation be structurally similar to the problem situation, although the situations may differ in surface features (e.g., one might involve the solar system and the other molecular structures). The subgoals in this approach are relating the steps in the original (familiar) domain to those in the transfer (problem) area. Students often use the analogy method to solve problems in textbooks. Examples are worked in the text (familiar domain), then students relate these steps to the problems they must solve.

Gick and Holyoak (1980, 1983) demonstrated the power of analogical problem solving. They presented learners with a difficult medical problem and, as an analogy, a solved military problem. Simply giving them the analogical problem did not automatically prompt them to use it. However, giving them a hint to use the military problem to solve the medical problem improved problem solving. Gick and Holyoak also found that giving students two analogue stories led to better problem solving than giving one story. However, having them summarize the analogue story, giving them the principle underlying the story while they read it, or providing them with a diagram illustrating the problem solution principle did not enhance problem solving. These results suggest that in an unfamiliar domain, students need guidance on the way to employ analogies and that multiple examples increase the likelihood of students' linking at least one example to the problem to be solved.

To be most effective, analogical problem solving requires good knowledge of the familiar and problem domains. Students often have enough difficulty using analogies to solve problems even when the solution strategy is highlighted. With inadequate knowledge, students are unlikely to see the relation between the problem and the analogue. Even assuming good knowledge, the analogy is most likely to fail when the familiar and problem domains are conceptually dissimilar. Learners may understand how fighting a battle (the military problem) is similar to fighting a disease (the medical problem), but they may not grasp other analogies (fighting a corporate takeover attempt).

Developmental evidence indicates that, despite its difficulties, children can employ analogical reasoning (Siegler, 1989). Teaching analogies to children—including those with learning disabilities—can improve their subsequent problem solving (Grossen, 1991). The use of case studies and case-based reasoning can help develop analogical thinking (Kolodner, 1997). Effective techniques for using analogies include having the adult teacher and child verbalize the solution principle that underlies the original and transfer problems, prompting children to recall elements of the original problem's causal structure, and presenting the two problems such that the causal structures proceed from most to least obvious (Crisafi & Brown, 1986). Other suggestions include using similar original and transfer problems, presenting several similar problems, and using pictures to portray causal relations.

This is not to suggest that all children can become experts at using analogies. The task is difficult, and children often draw inappropriate analogies. Compared with older students, younger ones require more hints, are more apt to be distracted by irrelevant perceptual features, and process information less efficiently (Crisafi & Brown, 1986). Children's success depends heavily on their knowledge about the original problem and their skill at encoding and making mental comparisons, which show wide individual differences (Siegler, 1989). Children learn problem-solving strategies better when they observe and explain them than when they merely observe (Crowley & Siegler, 1999).

Analogical problem solving is useful in teaching. Teachers often have students whose native language is not English. Teaching students in their native language is impossible. Teachers might relate this problem to teaching students who have difficulty learning. With the latter students, teachers would proceed slowly, use concrete experiences whenever possible, and provide much individual instruction. They might try the same tactics with non-English-language students, while simultaneously teaching them English words and phrases so they can follow along with the other students in class.

This analogy is appropriate because students with learning problems and students who speak little English have difficulties in the classroom. Other analogies might be inappropriate. Unmotivated students also have learning difficulties. Using them for the analogy, the teacher might offer the non-English-speaking students rewards for learning. This solution is apt to be less effective because the problem with non-English-speaking students is instructional rather than motivational.

Brainstorming.   Brainstorming is a general problem-solving strategy that is useful for formulating possible problem solutions (Mayer, 1992; Osborn, 1963). The steps in brainstorming are as follows:

- Define the problem.
- Generate as many solutions as possible without evaluating them.
- Decide on criteria for judging potential solutions.
- Use these criteria to select the best solution.

Successful brainstorming requires that participants withhold criticism of ideas until after all ideas are generated. In addition, brainstorming sessions often generate many ideas that build onto one another. Thus, "wild" and unusual ideas should be encouraged (Mayer, 1992).

As with analogical problem solving, the amount of knowledge one has about the problem domain affects the success of brainstorming because better domain knowledge allows one to generate more potential solutions and criteria for judging their feasibility. Brainstorming can be used individually, although the group interaction usually leads to more solutions.

Brainstorming lends itself well to many instructional and administrative decisions made in schools. Assume that a new school principal finds low staff morale. Staff members agree that better communication is needed. The grade-level leaders meet with the principal, and the group arrives at the following potential solutions: Hold a weekly meeting with staff, send out a weekly bulletin, post notices on a bulletin board, hold weekly meetings with grade-level leaders (after which they meet with teachers), send e-mail informational messages frequently, make announcements over the public address system. The group formulates two criteria: (a) minimally time-consuming for teachers and (b) minimally disrupting to classes. With the criteria in mind, they decide that the principal should send out a weekly bulletin and frequent e-mail messages and meet with grade-level leaders as a group. Although they will take time, meetings between the principal and grade-level leaders will be more focused than those between the principal and the entire staff.

Problem Solving and Learning

At the outset of this section we noted that although problem solving often is involved in learning, the concepts are not synonymous. According to a contemporary information processing view (Anderson, 1990, 1993), problem solving involves the acquisition, retention, and use of production systems, which are networks of condition-action sequences (rules) in which the conditions are the sets of circumstances that activate the system and the actions are the sets of activities that occur (Anderson, 1990; Andre, 1986). A production system consists of if-then statements. If statements (the condition) include the goal and test statements; then statements are the actions.

Productions are forms of procedural knowledge that include declarative knowledge and the conditions under which these forms are applicable. Productions are represented in LTM as propositional networks and are acquired in the same fashion as other procedural knowledge. Productions also are organized hierarchically with subordinate and superordinate productions. To solve two equations with two unknowns, one first represents one unknown in terms of the second unknown (subordinate production), after which one solves for the second unknown (production) and uses that value to solve for the first unknown (superordinate production).

Productions can be general or specific. Specific productions apply to content in well-defined areas. The preceding production is domain specific. In contrast, heuristics are general productions because they apply to diverse content. A means-ends analysis might be represented as follows (Anderson, 1990):

> IF the goal is to transform the current state into the goal state and D is the largest difference between the states
> THEN set as subgoals
>
> 1. To eliminate the difference D
> 2. To convert the resulting state into the goal state. (p. 243)

A second production will then need to be employed with the if-then statement, "If the goal is to eliminate the difference D." This sequence continues until the subgoals have been identified at a specific level; then domain-specific rules are applied. In short, general productions are broken down until the level at which domain-specific knowledge is applied. Production systems offer a means of linking general with specific problem-solving procedures. Other problem-solving strategies (e.g., analogical reasoning) also can be represented as productions.

Much learning in school is highly regulated and does not require problem solving. Problem solving is not applicable when students have a goal and a clear means for attaining it. When teachers move away from lockstep, highly regimented instruction and encourage more original and critical thinking by students, problem solving becomes more important. Fortunately, in recent years we have seen a movement in education to encourage problem solving by students, and experts feel that this trend will continue. In the meantime, students need to learn both general and specific problem-solving strategies so they can handle these added demands associated with learning.

Experts and Novices

Contemporary research addresses how experts and novices differ in problem solving. An *expert* is an individual who has attained a high competence level in problem solving. A *novice* is an individual who has some familiarity but generally performs poorly (not one who has no knowledge of problem solving).

Researchers have identified several differences between novices and experts (Anderson, 1990, 1993; Bruning, Schraw, & Ronning, 1995; Resnick, 1985). One difference involves the demands made on WM. Expert problem solvers do not activate large amounts of potentially relevant information; they identify key features of the problem, relate them to background knowledge, and generate one or a small number of potential solutions (Mayer, 1992). Experts reduce complex problems to manageable size by separating the problem space from the larger task environment, which includes the domain of facts and knowledge within which the problem is embedded (Newell & Simon, 1972). Coupled with the fact that experts can hold more information in WM (Chi, Glaser, & Farr, 1988), this reduction process retains relevant information, discards irrelevant information, fits within the limits of WM, and is accurate enough to allow a solution.

Experts often employ a working forward strategy by identifying the problem format and generating an approach to fit it (Mayer, 1992). This typically entails breaking the problem into parts and solving the parts sequentially (Bruning et al., 1995). Novice problem solvers, however, often attempt problem solving in piecemeal fashion, in part because of the poorer organization in their memories. They may use trial and error or try to work backward from what they are trying to find to the problem givens—an ineffective strategy if they are unaware of the substeps needed (Mayer, 1992). Their means-ends analyses often are based on surface features of problems. In mathematics, novices generate formulas from memory when confronted with word problems. Trying to store excess information in WM clutters their thinking (Resnick, 1985).

Experts and novices also differ in background domain-specific knowledge, although they appear to be comparably versed in knowledge of general problem-solving strategies (Elstein, Shulman, & Sprafka, 1978; Simon, 1979). Experts have more extensive and better-organized LTM structures in their area of expertise (Chi, Feltovich, & Glaser, 1981). The greater amount of knowledge experts can use in solving problems, the more likely they are to solve them and the better their memory organization facilitates efficiency.

Qualitative differences are evident in how knowledge is structured in memory (Chi, Glaser, & Rees, 1982). Experts' knowledge is more hierarchically organized. Chi et al. (1981) had expert and novice problem solvers sort physics textbook problems on any basis they wished. Novices grouped problems according to the type of apparatus employed (e.g., lever, beam), the words used in the problem, or the similarities in visual features. Experts classified problems based on the underlying physics principle needed to solve the problem (e.g., laws of motion, Newton's laws). This difference—experts grouping problems according to "deep structure" and novices relying more on surface features—can be striking (Hardiman, Dufresne, & Mestre, 1989). Interestingly, training of novices to recognize deep features improves their performances relative to those of untrained novices.

Novices typically respond to problems in terms of how they are presented; experts reinterpret problems to reveal an underlying structure, one that most likely matches their own LTM network (Resnick, 1985). Novices attempt to translate the given information directly into formulas and solve for the missing quantities. Rather than generate formulas, experts may initially draw diagrams to clarify the relations among problem aspects. They often construct a new version of the problem. By the time they are ready to perform calculations, they usually have simplified the problem and perform fewer calculations than novices. While working, experts monitor their performances better to assess goal progress and the value of the strategy they are using (Gagné et al., 1993).

Finally, experts spend more time planning and analyzing. They are more thoughtful and do not proceed until they have some strategy in mind. Moore (1990) found that experienced teachers spend more time planning than do less-experienced teachers, as well as more time exploring new classrooms. Such planning makes strategy implementation easier.

In summary, the differences between novice and expert problem solvers are many. Compared with novices, experts:

- Possess more declarative knowledge
- Have better hierarchical organization of knowledge
- Spend more time planning and analyzing
- Recognize problem formats more easily
- Represent problems at a deeper level
- Monitor their performances more carefully
- Understand better the value of strategy use

Implications for Instruction

The links between learning and problem solving suggest that students benefit from being taught problem-solving strategies. In addition, for information to be linked in memory, it is best to integrate problem solving with academic content rather than to teach problem solving with stand-alone programs.

Andre (1986) lists several suggestions that are derived from theory and research and that are useful for training students in problem-solving skills, especially as they represent productions in memory.

- **Provide students with metaphorical representations**. A concrete analogical passage given to students prior to an instructional passage facilitates learning from the target passage.
- **Have students verbalize during problem solving**. Verbalization of thoughts during problem solving can facilitate problem solutions and learning.
- **Use questions**. Ask students questions that require them to practice concepts they have learned; many such questions may be necessary.
- **Provide examples**. Give students many worked-out examples showing application of problem-solving strategies. Students may have difficulty seeing on their own how strategies apply to situations.
- **Coordinate ideas**. Show how productions and knowledge relate to one another and in what sequence they might need to be applied.
- **Use discovery learning**. Discovery learning often facilitates transfer and problem solving better than expository teaching. Discovery may force students to generate rules from examples. The same can be accomplished

through expository teaching, but discovery may lend itself better to certain content (e.g., science experiments).

- **Give a verbal description**. Providing students with a verbal description of the strategy and its rules for application can be helpful.
- **Teach learning strategies**. Learners may need assistance in using effective learning strategies. As discussed in Chapter 9, strategies help learning and problem solving.
- **Use small groups**. A number of studies have found that small-group learning helps develop students' problem-solving skills. Group members must be held accountable for their learning and all students must share in the work.
- **Maintain a positive psychological climate**. Psychological factors are important to effective problem solving. Minimize excessive anxiety among students and help to create a sense of self-efficacy among students for improving their skills (Chapter 3).

TRANSFER

Transfer is a critical topic for learning and often involves complex cognitive processes. *Transfer* refers to knowledge being applied in new ways, in new situations, or in old locations with different content. Transfer also explains how prior learning affects subsequent learning. The cognitive capability for transfer is important, because without it all learning would be situationally specific and much instructional time would be spent reteaching skills in new situations.

There are different types of transfer. *Positive transfer* occurs when prior learning facilitates subsequent learning. Thus, learning how to drive a car with standard transmission should facilitate learning to drive other cars with standard transmission. *Negative transfer* means that prior learning interferes with subsequent learning or makes it more difficult. Learning to drive a standard transmission car might have a negative effect on subsequently learning to drive a car with automatic transmission because one would be apt to hit the phantom clutch and possibly shift gears while the car is moving, which could ruin the transmission. *Zero transfer* means that one type of learning has no noticeable influence on subsequent learning. Learning to drive a standard transmission car should have no effect on learning to operate a computer.

Current cognitive conceptions of learning highlight the complexity of processes involved in transfer (Phye, 2001). Although some forms of simple skill transfer seem to occur automatically, much transfer requires higher-order thinking skills and beliefs about the usefulness of knowledge. This section begins with a brief overview of historical perspectives on transfer, followed by a discussion of cognitive views and the relevance of transfer to school learning.

Historical Views

Identical Elements.   Behavioral theories (Chapter 2) stress that transfer depends on identical elements or similar features (stimuli) among situations. Thorndike (1913b), for example, contended that transfer occurs when situations have identical elements (stimuli) and call for similar responses. A clear and known relation must exist between the original and transfer tasks, as is often the case between drill/practice and homework.

This view is intuitively appealing and holds some merit. Students who learn to solve the problem 602 − 376 = ? are apt to transfer that knowledge and also solve the problem 503 − 287 = ? We might ask, however, what elements are and how similar they must be to be considered identical. In subtraction, for example, do the same type of numbers need to be in the same column? Students who can solve the problem 42 − 37 = ? will not necessarily be able to solve the problem 7428 − 2371 = ?, even though the former problem is contained within the latter one. Findings such as this call into question the validity of the identical elements notion. Furthermore, even when identical elements exist, students must recognize them. If students believe no commonality exists between situations, no transfer will occur. So the identical elements position is inadequate to explain all transfer.

Mental Discipline. Also relevant to transfer is the *mental discipline* doctrine (Chapter 2), which holds that learning certain subjects (e.g., mathematics, the classics) enhances general mental functioning and facilitates learning of new content better than does learning other subjects. This view was popular in Thorndike's day and periodically reemerges in the form of recommendations for basic or core skills and knowledge (e.g., Hirsch, 1987).

Research by Thorndike (1924) provided no support for the mental discipline idea (Chapter 2). Instead, Thorndike concluded that the true factor improving new learning is students' beginning level of mental ability. Students who are more intelligent when they begin a course gain the most from the course. The intellectual value of studies reflects not how much they improve students' ability to think but rather how they affect students' interests and goals.

Generalization. Skinner (1953) propounded another view of transfer. According to operant conditioning theory, transfer involves *generalization* of responses from one discriminative stimulus to another. Thus, students might be taught to put their books away in their desks when the teacher rings a bell. If students go to another class and that teacher rings a bell, the response of putting things away might generalize to the new setting.

The notion of generalization, like identical elements, has intuitive appeal. Surely some transfer occurs through generalization, and it may even occur automatically. Students who are punished for misbehavior in one class may not misbehave in other classes. Once drivers learn to stop their cars at a red light, that response will generalize to other red lights regardless of location, weather, time of day, and so forth.

Nonetheless, the generalization position has problems. As with identical elements, we can ask what features of the situation are used in the generalization of responses. Situations share many common features, yet we respond only to some of them and disregard others. We respond to the red light regardless of many other features in the situation. At the same time, we might be more likely to run a red light when no other cars are around or when we are in a hurry. Our response is not fixed but rather depends on our cognitive assessment of the situation. The same can be said of countless other situations where generalization does not occur automatically. Cognitive processes are involved in most generalization as people determine whether responding in similar fashion is appropriate in that setting. The generalization position, therefore, is not really inaccurate but rather incomplete because it neglects the role of cognitive processes.

Activation of Knowledge in Memory

From a cognitive perspective, transfer involves activating knowledge in memory networks. It requires that information be cross-referenced with propositions linked in memory (Anderson, 1990; Gagné et al., 1993). The more links between bits of information in memory, the likelier that activating one piece of information will cue other information in memory. Such links can be made within and between networks.

The same process is involved in transfer of procedural knowledge and productions. Transfer occurs when knowledge and productions are linked in LTM with different content. Students must also believe that productions are useful in various situations. Transfer is aided by the uses of knowledge being stored with the knowledge itself. For example, learners may possess a production of skimming text. This may be linked in memory with other reading procedures (e.g., finding main ideas, sequencing), and may have various uses stored with it (e.g., skimming a newspaper to get the gist, skimming memos to determine meeting place and time). The more links in LTM and the more uses stored with skimming, the better the transfer. Such links are formed by having students practice skills in various contexts and by helping them understand the uses of knowledge.

This cognitive description of transfer fits much of what we know about cued knowledge. Where more LTM links are available, accessing information in different ways is possible. We may not be able to recall the name of Aunt Martha's dog by thinking about her (cuing the "Aunt Martha" network), but we might be able to recall the name by thinking about (cuing) breeds of dogs ("collie"). Such cuing is reminiscent of the experiences we periodically have of not being able to recall someone's name until we think about that person from a different perspective or in a different context.

At the same time, we still do not know many things about how such links form. Links are not automatically made simply by pointing out uses of knowledge to students or having them practice skills in different contexts. Different forms of transfer, governed by different conditions, appear to exist.

Types of Transfer

Recent evidence indicates that transfer is not a unitary cognitive phenomenon but rather is complex (Table 5.3). One distinction is between near and far transfer (Royer, 1986). *Near transfer* occurs when situations overlap a great deal, such as between the stimulus elements during instruction and those present in the transfer situation. An example is when fraction skills are taught and then students are tested on the

Table 5.3
Types of transfer.

Type	Characteristics
Near	Much overlap between situations; original and transfer contexts are highly similar.
Far	Little overlap between situations; original and transfer contexts are dissimilar.
Literal	Intact skill or knowledge transfers to a new task.
Figural	Use of some aspects of general knowledge to think or learn about a problem, such as with analogies or metaphors.
Low road	Transfer of well-established skills in spontaneous and possibly automatic fashion.
High road	Transfer involving abstraction through explicit conscious formulation of connections between situations.
Forward reaching	Abstracting behavior and cognitions from the learning context to one or more potential transfer contexts.
Backward reaching	Abstracting in the transfer context features of the situation that allow for integration with previously learned skills and knowledge.

content in the same format in which it was taught. In contrast, *far transfer* involves a transfer context much different from that in which original learning occurred. An example would be applying fraction skills in an entirely different setting without explicitly being told to do so. Thus, students might have to add parts of a recipe (1/2 cup milk and 1/4 cup water) to determine the amount of liquid without being told the task involves fractions.

Another distinction is between literal and figural transfer. *Literal transfer* involves transfer of an intact skill or knowledge to a new task (Royer, 1986). Literal transfer occurs when students use fraction skills in and out of school. *Figural transfer* refers to using some aspect of our general knowledge to think or learn about a particular problem. Figural transfer often involves using analogies, metaphors, or comparable situations. Figural transfer occurs when students encounter new learning and employ the same study strategies that they used to master prior learning in a related area. Figural transfer requires drawing an analogy between the old and new situations and transferring that general knowledge to the new situation.

Although some overlap exists, the forms of transfer involve different types of knowledge. Near and literal transfer involve primarily declarative knowledge and mastery of basic skills. Far and figurative transfer involve declarative and procedural knowledge, as well as conditional knowledge concerning the types of situations in which the knowledge may prove useful (Royer, 1986).

Salomon and Perkins (1989) distinguish low-road from high-road transfer. *Low-road transfer* refers to transfer of well-established skills in a spontaneous and perhaps automatic fashion. In contrast, *high-road transfer* is abstract and mindful; it "involves the explicit conscious formulation of abstraction in one situation that allows making a connection to another" (Salomon & Perkins, 1989, p. 118).

Low-road transfer occurs with skills and actions that have been practiced extensively in varied contexts. The behaviors tend to become performed automatically in response to characteristics of a situation that are similar to those of the situation in which they were acquired. Examples are learning to drive a car and then driving a different but similar car, brushing one's teeth with different toothbrushes and in different rooms, or solving math problems at school and at home. At times the transfer may occur in almost mindless fashion with little conscious awareness of what one is doing. The level of cognitive activity increases when some aspect of the situation differs and requires attention. Thus, most people have little trouble accommodating to cars they rent from agencies at airports and immediately turn knobs and push levers without reading instruction books. Only when features differ (e.g., the headlight control works differently or is in a different position from what one is used to) do people have to learn the features.

High-road transfer occurs when students learn a rule, principle, prototype, schema, and so forth, and then use it in a more general sense than how they learned it. Transfer is mindful because students do not apply the rule automatically. Rather, they examine the new situation and decide what strategies will be useful to apply. Abstraction is involved during learning and later when students perceive basic elements in the new problem or situation and decide to apply the skill, behavior, or strategy. We might say that low-road transfer primarily involves declarative knowledge and high-road transfer uses productions and conditional knowledge to a greater extent.

Salomon and Perkins (1989) distinguish two types of high-road transfer—forward reaching and backward reaching—according to where the transfer originates. *Forward-reaching transfer* occurs when one abstracts behavior and cognitions from the learning context to one or more potential transfer contexts. For example, while students are studying calculus, they might think about how the material might be pertinent in physics. Another example is while being taught in a class how a parachute works, students might think about how they will use the parachute in actually jumping from an airplane.

Forward-reaching transfer is proactive and requires self-monitoring of potential uses of skills and knowledge. It also requires some knowledge of potential contexts where knowledge might be useful. To determine potential uses of calculus, for example, learners must be familiar with other content knowledge of potential contexts in which knowledge might be useful. To determine potential uses of calculus, learners must be familiar with other content areas. Forward-reaching transfer is unlikely when students have little knowledge about potential transfer domains.

In *backward-reaching transfer*, students abstract in the transfer context features of the situation that allow for integration with previously learned ideas (Salomon & Perkins, 1989). While students are working on a physics problem, they might try to think of any situations in calculus that could be useful for solving the physics problem. Students who have difficulty learning new material employ backward-reaching transfer when they think back to other times when they experienced difficulty and ask what they did in those situations (e.g., seek help from friends, go to the library, reread the text, talk with the teacher). They then might be apt to implement one of those solutions in hopes of remedying their current difficulty.

Earlier we noted that cognitive transfer involves links of information in LTM such that the activation of a piece of information can cue other items. Presumably low-road transfer is characterized by relatively automatic cuing. A central distinction between the two forms is degree of *mindful abstraction,* or the volitional, metacognitively guided employment of nonautomatic processes (Salomon & Perkins, 1989). Mindful application requires that learners not simply act based on the first possible response but rather examine situational cues, define alternative strategies, gather information, and seek new connections between information. LTM cuing is not automatic with high-road transfer but rather deliberate and can result in links being formed in LTM as individuals think of new ways to relate knowledge and contexts.

Anderson, Reder, and Simon (1996) contend that transfer is more likely when learners attend to the cues that signal the appropriateness of using a particular skill. They then will be more apt to notice those cues on transfer tasks and employ the skill. In this sense, the learning and transfer tasks share *symbolic elements*. These shared elements are important in strategy transfer.

Strategy Transfer

Transfer applies to strategies as well as to skills and knowledge (Phye, 2001). An unfortunate finding of much research is that students learn strategies and apply them effectively but fail to maintain their use over time or generalize them beyond the instructional setting. Many factors impede strategy transfer (Borkowski & Cavanaugh, 1979; Paris et al., 1983; Pressley et al., 1990; Schunk, 1991; Schunk & Rice, 1993), including not understanding that the strategy is appropriate for different settings, not understanding how to modify its use with different content, believing that the strategy is not as useful for performance as other factors (e.g., time available), thinking that the strategy takes too much effort, or not having the opportunity to apply the strategy with new material.

Phye (1989, 1990, 1992, 2001; Phye & Sanders, 1992, 1994) developed a model useful for enhancing strategy transfer. During the initial acquisition phase, learners receive instruction and practice to include assessment of their metacognitive awareness of the uses of the strategy. At a later time, a retention phase includes further practice on training materials and recall measures. The third transfer phase occurs when participants attempt to solve new problems that have different surface characteristics but that require the same solution strategy practiced during training. Phye also stressed the role of learner motivation for transfer and ways to enhance motivation by showing learners uses of knowledge.

In one study in which adults worked on verbal analogy problems, some received corrective feedback during trials that consisted of identifying the correct solutions, whereas others were given advice concerning how to solve analogies. All students judged confidence in the correctness of solutions they generated. During training, corrective feedback was superior to advice in promoting transfer of problem-solving skills; however, on a delayed transfer task no difference occurred between conditions.

Regardless of condition, confidence in problem-solving capabilities bore a positive relation to actual performance.

Transfer of problem-solving strategies requires knowledge of the strategy plus conditional knowledge of the uses of the strategy, which is facilitated when learners explain the strategy as they acquire it (Crowley & Siegler, 1999). In addition, feedback about how the strategy helps improve performance facilitates strategy retention and transfer (Phye & Sanders, 1994; Schunk & Swartz, 1993a, 1993b). Phye's work provides a nice link of strategy transfer with information processing theory and highlights the important roles played by practice, corrective feedback, and motivational factors.

Instructional Applications

Although different forms of transfer may be distinct, they often work in concert. While working on a task, some behaviors may transfer automatically whereas others may require mindful application. For example, assume that Jeff is writing a short paper. In thinking through the organization, Jeff might employ high-road, backward-reaching transfer by thinking about how he organized papers in previous similar situations. Many aspects of the task, including word choice and spellings, will occur automatically (low-road transfer). As Jeff writes, he also might think about how this information could prove useful in other settings. Thus, if the paper is on some aspect of the Civil War, Jeff might think of how to use this knowledge in history class. Salomon and Perkins cite another example involving chess masters, who accumulate a repertoire of configurations from years of play. Although some of these may be executed rather automatically, expert play depends on mindfully analyzing play and potential moves. It is strategic and involves high-road transfer.

In some situations, low-road transfer could involve a good degree of mindfulness. With regard to strategy transfer, even minor variations in formats, contexts, or requirements can make transfer problematic among students, especially those who experience learning problems (Borkowski & Cavanaugh, 1979). Conversely, some uses of analogical reasoning can occur with little conscious effort if the analogy is relatively clear. A good rule is never to take transfer for granted; it must be directly addressed.

This raises the issue of how teachers might encourage transfer in students. We know that having students practice skills in varied contexts and ensuring that they understand different uses for knowledge builds links in LTM (Anderson, Reder, & Simon, 1996). Research shows that students do not automatically transfer strategies for the various reasons noted earlier in this chapter. Practice addresses some of these concerns but not others. Cox (1997) recommended that as students learn in many contexts they should determine what they have in common. More complex skills, such as comprehension and problem solving, will probably benefit most from this *situated cognition* approach (Griffin, 1995). Teachers may need to provide students with explicit strategy value feedback that links strategy use with improved performance and provides information about how the strategy will prove useful in that setting. Studies show that such feedback enhances strategy use, academic performance, and self-efficacy for performing well (Schunk & Rice, 1993).

Kathy Stone helps students build on the knowledge they already have learned. Mrs. Stone has her students recall the major points of each page of a story in their reading book before they write a summary paragraph about the story. She also reviews with them how to develop a complete paragraph. Building on former learning helps her children transfer knowledge and skills to a new activity.

In preparing for a class discussion about influential presidents of the United States, Jim Marshall sends a study sheet home with his students asking them to list presidents that they feel had a major impact on American history. He instructs them to not only rely on what has been discussed in class but also on knowledge they have from previous courses or other readings they have done. Mr. Marshall encourages students to pull the information together for the class discussion and incorporate the former learning into the learning that occurs from new material presented.

Establishing academic goals, the attainment of which requires careful deliberation and use of available resources, also should help students. By cuing students at appropriate times, teachers may help them use relevant knowledge in new ways. Teachers might ask a question such as, "What do you know that might help you in this situation?" Such cuing tends to be associated with greater generation of ideas. Especially important is the idea that teachers can serve as models for transfer. Modeling strategies that bring related knowledge to bear on a new situation encourages students to seek ways to enhance transfer in both forward- and backward-reaching fashion and feel more efficacious about doing so. Application 5.5 discusses teaching for transfer.

SELF-REGULATION

Information processing theories have evolved from their original formulations to incorporate self-regulatory processes. This section presents an information processing model of self-regulation and research and applications on learning strategies.

Model of Self-Regulation

Recall that information processing theories view learning as the encoding of information in LTM. Learners activate relevant portions of LTM and relate new knowledge to existing information in WM. Organized, meaningful information is easier to integrate with existing knowledge and more likely to be remembered.

From an information processing perspective, self-regulation is roughly equivalent to *metacognitive awareness* (Gitomer & Glaser, 1987). This awareness includes knowledge of the task (what is to be learned, when and how it is to be learned), as well as self-knowledge of personal capabilities, interests, and attitudes. Self-regulated learning requires learners to have a sound knowledge base comprising task demands, personal qualities, and strategies for completing the task.

Metacognitive awareness also includes procedural knowledge or productions that regulate learning of the material by monitoring one's level of learning, deciding when to take a different task approach, and assessing readiness for a test. Self-regulatory (metacognitive) activities are types of *control processes* (see Chapter 4) under the learner's direction. They facilitate processing and movement of information through the system.

The basic (superordinate) unit of self-regulation may be a *problem-solving production system*, in which the problem is to reach the goal and the monitoring serves to ascertain whether the learner is making progress. This system compares the present situation against a standard and attempts to reduce discrepancies.

An early formulation was Miller, Galanter, and Pribham's (1960) Test-Operate-Test-Exit (TOTE) model. The initial test phase compares the present situation against a standard. If they are the same, no further action is required. If they do not match, control is switched to the operate function to change behavior to resolve the discrepancy. One perceives a new state of affairs that is compared to the standard during the second test phase. Assuming that these match, one exits the model. If they do not match, further behavioral changes and comparisons are necessary.

Let us illustrate with Lisa, who is reading her economics text and stops periodically to summarize what she has read. She recalls information from LTM pertaining to what she has read and compares the information to her internal standard of an adequate summary. This standard also may be a production characterized by rules (e.g., be precise, include information on all topics covered, be certain of accuracy) developed through experiences in summarizing. Assuming that her summary matches her standard, she continues reading. If they do not match, Lisa evaluates where the problem lies (in her understanding of the second paragraph) and executes a correction strategy (rereads the second paragraph).

Information processing models differ, but two common features are comparisons of current activity against standards and steps taken to resolve discrepancies (Carver & Scheier, 1982). A key aspect of these models is knowledge of learning strategies, including their procedures and conditional knowledge of when and why to employ the strategies.

Learning Strategies

Learning strategies are cognitive plans oriented toward successful task performance (Pressley et al., 1990; Weinstein & Mayer, 1986). Strategies include activities such as selecting and organizing information, rehearsing material to be learned, relating new material to information in memory, and enhancing meaningfulness of material. Strategies also include techniques that create and maintain a positive learning climate—for example, ways to overcome test anxiety, enhance self-efficacy, appreciate the value of learning, and develop positive outcome expectations and attitudes (Weinstein & Mayer, 1986). Use of strategies is an integral part of self-regulated learning because strategies give learners better control over information processing (Winne, 2001).

Learning strategies assist encoding in each of its phases. Thus, learners initially attend to relevant task information and transfer it from the sensory register to WM. Learners also activate related knowledge in LTM. In WM, learners build connections (links) between new information and prior knowledge and integrate these links into LTM networks.

Table 5.4 outlines the steps in formulating and implementing a learning strategy. Initially learners analyze an activity or situation in terms of the activity's goal, aspects of the situation relevant to that goal, personal characteristics that seem to be important, and potentially useful self-regulated learning methods. Learners then might develop a strategy or plan along the following lines: "Given this task to be accomplished at this time and place according to these criteria and given these personal characteristics, I should use these procedures to accomplish the goal" (paraphrased from Snowman, 1986). Learners next implement the methods, monitor their goal progress, and modify the strategy when the methods are not producing goal progress. Guiding the implementation of these methods is metacognitive knowledge, which involves knowing that one must carry out the methods, why they are important, and when and how to perform them.

Self-regulated learning methods are specific procedures or techniques included in strategies to attain goals. The categories of learning methods shown in Table 5.4 are

Table 5.4
Steps in constructing and implementing a learning strategy.

Step	Learner Tasks
Analyze	Identify learning goal, important task aspects, relevant personal characteristics, and potentially useful learning techniques.
Plan	Construct plan: "Given this task _____ to be done _____ according to these criteria _____ and given these personal characteristics _____, I should use these techniques _____.
Implement	Employ tactics to enhance learning and memory.
Monitor	Assess goal progress to determine how well tactics are working.
Modify	Continue strategy use if assessment is positive; modify the plan if progress seems inadequate.
Metacognitive Knowledge	Guide operation of steps.

Source: Adapted from J. Snowman, 1986, Learning Tactics and Strategies, in G. D. Phye & T. Andre (Eds.), Cognitive classroom learning: Understanding, thinking, and problem solving (pp. 243–275). Orlando: Academic Press. Reprinted by permission.

interdependent (Weinstein & Mayer, 1986). For example, procedures that elaborate information also often rehearse and organize it. Methods that organize information may relieve one's stress about learning and help one cope with anxiety. Methods are not equally appropriate with all types of tasks. Rehearsal may be the procedure of choice when one must memorize simple facts, but organization is more appropriate for comprehension. The sections that follow discuss different procedures (Application 5.6).

Rehearsal. Repeating information verbatim, underlining, and summarizing are forms of *rehearsal*. Repeating information to oneself—aloud, subvocally (whispering), or covertly—is an effective procedure for tasks requiring rote memorization. For example,

---

APPLICATION 5.6
Learning Methods

Learning methods are useful at all grade levels. An elementary teacher might use rhyming schemes or catchy songs to teach the alphabet (the "ABC Song"). Kathy Stone uses familiar words to assist her third-grade students in learning the directions north, south, east, and west (e.g., the first letters in *west* spell "we").

At the junior or senior high school level, teachers may help students as they study for a unit test. In his history class, Jim Marshall shows students ways to organize material to be studied—the text, class notes, and supplementary readings. He also shows them how to create new notes that integrate material from the various sources. He even demonstrates how to create a time line and incorporate all the related material to provide a sequenced list of events covered in the unit.

In medical school, acronyms and pictures can help students memorize the terminology for parts of the body. When students learn the appropriate drugs to prescribe for various conditions, having them place the names of drugs, their uses, and their side effects into categories may assist with the learning.

Track coaches may help their broad jump and pole vault team members by asking them to close their eyes and slowly visualize every movement their bodies must make to accomplish the jumps. By visualizing their movements, team members can focus on specific positions they need to work on. Executing the actual jump happens so quickly that focusing on what one is doing is difficult, whereas the use of imagery helps to slow the action down.

Gina Brown uses a memory technique with her students to group psychologists who have similar views by developing a catchy phrase or acronym. For instance, when Dr. Brown introduces the major behaviorists she teaches her students: "The (Thorndike) Sisters (Skinner) Won't (Watson) Play (Pavlov) Together (Tolman)." This helps the undergraduates remember these people: They recall the sentence, then add the names.

to learn the names of the 50 state capitals, Janna might say the name of each state followed by the name of its capital. Rehearsal also can help learners memorize lines to a song or poem and learn English translations of foreign-language words.

Rehearsal that rotely repeats information does not link information with what one already knows. Nor does rehearsal organize information in hierarchical or other fashion. As a consequence, LTM does not store rehearsed information in any meaningful sense, and retrieval after some time is often difficult.

Rehearsal can be useful for complex learning, but it must involve more than merely repeating information. One useful rehearsal procedure is *underlining* (*highlighting*). This method, which is popular among high school and college students, improves learning if employed judiciously (Snowman, 1986). When too much material is underlined, underlining loses its effectiveness because less important material is underlined along with more important ideas. Underlined material should represent points most relevant to learning goals.

In *summarizing*—another popular rehearsal procedure—students put into their own words (orally or in writing) the main ideas expressed in the text. As with underlining, summarizing loses its effectiveness if it includes too much information (Snowman, 1986). Limiting the length of students' summaries forces them to identify main ideas.

The *reciprocal teaching* method of Palincsar and Brown (1984) includes summarization as a means for promoting reading comprehension (Chapter 9). Reciprocal teaching is based on Vygotsky's (1978) *zone of proximal development (ZPD)*, or the amount a student can learn given the proper instructional conditions (Chapter 7). Instruction begins with the teacher performing the activity, after which students and teacher perform together. Students gradually assume more responsibility and teach one another.

Palincsar and Brown taught children to summarize, question, clarify, and predict. Children periodically summarized what they read in the passage, asked teacher-type questions about main ideas, clarified unclear portions of text, and predicted what would happen next. Readers should note that these procedures are not unique to reading comprehension instruction; they are good problem-solving methods that can be used with effective results across domains (e.g., science, mathematics, social studies; Calfee & Drum, 1986).

Elaboration.   *Elaboration* procedures (imagery, mnemonics, questioning, and note taking) expand information by adding something to make learning more meaningful. Imagery (Chapter 4) adds a mental picture. Consider the definition of a turnip ("a biennial plant of the mustard family with edible hairy leaves and a roundish, light-colored fleshy root used as a vegetable"). One could memorize this definition through rote rehearsal or elaborate it by looking at a picture of a turnip and forming a mental image to link with the definition.

Mnemonics are popular elaboration methods (Weinstein, 1978). A mnemonic makes information meaningful by relating it to what one knows. Mnemonics take various forms (Table 5.5). *Acronyms* combine the first letters of the material to be remembered into a meaningful word. "HOMES" is an acronym for the five Great

Table 5.5
Learning methods.

Category	Types
Rehearsal	Repeating information verbatim
	Underlining
	Summarizing
Elaboration	Using imagery
	Using mnemonics: acronym, sentence, narrative story, pegword, method of loci, keyword
	Questioning
	Note taking
Organization	Using mnemonics
	Grouping
	Outlining
	Mapping
Comprehension Monitoring	Self-questioning
	Rereading
	Checking consistencies
	Paraphrasing
Affective	Coping with anxiety
	Holding positive beliefs: self-efficacy, outcome expectations, attitudes
	Creating a positive environment
	Managing time

Source: C. E. Weinstein & R. E. Mayer, 1986, The teaching of learning strategies, in M. C. Wittrock (Ed.), *Handbook of research on teaching* (3rd ed., pp. 315–327). New York: MacMillan. Reprinted by permission.

Lakes (Huron, Ontario, Michigan, Erie, Superior); "ROY G. BIV" for the colors of the spectrum (Red, Orange, Yellow, Green, Blue, Indigo, Violet). *Sentence mnemonics* use the first letters of the material to be learned as the first letters of words in a sentence. For example, "Every Good Boy Does Fine" is a sentence mnemonic for the notes on the treble clef staff (E, G, B, D, F), and "My Very Educated Mother Just Served Us Nine Pizzas" for the order of the planets from the sun (Mercury, Venus, Earth, Mars, Jupiter, Saturn, Uranus, Neptune, Pluto).

Also possible is combining material to be remembered into a *paragraph* or *narrative story.* This type of mnemonic might be useful when long lists have to be remembered (e.g., 50 state capitals). Student-generated acronyms, sentences, and stories are as effective as those supplied by others (Snowman, 1986).

The *pegword method* requires that learners first memorize a set of objects rhyming with integer names; for example, one-bun, two-shoe, three-tree, four-door, five-hive, six-sticks, seven-heaven, eight-gate, nine-wine, ten-hen. Then the learner generates an image of each item to be learned and links it with the corresponding object image. Thus, if Joan needs to buy some items at the grocery store (butter, milk, apples), she might imagine a buttered bun, milk in a shoe, and apples growing on a tree. To recall the shopping list, she recalls the rhyming scheme and its paired associates. Successful use of this technique requires that learners first learn the rhyming scheme.

To use the *method of loci*, learners imagine a familiar scene, such as a room in their house, after which they take a mental walk around the room and stop at each prominent object. Each new item to be learned is paired mentally with one object in the room. Assuming that the room contains (in order) a table, a lamp, and a television, and using the previous grocery list example, Joan might first imagine butter on the table, a milky-colored lamp, and apples on top of the television. To recall the grocery list, she mentally retraces the path around the room and recalls the appropriate object at each stop.

Atkinson and his colleagues developed the *keyword method* for learning foreign language vocabulary words (Atkinson, 1975; Atkinson & Raugh, 1975). For example, *pato* (pronounced "pot-o") is a Spanish word meaning "duck." Learners initially think of an English word (*pot*) that sounds like the foreign word (*pato*). Then they link an image of a pot with the English translation of the foreign word ("duck"); for example, a duck with a pot on its head. When the learners encounter *pato*, they recall the image of a duck with a pot on its head. Although the keyword method has been employed effectively with various types of academic content (Pressley, Levin, & Delaney, 1982), its success with young children often requires supplying them with the keyword and the picture incorporating the keyword and its English translation.

Mnemonic techniques incorporate several valid learning principles including rehearsal and relating new information to prior knowledge. Informal evidence indicates that most students have favorite memorization techniques, many of which employ mnemonics. Experiments that compare recall of students instructed in a mnemonic with recall of students not given a memory technique generally indicate that learning benefits from mnemonics instruction (Weinstein, 1978). Students must understand how to use the technique, which generally entails instruction.

Elaboration methods also are useful with complex learning tasks. Another technique is *questioning*, which requires that learners stop periodically as they read text and ask themselves questions. To address higher-order learning outcomes, learners might ask, "How does this information relate to what the author discussed in the preceding section?" (synthesis) or, "How can this idea be applied in a school setting?" (application).

Intuitively one might assume that questioning should improve comprehension, but research has not yielded strong support for this correlation (Snowman, 1986). To be effective, questions must reflect the types of desired learning outcomes. Questioning will not aid comprehension if questions address low-level, factual knowledge. Unfortunately, most research studies have used relatively brief passages of fewer than 1,500 words. With older students, questioning is most useful with longer passages. Among elementary children, rereading or reviewing (rehearsing) material is equally effective. This may be due to children's limited knowledge of how to construct good questions.

Note taking, another elaboration technique, requires learners to construct meaningful paraphrases of the most important ideas expressed in text. Note taking is similar to summarizing except that the former is not limited to immediately available information. While taking notes, students might integrate new textual material with other information in personally meaningful ways. To be effective, notes must not reflect verbatim textual information. Rotely copying material is a form of rehearsal and may improve recall, but it is not elaboration. The intent of note taking is to elaborate (integrate and apply) information. Students generally need instruction in how to take good notes for this method to be effective. Note taking works best when the notes include content highly relevant to the learning goals.

Organization.   The different types of organization techniques are mnemonics, grouping, outlining, and mapping. Mnemonics elaborate information and organize it in meaningful fashion. Acronyms, for example, organize information into a meaningful word. Information can be organized by grouping it before using rehearsal or mnemonics. If students are learning various mammal names, for instance, they might first group the names into common families (apes, cats, etc.) and then rehearse or use a mnemonic. Organization imposed by learners is an effective aid to recall; learners first recall the organizational scheme and then the individual components (Weinstein & Mayer, 1986).

Organization techniques are useful with complex material. A popular one is *outlining*, which requires that learners establish headings. Outlining improves comprehension, but as with other learning methods, students usually require instruction in how to construct a good outline. One way to teach outlining is to use a text with headings that are set off from the text or that appear in the margins, along with embedded (**boldface** or *italic*) headings interspersed throughout the text. Another way is to have students identify topic sentences and points that relate to each sentence. Simply telling students to outline a passage does not facilitate learning if students do not understand the procedure.

Mapping is an organizational technique that improves learners' awareness of text structure. Mapping involves identifying important ideas and specifying their interrelationship. Concepts or ideas are identified, categorized, and related to one another. The exact nature of the map varies depending on the content and types of relationships to be specified. The following steps are useful in teaching mapping:

- Discuss how different sentences in a paragraph relate to one another by giving the categories into which sentences will fit: main idea, example, comparison/contrast, temporal relationship, and inference.
- Model the application of this categorization with sample paragraphs.
- Give students guided practice on categorizing sentences and on explaining the reasons for their choices.

■ Have students practice independently on paragraphs. Once students acquire these basic skills, more complex textual material can be used (multiple paragraphs, short sections of stories or chapters) with new categories introduced as needed (e.g., transition; McNeil, 1987).

A *map* is conceptually akin to a *propositional network* because mapping involves creating a hierarchy, with main ideas or superordinate concepts listed at the top, followed by supporting points, examples, and subordinate concepts. Branching off from the main hierarchy are lines to related points, such as might be used if a concept is being contrasted with related concepts. Figure 5.2 shows a sample map.

Research indicates differential effectiveness for mapping as a means of improving comprehension (Snowman, 1986). The skill to discern some relationships is learned easily (main idea-example) and that to discern others is more difficult to acquire (cause-effect). Students often have difficulty linking ideas between sections or paragraphs. In teaching students to construct maps, having them first map each section or paragraph separately and then link the maps is helpful. Mapping is especially effective with students who experience difficulty integrating ideas (Holley, Dansereau, McDonald, Garland, & Collins, 1979).

Comprehension Monitoring. *Comprehension monitoring* helps learners determine whether they are properly applying declarative and procedural knowledge to material to be learned, evaluate whether they understand the material, decide whether their strategy is effective or whether a better strategy is needed, and know why strategy use

Figure 5.2
Cognitive map for "city."

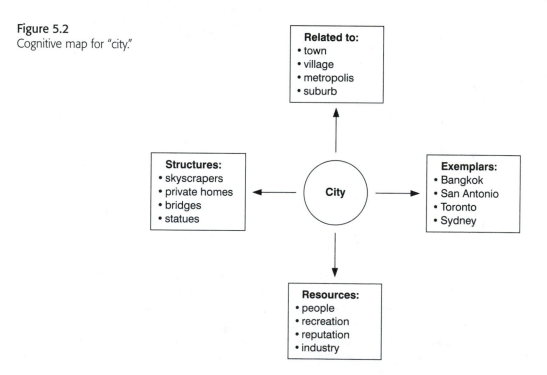

will improve learning. Teaching students comprehension monitoring is a central component of strategy-instruction programs (Baker & Brown, 1984; Borkowski & Cavanaugh, 1979; Paris et al., 1983). *Self-questioning*, *rereading*, *checking consistencies*, and *paraphrasing* are monitoring processes.

Some textual material periodically provides students with questions about content. Students who answer these questions as they read the material are engaging in self-questioning. When questions are not provided, students need to generate their own. As a means of training students to ask questions, teachers can instruct students to stop periodically while reading and ask themselves a series of questions (i.e., who, what, when, where, why, how).

Rereading is often accomplished in conjunction with self-questioning; when students cannot answer questions about the text or otherwise doubt their understanding, these cues prompt them to reread. Checking for consistencies involves determining whether the text is internally consistent; that is, whether parts of the text contradict others and whether conclusions that are drawn follow from what has been discussed. A belief that textual material is inconsistent serves as a cue for rereading to determine whether the author is inconsistent or whether the reader has failed to comprehend the content. Students who periodically stop and paraphrase material are checking their level of understanding. Being able to paraphrase is a cue that rereading is unnecessary (Paris & Oka, 1986).

A useful method to teach comprehension monitoring is Meichenbaum's (1986) *self-instructional training* (see Chapter 3). Cognitive modeling portrays a systematic approach to comprehension along with statements to self-check understanding and take corrective action as necessary. While presenting comprehension instruction to remedial readers, a teacher might verbalize the following (Meichenbaum & Asarnow, 1979):

> Well, I've learned three big things to keep in mind before I read a story and while I read it. One is to ask myself what the main idea of the story is. What is the story about? A second is to learn important details of the story as I go along. The order of the main events or their sequence is an especially important detail. A third is to know how the characters feel and why. So, get the main idea. Watch sequences. And learn how the characters feel and why. (p. 17)

Students learn to verbalize such statements and gradually fade them to a covert level. To remind learners what to think about, teachers might display key ideas on a poster board (e.g., get the main idea, watch sequences, learn how the characters feel and why).

Affective Techniques.   *Affective techniques* create a favorable psychological climate for learning (Weinstein & Mayer, 1986). These methods help one cope with anxiety, develop positive beliefs (self-efficacy, outcome expectations, attitudes), set goals, establish a regular time and place for studying, and minimize distractions (setting such rules as no talking on the phone and no watching television).

Affective techniques help learners focus and maintain attention on important task aspects, manage time effectively, and minimize anxiety. *Self-verbalization* helps keep students' attention on the academic task. At the outset of an academic activity, students might think to themselves, "This might be tough. I need to pay close attention to the teacher." If they notice their attention is waning, they might think, "Stop thinking about _____. I need to concentrate on what the teacher is saying."

Goal setting is an effective time-management strategy (Chapter 3). Learners who set overall learning goals and subdivide them into short-term goals are self-regulating their efforts by evaluating goal progress. In goal setting, students set time limits for accomplishing subgoals. The belief that they are making progress instills in them self-efficacy for learning (Schunk, 1989).

Anxiety about tests, grades, and failure interferes with learning. Students who ruminate about potential failure waste time and strengthen doubts about their capabilities. Anxiety-reduction programs employ systematic desensitization, modeling, and guided self-talk. Models verbalize positive achievement beliefs (e.g., "I know that if I work hard, I can do well on the test") rather than dysfunctional beliefs (e.g., "I can't pass the test"). Coping models, who initially are anxious but use effective self-regulated learning methods and persist until they perform better, are important therapeutic agents of change (Schunk, 1987).

For students who have difficulties taking tests, a specific program to teach test-taking skills may prove beneficial (Kirkland & Hollandsworth, 1980). These programs typically teach students to subdivide the test, establish time limits for each part, and not spend too long on any one question. To conquer negative thoughts while taking a test, students are taught relaxation techniques and ways to refocus attention on test items. Test performance and beliefs exert reciprocal effects. Experiencing some test success creates a sense of self-efficacy for performing well, which leads to more productive studying and better performance.

Critique of Strategy Instruction

The research literature on strategy instruction has expanded dramatically in recent years. Hattie, Biggs, and Purdie (1996) conducted an extensive review of interventions aimed at improving student learning. They concluded that most interventions were effective, and they obtained evidence for near transfer. When transfer is a goal, it is imperative that students understand the conditions under which the strategy is effective. The best self-regulated strategy instruction programs are those that are integrated with academic content and implemented in classrooms that support students' self-regulated learning (Butler, 1998a, 1998b; Perry, 1998; Winne, 2001).

As with other aspects of learning, strategy instruction is most effective when the methods are meaningful to students and they perceive them as valuable to use. The research literature contains many examples of strategy-instruction programs with immediate effects that did not endure over time or transfer beyond the learning context (Borkowski & Cavanaugh, 1979; Borkowski, Johnston, & Reid, 1987).

Pressley and his colleagues (Harris & Pressley, 1991; Pressley, Harris, & Marks, 1992; Pressley et al., 1990) argue that several factors should be taken into account when designing and implementing strategy-instruction programs. Strategies should not be foisted on students; teaching strategies in the hope that students will realize their benefits and use them is preferable. As Pressley and McCormick (1995) contend:

> Good strategy instruction sends the message that students can control how they do academically, with much gained by creatively applying the cognitive strategies that are taught to them. Good strategy instruction encourages student reflection, permitting powerful tools for reflective "meaning-getting" from texts, creation of reflective stances via writing, and reflective decision making about whether and how to use strategies they know to tackle new situations. (p. 515)

Strategy instruction is likely to be most effective when the constructivist nature of the acquisition and use of strategies is stressed (Goldin-Meadow et al., 1993). (We discuss constructivism in Chapter 7.) A key point is that students are motivated to construct understanding from inputs they receive. Good teaching complements this process because it provides rich inputs and the context for constructions to take place.

Pressley et al. (1992) highlight several recommended steps to follow in strategy instruction (Table 5.6). *Introducing a few strategies at a time* does not overload students, and the strategies can be coalesced into a large package to show how they interrelate. The advantage of *providing distributed practice on diverse tasks* is to facilitate transfer and maintenance. The importance of *teachers as models* cannot be underestimated, and we must remember that the modeling is rule governed; students learn strategies and how to modify them rather than rotely copying the model's actions (Rosenthal & Zimmerman, 1978). *Stressing the value of strategies* to students is necessary to encourage greater strategy use. Teachers can enhance perceived value with feedback showing how strategy use improves performance.

The importance of *feedback and personal teaching* is highlighted; teachers tailor feedback to individual student needs and teachers and students collaborate to work out understandings of strategies. Teachers and students also must *determine opportunities for transfer* through discussions, prompts to students, and opportunities to practice adapting strategies to new tasks. *Sustaining student motivation*, especially by

Table 5.6
Steps to follow in strategy instruction.

- Introduce a few strategies at a time
- Provide distributed practice on diverse tasks
- Have teachers serve as models
- Stress to students the value of strategy use
- Personalize feedback and teaching
- Determine opportunities for transfer
- Sustain student motivation
- Encourage habitual reflection and planning

Source: M. Pressley, K. R. Harris, & M. B. Marks, 1992, But good strategy instructors are constructivists! *Educational Psychology Review, 4*, pp. 10–11. Reprinted by permission.

highlighting empowerment that accompanies strategy learning, is necessary. Finally, teachers encourage *habitual reflection and planning*. They model reflection, provide opportunities for students to think through problems, and create an environment that values reflection more than simply completing assignments or arriving at correct answers.

Academic Studying

Much research has examined students' self-regulated learning during academic studying (Zimmerman, 1998). Many students have problems with studying, and research has revealed several weak areas (Weinstein & Palmer, 1990; Weinstein, Palmer, & Schulte, 1987). Materials increasingly are being published that help students develop better study habits (Kiewra & Dubois, 1998; Weinstein & Hume, 1998; Zimmerman et al., 1996), and courses are being integrated with content to assist students with self-regulated studying (Hofer, Yu, & Pintrich, 1998; Lan, 1998). The following section covers strategy instruction and time management.

Strategy Instruction.　Research has investigated how strategy instruction affects academic studying. Dansereau and his colleagues developed a strategy instruction program for college students (Dansereau, 1978; Dansereau, McDonald, Collins, Garland, Holley, Diekhoff, & Evans, 1979). The authors distinguished *primary strategies*, or those applied directly to the content, from *support strategies* that learners use to create and maintain a favorable psychological climate for learning. The latter include affective techniques and those used to monitor and correct ongoing primary strategies.

Effective studying requires that students comprehend, retain, retrieve, and use information. These are the primary elements of the Survey-Question-Read-Recite (Recall)-Review (SQ3R) method (Robinson, 1946), later modified to the SQ4R method with the addition of Reflection. When students use the SQ3R method, they first survey a text chapter by reading headings and boldface (or italics) print, after which they develop questions. Learners then read the text while keeping the questions in mind. After reading, students close the book and recall what they have read. They then open the book and review the material.

In Dansereau's program, students comprehend material by highlighting important ideas, recall material without referring to text, digest and expand the information, and review it. Expanding information means relating it to other information in LTM by creating links between memory networks. Students learn to ask themselves questions similar to the following: "Imagine you could talk to the author. What questions would you ask? What criticisms would you raise?", "How can the material be applied?", and "How could you make the material more understandable and interesting to other students?"

Dansereau's learning-strategy program moves beyond the SQ3R method because it includes support strategies such as goal setting, concentration management, and monitoring and diagnosing. Students learn to set daily, weekly, and longer-term goals by establishing schedules in a workbook. Learners monitor progress and adjust their work or goals as necessary if their performance does not match expectations. *Concentration management* is developed by helping students deal with frustration, anxiety, and anger. Use of *self-talk* is encouraged, and students can be *desensitized* by imagining anxiety-provoking situations when relaxing. *Monitoring* and *diagnosing* require that students determine in advance where they will stop in the text to assess their level of comprehension. As they reach each stop point, they *assess understanding* and *take corrective action* (e.g., rereading) as needed. Evaluations of the strategy-instructional program have shown that it improves academic behaviors and attitudes (Dansereau et al., 1979).

Dansereau (1988) modified this program for use in cooperative learning dyads. Each member of the pair took turns reading approximately 500 words of a 2,500-word passage. One member then served as recaller and orally summarized what was read; the other listened, corrected errors in recall, and elaborated knowledge by adding imagery and links to prior knowledge. Dansereau reported that this cooperative arrangement facilitated learning and transfer better than individual studying.

Strategic Use of Time.   Investigators from different theoretical traditions (e.g., social cognitive, information processing) increasingly are focusing on cognitive and behavioral processes students use to plan and manage academic learning time (Winne, 2001; Zimmerman, Greenberg, & Weinstein, 1994). Effective time management contributes to learning and achievement. Britton and Tesser (1991) found that the time management components of short-range planning and time attitudes were significant predictors of grade point average among college students. Effective use of time appears to be partly a function of use of goal setting and planning (Weinstein & Mayer, 1986). These procedures, in turn, prompt students to engage in other self-regulatory activities such as self-monitoring of progress. As noted earlier, time itself is an important dimension of self-regulation and can even be a performance outcome (e.g., how much time will I devote to this task?).

Various theories have been advanced to account for students' use of time (Zimmerman et al., 1994). In a social cognitive framework of triadic reciprocality, time use is assumed to depend on behavioral and environmental factors, along with personal learning strategies (Zimmerman, 1989). Behavioral influences include efforts to self-observe, self-evaluate, and self-react to performance outcomes. Environmental factors comprise use of planning aids such as watches, alarms, and appointment books. Personal influences involve goal setting, self-efficacy, attributions, and perceptions of strategy importance. Poor time management may reflect deficiencies in one or more of these areas.

Much research attests to the importance of these factors in effective studying (Zimmerman, 1998; Zimmerman et al., 1994). In addition, a growing body of research shows that students can learn to manage time more effectively. Weinstein et al. (1987) include time management as one of the areas of the Learning and Study Strategies Inventory (LASSI), a diagnostic and prescriptive self-report measure of strategic, goal-directed learning for students that focuses on thoughts, attitudes, beliefs, and behaviors that are related to academic success and can be altered. Completion of the LASSI or a similar instrument usually is necessary to ascertain the extent of a student's study problems.

Programs to facilitate better use of time typically include instruction and practice on topics such as becoming a strategic learner; the roles of goal setting and self-management; time-management planning; various study strategies including note taking, listening, underlining, summarizing, and coping with stress; test-taking strategies; and organizing a setting for learning.

One problem with study time is that students often do not realize how they really spend their time. A good assignment is to have students keep a time log for a week to show how much time they devoted to each task. Often they are surprised at how much time they wasted. Instruction must address ways to eliminate or reduce such waste.

Another common problem is failing to understand how long tasks take to complete. A student once informed me that she thought she would need about two hours to read eight chapters in her educational psychology textbook! A useful exercise is to have students estimate the amount of time various tasks will take and then to keep a log of the actual times and record these with the estimates to determine their accuracy.

Many times students need a change in work environment. Too often they try to study in places with distractions such as friends, telephones, televisions, refrigerators, stoves, video and audio equipment, and so forth. Some students may benefit from light music or noise in the background but almost everyone has difficulty concentrating when many potential distractions are present. Students should complete an inventory of study preferences and present study conditions to determine whether changes are necessary.

SUMMARY

Cognitive learning theories explain learning in terms of changes in cognitive processes. Elements of information processing apply to basic forms of learning but they assume greater significance in complex learning and in content-area learning (Chapter 9). This chapter covers theories and topics relevant to learning involving the operation of complex cognitive processes.

Conditional knowledge is knowing when and why to employ declarative and procedural knowledge. Simply knowing what to do and how to do it do not produce success. Students also must understand when knowledge and procedures are useful. Conditional knowledge most likely is stored in LTM as propositions linked with other declarative and procedural knowledge. Metacognition refers to deliberate, conscious control of mental activities. Metacognition includes knowledge and monitoring activities designed to ensure that tasks are completed successfully. Metacognition begins to develop around ages 5 to 7 and continues throughout schooling. One's metacognitive awareness depends on task, strategy, and learner variables. Even when learners are capable of monitoring task performances, they do not always do so. Educators have suggested that learners benefit from explicit instruction on metacognitive activities.

Concept learning involves higher-order processes of forming mental representations of critical attributes of categories. Current theories of concept learning emphasize analyzing features and forming hypotheses about concepts (feature analysis) as well as forming generalized images of concepts that include only some defining features (prototypes). Prototypes may be used to classify typical instances of concepts and feature analysis may be used for less typical ones. Models of concept acquisition and teaching have been proposed, and motivational processes also are involved in conceptual change.

A problem exists when one is trying to reach a goal but lacks a means for attaining it. Problem solving consists of an initial state, a goal, subgoals, and operations performed to attain the goal and subgoals. Current research examines the mental processes of learners engaged in problem solving and the different ways these processes operate in experts and novices. Problem solving has been viewed as reflecting trial and error, insight, and heuristics. These general approaches can be applied to academic content. As people gain experience in a domain, they acquire knowledge and production systems, or sets of rules to apply strategically to accomplish goals. Problem solving requires that one form a mental representation of the problem and apply a production to solve it. With well-defined problems and potential solutions that can be ordered in terms of likelihood, a generate-and-test strategy is useful. For more difficult or less well-defined problems, means-ends analysis is used, which requires establishing subgoals by working backward from the goal to the initial state or working forward from the initial state to the goal. Other problem-solving strategies involve analogies and brainstorming.

Research reveals many differences between experts and novices. Experts possess more domain-specific knowledge organized to reflect the underlying structure of the content. Experts form a more accurate problem representation and usually work forward. Novices often adopt a working backward strategy. Experts and novices do not differ much in their knowledge of problem-solving strategies.

Current cognitive conceptions highlight the complexity of transfer. Historical views of transfer include identical elements, mental discipline, and generalization. From a cognitive perspective, transfer involves activation of memory structures and occurs when information is linked. Distinctions are drawn between near and far, literal and figural, and low-road and high-road transfer. Some forms of transfer may occur automatically, but much is conscious and involves abstraction. Providing students with feedback on the usefulness of skills and strategies makes transfer more likely to occur.

From an information processing perspective, self-regulation is similar to metacognitive awareness, which includes task and personal knowledge. Self-regulated learning requires that learners understand task demands, their personal qualities, and strategies for completing the task. Metacognitive awareness also includes procedural knowledge, which helps one regulate learning of material, monitor level of learning, indicate when to take a different task approach, and assess test readiness. The basic (superordinate) unit of self-regulation may be a problem-solving production system in which the problem is to reach the goal and the monitoring checks each step to ascertain whether the learner is making progress. This system compares a present situation against a standard and attempts to reduce discrepancies.

Learning strategies are plans oriented toward successful academic performance. Strategies include activities such as selecting and organizing information, rehearsing material to be learned, relating new material to information in memory, enhancing the meaningfulness of material, and creating and maintaining a positive learning climate (ways to overcome test anxiety and enhance self-efficacy, outcome expectations, and attitudes). To construct a learning strategy, learners analyze the situation and their personal characteristics, devise a plan to accomplish the learning goal, implement the plan, monitor progress, and modify the plan as necessary. Metacognitive knowledge guides the operation of these steps. Learners select methods they believe will help them attain goals, such as rehearsal, elaboration, organization, comprehension monitoring, and affective techniques.

Simply knowing how to use strategies does not guarantee students will use them when not required to do so. An effective constructivist approach is for teachers and students to assist in formulating effective strategies for learning. Strategy instruction often is incorporated in programs designed to enhance academic studying and time management. Regardless of the domain, an important aspect is providing students with strategy value information linking improved performance with strategy use.

Cognition and Instruction

This chapter discusses instructional processes from a cognitive perspective. Instructional theory and research have changed dramatically in the last few years. Historically researchers examined topics such as behavioral objectives and programmed learning (Chapter 2). As the influence of behaviorism declined, researchers began to study the impact of learner, instructional, and contextual variables on one another and on learning in educational settings. Current instructional research investigates topics such as the influence of instructional variables on learners' cognitions, the role of individual differences in learning, and the interrelation of instructional and motivational variables during learning (Glaser, 1990). As technology becomes increasingly infused in instruction, researchers are examining how technological applications affect the design and delivery of instruction, the interactions among teachers and learners, and the ways that learners think about content, learning environments, and themselves (Jonassen, Peck, & Wilson, 1999).

This chapter builds on the preceding two. In Chapter 4 the components of cognitive information processing were discussed: attention, perception, encoding, memory, retrieval, and forgetting. Chapter 5 covered cognitive processes directly involved in learning: metacognition, concepts, problem solving, and transfer. Now we examine theories and models of instruction and instructional research that include cognitive processes.

The chapter begins by reviewing two cognitive perspectives that have been widely applied in classrooms: discovery learning and meaningful reception learning. These perspectives are historical in the sense that they preceded the cognitive viewpoints currently favored in education; they are, however, still much in vogue today.

We then review the instructional theory of Robert Gagné, which is one of the best known and most commonly applied. We see how Gagné's conditions of learning capture many learning principles discussed throughout this text. Following this section, some other instructional models are presented, along with their implications for teaching and learning. The remaining sections of the chapter address instruction with worked examples, research on teaching, learner characteristics, and technology and instruction.

The field of instructional technology has expanded greatly in recent years, and each advance in technology raises a question of how it affects learning. Technology is not a theory, nor is it necessarily cognitive in orientation; programmed instruction (Chapter 2) is a behavioral method that employs technology. Nonetheless, most researchers exploring technology in education hold a cognitive perspective and attempt to explain learning in terms of cognitive information processing. Readers interested in instructional design and implications for learning should consult sources that discuss these topics in greater depth (Ertmer & Newby, 1993; Grabe & Grabe, 1998a; Jonassen, 1996; Winn, 1990).

Chapter 1 included a section on the relation of learning and instruction, which stated that different theoretical perspectives on instruction share certain commonalities (see Table 1.4):

- Learners progress through stages or phases.
- Material should be organized and presented in small steps.
- Learners require practice, feedback, and review.
- Social models facilitate learning and motivation.
- Motivational and contextual factors influence learning.

Theories differ in the amount of emphasis they place on each of these, but the assumptions and principles of instructional theories address each point to some degree. Furthermore, each point is both intuitively plausible and substantiated by research.

When you finish studying this chapter, you should be able to do the following:

- Compare and contrast discovery learning and meaningful reception learning.

- Explain the major components of Gagné's instructional theory: learning outcomes, events, hierarchies, and phases.
- Describe the major assumptions and principles of Carroll's time model, mastery learning, inquiry teaching, and the Instructional Quality Profile.
- Explain the effects of worked examples on cognitive processing and discuss features of worked examples that promote learning.
- Summarize what research has identified as effective teacher practices in planning and instruction.
- Define "aptitude-treatment interaction" and explain how these interactions are important for learning.
- Describe some cognitive styles of learners and what they imply for instruction.
- Discuss the major functions of technology and some ways that technology has been infused into instruction.

DISCOVERY LEARNING

The Process of Discovery

Discovery learning refers to obtaining knowledge for oneself (Bruner, 1961). Discovery is important for cognitive learning—especially of complex forms—because it involves formulating and testing hypotheses rather than simply reading or listening to teacher presentations. Discovery is a type of *inductive reasoning,* because students move from studying specific examples to formulating general rules, concepts, and principles.

Discovery is a form of problem solving (Klahr & Simon, 1999; see Chapter 5); it is not simply letting students do what they want. Discovery is best handled as a "directed" activity: Teachers arrange activities in which students search, manipulate, explore, and investigate. Students learn new knowledge relevant to the domain and such general problem-solving skills as formulating rules, testing hypotheses, and gathering information (Bruner, 1961):

> Let it be clear what the act of discovery entails. It is rarely . . . that new facts are "discovered" in the sense of being encountered as Newton suggested in the form of islands of truth in an uncharted sea of ignorance. Or if they appear to be discovered in this way, it is almost always thanks to some happy hypotheses about where to

navigate. Discovery, like surprise, favors the well prepared mind. . . . Discovery, whether by a schoolboy going it on his own or by a scientist cultivating the growing edge of his field, is in its essence a matter of rearranging or transforming evidence in such a way that one is enabled to go beyond the evidence so reassembled to additional new insights. (p. 22)

Bruner's advice contradicts the notion that great discoveries are not planned or predicted but rather are accidents that happen to lucky people. Bruner's point is supported by how Pasteur developed the cholera vaccine (Root-Bernstein, 1988). Pasteur went on vacation during the summer of 1879. He had been conducting research on chicken cholera and left out germ cultures when he departed for 2 months.

Upon his return, he found that the cultures, though still active, had become avirulent; they no longer could sicken a chicken. So he developed a new set of cultures from a natural outbreak of the disease and resumed his work. Yet he found . . . that the hens he had exposed to the weakened germ culture still failed to develop cholera. Only then did it dawn on Pasteur that he had inadvertently immunized them. (p. 26)

The process of discovery often is contrasted with scientific inquiry, which relies on the use of logic and rational examination rather than being in the right place at the right time. In fact, much historical evidence reveals that discoveries typically are not flukes but rather a natural (albeit possibly unforeseen) consequence of a logical line of inquiry by the discoverer. Discoverers are not happy recipients of good fortune but rather cultivate it by expecting the unexpected. Pasteur did not leave the germ cultures unattended but rather in the care of his collaborator, Roux. When Pasteur returned from vacation, he inoculated chickens with the germs and they did not become sick.

But when the same chickens were later injected with a more virulent strain, they died. No discovery here . . . Pasteur did not even initiate his first successful enfeeblement experiment until a few months later. . . . He and Roux had tried to enfeeble the germs by passing them from one animal to another, by growing them in different media . . . and only after many such attempts did one of the experiments succeed. . . . For some time, the strains that failed to kill chickens were also too weak to immunize them. But by March of 1880, Pasteur had developed two cultures with the properties of vaccines. The trick . . . was to use a mildly acidic medium, not a strong one, and to leave the germ culture sitting in it for a long time. Thus, he produced an attenuated organism capable of inducing an immune response in chickens. The discovery . . . was not an accident at all; Pasteur had posed a question—Is it possible to immunize an animal with a weakened infectious agent?—and then systematically searched for the answer. (Root-Bernstein, 1988, p. 29)

This scenario supports the idea that discoveries may happen by chance but the discoverer often creates those circumstances. Most discoveries are not lucky occurrences. Students require background preparation (the well-prepared mind requires declarative, procedural, and conditional knowledge). Once students possess prerequisite knowledge, careful structuring of material allows them to discover important principles.

Teaching for Discovery

Teaching for discovery requires presenting questions, problems, or puzzling situations to resolve and encouraging learners to make intuitive guesses when they are uncertain. In leading a class discussion, teachers could ask questions that have no readily available answers and tell students that their answers will not be graded. Discoveries are not limited to activities within school. During a unit on ecology, students could discover why animals of a given species live in certain areas and not in others. Students might seek answers in classroom work stations, in the school media center, and on or off the school grounds. Teachers provide structure by posing questions and giving suggestions on how to search for answers. Greater teacher structure is beneficial when students are not familiar with the discovery procedure or require extensive background knowledge. Discovery actually can impede learning when students have no prior experience with the material or background information (Tuovinen & Sweller, 1999). Classroom examples of discovery learning are given in Application 6.1.

Teaching for discovery learning may not be appropriate with well-structured content that is easily presented. Students could discover which historical events occurred

---

APPLICATION 6.1
Discovery Learning

Learning becomes more meaningful when students explore their learning environments rather than listen passively to teachers. Kathy Stone uses guided discovery to help her third-grade children learn animal groups (e.g., mammals, birds, reptiles). Rather than providing students with the basic animal groups and examples for each, she asks students to provide the names of types of animals. Then she helps students classify the animals by examining their similarities and differences. Category labels are assigned once classifications are made. This approach is guided to ensure that classifications are proper, but students are active contributors as they discover the similarities and differences among animals

A high school chemistry teacher might use "mystery" liquids and have students discover the elements in each. The students could proceed through a series of experiments designed to determine if certain substances are present in a sample. By using the experimental process, students learn about the reactions of various substances to certain chemicals and also how to determine the contents of their mystery substance.

Gina Brown creates three different classroom scenarios that describe situations involving student learning and behaviors as well as teacher actions. Dr. Brown divides her educational psychology students into pairs and asks them to work through each scenario and discover which learning theories best describe the situations presented.

in which years, but this is trivial learning. If they arrived at the wrong answers, time would be wasted in reteaching the content. Discovery seems more appropriate when the learning process is important, such as with problem-solving activities that motivate students to learn and acquire the requisite skills. There are some drawbacks. Establishing discovery situations (e.g., growing plants) often takes time, and experiments might not work. Types of discovery learning situations that occur commonly in schools are role playing, independent or group projects, and computer simulations.

MEANINGFUL RECEPTION LEARNING

Meaningfulness and Expository Teaching

David Ausubel (1963, 1968; Ausubel & Robinson, 1969) developed a cognitive theory of *meaningful reception learning*. According to Ausubel (1968):

> The acquisition of subject-matter knowledge is primarily a manifestation of reception learning. That is, the principal content of what is to be learned is typically presented to the learner in more or less final form. Under these circumstances, the learner is simply required to comprehend the material and to incorporate it into his cognitive structure so that it is available for either reproduction, related learning, or problem solving at some future date. (p. 83)

Ausubel advocated using *expository teaching*, presenting information to students in an organized, meaningful fashion. The notion of expository teaching often is misunderstood:

> Few pedagogic devices in our time have been repudiated more unequivocally by educational theorists than the method of expository verbal instruction. It is fashionable in many quarters to characterize verbal learning as parrot-like recitation and rote memorization of isolated facts, and to dismiss it disdainfully as an archaic remnant of discredited educational tradition. (Ausubel, 1968, pp. 83–84)

The primary type of learning that occurs in classrooms differs fundamentally from associative and paired-associate learning. *Meaningful learning* refers to the learning of ideas, concepts, and principles by relating new information to knowledge in memory (Ausubel, 1977; Faw & Waller, 1976). Learning is meaningful when new material bears a systematic relation to relevant concepts in LTM; that is, new material expands, modifies, or elaborates information in memory. Meaningfulness also depends on personal variables such as age, background experiences, socioeconomic status, and educational background. Prior experiences determine whether students find learning meaningful.

In contrast to the inductive reasoning used in discovery learning, the Ausubel model advocates *deductive reasoning*: General ideas are taught first, followed by specific points. This model requires teachers to help students break ideas into smaller, related points and to link new ideas to similar content in memory. In information processing terms, the aims of the model are to expand propositional networks in memory by adding knowledge and to establish links between networks.

Meaningful reception learning requires much teacher-student interaction. Teachers verbally present new material, but student responses are continually solicited. Lessons must be well organized. Concepts are exemplified in diverse ways and build on one another so that students possess the requisite knowledge to benefit from the teaching.

Advance Organizers

Advance organizers, or broad statements presented at the outset of lessons, help to connect new material with prior learning. Organizers direct learners' attention to important concepts in material to be learned, highlight interrelationships among ideas presented, and link new material to what students know (Faw & Waller, 1976). Organizers also can be maps that are shown with accompanying text (Verdi & Kulhavy, 2002). Researchers assume that learners' cognitive structures are hierarchically organized so that inclusive concepts subsume subordinate ones. Organizers provide information at high levels in hierarchies.

Organizers can be expository or comparative. *Expository organizers* provide students with new knowledge needed to comprehend the lesson. Expository organizers include concept definitions and generalizations. *Concept definitions* state the concept, a superordinate concept, and characteristics of the concept. In presenting the concept of "warm-blooded animal," for example, a teacher might define it (i.e., animal whose internal body temperature remains relatively constant), relate it to superordinate concepts (animal kingdom), and give its characteristics (birds, mammals; see discussion of procedural knowledge in Chapter 4). *Generalizations* are broad statements of general principles from which hypotheses or specific ideas are drawn. A generalization appropriate for the study of terrain would be: "Less vegetation grows at higher elevations." Teachers can present examples of generalizations and ask students to think of others.

Comparative organizers introduce new material by drawing analogies with familiar material. Comparative organizers activate and link networks in LTM. If a teacher were giving a unit on the body's circulatory system to students who have studied communication systems, the teacher might relate the circulatory and communication systems with relevant concepts such as the source, medium, and target. For comparative organizers to be effective, students must have a good understanding of the material used as the basis for the analogy. Learners also must perceive the analogy easily. Difficulty perceiving analogous relationships impedes learning.

Ausubel's research shows that using organizers promotes learning over that which occurs without organizers (Ausubel, 1978); however, other studies have obtained conflicting results (Barnes & Clawson, 1975). Organizers seem most effective with lessons designed to teach how concepts are related (Mayer, 1984). If teachers stretch an analogy too far, students may not understand the connection. Organizers also are effective with difficult academic content when an analogy with familiar content is appropriate (Faw & Waller, 1976).

Another consideration is the developmental status of the learners. Organizers operate at general, abstract levels and require students to relate ideas mentally, which is beyond the capacity of young children. This deductive teaching approach works better with older students (Luiten, Ames, & Ackerson, 1980).

Evidence suggests that organizers aid transfer. Maps are effective organizers and lend themselves well to infusion in lessons via technology (Verdi & Kulhavy, 2002). Mayer (1979) reports research with college students who had no computer programming experience. Students were given programming materials to study; one group was given a conceptual model as an organizer, whereas the other group received the same materials without the model. The advance organizer group performed better on posttest items requiring transfer of learning to items different from those discussed in the instructional material. Organizers may help students relate new material to a broader set of experiences, which facilitates transfer (Application 6.2).

APPLICATION 6.2
Advance Organizers

Advance organizers help students connect new material with prior learning. Kathy Stone is teaching her students to develop comprehensive paragraphs. The students have been learning to write descriptive and interesting sentences. Mrs. Stone writes the students' sentences on the board and uses them as an organizer to show how to put sentences together to create a complete paragraph.

A middle school teacher might employ an organizer during geography. The teacher might begin a lesson on landforms (surfaces with characteristic shapes and compositions) by reviewing the definition and components of geography concepts previously discussed. The teacher could put the following points on the board to show that geography includes elements of the physical environment, human beings and the physical environment, and different world regions and their ability to support human beings.

The teacher could focus on elements of the physical environment and then move to landforms. The teacher could discuss types of landforms (e.g., plateaus, mountains, hills) by showing mock-ups and asking students to identify key features of each landform. This deductive approach gives students an overall framework or outline into which they can integrate new knowledge about the components.

In medical school an instructor teaching the effects of blood disorders might begin by reviewing the basic parts of blood (plasma, white and red cells, platelets). Then the teacher could list various categories of blood disease (anemia, bleeding and bruising, leukemia, bone marrow disease). The students can build on this outline by exploring the diseases in the different categories and by studying the symptoms and treatment for each condition.

CONDITIONS OF LEARNING

The instructional theory associated with Robert Gagné (1985) involves the *conditions of learning*, or the circumstances that prevail when learning occurs (Ertmer, Driscoll, & Wager, 2003). Two steps are critical in applying the theory. The first is to *specify the type of learning outcome;* Gagné identified five major types (discussed later). The second is to *determine the events of learning*, or factors that make a difference in instruction. Events are internal and external: Internal events include personal dispositions and cognitive processes; external events are instructional and are deliberately planned and arranged to promote learning. We consider these in turn.

Learning Outcomes

Gagné (1984) contended that learning is complex and that learners acquire capabilities that manifest themselves in different outcomes. Outcomes are distinct when learning requires different types of information processing and when learning enables different types of performances. The five types of learning outcomes are intellectual skills, verbal information, cognitive strategies, motor skills, and attitudes.

Intellectual skills include rules, procedures, and concepts. Previous chapters referred to intellectual skills as forms of procedural knowledge or production systems. This type of knowledge is employed in speaking, writing, reading, solving mathematical problems, and applying scientific principles to problems.

Verbal information, or declarative knowledge, is knowledge that something is the case. It is verbal because it is displayed verbally (in speaking or writing). Verbal information involves facts or meaningfully connected prose recalled verbatim (e.g., words to a poem or the "Star Spangled Banner"). Schemata, or organized networks of facts and events, are forms of verbal information.

Cognitive strategies are executive control processes. They include information processing skills such as attending to new information, deciding to rehearse information, elaborating, and using long-term memory (LTM) retrieval strategies. The problem-solving strategies discussed in Chapter 5 are examples of cognitive strategies.

Motor skills are developed through gradual improvements in the quality (smoothness, timing) of movements attained through practice. Whereas intellectual skills can be acquired abruptly, motor skills develop gradually with continued, deliberate practice (Ericsson et al., 1993). Intellectual skill development does not compare with the refinements in smoothness and timing found in motor-skill learning. Even practice conditions differ: Intellectual skills are practiced with different examples; motor-skill practice involves repetition of the same muscular movements.

Attitudes are internal beliefs that influence personal actions and that reflect characteristics such as generosity, honesty, and commitment to healthy living. Attitudes are inferred because they cannot be observed directly. Attitudes are learned, although unlike the preceding outcomes, they are not learned directly. Teachers can arrange proper conditions for learning intellectual skills, verbal information, cognitive strategies, and motor skills. Gagné believed that attitudes are learned indirectly through experiences and exposures to live and symbolic (televised, videotaped) models.

Learning Events

The five types of learning outcomes differ in their conditions: *Internal conditions* are prerequisite skills and cognitive processing requirements, whereas *external conditions* are environmental stimuli that support the learner's cognitive processes. One must specify as completely as possible both types of conditions when designing instruction to produce desired outcomes.

Internal conditions are learners' current capabilities, which the memory stores as knowledge. Gagné employed an information processing framework in which instructional cues from teachers and materials activate relevant knowledge in LTM (Gagné & Glaser, 1987). Internal conditions are important for designing learning hierarchies and instruction.

External conditions differ as a function of the learning outcome and the internal conditions. To teach students a classroom rule, a teacher might inform them of the rule and write it on the chalkboard. To teach students a strategy for checking their comprehension, a teacher might demonstrate the strategy and give students practice and feedback on its effectiveness. Proficient readers are instructed differently from those with decoding problems. Each phase of instruction is subject to alteration as a function of learning outcomes and internal conditions.

Learning Hierarchies

Learning hierarchies are organized sets of intellectual skills. The highest element in a hierarchy is the *target skill.* To devise a hierarchy, one begins at the top and asks what skills the learner must perform prior to learning the target skill or what skills are immediate prerequisites for the target skill. Then one asks the same question for each prerequisite skill, and so on down the hierarchy until one arrives at the skills the learner can perform now (Dick & Carey, 1985; Merrill, 1987). Figure 6.1 portrays a sample learning hierarchy.

Hierarchies are not linear orderings of skills. One often must apply two or more prerequisite skills to learn a higher-order skill with neither of the prerequisites dependent on the other. Nor are higher-order skills necessarily more difficult to learn than lower-order ones. Some prerequisites may be difficult to acquire; once learners have mastered the lower-order skills, learning a higher-order one may seem easier.

Phases of Learning

Instruction is a set of external events designed to facilitate internal learning processes. Table 6.1 shows the nine phases of learning grouped into the three categories (Gagné, 1985).

Preparation for learning includes introductory learning activities. During *attending,* learners focus on stimuli relevant to material to be learned (audiovisuals, written materials, teacher-modeled behaviors). The learner's *expectancy* orients the learner to the goal (learn a motor skill, learn to reduce fractions). During retrieval of relevant information from LTM, learners activate the portions relevant to the topic studied (Gagné & Dick, 1983).

Figure 6.1
Sample learning hierarchy.

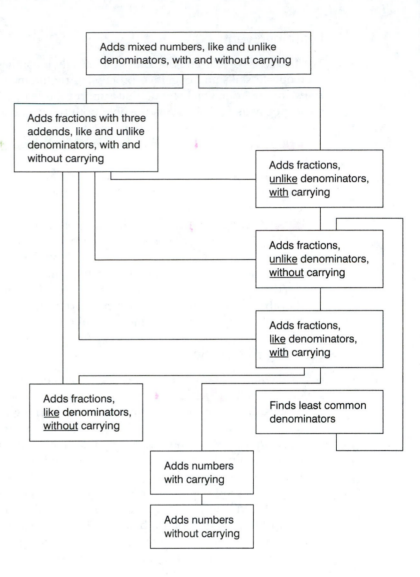

The main phases of learning are *acquisition* and *performance*. *Selective perception* means that the sensory register recognizes relevant stimulus features and transfers them to working memory (WM) for processing. *Semantic encoding* is the process whereby new knowledge is transferred to LTM. During *retrieval and responding*, learners retrieve new information from memory and make a response demonstrating learning. *Reinforcement* refers to feedback that confirms the accuracy of a student's response and provides corrective information as necessary.

Transfer of learning phases include cueing retrieval and generalizability. In *cueing retrieval*, learners receive cues signaling that previous knowledge is applicable in that situation. When solving word problems, for instance, a teacher might inform learners that their knowledge of right triangles is applicable. *Generalizability* is enhanced by

Table 6.1
Phases of learning (Gagné).

Category	Phase
Preparation for learning	Attending
	Expectancy
	Retrieval
Acquisition and performance	Selective perception
	Semantic encoding
	Retrieval and responding
	Reinforcement
Transfer of learning	Cueing retrieval
	Generalizability

providing learners the opportunity to practice skills with different content and under different circumstances (e.g., homework, spaced review sessions).

These nine phases are equally applicable for the five types of learning outcomes. Gagné and Briggs (1979) specified types of instructional events that might accompany each phase (Table 6.2). Instructional events enhancing each phase depend on the type of outcome. Instruction proceeds differently for intellectual skills than for verbal information.

Table 6.2
Instructional events accompanying learning phases (Gagné).

Phase	Instructional Event
Attending	Inform class that it is time to begin.
Expectancy	Inform class of lesson objective and type and quantity of performance to be expected.
Retrieval	Ask class to recall subordinate concepts and rules.
Selective perception	Present examples of new concept or rule.
Semantic encoding	Provide cues for how to remember information.
Retrieval and responding	Ask students to apply concept or rule to new examples.
Reinforcement	Confirm accuracy of students' learning.
Cueing retrieval	Give short quiz on new material.
Generalizability	Provide special reviews.

Gagné's theory incorporates each of the five elements mentioned at the beginning of this chapter:

■ Learning occurs in phases (Table 6.1).
■ Skills to be learned are acquired sequentially as set forth in the hierarchy; these are broken down into small steps.
■ Practice, feedback, and review are integral components of the system.
■ Social modeling is employed during the instructional phases (3–6).
■ Motivation is a function of learner's attitudes, and the external conditions of learning include contextual factors.

Furthermore, the theory represents a systematic combination of principles of learning and instruction. It highlights many of the ideas discussed in this text, including the structure and representation of knowledge, retrieval, practice, feedback, transfer, and motivation.

A potential downside is that developing learning hierarchies is difficult and time-consuming. The process requires the expertise of one with a firm grasp of the content domain to determine the successive prerequisite skills—the scope and sequence of instruction. Even a seemingly simple skill may have a complex hierarchy if learners must master several prerequisites. For those skills with less well-defined structures (e.g., creative writing), developing a hierarchy may be difficult. Another issue is that the system allows for little learner control because it prescribes how learners should proceed. The current educational emphasis on constructivism seems to be at odds with the basic assumptions of the theory.

Gagné's theory has made significant contributions to the study of learning and instruction (Ertmer et al., 2003). The theory provides a solid standard against which to gauge how well instructional theories incorporate principles of learning. We now turn to other instructional models that are less elaborate but also incorporate learning principles and specify instructional conditions to optimize learning, retention, and transfer.

MODELS OF INSTRUCTION

Over the years a large number of instructional models have been formulated. These vary in precision, theoretical orientation, and critical components. No attempt is made here to cover instructional models extensively, since that extends beyond the scope of this text. Rather, this section covers a small subset that was chosen to show how instructional principles link to learning.

Learning Time

Carroll (1963, 1965) formulated a model of school learning that places primary emphasis on the instructional variable of time spent learning. Carroll assumed that learning tasks can be specified clearly and that reliable means exist for determining whether students have learned the tasks.

The central premise is that students successfully learn to the extent that they spend the amount of time they need to learn. *Time* means academically engaged time, or time spent paying attention and trying to learn. This is a cognitive definition because it goes beyond a simple behavioral indicator of clock time. Within this framework, Carroll postulated factors that influence how much time learning requires and how much time is actually spent learning.

Time Needed for Learning.   One influence on this factor is *aptitude for learning the task*. Learning aptitude depends on the amount of prior task-relevant learning and on personal characteristics such as abilities and attitudes. A second, related factor is *ability to understand instruction*. This variable interacts with instructional method; for example, some learners comprehend verbal instruction well, whereas others benefit more from visual presentations.

Quality of instruction refers to how well the task is organized and presented to learners. Quality includes what learners are told about what they will learn and how they will learn it, the extent to which they have adequate contact with the learning materials, and how much prerequisite knowledge is acquired prior to learning the task. The lower the quality of instruction, the more time learners require to learn.

Time Spent in Learning.   *Time allowed for learning* is one influence on this factor. The school curriculum includes so much content that time allotted for a particular type of learning is less than optimal for some students. When teachers present material to the entire class at once, some learners are more likely to experience difficulty grasping it and require additional instruction. When students are ability grouped, the amount of time devoted to different content varies depending on the ease with which students learn.

A second influence is *time the learner is willing to spend learning*. Even when learners are given ample time to learn, they may not spend that time working productively. Whether due to low interest, high perceived task difficulty, or other factors, students may not be motivated to persist at a task for the amount of time they require to learn it. Carroll incorporated these factors into a formula to estimate the degree of learning for any student on a given task:

degree of learning = time spent/time needed

Ideally, students spend as much time as they need to learn (degree of learning = 1.0), but learners typically spend either more time (degree of learning > 1.0) or less time (degree of learning < 1.0) than they require.

Carroll's model highlights the importance of academic engaged time required for learning and the factors influencing time spent and time needed to learn. It does not offer specific prescriptions for how to correct inadequate student learning. The model incorporates valid psychological principles, but only at a general level as instructional or motivational factors. It does not explore cognitive engagement in depth. Carroll (1989) admitted that more research was needed to complete the details. Mastery learning researchers, who have systematically investigated the time variable, provide greater specificity.

Mastery Learning

Carroll's model predicts that if students vary in aptitude for learning a subject and if all receive the same amount and type of instruction, their achievement will differ. If the amount and type of instruction vary depending on individual differences among learners, then each student has the potential to demonstrate mastery; the positive relation between aptitude and achievement will disappear because all students will demonstrate equal achievement regardless of aptitudes.

These ideas form the basis of *mastery learning* (Anderson, 2003; Bloom, 1976; Bloom, Hastings, & Madaus, 1971). Mastery learning incorporates Carroll's ideas into a systematic instructional plan that includes defining mastery, planning for mastery, teaching for mastery, and grading for mastery (Block & Burns, 1977). Mastery learning contains cognitive elements, although its formulation seems quite basic compared with many current cognitive theories.

To *define mastery,* teachers prepare a set of objectives and a final (summative) exam. Level of mastery is established (e.g., where *A* students typically perform under traditional instruction). Teachers break the course into learning units mapped against course objectives.

Planning for mastery means teachers plan instructional procedures for themselves and students to include corrective feedback procedures (formative evaluation). Such evaluation typically takes the form of unit mastery tests that set mastery at a given level (e.g., 90%). Corrective instruction, which is used with students who fail to master aspects of the unit's objectives, is given in small-group study sessions, individual tutorials, and supplemental materials.

At the outset of *teaching for mastery,* teachers orient students to the mastery procedures and provide instruction using the entire class, small groups, or individual seatwork activities. Teachers give the formative test and certify which students achieve mastery. Students who fall short might work in small groups reviewing troublesome material, often with the aid of peer tutors who have mastered the material. Teachers allow students time to work on remedial materials along with homework.

Grading for mastery includes a summative (end-of-course) test. Students who score at or above the course mastery performance level receive *A* grades; lower scores are graded accordingly. Mastery learning has been most frequently applied at the elementary and secondary school levels, although colleges and universities have widely used Keller's Personalized System of Instruction (PSI; Chapter 2). Callahan and Smith (1990) found that PSI worked effectively with junior high gifted students.

The emphasis on student abilities as determinants of learning may seem uninteresting given that abilities generally do not change much as a result of instructional interventions. Bloom (1976) also stressed the *alterable variables* of schooling: cognitive entry behaviors (e.g., student skills and cognitive processing strategies at the outset of instruction), affective characteristics (e.g., interest, motivation), and specific factors influencing the quality of instruction (e.g., student participation, type of corrective feedback). Instructional interventions can improve these variables.

Reviews of the effect of mastery learning on student achievement are mixed. Block and Burns (1977) generally found mastery learning more effective than traditional forms of instruction. Kulik et al. (1990) examined more than 100 evaluations of mastery learning programs and found positive effects on academic performances and course attitudes among college, high school, and upper-grade elementary school learners. They also found that mastery learning may increase the time students spend on instructional tasks. In contrast, Bangert et al. (1983) found weaker support for mastery learning programs. They noted that mastery-based instruction was more effective at the college level than at lower levels. Its effectiveness undoubtedly depends on the proper instructional conditions (e.g., planning, teaching, grading) being established (Kulik et al., 1990).

Students participating in mastery instruction often spend more time in learning compared with learners in traditional classes (Block & Burns, 1977). Given that time is at a premium in schools, much mastery work—especially remedial efforts—must be accomplished outside of regular school hours. Most studies show smaller effects of mastery instruction on affective outcomes (e.g., interest in and attitudes toward the subject matter) than on academic outcomes.

An important premise of mastery learning is that individual differences in student learning decrease over time. L. Anderson (1976) found that when remedial students gained experience with mastery instruction, they gradually required less extra time to attain mastery because their entry-level skills improved. These results imply cumulative benefits of mastery learning. This point requires further research, but has important instructional implications. Some examples of mastery learning are given in Application 6.3.

Inquiry Teaching

Collins (1977; Collins & Stevens, 1983) formulated a theory of instruction based on the Socratic teaching method. The goals are to have students reason, derive general principles, and apply them to new situations. Appropriate learning outcomes include formulating and testing hypotheses, differentiating necessary from sufficient conditions, making predictions, and determining when making predictions requires more information.

This model seems particularly useful for developing an *intelligent computer-assisted instruction (CAI)* system. The actual implementation is one of intelligent one-to-one tutoring. The tutor repeatedly questions the student. Questions are guided by rules such as "Ask about a known case," "Pick a counterexample for an insufficient factor," "Pose a misleading question," and "Question a prediction made without enough information" (Collins, 1977). Rule-generated questions help students formulate general principles and apply them to specific problems.

The following is a sample dialogue between teacher (T) and student (S) on the topic of population density (the rules being applied are in parentheses; Collins, 1977):

T: In Northern Africa is there a large population density? (Rule 9: Pick a case with an extreme wrong value.)

S: In Northern Africa? I think there is.

APPLICATION 6.3
Mastery Learning

A mastery learning approach can be very beneficial in certain learning environments. For example, in a remedial reading group for secondary students, a well-organized mastery learning program would allow students to progress at their own rates. Students motivated to make rapid progress are not slowed down by this type of instruction, as might happen if they are placed in a traditional learning format. Whether teachers use existing mastery learning reading programs or develop their own, the key is to include a progression of activities from less difficult to more difficult. The program should have checkpoints at which the students interact with the teacher so that their progress is evaluated with reteaching or special assistance provided if needed.

Young children entering school for the first time come with a wide range of experiences and abilities. Mastery learning can help teachers deal more effectively with the varying abilities and developmental levels. Mastery learning techniques can be implemented by using learning centers and small groups. Children can be placed in the different centers and groups according to their current levels. Then they can move through various developmental levels according to their own readiness rates.

The mastery approach also can build students' self-efficacy for learning. As they note their progress in completing units, they are apt to believe they are capable of further learning. Enhancing self-efficacy is particularly important with remedial learners who have encountered school failures and doubt their capabilities to learn, as well as for young children who enter school with limited experiences and skills.

T: Well there is in the Nile valley, but elsewhere there is not. Do you have any idea why not? (Rule 12: Probe for a necessary factor.)

S: Because it's not good for cultivating purposes?

T: It's not good for agriculture?

S: Yeah.

T: And do you know why? (Rule 4: Ask for prior factors.)

S: Why?

T: Why is the farming at a disadvantage?

S: Because it's dry.

T: Right. (p. 353)

This instructional approach has limited classroom implementation potential because it is intended to be a plan for constructing CAI systems, which may not be easily accessed by students in schools. The applicability of the model is further limited because it represents a tutoring (one-to-one) system. Persons who serve as tutors require extensive training to pose appropriate questions in response to a student's level of thinking. With some modification, this approach might be highly appropriate with small groups of students.

Additional research is needed to specify the conditions under which inquiry teaching is beneficial. Good content-area knowledge is a prerequisite for problem-solving skills. Students who lack a decent understanding of basic knowledge are not likely to function well under an inquiry system designed to teach reasoning and application of principles. Other student characteristics (e.g., age, abilities) also may predict success under this model. Research should explore whether skills and strategies acquired through inquiry teaching transfer beyond the instructional context.

Instructional Quality Profile

The *Instructional Quality Profile (IQP)* is an instructional model that specifies procedures for analyzing quality of instruction with respect to instructional objectives and test items (Merrill, Reigeluth, & Faust, 1979; Merrill, Richards, Schmidt, & Wood, 1977). *Instructional quality* refers to "the degree to which instruction is effective, efficient, and appealing—that is, the degree to which it works in cost-effectively promoting student performance on a posttest and student affect toward learning" (Merrill et al., 1979, p. 165).

The IQP is used to analyze the quality of instruction in the six areas shown in Table 6.3, along with questions they address. The model is *prescriptive* because it specifies what one should do to obtain desired outcomes. Although the learning principles in

Table 6.3
Areas addressed by the Instructional Quality Profile.

Area	Question Addressed
Purpose-objective consistency	Is substance of the objectives consistent with purpose of the course?
Objective adequacy	Does objective contain characteristics that make it useful for guiding design of test items and instructional presentations?
Objective-test consistency	Are test items consistent with justified objectives?
Test adequacy	Do test items have characteristics necessary to ensure they will adequately test the objectives with which they are consistent?
Test-presentation consistency	Do instructional presentations provide information necessary for students to learn how to perform as required by the test?
Presentation adequacy	Have students been provided with complete, concise, easily studied, adequately illustrated, and sufficiently elaborated presentation to enable them to acquire desired performance efficiently?

the IQP are valid, their links to instruction often are not clear. Instructional principles tend to read like a checklist and readers must decide on their validity.

Outcomes deal with facts, concepts, procedures, and principles and have three major task levels: remember an instance, remember a generality, use a generality. Application of task levels to content types yields 10 cells (listed in parentheses): Remember an instance (fact, concept, procedure, principle), remember a generality (concept, procedure, principle), use a generality (concept, procedure, principle). Instructional presentations are judged adequate based on which strategies are employed. Some appropriate strategy components are the following (Merrill et al., 1979):

- **Feedback**: Give information on which answer is correct and why.
- **Isolation**: Separate critical information from other information and clearly label it as such.
- **Helps**: Add information to presentations to assist students in developing mastery (mnemonics, algorithms, attention-focusing devices).
- **Sampling**: Provide an adequate number of instances and practice items.
- **Divergence**: Provide instances and practice items that can differ in various ways.
- **Difficulty level**: Use a range of difficulty levels from easy to difficult.
- **Matching**: Match instances with noninstances on common properties (but not relevant to learning the concept or principle).

The IQP specifies precisely how to design instruction and tests consistent with the purpose and objectives. It operates on a micro level because it deals with content within a broader unit. Reigeluth has extended this idea to a macro level, or ways to organize topics within larger (course) units (Reigeluth, 1979; Reigeluth & Curtis, 1987; Reigeluth, Merrill, & Bunderson, 1978). This *Elaboration Theory of Instruction* contains points of overlap with the IQP, but one distinctive feature is the former's emphasis on "zooming." One begins with a general view of the content and moves to specific details, returning later to the general view (review, practice). This idea is similar to Ausubel's recommendation to present advance organizers and then specifics of instruction (discussed earlier in this chapter). From an information processing perspective, zooming activates a context in LTM, where new information is integrated into the slots.

Reigeluth's model also incorporates learning hierarchies. In designing instruction, the initial step is to use task analysis to determine which skills to teach and in what order. Content is assigned to different lessons, and instruction is designed for each lesson in the proper skill sequence. Elaboration Theory is prescriptive and contains many valid learning principles, as with those of the IQP; however, they often are not firmly linked with instructional prescriptions.

Instruction with Worked Examples

An instructional focus of many cognitive researchers is the role of worked examples. *Worked examples* typically present problem solutions in step-by-step fashion and often include accompanying diagrams. They portray an expert's problem-solving

---

Problem Statement: Find the Square Root of 7,225

Steps		Algorithm	
1.		$\sqrt{7225}$	
2.		$\sqrt{72.25}$	Mark off in units of two from the decimal point.
		$\dfrac{8}{}$	
3.		$\sqrt{72.25}$	Find the largest perfect square in the two numbers
	8 x 8	$\underline{64}$	to the left of the decimal. Subtract from 72 and
		825	"bring down" the next two numbers.
		$\dfrac{8}{}$	
4.		$\sqrt{72.25}$	Double the 8 and add a zero. Use the number (160)
		$\underline{64}$	as a trial divisor: 825 divided by 160 = 5, plus a
	160	825	remainder.
		$\dfrac{8\;5}{}$	
5.		$\sqrt{72.25}$	Substitute the 5 for the zero and multiply (165 x 5).
		$\underline{64}$	Product equals 825. Solution achieved.
		825	
	165 x 5	$\underline{825}$	

Figure 6.2
Sample worked example.
Source: Cognitive Psychology for Teachers by Glover, © Reprinted by permission of Pearson Education, Inc., Upper Saddle River, NJ.

model for learners to study before they begin to emulate it. A worked example is shown in Figure 6.2 (Glover, Ronning, & Bruning, 1990).

There is, of course, nothing new about using worked examples in teaching. Researchers of various theoretical bents advocate using modeled exemplars. Previously (Chapter 3) we considered the benefits of cognitive modeling and demonstration plus explanation (Rosenthal & Zimmerman, 1978; Schunk, 1981). From a motivational perspective, worked examples may help instill self-efficacy in learners for succeeding when they believe they understand the model and can apply the strategy themselves (Schunk, 1991). Worked examples also figure prominently in theories of concept acquisition (Bruner et al., 1956).

What is new is the link of worked examples to cognitive learning principles, especially for complex forms of learning, such as algebra, physics, and geometry (Atkinson, Derry, Renkl, & Wortham, 2000). Applying the novice-expert model (Chapter 9), researchers have found that experts typically focus on deeper (structural) aspects of problems and that novices more often deal with surface features. Practice alone is less effective in promoting skills than is practice coupled with worked examples (Atkinson et al., 2000).

Worked examples seem most beneficial with students in the early stages of skill acquisition, as opposed to proficient learners who are refining skills. Its applicability is seen clearly in the four-stage model of skill acquisition within the ACT-R framework

(Anderson, Fincham, & Douglass, 1997; see Chapter 4). In stage 1 learners use analogies to relate examples to problems to be solved. In stage 2 they develop abstract declarative rules through practice. During stage 3, performance becomes quicker and smoother as aspects of problem solution become automatized. By stage 4 learners have in memory many types of problems and can retrieve the appropriate solution strategy quickly when confronted with a problem. Use of worked examples is best suited for stage 1 and early stage 2 learners. During later stages, people benefit from practice to hone their strategies, although even at advanced stages studying solutions of experts can be helpful.

From an instructional perspective certain issues are critical. One is how to integrate the components of an example, such as diagram, text, aural information, and subgoals. It is imperative that a worked example not overload the learner's WM, which multiple sources of information presented simultaneously can do. Research supports the prediction that dual presentation facilitates learning better than single-mode presentation (Atkinson et al., 2000; Mayer, 1997; see the technology section later in this chapter). This result is consistent with dual-coding theory (Paivio, 1986; see Chapter 4), with the caveat that too much complexity is not desirable. Similarly, examples intermixed with subgoals help create deep structures and facilitate learning.

A key point is that examples that include multiple presentation modes should be unified so that learners' attention is not split across nonintegrated sources. Aural and verbal explanations should indicate to which aspect of the example they refer, so learners do not have to search on their own. Subgoals should be clearly labeled and visually isolated in the overall display.

A second issue concerns how examples should be sequenced during an instructional unit. Research supports the conclusions that two examples are superior to a single one, that varied examples are better than two of the same type, and that intermixing examples and practice is more effective than a lesson that presents examples followed by practice problems (Atkinson et al., 2000).

Chi, Bassok, Lewis, Reimann, and Glaser (1989) found that students who provide *self-explanations* while studying examples subsequently achieve at higher levels compared with students who do not self-explain. Presumably the self-explanations help students understand the deep structure of the problems and thereby encode it more meaningfully. Self-explanation also is a type of rehearsal, and the benefit of rehearsal on learning is well established. The implication for instruction is to encourage students to self-explain while studying worked examples; for example, by verbalizing subgoals.

In summary, there are several features that when incorporated with worked examples help learners create cognitive schemas to facilitate subsequent achievement (Table 6.4). These instructional strategies are best employed during the early stages of skill learning. Through practice, these initial cognitive representations should evolve into the refined schemas that experts employ.

The worked examples literature lends itself to integration with findings from other research traditions. For example, verbalization is a key part of self-instructional training (Chapter 3). From a social cognitive perspective, verbalization can help to build self-efficacy and motivation as learners become aware that they understand a

Table 6.4
Suggestions for using worked examples in instruction.

- Present examples in close proximity to problems students will solve.
- Present multiple examples showing different types of problems.
- Present information in different modalities (aural, visual).
- Indicate subgoals in examples.
- Ensure that examples present all information needed to solve problems.
- Teach students to self-explain examples and encourage self-explanations.
- Allow sufficient practice on problem types so students refine skills.

strategy for solving problems. Atkinson et al. (2000) discuss the need to provide incentives for students to self-explain. The modeling literature (Chapter 3) suggests that peer models who demonstrate solution strategies and verbalize cognitive explanations can be especially effective teachers and raise observers' self-efficacy. Thus, although this material on worked examples is based on Anderson's ACT-R theory and reflects an information processing approach to skill learning (Lee & Anderson, 2001), its principles align well with other cognitive and motivational theories discussed in this text.

RESEARCH ON TEACHING

Years ago teaching was viewed in the narrow sense of teacher activities that led to student learning; specifically, presenting instruction and having students practice applying skills. Learning was unidirectional: Teachers influenced students. An important part of the teacher's job was to arrange the environment properly so students could respond and be reinforced. Much learning could occur even with little teacher-student interaction (Keller, 1968). This is a behavioral view of learning because it does not address cognitive processes.

This picture of teaching has changed dramatically. Today we know that practically everything teachers do can affect student learning, that learning is a complex process, and that learning involves reciprocal interactions among teachers and instructional activities, learners' cognitive processes and behaviors, and facets of the instructional environment (Oser & Baeriswyl, 2001; Pintrich & Schunk, 2002). Compared with earlier behaviorally oriented research, current investigations examine cognitive teaching factors in depth. The following section covers two aspects of teaching that have been extensively researched and that have important effects on student learning: planning and decision making, and instructional practices.

Teacher Planning and Decision Making

Planning Models. Planning and decision making are critical to teaching and student learning. Early models of planning were highly prescriptive because they specified clearly what teachers should do to promote student learning (Clark & Yinger, 1979).

These models included steps such as specifying learning objectives, selecting teacher and student activities, organizing instruction, and determining methods of evaluation.

In contrast to these linear models, a different type of model views planning as beginning with teacher decisions about what types of activities to use. Within this context, objectives arise and are integrated with activities. The means and ends of teaching become integrated, which means that goals are not completely specified initially.

Recent research has placed greater emphasis on exploring teachers' thought processes before, during, and after teaching to examine teacher planning at different times (Clark & Peterson, 1986). Planning is not confined to what teachers do prior to instruction; rather, it is a continuous process. This view reflects a cognitive information processing approach, which stresses the receiving, organizing, and encoding of information in memory (Gagné et al., 1993).

Research using a variety of methods including teacher verbal reports and think-alouds shows that teacher planning strongly reflects student characteristics such as needs, abilities, and motivational variables (Clark & Peterson, 1986). Teachers are concerned with how to foster attainment of learning objectives given their students' abilities and with how their students will receive instruction and activities. When teachers take interest value into account, student activities often do not follow logically from specification of objectives and the latter is not always important in planning.

Motivational concerns are important in teachers' decisions about planning. Clark and Yinger (1979) asked teachers to view videotaped segments of their teaching and recall what they were thinking about at the time. Teachers considered using alternative teaching strategies only when instruction was not functioning well. The main cue to assess instructional effectiveness was students' involvement and participation, which are motivational variables. Teachers considered changing approaches when they noticed that student motivation was lagging.

Teachers often do not follow a linear planning model because they do not plan lessons strictly in line with stated objectives. They often begin by considering the setting and content and then think about motivational concerns (e.g., student involvement and participation). When they deviate from their plans during teaching, they often do so because of motivational problems. Teachers and students influence one another. Teachers affect student motivation and learning through planning, but student reactions to instruction cause teachers to rethink their approach and implement what they believe are better strategies for learning.

Instructional Grouping.   Another critical aspect of planning is *grouping for instruction* (see Chapter 8). Three types of grouping structures are competitive, cooperative, and individualistic (Ames, 1984; Deutsch, 1949; Johnson & Johnson, 1974; Slavin, 1983). *Competitive structures* negatively link individuals' goals so that if Liz attains her goal, then the chances of others attaining their goals are lowered. In *cooperative structures*, by contrast, individuals' goals are positively linked such that Liz can attain her goal only if others attain theirs. *Individualistic structures* have no link between individuals' goals.

Structures can affect learning and motivation in many ways. They help to provide cues about students' capabilities (Ames, 1984). Competitive structures highlight the importance of ability and promote social comparisons with others. Motivation and learning improve when students believe they are performing better than others but may decline if they perceive their work as poorer. In competitive situations a few students regularly receive most of the rewards, which is not motivating for all students.

In individualistic structures, students compare their present work with previous efforts to determine progress (Ames, 1984). The perception of self-improvement substantiates self-efficacy for learning and enhances motivation and learning (Schunk, 1989).

In cooperative structures, students share in successes of the group. Ames (1981) compared the effects of competitive and cooperative structures on children's self-evaluations. In cooperative groups, the outcome affected students' perceptions of their abilities and feelings of satisfaction. Group success alleviated negative self-perceptions resulting from poor individual performance and group failure lowered positive self-perceptions of students who performed well. Failure in competitive situations has a stronger effect on self-perceptions than does failure in noncompetitive situations. In cooperative groups, low achievers share in the group success as much as high achievers. At the same time, when cooperative groups fail, dissatisfaction can be high regardless of individual performance. For low achievers, successful cooperative groups can build self-confidence; unsuccessful ones, however, can have the same type of negative effect on self-efficacy as failure under competitive conditions (Ames & Felker, 1979).

Whether teachers should use competitive, cooperative, or individualistic structures for particular activities depends on several factors, including the purpose of instruction, ease of grouping, type of activity, potential effects of success and failure under different arrangements, and amount of social cohesiveness that exists. Regardless of structure, planning activities at which students can succeed with diligent effort to enhance their self-perceptions, motivation, and learning is important.

Instructional Practices

Effective Teaching.   Much research has investigated how teaching practices affect student achievement. In several large-scale studies, some teachers were trained to implement specific instructional procedures, whereas others taught in their regular manner. These studies generally showed that trained teachers produce higher achievement (Brophy & Good, 1986). Rosenshine and Stevens (1986) summarized how successful instructors teach well-structured material (Table 6.5).

Although much research on teaching has not examined how teaching practices affect information processing, these suggestions can be linked with learning theory and research (Anderson, 1990; Gagné et al., 1993; Winne, 2001). Given that WM is limited in capacity, teachers should not present too much new information at once or require unduly complex cognitive processing by students. One means of assisting students to integrate new information into LTM networks is to cue relevant prior information from memory by reviewing it during a lesson overview. When skills are

Table 6.5
Principles for teaching
structured content.

- Begin lesson with brief review of prior prerequisite learning.
- Provide short statement of objectives.
- Present material in short steps with student practice after each step.
- Give clear explanations and demonstrations.
- Provide for much student practice of new learning.
- Ask questions and check for understanding by all students.
- Monitor students during guided practice.
- Provide feedback and corrective instruction as necessary.
- Give clear directions for seatwork; monitor as necessary.

well established, many aspects of skilled performance occur automatically (e.g., decoding in good readers). Student practice facilitates automaticity so that eventually executing mental processes requires little effort (Rosenshine & Stevens, 1986). Practice is a form of rehearsal that also helps to organize and store information in memory. Automatic processing helps clear space in WM for new material. Clear explanations and demonstrations ensure that students understand the content. Asking students questions, checking for understanding, monitoring their work, and providing corrective feedback ensure proper learning and allow for correction of errors before faulty learning becomes established.

Presenting material in small steps is helpful for children because of developmental limitations in information processing capability, for students with learning problems who may have difficulty processing information and can become easily overloaded, and for students of any age during the early stages of learning. Younger students need more practice and feedback; with development, the amount of presentation time can increase relative to practice because older students rehearse and encode information better (Pintrich & Schunk, 2002). Organizing information hierarchically so that memory networks can be developed through teaching is desirable.

By integrating learning research with research on teaching, one can say that teaching practices facilitate learning if they:

- Break material to be learned into small steps.
- Give learners practice on each step before introducing complexity.
- Assist encoding by relating new information to prior knowledge.
- Give additional practice to facilitate automatic processing.

This instructional approach works best with well-structured content taught step by step (e.g., factual knowledge, mathematical algorithms, mechanics of writing letters, English grammar). The approach is not as applicable with less-structured content (e.g., composition writing, discussions of social issues). In applying this approach, one must consider student developmental level and other potential limiting factors.

Teaching Functions.   Rosenshine and Stevens (1986) developed the following list of six teaching functions based on information processing research and research on teaching:

- Review and check previous day's work; reteach if necessary.
- Present new material.
- Give students guided practice; check for understanding.
- Offer feedback; reteach if necessary.
- Give students independent practice.
- Review at spaced intervals (weekly, monthly).

These steps are typically part of instructional models (Hunter, 1982). One research challenge is to explore links between teaching practices and learning principles, especially those involving learners' cognitive processes (Winne, 2001). For example, during the lesson focus phase, teachers cue knowledge and relate it to the lesson purpose. Learning research suggests that cued information is activated in students' memories and that links are formed with the lesson content.

Another area for research is to determine ways to implement effective instructional models. Independent practice, for example, can occur when students work alone or in small groups. Research on cooperative learning shows that small groups operate best when each group member is responsible for some aspect of the task (Slavin, 1983). Research might determine how to subdivide tasks during independent practice to facilitate learning and self-efficacy among group members.

LEARNER CHARACTERISTICS

Theories and models of instruction consider characteristics of learners and teachers that affect instruction and student learning. This section looks at some of these qualities, including learner aptitudes, cognitive styles, and information processing capabilities. The section concludes with suggestions for adapting instruction to individual student differences.

Aptitude-Treatment Interactions

Aptitude-treatment interactions reflect the principle of tailoring instruction to important student characteristics (Snow, Corno, & Jackson, 1996). *Aptitudes* are student characteristics—for example, abilities, attitudes, personality variables, and demographic factors (age, sex, ethnic background). *Treatments* are forms of instruction or sets of conditions associated with instruction. *Aptitude-treatment interactions (ATIs)* refer to differences in student outcomes (e.g., achievement, attitudes) as a function of the interaction (combination) of instructional conditions (treatments) with student characteristics (aptitudes). ATI research examines how individual differences in aptitudes predict students' responses to forms of instruction.

For example, suppose that Karen wanted to know whether large- or small-group instruction (the treatment) produced better achievement in social studies among seventh graders, and whether large- and small-group instruction was differentially effective among boys and girls (the aptitude). Karen could randomly assign boys and girls to either a large- or a small-group instructional condition. Assuming that Karen could equate the instructional content between the large- and small-group conditions, she could test the students following the instructional unit to determine whether (a) a difference existed between large and small groups, (b) a difference existed between boys and girls, and (c) class format interacted with student gender (e.g., girls did equally well under either form of instruction but boys did significantly better in small groups than in large groups). A significant (c) finding would constitute an ATI.

The hypothesis that instructional conditions affect student outcomes differently depending on students' attributes is intuitively plausible (Corno & Snow, 1986). Good teachers know that students need to be treated differently depending on their needs and that any type of instruction will not be equally effective with all students.

ATI research was very active in the years following the information processing breakthrough (mid-1960s to 1980s), but ATI research has declined in recent years. We know that student abilities are important predictors of achievement (Kyllonen & Stephens, 1990; Lohman, 1989) and a wealth of evidence obtained ATIs (Cronbach & Snow, 1977). One reason for the research decline is that many ATI findings have not been replicated in subsequent studies (Cronbach & Snow, 1977). Findings that cannot be replicated may not be reliable. In addition, complex interactions involving three or more variables are difficult to interpret and apply in classes to improve teaching and learning.

Tobias (1989) noted that inconsistent ATI results may reflect the idea that treatments require different forms of cognitive processing that may not be inherently linked with other student aptitudes. For example, if Karen obtained an ATI, it implies that the type of cognitive processing required in large- and small-group settings differs; however, the results do not imply that all boys process information better in small groups. Wide individual differences occur in any outcome measure. Tobias also recommended including more affective (motivational) variables in ATI studies to determine how these interact with treatments and other aptitudes to influence results. Snow et al. (1996) discussed at length research on the interplay of aptitudes and affective variables.

Cognitive Styles

Many researchers interested in learner characteristics have explored cognitive styles. *Cognitive styles* (or *learning styles*) are stable individual variations in perceiving, organizing, processing, and remembering information (Shipman & Shipman, 1985; Sigel & Brodzinsky, 1977). Messick (1994) defined them as, "modes of perceiving, remembering, thinking, problem solving, and decision making, reflective of information-processing regularities that develop in congenial ways around underlying personality trends" (p. 122). Styles are people's preferred ways to process information (Sternberg & Grigorenko, 1997); they are not synonymous with abilities. Abilities refer to capacities to execute skills; cognitive styles are habitual ways of processing information.

Styles are inferred from consistent individual differences in organizing and processing information on different tasks (Messick, 1984). To the extent that styles affect cognition, affects, and behavior, they help link cognitive, affective, and social functioning (Messick, 1994). In turn, stylistic differences are associated with differences in learning and receptivity to various forms of instruction (Messick, 1984).

The three major styles discussed below—field dependence-independence, categorization, cognitive tempo—have substantial research bases and educational implications. Other styles include *leveling* or *sharpening* (blurring or accentuating differences among stimuli), *risk taking* or *cautiousness* (high or low willingness to take chances to achieve goals), and *sensory modality preference* (enactive or kinesthetic, iconic or visual, symbolic or auditory; Sternberg & Grigorenko, 1997; Tobias, 1994).

Cognitive styles provide important information about cognitive development. One also can relate cognitive styles to larger behavioral patterns to study personality development. Educators investigate styles to devise complementary learning environments and to teach students more adaptive styles to enhance learning and motivation.

Field Dependence-Independence. *Field dependence-independence* (also called *psychological differentiation, global* and *analytical functioning*) refers to the extent that one depends on or is distracted by the context or perceptual field in which a stimulus or event occurs (Sigel & Brodzinsky, 1977; Sternberg & Grigorenko, 1997). The construct was identified and principally researched by Witkin and his colleagues (Witkin, 1969; Witkin, Moore, Goodenough, & Cox, 1977).

Various measures determine reliance on perceptual context. One is the Rod-and-Frame test, in which the individual attempts to align a tilted luminous rod in an upright position within a tilted luminous frame—inside a dark room with no other perceptual cues. Field independence originally was defined as the ability to align the rod upright using only an internal standard of upright. Other measures are the Embedded Figures test, in which one attempts to locate a simpler figure embedded within a more complex design, and the Body Adjustment test, in which the individual sits in a tilted chair in a tilted room and attempts to align the chair upright. Participants who can easily locate figures and align themselves upright are classified as field independent (Application 6.4).

Young children primarily are field dependent, but an increase in field independence begins during preschool and extends into adolescence. Children's individual preferences remain reasonably consistent over time (Sigel & Brodzinsky, 1977). The data are less clear on gender differences. Although some data suggest that older male students are more field independent than older female students, research on children shows that girls are more field independent than boys. Whether these differences reflect cognitive style or some other construct that contributes to test performance (e.g., activity-passivity) is not clear.

Witkin et al. (1977) noted that field dependent and independent learners do not differ in learning ability but may respond differently to learning environments and content. Because field dependent persons may be more sensitive to and attend carefully to aspects of the social environment, they are better at learning material with social content; however, field independent learners can easily learn such content

APPLICATION 6.4
Field Dependence and Independence

Elementary teachers must be careful to address the cognitive differences of their children in designing classroom activities, particularly because young children are more field dependent (global) than field independent (analytical). For the primary child, emphasis should be placed on designing activities that address global understanding, while at the same time taking analytical thinking into account.

For example, when Kathy Stone implements a unit on the neighborhood she and her children might initially talk about the entire neighborhood and all the people and places in it (global thinking). The children might build replicas of their homes, the school, churches, stores, and so forth—which could tap analytical thinking—and place these on a large floor map to get an overall picture of the neighborhood (global). Children could think about people in the neighborhood and their major features (analytical thinking), and then put on a puppet show portraying them interacting with one another without being too precise about exact behaviors (global). Mrs. Stone could show a real city map to provide a broad overview (global) and then focus on that section of the map detailing their neighborhood (analytical).

Secondary teachers can take cognitive style differences into account in lesson planning. In teaching about the Civil War, Jim Marshall should emphasize both global and analytical styles by discussing overall themes and underlying causes of the war (e.g., slavery, economy) and by creating lists of important events and characters (e.g., Lincoln, Lee, Battle of Fredericksburg, Appomattox). Student activities can include discussions of important issues underlying the war (global style) and making time lines showing dates of important battles and other activities (analytical style). If Mr. Marshall were to stress only one type of cognitive style, students who process information differently may doubt their ability to understand material, which will have a negative impact on self-efficacy and motivation for learning.

when it is brought to their attention. Field dependent learners seem sensitive to social reinforcement (e.g., teacher praise) and criticism. Field independent persons are more likely to impose structure when material lacks organization; field dependent learners consider material as it is. With poorly structured material, field dependent learners may be at a disadvantage. They use salient features of situations in learning, whereas field independent learners also consider less-salient cues. The latter students may be at an advantage with concept learning when relevant and irrelevant attributes are contrasted.

These differences suggest ways for teachers to alter instructional methods. If field dependent learners miss cues, teachers should highlight them to help students distinguish relevant features of concepts. This may be especially important with beginning readers as they focus on letter features. Evidence indicates that field dependent learners have more trouble during early stages of reading (Sunshine & DiVesta, 1976).

Categorization Style. *Categorization style* refers to criteria used to perceive objects as similar to one another (Sigel & Brodzinsky, 1977). Style is assessed with a grouping task in which one must group objects on the basis of perceived similarity. This is not a cut-and-dried task because objects can be categorized in many ways. From a collection of animal pictures, one might select a cat, dog, and rabbit and give as the reason for the grouping that they are mammals, have fur, run, and so forth. Categorization style reveals information about how the individual prefers to organize information.

Three types of categorization styles are relational, descriptive, and categorical (Kagan, Moss, & Sigel, 1960). A *relational (contextual) style* links items on a theme or function (e.g., spatial, temporal); a *descriptive (analytic) style* involves grouping by similarity according to some detail or physical attribute; a *categorical (inferential) style* classifies objects as instances of a superordinate concept. In the preceding example, "mammals," "fur," and "run," reflect categorical, descriptive, and relational styles, respectively.

Preschoolers' categorizations tend to be descriptive; however, relational responses of the thematic type also are prevalent (Sigel & Brodzinsky, 1977). Researchers note a developmental trend toward greater use of descriptive and categorical classifications along with a decrease in relational responses.

Style and academic achievement are related, but the causal direction is unclear (Shipman & Shipman, 1985). Reading, for example, requires perception of analytic relations (e.g., fine discriminations); however, the types of discriminations made are as important as the ability to make such discriminations. Students are taught the former. Style and achievement may reciprocally influence each other. Certain styles may lead to higher achievement, and the resulting rewards, perceptions of progress, and self-efficacy may reinforce one's continued use of the style.

Cognitive Tempo. *Cognitive (conceptual, response) tempo* has been extensively researched by Kagan and his associates (Kagan, 1966; Kagan, Pearson, & Welch, 1966). Kagan was investigating styles of categorization when he observed that some children responded rapidly and that others were more thoughtful and took their time. Cognitive tempo refers to the willingness "to pause and reflect upon the accuracy of hypotheses and solutions in a situation of response uncertainty" (Shipman & Shipman, 1985, p. 251).

Kagan developed the Matching Familiar Figures (MFF) test to use with children. The MFF is a 12-item match-to-standard test in which a standard figure is shown with six possible matches, one of which is perfect. The dependent variables are time to the first response on each item and total errors across all items. Reflective children score above the median on time (longer) but below the median on errors (fewer), whereas impulsive children show the opposite pattern. Two other groups of children are fast-accurate (below the median on both measures) and slow-inaccurate (above the median on both measures).

Children become more reflective with development, particularly in the early school years (Sigel & Brodzinsky, 1977). Evidence suggests different rates of development for boys and girls, with girls showing greater reflectivity at an earlier age. A moderate positive correlation between scores over a 2-year period indicates reasonable stability (Brodzinsky, 1982; Messer, 1970).

Differences in tempo are unrelated to intelligence scores but correlate with school achievement. Messer (1970) found that children not promoted to the next grade were more impulsive than peers who were promoted. Reflective children tend to perform better on moderately difficult perceptual and conceptual problem-solving tasks and make mature judgments on concept attainment and analogical reasoning tasks (Shipman & Shipman, 1985). Reflectivity bears a positive relationship to prose reading, serial recall, and spatial perspective-taking (Sigel & Brodzinsky, 1977). Impulsive children often are less attentive and more disruptive than reflective children, oriented toward quick success, and demonstrate low performance standards and mastery motivation (Sternberg & Grigorenko, 1997).

Given the educational relevance of cognitive tempo, many have suggested training children to be less impulsive. The Meichenbaum and Goodman (1971) study (Chapter 3) found that self-instructional training decreased errors among impulsive children. Modeled demonstrations of reflective cognitive style, combined with student practice and feedback, seem important as a means of change.

Critique. Cognitive styles seem important for teaching and learning, and a fair amount of research exists that may help guide future efforts and attempts by practitioners to apply findings to improve students' adaptive functioning. At the same time, research on the topic has declined in recent years, and the literature often seems disorganized, which makes attempting to draw conclusions difficult (Miller, 1987). The distinction between cognitive styles and abilities is tenuous and controversial (Tiedemann, 1989); field independence may be synonymous with aspects of intelligence (Sternberg & Grigorenko, 1997). If styles really are ability-driven, then attempts to alter styles may meet with much less success than if styles are acquired and subject to change. More-recent research has investigated the organization of styles within information processing frameworks and within the structure of human personality (Messick, 1994; Sternberg & Grigorenko, 1997). These directions may help revive interest in the topic and suggest ways of developing styles in students that facilitate learning.

Learners' Resource Allocations

Learners differ in their limits on information processing capabilities, which has direct implications for instruction. People are limited in how much information they can attend to, rehearse, store in WM, transfer to LTM, and so forth (Chapters 4 and 5). These differences are more apparent in children, but learners of any age demonstrate them.

The *resource allocation model* is a framework that addresses this issue (Kanfer & Ackerman, 1989; Kanfer & Kanfer, 1991). This model posits that attention is the key cognitive process; through attention, other factors such as abilities, motivation, self-regulation, and perceived task demands, affect performance. Attention is a limited resource and is allocated to activities as a function of motivation and self-regulation. *Distal processes* refer to task-related goals and limit total resource availability. *Proximal processes* direct attention to on-task, off-task, or self-regulatory activities. Allocations are adjusted based on feedback about effectiveness. When task demands are high (e.g., difficult goals), people allocate greater attention to the task; conversely, when demands are lower, they may shift some attention away from the task and to other activities. Self-regulation is a central means for producing changes in resource allocation.

Research by Kanfer and others shows how conditions can affect attention allocation. Kanfer and Ackerman found that task-specific confidence in capabilities (a measure analogous to self-efficacy) is associated with higher levels of self-regulatory activity and affects resource allocations. As Wood and Bandura (1989) and Jourden, Bandura, and Banfield (1991) have shown, self-efficacy bears an important relation to conceptions of ability; thus, the latter construct may indirectly affect allocation of attention.

The resource allocation model suggests that teachers should make attentional demands appropriate for students during learning and minimize competing conditions (e.g., distractions). Because motivational factors also are important (e.g., efficacy, perceived value), instruction should help build these outcomes to ensure continued allocation of attention to learning tasks. Although the theory needs considerable clarification, it offers a unique perspective for linking instruction and learning.

Adapting Instruction

Ideally the conditions of instruction will match the learners' characteristics; however, this match often does not occur. Learners may need to adapt their learning styles and preferred modes of working to instructional conditions involving content and teaching methods. Self-regulation methods help learners adapt to changing instructional conditions.

Conversely, instructional conditions can be tailored to individual differences to provide equal learning opportunities for all students despite differences in aptitudes, styles, and so forth (Corno & Snow, 1986; Snow et al., 1996). Macroadaptation occurs at the system or course level, microadaptation at the lesson or segment level.

Macroadaptation.   An example of macroadaptation is a college course that uses the Keller Plan (Chapter 2). By allowing students to proceed at their own pace and recycle through material as needed, such courses take into account individual differences in learning ability. Mastery learning programs at the elementary and secondary levels attempt the same.

Two other examples of macro-level adaptive programs are Individually Guided Education (IGE) and the Adaptive Learning Environments Model (ALEM). Under an IGE program, a school determines instructional objectives for each student based on aptitude profiles (e.g., reading, mathematics, motivation). Instruction varies along different dimensions: teacher attention and guidance, amount of time spent interacting with other students and technology, and amount of instruction provided in whole-class and small-group settings (Corno & Snow, 1986). Repeated formative evaluations show how well each student has mastered the objectives, and remedial instruction is given as necessary.

ALEM is designed for elementary students (Wang, 1980). Student assignments in reading and mathematics are individualized according to assessments of entry-level competencies. Quantity and quality of instruction vary depending on student abilities. ALEM makes use of parent involvement, team teaching, and group learning.

Microadaptation.   Individual teachers make adaptations with their students during lessons. They provide remedial instruction to students who have difficulty grasping new material. Teachers control many aspects of the instructional environment, which they can tailor to student differences. These aspects include organizational structure (whole-class, small-group, individual), regular and supplementary materials, use of technology, type of feedback, and type of material presented (tactile, auditory, visual).

Microadaptation occurs when students work on computer programs that provide additional instruction and practice. Decisions on these individual adaptations often are spontaneous and based on teachers' perceptions of how students react to material. For systematic adaptations, teachers might use measures of ability and motivation during instructional planning to tailor instruction to individual differences (Corno & Snow, 1986).

TECHNOLOGY AND INSTRUCTION

In the last few years there has been a rapid infusion of technology into instruction (Bonk & King, 1998; Cognition and Technology Group at Vanderbilt, 1996; Fisher, Dwyer, & Yocam, 1996; Grabe & Grabe, 1998a; Jonassen et al., 1999). Technology often is equated with equipment (e.g., computers, CDs, DVDs, VCRs), but its meaning is much broader. *Technology* refers to the designs and environments that engage learners (Jonassen et al., 1999). Research on the effects of technology on learning is increasing, as are efforts to remove barriers to infusing technology into instruction (Ertmer, 1999).

It seems clear that technology has the potential to facilitate instruction in ways that formerly were unimaginable. For example, not long ago technological classroom applications were limited to movies, televisions, slide projectors, radios, and the like. Today students can experience simulations of environments and events that they never could in regular classes, receive instruction from and communicate with others at long distances, and interact with large knowledge bases and expert tutoring systems. A challenge for researchers is to determine how technology affects learners' cognitive processes during encoding, retention, transfer, and so forth.

This section covers some of the ways that technology is used in instruction with special emphasis on the link between technology and learning. This material is not a practical guide on how to use technology. Readers interested in this topic should consult books and journals devoted to technology.

Functions of Technology

Technology comprises many applications, but clearly computers figure in many of them. When the computer revolution in education began in the 1980s, a prominent focus area was *computer literacy* (Seidel, Anderson, & Hunter, 1982). At a general level, computer literacy means "the minimum knowledge, know-how, familiarity, capabilities, abilities, and so forth, about computers essential for a person to function well in the contemporary world" (Bork, 1985, p. 33). More specifically, computer literacy can refer to:

- Ability to control and program a computer
- Ability to employ preprogrammed computer packages for personal, academic, or business uses
- Knowing about available hardware and software packages
- Understanding how computers affect individuals, nations, and the world at large
- Knowing how to perform constructive actions with a computer.

Computer literacy is not the major issue that it was formerly, in large part because computers are more readily available and many students learn to use a computer without school instruction (Jonassen, 1996). Currently most educators instead focus on the roles that computers play in teaching and learning. Although computer learning is not a theory of learning, we might ask whether computers improve school achievement more than traditional instruction and whether computers help develop thinking or problem-solving skills better than other modes of instruction.

There is much debate on this topic (Oppenheimer, 1997), with proponents claiming they do and critics asserting they do not. Comparing learning via computers with learning from traditional instruction can be misleading because other factors (e.g., content, teacher-student interaction) also may differ. Rather than focusing on this debate we will discuss the functions of technology and what research shows about their effectiveness.

Some years ago Taylor (1980) identified three educational roles for computers: tutor, tool, and tutee. I broaden these roles to include all technological applications. Technology as *tutor* presents material to be learned or reviewed, along with evaluative feedback, and decides what material to present next (e.g., expert tutor, software programs). Applications such as videotapes, slides, television, word processing, data analysis, multimedia construction, and computer conferencing represent the *tool* role. Technology functions as *tutee* when students instruct it what to do (e.g., programming, merging files, creating a website). These functions do not have clear-cut boundaries; for example, while engaged in word processing (a tool function) students may instruct a Web browser to locate information to be incorporated into the text (a tutee function).

Jonassen et al. (1999) presents a dynamic perspective on the role of technology in learning. The maximum benefits of technology derive when it energizes and facilitates thinking and knowledge construction. In this reconceptualization, technology can serve the functions shown in Table 6.6. The technological applications relevant to learning described in the next section are differentially effective in accomplishing these functions.

Table 6.6
Functions of technology.

- *Tool* to support knowledge construction.

- *Information vehicle* for exploring knowledge to support learning by constructing.

- *Context* to support learning by doing.

- *Social medium* to support learning by conversing.

- *Intellectual partner* to support learning by reflecting.

Source: From *Learning with Technology: A Constructivist Perspective*, by D. H. Jonassen, K. L. Peck, and B. G. Wilson, 1999, Upper Saddle River, NJ: Merrill/Prentice Hall. Reprinted with permission.

Technological Applications

Computer-Based Instruction.   Chapter 2 discussed computer-based instruction (CBI) or computer-assisted instruction (CAI) in the context of operant conditioning. Until recently, CBI was the most common application of computer learning in schools (Jonassen, 1996). CBI is often used for drills and tutorials. Drill programs are easy to write; because they review information, the student proceeds in linear fashion. Tutorials are interactive; they present information and feedback to students and respond based on students' answers. Branching programs are examples of tutorials (Chapter 2).

Studies investigating CBI in college courses yield beneficial effects on students' achievement and attitudes (Kulik et al., 1980). Several CBI features are firmly grounded in learning theory and research (Lepper, 1985). Computers command students' attention and provide immediate response feedback. Feedback can be of a type not often given in the classroom, such as how students' present performances compare with their prior performances (to show progress in learning). Computers individualize content and rate of presentation.

Although drills and tutorials place strict limitations on how students can interact with the material, one advantage of CBI is that many programs allow personalization; students enter information about themselves, parents, and friends, which is then included in the instructional presentation. Personalization can produce higher achievement than other formats (Anand & Ross, 1987; Ross et al., 1985). Anand and Ross (1987) gave elementary schoolchildren instruction in dividing fractions according to one of three problem formats (abstract, concrete, personalized), shown with sample problems:

- (Abstract) There are three objects. Each is cut in half. In all, how many pieces would there be?
- (Concrete) Billy had three candy bars. He cut each one of them in half. In all, how many pieces of candy did Billy have?
- (Personalized for student named Joseph) Joseph's teacher, Mrs. Williams, surprised him on December 15 when she presented Joseph with three candy bars. Joseph cut each one of them in half so that he could share the birthday gift with his friends. In all, how many pieces of candy did Joseph have? (pp. 73–74)

The personalized format led to better learning and transfer than the abstract format and to more positive attitudes toward instruction than the concrete format. Personalizing instruction may improve meaningfulness and allow easy integration into LTM networks. This issue needs further investigation.

Simulations and Games.   *Simulations* represent real or imaginary situations that cannot be brought into the learning setting. Examples are programs simulating the flights of aircraft, underwater expeditions, and life in a fictional city. Learners can build memory networks better when they have tangible referents during learning. *Games* are designed to create an enjoyable learning context by linking material with sport, adventure, or fantasy. Games can emphasize thinking skills and problem solving but also can be used to teach specific content (e.g., basketball game to teach fractions).

Lepper and his colleagues (Lepper, 1985; Lepper & Hodell, 1989) suggest that games also influence learning via increased motivation. Motivation is greater when an *endogenous* (natural) relationship exists between the content and the means ("special effects") by which the game or simulation presents the content. Fractions are endogenously related to a basketball game, for example, when students are asked to determine how much of the court is covered by players dribbling down the floor. From an information processing perspective, an endogenous relationship enhances meaningfulness and LTM coding and storage. In many games and simulations, however, the relation between content and means is arbitrary, such as when a student's correct response to a question produces fantasy elements (e.g., cartoon characters). When the relation is arbitrary, the game does not produce better learning than traditional instruction, although the former may be more interesting.

As a type of computer-based environment, simulations seem well suited for discovery learning. In their review of studies using computer simulations in discovery learning, de Jong and van Joolingen (1998) concluded that simulations were more effective than traditional instruction in inculcating students' "deep" (intuitive) cognitive processing. Simulations also may be beneficial for learning problem-solving skills. Woodward, Carnine, and Gersten (1988) found that the addition of computer simulations to structured teaching produced problem-solving gains for special education high school students compared with traditional instruction alone. The authors noted, however, that the mechanism producing these results was unclear and the results may not generalize to stand-alone computer simulations.

Programming.   Computer science courses teach programming skills, which are useful in various occupations. From a learning perspective, programming may aid the development of students' thinking, reasoning, and problem-solving skills in ways not possible with standard educational curricula (Jonassen, 1996; Lepper, 1985). Learning to program helps one acquire general problem-solving skills such as formalizing a conceptual model, breaking a larger problem into subproblems, employing a flow chart to determine alternatives, and isolating and correcting conceptual and computational errors (debugging). Programming also exposes children to concepts ordinarily associated with higher-level mathematics (variables, geometric functions), which can be "revisited" periodically during schooling (Bruner, 1960).

Years ago Papert (1980), a leading computer proponent, described the philosophy of the programming language *LOGO*, which is explicitly designed for children. Through "turtle geometry," children create unusual geometric designs and cartoon drawings by using a small number of simple commands (e.g., "forward," "back," "left turn"). The effects provide children with immediate feedback of efforts to control the environment. In addition, children form commands by using subroutines, or sets of commands that produce given configurations. Rather than simply giving the computer a list of instructions, learners combine standard commands with their unique ones.

Empirical evidence is mixed regarding how well computer programming develops thinking and problem-solving skills (Grabe & Grabe, 1998a; Lepper, 1985; Oppenheimer, 1997; Palumbo, 1990). With respect to LOGO, research shows that children typically are product oriented and want to generate effects. These outcomes are antithetical to the type of reasoned analysis and careful construction of subroutines required for programming (Grabe & Grabe, 1998a). Although some critics argue that programming results in no learning benefits, Clements and Gullo (1984) obtained positive effects. Six-year-olds were assigned to a programming group or a CBI condition and participated in two 40-minute sessions for 12 weeks. The programming group received training on LOGO; the CBI group worked on commercial software dealing with reading and mathematics. On a posttest, the programming condition scored higher on measures of reflectivity (cognitive style), divergent thinking (fluency, originality), and metacognition (awareness of comprehension failure).

Research has obtained advantages for programming on measures of social behaviors while children worked in pairs during problem solving (conflict resolution, self-directed work, rule determination), but no advantage for programming on reading or mathematics achievement tests (Clements, 1986; Clements & Nastasi, 1988). Evidence also shows that collaborative efforts among students working on LOGO encourage positive social behaviors and constructive attempts to resolve conflicts (Nastasi, Clements, & Battista, 1990). With respect to creativity, Clements (1991, 1995) found that LOGO enhanced creativity in both the verbal and figural domains. Clements (1995) noted, however, that creativity enhancement depends on teacher efforts and that many teachers find it difficult to create a school environment that fosters creativity.

Multimedia.   *Multimedia* refers to technology that combines the capabilities of computers with other media such as film, video, sound, music, and text (Galbreath, 1992). Multimedia learning occurs when students interact with information presented in more than one mode (e.g., words and pictures; Mayer, 1997). The capabilities of computers to interface with other media have advanced rapidly. Video streaming, CDs, and DVDs can be used with computers for instructional purposes (Hannafin & Peck, 1988).

Multimedia have important implications for teaching because they offer many possibilities for infusing technology into instruction (Dede, 1992; Galbreath, 1992; Hirschbuhl, 1992; Jonassen, 1989; Kozma, 1991). At the same time, research evidence provides only lukewarm support for the benefits of multimedia for learning. In his review of research studies, Mayer (1997) found that multimedia enhanced students' problem solving and transfer; however, effects were strongest for students with little prior knowledge and high spatial ability. Dillon and Gabbard (1998) also concluded from their review that effects depended in part on ability: Students with lower general ability had the greatest difficulty with multimedia. Learning style was important: Students willing to explore obtained the greatest benefits. Multimedia seems especially advantageous on specific tasks requiring rapid searching through information.

Mayer and his colleagues have conducted extensive research on the conditions favoring learning from multimedia. When verbal and visual (e.g., narration and animation) information are combined during instruction, students benefit from dual coding (Paivio, 1986; Chapter 4). The simultaneous presentation helps learners form connections between words and pictures because they are in WM at the same time (Mayer, Moreno, Boire, & Vagge, 1999). Some instructional devices that assist multimedia learning are text signals that emphasize the structure of the content and its relationship to other material (Mautone & Mayer, 2001), personalized messages that address students and make them feel as participants in the lesson (Moreno & Mayer, 2000), allowing learners to exercise control over the pace of instruction (Mayer & Chandler, 2001), and animations that include movement and simulations (Mayer & Moreno, 2002).

Maximal benefits of multimedia require that some logistical and administrative issues be addressed. Interactive capabilities are expensive to develop and produce. Costs prohibit many school systems from purchasing components. Interactive video may require additional instruction time because programs present more material and require greater student time in responding. Compared with video alone, students might demonstrate higher achievement with interactive video, but if the latter requires increased instruction time, it offers no advantage in the amount learned per unit of time (Schaffer & Hannafin, 1986). Many interactive systems are bulky and require a permanent workstation, which can be a problem given that space often is at a premium in schools.

Such elaborate technology may seem overwhelming to many teachers and students, who will require extensive training. The equipment requires maintenance and upgrading, which are problematic when budgets are tight. Although the jury is still out on the effects on student learning of multimedia, clearly it can alter classroom life and complement instruction on a variety of topics.

Networking and Distance Learning.   Another technological application is *microcomputer networking*. Networks connect microcomputers to one another and to central peripherals (e.g., printers, storage devices). Networking allows schools to be connected with one another and with devices inside and outside of the district. Networking offers several advantages. Students have easy access to computers in their schools. Computer processing takes place in the microcomputer rather than in larger (mainframe) computers. Microcomputers are portable; permanent workstations are not required. Centralized peripheral devices help contain costs. One disadvantage is that when a system becomes excessively large it requires full-time supervision.

Distance learning (distance education) occurs when instruction that originates in one location is transmitted to students at one or more remote sites. If interactive capabilities exist, then two-way feedback and discussions become part of the learning experience. Distance learning saves time, effort, and money because instructors and students do not have to make long journeys to classes. Universities, for example, can recruit graduate students from a wide geographical area. There is less concern about the students traveling great distances to attend classes because they are held at a local site (e.g., school district building). Districts can conduct in-service programs by transmitting from a central site to all of the schools. Distance learning sacrifices face-to-face contact with instructors, although if two-way interactive video is used the interactions are real-time (*synchronous*).

Another networking application is the *electronic bulletin board* (*conference*). People networked with computers can post messages, but more important for learning can be part of a discussion (chat) group. Participants ask questions and raise issues, as well as respond to the comments of others. A fair amount of research has examined whether such e-mail exchanges facilitate writing skill acquisition (Fabos & Young, 1999). Whether this *asynchronous* means of telecommunication exchange promotes learning any better than face-to-face interaction is problematic; much of the research is conflicting or inconclusive (Fabos & Young, 1999). More research is needed. We can say, however, that telecommunication has the benefit of convenience in that people can respond at any time, not just when they are gathered together. The receptive learning environment may indirectly promote learning.

As forms of *computer-mediated communication (CMC)*, distance learning and computer conferencing greatly expand the possibilities for learning through social interaction. Research should determine whether certain personal characteristics of learners and types of instructional content enhance the benefits of CMC on learning and motivation.

E-Learning.   *E-learning* refers to learning through electronically delivered means. The term often is used generally to refer to any type of electronic communication (e.g., videoconferencing); however, here it is used in the narrower sense of Internet (Web-based) instruction.

The *Internet* is an international collection of computer networks. It is a system of shared resources that no one owns. Each computer in the network has a unique address. The Internet provides access to other people (users) through e-mail and conferences (chat rooms), files, and the World Wide Web (WWW)—a multicomputer interactive multimedia resource. It also stores information that can be copied for personal use (Grabe & Grabe, 1998b).

The Internet is a wonderful resource for information, but we must assess its role in learning. On the surface, the Internet has advantages. Web-based instruction provides students with access to more resources in less time than is possible in traditional ways; however, more resources do not automatically mean better learning. The latter is accomplished only if students acquire new skills, such as methods for conducting research on a topic or critical thinking about the accuracy of material on the Web. Web resources also can promote learning when students take information from the Web and incorporate it into classroom activities (e.g., discovery learning).

Teachers can assist the development of students' Internet skills with a scaffolding approach. Students must be taught search strategies (e.g., ways to use browsers), but teachers also might conduct the initial Web search and provide students the names of helpful websites. Grabe and Grabe (1998b) offer other suggestions.

Web-based learning is commonly incorporated into traditional instruction as a *blended* model of instruction (i.e., some face-to-face instruction and the rest via e-learning). Web-based learning also is useful in conjunction with multimedia projects. In many teacher preparation programs preservice teachers use the Web to obtain resources and then selectively incorporate these into multimedia projects as part of lesson designs.

A danger in students using the Internet is that the large array of information available could inculcate the belief that everything is important and reliable. Students then may engage in "associative writing" (Chapter 9) by trying to include too much information in reports and papers. To the extent that e-learning helps teach students the higher-level skills of analysis and synthesis, they will acquire strategies for determining what is important and merging information into a coherent product.

Virtual Reality.   *Virtual reality* refers to a computer-based technology that incorporates input and output devices and allows students to experience and interact with an artificial environment as if it were the real world (Middleton, 1992). Virtual-reality systems present a 360° environment that includes lifelike and fantasy elements (i.e., a real world or a fantasy world). Specialized input and output are accomplished through devices for moving in space (e.g., gloves, treadmill, stationary bicycle, bodysuit), mounted displays for visualization, and audio receivers to transmit three-dimensional sound. A feeling of presence in the world is important, so sensors worn by participants (i.e., in bodysuits or data gloves) inform the system of their location, which then varies spatial and audio feedback. Critical features include *flexibility* (ability to present real and unreal worlds), *presence* (sensors and the three-dimensional environment provide users with a sense of being there), *control and interaction* (users can exert control over features of the environment), and *feedback* (users receive sophisticated tactile and temperature feedback).

Although virtual reality is still developing and not commonly used in education, several of its features may enhance learning (Lanier, 1992; Middleton, 1992). Because the world can be changed to meet individual users' needs, it is well designed to accommodate instructional scaffolding and to serve as a medium for apprenticeships. It allows learners to experience phenomena that they cannot in traditional classrooms (e.g., inside of a machine, underground environment). A third application is with physical skills. A virtual-reality world facilitates learning a physical skill because motion can be slowed. This is important for many skills that occur quickly and are difficult to grasp (e.g., juggling), and also for physical therapy patients who are relearning skills (Lanier, 1992). The hope is that virtual reality will stimulate creative thinking by allowing people to test problem solutions in ways not usually possible. Research in this area could foster new teaching methods.

Critique.   From the preceding evidence, we might conclude that technology can enhance learning compared with traditional instruction. However, comparing technologically enhanced instruction with conventional instruction can present misleading results (Oppenheimer, 1997). No one instructional medium is consistently superior to others, regardless of content, learners, or setting (Clark & Salomon, 1986). Many research studies about computers suffer from methodological problems involving inadequate comparison groups and the introduction of novelty (Oppenheimer, 1997). When computer learning shows advantages over traditional instruction, it may be because computers present better-prepared materials and implement more effective instructional design strategies. Technology is not a cause of learning; rather, it is a means for applying principles of effective instruction and learning.

Clark and Salomon (1986) recommended that researchers determine the conditions under which computers facilitate instruction and learning. This is still true today and may be said for technology in general. The history of educational reform is littered with changes being adopted prior to any convincing evidence of their effectiveness. Use of technology should depend on the learning goals. Although technology has the potential to foster different learning goals, it may not be the best way to promote student interaction through peer teaching, group discussions, or cooperative learning. Application 6.5 gives some suggestions for infusing technology into classroom instruction.

Even when its use seems beneficial, technology has the disadvantage of not allowing for incidental learning as might occur when a teacher or student mentions in class an anecdote related to the material being studied. Although most Web information is reasonably up-to-date, it may need to be supplemented to relate material to current events; after students gather information from the Web on the history and geography of a world region, the teacher and students could discuss the current political situation in the area.

Promising evidence suggests that technological applications can enhance learning, but more research evaluating their effectiveness is necessary. Some research shows that computer-based problem-solving is differentially effective for male and female students (Littleton, Light, Joiner, Messer, & Barnes, 1998). Exploring gender and ethnic differences should be a research priority.

Another area that needs to be addressed is the motivational effects of technology on teachers and students (Ertmer, 1999; Lepper & Gurtner, 1989). Lepper and Malone (1987) noted that computers can focus attention on the task through motivational enhancements, maintain level of arousal at an optimal level, and direct students to engage in task-directed information processing rather than attend to focusing on irrelevant task aspects. The idea is that effective motivational principles can enhance *deep* (rather than shallow) *processing* (Hooper & Hannafin, 1991).

Future Directions

Technological developments occur rapidly, and research is sure to accelerate. As technology becomes more elaborate, it will offer a far greater range of instructional possibilities. We will be able to access and create knowledge in new, sophisticated ways. Research will explore the effects of these developments on student learning, as well as effective ways to infuse technology into instruction.

At a basic research level, investigations on artificial intelligence (AI) may provide important insights into human learning, thinking, and problem solving. *Artificial intelligence* refers to computer programs that simulate human abilities to infer, evaluate,

APPLICATION 6.5
Technology and Learning

Technological applications can be applied effectively to help improve student learning. Jim Marshall works with an American history teacher in a neighboring high school in developing a Civil War computer simulation. The classes draw straws to determine which class will be the Union and which the Confederacy. The students in each class then study the battles of the Civil War and look for information about the terrain, the weather at the time of each battle, the number of soldiers involved, and the leadership abilities of the individuals in charge. The students in both classes then simulate the battles on the computer, interacting with each other, using the data, trying to see if they might change the outcome of the original battle. When students make a strategic move, they have to defend and support their move with historical data.

Gina Brown uses streaming video and the Web to have her students study and reflect on educational psychology principles applied in classrooms. As students observe the video of an elementary class lesson, they stop the video and enter responses to relate educational practices to psychological principles they have been discussing in class. Then students are able to interact with other students and Dr. Brown to share thoughts on the lesson observed. Dr. Brown also has a fictional classroom set up on a website. She poses questions to her students (e.g., "How might the teacher use authentic assessment in science?"), after which they go to the website, read and reflect, and construct a response that is distributed to Dr. Brown and all other students. Thus, everyone can respond and interact with others.

Kathy Stone uses her computers for various activities in her third-grade class, but one of the fun activities that incorporates creative writing abilities and word-processing skills becomes a class project each month. At the beginning of each month, Mrs. Stone starts a story on the computer entitled, "The Adventures of Mrs. Stone's Class." Children have the opportunity to add to the story as often as they wish. At the end of the month they print the story and read it aloud in class. The computer provides a unique means for constructing a story collaboratively.

reason, solve problems, understand speech, and learn (Trappl, 1985). John McCarthy coined the term in 1956 as a conference theme. Other terms found in the literature (e.g., machine intelligence, intelligent CAI) are roughly synonymous.

AI has three important aspects or goals. First, computers can be programmed to behave in an intelligent manner. These expert systems are increasingly used to solve problems and provide instruction in various domains. A second aspect involves programming computers to simulate human learning and other thought processes with the goal of understanding the operation of the mind. The third aspect (robotics) investigates how machines can be programmed to perform tasks.

Expert systems are large computer programs that supply the knowledge and problem-solving processes of one or more experts (Anderson, 1990; Fischler & Firschein, 1987; Trappl, 1985). Analogous to human consultants, expert systems have been applied to diverse fields such as medicine, chemistry, electronics, and law. Expert systems have a vast knowledge base consisting of declarative knowledge (facts) and procedural knowledge (system of rules used to draw inferences). An interface poses questions to users and gives recommendations or solutions. A common application of expert systems is to teach by providing expertise to students (Park, Perez, & Seidel, 1987). Instruction often employs guided discovery; students formulate and test hypotheses and experience consequences.

Future expert systems will be applied to a wider array of domains (Self, 1988). One challenge is to improve systems' capabilities to understand natural languages, especially speech. Although expert systems can perform pattern-recognition tasks, most of these tasks involve only visual stimuli. Machines can be programmed to understand a particular human voice. The use of *assistive technology* in education is expanding, as students with disabilities are integrated as much as possible in regular classroom instruction. Expert systems should enhance the capabilities of computers such that they will be accessible to all learners (e.g., auditory, visual, multiple handicaps).

Technology holds exciting possibilities for helping us *understand human thought processes*. This application involves programming computers with some knowledge and rules that allow them to alter and acquire new knowledge and rules based on experiences (Anderson, 1990; Shallis, 1984). In concept learning, for example, a computer might be programmed with an elementary rule and then be exposed to instances and noninstances of the concept. The program modifies itself by storing the new information in memory and altering its rule. Learning also can occur from exposure to case histories. A computer can be programmed with facts and case histories of a disease. As the computer analyzes these histories, it alters its memory to incorporate the etiology, symptoms, and course of the disease. When the computer acquires an extensive knowledge base for a particular disease, it can diagnose future cases with precision.

Technological progress is likely in additional content areas and in the domain of information processing. Computers are built to process information sequentially; humans can process information in parallel (e.g., think of one thing while attending to something else). In a computer, parallel processing can occur by initially dividing a task into subgoals and then assigning subgoals to different processors that are linked. This type of computer activity might provide insight into how pieces of information become linked in thought to provide integrated knowledge.

Robotics is the study of ways to program machines to perform tasks. Robots often conjure up images of humanlike forms in science fiction novels, but most robots in use today are either boxes with mechanical arms and grippers or normal-looking machines (e.g., forklift trucks) without operators. Robots contain sensors that detect light, pressure, sound, and distances, which provide feedback on location of the robot relative to aspects of its environment. Mechanical hands, arms, wheels, and other devices are used to operate on the environment. The computer may be inside the robot or a mainframe computer linked to the robot by electric wire, cable, or radio. The typical industrial robots can move freely but cannot think or reason. Robots are insensitive to adverse working conditions involving noise, dust, and dangers; they also do not take long lunch breaks or complain about salaries or working conditions! Future research will most likely focus on making them more economical to build and operate and versatile in task performance.

SUMMARY

This chapter discusses theories of instruction, with particular emphasis on their links to principles of cognitive information processing. Instructional theory historically involved the design of instruction, but with the decline of behaviorism, the focus has broadened to how learner, instructional, and contextual variables operate in educational contexts. Current instructional research investigates the influence of instructional variables on learners' cognitions, how learners construct knowledge, the role of individual differences in learning, and the impact of motivational variables on learning.

Discovery learning allows students to obtain knowledge for themselves through problem solving. Discovery learning is a type of inductive reasoning. It requires that teachers arrange activities such that students can form and test hypotheses; it is not simply letting students do what they want.

Meaningful reception learning of facts, concepts, and principles occurs by relating new information to knowledge in memory. Expository teaching presents information in an organized fashion so it can be incorporated into memory networks. This is a deductive approach: The key is to build hierarchical memory structures where general concepts subsume specific ideas. Advance organizers, or broad statements that introduce lessons, help make learning meaningful. Organizers direct students' attention to important material, highlight interrelations among ideas, and link material to what students know.

Gagné postulated an instructional theory emphasizing the conditions of learning, or the circumstances that prevail when learning occurs. Types of learning outcomes are intellectual skills, verbal information, cognitive strategies, motor skills, and attitudes. Events of learning are factors that make a difference in instruction. Internal events are learners' current capabilities, personal dispositions, and ways of processing information. External events are instructional factors (material, mode of presentation) that support students while they are learning. In designing instruction for intellectual skills, the use of a learning hierarchy specifying component skills and prerequisites is helpful. Some other perspectives on instruction incorporating cognitive elements include the time model, mastery learning, inquiry teaching, and the Instructional Quality Profile.

A recent advance in cognitive instruction involves the use of worked examples in teaching. Worked examples portray an expert's problem-solving model for learners to study before they begin work on their own. Worked examples seem particularly helpful during the early stages of learning when students are acquiring skills.

Research shows that presenting more than one worked example is better than only a single example, that examples should portray different types of problems, that examples should not overload learners' WM, that learners should be encouraged to self-explain solutions, and that interspersing examples with practice is more effective than a lesson where examples are first presented followed by practice problems.

Research on teaching shows that teachers' cognitive planning and decision making exert important effects on student learning. An effective instructional model includes components such as specifying learning goals, explaining and demonstrating concepts, monitoring student guided practice, having students practice independently, and arranging spaced reviews of material.

The role of learner characteristics in teaching is receiving increased emphasis. Aptitude-treatment interactions involve instructional variables that are differentially effective depending on student characteristics. Cognitive styles are stable variations in perceiving, organizing, processing, and remembering information. Styles serve as bases for adapting instruction to individual differences. Individual differences in learners' attentional allocations also affect instructional effectiveness and student learning. Teachers often must adapt instruction to student individual differences. Macroadaptations are made at the system or course level, microadaptations at the lesson or segment level.

Technology is assuming an increasingly important role in learning and instruction. A central technological component is the computer. Computer literacy, once a primary focus, has given way to technological applications that assist student learning. Some common applications in schools involve CBI, simulations and games, programming, multimedia, networking, e-learning, and virtual reality. Research evidence on the effects of technology on learning generally is positive with benefits being obtained for metacognition, deep processing, and problem solving. As technological innovation continues, it is important that researchers determine how technological advances affect student learning and explore artificial intelligence as a means of understanding human thought.

7 Constructivism

Constructivism is a psychological and philosophical perspective contending that individuals form or construct much of what they learn and understand (Bruning, Schraw, & Ronning, 1999). A major influence on the rise of constructivism has been theory and research in human development, especially the theories of Piaget and Vygotsky. Human development is the subject of Chapter 10; however, the present chapter covers Vygotsky's theory because it forms a cornerstone of the constructivist movement. The emphasis that Vygotsky placed on the role of social mediation of knowledge construction is central to many forms of constructivism.

In recent years constructivism increasingly has been applied to learning and teaching. The history of learning theory reveals a shift away from environmental influence and toward human factors as explanations for learning. This shift began with the advent of cognitive psychology, which disputed the claim of reinforcement theories that stimuli, responses, and consequences were adequate to explain learning. Cognitive theories place great emphasis on learners' information processing as a central cause of learning. Yet, despite the elegance of cognitive learning theories, some researchers have felt that these theories fail to capture the complexity of human learning. This point is underscored by the fact that some cognitive perspectives use behavioral terminology such as the "automaticity" of performance and "forming connections" between items in memory.

Today a number of learning researchers have shifted even more toward a focus on learners. Rather than talk about how knowledge is acquired, they speak of how it is constructed. Although these researchers differ in their emphasis on factors that affect learning and learners' cognitive processes, the theoretical perspectives they espouse may be loosely grouped and referred to as *constructivism.*

This chapter begins by providing an overview of constructivism to include a description of its key assumptions and the different types of constructivist theories. Vygotsky's theory is described next, with emphasis on those aspects relevant to learning. The critical roles of social processes and private speech are discussed, followed by coverage of motivation and self-regulation from a constructivist perspective. The chapter concludes with a discussion of constructivist learning environments, including its key features, examples of instructional methods, and the components of reflective teaching.

When you finish studying this chapter, you should be able to do the following:

- Discuss the major assumptions and various types of constructivism.
- Explain the key principles of Vygotsky's sociocultural theory and implications for teaching in the zone of proximal development.
- Explain the function of private speech for learning and self-regulation.
- Discuss how classroom structure and TARGET variables affect student motivation.

- Describe how teacher expectations are formed and how they can affect teachers' interactions with students.
- Discuss self-regulation from a constructivist perspective to include the role of students' implicit theories.
- List the key features of constructivist learning environments and the major

- components of the APA learner-centered principles.
- Describe how class discussions, peer tutoring, and cooperative learning can be structured to reflect constructivist principles.
- Explain how teachers might become more reflective and thereby enhance student achievement.

CONSTRUCTIVIST ASSUMPTIONS AND PERSPECTIVES

Many learning researchers have questioned some of cognitive psychology's assumptions about learning and instruction because they believed these assumptions could not completely explain students' learning and understanding. These questionable assumptions are as follows (Greeno, 1989):

- Thinking resides in the mind rather than in interaction with persons and situations.
- Processes of learning and thinking are relatively uniform across persons, and some situations foster higher-order thinking better than others.
- Thinking derives from knowledge and skills developed in formal instructional settings more than on general conceptual competencies that result from one's experiences and innate abilities.

Constructivists do not accept these assumptions because of evidence that thinking takes place in contexts and that cognitions are largely constructed by individuals as a function of their experiences in situations. Constructivist accounts of learning and development highlight the contributions of individuals to what is learned. Social constructivist models further emphasize the importance of social interactions in acquisition of skills and knowledge. We now examine further what constructivism is, its assumptions, and its forms.

Overview

What Is Constructivism? Strictly speaking, constructivism is not a theory but rather an *epistemology,* or philosophical explanation about the nature of learning (Simpson, 2002). As discussed in Chapter 1, a theory is a scientifically valid explanation for learning. Theories allow for hypotheses to be generated and tested. Constructivism does not propound that learning principles exist and are to be discovered and tested, but rather that learners create their own learning.

Nonetheless, this text refers to "constructivist theories" to maintain consistency with other perspectives and because constructivism makes general predictions that can be operationalized and tested. Although the latter predictions are general and thus open to different interpretations (i.e., what does it mean that learners construct their own learning?), they could be the focus of research.

Constructivist theorists reject the notion that scientific truths exist and await discovery and verification. They argue that no statement can be assumed as true but rather should be viewed with reasonable doubt. The world can be mentally constructed in many different ways, so no theory has a lock on the truth. This is true even for constructivism; there are many varieties and no one version should be assumed to more correct than any other (Simpson, 2002).

Rather than viewing knowledge as truth, constructivists construe it as a working hypothesis. Knowledge is not imposed from outside people but rather formed inside them. A person's constructions are true to that person but not necessarily to anyone else. This is because people produce knowledge based on their beliefs and experiences, which differ from person to person. All knowledge, then, is subjective and personal and a product of our cognitions (Simpson, 2002).

Assumptions.   Constructivism highlights the interaction of persons and situations in the acquisition and refinement of skills and knowledge. Constructivism contrasts with behavioral views of learning that stress the influence of the environment on the person; constructivism contrasts also with classical information processing theory, which places the locus of learning within the mind with little attention to the context in which it occurs. It shares with social cognitive theory (Bandura, 1986, 1997) the assumption that persons, behaviors, and environments interact in reciprocal fashion.

A basic assumption of constructivism is that people are active learners and must construct knowledge for themselves (Geary, 1995). To understand material well, learners must discover the basic principles for themselves. Constructivists differ in the extent to which they ascribe this function entirely to learners. Some believe that mental structures come to reflect reality, whereas others (radical constructivists) believe that the individual's mental world is the only reality. Constructivists also differ in how much they ascribe the construction of knowledge to social interactions with teachers, peers, parents, and others.

Many of the principles, concepts, and ideas discussed in this text reflect the idea of constructivism, including cognitive processing, expectations, values, and perceptions of self and others (Derry, 1996). Thus, although constructivism seems to be a recent arrival on the learning scene, its basic premise that learners construct understandings underlies many learning principles. This is the epistemological aspect of constructivism. Some constructivist ideas are not as well developed as those of other theories discussed in this text, but constructivism has affected theory and research in learning and development.

Constructivism also has influenced educational thinking about curriculum and instruction. It underlies the emphasis on the integrated curriculum in which students study a topic from multiple perspectives. For example, in studying hot-air balloons, students might read about them, write about them, learn new vocabulary words, visit one (hands-on experience), study the scientific principles involved, draw pictures of them, and learn songs about them. Constructivist ideas also are found in many professional standards and affect design of curriculum and instruction, such as the learner-centered principles developed by the American Psychological Association (discussed later) and the Professional Standards for Teaching Mathematics (National Council of Teachers of Mathematics, 1991).

Another constructivist assumption is that teachers should not teach in the traditional sense of delivering instruction to a group of students. Rather, they should structure situations such that learners become actively involved with content through manipulation of materials and social interaction. Activities include observing phenomena, collecting data, generating and testing hypotheses, and working collaboratively with others. Classes visit sites outside of the classroom. Teachers from different disciplines plan the curriculum together. Students are taught to be self-regulated and take an active role in their learning by setting goals, monitoring and evaluating progress, and going beyond basic requirements by exploring interests (Bruning et al., 1999; Geary, 1995).

Perspectives

Constructivism is not a unified theory but rather has different perspectives (see Table 7.1; Bruning et al., 1999; Moshman, 1982; Phillips, 1995). *Exogenous constructivism* refers to the idea that the acquisition of knowledge represents a reconstruction of structures that exist in the external world. This view posits a strong influence of the external world on knowledge construction, such as by experiences, teaching, and exposure to models. Knowledge is accurate to the extent it reflects that reality. Contemporary information processing theories reflect this notion in concepts such as schemata, productions, and memory networks.

In contrast, *endogenous constructivism* emphasizes the coordination of cognitive actions (Bruning et al., 1999). Mental structures are created out of earlier structures, not directly from environmental information; therefore, knowledge is not a mirror of the external world acquired through experiences, teaching, or social inter-

Table 7.1
Perspectives on constructivism.

Perspective	Premises
Exogenous	The acquisition of knowledge represents a reconstruction of the external world. The world influences beliefs through experiences, exposure to models, and teaching. Knowledge is accurate to the extent it reflects external reality.
Endogenous	Knowledge derives from previously acquired knowledge and not directly from environmental interactions. Knowledge is not a mirror of the external world; rather, it develops through cognitive abstraction.
Dialectical	Knowledge derives from interactions between persons and their environments. Constructions are not invariably tied to the external world nor wholly the workings of the mind. Rather, knowledge reflects the outcomes of mental contradictions that result from one's interactions with the environment.

actions. Knowledge develops through the cognitive activity of abstraction and follows a generally predictable sequence. Piaget's (1970) theory of cognitive development (discussed in Chapter 10) fits this framework.

Between these extremes lies *dialectical* constructivism, which holds that knowledge derives from interactions between persons and their environments. Constructions are not invariably bound to the external world nor are they wholly the result of the workings of the mind; rather, they reflect the outcomes of mental contradictions that result from interactions with the environment. This perspective has become closely aligned with many contemporary theories. For example, it is compatible with Bandura's (1986) social cognitive theory (Chapter 3) and with many motivation theories (Chapter 8). The developmental theories of Bruner (discussed in Chapter 10) and Vygotsky (discussed in this chapter) also emphasize the influence of the social environment.

Each of these perspectives has merit and is potentially useful for research and teaching. Exogenous views are appropriate when we are interested in determining how accurately learners perceive the structure of knowledge within a domain. The endogenous perspective is relevant to explore how learners develop from novices through greater levels of competence (Chapter 9). The dialectical view is useful for designing interventions to challenge children's thinking and for research aimed at exploring the effectiveness of social influences such as exposure to models and peer collaboration.

Situated Cognition

A core premise of constructivism is that cognitive processes (including thinking and learning) are situated (located) in physical and social contexts (Anderson, Reder, & Simon, 1996; Greeno et al., 1998). *Situated cognition* (or *learning*) involves relations between a person and a situation; cognitive processes do not reside solely in one's mind (Greeno, 1989).

The idea of person-situation interaction is not new. Most contemporary theories of learning and development assume that beliefs and knowledge are formed as people interact in situations. This emphasis contrasts with the classical information processing model that highlights the processing and movement of information through mental structures (e.g., sensory registers, WM, LTM). Information processing downplays the importance of situations once environmental inputs are received. Research within a variety of disciplines—including cognitive psychology, social cognitive learning, and specific content domains (e.g., reading, mathematics)—shows this to be a limited view and that thinking involves an extended reciprocal relation with the context (Bandura, 1986; Greeno, 1989).

Research highlights the importance of exploring situated cognition as a means of understanding the development of competence in domains such as literacy, mathematics, and science (Cobb, 1994; Driver, Asoko, Leach, Mortimer, & Scott, 1994; Lampert, 1990; see Chapter 9). Situated cognition also is relevant to motivation (Chapter 8). As with learning, motivation is not an entirely internal state as posited by classical views or wholly dependent on the environment as predicted by reinforcement theories (Chapter 2). Rather, motivation depends on cognitive activity in interaction with sociocultural and instructional factors, which include language and forms of assistance such as scaffolding of information (Sivan, 1986).

Situated cognition addresses the intuitive notion that many processes interact to produce learning. We know that motivation and instruction are linked: Good instruction can raise motivation for learning and motivated learners seek effective instructional environments (Schunk, 1991). A further benefit of the situated cognition perspective is that it leads researchers to explore cognition in authentic learning contexts such as schools, workplaces, and homes, many of which involve mentoring or apprenticeships.

Research on the effectiveness of situated learning is recent, but results are promising. Griffin (1995) compared traditional (in-class) instruction on map skills with a situated learning approach in which college students received practice in the actual environments depicted on the maps. The situated learning group performed better on a map-skill assessment. Although Griffin found no benefit of situated learning on transfer, the results of situated learning studies should be highly generalizable to similar contexts.

The situative idea also is pertinent to how learning occurs (Greeno et al., 1998). Students exposed to a certain procedure for learning a subject experience situated cognition for that method; in other words, that is how this content is learned. For example, if students repeatedly receive mathematics instruction taught in didactic fashion by a teacher explaining and demonstrating, followed by their engaging in independent problem solving at their desks, then mathematics learning is apt to become situated in this context. The same students might have difficulty adjusting to a new teacher who favors using guided discovery by collaborative peer groups.

The instructional implication is that teaching methods should reflect the outcomes we desire in our learners. If we are trying to teach them inquiry skills, the instruction must incorporate inquiry activities. The method and the content must be properly situated.

Situated cognition fits well with the constructivist idea that context is an inherent part of learning. Especially in subject domains (Chapter 9), this idea increasingly has been shown to be valid. Nonetheless, extending the idea of situated learning too far may be erroneous. As Anderson, Reder, and Simon (1996) show, there is plenty of empirical evidence for contextual independence of learning and transfer of learning between contexts. Rather than being at an impasse over knowing whether learning is situated, researchers need to explore the issue in greater depth. We need more information on which types of learning proceed best when they are firmly linked to contexts and when it is better to teach broader skills and show how they can be applied in different contexts.

Contributions and Applications

Constructivism has only recently been applied to the field of learning, so research exploring constructivist assumptions about learning is in its infancy. Another factor that makes determining the contributions of constructivism difficult is that the approach is not a unified one that offers specific hypotheses to be tested. Bereiter

(1994) accurately noted that the claim that "students construct their own knowledge" is not falsifiable but rather is true of all cognitive learning theories. Cognitive theories view the mind as a repository of beliefs, values, expectations, schemata, and so forth, so any feasible explanation of how those thoughts and feelings come to reside in the mind must assume that they are formed there. For example, social cognitive theory emphasizes the roles of expectations (e.g., self-efficacy, outcome) and goals; these beliefs and cognitions do not arise from nowhere but, rather, are constructed by learners.

Constructivism eventually must be evaluated not on whether any of its premises are true or false. Rather, it seems imperative to determine the process whereby students construct knowledge and what social, developmental, and instructional factors may influence that process. Research also is needed on when situational influences have greater effects on mental processes. A drawback of many forms of constructivism is the emphasis on *relativism* (Phillips, 1995), or the idea that all forms of knowledge are justifiable because they are constructed by learners, especially if they reflect societal consensus. Educators cannot accept this premise in good conscience because education demands that we inculcate values such as honesty, fairness, and responsibility in our students regardless of whether societal constituencies deem them important.

Furthermore, nature may constrain our thinking more than we wish to admit. For example, research suggests that some mathematical competencies—such as one-to-one correspondence and being able to count—are not constructed but rather largely genetically driven (Geary, 1995; Gelman & Gallistel, 1978; see Chapter 9). Far from being relative, some forms of knowledge may be universally endogenous. Acquisition of other competencies (e.g., multiplying, word processing) requires environmental input. Research will help to establish the scope of constructivist processes in the sequence of competency acquisition and how these processes change as a function of developmental level (Muller, Sokol, & Overton, 1998).

Constructivist perspectives have important implications for instruction and curriculum design (Phillips, 1995). The most straightforward recommendations are to involve students actively in their learning and to provide experiences that challenge their thinking and force them to rearrange their beliefs. Constructivism also underlies the current emphasis on *reflective teaching* (discussed later in this chapter). Social constructivist views such as Vygotsky's stress that social group learning and peer collaboration are useful. As students model for and observe each other, they not only teach skills but also experience higher self-efficacy for learning (Schunk, 1987). Application 7.1 gives constructivist applications. We now turn to a more in-depth examination of constructivism and its applications to human learning.

VYGOTSKY'S SOCIOCULTURAL THEORY

Vygotsky's theory is a constructivist perspective that emphasizes the social environment as a facilitator of development and learning. We discuss the background of the theory and its key assumptions and principles.

APPLICATION 7.1
Constructivism and Teaching

Constructivism emphasizes integrated curricula and having teachers use materials in such a way that learners become actively involved. Kathy Stone implements various constructivist ideas in her third-grade classroom using integrated units. In the fall she presents a unit on pumpkins. In social studies children learn where pumpkins are grown and about the products made from pumpkins. They also study the uses of pumpkins in history and the benefits of pumpkins to early settlers.

Mrs. Stone takes her class on a field trip to a pumpkin farm, where they learn how pumpkins are grown. Each student selects a pumpkin and brings it back to class. The pumpkin becomes a valuable learning tool. In mathematics the students estimate the size and weight of their pumpkins and then measure and weigh them. They establish class graphs by comparing all the pumpkins by size, weight, shape, and color. They also estimate the number of seeds they think Mrs. Stone's pumpkin has, and then they count the seeds when she cuts open her pumpkin. As another class activity, the students make pumpkin bread with Mrs. Stone's pumpkin. For art they design a shape for the carving of their pumpkins, and then with Mrs. Stone's assistance they carve them. In language arts they write a story about pumpkins. They also write a thank-you letter to the pumpkin farm. For spelling Mrs. Stone uses words that they have used in the study of pumpkins. These examples illustrate how Mrs. Stone integrates the study of pumpkins across the curriculum.

Background

Perhaps no theorist has influenced modern constructivist thinking more than Lev Semenovich Vygotsky, who was born in Russia in 1896. He studied various subjects in school, including psychology, philosophy, and literature, and received a law degree from Moscow Imperial University in 1917.

Following graduation, he returned to his hometown of Gomel', which was beset with problems stemming from German occupation, famine, and civil war. Two of his brothers died, and he contracted tuberculosis—the disease that eventually killed him. He taught courses in psychology and literature, wrote literary criticism, and edited a journal. He also worked at a teacher training institution, where he founded a psychology laboratory and wrote an educational psychology book (Tudge & Scrimsher, 2003).

A critical event in Vygotsky's life occurred in 1924 at the Second All-Russian Congress of Psychoneurology in Leningrad. Prevailing psychological theory at that time neglected subjective experiences in favor of Pavlov's conditioned reflexes and behaviorism's emphasis on environmental influences. Vygotsky presented a paper ("The Methods of Reflexological and Psychological Investigation") in which he criticized the dominant views and spoke on the relation of conditioned reflexes to human consciousness and behavior. Pavlov's experiments with dogs (Chapter 2) and Gestalt theorist Köhler's studies with apes (Chapter 5) erased many distinctions between animals and humans.

Vygotsky contended that, unlike animals that react only to the environment, humans have the capacity to alter the environment for their own purposes. This adaptive capacity distinguishes humans from lower forms of life. His speech made such an impression on one listener—Alexander Luria (discussed later in this chapter)—that he was invited to join the prestigious Institute of Experimental Psychology in Moscow. He helped to establish the Institute of Defektology, the purpose of which was to study ways to help handicapped individuals. Until his death from tuberculosis in 1934, he wrote extensively on the social mediation of learning and the role of consciousness, often in collaboration with colleagues Luria and Leontiev (Rohrkemper, 1989).

Understanding Vygotsky's position requires keeping in mind that he was a Marxist and that his views represented an attempt to apply Marxist ideas of social change to language and development (Rohrkemper, 1989). After the 1917 Russian Revolution, an urgency among the new leaders produced rapid change in the populace. Vygotsky's strong sociocultural theoretical orientation fit well with the revolution's goals of changing the culture to a socialist system.

Although Vygotsky had some access to Western society (writers such as Piaget; Tudge & Winterhoff, 1993), little of what Vygotsky wrote was published during his brief lifetime or for some years following his death. Unfortunately, a negative political climate prevailed in the former Soviet Union; among other things, the Communist Party curtailed psychological testing and publications. Although Vygotsky was a Marxist, he propounded revisionist thinking (Bruner, 1984). He moved from a Pavlovian view of psychology focusing on reflexes to a cultural-historical perspective that stressed language and social interaction (Tudge & Scrimsher, 2003). Some of Vygotsky's writings were at odds with Stalin's views and because of that were not published. References to his work were banned in the Soviet Union until the 1980s (Tudge & Scrimsher, 2003). In recent years Vygotsky's writings have been increasingly translated and circulated, which has expanded their impact in fields such as education, psychology, and linguistics.

Basic Principles

One of Vygotsky's central contributions to psychological thought was his emphasis on socially meaningful activity as an important influence on human consciousness (Kozulin, 1986; Tudge & Winterhoff, 1993). Vygotsky attempted to explain human thought in new ways. He rejected introspection (Chapter 1) and raised many of the same objections as the behaviorists (Chapter 2). He wanted to abandon explaining states of consciousness by referring to the concept of consciousness; similarly, he rejected behaviorist explanations of action in terms of prior actions. Rather than discarding consciousness (which the behaviorists did) or the role of the environment (which the introspectionists did), he sought a middle ground of taking environmental influence into account through its effect on consciousness.

Vygotsky's theory stresses the interaction of interpersonal (social), cultural-historical, and individual factors as the key to human development (Tudge & Scrimsher, 2003). Interactions with persons in the environment (e.g., apprenticeships, collaborations) stimulate developmental processes and foster cognitive growth. But interactions are not useful in a traditional sense of providing children with information. Rather, children transform their experiences based on their knowledge and characteristics and reorganize their mental structures.

The cultural-historical aspects of Vygotsky's theory illuminate the point that learning and development cannot be dissociated from their context. The way that learners interact with their worlds—with the persons, objects, and institutions in it—transforms their thinking. The meanings of concepts change as they are linked with the world. Thus, "school" is not simply a word or a physical structure but also an institution that seeks to promote learning and citizenship.

Finally, there are the individual, or inherited factors, that affect development. Vygotsky was very interested in children with mental and physical disabilities. He believed that their inherited characteristics produced different learning trajectories than those of children without such challenges.

Of these three influences, the one that has received the most attention—at least among Western researchers and practitioners—is the interpersonal. Vygotsky considered the social environment critical for learning and thought that social interactions transformed learning experiences. Social activity is a phenomenon that helps explain changes in consciousness and establishes a psychological theory that unifies behavior and mind (Kozulin, 1986; Wertsch, 1985).

The social environment influences cognition through its "tools"—that is, its cultural objects (e.g., cars, machines) and its language and social institutions (e.g., schools, churches). Social interactions help to coordinate the three influences on development. Cognitive change results from using cultural tools in social interactions and from internalizing and mentally transforming these interactions (Bruning et al., 1999). Vygotsky's position is a form of dialectical constructivism because it emphasizes the interaction between persons and their environments. *Mediation* is the key mechanism in development and learning:

> All human psychological processes (higher mental processes) are mediated by such psychological tools as language, signs, and symbols. Adults teach these tools to children in the course of their joint (collaborative) activity. After children internalize these tools they function as mediators of the children's more advanced psychological processes. (Karpov & Haywood, 1998, p. 27)

Vygotsky's most controversial contention was that all higher mental functions originated in the social environment (Vygotsky, 1962). This is a very powerful claim that has a good degree of truth to it. The most influential process involved is language. Vygotsky thought that a critical component of psychological development was mastering the external process of transmitting cultural development and thinking through symbols such as language, counting, and writing. Once this process was mastered, the next step involved using these symbols to influence and self-regulate thoughts and actions. Self-regulation uses the important function of private speech (discussed later in this chapter).

Table 7.2
Key points in Vygotsky's theory.

- Social interactions are critical; knowledge is co-constructed between two or more people.

- Self-regulation is developed through internalization (developing an internal representation) of actions and mental operations that occur in social interactions.

- Human development occurs through the cultural transmission of tools (language, symbols).

- Language is the most critical tool. Language develops from social speech, to private speech, to covert (inner) speech.

- The zone of proximal development is the difference between what children can do on their own and what they can do with assistance from others. Interactions with adults and peers in the ZPD promote cognitive development.

Source: From *Child and Adolescent Development for Educators*, 2nd ed. (pp. 169–170), by J. L. Meece, 2002, New York: McGraw-Hill.

In spite of this impressive theorizing, Vygotsky's claim appears to be too strong. Research evidence shows that young children mentally figure out much knowledge about the way the world operates long before they have an opportunity to learn from the culture in which they live (Bereiter, 1994). Children also seem biologically predisposed to acquire certain concepts (e.g., understanding that adding increases quantity), which does not depend on the environment (Geary, 1995). Although social learning affects knowledge construction, the claim that all learning derives from the social environment seems overstated. Nonetheless, we know that learners' cultures are critical and need to be considered in explaining learning and development. A summary of major points in Vygotsky's (1978) theory appears in Table 7.2.

Zone of Proximal Development

A key concept is the *zone of proximal development (ZPD)*, defined as "the distance between the actual developmental level as determined by independent problem solving and the level of potential development as determined through problem solving under adult guidance or in collaboration with more capable peers" (Vygotsky, 1978, p. 86). The ZPD represents the amount of learning possible by a student given the proper instructional conditions (Day, 1983). It is largely a test of a student's developmental readiness or intellectual level in a specific domain (Campione, Brown, Ferrara, & Bryant, 1984) and can be viewed as an alternative to the conception of intelligence (Belmont, 1989). In the ZPD, a teacher and learner (adult/child, tutor/tutee, model/observer, master/apprentice, expert/novice) work together on a task that the learner could not perform independently because of the difficulty level. The ZPD reflects the Marxist idea of collective activity, in which those who know more or are more skilled share that knowledge and skill to accomplish a task with those who know less (Bruner, 1984).

Cognitive change occurs in the ZPD as teacher and learner share cultural tools, and this culturally mediated interaction produces cognitive change when it is internalized in the learner (Bruning et al., 1999; Cobb, 1994). Working in the ZPD requires a good deal of guided participation (Rogoff, 1986); however, children do not acquire cultural knowledge passively from these interactions, nor is what they learn necessarily an automatic or accurate reflection of events. Rather, learners bring their own understandings to social interactions and construct meanings by integrating those understandings with their experiences in the context. The learning often is sudden, in the Gestalt sense of insight, rather than reflecting a gradual accretion of knowledge (Wertsch, 1984).

For example, assume that a teacher (Trudy) and a child (Laura) will work on a task (making a picture of mom, dad, and Laura doing something together at home). Laura brings to the task her understandings of what the people and the home look like and of the types of things they might work on, combined with knowledge of how to draw and make pictures. Trudy brings the same understandings plus knowledge of conditions necessary to work on various tasks. Suppose they decide to make a picture of the three working in the yard. Laura might draw a picture of dad cutting grass, mom trimming shrubs, and Laura raking the lawn. If Laura were to draw herself in front of dad, Trudy would explain that Laura must be behind dad to rake up the grass left behind by dad's cutting. During the interaction, Laura modifies her beliefs about working in the yard based on her current understanding and on the new knowledge she constructs.

Despite the importance of the ZPD, the overarching emphasis it has received in Western cultures has served to distort its meaning and downplay the complexity of Vygotsky's theory. As Tudge and Scrimsher (2003) explain:

> Moreover, the concept itself has too often been viewed in a rather limited way that emphasized the interpersonal at the expense of the individual and cultural-historical levels and treats the concept in a unidirectional fashion. As if the concept were synonymous with "scaffolding," too many authors have focused on the role of the more competent other, particularly the teacher, whose role is to provide assistance just in advance of the child's current thinking. . . . The concept thus has become equated with what sensitive teachers might do with their children and has lost much of the complexity with which it was imbued by Vygotsky, missing both what the child brings to the interaction and the broader setting (cultural and historical) in which the interaction takes place. (p. 211)

The influence of the cultural-historical setting is seen clearly when we consider that Vygotsky felt that schooling was important not because it was where children were scaffolded but, rather, because it allowed them to develop greater awareness of themselves, their language, and their role in the world order. Participating in the cultural world transforms mental functioning rather than simply accelerate processes that would have developed anyway. Broadly speaking, therefore, the ZPD refers to new forms of awareness that occur as people interact with their societies' social institutions. The culture affects the course of one's mental development. It is unfortunate that in most discussions of the ZPD, it is conceived so narrowly as an expert teacher providing learning opportunities for a student (although that is part of it).

Applications

Having stressed the broad generality of Vygotsky's theory, we must emphasize that his ideas lend themselves to many educational applications (Karpov & Haywood, 1998). The field of self-regulation (discussed later in this chapter) has been strongly influenced by the theory. Self-regulation requires metacognitive mediators such as planning, checking, and evaluating. This section and Application 7.2 discuss other examples.

Helping students acquire cognitive mediators (e.g., signs, symbols) through the social environment can be accomplished in many ways. A common application involves the concept of *instructional scaffolding*, which refers to the process of controlling task elements that are beyond the learners' capabilities so that they can focus on and master those features of the task that they can grasp quickly (Bruning et al., 1999). To use an analogy of scaffolding employed in construction projects, instructional scaffolding has five major functions: provide support, function as a tool, extend the range of the learner, permit the attainment of tasks not otherwise possible, and use selectively only as needed.

In a learning situation, a teacher initially might do most of the work, after which the teacher and the learners share responsibility. As learners become more competent,

---

APPLICATION 7.2
Vygotsky's Theory

Vygotsky postulated that one's interactions with the environment contribute to success in learning. The experiences one brings to a learning situation can greatly influence the outcome.

Ice skating coaches may work with advanced students who have learned a great deal about ice skating and how their bodies perform on the ice. Students bring with them their own concepts of balance, speed, movement, and body control based on their prior experiences in skating. Coaches take the strengths and weaknesses of these students and help them learn to alter various movements to improve their performances. For example, a skater who has trouble completing a triple axle toe loop has the height and speed needed to complete the jump, but the coach notices that she turns her toe at an angle during the spin that alters the smooth completion of the loop. After the coach points this out to the skater and helps her learn to alter that movement, she is able to successfully complete the jump.

Veterinary students who have grown up on farms and have experienced births, illnesses, and care of various types of animals bring valuable knowledge to their training. Veterinary instructors can use these prior experiences to enhance students' learning. In teaching students how to treat an injured hoof of a cow or horse, the instructor might call on some of these students to discuss what they have observed and then build on that knowledge by explaining the latest and most effective methods of treatment.

the teacher gradually withdraws the scaffolding so learners can perform independently (Campione et al., 1984). The key is to ensure that the scaffolding keeps learners in the ZPD, which is raised as they develop capabilities. Students are challenged to learn within the bounds of the ZPD.

It is critical to understand that scaffolding is not a formal part of Vygotsky's theory; however, it does fit nicely within the ZPD. Scaffolding is part of Bandura's (1986) participant modeling technique (Chapter 3), in which a teacher initially models a skill, provides support, and gradually reduces aid as learners develop the skill. The notion also bears some relation to shaping (Chapter 2), as instructional supports are used to guide learners through various stages of skill acquisition.

Scaffolding is appropriate when a teacher wants to provide students with some information or to complete parts of tasks for them so that they can concentrate on the part of the task they are attempting to master. Thus, if Kathy Stone were working with her third-grade children on organizing sentences in a paragraph to express ideas in a logical order, she might assist the students by initially giving them the sentences with word meanings and spellings so that these needs would not interfere with their primary task. As they became more competent in sequencing ideas, she might have students compose their own paragraphs while still assisting with word meanings and spellings. Eventually students will assume responsibility for these functions.

Another application that reflects Vygotsky's ideas is *reciprocal teaching*. This technique is discussed and exemplified in Chapter 9 in conjunction with reading. Reciprocal teaching involves an interactive dialogue between a teacher and small group of students. Initially the teacher models the activities, after which teacher and students take turns being the teacher. If students are learning to ask questions during reading comprehension, the instructional sequence might include the teacher modeling a question-asking strategy to check on his or her own level of understanding. From a Vygotskian perspective, reciprocal teaching comprises social interaction and scaffolding as students gradually develop skills.

An important application area is *peer collaboration*, which reflects the notion of collective activity (Bruner, 1984). When peers work on tasks cooperatively, the shared social interactions can serve an instructional function. Research shows that cooperative groups are most effective when each student has assigned responsibilities and all must attain competence before any are allowed to progress (Slavin, 1983). The current emphasis on using peer groups for learning in fields such as mathematics, science, and language arts (Cobb, 1994; Cohen, 1994; DiPardo & Freedman, 1988; Geary, 1995) attests to the recognized impact of the social environment during learning.

Finally, an application relevant to Vygotsky's theory and to the topic of situated cognition (discussed in a prior section) is the notion of social guidance through *apprenticeships* (Radziszewska & Rogoff, 1991; Rogoff, 1990). In apprenticeships, novices work closely with experts in joint work-related activities. Apprenticeships fit well with the ZPD because they occur in cultural institutions (e.g., schools, agencies) and thus help to transform learners' cognitive development. On the job, apprentices operate within a ZPD because they often work on tasks beyond their capabilities. By working with experts, novices develop a shared understanding of important processes and integrate this with their current understandings. Apprenticeships represent a type of dialectical constructivism that depends heavily on social interactions.

As noted above, a critical aspect of apprenticeships is that instruction is set within a particular cultural context. Childs and Greenfield (1981) described the teaching of weaving in the Zincantecan culture of Mexico. Young girls observed their mothers and other older women weave from the time they were born, so when instruction began, they already had been exposed to many models. In the early phases of instruction, the adult spent more than 90% of the time weaving with the child, but this dropped to 50% after weaving one garment. The adult then worked on the more difficult aspects of the task. The adult's participation dropped to less than 40% after completion of four garments. This instructional procedure exemplifies close social interaction and scaffolding operating within the ZPD.

Apprenticeships are used in many areas of education. Student teachers work with cooperating teachers in schools, and once on the job often are paired with experienced teachers for mentoring. Counselor trainees serve internships under the direct guidance of a supervisor. On-the-job training programs use the apprentice model as students acquire skills while in the actual work setting and interacting with others. There is much emphasis on expanding youth apprenticeships, especially for non-college-bound adolescents (Bailey, 1993). Future research should evaluate the factors that influence the success of apprenticeships as a means of fostering skill acquisition in students of various ages.

Critique

It is difficult to evaluate the contributions of Vygotsky's theory to the fields of human development and learning (Tudge & Scrimsher, 2003). His works were not circulated for many years, and translations have only recently become available. Even so, only a small number of sources exist (Vygotsky, 1978, 1987). Researchers and practitioners have tended to zero in on a single concept (the ZPD) without placing it in a larger theoretical context that is centered around cultural influence.

Another problem is that when applications of Vygotsky's theory are discussed, they often are not part of the theory but rather seem to fit with it. The term *scaffolding*, for example, was introduced by Wood, Bruner, and Ross (1976), who presented it as a way for teachers to structure learning environments. As such, it has little relation to the dynamic ZPD that Vygotsky wrote about. Although *reciprocal teaching* also is not a Vygotskian concept, the term captures much better this sense of dynamic, multidirectional interaction.

Given these issues, there has been little debate on the adequacy of the theory. Debate that has ensued often has focused on "Piaget versus Vygotsky," contrasting their presumably discrepant positions on the course of human development (Duncan, 1995; although on many points they do not differ, see Chapter 10). While such debates may illuminate differences and provide testable research hypotheses, they are not helpful to educational practitioners seeking solid methods for improving children's learning.

Possibly the most significant implication of Vygotsky's theory for education is that the cultural-historical context is relevant to all forms of learning because learning does not occur in isolation. Student-teacher interactions are part of that context. Research has identified, for example, different interaction styles between Hawaiian, Anglo, and Navajo children (Tharp, 1989; Tharp & Gallimore, 1988). Whereas the Hawaiian culture encourages collaborative activity and more than one student talking at once, Navajo children are less acculturated to working in groups and more likely to wait to talk until the speaker is finished. Thus, the same instructional style would not be equally beneficial for all cultures. This point is especially noteworthy given that many schools are seeing a large influx of Asian and Hispanic American children.

SOCIAL PROCESSES AND PRIVATE SPEECH

A central premise of constructivism is that learning involves transforming and internalizing the social environment. Language plays a key role. This section discusses a central mechanism—private speech—that serves to perform these critical transforming and internalizing processes.

Private Speech

Private speech refers to the set of speech phenomena that has a self-regulatory function but is not socially communicative (Fuson, 1979). Various theories—including constructivism, cognitive-developmental, and social cognitive—establish a strong link between private speech and the development of self-regulation (Berk, 1986; Frauenglass & Diaz, 1985; Harris, 1982).

The historical impetus derives in part from work by Pavlov (1927). Recall from Chapter 2 that Pavlov distinguished the first (perceptual) from the second (linguistic) signal systems. Pavlov realized that animal conditioning results do not completely generalize to humans; human conditioning often occurs quickly with one or a few pairings of conditioned stimulus and unconditioned stimulus, in contrast to the multiple pairings required with animals. Pavlov believed that conditioning differences between humans and animals are largely due to the human capacity for language and thought. Stimuli may not produce conditioning automatically; people interpret stimuli in light of their prior experiences. Although Pavlov did not conduct research on the second signal system, subsequent investigations have validated his beliefs that human conditioning is complex and language plays a mediational role.

The Soviet psychologist Luria (1961) focused on the child's transition from the first to the second signal system. Luria postulated three stages in the development of verbal control of motor behavior. Initially, the speech of others is primarily responsible for directing the child's behavior (ages $1\frac{1}{2}$ to $2\frac{1}{2}$). During the second stage (ages 3 to 4), the child's overt verbalizations initiate motor behaviors but do not necessarily inhibit them. In the third stage, the child's private speech becomes capable of initiating, directing, and inhibiting motor behaviors (ages $4\frac{1}{2}$ to $5\frac{1}{2}$). Luria believed this private, self-regulatory speech directs behavior through neurophysiological mechanisms.

The mediational and self-directing role of the second signal system is embodied in Vygotsky's theory. Vygotsky (1962) believed private speech helps develop thought by organizing behavior. Children employ private speech to understand situations and surmount difficulties. Private speech occurs in conjunction with children's interactions in the social environment. As children's language facility develops, words spoken by others acquire meaning independent of their phonological and syntactical qualities. Children internalize word meanings and use them to direct their behaviors.

Vygotsky hypothesized that private speech follows a curvilinear developmental pattern: Overt verbalization (thinking aloud) increases until ages 6 to 7, after which it declines and becomes primarily covert (internal) by ages 8 to 10. However, overt verbalization can occur at any age when people encounter problems or difficulties. Research shows that although the amount of private speech decreases from approximately ages 4 or 5 to 8, the proportion of private speech that is self-regulating increases with age (Fuson, 1979). In many research investigations, the actual amount of private speech is small, and many children do not verbalize at all. Thus, the developmental pattern of private speech seems more complex than originally hypothesized by Vygotsky.

Verbalization and Achievement

Verbalization of rules, procedures, and strategies can improve student learning. Although Meichenbaum's (1977, 1986) *self-instructional training* procedure is not rooted in constructivism, it recreates the overt-to-covert developmental progression of private speech. Types of statements modeled are *problem definition* ("What is it I have to do?"), *focusing of attention* ("I need to pay attention to what I'm doing"), *planning and response guidance* ("I need to work carefully"), *self-reinforcement* ("I'm doing fine"), *self-evaluation* ("Am I doing things in the right order?"), and *coping* ("I need to try again when I don't get it right"). Teachers can use self-instructional training to teach learners cognitive and motor skills, and it can create a positive task outlook and foster perseverance in the face of difficulties (Meichenbaum & Asarnow, 1979). The procedure need not be scripted; learners can construct their own verbalizations.

Verbalization seems most beneficial for students who often experience difficulties and perform in a deficient manner (Denney, 1975; Denney & Turner, 1979). Teachers have obtained benefits with children who do not spontaneously rehearse material to be learned, impulsive learners, students with learning disabilities and mental retardation, and learners who require remedial experiences (Schunk, 1986). Verbalization helps students with learning problems work at tasks systematically (Hallahan et al., 1983). It forces students to attend to tasks and to rehearse material, both of which enhance learning. Verbalization does not seem to facilitate learning when students can handle task demands adequately without verbalizing. Because verbalization constitutes an additional task, it might interfere with learning by distracting children from the task at hand.

Research has identified the conditions under which verbalization promotes performance. Denney (1975) modeled a performance strategy for 6-, 8-, and 10-year-old normal learners on a 20-question task. The 8- and 10-year-olds who verbalized the model's strategy as they performed the task scored no higher than children who did not verbalize. Verbalization interfered with the performance of 6-year-olds. Children verbalized specific statements (e.g., "Find the right picture in the fewest questions"); apparently performing this additional task proved too distracting for the youngest children. Denney and Turner (1979) found that among normal learners ranging in age from 3 to 10 years, adding verbalization to a strategy modeling treatment resulted in no benefits on cognitive tasks compared with modeling alone. Participants constructed their own verbalizations, which might have been less distracting than Denney's (1975) specific statements. Coates and Hartup (1969) found that 7-year-olds who verbalized a model's actions during exposure did not subsequently produce them better than children who passively observed the behaviors. The children regulated their attention and cognitively processed the model's actions without verbalizing.

Berk (1986) studied first and third graders' spontaneous private speech. Task-relevant overt speech was negatively related and faded verbalization (whispers, lip movements, muttering) was positively related to mathematical performance. These results were obtained for first graders of high intelligence and third graders of average intelligence; among third graders of high intelligence, overt and faded speech showed no relationship to achievement. For the latter students, internalized self-guiding speech apparently is the most effective.

Keeney, Cannizzo, and Flavell (1967) pretested 6- and 7-year-olds on a serial recall task and identified those who failed to rehearse prior to recall. After these children learned how to rehearse, their recall matched that of spontaneous rehearsers. Asarnow and Meichenbaum (1979) identified kindergartners who did not spontaneously rehearse on a serial recall test. Some were trained to use a rehearsal strategy similar to that of Keeney et al., whereas others received self-instructional training. Both treatments facilitated recall relative to a control condition, but the self-instructional treatment was more effective. Taylor and his colleagues (Taylor, Josberger, & Whitely, 1973; Whitely & Taylor, 1973) found that educable mentally retarded children who were trained to generate elaborations between word associate pairs recalled more associates if they verbalized their elaborations than if they did not. In the Coates and Hartup (1969) study, 4-year-olds who verbalized a model's actions as they were being performed later reproduced them better than children who merely observed the model.

Schunk (1982b) instructed students who lacked division skills. Some students verbalized explicit statements (e.g., "check," "multiply," "copy"), others constructed their own verbalizations, a third group verbalized the statements and their own verbalizations, and students in a fourth condition did not verbalize. Self-constructed verbalizations—alone or combined with the statements—led to the highest division skill.

In summary, verbalization is more likely to promote student achievement if it is relevant to the task and does not interfere with performance. Higher proportions of task-relevant statements produce better learning (Schunk & Gunn, 1986). Private speech follows an overt-to-covert developmental cycle, and speech becomes internalized earlier in students with higher intelligence (Berk, 1986; Frauenglass & Diaz, 1985). Allowing students to construct their verbalizations—possibly in conjunction with verbalizing steps in a strategy—is more beneficial than limiting verbalizing to specific statements. To facilitate transfer and maintenance, overt verbalization should eventually be faded to whispering or lip movements and then to a covert level.

These benefits of verbalization do not mean that all students ought to verbalize while learning. That practice would result in a loud classroom and distract many students! Rather, verbalization could be incorporated into instruction for students having

APPLICATION 7.3
Self-Verbalization

A teacher might use self-verbalization (self-talk) in a special education resource room or at a work station separated from other students in a regular classroom to assist students having difficulty attending to material and mastering skills. When Mrs. Stone introduces long division to her third-grade students, she uses verbalization to help those children who cannot remember the steps to complete the procedure. She works individually with the students by verbalizing and applying the following steps:

- Will (number) go into (number)?
- Divide.
- Multiply: (number) × (number) = (number).
- Put down the answer.
- Subtract: (number) − (number) = (number).
- Bring down the next number.
- Repeat steps.

Use of self-talk helps students stay on task and builds their self-efficacy to work systematically through the long process. Once they begin to grasp the content, it is to their advantage to fade verbalizations to a covert (silent) level so they can work more rapidly.

Self-verbalization also can help students who are learning various sport skills and strategies. Thus, they might verbalize what is happening and what moves they should make. A tennis coach, for example, might encourage students to use self-talk during practice matches: "high ball—overhand return," "low ball—underhand return," "cross ball—backhand return."

Aerobic and dance instructors often use self-talk during practice. A ballet teacher might have young students repeat "paint a rainbow" for a flowing arm movement, and "walk on eggs" to get them to move lightly on their toes. Participants in aerobic exercise classes also might verbalize movements (e.g., "bend and stretch," "slide right and around") as they perform them.

difficulties learning. A teacher or classroom aide could work with such students individually or in groups to avoid disrupting the work of other class members. Application 7.3 shows some ways to integrate verbalization into learning.

Socially Mediated Learning

Many forms of constructivism, and Vygotsky's theory in particular, stress the idea that learning is a socially mediated process. This focus is not unique to constructivism; many other learning theories emphasize social processes as having a significant impact on learning. Bandura's (1986, 1997) social cognitive theory (Chapter 3), for example, high-lights the reciprocal relations among learners and social environmental influences, and much research has shown that social modeling is a powerful influence on learning (Rosenthal & Zimmerman, 1978; Schunk, 1987). In Vygotsky's theory, however, social mediation of learning is the central construct (Karpov & Haywood, 1998). All learning is mediated by tools such as language, symbols, and signs. Children acquire these tools during their social interactions with others. They internalize these tools and then use them as mediators of more advanced learning (i.e., higher cognitive processes such as concept learning and problem solving).

The centrality of social mediation is apparent in self-regulation and constructivist learning environments (discussed later). For now, let us examine how social media-tion influences concept acquisition. Young children acquire concepts spontaneously by observing their worlds and formulating hypotheses. For example, they hear the noise that cars make and the noise that trucks make, and they may believe that bigger objects make more noise. They have difficulty accommodating discrepant observations (e.g., a motorcycle is smaller than a car or truck but may make more noise that either).

In the context of social interactions, children are taught concepts by others (e.g., teachers, parents, older siblings). This is often a fairly direct process; thus, teachers teach children the difference between squares, rectangles, triangles, and circles. Borrowing from cognitive psychology, such concepts are internalized as declarative knowledge. Thus, children use the tools of language and symbols to internalize these concepts.

It is, of course, possible to learn concepts on one's own without social interac-tions with others. But even such independent learning is, in a constructivist sense, socially mediated, because it involves the tools (language, signs, symbols) that have been acquired through previous social interactions. Further, a certain amount of la-beling is needed. Children may learn a concept but not have a name for it ("What do you call a thing that looks like _____?"). Such labeling involves language and will likely be supplied by another person.

Tools not only are useful for learning but also for teaching. Children teach one another things they have learned. Vygotsky (1962, 1978) believed that by being used for social purposes, tools exerted powerful influences on others.

These points have interesting implications for instruction. Earlier (Chapter 6) we considered two different instructional approaches: guided discovery and expository teaching. Both methods are employed in school, but typically for the lower-level, more-basic type of knowledge that serves as the foundation for higher mental processes. Once children have acquired basic concepts, they can engage in inde-pendent learning to "discover" more-advanced principles. This does not have to in-volve children working alone; rather, they can work collaboratively. But it does sug-gest that students must be well prepared with the basic tools, and this teaching can be quite direct. There is no need for students to "discover" the obvious, or what they can be easily taught. Constructed discoveries are thus the result of basic learning, not their cause (Karpov & Haywood, 1998).

The implication is that teachers must prepare students to engage in discovery by teaching them the tools to do so and then provide opportunities for it. Some class-room applications of socially mediated learning are discussed in Application 7.4.

APPLICATION 7.4
Socially Mediated Learning

Socially mediated learning is appropriate for students of all ages. Gina Brown knows that success in teaching depends in part on understanding the culture of the communities served by the school. She obtains consent from the schools where her students are placed and from the appropriate parents and she assigns each of her students to be a "buddy" of a school child. As part of their placements, her students spend extra time with their assigned buddies—for example, working one-to-one, eating lunch with them, riding home on the school bus with them, and visiting them in their homes. She pairs her students and the members of each dyad meet regularly to discuss the culture of their assigned buddies. Thus, they might discuss what their buddies like about school, what their parents or guardians do, and characteristics of the neighborhoods where their buddies live. She meets regularly with each dyad to discuss the implications of the cultural variables for school learning. Through social interactions with buddies, her, and other class members, Gina's students develop better understanding of the role of culture in schooling.

Historical events typically are open to multiple interpretations, and Jim Marshall uses social mediation to develop his students' thinking about events. As part of a unit on post-World War II changes in American life, he organizes students into five teams. Each team is assigned a topic: medicine, transportation, education, technology, suburbs. Teams prepare a presentation on why their topic represents the most significant advance in American life. Students on each team work together to prepare the presentation, and each member presents part of it. After the presentations are finished, Jim leads a discussion with the class. He tries to get them to see how advances are interrelated; for example, technology influences medicine, transportation, and education; more automobiles and roads lead to growth in suburbs; better education results in preventative medicine. Social mediation through discussions and presentations helps students gain deeper understanding of changes in American life.

MOTIVATION

Constructivism is primarily a theory of human development that in recent years has been applied to learning. One who reads the constructivist literature will find little mention of motivation. Nonetheless, constructivism seems applicable to motivation, and some motivational principles explored by researchers in other theoretical traditions fit well (Sivan, 1986). Aspects of motivation especially relevant to constructivism include contextual factors, implicit theories, and teachers' expectations.

Contextual Factors

Organization and Structure.   Constructivism stresses contextual specificity and notes the importance of taking the context of learning environments into account in attempting to explain behavior. A topic highly relevant to constructivism is *organization and structure of learning environments*—that is, how students are grouped for instruction, how work is evaluated and rewarded, how authority is established, and how time is scheduled. Many researchers and practitioners believe that learning environments are complex and that to understand learning we must take into account many factors and how they interact with one another (i.e., one factor might supplement or detract from the influence of another factor; Marshall & Weinstein, 1984).

An important aspect of organization is *dimensionality* (Rosenholtz & Simpson, 1984). *Unidimensional* classrooms include a small number of activities that address a limited range of student abilities. *Multidimensional* classrooms have more activities and allow for greater diversity in student abilities and performances. Multidimensional classes are more compatible with constructivist tenets about learning.

Classroom characteristics that indicate dimensionality include differentiation of task structure, student autonomy, grouping patterns, and salience of formal performance evaluations (Table 7.3). Unidimensional classrooms have *undifferentiated task structures*. All students work on the same or similar tasks and instruction employs a small number of materials and methods (Rosenholtz & Simpson, 1984). The more undifferentiated the structure, the more likely the daily activities will produce consistent performances from each student and the greater the probability that students will socially compare their work with that of others to determine relative standing. Structures become *differentiated* (and classrooms become multidimensional) when students work on different tasks at the same time.

Autonomy refers to the extent to which students have choices about what to do and when and how to do it. Classrooms are unidimensional when autonomy is low, which can hinder self-regulation and stifle motivation. Multidimensional classrooms offer students more choices, which can enhance intrinsic motivation.

Table 7.3
Characteristics of dimensionality.

Characteristic	Unidimensional	Multidimensional
Differentiation of task structure	Undifferentiated; students work on same tasks	Differentiated; students work on different tasks
Student autonomy	Low; students have few choices	High; students have choices
Grouping patterns	Whole class; students grouped by ability	Individual work; students not grouped by ability
Performance evaluations	Students graded on same assignments; grades are public; much social comparison	Students graded on different assignments; less public grading and social comparison

With respect to *grouping patterns*, social comparisons become more prominent when students work on whole-class activities or are grouped by ability. Comparisons are not as prevalent when students work individually or in mixed-ability groups. Grouping contributes to classroom multidimensionality and affects motivation and learning. Grouping has added influence over the long term if groups remain intact and students understand they are bound to the groups regardless of how well they perform.

Salience of formal *performance evaluations* refers to the public nature of grading. Unidimensional classrooms grade students on the same assignments and grades are public, so everyone knows the grade distribution. Those receiving low grades may not be motivated to improve. As grading becomes less public or as grades are assigned for different projects (as in multidimensional classes), grading can motivate a higher proportion of students, especially those who believe they are progressing and capable of further learning (Pintrich & Schunk, 2002).

Unidimensional classrooms have high visibility of performance (Rosenholtz & Rosenholtz, 1981), which can motivate high achievers to learn but often has a negative effect on everyone else. Multidimensional classrooms are more likely to motivate all students because they feature more differentiation, greater autonomy, less ability grouping, and more flexibility in grading with less public evaluation.

TARGET.   Classrooms include other factors that can affect learners' perceptions, motivation, and learning. Some of these, as shown in Table 7.4, can be summarized by the acronym *TARGET*: task design, distribution of authority, recognition of students, grouping arrangements, evaluation practices, and time allocation (Epstein, 1989).

The *task* dimension involves the design of learning activities and assignments. Chapter 8 discusses ways to structure tasks to promote a mastery (learning) goal orientation in students—for example, by making learning interesting, using variety and challenge, assisting students to set realistic goals, and helping students develop organizational, management, and other strategic skills (Ames, 1992a, 1992b). Task structure is a distinguishing feature of dimensionality. In unidimensional classes, students use

Table 7.4
TARGET factors affecting motivation and learning.

Factor	Characteristics
Task	Design of learning activities and assignments
Authority	Extent that students can assume leadership and develop independence and control over learning activities
Recognition	Formal and informal use of rewards, incentives, praise
Grouping	Individual, small group, large group
Evaluation	Methods for monitoring and assessing learning
Time	Appropriateness of workload, pace of instruction, time allotted for completing work

the same materials and have the same assignments, so variations in ability can translate into motivational differences. In multidimensional classes, students may not all work on the same task and thereby have fewer opportunities for social comparisons.

Authority refers to whether students can assume leadership and develop independence and control over learning activities. Teachers foster authority by allowing students to participate in decisions, giving them choices and leadership roles, and teaching them skills that allow them to take responsibility for learning. Self-efficacy tends to be higher in classes that allow students some measure of authority (Ames, 1992a, 1992b).

Recognition, which involves the formal and informal use of rewards, incentives, and praise, has important consequences for motivated learning (Schunk, 1989). Ames (1992a, 1992b) recommends that teachers help students develop mastery goal orientations by recognizing progress, accomplishments, effort, and self-directed strategy use; providing opportunities for all learners to earn rewards; and using private forms of recognition that avoid comparing students or emphasizing the difficulties of others.

The *grouping* dimension focuses on students' ability to work with others. Teachers should use heterogeneous cooperative groups and peer interaction where possible to ensure that differences in ability do not translate into differences in motivation and learning. Low achievers especially benefit from small-group work because contributing to the group's success engenders feelings of self-efficacy. Group work also allows more students to share in the responsibility for learning so a few students do not do all of the work. At the same time, individual work is important because it provides for clear indicators of learning progress.

Evaluation involves methods for monitoring and assessing student learning; for example, evaluating students for individual progress and mastery, giving students opportunities to improve their work (e.g., revise work for a better grade), using different forms of evaluation, and conducting evaluations privately. Although normative grading systems are common in schools (i.e., students compared to one another), such normative comparisons can lower self-efficacy among students who do not perform as well as their peers.

Time involves the appropriateness of workload, pace of instruction, and time allotted for completing work (Epstein, 1989). Effective strategies for enhancing motivation and learning are to adjust time or task requirements for those having difficulty and allowing students to plan their schedules and timelines for making progress. Giving students greater control over their time helps allay anxiety about completing work and can promote use of self-regulatory strategies and self-efficacy for learning (Schunk & Zimmerman, 1994; Zimmerman et al., 1994). Application 7.5 gives some classroom applications of TARGET.

Implicit Theories

Constructivist theories call attention to many facets of motivation, including the cognitive and the affective. A central premise of many contemporary theories of learning and motivation, and one that fits nicely with constructivist assumptions, is that

> **APPLICATION 7.5**
> ## Applying TARGET in the Classroom
>
> Incorporating TARGET components into a unit can positively affect motivation and learning. As Kathy Stone develops a unit on deserts, she plans part of the unit but also involves her students in planning activities. Mrs. Stone sets up learning centers, plans reading and research assignments, organizes large- and small-group discussions, and designs unit pre- and posttests as well as tasks for checking mastery throughout the unit. The class helps Mrs. Stone plan a field trip to a nearby desert, develop small-group project topics, and decide how to create a desert in the classroom. Mrs. Stone and the students then develop a calendar and timeline for working on and completing the unit. Notice in this example how Mrs. Stone incorporates motivational components into the TARGET classroom features: task, authority, recognition, grouping, evaluation, and time.

people hold *implicit theories* about issues such as how they learn, what contributes to school achievement, and how motivation affects performance. Learning and thinking occur in the context of learners' beliefs about cognition, which differ as a function of personal, social, and cultural factors (Greeno, 1989).

Research shows that implicit theories about such processes as learning, thinking, and ability influence how students engage in learning and their views about what leads to success in and outside of the classroom (Duda & Nicholls, 1992; Dweck, 1991, 1999; Dweck & Leggett, 1988; Nicholls, Cobb, Wood, Yackel, & Patashnick, 1990; Nicholls, Patashnick, & Nolen, 1985; Nicholls & Thorkildsen, 1989). Motivation researchers have identified two distinct implicit theories about the role of ability in achievement: entity theory and incremental theory. Students may view their abilities as representing fixed traits over which they have little control (*entity theory*) or as a set of skills that they can improve through learning (*incremental theory*; Dweck, 1999; Dweck & Leggett, 1988). These perspectives influence motivational patterns and ultimately learning and achievement. Wood and Bandura (1989) found that adults who view managerial skills as capable of being developed use better strategies, hold higher self-efficacy for success, and set more challenging goals than those who believe such skills are relatively fixed and not capable of being altered.

Students who believe that abilities are relatively fixed are apt to be discouraged if they encounter difficulty in school because they think they can do little to alter their status. Such discouragement results in low self-efficacy (Chapter 3), which can affect school learning adversely (Schunk, 1991). Conversely, students who believe they have control over their learning capabilities are less apt to give up when they encounter difficulty and instead alter their strategy, seek assistance, consult additional sources of information, or engage in other self-regulatory strategies (Zimmerman, 1994, 1998; Zimmerman & Martinez-Pons, 1992).

Evidence also shows that implicit theories can affect the way that learners process information (Graham & Golan, 1991). Students who believe that learning outcomes are under their control may expend greater mental effort, rehearse more, use organizational strategies, and employ other tactics to improve learning. In contrast, students who hold a fixed view may not expend the same type of effort.

Students differ in how they view kinds of classroom learning. Nicholls and Thorkildsen (1989) found that elementary school students perceived learning substantive matters (e.g., mathematical logic, facts about nature) as more important than learning intellectual conventions (e.g., spelling, methods of representing addition). Students also saw didactic teaching as more appropriate for teaching of conventions than for matters of logic and fact. Nicholls et al. (1985) found that high school students held definite beliefs about what types of activities should lead to success. *Task orientation,* or a focus during learning on mastery of the task, was positively associated with student perceptions that success in school depends on being interested in learning, working hard, trying to understand (as opposed to memorizing), and working collaboratively. (Goal orientations are discussed in more depth in Chapter 8.)

Implicit theories undoubtedly are formed as children encounter a variety of socialization influences. Dweck and her colleagues have found evidence for implicit theories in children as young as $3\frac{1}{2}$ years (Dweck, 1999). Early on, children are socialized by significant others about right and wrong, good and bad. Through what they are told and what they observe, they form early implicit theories about rightness, badness, and the like. At achievement tasks, praise and criticism from others serve as strong influences about what produced good and poor outcomes (e.g., "You worked hard and got it right," "You don't have what it takes to do this right"). As with other beliefs, these may be situated within contexts; teachers and parents may stress different causes of achievement (effort and ability). By the time children enter school, they hold a wide range of implicit theories that they have constructed and that cover most situations.

Research findings such as those summarized in this section have profound implications for teaching and learning because they show that asking whether one understands a fact or principle is insufficient (Greeno, 1989). The premise that learning requires providing students with information to build propositional networks is incomplete. Of greater importance may be how children refine, modify, combine, and elaborate their conceptual understandings as a function of experience. Those understandings will be situated in the context of a personal belief system and will include beliefs about the usefulness and importance of knowledge, how it relates to what else one knows, and in what situations it may be appropriate. Research should determine how students form implicit theories, how these theories change as a consequence of cognitive development, and how learners resolve inconsistencies (e.g., students who believe ability is fixed but whose teachers provide feedback linking higher achievement with greater effort).

Teachers' Expectations

A motivational topic that has attracted much research and applied attention and that integrates nicely with constructivism is *teachers' expectations*. Theory and research suggest teachers' expectations for students relate to teacher actions and student achievement outcomes (Braun, 1976; Cooper & Good, 1983; Cooper & Tom, 1984; Dusek, 1985).

The impetus for exploring expectations came from a study by Rosenthal and Jacobson (1968), who gave elementary school students a test of nonverbal intelligence at the start of the academic year. Teachers were told that this test predicted which students would bloom intellectually during the year. The researchers actually randomly identified 20% of the school population as bloomers and gave these names to the teachers. Teachers were not aware of the deception: The test did not predict intellectual blooming and names bore no relation to test scores. Teachers taught in their usual fashion and students were retested one semester, 1 year, and 2 years later. For the first two tests, students were in the classes of teachers given bloomers' names; for the last test, students were in new classes with teachers who did not have these names.

After the first year, significant differences in intelligence were seen between bloomers and control students (those not identified as bloomers); differences were greater among children in the first and second grades. During the subsequent year, these younger children lost their advantage, but bloomers in upper grades showed an increasing advantage over control students. Differences were greater among average achievers than among high or low achievers. Similar findings were obtained for grades in reading. Overall the differences between bloomers and control students were small, both in reading and on the intelligence test.

Rosenthal and Jacobson concluded that teacher expectations can act as *self-fulfilling prophecies* because student achievement comes to reflect the expectations. They suggested that results are stronger with young children because they have close contact with teachers. Older students may function better after they move to a new teacher.

This study is controversial: It has been criticized on conceptual and methodological grounds, and many attempts at replication have not been successful (Cooper & Good, 1983; Elashoff & Snow, 1971; Jensen, 1969). Brophy and Good (1974) contend that early in the school year teachers form expectations based on initial interactions with students and information in records. Teachers then may begin to treat students differently consistent with these expectations. Teacher behaviors are reciprocated; for example, teachers who treat students warmly are apt to receive warmth in return. Student behaviors begin to complement and reinforce teacher behaviors and expectations. Effects will be most pronounced for rigid and inappropriate expectations. When they are appropriate or inappropriate but flexible, student behavior may substantiate or redefine expectations. When expectations are inappropriate or not easily changed, student performance might decline and become consistent with expectations.

Once teachers form expectations, they may convey them to students through socioemotional climate, verbal input, verbal output, and feedback (Rosenthal, 1974).

Socioemotional climate includes smiles, head nods, eye contact, and supportive and friendly actions. Teachers create a warmer climate for students for whom they hold high expectations than for those for whom expectations are lower (Cooper & Tom, 1984). *Verbal input,* or opportunities to learn new material and difficulty of material, varies when high-expectation students have more opportunities to interact with and learn new material and be exposed to more difficult material. *Verbal output* refers to number and length of academic interactions. Teachers engage in more academic interchanges with high- than with low-expectation students (Brophy & Good, 1974). They also are more persistent with highs and get them to give answers by prompting or rephrasing questions. *Feedback* refers to use of praise and criticism. Teachers praise high-expectation students and criticize low-expectation students more (Cooper & Tom, 1984).

Although these factors are genuine, wide differences exist between teachers (Pintrich & Schunk, 2002). Some teachers consistently encourage lower achievers and treat them much like the patterns described above for high achievers (e.g., give more praise, get them to answer more questions). Teachers have expectations for students; the real issue is whether these expectations become negatively self-fulfilling for some and how they do so. Appropriate expectations can improve learning. Tailoring difficulty of material and level of questioning to students based on their prior performances (which are correlated with teacher expectations) seems instructionally appropriate. Expecting all students to learn with requisite effort also seems reasonable. Greatly distorted expectations are not credible and typically have little effect on learning. Most teachers at the elementary level (when expectation effects may be strongest) hold positive expectations for students, provide for a lot of successes, and use praise often (Brophy & Good, 1974).

It seems likely that students construct theories about what their teachers think and expect of them. Whether or how these theories influence their achievement actions is less predictable. Our beliefs about what others expect of us may motivate ("She thinks I can do it, so I'll try"), demotivate ("She thinks I can't do it, so I won't try"), or lead us to act contrary to our theories ("She thinks I can't do it, so I'll show her I can"). The best advice is to expect that all students can succeed and provide support for them to do so, which should help them construct appropriate expectations for themselves. Application 7.6 gives some suggestions for conveying positive expectations to students.

SELF-REGULATION

Constructivist researchers have written about self-regulation, which seems natural given that a central assumption is that learners construct not only knowledge but also ways for acquiring and applying it. There are various sources for constructivist accounts of self-regulation, including cognitive-developmental theory (see Chapter 10), precursors of contemporary cognitive theories (e.g., Gestalt psychology, memory; see Chapter 4), and Vygotsky's theory (Paris & Byrnes, 1989). Regardless of the

APPLICATION 7.6
Teacher Expectations

Expectations that teachers hold for students can positively and negatively affect their interactions with students. Teachers might incorporate some of the following actions into classroom practices:

- Enforce rules fairly and consistently.
- Assume that all students can learn and convey that expectation to them.
- Do not form differential student expectations based on qualities unrelated to performance (e.g., gender, ethnicity, parents' background).
- Do not accept excuses for poor performance.
- Realize that upper limits of student ability are unknown and not relevant to school learning.

A college English professor told her class that they would be expected to do a lot of writing throughout the semester. Some of the students looked apprehensive and the professor tried to assure them that it was a task they could do. "We can all work together to improve our writing. I know some of you have had different experiences in high school with writing, but I will work with each of you and I know by the end of the semester you will be writing well."

One student waited after class and told the professor that he had been in a special education class in school and said, "I can hardly write a good sentence; I don't think you can make a writer out of me." To which the professor replied, "Well, sentences are a good place to begin. I'll see you Wednesday morning in class."

Table 7.5
Constructivist assumptions of self-regulation.

- There is an intrinsic motivation to seek information.
- Understanding goes beyond the information given.
- Mental representations change with development.
- There are progressive refinements in levels of understanding.
- There are developmental constraints on learning.
- Reflection and reconstruction stimulate learning.

source, constructivist views of self-regulation rest on certain assumptions, as shown in Table 7.5 (Paris & Byrnes, 1989).

Two key points underlying these assumptions are that sociocultural influences are critical and that people form implicit theories about themselves, others, and how to best manage demands. These are discussed in turn.

Sociocultural Influences

Vygotsky's theory of human development is constructivist and lends itself well to self-regulation. Recall from our earlier discussion that Vygotsky believed that people and their cultural environments constituted an interacting social system. Through their communications and actions, people in children's environments taught children the tools (e.g., language, symbols, signs) they needed to acquire competence. Using these tools within the system, learners develop higher-level cognitive functions, such as concept acquisition and problem solving. As Vygotsky used the term *higher mental function,* he meant a consciously directed thought process. In this sense, self-regulation may be thought of as a higher mental function (Henderson & Cunningham, 1994).

In the Vygotskian view, self-regulation includes the coordination of such mental processes as memory, planning, synthesis, and evaluation (Henderson & Cunningham, 1994). These coordinated processes do not operate independently of the context in which they are formed. Indeed, the self-regulatory processes of an individual reflect those that are valued and taught within the person's culture.

Vygotsky believed that people came to control their own deliberate actions (i.e., learned to self-regulate). The primary mechanisms affecting self-regulation are language and the zone of proximal development (ZPD).

Kopp (1982) provided a useful framework for understanding the development of the self-regulatory function of speech. In her view, self-regulation involves a transition from responding to the commands of others to the use of speech and other cognitive tools to plan, monitor, and direct one's activities.

Self-regulation also depends on learners being aware of socially approved behaviors (Henderson & Cunningham, 1994). The meaning of actions depends on both the context and the tools (language, signs, and symbols) used to describe the actions. Through interactions with adults in the ZPD, children make the transition from behaviors regulated by others to behaviors regulated by themselves (self-regulation).

Wertsch (1979) described four stages of intersubjectivity that correspond to the degrees of responsibility held by parties in a social context. Initially the child does not understand the adult's words or gestures, so there is no intersubjectivity. With maturation of the child and greater sensitivity of the adult to the child's situation, a shared understanding of the situation develops, although responsibility for regulating behavior still lies with the adult. In the third phase, the child learns the relation between speech and activity and takes responsibility for the task. During the third phase, private speech is commonly used to self-regulate behavior. As this speech is internalized to self-directed thought, intersubjectivity becomes complete and self-regulation occurs independently.

It is noteworthy that even after the teacher is no longer present, the child's self-regulatory activity will reflect the teacher's influence. Although the action is self-directed, it is the internalized regulation of the other's influence. Often the child may repeat the same words used by the adult. In time, the child's self-regulatory activity becomes idiosyncratic, but early on it will largely reflect the adult influence.

Implicit Theories of Self-Regulation

As was discussed in the preceding section on motivation, implicit theories are an inherent feature of constructivist accounts of learning, cognition, and motivation. Students also construct theories about self-regulated learning. These theories exist along with theories about others and their worlds, so self-regulated learning theories are highly contextualized (Paris, Byrnes, & Paris, 2001).

A major type of implicit theory involves children's beliefs about their academic abilities. Children who experience learning problems and who believe that these problems reflect poor ability are apt to demonstrate low motivation to succeed. The beliefs that effort leads to success and that learning produces higher ability are positively related to effective self-regulation (see Chapter 8).

Children also develop theories about their competence relative to their peers. Through social comparisons with similar others, they formulate perceptions of ability and of their relative standing within their class. They also begin to differentiate their perceptions by subject area and to ascertain how smart they are in subjects such as reading and mathematics.

In line with these beliefs, children formulate theories about what contributes to success in different domains. Self-regulatory strategies may be general in nature, such as taking notes and rehearsing information to be learned, or they may be idiosyncratic to a particular area. Whether these strategies truly are useful is not the point. Because they are constructed, they may be misleading.

Learners also develop theories about agency and control that they have in academic situations. For example, they may feel self-efficacious (Chapter 3) and believe that they are capable of learning what is being taught in school. Conversely, they may entertain serious doubts about their learning capabilities. Again, these beliefs may or may not accurately capture reality. Research has shown, for example, that children often feel highly self-efficacious about successfully solving mathematical problems even after being given feedback showing that they had failed most or all of the problems they attempted to solve (Bandura & Schunk, 1981). The correspondence between self-efficacy judgments and actual performance can be affected by many factors (Bandura, 1997).

Another class of theories involves schooling and academic tasks (Paris et al., 2001). These theories contain information about the content and skills taught in school and what is required to learn the content and skills. To this end, students formulate goals for schooling, which may not be consistent with those of teachers and parents. For example, students' school goals may be to perform well, make friends, or stay out of trouble. For a subject area (e.g., reading), students may have a goal of understanding the text or simply verbalizing the words on a page. A goal of writing may be to fill the lines on a page or create a short story.

From a constructivist perspective, therefore, self-regulation involves individuals constructing theories about themselves (abilities, capabilities, typical effort, and so forth), others, and their environments. These theories are constructed partly through direct instruction from others (teachers, peers, and parents) but also largely through their reflections about their performances, environmental effects, and responses from others. Theories are constructed using the tools (language, signs, and symbols), and in social contexts often through instruction in the ZPD.

The goal is for students to construct a self-identity as students. Their beliefs are influenced by parents, teachers, and peers and may include stereotypes associated with gender, culture, and ethnic background. As Paris et al. (2001) contend, the separation of identity development and self-regulated learning is impossible because achievement behaviors are indicators of who students believe they are or who they want to become. Strategies cannot be taught independently of goals, roles, and identities of students. In other words, self-regulation is intimately linked with personal development.

Children are intrinsically motivated to construct explanatory frameworks and understand their educational experiences (Paris et al., 2001). When they are successful, they construct theories of competence, tasks, and themselves that aid learning and usage of adaptive learning strategies. But when they are not successful, they may construct inappropriate goals and strategies. To use terminology from cognitive psychology, implicit theories include declarative and conditional knowledge that underlie procedural knowledge. In short, self-regulation is heavily dependent on how children perceive themselves and achievement tasks.

CONSTRUCTIVIST LEARNING ENVIRONMENTS

Learning environments created to reflect constructivist principles look quite different from traditional classrooms. This section discusses some critical features of constructivist learning environments pertaining to learning and teaching.

Key Features

Learning in a constructivist setting is not allowing students to do whatever they want. Rather, constructivist environments should create rich experiences that encourage students to learn.

Some of the ways that constructivist classrooms differ from traditional classrooms are as follows (Brooks & Brooks, 1999). In traditional classes, basic skills are emphasized. Curriculum, which is presented in small parts, uses textbooks and workbooks. Teachers generally disseminate information to students didactically and seek correct answers to questions. Assessment of student learning is distinct from teaching and usually done through testing. Students often work alone.

In constructivist classrooms, the curriculum focuses on big concepts. Activities typically involve primary sources of data and manipulative materials. Teachers generally interact with students by seeking their questions and points of view. Assessment is authentic; it is interwoven with teaching and includes teacher observations and student portfolios. Students often work in groups.

Some guiding principles of constructivist learning environments are shown in Table 7.6 (Brooks & Brooks, 1999). One principle is that teachers should *pose problems of emerging relevance* to students, where relevance is preexisting or emerges

Table 7.6
Guiding principles of constructivist learning environments.

- Pose problems of emerging relevance to students.

- Structure learning around primary concepts.

- Seek and value students' points of view.

- Adapt curriculum to address students' suppositions.

- Assess student learning in the context of teaching.

Source: From *In Search of Understanding: The Case for Constructivist Classrooms* (p. 33) by J. G. Brooks and M. G. Brooks, 1999, Alexandria, VA: Association for Supervision and Curriculum Development.

through teacher mediation. Thus, a teacher might structure a lesson around questions that challenge students' preconceptions. This takes time, which means that other critical content may not be covered. Relevance is not established by threatening to test students but, rather, by stimulating their interest and helping them discover how the problem affects their lives.

A second principle is that *learning should be structured around primary concepts.* This means that teachers design activities around conceptual clusters of questions and problems so that ideas are presented holistically rather than in isolated fashion (Brooks & Brooks, 1999). Being able to see the whole helps to understand the parts.

Holistic teaching does not necessarily require sacrificing content, but it does involve structuring content differently. A piecemeal approach to teaching history is to present information chronologically as a series of events. In contrast, a holistic method involves presenting themes that recur in history (e.g., economic hardship, disputes over territory) and then structuring content so that students can discover these themes in different eras. Students then can see that although environmental features change over time (e.g., armies—air forces; farming—technology), the themes remain the same.

Holistic teaching also can be done across subjects. In the middle school curriculum, for example, the theme of "courage" can be explored in social studies (e.g., courage of people to stand up and act based on their beliefs when these conflicted with governments), language arts (e.g., characters in literature who displayed courage), and science (e.g., courage of scientists who disputed prevailing theories). An integrated curriculum in which teachers plan units together reflects this holism.

Third, it is important to *seek and value students' points of view.* Trying to understand students' perspectives is essential for planning activities that are challenging and interesting. This requires that teachers ask questions, stimulate discussions, and listen to what students say. Teachers who make little effort to understand what students think fail to capitalize on the role of their experiences in learning. This is not to suggest that teachers should analyze every student utterance; that is not necessary, nor is there time to do it. Rather, teachers should try to learn students' conceptions of a topic.

With the current emphasis on achievement test scores, it is easy to focus only on students' correct answers. Constructivist education, however, requires that— where feasible—we go beyond the answer and learn how the students arrived at that answer. Teachers do this by asking students to elaborate on their answers. Thus, they might ask a student, "How did you arrive at that answer?" or "Why do you think that?" It is possible for a student to arrive at a correct answer through faulty reasoning and, conversely, to answer incorrectly but engage in sound thinking. Students' perspectives on a situation or theories about a phenomenon help teachers in curriculum planning.

Fourth, we should *adapt curriculum to address students' suppositions.* This means that curricular demands on students should align with the beliefs they bring to the classroom. When there is a gross mismatch, lessons will lack meaning for students. This does not mean that alignment must be perfect. In fact, demands that are slightly above students' present capabilities (i.e., within the zone of proximal development) produce challenge and learning.

When students' suppositions are incorrect, the typical response is to inform them of such. Instead, constructivist teaching challenges students to discover the information. Consider the following dialogue from a first-grade lesson on measurement and equivalence. Children were using a balance to determine how many plastic links equaled one metal washer in weight (Brooks & Brooks, 1999, p. 73).

Teacher: How many links does it take to balance one washer?

Anna: (After a few seconds of experimenting) Four.

Teacher: If I placed one more washer on this side, how many more links do you think we would need to balance it?

Anna: One.

Teacher: Try it.

Rather than simply tell Anna that her answer is wrong, the teacher challenged Anna to discover the correct answer. Anna placed another link in the balance tray and saw that it did not balance. She placed a second and third link in the tray, and finally a fourth, at which time there was balance. The teacher then asked her how many it took to balance a washer.

Anna: Four.

Teacher: And how many to balance two washers?

Anna: (Counting) Eight.

Teacher: If I put one more washer on this side, how many more links will you need to balance it?

Anna: (Pondered and looked quizzically at the teacher) Four.

Teacher: Try it.

Anna: (After successfully balancing with four links) Each washer is the same as four links.

Teacher: Now, let me give you a really hard question. If I took four links off of the balance, how many washers would I need to take off in order to balance it?

Anna: One!

Notice that after Anna answered "four" correctly, the teacher did not respond by saying "correct" but rather continued to question her. This example shows how the teacher modified the lesson based on Anna's suppositions and how she challenged Anna to discover the correct principle.

Finally, constructivist education requires that we *assess student learning in the context of teaching*. This point runs counter to the typical situation in classrooms where most assessments of student learning occur disconnected from teaching—for example, end-of-grade tests, end-of-unit exams, pop quizzes. Although the content of these assessments may align well with learning objectives addressed during instruction, the assessment occasions are separate from teaching.

In a constructivist environment assessment occurs continuously during teaching and is an assessment of both students and teacher. In the preceding example, Anna's learning was being assessed throughout the sequence, as was the success of the teacher in designing an activity and guiding Anna to understand the concept.

Of course, assessment methods must reflect the type of learning. Constructivist environments are best designed for meaningful, deep-structure learning, not for superficial understanding. True-false and multiple-choice tests may be inappropriate to assess learning outcomes. Authentic forms of assessment may require students to write reflective pieces discussing what they learned and why this knowledge is useful in the world or to demonstrate and apply skills they have acquired.

Constructivist assessment is less concerned about right and wrong answers than about next steps after students answer. This type of authentic assessment, which occurs during teaching and learning, guides instructional decisions. Authentic assessment is difficult, because it forces teachers to design activities to get student feedback and alter instruction as needed. It is much easier to design and score a multiple-choice test, but encouraging teachers to teach constructively and then assess separately in a traditional manner sends a mixed message. Given the present emphasis on accountability, we may never move completely to authentic assessment, but encouraging authentic assessment facilitates curricular planning and provides for more-interesting lessons than drilling students to pass tests.

APA Learner-Centered Principles

The American Psychological Association developed a set of learner-centered psychological principles (American Psychological Association Work Group of the Board of Educational Affairs, 1997). These principles (Table 7.7), which reflect a constructivist learning approach, were developed as guidelines for school design and reform.

The principles are grouped into four major categories: cognitive and metacognitive factors, motivational and affective factors, developmental and social factors, and individual differences. Cognitive and metacognitive factors involve the nature of the learning process, learning goals, construction of knowledge, strategic thinking, thinking about thinking, and the content of learning. Motivational and affective factors reflect motivational and emotional influences on learning, the intrinsic motivation to learn, and the effects of motivation on effort. Developmental and social factors include developmental and social influences on learning. Individual differences comprise individual difference variables, learning and diversity, and standards and assessment.

Table 7.7

Cognitive and Metacognitive Factors

1. *Nature of the learning process.* The learning of complex subject matter is most effective when it is an intentional process of constructing meaning from information and experience.

2. *Goals of the learning process.* The successful learner, over time and with support and instructional guidance, can create meaningful, coherent representations of knowledge.

3. *Construction of knowledge.* The successful learner can link new information with existing knowledge in meaningful ways.

4. *Strategic thinking.* The successful learner can create and use a repertoire of thinking and reasoning strategies to achieve complex learning goals.

5. *Thinking about thinking.* Higher-order strategies for selecting and monitoring mental operations facilitate creative and critical thinking.

6. *Context of learning.* Learning is influenced by environmental factors, including culture, technology, and instructional practices.

Motivational and Affective Factors

7. *Motivational and emotional influences on learning.* What and how much is learned is influenced by the learner's motivation. Motivation to learn, in turn, is influenced by the individual's emotional states, beliefs, interests and goals, and habits of thinking.

8. *Intrinsic motivation to learn.* The learner's creativity, higher-order thinking, and natural curiosity all contribute to motivation to learn. Intrinsic motivation is stimulated by tasks of optimal novelty and difficulty, tasks that are relevant to personal interests, and tasks that provide for personal choice and control.

9. *Effects of motivation on effort.* Acquisition of complex knowledge and skills requires extended learner effort and guided practice. Without learners' motivation to learn, the willingness to exert this effort is unlikely without coercion.

Development and Social Factors

10. *Developmental influences on learning.* As individuals develop, there are different opportunities and constraints for learning. Learning is most effective when differential development within and across physical, intellectual, emotional, and social domains is taken into account.

11. *Social influences on learning.* Learning is influenced by social interactions, interpersonal relations, and communication with others.

Individual Differences Factors

12. *Individual differences in learning.* Learners have different strategies, approaches, and capabilities for learning that are a function of prior experience and heredity.

13. *Learning and diversity.* Learning is most effective when differences in learners' linguistic, cultural, and social backgrounds are taken into account.

14. *Standards and assessment.* Setting appropriately high and challenging standards and assessing the learner as well as learning progress—including diagnostic, process, and outcome assessment—are integral parts of the learning process.

Source: APA Work Group of the Board of Educational Affairs, 1997. American Psychological Association, Washington, DC. Copyright © 1997 by the American Psychological Association. Reprinted with permission.

> **APPLICATION 7.7**
> *Learner-Centered Principles*
>
> ---
>
> Jim Marshall applies many of the APA learner-centered principles in his history classes. He knows that many students are not intrinsically motivated to learn history and take it only because it is required. He thus builds into the curriculum strategies to enhance interest. He makes use of tapes, field trips, and class reenactments of historical events to link history better with real-world experiences. Jim also does not want students to simply memorize content but rather learn to think critically. He teaches them a strategy to use to analyze historical events that includes key questions such as, "What preceded the event?", "How might it have turned out differently?", and "How did this event influence future developments?" Because he likes to focus on historical themes (e.g., economic development, territorial conflict), he has students apply these themes throughout the school year to different historical periods.
>
> Being a psychologist herself, Gina Brown is familiar with the APA principles and incorporates them into her teaching. She knows that her students must have a good understanding of developmental, social, and individual difference variables if they are to be successful teachers. For their field placements Gina ensures that students work in a variety of settings. Thus, students are assigned at different times to classes with younger and older students. She also ensures that students have the opportunity to work in classes where there is diversity in ethnic and socioeconomic backgrounds of students and with teachers who use methods utilizing social interactions (e.g., cooperative learning, tutoring). Gina understands the importance of students' reflections on their experiences as they construct meaning of teaching. They write journals on the field placement experiences and share these in class. She helps students understand how to link these experiences to topics they study in the course (e.g., development, motivation, learning).

Application 7.7 illustrates some ways to apply these learner-centered principles in learning environments. In considering their application, teachers should keep in mind the purpose of the instruction and the uses to which it will be put. Teacher-centered instruction will often be the appropriate means of instruction, and, indeed, often it is the most efficient. But when deeper student understanding is desired—along with greater student activity—the principles offer sound guidelines.

Instructional Methods

The educational literature is replete with examples of instructional methods that reflect constructivist principles. Some of the better-known methods are summarized in this section. (Reciprocal teaching, which also is based on constructivist principles, is discussed in Chapter 9.)

Several commonalities are evident in these methods. One is that the teacher is not always the center of the instruction. Rather, environments are designed so that students have an active role in learning—mentally, physically, socially, and emotionally.

Another common feature is diverse instructional formats—small groups, activity centers, peer collaboration, reciprocal teaching, cooperative learning, scaffolding, and apprenticeships. Students are expected to take responsibility for their learning and contribute to the instruction and conversations. Differentiated classroom structure means that not all students may be working on the same task at the same time. In a class some students might be in a small group, others at the media center, and still others in a reading group with the teacher.

A third common feature is that learning tasks involve real-world problems rather than the artificial ones found in textbooks. For example, in a science class students may be given the assignment of devising a plan to save energy in their community. In history, students could develop World War II scenarios if the Normandy invasion had been unsuccessful.

Fourth, the environment should provide multiple representations of content. Assignments may require students to discuss material, read books, search the Web, make graphs and charts, develop a PowerPoint demonstration, and so forth. Such planning is difficult; it is much easier to design a lesson and present it to the class as a whole. In a constructivist environment, the teacher designs multiple activities for students to engage in and ensures that each student is exposed to different activities.

Constructivism does not absolve the teacher of responsibility. In some ways, it places greater demands on the teacher. Even in situations in which students work largely on their own without direct teacher intervention (e.g., guided discovery), the teacher must ensure that students are properly prepared with the skills they will need and that necessary materials are available.

Class Discussions.   Class discussions are useful when the objective is to acquire greater conceptual understanding or multiple sides of a topic. The topic being discussed is one for which there is no clear right answer but rather involves a complex or controversial issue. Students enter the discussion with some knowledge of the topic and are expected to gain understanding as a result of the discussion.

Discussions lend themselves to various disciplines, such as history, literature, science, and economics. Regardless of the topic, it is critical that a class atmosphere be created that is conducive to free discussion. Students likely will have to be given rules for the discussion (e.g., do not interrupt someone who is speaking, keep arguments to the topic being discussed, do not personally attack other students). If the teacher is the facilitator of the discussion, then he or she must support multiple viewpoints, encourage students to share, and remind students of the rules when they are violated. Teachers also can ask students to elaborate on their opinions (e.g., "Tell us why you think that.").

When class size is large, small-group discussions may be preferable to whole-class ones. Students reluctant to speak in a large group may feel less inhibited in a smaller one. Teachers can train students to be facilitators of small-group discussions.

A variety of the discussion is the *debate*, in which students selectively argue sides of an issue. This requires preparation by the groups and, likely, some practice if they will be giving short presentations on their sides. Teachers enforce rules of the debate and ensure that all team members participate. A larger discussion with the class can follow, which allows for points to be reinforced or new points brought up.

Peer Tutoring.   *Peer tutoring* occurs when a student who has learned a skill or concept teaches it to one who has not. Peer tutoring provides an alternative to traditional teaching.

Peer tutoring captures many of the principles of constructive teaching. It ensures that students are active in the learning process. Both tutor and tutee freely participate. There is some evidence that peer tutoring can lead to greater achievement gains than traditional instruction (Fuchs, Fuchs, Mathes, & Simmons, 1997). The one-to-one context may encourage tutees to ask questions that they might be reluctant to ask in a large class.

Peer tutoring also encourages cooperation among students and helps to diversify the class structure. A teacher might split the class into small groups and tutoring groups while continuing to work with a different group. The content of the tutoring is tailored to the specific needs of the tutee.

Teachers likely will need to instruct peer tutors to ensure that they possess the requisite academic and tutoring skills. It also should be clear what the tutoring session is expected to accomplish. A specific goal is preferable to a general one—thus, "Work with Mike to help him understand how to regroup from the 10s column," rather than "Work with Mike to help him get better in subtraction."

Cooperative Learning.   Cooperative learning is frequently used in classrooms. Unfortunately, when it is not properly structured, the cooperative groups can lead to poorer learning compared with whole-class instruction.

In cooperative learning the objective is to develop in students the ability to work collaboratively with others. The task should be one that is too extensive for a single student to complete in a timely fashion. The task also should lend itself well to a group, such as by having components that can be completed by individual students who then merge their individual work into a final product.

There are certain principles that when followed help cooperative groups be successful. One is to form groups with students who are likely to work together well and who can develop and practice cooperative skills. This does not necessarily mean allowing students to choose groups, since they may select their friends and some students may be left without a group. It also does not necessarily mean heterogeneous grouping, where different ability levels are represented. Although that strategy often is recommended, research shows that high-achieving peers do not always benefit from being grouped with lower achievers (Hogan & Tudge, 1999). Whatever the means of grouping, teachers should ensure that each group can succeed with reasonable effort.

Groups also need guidance on what they are to accomplish—what is the expected product—as well as the expected mode of behavior. The task should be one that requires interdependence; no group member should be able to accomplish most of the entire task single-handedly. Ideally, the task also will allow for different approaches. For example, to address the topic of "Pirates in America," a group of middle school students might give a presentation, use posters, conduct a skit, and involve class members in a treasure hunt.

Finally, it is important to ensure that each group member is accountable. If grades are given, it is necessary for group members to document what their overall contributions were to the group. A group in which only two members do most of the work but everyone receives an "A" is likely to breed resentment.

Two well-known variations of cooperative learning are the jigsaw method and STAD (student-teams-achievement divisions). In the *jigsaw method,* teams work on material that is subdivided into parts. After each team studies the material, each team member takes responsibility for one part. The team members from each group meet together to discuss their part, after which they return to their teams to help other team members learn more about their part (Slavin, 1994). This jigsaw method (and there are other variations) combines many desirable features of cooperative learning, including group work, individual responsibility, and clear goals.

STAD groups study material after it has been presented by the teacher (Slavin, 1994). Group members practice and study together but are tested individually. Each member's score contributes to the overall group score, but because scores are based on improvement, each group member is motivated to improve because individual improvements raise the overall group score. Although STAD is a form of cooperative learning, it seems best suited for material with well-defined objectives or problems with clear answers—for example, mathematical computations and social studies facts. Given its emphasis on improvement, STAD will not work as well where conceptual understanding is involved because student gains may not occur quickly.

Reflective Teaching

Reflective teaching is based on thoughtful decision making that takes into account knowledge about students, the context, psychological processes, learning and motivation, and knowledge about oneself. Although reflective teaching is not part of any constructivist perspective on learning, its premises are based on the assumptions of constructivism (Armstrong & Savage, 2002).

Components.   Reflective teaching stands in stark contrast to traditional conceptions of teaching in which a teacher prepares a lesson, presents it to a class, gives students assignments and feedback, and evaluates their learning. Reflective teaching assumes that teaching cannot be reduced to one method to apply to all students. Each teacher brings a unique set of personal experiences to teaching. How teachers interpret situations will differ depending on their experiences and perceptions of the situation. Professional development requires that teachers reflect on their beliefs and theories about students, content, context, and learning and check the validity of these beliefs and theories against reality.

Table 7.8
Components of reflective teaching decisions.

- Sensitive to the context

- Guided by fluid planning

- Informed by professional and personal knowledge that is critically examined

- Enhanced by formal and informal professional growth opportunities

Source: From *Reflective Teaching: The Study of Your Constructivist Practices*, 2nd ed., by J. G. Henderson, 1996, Englewood Cliffs, NJ: Merrill/Prentice Hall.

Henderson (1996) lists four components of reflective teaching that involve decision making (Table 7.8). Teaching decisions must be sensitive to the context. The context includes the school, content, students' backgrounds, time of the year, educational expectations, and the like. Fluid planning means that instructional plans must be flexible and change as conditions warrant. When students do not understand a lesson, it makes little sense to reteach it in the same way. Rather, the plan must be modified to aid student understanding.

Henderson's model puts emphasis on teacher personal knowledge. Teachers should be aware of why they do what they do and be keen observers of situations. They must reflect on and process a wide variety of information about situations. Teachers must have reasons for what they do.

Finally, decisions are strengthened by professional growth opportunities. Teachers must have a strong knowledge base from which to draw to engage in flexible planning and tailor lessons to student and contextual differences. There is no substitute for strong professional development among teachers.

Reflective teachers are characterized as active persons who seek solutions to problems rather than wait for others to tell them what to do. They persist until they find the best solution rather than settle for one that is less than satisfactory. They are ethical and put students' needs above their own; they ask what is best for students rather than what is best for them. Reflective teachers also thoughtfully consider evidence by mentally reviewing classroom events and revising their practices to better serve students' needs (Armstrong & Savage, 2002).

In summary, reflective teachers (Armstrong & Savage, 2002):

- Use context considerations
- Use personal knowledge
- Use professional knowledge
- Make fluid plans
- Commit to formal and informal professional growth opportunities

We can see assumptions of constructivism that underlie these points. Constructivism places heavy emphasis on the context of learning because learning is situated. People construct knowledge about themselves (e.g., their capabilities, interests, attitudes) and about their profession from their experiences. Teaching is not a lock-step function that proceeds immutably once a lesson is designed. And finally, there is no "graduation" from teaching. Conditions always are changing, and teachers must stay at the forefront in terms of content, psychological knowledge of learning and motivation, and student individual differences.

Becoming a Reflective Teacher.   What types of experiences are useful to help improve teachers' reflective capabilities? Being a reflective teacher is a skill, and like other skills it requires instruction and practice. The following suggestions seem useful in developing this skill.

Being a reflective teacher requires good *personal knowledge*. Teachers have beliefs about their teaching competencies to include subject knowledge, pedagogical knowledge, and student capabilities. To develop personal knowledge, teachers reflect on and assess these beliefs. Self-questioning is helpful. For example, teachers might ask themselves: "What do I know about the subjects I teach? How confident am I that I can teach these subjects so that students can acquire skills? How confident am I that I can establish an effective classroom climate that facilitates learning? What do I believe about how students can learn? Do I hold biases (e.g., that students from some ethnic or socioeconomic backgrounds cannot learn as well as other students)?"

Personal knowledge is important because it forms the basis from which to seek improvement. Thus, teachers who feel they are not well skilled in using technology to teach social studies can seek out professional development to aid them. If they find that they have biases, they can employ strategies so that their beliefs do not cause negative effects. Thus, if they believe that some students cannot learn as well as others, they can seek ways to help the former students learn better.

Being a reflective teacher also requires *professional knowledge*. Effective teachers are well skilled in their disciplines, understand classroom management techniques, and have knowledge about human development. Teachers who reflect on their professional knowledge and recognize deficiencies can correct them, such as by taking university courses or participating in staff development sessions on those topics.

Like other professionals, teachers must keep abreast of current developments in their fields. They can do this by belonging to professional organizations, attending conferences, subscribing to journals and periodicals, and discussing issues with colleagues.

Third, reflective teaching means *planning and assessing*. When reflective teachers plan, they do so with the goal of reaching all students. Many good ideas for lesson plans can be garnered by discussing them with colleagues and consulting practitioner journals. When students have difficulty grasping content presented in a certain way, reflective teachers consider other methods for attaining the same objective.

Assessment works together with planning. Reflective teachers ask how they will assess students' learning outcomes. To gain further knowledge of assessment methods, teachers may need to take courses or participate in staff development. The authentic methods that have come into vogue in recent years offer many possibilities for assessing outcomes, but teachers may need to consult with assessment experts and receive training on their use.

SUMMARY

Constructivism is an epistemology, or philosophical explanation about the nature of learning. Constructivist theorists reject the idea that scientific truths exist and await discovery and verification. Knowledge is not imposed from outside people but, rather, formed inside them. Learners construct their own understandings of knowledge; it is not acquired automatically. Constructivist approaches vary from those that postulate complete self-construction, through those that hypothesize socially mediated constructions, to those that argue that constructions match reality. Constructivism calls our attention to the fact that we must structure teaching and learning experiences to challenge students' thinking so that they will be able to construct new knowledge. A core premise of constructivism is that cognitive processes are situated (located) in physical and social contexts. The concept of situated cognition highlights these relations between persons and situations.

Vygotsky's sociocultural theory emphasizes the social environment as a facilitator of development and learning. The social environment influences cognition through its tools—cultural objects, language, symbols, and social institutions. Cognitive change results from using these cultural tools in social interactions and from internalizing and transforming these interactions. A key concept is the zone of proximal development, which represents the amount of learning possible by a student given proper instructional conditions. It is difficult to evaluate the contributions of Vygotsky's theory to the field of learning because research testing its predictions is recent and many educational applications that fit with the theory are not part of it. Applications that reflect Vygotsky's ideas are instructional scaffolding, reciprocal teaching, peer collaboration, and apprenticeships.

Private speech is speech that has a self-regulatory function but is not socially communicative. Vygotsky believed that private speech develops thought by organizing behavior. Children employ private speech to understand situations and surmount difficulties. Private speech becomes covert with development, although overt verbalization can occur at any age. Verbalization can promote student achievement if it is relevant to the task and does not interfere with performance. Self-instructional training is useful for helping individuals verbally self-regulate their performances.

Vygotsky's theory contends that learning is a socially mediated process. Children learn many concepts during social interactions with others. Structuring learning environments to promote these interactions facilitates learning.

Aspects of motivation relevant to constructivism include contextual factors, implicit theories, and teachers' expectations. Multidimensional classrooms, which have many activities and allow for greater diversity in student performances, are more compatible with constructivism than are unidimensional classes. Characteristics that indicate dimensionality are differentiation of task structure, student autonomy, grouping patterns, and salience of performance evaluations. The TARGET variables (task, authority, recognition, grouping, evaluation, and time) affect learners' motivation and learning.

Students hold implicit theories about such issues as how they learn and what contributes to achievement. Implicit theories are formed during socialization practices and self-reflection and influence students' motivation and learning. Incremental the-orists believe that skills can be increased through effort. Entity theorists view their abilities as fixed traits over which they have little control. Research shows that stu-dents who believe learning is under their control expend greater effort, rehearse more, and use better learning strategies. Teachers convey their expectations to stu-dents in many ways. Teachers' expectations influence teacher-student interactions, and some research shows that under certain conditions expectations may affect stu-dent achievement. Teachers should expect all students to succeed and provide sup-port for them to do so.

Self-regulation includes the coordination of mental processes, such as memory, planning, synthesis, and evaluation. Vygotsky believed that language and the zone of proximal development were critical for the development of self-regulation. In Kopp's theory, self-regulation involves a transition from responding to others to us-ing speech and other tools to plan, monitor, and direct one's activities. Self-regula-tion also involves learning the meanings of actions, which are affected by contexts and tools. As with motivation, learners develop implicit theories of self-regulation that address their competence relative to peers, what produces success in different domains, and how much control they have in academic situations. From a con-structivist perspective, identity development and self-regulation cannot be separated because self-identity includes being a student.

The goal of constructivist learning environments is to provide rich experiences that encourage students to learn. Constructivist classrooms teach big concepts using much student activity, social interaction, and authentic assessments. Students' ideas are avidly sought, and, compared with traditional classes, there is less emphasis on superficial learning and more emphasis on deeper understanding. The APA learner-centered principles, which address various factors (cognitive, metacognitive, motiva-tional, affective, developmental, social, and individual difference), reflect a construc-tivist learning approach. Some widely practiced instructional methods that fit well with constructivism are class discussions, peer tutoring, and cooperative learning.

Reflective teaching is thoughtful decision making that considers such factors as students, contexts, psychological processes, learning, motivation, and self-knowl-edge. The premises of reflective teaching are based on constructivist principles. Be-coming a reflective teacher requires the development of personal and professional knowledge, planning strategies, and assessment skills.

Motivation

We have seen throughout this text that much human learning—regardless of domain or content area—has common features. For one, it begins with a certain knowledge and skill that learners bring to the situation, which expand and refine as a function of learning. For another, it involves the use of cognitive strategies and processes such as attention, perception, rehearsal, organization, elaboration, storage, and retrieval.

This chapter discusses motivation—a topic intimately linked with learning. *Motivation* is the process of instigating and sustaining goal-directed behavior (Pintrich & Schunk, 2002). This is a cognitive definition because it postulates that learners set goals and employ cognitive processes (e.g., planning, monitoring) and behaviors (e.g., persistence, effort) to attain their goals. Although behavioral views of motivation are reviewed, the bulk of this chapter is devoted to cognitive perspectives.

As with learning, motivation is not observed directly but rather inferred from behavioral indexes such as verbalizations, task choices, and goal-directed activities. Motivation is an explanatory concept that helps us understand why people behave as they do.

Although some simple types of learning can occur in the absence of motivation, motivation plays an important role in learning. Students motivated to learn attend to instruction and engage in such activities as rehearsing information, relating it to previously acquired knowledge, and asking questions. Rather than

quit when they encounter difficult material, motivated students expend greater effort. They choose to work on tasks when they are not required to do so; in their spare time they read books on topics of interest, solve problems and puzzles, and work on computer projects. In short, motivation engages students in activities that facilitate learning.

An active area of current interest is neurophysiological research (Byrnes & Fox, 1998), which is covered in Chapter 10. Investigators are examining how changes in brain waves, hormones, and neurochemical activities relate to behavior. This research holds promise for making significant contributions in understanding motivational processes.

We begin by presenting a generic model of *motivated learning*, or the motivation to acquire skills and strategies, as distinct from the motivation to complete activities. Some historical views of motivation are covered, and the remainder of the chapter covers cognitive perspectives. Key motivational processes are explained and linked to learning. Topics covered are achievement motivation theory, attribution theory, social cognitive theory, goal theory, perceptions of control, self-concept, and intrinsic motivation. The chapter concludes by discussing the relation of motivation to self-regulation.

When you finish studying this chapter, you should be able to do the following:

■ Sketch a model of motivated learning and explain its major components.

- Briefly discuss some important historical theories of motivation: drive, conditioning, cognitive consistency, humanistic.

- Explain the major features in a current model of achievement motivation.

- Discuss the causal dimensions in Weiner's attribution theory and the effects they have in achievement situations.

- Explain how the social cognitive processes of goals and expectations can be formed and interact to affect motivation.

- Distinguish between learning (process) and performance (product) goals and

- explain how they can influence motivation and learning.

- Explain the potential effects of perceived control on learning, behavior, and emotions.

- Define self-concept and explain the major factors that affect its development.

- Distinguish intrinsic from extrinsic motivation and the conditions under which rewards may increase or decrease intrinsic motivation.

- Discuss how different motivational variables relate to self-regulation.

MODEL OF MOTIVATED LEARNING

Table 8.1 depicts a model of motivated learning (Pintrich & Schunk, 2002; Schunk, 1995). The model is generic and is not intended to reflect any one particular theoretical perspective. It is a cognitive model because it views motivation arising largely from thoughts and beliefs. The model portrays three phases: pretask, during task, posttask. This is a convenient way to think about the changing role of motivation during learning.

Pretask

Several variables influence students' incoming motivation for learning. Students enter tasks with various goals, such as learn the material, perform well, be the first one to finish, and so on. Not all goals are academic. As Wentzel (1992, 1996) has shown, students have social goals that can integrate with their academic ones. During a group activity, Ben may want to learn the material but also become friends with Tina.

Students enter with various *expectations*. As discussed in Chapter 3, expectations may involve capabilities for learning (self-efficacy) and perceptions of the consequences of learning (outcome expectations). Students have differing perceptions of the *value*, or perceived importance, of learning. Wigfield and Eccles (1992) distinguished different values, which are explained later.

Students differ in their *affects* associated with learning. They may be excited, anxious, or feel no particular emotion. These affects may relate closely to students' *needs*, which some theories postulate to be important.

Finally, we expect that the social support in students' lives will vary. *Social support* includes the types of assistance available at school from teachers and peers, as well as help and encouragement from parents and significant others in students' lives. Learning often requires that others provide time, money, effort, transportation, and so forth.

Table 8.1
Model of motivated learning.

Pretask	During Task	Posttask
Goals	Instructional variables Teacher	Attributions
Expectations Self-efficacy Outcome	Feedback Materials Equipment	Goals Expectations
Values	Contextual variables Peers	Affects
Affects	Environment	Values
Needs	Personal variables Knowledge construction	Needs
Social support	Skill acquisition Self-regulation Choice of activities Effort Persistence	Social support

During Task

Instructional, contextual, and personal variables come into play during learning. *Instructional variables* include teachers, forms of feedback, materials, and equipment. Although these variables typically are viewed as influencing learning, they also affect motivation. For instance, teacher feedback can encourage or discourage; instruction can clarify or confuse; materials can provide for many or few successes.

Contextual variables include social and environmental resources. Factors such as location, time of day, distractions, temperature, ongoing events, and the like can enhance or retard motivation for learning. Many investigators have written about how highly competitive conditions can affect motivation (Ames, 1992a; Meece, 1991). Students' social comparisons of ability with peers directly link to motivation.

Personal variables include those associated with learning, such as knowledge construction and skill acquisition, self-regulation variables, and motivational indexes (choice of activities, effort, persistence). Students' perceptions of how well they are learning and of the effects of instructional, contextual, and personal variables influence motivation for continued learning.

Posttask

Posttask denotes the time when the task is completed and periods of self-reflection when students pause during the task and think about their work. The same variables important prior to task engagement are critical during self-reflection with the addition of *attributions* (perceived causes of outcomes). All of these variables, in cyclical fashion, affect future motivation and learning. Students who believe that they are progressing toward their learning goals and make positive attributions for success are apt to sustain their self-efficacy for learning, outcome expectations, perceived value, and positive emotional climate. Factors associated with instruction, such as teacher feedback, provide information about goal progress and outcome expectations. Thus, students who expect to do well and receive positive outcomes from learning are apt to be motivated to continue to learn assuming they believe they are making progress and can continue to do so by using effective learning strategies.

We now turn to a discussion of historical perspectives on motivation. Whereas some variables included in historical theories are not relevant to the preceding model, historical views helped set the stage for current cognitive conceptions and several historical ideas have contemporary relevance.

HISTORICAL PERSPECTIVES

Much early work examined the idea that motivation results primarily from *instincts*. Ethologists, for example, based their ideas on Darwin's theory, which postulates that instincts have survival value for organisms. Energy builds within organisms and releases itself in behaviors designed to help species survive. Others have emphasized the individual's need for *homeostasis*, or optimal levels of physiological states. Still another perspective involves *hedonism*, or the idea that humans seek pleasure and avoid pain. Although each of these views may explain some instances of human motivation, they are inadequate to account for a wide range of motivated activities, especially those that occur during learning. Readers interested in these views should consult other sources (Petri, 1986; Pintrich & Schunk, 2002; Weiner, 1992).

Let us now take a look at four historical perspectives on motivation: drive theory, conditioning theory, cognitive consistency theory, humanistic theory.

Drive Theory

Drive theory originated as a physiological theory; eventually, it was broadened to include psychological needs. Woodworth (1918) defined *drives* as internal forces that sought to maintain homeostatic body balance. When an organism is deprived of an essential element (e.g., food, air, water), this activates a drive that causes the organism to respond. The drive subsides when the element is obtained.

Much of the research that tested predictions of drive theory was conducted with laboratory animals (Richter, 1927; Woodworth & Schlosberg, 1954). In these experiments, animals often were deprived of food or water for some time and their behaviors to get food or water were assessed. For example, rats might be deprived of food for varying amounts of time and placed in a maze. The time that it took them to run to the end to receive food was measured. Not surprisingly, response strength (running speed) normally varied directly with the number of prior reinforcements and with longer deprivation up to 2 to 3 days, after which it dropped off because the animals became progressively weaker.

Hull (1943) broadened the drive concept by postulating that physiological deficits were primary needs that instigated drives to reduce the needs. *Drive (D)* was the motivational force that energized and prompted organisms into action. Behavior that obtained reinforcement to satisfy a need resulted in *drive reduction*. This process is as follows:

Need → Drive → Behavior

Hull (1943) defined *motivation* as the "initiation of learned, or habitual, patterns of movement or behavior" (p. 226). He believed that innate behaviors usually satisfied primary needs and that learning occurred only when innate behaviors proved ineffective. *Learning* represented the organism's adaptation to the environment to ensure survival.

Hull also postulated the existence of *secondary reinforcers* because much behavior was not oriented toward satisfying primary needs. Stimulus situations (e.g., work to earn money) acquired secondary reinforcing power by being paired with primary reinforcement (e.g., money buys food).

Drive theory generated much research as a consequence of Hull's writings (Weiner, 1992). As an explanation for motivated behavior, drive theory seems best applied to immediate physiological needs. If Mike were lost in a desert, he would be primarily concerned with finding food, water, and shelter; if Sherrie fell into shark-infested waters, she would need physical safety.

Drive theory is not an ideal explanation for much human motivation. Needs do not always trigger drives oriented toward need reduction. Students hastily finishing an overdue term paper may experience strong symptoms of hunger, yet they may not stop to eat because the desire to complete an important task outweighs a physiological need. Conversely, drives can exist in the absence of biological needs. A sex drive can lead to promiscuous behavior even though sex is not immediately needed for survival.

Although drive theory may explain some behaviors directed toward immediate goals, many human behaviors reflect long-term goals: find a job, obtain a college degree, sail around the world. People are not in a continuously high drive state while pursuing these goals. They typically experience periods of high, average, and low motivation. High drive is not conducive to performance over lengthy periods and especially on complex tasks (Broadhurst, 1957; Yerkes & Dodson, 1908). In short, drive theory does not offer an adequate explanation for academic motivation.

Conditioning Theory

Conditioning theory (Chapter 2) explains motivation in terms of responses elicited by stimuli (classical conditioning) or emitted in the presence of stimuli (operant conditioning). In the *classical conditioning model*, the motivational properties of an unconditioned stimulus (UCS) are transmitted to the conditioned stimulus (CS) through repeated pairings. Conditioning occurs when the CS elicits a conditioned response

(CR) in the absence of the UCS. This is a passive view of motivation, because it postulates that once conditioning occurs, the CR is elicited when the CS is presented. As discussed in Chapter 2, conditioning is not an automatic process but, rather, depends on information conveyed to the individual about the likelihood of the UCS occurring when the CS is presented.

In *operant conditioning*, motivated behavior is an increased rate of responding or a greater likelihood that a response will occur in the presence of a stimulus. Skinner (1953) contended that internal processes accompanying responding are not necessary to explain behavior. Individuals' immediate environment and their history must be examined for the causes of behavior. Labeling a student "motivated" does not explain why the student works productively. The student is productive because of prior reinforcement for productive work and because the current environment offers effective reinforcers.

Ample evidence shows that reinforcers influence what people do; however, what affects behavior is not reinforcement but, rather, beliefs about reinforcement. People engage in activities because they believe they will be reinforced and value that reinforcement (Bandura, 1986). When reinforcement history conflicts with current beliefs, people act based on their beliefs (Brewer, 1974). By omitting cognitive elements, conditioning theories offer an incomplete account of human motivation.

Cognitive Consistency Theory

Cognitive consistency theory assumes that motivation results from interactions of cognitions and behaviors. Views within this tradition are *homeostatic*: When tension occurs among elements, the problem needs to be resolved by making cognitions and behaviors consistent with one another. Two prominent perspectives are balance theory and dissonance theory.

Balance Theory.   Heider's (1946) *balance theory* postulates that a tendency exists to cognitively balance relations among persons, situations, and events. The basic situation involves three elements, and relations can be positive or negative.

For example, assume the three elements are Janice (teacher), Ashley (student), and chemistry (subject). Balance exists when relations among all elements are positive; Ashley likes Janice, Ashley likes chemistry, Ashley believes Janice likes chemistry. Balance also exists with one positive and two negative relations: Ashley does not like Janice, Ashley does not like chemistry, Ashley believes Janice likes chemistry (Figure 8.1).

Cognitive imbalance exists with one negative and two positive relations (Ashley likes Janice, Ashley does not like chemistry, Ashley believes Janice likes chemistry) and when all relations are negative. Balance theory predicts no tendency to change relationships exists when the triad is balanced, but people will try (cognitively and behaviorally) to resolve conflicts when imbalance exists. For example, Ashley might decide that because she likes Janice and Janice likes chemistry, maybe chemistry is not so bad after all (i.e., Ashley changes her attitude about chemistry).

That people seek to restore cognitive imbalance is intuitively plausible, but balance theory contains problems. It predicts when people will attempt to restore bal-

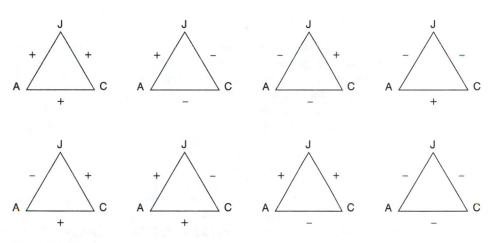

Figure 8.1
Predictions of balance theory.

Note: J = Janice (chemistry teacher); A = Ashley (student); C = chemistry. The symbols + and − stand for "likes" and "does not like," respectively, so that the top left balance can be read as follows: Ashley likes Janice, Ashley likes chemistry, Ashley believes Janice likes chemistry.

ance but not how they will do it. Ashley might change her attitude toward chemistry, but she also could establish balance by disliking chemistry and Janice. The theory also does not adequately take into account the importance of imbalanced relationships. People care very much when imbalance exists among people and situations they value, but they may make no effort to restore balance when they care little about the elements.

Cognitive Dissonance. Among the most elegant consistency theories is Festinger's (1957) *cognitive dissonance*, which postulates that individuals attempt to maintain consistent relations among their beliefs, attitudes, opinions, and behaviors. Relations can be consonant, irrelevant, or dissonant. Two cognitions are *consonant* if one follows from or fits with the other (e.g., "I have to give a speech in Los Angeles tomorrow morning at 9," and "I'm flying there today"). Many beliefs are *irrelevant* to one another—for example, "I like chocolate," and "There is a hickory tree in my yard." *Dissonant* cognitions exist when one follows from the opposite of the other. The following cognitions are dissonant because the second follows from the opposite of the first: "I don't like Deborah," and "I bought Deborah a gift." Dissonance is tension with drive-like properties leading to reduction. Dissonance should increase as the discrepancy between cognitions increases. Assuming I bought Deborah a gift, the cognition "I dislike Deborah" ought to produce more dissonance than "Deborah and I are acquaintances."

Cognitive dissonance theory also takes the importance of the cognitions into account. Large discrepancies between trivial cognitions do not cause much dissonance. "Yellow is not my favorite color" and "I drive a yellow car" will not produce much dissonance if car color is not important to me.

Dissonance can be reduced in various ways:

- Change a discrepant cognition ("Maybe I actually like Deborah").
- Qualify cognitions ("The reason I do not like Deborah is because 10 years ago she borrowed $100 and never repaid it. But she's changed a lot since then and probably would never do that again").
- Downgrade the importance of the cognitions ("It's no big deal that I gave Deborah a gift; I give gifts to lots of people for different reasons").
- Alter behavior ("I'm never giving Deborah another gift").

Dissonance theory calls attention to how cognitive conflicts can be resolved (Aronson, 1966). The idea that dissonance propels us into action is appealing. By dealing with discrepant cognitions, the theory is not confined to triadic relations as is balance theory. But dissonance and balance theories share many of the same problems. The dissonance notion is vague and difficult to verify experimentally. To predict whether cognitions will conflict in a given situation is problematic, because they must be salient and important. The theory does not predict how dissonance will be reduced—by changing behavior or by altering thoughts. These problems suggest that additional processes are needed to explain human motivation; see Shultz and Lepper (1996) for a model that may reconcile discrepant findings from dissonance research and integrate dissonance better with other motivational variables.

Humanistic Theory

Humanistic theory as applied to learning is largely constructivist (see Chapter 7) and emphasizes cognitive and affective processes. Humanistic theories emphasize people's capabilities and potentialities as they make choices and seek control over their lives. They do not explain behavior in terms of reinforcing responses to environmental stimuli.

Humanistic theories make certain assumptions (Pintrich & Schunk, 2002). One assumption is that the study of persons is *holistic*: To understand people, we must study their behaviors, thoughts, and feelings (Weiner, 1992). Humanists disagree with behaviorists who study individual responses to discrete stimuli. Humanists emphasize individuals' self-awareness.

A second assumption is that human choices, creativity, and self-actualization are important areas to study (Weiner, 1992). To understand people, researchers should not study lower organisms but, rather, people who are psychologically functioning and attempting to be creative and attempting to maximize their capabilities and potential. Motivation is important for attaining basic needs, but greater choices are available when attempting to maximize one's potential.

Well-known humanistic theories include those of Abraham Maslow and Carl Rogers. Maslow's theory, which emphasizes motivation to develop one's full potential, is discussed next, followed by Rogers's theory, which addresses both learning and instruction.

Hierarchy of Needs. Maslow (1968, 1970) believed that human actions are unified by being directed toward goal attainment. Behaviors can serve several functions simultaneously; for example, attending a party could satisfy needs for self-esteem and social interaction. Maslow felt that conditioning theories did not capture the complexity of human behavior. To say that one socializes at a party because one has previously been reinforced for doing so fails to take into account the current role that socialization plays for the person.

Most human action represents a striving to satisfy needs. Needs are *hierarchical* (Figure 8.2). Lower-order needs have to be satisfied adequately before higher-order needs can influence behavior. *Physiological needs,* the lowest on the hierarchy, concern necessities such as food, air, and water. These needs are satisfied for most people most of the time, but they are prepotent when they are not satisfied. *Safety needs,* which involve environmental security, dominate during emergencies: People fleeing from rising waters will abandon valuable property to save their lives. Safety needs are also manifested in activities such as saving money, securing a job, and taking out an insurance policy (Petri, 1986).

Once physiological and safety needs are adequately met, *belongingness (love) needs* become important. These needs involve having intimate relationships with others, belonging to groups, and having close friends and acquaintances. A sense of belonging is attained through marriage, personal commitments, volunteer groups,

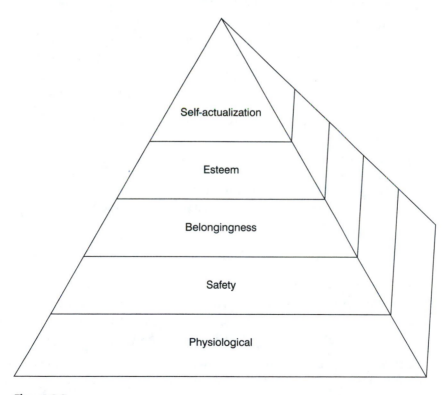

Figure 8.2
Maslow's hierarchy of needs.
Source: Motivation and Personality by Maslow, ©. Reprinted by permission of Pearson Education, Inc., Upper Saddle River, NJ.

clubs, churches, and the like. *Esteem needs* comprise self-esteem and esteem from others. These needs manifest themselves in high achievement, independence, competent work, and recognition from others.

The first four needs are *deprivation needs:* Their lack of satisfaction produces deficiencies that motivate people to satisfy them. Severe or prolonged deficiencies can lead to mental problems (Maslow, 1968): "Most neuroses involved, along with other complex determinants, ungratified wishes for safety, for belongingness and identification, for close love relationships and for respect and prestige" (p. 21).

At the highest level is the *need for self-actualization,* or the desire for self-fulfillment. Self-actualization manifests itself in the need to become everything that one is capable of becoming. Behavior is not motivated by a deficiency but rather by a desire for personal growth (Maslow, 1968):

> Healthy people have sufficiently gratified their basic needs for safety, belongingness, love, respect, and self-esteem so that they are motivated primarily by trends to self-actualization [defined as ongoing actualization of potentials, capacities and talents, as fulfillment of mission (or call, fate, destiny, or vocation), as a fuller knowledge of, and acceptance of, the person's own intrinsic nature, as an unceasing trend toward unity, integration or synergy within the person]. (p. 25)

Although most people go beyond the deficiency needs and strive toward self-actualization, few people ever fully reach this level—perhaps 1% of the population (Goble, 1970). Self-actualization can be manifested in various ways:

> The specific form that these needs will take will of course vary greatly from person to person. In one individual it may take the form of the desire to be an ideal mother, in another it may be expressed athletically, and in still another it may be expressed in painting pictures or in inventions. At this level, individual differences are greatest. (Maslow, 1970, p. 46)

A strong motive to achieve in or out of school is another manifestation of self-actualization (Application 8.1).

Maslow informally studied personal acquaintances and historical figures. Characteristics of self-actualized individuals include an increased perception of reality, acceptance (of self, others, nature), spontaneity, problem-centering, detachment and desire for privacy, autonomy and resistance to enculturation, freshness of appreciation and richness of emotional reaction, frequency of peak experiences (loss of self-awareness), and identification with the human species (Maslow, 1968).

When self-actualized persons attempt to solve important problems, they look outside of themselves for a cause and dedicate their efforts to solving it. They also display great interest in the means for attaining their goals. The outcome (righting a wrong or solving a problem) is as important as the means to the end (the actual work involved).

Critique. Maslow's hierarchy is a useful general guide for understanding behavior. It demonstrates how unrealistic teachers and parents are to expect students to learn well in school if they are suffering from physiological or safety deficiencies. The hierarchy provides teachers with clues concerning why students act as they do. Teachers stress intellectual achievement, but many adolescents are preoccupied with belongingness and esteem.

APPLICATION 8.1
Maslow's Hierarchy

Maslow's hierarchy can help teachers understand students and create an environment to enhance learning. It is unrealistic to expect students to show interest in classroom activities if they are suffering from physiological or safety deficiencies. Children who come to school without having had breakfast and who have no lunch money cannot focus properly on classroom tasks. Teachers can work with counselors, principals, and social workers to assist children's families or to have children approved for free or reduced-cost meal programs.

Some students will have difficulty working on tasks with nearby distractions (e.g., movement, noise). Teachers can meet with parents to assess whether home conditions are disruptive. Disruption at home can result in an unfilled safety need—a desire to feel more secure about learning. Teachers can urge parents to provide a favorable home environment for studying, ensure few classroom distractions, and teach students skills for coping with them (e.g., how to concentrate and pay close attention to academic activities).

Some high schools have problems with violence and pressures associated with gang behaviors. If students are afraid that they may be physically harmed or often must deal with pressures to join a gang, concentrating on academic tasks may be impossible. Teachers and administrators might consider working with students, parents, community agencies, and law enforcement officials to develop effective strategies for eliminating the safety concerns. These issues must be addressed in order to create an atmosphere conducive for learning. Once the appropriate atmosphere is created, teachers should provide activities that students can complete successfully. The established goals and expectations set must be attainable.

At the same time, the theory has problems. One is conceptual vagueness; what constitutes a deficiency is not clear. What one person considers a deficiency in some area, another person may not. Another problem is that lower-order needs are not always prepotent. People commonly risk their safety to rescue others from danger. Third, research on the qualities of self-actualized individuals has yielded mixed results (Petri, 1986). Apparently, self-actualization can take many forms and be manifested at work, school, home, and so forth. How it may appear and how it can be influenced are unclear. Despite these problems, the idea that people strive to feel competent and lead self-fulfilling lives is a central notion in many theories of motivation (Pintrich & Schunk, 2002).

Actualizing Tendency. Rogers was an internationally known psychotherapist whose approach to counseling is known as *client-centered therapy*. According to Rogers (1963), life represents an ongoing process of personal growth or achieving wholeness.

This process is the *actualizing tendency,* which is a motivational construct and presumably innate (Rogers, 1963). Rogers considered this motive the only fundamental one from which all others (e.g., hunger, thirst) derive. The actualizing tendency is oriented toward personal growth, autonomy, and freedom from control by external forces:

> We are, in short, dealing with an organism which is always motivated, is always "up to something," always seeking. So I would reaffirm . . . my belief that there is one central source of energy in the human organism; that it is a function of the whole organism rather than some portion of it; and that it is perhaps best conceptualized as a tendency toward fulfillment, toward actualization, toward the maintenance and enhancement of the organism. (p. 6)

The environment can affect the actualizing tendency. Our experiences and interpretations of them foster or hinder attempts at growth. With development, individuals become more aware of their own being and functioning (*self-experience*). This awareness becomes elaborated into a self-concept through interactions with the environment and significant others (Rogers, 1959). The development of self-awareness produces a need for *positive regard,* or feelings such as respect, liking, warmth, sympathy, and acceptance. We experience positive regard for others when we have these feelings about them. We perceive ourselves as receiving positive regard when we believe that others feel that way about us. This relation is reciprocal: When people perceive themselves as satisfying another's need for positive regard, they experience satisfaction of their need for positive regard.

People also have a need for *positive self-regard,* or positive regard that derives from self-experiences (Rogers, 1959). Positive self-regard develops when people experience positive regard from others, which creates a positive attitude toward oneself. A critical element is receiving *unconditional positive regard,* or attitudes of worthiness and acceptance with no strings attached. Unconditional positive regard is what most parents feel for their children. Parents value or accept ("prize") their children all the time, even though they do not value or accept all of their children's behaviors. People who experience unconditional positive regard believe they are valued regardless of what they do. The actualizing tendency grows because people accept their own experiences, and their perceptions of themselves are consistent with the feedback they receive.

Problems occur when people experience *conditional regard*, or regard contingent on certain actions. People act in accordance with these conditions of worth when they seek or avoid experiences that they believe are more or less worthy of regard. Conditional regard creates tension because people feel accepted and valued only when they behave appropriately. To protect themselves, people may selectively perceive or distort experiences or block out awareness.

Educational Implications.   Carl Rogers discussed education in his book *Freedom to Learn* (Rogers, 1969). Meaningful, experiential learning has relevance to the whole person, has personal involvement (involves learners' cognitions and feelings), is self-initiated (impetus for learning comes from within), is pervasive (affects learners' behavior, attitudes, and personality), and is evaluated by the learner (according to whether it is meeting needs or leading to goals). Meaningful learning contrasts with meaningless learning that does not lead to learners being invested in their learning, is initiated by others, does not affect diverse aspects of learners, and is not evaluated by learners according to whether it is satisfying their needs.

Rogers (1969) believed people have a natural potentiality for learning and are eager to learn:

> I become very irritated with the notion that students must be "motivated." The young human being is intrinsically motivated to a high degree. Many elements of his environment constitute challenges for him. He is curious, eager to discover, eager to know, eager to solve problems. A sad part of most education is that by the time the child has spent a number of years in school this intrinsic motivation is pretty well dampened. (p. 131)

Students perceive meaningful learning as relevant because they believe it will enhance their selves. Learning requires active participation combined with self-criticism and self-evaluation by learners and the belief that learning is important. Readers should note that other views—especially social cognitive and expectancy-value theories—also emphasize these points.

Rogers said that learning that can be taught to others was of little value. Rather than imparting learning, the primary job of teachers is to act as *facilitators* who establish a classroom climate oriented toward significant learning and help students clarify their goals. Facilitators arrange resources so that learning can occur and, because they are resources, share their feelings and thoughts with students.

Instead of spending a lot of time writing lesson plans, facilitators should provide resources for students to use to meet their needs. Individual contracts are preferable to lockstep sequences in which all students work on the same material at the same time. Contracts allow students considerable freedom (i.e., self-regulation) in deciding on goals and timelines. Freedom itself should not be imposed; students who want more teacher direction should receive it. Rogers advocated greater use of inquiry, simulations, programmed instruction, and self-evaluation as ways to provide freedom. Application 8.2 offers suggestions for applying humanistic principles.

Rogers's theory has seen wide psychotherapeutic application. The focus on helping people strive for challenges and maximize their potential is important for motivation and learning. The theory is developed only in general terms and the meanings of several constructs are unclear. Additionally, how one might assist students to develop self-regard is not clear. Still, the theory offers teachers many good principles to use to enhance learner motivation. We now turn to achievement motivation theory, which has direct relevance to student motivation.

ACHIEVEMENT MOTIVATION

Achievement motivation refers to striving to be competent in effortful activities (Elliot & Church, 1997). Murray (1938) identified the achievement motive, along with other physiological and psychological needs contributing to personality development. Motivation to act presumably results because of a desire to satisfy needs. Over the years achievement motivation has been heavily researched, with results that bear on learning.

APPLICATION 8.2
Humanistic Teaching

Humanistic principles are highly relevant to classrooms. Some important principles that can be built into instructional goals and practices are:

- Show positive regard for students.
- Separate students from their actions.
- Encourage personal growth by providing students with choices and opportunities.
- Facilitate learning by providing resources and encouragement.

Jim Marshall employed all four of these principles with Tony, a student in his American history class who was known to be one of the neighborhood troublemakers. Other teachers in the building told Mr. Marshall negative things about Tony. Mr. Marshall noticed, however, that Tony seemed to have an outstanding knowledge of American history. Undaunted by Tony's reputation among others, Mr. Marshall often called on him to share in the classroom, provided him with a variety of project opportunities and resources, and praised him to further develop his interest in history. At the end of the semester, Mr. Marshall worked with Tony to prepare a project for the state history fair, after which Tony submitted it and won second place.

Murray (1936) devised the *Thematic Apperception Test* (*TAT*) to study personality processes. The TAT is a projective technique in which an individual views a series of ambiguous pictures and for each makes up a story or answers a series of questions. McClelland and his colleagues adapted the TAT to assess the achievement motive (McClelland, Atkinson, Clark, & Lowell, 1953). Researchers showed respondents pictures of individuals in unclear situations and asked questions such as "What is happening?", "What led up to this situation?", "What is wanted?", and "What will happen?" They scored responses according to various criteria and categorized participants on strength of achievement motive. Although many experimental studies have employed the TAT, it suffers from problems that include low reliability and low correlation with other achievement measures. In recent years, researchers have devised other measures of achievement motivation (Weiner, 1992).

The following section discusses the historical foundations of achievement motivation theory. Later some contemporary perspectives on achievement motivation are presented.

Expectancy-Value Theory

John W. Atkinson (Atkinson, 1957; Atkinson & Birch, 1978; Atkinson & Feather, 1966; Atkinson & Raynor, 1974, 1978) developed an *expectancy-value theory of achievement motivation.* The basic idea of this and other expectancy-value theories is that behavior depends on how much individuals *value* a particular outcome (goal, reinforcer) and their *expectancy* of attaining that outcome as a result of performing given behaviors. People judge the likelihood of attaining various outcomes. They are not motivated to attempt the impossible, so they do not pursue outcomes perceived as unattainable. Even a positive outcome expectation does not produce action if the outcome is not valued. An attractive outcome, coupled with the belief that it is attainable, motivates people to act.

Atkinson postulated that achievement behaviors represent a conflict between approach (*hope for success*) and avoidance (*fear of failure*) tendencies. Achievement actions carry with them the possibilities of success and failure. Key concepts are as follows: the *tendency to approach an achievement-related goal* (T_s), the *tendency to avoid failure* (T_{af}), and the *resultant achievement motivation* (T_a). T_s is a function of the *motive to succeed* (M_s), the *subjective probability of success* (P_s), and the *incentive value of success* (I_s):

$$T_s = M_s \times P_s \times I_s$$

Atkinson believed that M_s (*achievement motivation*) is a stable disposition, or characteristic trait of the individual, to strive for success. P_s (the individual's estimate of how likely goal attainment is) is inversely related to I_s: Individuals have a greater incentive to work hard at difficult tasks than at easy tasks. Greater pride is experienced in accomplishing difficult tasks.

In similar fashion, the *tendency to avoid failure* (T_{af}) is a multiplicative function of the *motive to avoid failure* (M_{af}), the *probability of failure* (P_f), and the *inverse of the incentive value of failure* ($-I_f$):

$$T_{af} = M_{af} \times P_f \times (-I_f)$$

The *resultant achievement motivation* (T_a) is represented as follows:

$$T_a = T_s - T_{af}$$

Notice that simply having a high hope for success does not guarantee achievement behavior because the strength of the motive to avoid failure must be considered. The best way to promote achievement behavior is to combine a strong hope for success with a low fear of failure (Application 8.3).

This model predicts that students high in resultant achievement motivation will choose tasks of intermediate difficulty; that is, those they believe are attainable and will produce a sense of accomplishment. These students should avoid difficult tasks for which successful accomplishment is unlikely, as well as easy tasks for which success, although guaranteed, produces little satisfaction. Students low in resultant achievement motivation are more apt to select either easy or difficult tasks. To accomplish the former, students have to expend little effort to succeed. Although accomplishing the latter seems unlikely, students have an excuse for failure—the task is so difficult that no one can succeed at it. This excuse gives these students a reason for not expending effort because even great effort is unlikely to lead to success.

APPLICATION 8.3
Achievement Motivation

Atkinson's theory has implications for teaching and learning. If an academic assignment is perceived as too hard, students may not attempt it or may quit readily because of high fear of failure and low hope for success. Lowering fear of failure and raising hope for success enhance motivation, which can be done by conveying positive expectations for learning to students and by structuring tasks so students can successfully complete them with reasonable effort. Viewing an assignment as too easy is not beneficial: Higher achieving students may become bored with material they feel is not challenging. If lessons are not planned to meet the varying needs of students, the desired achievement behaviors will not be displayed.

In working on division, some of Kathy Stone's third-grade students are still having difficulty with multiplication. They may need to spend the majority of their time learning facts and using manipulatives to reinforce learning of new concepts. Success on these activities in a nonthreatening classroom environment builds hope for success and lowers fear of failure. Students who are proficient in multiplication, have mastered the division algorithm, and understand the relationship between multiplication and division do not need to spend lots of class time on review. Instead, they can be given a brief review and then guided into more difficult skills, which maintains challenge and produces optimal achievement motivation.

College professors such as Gina Brown should become more familiar with the research knowledge and writing skills of their students prior to assigning a lengthy paper or research project. Student background factors (e.g., type of high school attended, expectations and guidance of former teachers) can influence student confidence for completing such challenging tasks. Dr. Brown should seek students' input regarding their past research and writing experiences and should highlight model research and writing projects in the classroom. When making assignments, she might begin with short writing tasks and by having students critique various research projects. Then Dr. Brown can provide students with detailed input and feedback regarding the effectiveness of their writing. Throughout the semester assignments can become longer and more challenging. This approach helps to build hope for success and diminish fear of failure, which collectively raise achievement motivation and challenge students to set more difficult goals.

Research on task difficulty preference as a function of level of achievement motivation has yielded conflicting results (Cooper, 1983; Ray, 1982). In systematic studies of task difficulty by Kuhl and Blankenship (1979a, 1979b), individuals repeatedly chose tasks. These researchers assumed that fear of failure would be reduced following task success, so they predicted the tendency to choose easy tasks would diminish over time.

They expected this change to be most apparent among subjects for whom $M_{af} > M_s$. Kuhl and Blankenship found a shift toward more difficult tasks for participants in whom $M_{af} > M_s$, as well as for those in whom $M_s > M_{af}$. Researchers found no support for the notion that this tendency would be greater in the former participants.

These findings make sense when interpreted differently. Repeated success builds perceptions of competence (self-efficacy). People then are more likely to choose difficult tasks because they feel capable of accomplishing them. In short, people choose to work on easy or difficult tasks for many reasons, and Atkinson's theory may have overestimated the strength of the achievement motive.

Classical achievement motivation theory has generated much research. One problem with a global achievement motive is that it rarely manifests itself uniformly across different achievement domains. Students typically show greater motivation to perform well in some content areas than in others. Because the achievement motive varies with the domain, how well such a global trait predicts achievement behavior in specific situations is questionable. Some theorists (Elliot & Church, 1997; Elliot & Harackiewicz, 1996) proposed an integration of classical theory with goal theory; the latter is discussed later in this chapter.

Familial Influences

It is plausible that achievement motivation depends strongly on factors in children's homes. An early investigation studied parents' interactions with their sons (Rosen & D'Andrade, 1959). Children were given tasks and parents could interact in any fashion. Parents of boys with high achievement motivation interacted more, gave more rewards and punishments, and held higher expectations for their children than parents of boys with low achievement motivation. The authors concluded that parental pressure to perform well is a more important influence on achievement motivation than parental desire for child independence.

Subsequent research has yielded conflicting findings (Weiner, 1992). For example, Stipek and Ryan (1997) found that whereas economically disadvantaged preschoolers scored lower than advantaged children on cognitive measures, researchers found virtually no differences between these groups on motivation measures.

Attempts to identify parental behaviors that encourage achievement strivings are complicated because parents display many behaviors with their children. Determining which behaviors are most influential is difficult. Thus, parents may encourage their children to perform well, convey high expectations, give rewards and punishments, respond with positive affect (warmth, permissiveness), and encourage independence. These behaviors also are displayed by teachers and other significant persons in a child's life, which complicates determining the precise nature of familial influence. Another point is that although parents influence children, children also influence parents (Feld, 1967). Parents help children develop achievement behaviors when they encourage preexisting tendencies in their children; for example, children develop independence through interactions with peers and then are praised by parents. Additional research is needed on the role of the family in developing achievement motivation.

Fear of Success

As originally conceptualized by Atkinson and his colleagues, the achievement motive manifests itself in behaviors such as competition, independence, and "moving up the ladder of success." In Western societies, these behaviors have been historically and stereotypically associated with success among men but less so among women. Many men and women view these behaviors as incompatible with the basic notion of femininity. Not surprising, therefore, some research shows that Atkinson's theory predicts achievement behaviors better for men than women (Petri, 1986). Due to cultural beliefs and social practices, achievement motivation may be more complex among women.

This notion has been captured in the construct *fear of success*, or the motive to avoid success (M_{as}; Horner, 1972, 1978). Fear of success is a stable motivational disposition manifested by anxiety that inhibits achievement behavior. Fear of success arises from anticipated negative consequences of success in competitive achievement situations, such as rejection by others and loss of one's self-esteem and sense of femininity. Compared with men, women typically experience greater anxiety in competitive activities, including those involving intellectual achievement. The motive presumably is acquired early in life as a function of training in sex role standards (Horner, 1978), although the strength of fear of success among women varies widely. The motive inhibits behavior in achievement situations and can lead women to avoid competitive settings or to perform poorly.

Horner (1978) investigated fear of success by including a verbal item at the end of the TAT. For women, the item was: "After the first term finals, Anne finds herself at the top of her medical school class." For men, "John" was substituted for "Anne." Participants' responses were scored to determine the extent of perceived negative consequences and anxiety as a result of the success. The results showed that 62% of the women expressed fear of success compared with 10% of the men.

Other research has yielded conflicting results (Zuckerman & Wheeler, 1975). Hoffman (1974) found that a greater proportion of men demonstrated fear of success than women. Breedlove and Cicirelli (1974) found that fear of success among women was greater in nontraditional settings (e.g., medical school class) than in traditional ones (e.g., elementary education class). These inconsistent findings do not disprove Horner's ideas about fear of success, but they question whether fear of success is a stable motive and confined to women. Furthermore, the motive may be highly situationally specific and easily affected by task conditions. To the extent that fear of success reflects people's perceptions concerning acceptable behavior, one should expect these perceptions to change as societal traditions change. Compared with only a few years ago, women today occupy a greater proportion of professional and managerial positions. We might expect that the emphasis on competitiveness in classical achievement motivation theory is becoming more typical of women's achievement behavior. Although fear of success is of interest, its theoretical and practical usefulness is uncertain.

Contemporary Model of Achievement Motivation

The classical view of achievement motivation contrasts sharply with theories that stress needs, drives, and reinforcers. Atkinson and others moved the field of motivation away from a simple stimulus-response ($S \rightarrow R$) perspective to a cognitive and more complex model. Early achievement motivation theory stressed the person's perceptions and beliefs as influences on behavior, which shifted the focus of motivation from inner needs and environmental factors to the subjective world of the individual.

An important contribution was emphasizing both expectancies for success and perceived value of engaging in the task as factors affecting achievement behavior. Contemporary models of achievement motivation have continued with this type of subjective emphasis and, in addition, have incorporated other important cognitive variables into the models such as goals and perceptions of capabilities. Current models also place greater emphasis on contextual influences on achievement motivation, realizing that people alter their motivation depending on perceptions of their current situations.

This section considers a contemporary theoretical perspective on achievement motivation as espoused by Eccles and Wigfield. In the following section, another current view of achievement motivation—self-worth theory—is presented (Covington, 1984, 1992). Collectively, these two approaches represent valuable attempts to refine achievement motivation theory to incorporate additional elements.

Figure 8.3 shows the contemporary model (Eccles, 1983; Wigfield, 1994; Wigfield & Eccles, 1992, 2000, 2002). The processes shown in the middle are internal to the individual, whereas the boxes on the left and right are in the external world. Beginning

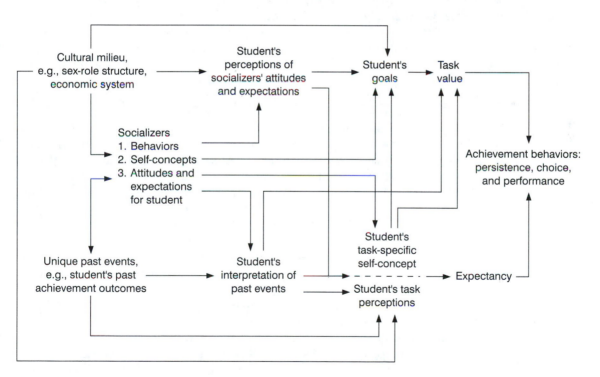

Figure 8.3

Contemporary model of achievement motivation.

Source: From *Achievement and Achievement Motives: Psychological and Sociological Approaches* by Janet T. Spence. © 1983 by W. H. Freeman and Company. Used with permission.

on the left, we see that various factors in the social world affect the types of cognitive processes and motivational beliefs that students possess. These social influences include factors associated with the culture, the behaviors of important socialization influences in the individual's environment, and past performance outcomes.

Students' initial cognitive processes in an achievement situation involve their perceptions of their environment and their interpretations for past events (attributions, or perceived causes of outcomes, are discussed later in this chapter). This model is task-specific: Students' cognitive processes will pertain to the context and include perceptions of the same or similar situations in the past. Students' initial motivational beliefs center on goals, task-specific self-concept, and perceptions of task difficulty. More is said about goals later in this chapter, but the point is that students' goals may not coincide with those of teachers, parents, and significant others.

Task-specific self-concepts are students' perceptions of their ability or competence in different domains. These perceptions are task-specific and vary greatly by domain; thus, students may feel highly competent in mathematics and English composition but less able in English grammar and science classes. Task-specific self-concept bears a close relation to Bandura's (1986) notion of self-efficacy (see Chapter 3 and later in this chapter); however, task-specific self-concept is more reflective of one's perceived ability whereas self-efficacy incorporates perceptions of various factors such as ability, effort, task difficulty, help from others, similarity to models, and so forth.

Perceptions of task difficulty refer to judgments of how difficult the task is to accomplish. Task difficulty is always considered relative to perceived capabilities; the actual difficulty level is less important than people's beliefs about whether they are capable enough to overcome the challenges and master the task.

The task value and expectancy constructs come next in the model. *Value* refers to the perceived importance of the task, or the belief about why one should engage in the task. The overall value of any task depends on three components. *Attainment value* is the importance of doing well on the task; this importance may be accorded because the task conveys important information about the self, provides a challenge, or offers the opportunity to fulfill achievement or social needs. *Intrinsic* or *interest value* refers to the inherent, immediate enjoyment one derives from the task. This construct is roughly synonymous with *intrinsic motivation* discussed later in this chapter. *Utility value* relates to task importance relative to a future goal (e.g., taking a course because it is necessary to attain a career goal).

The *expectancy* construct refers to the individual's perceptions concerning the likelihood of future task success. This construct is not synonymous with perceived competence; rather, it bears some resemblance to Bandura's (1986) outcome expectation in the sense that it is forward looking and reflects the person's perception of doing well in the future. It also contrasts with task-specific self-concept, which involves current beliefs about perceived ability. Research shows that higher expectancies for success are positively related to achievement behaviors, including choice of tasks, effort, persistence, and actual achievement (Bandura, 1986, 1997; Eccles, 1983; Eccles & Wigfield, 1985; Wigfield, 1994).

Research by Eccles, Wigfield, and others demonstrates support for many of the relations depicted in the model. Studies have used both cross-sectional and longitudinal designs that assess the beliefs and achievement of upper elementary and junior high students over time. A general finding across several studies is that expectancies and task-specific self-concepts are mediators between environmental contexts and achievement, as proposed by the model. These findings have good generalizability because the studies use students in actual classrooms and follow them over lengthy periods (Eccles, 1983). A challenge for the future is to explore in greater depth the links between variables and determine how these vary depending on the classroom context and variables associated with students (e.g., developmental status, ability level, gender).

Self-Worth Theory

Atkinson's theory predicts that achievement behavior results from an emotional conflict between hope for success and fear of failure. This notion is intuitively appealing. Thinking about beginning a new job or taking a difficult course produces anticipated satisfaction from being successful as well as anxiety over the possibility of failing.

Self-worth theory refines this idea by combining the emotional aspect with cognitive factors (Beery, 1975; Covington, 1983, 1984, 1992; Covington & Beery, 1976; Covington & Dray, 2002). This theory assumes that success is valued and that failure, or the belief that one has failed, should be avoided because it implies low ability. People want to be viewed as able, but failure creates feelings of unworthiness. To preserve a basic sense of self-worth, individuals must feel able and demonstrate that ability often to others. The key is to be perceived as able by oneself and by others.

One means of avoiding failure is to pursue easy goals that guarantee success. Another means is to cheat, although cheating is problematic. Shannon might copy answers from Yvonne, but if Yvonne does poorly, then Shannon will too. Shannon also might get caught copying answers by her teacher. Another way to avoid failure is to escape from a negative situation. Students who believe they will fail a course are apt to drop it; those who are failing several courses may quit school.

Strangely, students can avoid the perception of low ability through deliberate failure. One can pursue a difficult goal, which increases the likelihood of failure (Covington, 1984). Setting high aspirations is valued in our society, and failing to attain them does not automatically imply low ability. A related tactic is to blame failure on low effort: One could have succeeded if circumstances had allowed one to expend greater effort. Kay cannot be faulted for failing an exam for which she did not properly study, especially if she had a job and had inadequate study time.

Expending effort carries risk. High effort that produces success maintains the perception of ability, but high effort that results in failure implies low ability. Low effort also carries risk because teachers routinely stress effort and criticize students for not expending effort (Weiner & Kukla, 1970). Effort is a "double-edged sword" (Covington & Omelich, 1979). Excuses can help students maintain the perception of ability. The following are common excuses: "I would have done better had I been able to study more," "I didn't work hard enough" [when in fact the student worked very hard], or "I was unlucky—I studied the wrong material."

Self-worth theory stresses perceptions of ability as the primary influences on motivation. Research shows that perceived ability bears a strong positive relationship to students' expectations for success, motivation, and achievement (Eccles & Wigfield, 1985). That effect, however, seems most pronounced in Western societies. Cross-cultural research shows that effort is more highly valued as a contributor to success among students from China and Japan than it is among students from the United States (Stipek, 1998).

Another problem with self-worth theory is that perceived ability is only one of many influences on motivation, as this chapter makes clear. Self-worth predictions depend somewhat on students' developmental levels: Older students perceive ability to be a more important influence on achievement than younger students (Harari & Covington, 1981; Pintrich & Schunk, 2002). Young children have no clear differentiation between effort and ability (Nicholls, 1978, 1979). At approximately age 8, they begin to distinguish the concepts and realize that their performances do not necessarily reflect their abilities. With development, students increasingly value ability while somewhat devaluing effort (Harari & Covington, 1981). Teachers and adolescents will work at cross-purposes if teachers stress working harder while adolescents (believing that hard work implies low ability) attempt to shy away from expending effort. A mature conception eventually emerges in which successes are attributed to a combination of ability and effort. Despite these limitations, self-worth theory captures the all-too-common preoccupation with ability and its negative consequences.

Task and Ego Involvement

Achievement motivation theories have shifted their focus away from general achievement motives to task-specific beliefs. Later we discuss goal theory, which stresses the roles of goals, conceptions of ability, and motivational patterns in achievement contexts. In this section we discuss task and ego involvement, which are types of motivational patterns that derive largely from work in achievement motivation (Pintrich & Schunk, 2002).

Task involvement stresses learning as a goal. Task-involved students "forget about themselves" and focus on task demands: solve the problem, balance the equation, write the book report. Learning is valued as an important goal. In contrast, *ego involvement* is a type of self-preoccupation. Ego-involved students want to avoid looking incompetent. Learning is valued not for itself but only as a means to avoid appearing incapable (Nicholls, 1983, 1984).

Task and ego involvement reflect different beliefs about ability and effort (Jagacinski & Nicholls, 1984, 1987). Ego-involved students perceive ability as synonymous with *capacity*. Ability is a relatively fixed quantity assessed by comparisons with others (norms). The role of effort is limited; effort can improve performance only to the limit set by ability. Success achieved with great effort implies high ability only if others require more effort to attain the same performance or if others perform less well with the same effort. Task-involved students perceive ability as close in meaning to *learning* such that more effort can raise ability. Students feel more competent if they expend greater effort to succeed, because learning is their goal and implies greater ability. Feelings of competence arise when students' current performance is seen as an improvement over prior performance.

Ego and task involvement are not fixed characteristics. Nicholls (1983) suggested they are affected by conditions in school. Ego involvement is engendered by competition, which fosters self-evaluation of abilities relative to those of others. Task involvement is promoted under individual learning conditions. Students evaluate their own progress relative to how they, rather than others, performed previously. Task involvement also is enhanced by cooperative learning conditions (students in a group collectively work on tasks). In support of these predictions, Ames (1984) found that students placed greater emphasis on ability as a determinant of outcomes in competitive contexts but stressed effort in noncompetitive (cooperative, individual) situations.

Certain classroom features foster ego involvement (Nicholls, 1979). Students typically compete for teacher attention, privileges, and grades. Elementary and middle-grades students often are grouped for reading and mathematics instruction based on ability differences; secondary students are "tracked." Teacher feedback may unwittingly foster ego involvement (e.g., "Tommy, finish your work; everyone else is done"), as can teacher introductions to a lesson (e.g., "This is hard material; some of you may have trouble learning it"). Much research has examined how instructional and social factors affect students' motivational involvement (Ames, 1987, 1992a; Brophy, 1985; Meece, 1991).

Achievement Motivation Training

Achievement motivation training aims to help students develop thoughts and behaviors typical of learners high in achievement motivation (de Charms, 1968, 1984). De Charms (1976) initially trained teachers, who then worked with students. The goal was to help students develop personal responsibility for their learning outcomes.

The teacher training included self-study of academic motivation, realistic goal setting, development of concrete plans to accomplish goals, and evaluation of goal progress. Student motivation training was integrated with academic content. Classroom activities included self-study of academic motives, achievement motivation thinking, development of self-concept, realistic goal setting, and personal responsibility training. During a spelling activity designed to teach goal setting, students could choose to learn easy, moderate, or difficult words. To teach personal responsibility, teachers had students write stories about achievement, which were then used in a classroom essay contest. The results showed that training raised teachers' and students' motivation, halted the trend among low achievers to fall increasingly behind their peers in achievement, and reduced student absenteeism and tardiness.

Integrating achievement motivation training with academic content instruction, rather than including it as an add-on activity with special content, seems imperative. The danger of the latter approach is that students may not learn how the training applies in regular achievement domains.

Alderman (1985, 1999) recommends several useful components of motivation training. One is having teachers assist students to set realistic goals and provide feedback concerning their goal progress. Another aspect is self-study to examine one's motives for learning and to develop personal responsibility. The distinction between task and ego involvement (discussed earlier) seems useful. A series of questions helps students examine how they feel about tasks and what they see as their goals (e.g., learning versus pleasing others). Attributional training (discussed in the next section) also is relevant. One means of teaching personal responsibility is to help students place greater emphasis on effort as a cause of outcomes rather than blaming others when they fail or believing they were lucky when they succeed. As students experience successes, they should develop increased self-efficacy for continued learning and assume greater control of their learning.

Alderman (1985) applied these ideas to a senior high girls' physical education class. On the first day of class, students completed a self-evaluation of their health and physical fitness status and competence and interest in various activities, and they set fitness goals. They took weekly self-tests in different activities (e.g., aerobics, flexibility, strength, and posture). At the end of the first grading period, students set goals for the final exam. They had various ways to accomplish the aerobic goal (running, walking, and jumping rope). The teacher met with individual students to assess goals and made suggestions if these did not seem realistic. Students established practice schedules of at least three times a week for 9 weeks and kept a record of practices. Following the final exam, students completed a self-evaluation of what they had learned. Alderman noted: "To the instructor, the most striking comment made by students on the final self-evaluation was, 'I learned to set a goal and accomplish it'" (p. 51).

ATTRIBUTION THEORY

Attribution theory has been widely applied to the study of motivation (Pintrich & Schunk, 2002). *Attributions* are perceived causes of outcomes. *Attribution theory* explains how people view the causes of their behaviors and those of others (Weiner, 1985, 1992). The theory assumes that people are inclined to seek information to form attributions. The process of assigning causes is presumably governed by rules, and much attributional research has addressed how rules are used. From a motivational perspective, attributions are important because they influence beliefs, emotions, and behaviors.

Before discussing attributions in achievement settings, some relevant background material will be described. Rotter's *locus of control* and Heider's *naïve analysis of action* incorporate important attributional concepts.

Locus of Control

A central tenet of most cognitive motivation theories is that people seek to control important aspects of their lives. According to Rotter (1966), people believe that outcomes occur independently of how they behave (*external locus of control*) or that outcomes are highly contingent on their behavior (*internal locus of control*):

> When a reinforcement is perceived by the subject as following some action of his own but not being entirely contingent upon his action, then, in our culture, it is typically perceived as the result of luck, chance, fate, as under the control of powerful others, or as unpredictable because of the great complexity of the forces surrounding him. When the event is interpreted in this way by an individual, we have labeled this a belief in external control. If the person perceived that the event is contingent upon his own

behavior or his own relatively permanent characteristics, we have termed this a belief in internal control. (p. 1)

Rotter conceptualized locus of control as a *generalized expectancy* concerning whether responses influence the attainment of outcomes (e.g., successes, rewards); however, other investigators have noted that locus of control may vary depending on the situation (Phares, 1976). It is not unusual to find students who generally believe they have little control over academic successes and failures but also believe they can exert much control in a particular class because the teacher and peers are helpful and because they like the instructional content.

Locus of control is important in achievement contexts because expectancy beliefs are hypothesized to affect behavior. Students who believe they have control over their successes and failures should be more inclined to engage in academic tasks, expend effort, and persist than students who believe their behaviors have little impact on outcomes. In turn, effort and persistence promote achievement (Lefcourt, 1976; Phares, 1976).

Regardless of whether locus of control is a general disposition or is situationally specific, it reflects *outcome expectations* (beliefs about the anticipated outcomes of one's actions). Outcome expectations are important determinants of achievement behaviors, but they alone are insufficient (Bandura, 1982b, 1997). Students may not work on tasks because they do not expect competent performances to produce favorable results (negative outcome expectation), as might happen if they believe the teacher dislikes them and will not reward them no matter how well they do. Positive outcome expectations do not guarantee high motivation; students may believe that hard work will produce a high grade but will not work hard if they doubt their capability to put forth the effort (low self-efficacy).

These points notwithstanding, self-efficacy and outcome expectations usually are related (Bandura, 1986, 1997). Students who believe they are capable of performing well (high self-efficacy) expect positive reactions from their teachers following successful performances (positive outcome expectation). Outcomes, in turn, validate self-efficacy because they convey that one is capable of succeeding.

Naïve Analysis of Action

The origin of attribution theory is generally ascribed to Fritz Heider (1958), who referred to his theory as a *naïve analysis of action*. *Naïve* means that the average individual is unaware of the objective determinants of behavior. Heider's theory examines what ordinary people believe are the causes of important events in their lives.

Heider postulated that people attribute causes to internal or external factors. He referred to these factors, respectively, as the *effective personal force* and the *effective environmental force*, as follows:

$$\text{Outcome} = \text{personal force} + \text{environmental force}$$

Internal causes are within the individual: needs, wishes, emotions, abilities, intentions, and effort. The *personal force* is allocated to two factors: *power* and *motivation*. Power refers to abilities and motivation (trying) to intention and exertion:

$$\text{Outcome} = \text{trying} + \text{power} + \text{environment}$$

Collectively, power and environment constitute the *can factor*, which, combined with the *try factor*, is used to explain outcomes. One's power (or ability) reflects the environment. Whether Beth can swim across a lake depends on Beth's swimming ability relative to the forces of the lake (current, width, and temperature). Similarly, Matt's success or failure on a test depends on his ability relative to the difficulty of the test, along with his intentions and efforts in studying. Assuming that ability is sufficient to conquer environmental forces, then trying (effort) affects outcomes.

Heider sketched a framework for how people view significant events in their lives. Unfortunately, this framework has provided researchers with few empirically testable hypotheses. Later investigators have clarified his ideas and conducted attributional research testing refined hypotheses.

Attribution Theory of Achievement

In achievement settings, the search for causes elicits the following types of questions: "Why did I do well (poorly) on my social studies test?", and "Why did I get an A (D) in biology?" A series of studies by Weiner and his colleagues provided the empirical base for developing an attribution theory of achievement (Weiner, 1974, 1979, 1985, 1992; Weiner et al., 1971; Weiner, Graham, Taylor, & Meyer, 1983; Weiner & Kukla, 1970). This section discusses Weiner's theory in depth.

Causal Factors.   Guided by Heider's work, Weiner et al. (1971) postulated that students attribute their academic successes and failures largely to ability, effort, task difficulty, and luck. These authors assumed that these factors were given general weights, and that for any given outcome one or two factors would be judged as primarily responsible. For example, if Kara received an A on a social studies test, she might attribute it mostly to ability ("I'm good in social studies") and effort ("I studied hard for the test"), somewhat to task difficulty ("The test wasn't too hard"), and very little to luck ("I guessed right on a couple of questions"; Table 8.2).

Weiner et al. (1971) did not imply that ability, effort, task difficulty, and luck were the only attributions students use to explain their successes and failures, but rather that they are commonly given by students as causes of achievement outcomes. Subsequent research identified other attributions: other people (teachers, students), mood, fatigue, illness, personality, physical appearance (Frieze, 1980; Frieze, Francis, & Hanusa, 1983). Of the four attributions identified by Weiner et al. (1971), luck gets relatively less emphasis. Luck is a more important attribution in games of chance. Frieze et al. (1983) have shown that task conditions are associated with particular attributional patterns. Exams tend to generate effort attributions, whereas art projects are ascribed to ability and effort.

Causal Dimensions.   An attribution theory requires integrating causes into a framework highlighting their similarities and differences. Drawing on the work of Heider (1958) and Rotter (1966), Weiner et al. (1971) originally represented causes along two dimensions: (a) internal or external to the individual, and (b) relatively stable or

Table 8.2
Sample attributions for grade on mathematics exam.

Grade	Attribution	Example
High	Ability	I'm good in math.
	Effort	I studied hard for the exam.
	Ability + Effort	I'm good in math, and I studied hard for the exam.
	Task ease	It was an easy test.
	Luck	I was lucky; I studied the right material for the exam.
Low	Ability	I'm no good in math.
	Effort	I didn't study hard enough.
	Ability + Effort	I'm no good in math, and I didn't study hard enough.
	Task difficulty	The test was impossible; nobody could have done well.
	Luck	I was unlucky; I studied the wrong material for the exam.

unstable over time (Table 8.3). Ability is internal and relatively stable. Effort is internal but unstable; one can alternatively work diligently and lackadaisically. Task difficulty is external and relatively stable because task conditions do not vary much from moment to moment; luck is external and unstable—one can be lucky one moment and unlucky the next.

Weiner (1979) added a third causal dimension: controllable or uncontrollable by the individual (see Table 8.3). Although effort is generally viewed as internal and unstable (immediate effort), a general effort factor (typical effort) also seems to exist: People are characteristically lazy or hardworking. Effort is considered to be controllable; mood factors (to include fatigue and illness) are not. The classification in Table 8.3 has some problems (e.g., the usefulness of including both immediate and typical effort, the question of whether an external factor can be controllable), but it has served as a framework to guide research and attributional intervention programs.

In forming attributions, people use situational cues, the meanings of which they have learned via prior experiences (Schunk, 1994; Weiner et al., 1971). Salient cues for ability attributions are success attained easily or early in the course of learning,

Table 8.3
Weiner's model of causal attribution.

	Internal		External	
	Stable	**Unstable**	**Stable**	**Unstable**
Controllable	Typical effort	Immediate effort	Teacher bias	Help from others
Uncontrollable	Ability	Mood	Task difficulty	Luck

as well as many successes. With motor skills, an important effort cue is physical exertion. On cognitive tasks, effort attributions are credible when we expend mental effort or persist for a long time to succeed. Task difficulty cues include task features; for example, reading passages with fewer or easier words indicate easier tasks than those with more words or more difficult words. Task difficulty also is judged from social norms. If everyone in class fails a test, failure is more likely attributed to high task difficulty; if everyone makes an A, then success may be attributed to task ease. A prominent cue for luck is random outcomes; how good students are (ability) or how hard they work (effort) has no obvious connection to how well they do.

Attributional Consequences. Attributions affect expectations for subsequent successes, achievement behaviors, and emotional reactions (Weiner, 1979, 1985, 1992). The *stability* dimension is thought to influence *expectancy of success*. Assuming that task conditions remain much the same, attributions of success to stable causes (high ability, low task difficulty) should result in higher expectations of future success than attributions to unstable causes (immediate effort, luck). Students may be uncertain whether they can sustain the effort needed to succeed or whether they will be lucky in the future. Failure ascribed to low ability or high task difficulty is apt to result in lower expectations for future success than failure attributed to insufficient effort or bad luck. Students may believe that increased effort will produce more favorable outcomes or that their luck may change in the future.

The *locus* dimension is hypothesized to influence *affective reactions*. One experiences greater pride (shame) after succeeding (failing) when outcomes are attributed to internal causes rather than to external ones. Students experience greater pride in their accomplishments when they believe they succeeded on their own (ability, effort) than when they believe external factors were responsible (teacher assistance, easy task).

The *controllability* dimension has diverse effects (Weiner, 1979). Feelings of control seem to promote choosing to engage in academic tasks, effort and persistence at difficult tasks, and achievement (Bandura, 1986; Dweck & Bempechat, 1983; Monty & Perlmuter, 1987; Wang, 1983). Students who believe they have little control over academic outcomes hold low expectations for success and display low motivation to succeed (Licht & Kistner, 1986).

Individual Differences. Some research indicates that attributions may vary as a function of gender and ethnic background. With respect to gender, a common finding (although there are exceptions) is that in subjects such as mathematics and science, girls tend to hold lower expectancies for success than do boys (Bong & Clark, 1999; Meece & Courtney, 1992; Meece, Parsons, Kaczala, Goff, & Futterman, 1982). What is not clear is whether this difference is mediated by different attributions, as might be predicted by attributional theories. Some studies have found that women are more likely to attribute success to external causes (e.g., good luck, low task difficulty) or unstable causes (effort) and attribute failure to internal causes (low ability; Eccles, 1983; Wolleat, Pedro, Becker, & Fennema, 1980); however, other research has not yielded differences (Diener & Dweck, 1978; Dweck & Repucci, 1973). Eccles (1983) notes the difficulties of attempting to make sense of this research because of differences in participants, instruments, and methodologies.

With respect to ethnic differences, some early research suggested that African American students used information about effort less often and less systematically than did Anglo American students and were more likely to use external attributions and hold an external locus of control (Friend & Neale, 1972; Weiner & Peter, 1973). Graham (1991, 1994) reexamined these findings and concluded that although many studies show greater externality among African American students, researchers often have not controlled for social class; thus, African American students were overrepresented in lower socioeconomic backgrounds. When the effect of social class is controlled, researchers find few, if any, ethnic differences (Graham, 1994; Pajares & Schunk, 2001), and some research yields a more adaptive attributional pattern among African American students who place greater emphasis on low effort as a cause of failure (Graham & Long, 1986; Hall, Howe, Merkel, & Lederman, 1986). Research investigating ethnic differences in achievement beliefs has not yielded reliable differences (Graham & Taylor, 2002). The issue is complex, but the inconsistent results suggest that more research is needed before conclusions are drawn.

Attribution Change Programs

Attribution change programs attempt to enhance motivation by altering students' attributions for successes and failures. Students commonly have some difficulties when learning new material. Some learners attribute these problems to low ability. Students who believe they lack the requisite ability to perform well may work at tasks in a lackadaisical fashion, which retards skill development. Researchers have identified students who fit this attributional pattern and have trained them to attribute failure to controllable factors (e.g., low effort, improper strategy use) rather than to low ability. Effort has received special attention; students who believe that they fail largely because of low ability may not expend much effort to succeed. Because effort is under volitional control, teaching students to believe that prior difficulties resulted from low effort may lead them to work harder with the expectation that it will produce better outcomes (Application 8.4).

In an early study, Dweck (1975) identified children who had low expectations for success and whose achievement behaviors deteriorated after they experienced failure (e.g., low effort, lack of persistence). Dweck presented the children with arithmetic problems (some of which were insolvable) to assess the extent of performance decline following failure. Children largely attributed their failures to low ability. During training, children solved problems with a criterion number set for each trial. For some (*success-only*) children, the criterion was set at or below their capabilities as determined by the pretest. A similar criterion applied on most trials for *attribution retraining* children, but on some trials the criterion was set beyond their capabilities. When these children failed, they were told they did not try hard enough. On the posttest, success-only children continued to show deterioration in performance following failure, whereas attribution-retraining children showed less impairment. Success-only children continued to stress low ability; attribution-retraining students emphasized low effort.

Dweck did not assess self-efficacy or expectancies for success, so the effect of attributions on expectancies could not be determined. Other investigations have

APPLICATION 8.4
Attributional Feedback

Providing effort attributional feedback to students for their successes promotes achievement expectancies and behaviors, but the feedback must be perceived as credible. When a student is having trouble mastering difficult multiplication problems, the teacher can use past student successes and attributional feedback to build confidence in learning. If the student has mastered addition and multiplication concepts and facts, the teacher might say, "I know these new problems look hard, but you can learn how to work them because you know all the things you need to know. You just need to work hard and you'll do fine."

As the student works, the teacher can interject comments similar to the following:

- "You're doing well; you completed the first step. I was sure you knew your multiplication facts. Keep working hard."
- "Wow! Look at that! You did those so quickly. I knew you could do that because you're working hard."
- "You did it! You got it right because you worked hard."

In a nursing program an instructor should give the future nurses positive and accurate feedback regarding their administration of various clinical procedures and their effectiveness in interacting with patients. For example, after a trainee has completed the drawing of blood for testing purposes, the instructor might say:

- "I'm glad to see you used all the correct safety procedures in handling the blood. You know what to do."
- "You did a great job of explaining the procedure to the patient before starting the process. You are really good at giving explanations!"
- "You completed the procedure very calmly and with a smile. You have real talent at this."

These types of remarks reflect positive attributional feedback concerning students' competencies, which can raise their self-efficacy and motivation for further learning.

shown that teaching students to attribute failures to low effort enhances effort attributions, expectancies, and achievement behaviors (Andrews & Debus, 1978; Chapin & Dyck, 1976).

Providing effort-attributional feedback to students for their successes also promotes achievement expectancies and behaviors (Schunk, 1982a; Schunk & Cox, 1986; Schunk & Rice, 1986). In the context of subtraction instruction, Schunk (1982a) found that linking children's prior achievements with effort (e.g., "You've been working hard") enhanced task motivation, perceived competence, and skill acquisition better than linking their future achievement with effort (e.g., "You need to work hard") or not providing effort feedback. For effort feedback to be effective, students must believe that it is credible. Feedback is credible when students realistically have to work hard to succeed, as in the early stages of learning.

Effort feedback may be especially useful for students with learning problems. Schunk and Cox (1986) provided subtraction instruction and practice opportunities to middle school students with learning disabilities. Some students received effort feedback ("You've been working hard") during the first half of a multisession instructional program, others received it during the second half, and learners in a third condition did not receive effort feedback. Each type of feedback promoted self-efficacy, motivation, and skill acquisition better than no feedback. Feedback during the first half of the program enhanced students' effort attributions for successes. Given students' learning disabilities, effort feedback for early or later successes may have seemed credible.

Young children attribute successes to effort, but by age 8 they begin to form a distinct conception of ability and continue to differentiate the concepts up to about age 12 (Nicholls, 1978, 1979; Nicholls & Miller, 1984). Ability attributions become increasingly important, whereas the influence of effort as a causal factor declines (Harari & Covington, 1981). During arithmetic instruction and practice, Schunk (1983a) found that providing children with ability feedback for prior successes (e.g., "You're good at this") enhanced perceived competence and skill better than providing effort feedback or ability-plus-effort (combined) feedback. Children in the latter condition judged effort expenditure greater than ability-only children and apparently discounted some of the ability information in favor of effort. In a follow-up study using a similar methodology (Schunk, 1984b), ability feedback given when children succeeded early in the course of learning enhanced achievement outcomes better than early effort feedback regardless of whether the ability feedback was continued or discontinued during the later stages of learning.

The *structure* of classroom activities conveys attributional information (Ames, 1992a, 1992b). Students who compete for grades and other rewards are more likely to compare their ability among one another. Students who succeed under *competitive* conditions are more likely to emphasize their abilities as contributing to their successes; those who fail believe they lack the requisite ability to succeed. These conditions create an ego-involved motivational state. Students begin to ask themselves, "Am I smart?" (Ames, 1985).

Cooperative or *individualistic* reward structures, on the other hand, minimize ability differences. Cooperative structures stress student effort when each student is responsible for completing some aspect of the task and for instructing other group members on that aspect, and when the group is rewarded for its collective performance. In individualistic structures, students compare their current work with their prior performances. Students in individualistic structures focus on their efforts ("Am I trying hard enough?") and on learning strategies for enhancing their achievement ("How can I do this?").

The current educational emphasis on *inclusion* means that students with high-incidence (e.g., learning) disabilities and low-incidence (e.g., severe) disabilities are grouped with other learners in the regular classroom as much as possible. In inclusive classrooms learners often work on tasks cooperatively. Research on the effectiveness of inclusive classrooms is in its infancy (McGregor & Vogelsberg, 1998), but related research shows that grouping is a beneficial practice as long as the group succeeds (Ames, 1984). Group success enhances the self-evaluations of poor performers. Cooperative groups comprising students with and without learning disabilities function well if they are first taught how to work in small groups (Bryan, Cosden, & Pearl, 1982). When group members do not work well together, the performances and self-evaluations of students with and without learning disabilities suffer (Licht & Kistner, 1986). Furthermore, if the group fails, students may blame the slower learners (often unfairly), which negatively affects self-efficacy and motivation of group members.

Attribution theory has had a tremendous impact on motivation theory, research, and practice. To ensure an optimal level of motivation, students need to make facilitative attributions concerning the outcomes of achievement behaviors. Dysfunctional judgments about abilities, the importance of effort and strategies, and the role of significant others can lead to low levels of motivation and learning.

Social cognitive theory provides another important cognitive perspective on motivation, and much of Chapter 3 is relevant to motivation as well as to learning. The next section provides a brief recap.

SOCIAL COGNITIVE THEORY

Although different perspectives on motivation have relevance to learning, social cognitive theorists have directed considerable attention to the relation between motivation and learning (Bandura, 1986, 1997; Pajares, 1996; Pajares & Miller, 1994, 1995; Pajares & Schunk, 2001, 2002; Pintrich & Schrauben, 1992; Schunk, 1989, 1991). In social cognitive theory, *goals* and *expectations* are important learning mechanisms. Bandura (1986, 1991, 1997) views motivation as goal-directed behavior instigated and sustained by people's expectations concerning the anticipated outcomes of their actions and their self-efficacy for performing those actions. Attributions and other cognitions (e.g., values, perceived similarity) influence motivation in part through their effects on goals and expectations.

Goals and Expectations

Goal setting and *self-evaluation of goal progress* constitute important motivational mechanisms (Bandura, 1977b, 1986, 1991). The perceived negative discrepancy between a goal and current performance creates an inducement for change. As people work toward goals, they note their progress and sustain their motivation.

Goal setting works in conjunction with outcome expectations and self-efficacy. People act in ways they believe will help attain their goals. A sense of self-efficacy for performing actions to accomplish goals is necessary for goals to affect behavior (see Chapter 3). Thus, assume that Allison wants teacher praise (goal) and believes she will earn it if she volunteers correct answers (positive outcome expectation). But she may not volunteer answers if she doubts her capabilities to give correct ones (low self-efficacy).

Unlike conditioning theorists who believe that reinforcement is a response strengthener, Bandura (1986) contends that reinforcement informs people about the likely outcomes of behaviors and motivates them to behave in ways they believe will result in positive consequences. People form expectations based on their experiences, but another important source of motivation is observation of models. Social comparisons exert profound effects on student motivation.

Social Comparison

Social comparison is the process of comparing ourselves with others. Festinger (1954) hypothesized that when objective standards of behavior are unclear or unavailable, people evaluate their abilities and opinions through comparisons with others. He also noted that the most accurate self-evaluations derive from comparisons with those similar in the ability or characteristic being evaluated. The more alike observers are to models, the greater the probability that similar actions by observers are socially appropriate and will produce comparable results (Schunk, 1987).

Model-observer similarity in competence can improve learning (Braaksma, Rijlaarsdam, & van den Bergh, 2002). This effect on learning may result largely from the motivational effects of vicarious consequences, which depend on self-efficacy. Observing similar others succeed raises observers' self-efficacy and motivates them to try the task because they are apt to believe that if others can succeed, they will too. Observing similar others fail can lead people to believe they also lack the competencies to succeed, which dissuades them from attempting the behavior. Similarity may be especially influential in situations in which individuals have experienced difficulties and possess self-doubts about performing well (Application 8.5).

Developmental level is important in social comparison. The ability to use comparative information depends on higher levels of cognitive development and on experience in making comparative evaluations (Veroff, 1969). Festinger's hypothesis may not apply to children younger than 5 or 6, because they tend not to relate two or more elements in thought and are egocentric in that the "self" dominates their cognitive focus (Higgins, 1981). This does not mean that young children cannot evaluate themselves relative to others, only that they may not automatically do so. Children show increasing interest in comparative information in elementary school, and by fourth grade they regularly use this information to form self-evaluations of competence (Ruble, Boggiano, Feldman, & Loebl, 1980; Ruble, Feldman, & Boggiano, 1976).

The meaning and function of comparative information change with development, especially after children enter school. Preschoolers actively compare at an overt level (e.g., amount of reward). Other social comparisons involve how one is similar to and different from others, and competition based on a desire to be better than others without involving self-evaluation (e.g., "I'm the general; that's higher than the captain"; Mosatche & Bragioner, 1981). Later social comparisons shift to a concern for how to perform a task (Ruble, 1983). First graders engage in peer comparisons—often to obtain correct answers from peers. Providing comparative information to young children increases motivation for practical reasons. Direct adult evaluation of children's capabilities (e.g., "You can do better") influences children's self-evaluations more than comparative information.

APPLICATION 8.5
Social Comparison

Teachers can use social comparison as a motivation tool for improving behavior and effort in completing assigned tasks. As Kathy Stone works with a small reading group, complimenting students for appropriate displays of behavior emphasizes expected behaviors and instills a sense of self-efficacy in students for performing accordingly. Mrs. Stone might say:

- "I really like the way Adrian is sitting quietly and waiting for all of us to finish reading."
- "I like the way Carrie read that sentence clearly so we could hear her."

Observing student successes leads other students to believe they are capable of succeeding. A teacher might ask a student to go to the chalkboard and match contractions with the original words. Because the students in the group have similar abilities, the successes of the student at the board should raise self-efficacy in the others.

A swimming coach might group swimmers with similar talents and skills when planning for general practice and especially for simulated competitions. With students of like skills in the same group, a coach can use social comparison while working on improving certain movements and speed. The coach might say:

- "Dan is really working to keep his legs together with very little bending and splashing as he moves through the water. Look at the extra momentum he is gaining from this movement. Good job, Dan!"
- "Joel is doing an excellent job of cupping his hands in a way that acts like a paddle and that pulls him more readily through the water. Good work!"

Teachers and coaches should be judicious in their use of social comparison. Students who serve as models must succeed and be perceived by others as similar in important attributes. If models are perceived as dissimilar (especially in underlying abilities) or if they fail, social comparisons will not positively motivate observers.

As has been mentioned often in this text, comparing one's current and prior performances (temporal comparison) and noting progress enhances self-efficacy and motivation. Developmentally this capability is present in young children; however, they may not employ it. R. Butler (1998) found among children ages 4 to 8 that temporal comparisons increased with age but that children most often attended only to their last outcome. In contrast, children frequently employed social comparisons and evaluated their performances higher if they exceeded those of peers. Butler's results suggest that teachers need to assist children in making temporal comparisons, such as by showing children their prior work and pointing out areas of improvement.

In summary, with its emphasis on goals, expectations, and related cognitive processes, social cognitive theory offers a useful perspective on motivation. Application 8.6 gives some classroom applications of social cognitive principles. We now turn to goal theory, a relatively recent perspective on motivation that uses social cognitive principles as well as ideas from other theories.

GOAL THEORY

Goal theory represents a relatively new conception of human motivation, although it incorporates many variables hypothesized to be important by other theories (Pintrich & Schunk, 2002). Goal theory postulates that important relations exist among goals, expectations, attributions, conceptions of ability, motivational orientations, social and self comparisons, and achievement behaviors (Ames, 1992a, 1992b; Blumenfeld, 1992; Pintrich, 2000a, 2000b; Pintrich & Zusho, 2002; Weiner, 1990).

Although goal theory bears some similarity to the goal-setting theory discussed in Chapter 3 (Bandura, 1988; Locke & Latham, 1990), important differences exist. Educational and developmental psychologists developed goal theory to explain and predict achievement behavior, especially in the classroom. Goal-setting theory, in contrast, has drawn from various disciplines, including social psychology, management, and clinical and health psychology. A central construct in goal theory is *goal orientation*, which refers to the purpose and focus of an individual's engagement in achievement activities. Goal-setting theory is more concerned with how goals are established and altered and with the role of their properties (e.g., specificity, difficulty, and proximity) in instigating and directing behavior. Third, goal theory considers a wide array of variables in explaining goal-directed behavior, some of which may not directly involve goals (e.g., comparisons with others). Goal-setting theory typically considers a more restricted set of influences on behavior.

Goal Orientations

A central feature of goal theory is its emphasis on how different types of goals can influence behavior in achievement situations (Pintrich & Schunk, 2002). Goal orientations may be thought of as students' reasons for engaging in academic tasks (Anderman, Austin, & Johnson, 2002). Researchers have identified different orientations.

One distinction is between learning and performance goals (Dweck, 1991, 1999, 2002; Dweck & Leggett, 1988; Elliott & Dweck, 1988; Schunk, 1996; Schunk & Swartz, 1993a, 1993b). A *learning goal* refers to what knowledge, behavior, skill, or strategy students are to acquire; a *performance goal* denotes what task students are to complete. Other types of goals mentioned in the literature that are conceptually similar to learning goals include *mastery, task-involved,* and *task-focused goals* (Ames & Archer, 1987; Butler, 1992; Meece, 1991; Nicholls, 1984); synonyms for performance goals include *ego-involved* and *ability-focused goals.*

APPLICATION 8.6
Social Cognitive Theory

Students enter learning situations with a sense of self-efficacy for learning based on prior experiences, personal qualities, and social support mechanisms. Teachers who know their students well and incorporate various educational practices can positively affect motivation and learning.

Material presented in a way that students are able to comprehend fosters high self-efficacy for learning. Some students learn best from large group lectures and others from small group discussions. If a college English teacher is introducing a unit on the major works of William Shakespeare, the instructor might initially give a lecture providing background on Shakespeare's life and literary reputation. Then the professor could divide the students into small groups to review and discuss what had been introduced. This process would help build the self-efficacy of both students who learn well in large groups and those who do better in small groups.

As the instructor moves through the unit and introduces the major periods of Shakespeare's dramatic career, activities, exercises, and assignments need to be developed that provide students with performance feedback. Progress made toward the acquisition of basic facts about Shakespeare and his works can be assessed through short tests or self-checked assignments. Individual student growth as it relates to understanding specific Shakespearean works can be provided through written comments on essays and papers and through verbal comments during class discussions.

Students should be encouraged to share their own insights and frustrations in working with interpretations of various Shakespearean plays. Guiding students to serve as models during the analysis and discussion of the plays should promote efficacy better than will having a professor who has built his or her career studying Shakespeare's works provide the interpretation.

In working with students to develop goals toward learning the material and understanding Shakespeare and his works, the instructor could help each student focus on short-term and specific goals. For example, the professor might have students read a portion of one major work and practice writing a critique, after which they could discuss their analyses with one another. Breaking the material into short segments helps to instill self-efficacy for eventually mastering it. Commenting on the quality of the critiques by students is more beneficial than rewarding them for just reading a certain number of plays. Being able to interpret Shakespeare's work is more difficult than simply reading, and rewarding students for progress on difficult assignments strengthens self-efficacy.

Although these goal orientations at times may be related (e.g., learning produces faster performance), the importance of these goals for achievement behavior and learning stems from the effects they can have on learners' beliefs and cognitive processes (Pintrich, 2000a). Learning goals focus students' attention on processes and strategies that help them acquire capabilities and improve their skills (Ames, 1992a). The task focus motivates behavior and directs and sustains attention on task aspects critical for learning. Students who pursue a learning goal are apt to feel self-efficacious for attaining it and be motivated to engage in task-appropriate activities (e.g., expend effort, persist, and use effective strategies; Bandura, 1986; Schunk, 1989). Self-efficacy is substantiated as they work on the task and assess their progress (Wentzel, 1992). Perceived progress in skill acquisition and self-efficacy for continued learning sustain motivation and enhance skillful performance (Schunk, 1996; Figure 8.4a).

In contrast, performance goals focus attention on completing tasks (Figure 8.4b). Such goals may not highlight the importance of the processes and strategies underlying task completion or raise self-efficacy for acquiring skills (Schunk & Swartz, 1993a, 1993b). As students work on tasks, they may not compare their present and past performances to determine progress. Performance goals can lead to social comparisons of one's work with that of others to determine progress. Social comparisons can result in low perceptions of ability among students who experience difficulties, which adversely affect task motivation (Schunk, 1996).

Research supports these ideas. During science lessons, Meece, Blumenfeld, and Hoyle (1988) found that students who emphasized task-mastery goals reported more active cognitive engagement characterized by self-regulatory activities (e.g., reviewing material not understood). Intrinsic motivation (discussed later in this chapter) related positively to goals stressing learning and understanding.

Elliott and Dweck (1988) gave children feedback indicating they had high or low ability, along with instructions highlighting a learning goal of developing competence or a performance goal of appearing competent. Learning-goal children sought to increase competence by choosing challenging tasks and using problem-solving strategies. Performance-goal children who received high-ability feedback persisted at the task but also avoided challenging tasks that might have entailed public errors. Performance-goal children given low-ability feedback selected easier tasks, did not persist to overcome mistakes, and displayed negative affect.

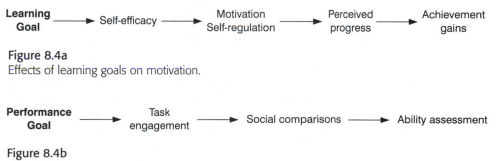

Figure 8.4a
Effects of learning goals on motivation.

Figure 8.4b
Effects of performance goals on motivation.

During reading comprehension instruction, Schunk and Rice (1989) found that with children deficient in reading skills, a process goal (e.g., learning to use a comprehension strategy) and a product (e.g., performance) goal (e.g., answering questions) led to higher self-efficacy than did a general goal of working productively; however, the process and product conditions did not differ. Schunk and Rice (1991) found that combining a process goal with feedback on progress toward the goal of learning to use a strategy promoted self-efficacy and skill better than process and product goal conditions. These two studies suggest that without progress feedback, learning goals may not be more effective than performance goals among students with reading problems.

Schunk and Swartz (1993a, 1993b) provided children in regular and gifted classes with a process goal of learning to use a paragraph-writing strategy or a product (performance) goal of writing paragraphs. Half of the process-goal students periodically received feedback on their progress in learning the strategy. Schunk and Swartz found that the process goal with feedback was the most effective and that the process goal with or without feedback led to higher achievement outcomes than did the product goal.

Schunk (1996) provided fourth graders with instruction and practice on fractions, along with either a learning goal (e.g., learning how to solve problems) or a performance goal (e.g., solving problems). In the first study, half of the students in each goal condition evaluated their problem-solving capabilities. The learning goal with or without self-evaluation and the performance goal with self-evaluation led to higher self-efficacy, skill, motivation, and task orientation than did the performance goal without self-evaluation. In the second study, all students in each goal condition evaluated their progress in skill acquisition. The learning goal led to higher motivation and achievement outcomes than did the performance goal. These findings were replicated with college students by Schunk and Ertmer (1999), who found that self-efficacy for applying computer skills was enhanced when students received a process (learning) goal and an opportunity to evaluate their learning progress.

Investigators have begun to examine further distinctions in the mastery-performance dichotomy. Drawing on the work of Carver and Scheier (1998), Linnenbrink and Pintrich (2002) proposed classifying mastery and performance goals according to whether they involve approach or avoidance. They further hypothesized that in this fourfold scheme, goals have different emotional consequences. Approach mastery goals are predicted to lead to positive affect, whereas both types of avoidance goals are expected to result in negative affect. Linnenbrink and Pintrich report support for these predictions. The role of affect in goal choice and outcomes often is not addressed, yet the emotional consequences of motivation for schooling are important (Meyer & Turner, 2002).

Goal orientations also play a key role in self-regulation (discussed later in this chapter), because they provide a framework within which learners interpret and react to events (Dweck & Leggett, 1988; Meece, 1994). Students who develop and maintain high self-efficacy for learning have higher expectancies for success, greater perceived control over learning, and more intrinsic interest in learning (Covington, 1992; Eccles, 1983; Harter & Connell, 1984). Students are more likely to adopt a task/learning-goal orientation when they believe they can improve their ability through expending effort (Dweck & Leggett, 1988; Meece, 1994; Nicholls & Miller, 1984). Purdie, Hattie, and Douglas (1996) found among Australian and Japanese students that a conception of learning as understanding was related to greater use of learning strategies. In contrast to this incremental conception of ability, students with a fixed conception believe that effort will improve ability only to a set limit. Effort becomes less important when ability is fixed.

Various achievement goal patterns can affect self-regulatory efforts. Providing students with feedback stressing a learning-goal orientation can enhance self-effi-cacy, motivation, self-regulatory activities, and achievement more than providing feedback emphasizing performance goals (Schunk & Swartz, 1993a, 1993b). Achievement goals affect students' task persistence and effort expenditure (Elliott & Dweck, 1988; Stipek & Kowalski, 1989). Under performance-oriented conditions, children with low perceived ability experience performance deterioration when they begin to fail (Meece, 1994); however, this pattern is not found among learning-ori-ented children regardless of perceived ability and among performance-oriented stu-dents with high perceived ability. Ames and Archer (1988) found that classroom mas-tery (learning) goal orientation relates positively to students' reported use of effective learning strategies and effort attributions.

Research also shows that achievement goals can affect how students study and what they learn. Learning-oriented students tend to use deep processing strategies that enhance conceptual understandings and that require cognitive effort (e.g., inte-grating information, monitoring comprehension) (Graham & Golan, 1991; Nolen, 1988, 1996; Pintrich & Garcia, 1991). In contrast, ego-oriented goal patterns are as-sociated with such short-term and surface-level processing strategies as rehearsal and memorization (Graham & Golan, 1991; Meece, 1994).

Factors in the home and school can affect the role of learning-goal orientation in self-regulation. Learning situations that emphasize self-improvement, discovery of new information, and usefulness of learning material can promote a learning-goal orientation (Ames & Archer, 1988; Graham & Golan, 1991; Jagacinski & Nicholls, 1984). In contrast, interpersonal competition, tests of intellectual skills, and norma-tive evaluations can enhance performance goals.

In sum, evidence demonstrates that a learning-goal orientation facilitates achievement motivation, beliefs, and skill acquisition, better than a performance-goal orientation. Let us consider a mechanism that may explain such effects.

Conceptions of Ability

Several investigators (Dweck, 1986, 1991, 1999; Dweck & Leggett, 1988; Nicholls, 1983, 1984) suggest that goal orientation is intimately related to one's theory about the nature of intelligence (ability), including whether it changes over time. Dweck (1991) proposed two theories of intelligence: entity and incremental. People who hold an *entity theory* believe that intelligence is relatively fixed, stable, and un-changing over time and with conditions. Effort helps to reach one's limit, not for pro-gressing much beyond it. Difficulties are viewed as obstacles, can lower self-efficacy, and lead students to display ineffective strategies and give up or work halfheartedly.

In contrast, people who hold an *incremental theory* roughly equate intelligence with learning. Students believe that intelligence can change and increase with experience, effort, and learning. An upper limit of intelligence—if it exists—is sufficiently high and does not preclude one from working harder to improve. Difficulties are viewed as challenges and can raise self-efficacy if students mobilize effort, persist at the task, and use effective strategies.

With some exceptions, students who hold an incremental view of intelligence are more likely to believe that learning will raise their overall ability and thus should be more likely to adopt learning goals. Conversely, students holding an entity view may be less likely to adopt learning goals because they believe that learning will not raise their overall level of ability. These predictions have received research support (Dweck, 1991, 1999).

Research also shows important relations among conceptions of ability, motivation, and achievement outcomes. Wood and Bandura (1989) had adults engage in a managerial decision-making task and told them that decision-making ability was fixed (reflecting their basic cognitive capabilities) or incremental (developed through practice). As we will see in the next section, these ability conceptions often are associated with ego and task orientations, respectively (Dweck & Leggett, 1988; Jagacinski & Nicholls, 1984; Nicholls, 1983). Incremental decision makers maintained high self-efficacy, set challenging goals, applied rules efficiently, and performed better; entity participants showed a decline in self-efficacy. Jourden, Bandura, and Banfield (1991) obtained similar results among college students performing a pursuit-rotor tracking task. Subjects led to believe that performance was an acquirable skill showed increased self-efficacy, positive self-reactions to their performance, and greater skill acquisition and task interest; those led to believe that performance reflected inherent aptitude showed no gain in self-efficacy, little increase in skill and interest, and negative self-reactions. Bempechat, London, & Dweck (1991) found important relations between theories of intelligence and achievement beliefs and behaviors in K–5 children.

While these results are promising, further research is warranted. In particular, researchers should examine the process whereby goal orientations become linked with conceptions of ability and how, in turn, these beliefs affect motivation and other achievement outcomes. These results suggest that teachers might help students alter their beliefs about limits to their abilities and the usefulness of effort as a means to improve their motivation. Giving students progress feedback showing how their skills have improved (i.e., how much they have learned), along with information showing that effort has helped to produce learning, can raise self-efficacy and motivate students to improve skills further.

Implications for Teaching

Goal theory and research suggest several ways that teachers can foster a productive learning orientation. One suggestion is to use more collaborative student activities. Duda and Nicholls (1992) found for both sport and schoolwork that task orientation related to high school students' beliefs that success depends on effort and collaboration with peers, whereas ego orientation was associated with beliefs that success is due to high ability and attempting to perform better than others. Goal orientations and beliefs about success were not strongly related to perceived ability. Perceived ability related better to satisfaction in sport than in school; the opposite pattern was obtained for task orientation.

Another suggestion derives from research showing that female students hold a less adaptive pattern of attributions than do male students (i.e., female students are more helpless oriented, as discussed later in this chapter; Dweck, Davidson, Nelson, & Enna, 1978). Female students might be more performance-goal oriented and more likely to endorse an entity conception of ability. Some research shows that high-ability female students are more likely than comparable male students to endorse an entity theory (Dweck, 1991). Teachers may need to tailor feedback to show girls how their efforts are promoting their performance and their corresponding abilities (see the previous section on attributional feedback.)

Perhaps the best way to promote a learning-goal orientation is to help students adopt learning goals. Teachers can stress acquiring skills, learning new strategies, developing problem-solving methods, and so forth. They also can de-emphasize goals such as completing work, finishing earlier than other students, and rechecking work. Assignments should involve learning; when students practice skills, teachers can stress the reasons for the practice (e.g., to retard forgetting) and inform students that skillful practice shows skills have been retained (i.e., recast practice in terms of skill acquisition). Application 8.7 gives some other suggestions for instilling a task orientation, incremental ability conception, and focus on learning goals in students.

PERCEPTIONS OF CONTROL

We have seen that cognitive conceptions of motivation differ in many ways, including which constructs are important, how they affect motivation, and how motivation can be enhanced and optimized. At the same time, cognitive perspectives are unified in their belief that *perceived control* over task engagement and outcomes is a critical influence on motivation (Pintrich & Schunk, 2002). Earlier, two perspectives on control were discussed: Rotter's (1966) *locus of control* and de Charms's (1968) achievement motivation training. Weiner's (1985) *attribution theory* also includes a controllability dimension.

Perceived control is revisited here both because it is critical to understanding human motivation and because it forms the core of the belief system known as *learned helplessness*, which is a psychological perspective on behavior relevant to academic motivation. Later in this chapter we will see how perceptions of control are important determinants of intrinsic motivation.

Control Beliefs

People might believe that they have greater or lesser amounts of control over many types of situations and circumstances. Recall that Bandura (1986; Chapter 3) distinguished between *self-efficacy* and *outcome expectations*; the former refers to perceived

APPLICATION 8.7
Learning Goal Orientation

Promoting a learning goal orientation in the classroom can foster efficacy and enhance learning. In working with her third-grade students on multiplication, Kathy Stone might introduce the unit by saying, "Boys and girls, today we are going to learn some things about putting numbers together that will make you much better math students." Then Mrs. Stone could emphasize acquisition of skills ("As we work today, you are going to learn how to multiply numbers together"), learning of new strategies ("We are going to use these manipulatives to help us figure out different ways to group numbers together and multiply"), and development of problem-solving methods ("I want all of you to put on your thinking caps as we work to figure out different numbers you can multiply together to make 20"). It is important to stress these goals and de-emphasize goals such as completing work and finishing before other students.

Working together in a large group, in small groups, or in pairs to solve problems helps to diminish competition and allow students to focus more on learning rather than on completing a certain amount of work. In working with first-year law students on cases dealing with child abuse, an instructor could pair students to help one another locate prior related cases and encourage them with statements such as, "I want you to put your efforts toward learning how to research a case," and "I want you to work to prepare precise short and direct opening statements." These types of statements focus students on goals for the task at hand; students can then assess learning progress against these statements.

capabilities to learn or perform behaviors and the latter to beliefs about the consequences of actions. Perceived control is central to both of these expectations. People who believe they can control what they learn and perform, as well as the consequences of their actions, are more apt to initiate and sustain behaviors directed toward those ends than are individuals who hold a low sense of control over their capabilities and outcomes of their actions.

Skinner, Wellborn, and Connell (1990) distinguished three types of beliefs that contribute to perceived control and are important in school. *Strategy beliefs* are expectations about factors that influence success in school (e.g., ability, effort, other persons, luck, and unknown factors). *Capacity beliefs* refer to personal capabilities with respect to ability, effort, others, and luck. For example, a strategy belief might be, "The best way for me to get good grades is to work hard"; a capacity belief could be, "I cannot seem to work very hard in school." *Control beliefs* are expectations about one's chances of doing well in school without reference to specific means (e.g., "I can do well in school if I want to").

Similar to Bandura's model in which self-efficacy and outcome expectations make up an individual's perceived control system, Skinner et al. described a three-part system of perceived control. Their research showed that these beliefs influence academic performance by promoting or decreasing active engagement in learning and that teachers contributed to students' perceptions of control by providing *contingency* (clear and consistent guidelines and feedback) and *involvement* (interest in and dedication of resources to students).

Evidence also indicates that when people think they have control over their environment, they tolerate aversive stimuli better and perform at a higher level. Glass and Singer (1972) had adults work on tasks and periodically exposed them to a loud, irritating noise. No-control participants could not control the sound. Researchers told perceived direct-control participants they could terminate the noise by pushing a button but advised them not to do so unless they needed to. Researchers told perceived indirect-control participants that pushing a button would send a signal to a confederate who could terminate the noise; the experimenter also advised these participants not to push unless they needed to. Perceived control (direct or indirect) led to significantly longer persistence and fewer errors compared with no perceived control. Perceived-control individuals judged the noise as less aversive than did no-control participants. Let us now consider learned helplessness, which represents one of the most elegant psychological formulations highlighting perceptions of control.

Learned Helplessness

Learned helplessness refers to a psychological state involving a disturbance in motivation, cognitive processes, and emotions due to previously experienced uncontrollability (Maier & Seligman, 1976; Seligman, 1975). Learned helplessness results from perceived independence between responses and outcomes. Helplessness was identified in laboratory studies in which dogs given inescapable shocks were moved to another location, where they could avoid shocks by jumping a hurdle. The prior inescapable shocks conditioned the dogs; they made little attempt to escape in the new setting but, rather, passively endured the shock. Dogs not previously exposed to inescapable shock easily learned to escape.

One manifestation of helplessness is *passivity*. People may do nothing when they believe they have no control over a situation. Passivity does not depend on the outcome; uncontrollable rewards produce *learned laziness* (Engberg, Hansen, Welker, & Thomas, 1972). Helplessness also *retards learning*. People and animals exposed to uncontrollable situations may never learn adaptive responses or may learn them more slowly than those not exposed to uncontrollability. Helplessness has *emotional manifestations*. Prior uncontrollable situations may initially make one respond more aggressively, but eventually behavior becomes less assertive.

Learned helplessness has been applied in diverse clinical contexts (Fincham & Cain, 1986). Seligman (1975) proposed helplessness as an explanation for *reactive depression* brought about by sudden, dramatic changes in one's life (e.g., death of loved one, divorce, or loss of job). This explanation is intuitively plausible because people typically feel helpless in these situations. At the same time, many depressed people blame themselves for the negative events in their lives. Alex may believe, for example, that he was fired because he continually was late to work and could have avoided being fired had he arrived a few minutes earlier each day. Feeling personally responsible for negative events is incompatible with the notion that helplessness results from perceived lack of control.

Seligman's original model of learned helplessness was reformulated to incorporate an *attributional perspective* (Abramson, Seligman, & Teasdale, 1978). The reformulated model postulates that explanations (attributions) for outcomes influence future expectancies of outcomes and reactions to them. Explanations vary along three dimensions: *stable-unstable*, *global-specific*, and *internal-external*. One who attributes negative outcomes to stable causes (e.g., "I always arrive late for everything") is more likely to expect bad events in the future and may acquire helplessness than is one who makes attributions to unstable causes (e.g., "I arrived late when the weather was bad"). Causes can affect many areas of one's life (global) or only one area (specific). Students may believe they lack ability in all school subjects or only in one subject. Global attributions are more likely to produce helplessness. Causes for negative events may be internal to the person (low intelligence) or external (the teacher gives unfair tests). Internal attributions are apt to result in helplessness. Collectively, people most prone to helplessness are those who typically explain negative events with internal, global, and stable attributions (e.g., "I do poorly in school because I'm not very smart").

Students with Learning Problems

Learned helplessness characterizes many students with learning problems who enter a vicious cycle in which negative beliefs reciprocally interact with academic failures (Licht & Kistner, 1986). For various reasons, students fail in school, and they begin to doubt their learning capabilities and view academic successes as uncontrollable. These beliefs produce frustration and giving up readily on tasks. Lack of effort and persistence contributes to further failures, which reinforce negative beliefs. Eventually, students interpret their successes as externally caused: The task was easy; they were lucky; the teacher helped them. They attribute failures to low ability (internal, global, stable), which negatively affects self-efficacy, motivation, and achievement (Nolen-Hoeksema, Girgus, & Seligman, 1986).

Compared with normal learners, students with learning problems hold lower expectations for success, judge themselves lower in ability, and emphasize lack of ability as a cause of failure (Boersma & Chapman, 1981; Butkowsky & Willows, 1980; Chapman, 1988; Palmer, Drummond, Tollison, & Zinkgraff, 1982). Such students often do not attribute failure to low effort (Andrews & Debus, 1978; Dweck, 1975; Pearl, Bryan, & Donohue, 1980; Schunk, 1989). They give up readily when they encounter difficulties, cite uncontrollable causes for successes and failures, and hold low perceptions of internal control over outcomes (Johnson, 1981; Licht & Kistner, 1986). Students may even generalize these negative beliefs to situations in which they previously have not failed.

Dweck integrated learned helplessness into a model of achievement motivation (Dweck, 1986, 1999; Dweck & Leggett, 1988). Ego involvement characterizes helpless students. Their school goals are to complete tasks and avoid negative judgments of their competence. They believe that intelligence is a fixed quantity. They avoid challenges, display low persistence in the face of difficulty, hold low perceptions of their capabilities, and may experience anxiety while engaged in tasks (Diener & Dweck, 1978, 1980). In contrast, mastery-oriented students display a task-involved achievement pattern. They believe intelligence can improve, and their school goals are to learn and become more competent. They hold high perceptions of their learning capabilities, frequently seek challenges, and persist at difficult tasks.

Mastery-oriented and helpless students often do not differ in intellectual ability. Although helpless students may possess cognitive skill deficits, these alone do not cause failure. Not all students with learning problems enter this cycle; some continue to feel confident and display positive attributional patterns. One factor that may be important is frequency of failure: Students who fail in many school subjects are especially susceptible. Reading deficits are particularly influential, presumably because poor reading skills affect learning in many content areas. Reading deficits can promote negative beliefs even in areas that involve little or no reading (e.g., mathematics; Licht & Kistner, 1986).

Variables associated with the instructional environment either prevent students with learning problems from entering this cycle or help them overcome it (Friedman & Medway, 1987). Attributional feedback can alter students' maladaptive achievement beliefs and behaviors. Teachers also need to give students tasks they can accomplish and feedback highlighting progress toward learning goals (Schunk, 1989; Stipek, 2002). Stipek and Kowalski (1989) found that teaching students task strategies facilitated academic performance among children who de-emphasized the role of effort.

We will now examine an important influence on motivation—self-concept, which has received much attention by researchers and practitioners as they attempt to understand student motivation and achievement.

SELF-CONCEPT

For many years psychologists and educators have studied self-concept, stimulated in large part by attempts to understand human personality and functioning. Although educators often believed that self-concept related positively to academic achievement, theoretical and research evidence to support this claim was missing.

This situation has been dramatically altered as theory and research on self-concept have undergone a resurgence (Hattie, 1992). Teachers are concerned with issues such as how self-concept relates to motivation and learning, how self-concept can be improved, and how social and instructional factors influence self-concept. This section provides an overview of the makeup of the self-concept and its role in academic motivation.

Dimensions and Development

Self-concept refers to one's collective self-perceptions: (a) formed through experiences with, and interpretations of, the environment, and (b) heavily influenced by reinforcements and evaluations by significant other persons (Shavelson & Bolus,

1982). Self-concept is multidimensional and comprises elements such as self-confidence, self-esteem, self-concept stability, and self-crystallization (Pajares & Schunk, 2001, 2002; Rosenberg & Kaplan, 1982). *Self-esteem* is one's perceived sense of self-worth, or whether one accepts and respects oneself. Self-esteem is the evaluative component of self-concept. *Self-confidence* denotes the extent to which one believes one can produce results, accomplish goals, or perform tasks competently (analogous to self-efficacy). Self-esteem and self-confidence are related. The belief that one is capable of performing a task competently can raise self-esteem. High self-esteem might lead one to attempt difficult tasks, and subsequent success enhances self-confidence.

Self-concept stability refers to the ease or difficulty of changing the self-concept. Stability depends in part on how crystallized or structured beliefs are. Beliefs become crystallized with development and repeated similar experiences. By adolescence, individuals have relatively well-structured perceptions of themselves in areas such as intelligence, sociability, and sports. Brief experiences providing evidence that conflicts with personal beliefs may not have much effect. Conversely, self-concept is modified more easily when people have poorly formed ideas about themselves, usually because they have little or no experience.

The development of self-concept proceeds from a concrete view of oneself to a more abstract one (Montemayor & Eisen, 1977). Young children perceive themselves concretely; they define themselves in terms of their appearance, actions, name, possessions, and so forth. Children do not distinguish among behaviors and underlying abilities or personal characteristics. They also do not have a sense of enduring personality because their self-concepts are diffuse and loosely organized. They acquire a more abstract view with development and as a function of schooling. As they develop separate conceptions of underlying traits and abilities, their self-concepts become better organized and more complex.

Development also produces a differentiated self-concept. Although most investigators postulate the existence of a general self-concept, evidence indicates that it is hierarchically organized (Marsh & Shavelson, 1985; Pajares & Schunk, 2001, 2002; Shavelson & Bolus, 1982). A general self-concept tops the hierarchy and specific sub-area self-concepts fall below. Self-perceptions of specific behaviors influence sub-area self-concepts (e.g., math, social studies), which in turn combine to form the academic self-concept. For example, Chapman and Tunmer (1995) found that children's reading self-concept comprised perceived competence in reading, perceived difficulty with reading, and attitudes toward reading. General self-concept comprises self-perceptions in the academic, social, emotional, and physical domains. Vispoel (1995) examined artistic domains and found evidence for the multifaceted nature of self-concept but less support for the hierarchical framework.

Experiences that help form the self-concept emanate from personal actions and vicarious (modeled) experiences. The role of social comparison is important, especially in school (see discussion earlier in this chapter).

Evidence indicates that self-concept is not passively formed but rather is a dynamic structure that mediates significant intrapersonal and interpersonal processes (Cantor & Kihlstrom, 1987). Markus and colleagues (Markus & Nurius, 1986; Markus & Wurf, 1987) hypothesized that the self-concept is made up of self-schemas or generalizations formed through experiences. These schemas process personal and social information much as academic schemas process cognitive information. The multidimensional nature of self-concept is captured by the notion of *working self-concept*, or self-schemas that are mentally active at any time (presently accessible self-knowledge). Thus, a stable core (general) self-concept exists, surrounded by domain-specific self-concepts capable of being altered.

Self-Concept and Learning

Many educators believe that self-concept is positively related to school learning. Students who are confident of their learning abilities and feel self-worthy display greater interest and motivation in school, which enhances achievement. Higher achievement, in turn, validates self-confidence for learning and maintains high self-esteem.

Although plausible, these ideas are not consistently supported by research. Wylie (1979) reviewed many research studies. The general correlation between academic achievement measures (grade point averages) and measures of self-concept was $r = +.30$, which is a moderate and positive relation suggesting a direct correspondence between the two. Correlation does not employ causality, so it cannot be determined whether self-concept influences achievement, achievement influences self-concept, each influences the other, or each is influenced by other variables (e.g., factors in the home). Wylie found somewhat higher correlations when standardized measures of self-concept were employed and lower correlations with researcher-developed measures. That higher correlations were obtained between achievement and academic self-concept than between achievement and overall self-concept supports the hierarchical organization notion. The highest correlations with achievement have been found with domain-specific self-concepts (e.g., in areas such as English or mathematics).

It seems reasonable to assume that self-concept and learning affect one another. Given the general nature of self-concept, brief interventions designed to alter it may not have much effect. Rather, interventions tailored to specific domains may alter domain-specific self-concepts, which can extend up the hierarchy and influence higher-level self-concepts.

Indeed, the research literature supports this proposition. The moderate relation between self-concept and achievement found in research studies may result because general self-concept measures were used. Conversely, when domain-specific self-concept measures are compared with achievement in that domain, the relation is strong and positive (Pajares & Schunk, 2001). As self-concept is defined more specifically, it increasingly resembles self-efficacy, and there is much evidence showing that self-efficacy predicts achievement (Bandura, 1997; Pajares, 1996; Schunk, 1995; see Chapter 3). Future research will help to clarify the relation between self-concept and achievement.

Many of the suggestions made in this chapter have relevance for influencing self-concept. Teachers who show students they are capable of learning and have made academic progress, provide positive feedback, use models effectively, and minimize negative social comparisons can help develop students' self-concepts (see Chapter 3 for ways to enhance self-efficacy).

INTRINSIC MOTIVATION

Earlier it was noted that different theories predict that motivation arises in part from a desire to control the environment, which has been labeled *mastery, competence, effectance*, and *intrinsic motivation*. Although theories differ on many points, they agree that intrinsic motivation involves a desire to engage in an activity for no obvious reward except task engagement itself (Deci, 1975). The importance of intrinsic motivation for learning is underscored by research showing that interest in learning relates positively to cognitive processing and achievement (Alexander & Murphy, 1998; Schiefele, 1996). We now examine in depth a few perspectives on intrinsic motivation.

Theoretical Perspectives

Effectance Motivation.   In a seminal paper, White (1959) defined effectance motivation as:

> Fitness or ability, and the suggested synonyms capability, capacity, efficiency, proficiency, and skill. It is therefore a suitable word to describe such things as grasping and exploring, crawling and walking, attention and perception, language and thinking, manipulating and changing the surroundings, all of which promote an effective—a competent—interaction with the environment. The behavior . . . is directed, selective, and persistent, and it is continued not because it serves primary drives, which indeed it cannot serve until it is almost perfected, but because it satisfies an intrinsic need to deal with the environment. (pp. 317–318)

Effectance motivation is seen in young children as they interact with environmental features that catch their attention. A youngster may reach out and grab an object, turn it over, and push it away in an effort to control it. Effectance motivation is undifferentiated in young children; it is directed toward all aspects of the environment. With development, motivation becomes increasingly specialized. Once children enter school, they manifest effectance motivation in achievement behaviors in various school subjects.

Effectance motivation arises when biological motives are satisfied; it also facilitates future need satisfaction. Taking the top off of a jar initially satisfies the effectance motive, but in so doing the child learns that cookies are in the jar. This knowledge is used in the future to satisfy hunger.

Mastery Motivation.   The notion of effectance motivation is intuitively appealing. At the same time, its generality limits the search for its causes and its effectiveness as an explanatory mechanism of actions. Furthermore, the way to influence such a global construct, and thereby improve academic motivation, is unclear.

Harter (1978, 1981) attempted to specify the antecedents and consequences of effectance motivation in a developmental model of *mastery motivation*. Whereas White focused on success, Harter took success and failure into account. Harter also stressed the roles of socializing agents and rewards, the process whereby children *internalize* mastery goals and develop a self-reward system, and the important correlates of effectance motivation (e.g., perceived competence and control; Figure 8.5).

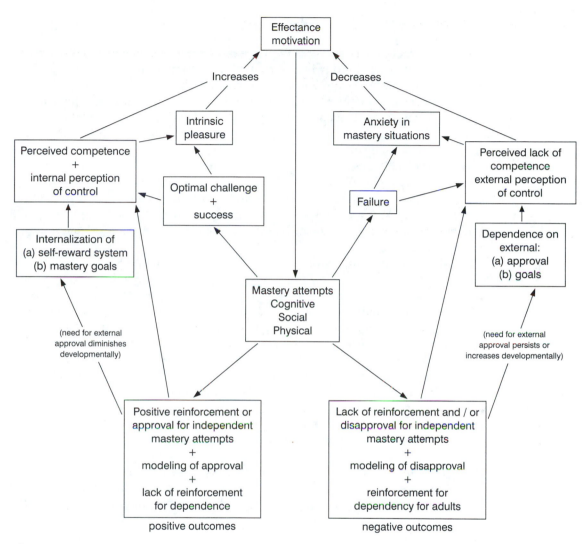

Figure 8.5

Model of mastery motivation.

Source: "A Model of Mastery Motivation in Children: Individual Differences and Developmental Change," by S. Harter, 1981. In W. A. Collins (Ed.), *Aspects on the Development of Competence: The Minnesota Symposia on Child Psychology* (Vol. 14, pp. 215–255). Copyright © 1981 by Lawrence Erlbaum Associates. Used by permission.

The left side of the model portrays success and is somewhat similar to White's formulation. Effectance motivation can trigger mastery attempts. White considered the motive generic, but Harter differentiated it according to domain (school, peers, athletics). Most behaviors will involve optimally challenging tasks. Successes will produce intrinsic pleasure and perceptions of competence and control, which in turn strengthen effectance motivation.

The bottom part highlights the role played by socializing agents. Some positive reinforcement for mastery attempts is necessary to develop and maintain motivation. Much of this reinforcement comes from primary caregivers, and eventually a self-reward system is internalized, which allows children to reinforce themselves for mastery attempts. Children acquire mastery goals through observation (social learning), and internalization becomes more complete with development. In support of these points, research shows that children from homes in which learning opportunities and activities are emphasized display higher intrinsic motivation for learning (Gottfried, Fleming, & Gottfried, 1998).

On the left side of the model are positive outcomes that result when social environments satisfy children's natural desires. The right side portrays negative outcomes, or the development of extrinsically oriented individuals. Unsuccessful mastery attempts, coupled with a nonresponsive environment, can lead to low perceptions of competence, an external locus of control, and anxiety. Effectance motivation ebbs if children increasingly depend on others to set goals and reward actions.

Research supports many of the propositions of the model. For example, intrinsic motivation relates positively to perceived competence and internal control (Harter, 1981; Harter & Connell, 1984). Social models are important sources of mastery behavior and learning (Bandura, 1986, 1997; Schunk, 1987). Perceived competence relates positively to intrinsic motivation (Gottfried, 1985, 1990). At the same time, the model relies heavily on socializing agents. They are important, but research has identified other ways to foster mastery behavior, including setting learning goals, providing attributional feedback, and teaching self-regulatory strategies (Ames, 1992a; Pintrich & Schrauben, 1992; Schunk, 1989; Zimmerman, 1989). Relatively little attention has been paid to educational implications of the theory—for example, how students can be taught to adopt an intrinsic orientation toward school. The theory must be broadened to address these points (Pintrich & Schunk, 2002).

Incongruity and Arousal. Some investigators postulate that intrinsic motivation reflects an inherent need for a moderate amount of environmental stimulation. Hunt (1963) argued that exploratory behaviors and curiosity are intrinsically motivated and result from incongruity between prior experiences and new information. People extract information from the environment and compare it to internal representations. When incongruity exists between the input and internal knowledge or expectation, people become intrinsically motivated to reduce the incongruity. Hunt postulated that people require an optimal level of incongruity. When deprived of that level, they seek situations that provide it. Too much incongruity proves frustrating and triggers a drive to reduce frustration. Although Hunt's views have intuitive. merit, they have been criticized because "optimal level of incongruity" is vague and how much incongruity is required to trigger motivation is not clear (Deci, 1975).

Berlyne (1960, 1963) similarly hypothesized that an optimal level of physiological incongruity (stimulation to the nervous system) is necessary and adaptive. If it becomes too low, people are intrinsically motivated to increase it; conversely, they are motivated to reduce it if it becomes too great. Berlyne's "arousal potential" may be interpreted as being approximately equivalent on a physiological level to Hunt's psychological incongruity. *Collative properties* of stimuli involving their novelty, ambiguity, incongruity, and surprise affect arousal and motivate people to explore the objects.

Although the notions of arousal and incongruity seem intuitively sensible, the idea of an optimal level of arousal or incongruity is vague and it is unclear how much is needed to stimulate motivation. Practically speaking, we know novelty and surprise raise student interest, but how much of either is optimal? Too much may lead to frustration and attempts to escape from the situation or diminish the level.

Self-Determination.   Deci and colleagues (Deci, 1980; Deci & Porac, 1978; Deci & Ryan, 1991; Grolnick, Gurland, Jacob, & Decourcey, 2002; Ryan, Connell, & Deci, 1985) postulated that intrinsic motivation is an innate human need and originates in infants as an undifferentiated need for competence and *self-determination*. As children develop, the need differentiates into specific areas (e.g., athletics, academics), and environmental interactions influence the direction of differentiation.

This self-determination view emphasizes the internalization of social values and mores. Society contains many extrinsic rewards and controls that may not fit with children's quest for self-determination but produce good behavior and social functioning. With development, these external motivators may become an internalized part of the self-regulatory system (see later in this chapter).

Motivation is conceptualized as a continuum: Intrinsic and extrinsic motivation anchor the ends and in the middle are behaviors that originally were extrinsically motivated but have become internalized and now are self-determined. For instance, students may want to avoid some academic activities but they work on them to obtain rewards and avoid teacher punishment. As skills develop and students believe they are becoming more competent, they perceive a sense of control and self-determination over learning. The activities become more intrinsically motivating, and positive social reinforcers (e.g., praise, feedback) assist the process.

Deci's position is thought-provoking and has generated much research. It also has implications for educational practice because it stresses the role of self-determination in learning. Many points in the model are not clearly specified, but research continues to test its ideas.

Overjustification and Reward

Lepper and Hodell (1989) believe there are four *sources of intrinsic motivation*: challenge, curiosity, control, and fantasy. With the exception of fantasy, the perspectives on intrinsic motivation discussed earlier support the importance of these sources. Fantasy contexts (e.g., involving role playing, simulations) seem well designed to heighten intrinsic motivation. Despite their differences, the various perspectives contend that intrinsic motivation is a strong, positive force in people's lives.

We typically think of intrinsic motivation increasing, but it also can diminish. Research discussed in this section shows that engaging in an intrinsically interesting activity to obtain an extrinsic reward can undermine intrinsic motivation (Lepper &

Greene, 1978). This finding has important educational implications given the prevalence of rewards.

When people are *intrinsically motivated*, they engage in an activity as an end in itself. Csikszentmihalyi (1975) studied persons who engaged in intrinsically motivating activities and found that their experiences reflected total involvement or flow with the activities. *Flow* is a personal process and reflects *emergent motivation* stemming from the discovery of new goals and rewards as a consequence of interacting with the environment (Csikszentmihalyi & Rathunde, 1993; Meyer & Turner, 2002).

In contrast, *extrinsic motivation* involves engaging in an activity for reasons external to the task. This activity is a means to some end: an object, a grade, feedback or praise, or being able to work on another activity. Students are extrinsically motivated if they try to perform well in school primarily to please their parents, earn high grades, or receive teacher approval.

Intrinsic reasons for working on a task are internal to it. The reward comes from working on the task; the task is both the means and the end. The rewards for intrinsic motivation may be feelings of competence and control, self-satisfaction, task success, or pride in one's work.

We commonly engage in activities for both intrinsic and extrinsic reasons. Many students like to feel competent in school and experience pride for a job done well, but they also desire teacher praise and good grades. Rewards are not inherently extrinsically motivating. Deci (1975) contended that rewards have an *informational* and a *controlling* aspect. Reward systems may be primarily structured to convey information about one's capabilities or to control one's behavior, and the relative salience of each (information or control) influences subsequent behavior. A salient informational aspect indicating successful performance should promote feelings of competence, whereas a salient controlling aspect can lead to perceptions of the reward as the cause of the behavior.

For example, suppose that in a classroom reward system the more work students accomplish, the more points they earn. Although students will want to work to earn points (because the points can be exchanged for privileges), the points convey information about their capabilities: The more points students earn, the more capable they are. In contrast, if points are given simply for time spent on a task regardless of output, the task may be viewed primarily as a means to an end. The points convey nothing about capabilities; students are more likely to view the rewards as controlling their task engagement. Expected, tangible rewards offered to students for simply doing a task diminish intrinsic motivation (Cameron & Pierce, 1994).

Lepper postulates that the perception of reward influences students' intrinsic motivation (Lepper, 1983; Lepper & Greene, 1978). Motivation is largely a function of one's perceptions for engaging in the task. When external constraints are salient, unambiguous, and sufficient to explain the behavior, individuals attribute their behaviors to those constraints. If external constraints are viewed as weak, unclear, or psychologically insufficient to account for their behavior, people are more likely to attribute their actions to their desires or personal dispositions.

In a classic experiment (Lepper, Greene, & Nisbett, 1973), preschoolers were observed during free play. Those who spent a lot of time drawing were selected for the study and assigned to one of three conditions. In the expected-award group, children were offered a good player certificate if they drew a picture. Unexpected-award children were not offered the certificate, but unexpectedly received it after they drew a picture. No-award children were not offered the award and did not receive it. Two weeks later children were again observed during free play.

The expected-award children engaged in drawing for a significantly shorter time following the experiment than they had prior to the study, whereas the other two conditions showed no significant change. Expected-award children spent less time drawing following the study compared with the other conditions. It was not the reward itself that was important but rather the contingency. Lepper et al. (1973) postulated the *overjustification hypothesis*: Engaging in an intrinsically interesting activity under conditions that make it salient as a means to an end (reward) decreases subsequent interest in that activity. The overjustification hypothesis has been supported in experimental investigations with different tasks and participants of all ages (Lepper & Greene, 1978; Lepper & Hodell, 1989).

Rewards need not have detrimental effects on performance. Rewards can help develop skills, self-efficacy, and interest when they are linked to one's actual performance and convey that one is making progress in learning. Offering children rewards based on the amount of work they accomplish during learning activities increases self-efficacy, motivation, and skill acquisition compared with offering rewards merely for task participation or not offering rewards (Schunk, 1983e). During a subtraction instruction program, Bandura and Schunk (1981) found that higher self-efficacy related positively to the amount of intrinsic interest children subsequently showed in solving arithmetic problems.

Thus, when rewards convey that one has learned, they can increase self-efficacy and intrinsic motivation. As a form of reward, grades can function in the same way. A grade that improves shows that one is performing better in the subject, which promotes self-efficacy and motivation for further learning. Unfortunately, research shows that children's intrinsic motivation in learning declines with development (Lepper, Sethi, Dialdin, & Drake, 1997), although other research shows that interest and self-efficacy are related positively in elementary and middle-grades students (Tracey, 2002). Application 8.8 demonstrates ways to enhance and sustain intrinsic motivation.

MOTIVATION AND SELF-REGULATION

Motivation is intimately linked with self-regulation. People motivated to attain a goal engage in self-regulatory activities they believe will help them (e.g., organize and rehearse material, monitor learning progress and adjust strategies). In turn, self-regulation promotes learning, and the perception of greater competence sustains motivation and self-regulation to attain new goals (Schunk & Ertmer, 2000).

The link between motivation and self-regulation is seen clearly in theoretical models (Pintrich, 2000b; Zimmerman, 2000). Pintrich's model is heavily motivation dependent, since motivation underlies learners' setting and pursuit of goals and also is a focus of their self-regulation as they engage in tasks. In Zimmerman's model, motivation enters at all phases: forethought (self-efficacy, outcome expectations, interest,

APPLICATION 8.8
Intrinsic Motivation

Intrinsic motivation involves perceptions of control and competence. Individuals develop perceived competence by mastering difficult situations. If elementary teachers are helping slower students complete assigned tasks in an allotted time, they may begin by offering a reward (extrinsic motivator) and work toward building student pride in their accomplishments (intrinsic motivator). Initially teachers might reward students for increased output with time on the computer, verbal praise, or special notes home to parents. Gradually teachers could reward intermittently and then decrease it to allow students to focus more on their accomplishments. The ability to complete tasks in the appropriate time span provides students with information about their capabilities and their ability to control situations. When pride from successfully completing tasks becomes a reward, students are intrinsically motivated to continue to display the new behavior.

High school and college students often are motivated to achieve in school primarily to earn a good grade (extrinsic motivator). Teachers and professors should attempt to show the connection with what is being taught in each course with the "real" world and to link each student's accomplishments with his or her ability to be successful in that world. Instructors must work to move students toward wanting to learn for the sake of learning and to be able to better address future challenges (intrinsic motivator). Thus, subjects such as chemistry, physics, and biology are not stale subjects studied in artificial laboratories but have direct relevance to what we eat, what we wear, what we do, and how we conduct our daily lives. The field experience component of Gina Brown's educational psychology class allows students to observe applications of teaching and learning principles during actual teaching. Enhanced perceived value of learning strengthens intrinsic motivation to learn.

value, goal orientations), performance control (attention focusing, self-monitoring), and self-reflection (self-evaluation and causal attributions).

Additional evidence of this link is seen in research by Wolters and his colleagues (Wolters, 1998, 1999; Wolters, Yu, & Pintrich, 1996). In these studies, the researchers determined how various strategies designed to maintain optimal task motivation (e.g., expend effort, persist, make the task interesting, and self-reward) related to self-regulatory strategy use during learning (e.g., rehearsal, elaboration, planning, monitoring, and organization). Multiple regression analyses revealed that motivation regulation activities were predictive of self-regulation. Adopting a learning-goal orientation was associated with higher self-efficacy, task value, and achievement.

One aspect of self-regulation that is drawing increased research attention is *volition*, which is discussed in the next section. Some researchers define volition as part of a larger self-regulatory system that includes motivation and other cognitive processes (Corno, 1993; Snow, 1989). Many other motivational components are receiving research attention for their role in self-regulation—for example, goal properties, goal orientations, self-efficacy, attributions, values, self-schemas, and help seeking. Earlier, the roles of goal properties, goal orientations, self-efficacy, and attributions were considered; the remainder of this section discusses volition and the latter three influences.

Volition

Volition has been of interest for a long time. Early psychologists drew on the writings of Plato and Aristotle (Chapter 1) and conceived of the mind as comprising knowing (cognition), feeling (emotion), and willing (motivation). The will reflected one's desire, want, or purpose; volition was the act of using the will (Pintrich & Schunk, 2002).

Philosophers and psychologists disagreed over whether volition was an independent process or a by-product of other mental processes (e.g., perceptions). Wundt thought volition was a central, independent factor in human behavior, which presumably accompanied such processes as attention and perception and helped translate thoughts and emotions into actions. William James (1890, 1892) also believed that volition was the process of translating intentions into actions and had its greatest effect when different intentions competed for action. Volition worked to execute intended actions by activating mental representations of them, which served as guides for behavior.

Ach (1910) pioneered the experimental study of volition. Ach considered volition the process of dealing with implementing actions designed to attain goals. This is a narrow view of motivation because it does not address the process whereby people formulate goals and commit themselves to attaining them (Heckhausen, 1991; Pintrich & Schunk, 2002). Processes that allow goals to be translated into action are *determining tendencies*; they compete with previously learned association tendencies to produce action even when the action conflicts with prior associations.

The conceptual basis for contemporary work derives from *action control theory* by Heckhausen (1991) and Kuhl (1984). These theorists proposed differentiating *predecisional processing* (cognitive activities involved in making decisions and setting goals) from *postdecisional processing* (activities engaged in subsequent to goal setting). Predecisional analyses involve decision making and are motivational; postdecisional analyses deal with goal implementation and are volitional. Volition mediates the relation between goals and actions to accomplish them. Once students move from planning and goal setting to implementation of plans, they cross a metaphorical Rubicon that protects goals by self-regulatory activities rather than reconsidering or changing them (Corno, 1993).

Debate continues over whether motivation and volition are separate constructs or whether the latter is part of the former. Nonetheless, separating pre- from postdecisional processes seems worthwhile. Some motivational indexes used in studies of performance are not useful in learning. Choice of activities is a common index, yet in school students often do not choose to engage in tasks. There often is little predecisional activity by students. In contrast, postdecisional activity offers more latitude, especially if multiple ways are available to accomplish tasks or deal with distractions. Choice is an integral component of self-regulation (Zimmerman, 1994, 1998, 2000), but students still can have many choices available even when they do not choose whether to work on a task. Volitional activities presumably direct and control information processing, affects, and behaviors directed toward accomplishing goals (Corno, 1993).

Corno (1989, 1993, 1994; Corno & Kanfer, 1993) has written extensively about the role of volition in self-regulation:

> Volition can be characterized as a dynamic system of psychological control processes that protect concentration and directed effort in the face of personal and/or environmental distractions, and so aid learning and performance. (Corno, 1993, p. 16)

It is useful to distinguish two aspects of volitional function with respect to self-regulation: action control and volitional style (Corno, 1994). The *action-control* function refers to potentially modifiable regulatory skills or strategies. This function would include the focus of many interventions aimed at enhancing self-regulation, such as metacognitive monitoring (self-observation), self-arranged contingencies, redesign of tasks, strategies of emotion control, and management of environmental resources. Kuhl (1985) proposed a taxonomy of volitional strategies; Corno (1993) discussed two such strategies with educational examples (Table 8.4). Many examples are available of successful training efforts for action-control strategies (Corno, 1994).

A second function, *volitional style*, refers to stable, individual differences in volition, as opposed to the specific skills and strategies involved in action control. Volitional style is dispositional and refers to aspects of personality that should be less amenable to change through instruction—for example, impulsiveness, conscientiousness, and dependability (Snow, 1989). Corno (1994) cited research showing the predictive value of dispositions for various student academic outcomes.

The case for treating volition as a separate construct has some merit. One problem with separating goal setting from implementation stems from research showing that learners adjust or set new goals during task performance (Locke & Latham, 1990). Another concern is how such motivationally germane processes as attributions and self-efficacy relate to volition. Much research is needed in this area.

Values

A central component of motivation that relates to self-regulation is the *value* students ascribe to learning. Students who do not value what they are learning are not motivated to improve or exercise self-regulation over their activities.

Wigfield (1994) discussed the process whereby valuing a task can lead to greater self-regulatory efforts. Values have a direct link to such achievement behaviors as persistence, choice, and performance. Values may relate positively to many self-regulating processes such as self-observation, self-evaluation, and goal setting. For instance, students who value history are apt to study for history tests diligently, set goals for their learning, monitor their learning progress, not be overcome by obstacles, and adjust their strategies as needed. In contrast, students who do not value history should be less likely to engage in these activities at the same level.

Table 8.4
Examples of volitional control strategies.

Motivation Control

- Set contingencies for performance that can be carried out mentally (e.g., self-reward).

- Escalate goals by prioritizing and imagining their value.

- Visualize doing the work successfully.

- Uncover ways to make the work more fun or challenging.

- Immerse yourself in plans for achieving goals.

- Self-instruct.

- Analyze failure to direct a second try.

Emotion Control

- Count to 10 in your head.

- Control breathing so it is slow, steady, and deep.

- Generate useful diversions (e.g., sing to yourself).

- Visualize doing the work successfully and feeling good about that (change the way you respond emotionally to the task).

- Recall your strengths and your available resources.

- Consider any negative feelings about the experience and ways to make it more reassuring.

Source: From "The Best-Laid Plans: Modern Conceptions of Volition and Educational Research," by L. Corno, 1993, *Educational Researcher, 22* (2), p. 16. Copyright 1993 by American Educational Research Association. Reprinted by permission.

Other research supports the idea that valuing achievement tasks relates to the productive use of cognitive learning strategies, perceived self-regulation, and academic performance (Pintrich & De Groot, 1990; Wigfield, 1994). Pokay and Blumenfeld (1990) found that students' valuing of mathematics led to their using different cognitive strategies, and in turn, strategy use influenced mathematics performance. Wigfield noted that task values may relate positively to the strategies of volitional action control proposed by Kuhl (1985).

Unfortunately, research shows that children often value academic tasks less as they get older (Eccles & Midgley, 1989). Many ways to enhance student motivation relate directly to perceptions of task value, including showing students how tasks are important in their lives and how they help them attain their goals. Linking learning to real-world phenomena improves perceptions of value. Teachers should incorporate methods for enhancing perceived value into their planning to ensure benefits for learning and self-regulation.

Self-Schemas

Self-schemas are "cognitive manifestations of enduring goals, aspirations, motives, fears, and threats" (Markus & Nurius, 1986, p. 954). They include cognitive and affective evaluations of ability, volition, and personal agency. They essentially are conceptions of ourselves in different situations or what we might be. The theoretical importance of self-schemas is that they presumably mediate the link between situations and behavior. Individuals act in part based on perceptions of their selves. Self-concept includes many self-schemas, only some of which are active at a given time. Those active at any time are *working self-concepts*. Self-schemas have an affective dimension (self-conceptions are positive and negatively valued), a temporal dimension (experiences result in concepts of past, present, and future possible selves), an efficacy dimension (beliefs about what we can do to attain our selves), and a value dimension (importance or centrality of the self to the individual).

As organized knowledge structures, possible selves are ways to network multiple motivational beliefs at a higher level (Garcia & Pintrich, 1994). Thus, goals are important motivational processes, and self-schemas are organized knowledge structures that link multiple goals. Self-schemas may provide a link between motivation and strategy use. If persons have ideas about what they can be and what they can do, then possible selves can serve as guides for action and contain strategies to be implemented.

Possible selves can play an important role in self-regulation because the notion of what one might become underlies use of self-regulatory strategies (Garcia & Pintrich, 1994). Individuals regulate their behaviors to approximate or become their possible selves and to avoid becoming negative possible selves. People must understand what to do to become their possible selves. Garcia and Pintrich discussed motivational strategies that individuals may use to attain selves and protect their sense of self-worth. Although research on self-schemas is in the early stage, initial results are promising and support the claim that self-schemas serve to link motivation and self-regulation.

Help Seeking

Help seeking is a way to regulate the social environment to promote learning. Self-regulated learners are likely to ask for assistance when they confront difficult tasks and perceive the need for help (Newman, 1994, 2002). In particular, high achievers often seek help from teachers and peers (Zimmerman & Martinez-Pons, 1990).

Newman (1994) proposed a model in which adaptive help seeking:

- Occurs following a student's lack of understanding.
- Includes the student considering the need for help, the content of the request, and the request target.
- Involves expressing the need for help in the most suitable fashion given the circumstances.
- Requires that the help seeker receive and process help in a way that will optimize the probability of success in later help-seeking attempts.

Help seeking is a relatively complex activity that includes more than the verbal request for assistance. Motivational factors come into play. Many motivational processes have been investigated for their relation to help seeking, especially the roles of self-efficacy and goal setting. Students with higher self-efficacy for learning are more apt to seek help than are those with lower efficacy (Ryan, Gheen, & Midgley, 1998). Students with a task goal orientation are more likely to seek assistance to determine the correctness of their work, whereas ego-involved students may seek help to determine how their work compares with that of others (Newman & Schwager, 1992; Ryan et al., 1998).

This research suggests that different motivational patterns can prompt various forms of help seeking. From the perspective of self-regulation, the most adaptive type of help seeking is that which provides feedback on learning and progress. Teachers can work with students to encourage their seeking assistance and for reasons related to the development of their academic skills.

SUMMARY

Motivation refers to the process of instigating and sustaining goal-directed behavior. Some early views on motivation were drive theory, conditioning theory, cognitive consistency theory, and humanistic theory. Each of these contributed to the understanding of motivation, but none was adequate to explain human motivated behavior. Most current theories view motivation as deriving from cognitive processes, although these theories differ in the importance ascribed to various cognitions. Models of motivated learning assume that motivation operates before, during, and after learning.

Atkinson's achievement motivation theory postulates that need for achievement is a general motive leading individuals to perform their best in achievement contexts. Achievement behavior represents an emotional conflict between hope for success and fear of failure. Horner broadened the theory to include fear of success. Eccles and Wigfield developed an expectancy-value theory of achievement motivation that surmounts many problems of older views. The self-worth theory of Covington and his colleagues hypothesizes that achievement behavior is a function of students' efforts to preserve the perception of high ability among themselves and others. Other researchers focus on motivational states such as task and ego involvement. Much work also has been done on achievement motivation training.

Attribution theory, a systematic cognitive view of motivation, incorporates Rotter's locus of control and many elements of Heider's naïve analysis of action. Weiner's attribution theory, which is relevant in achievement settings, categorized attributions along three dimensions: internal-external, stable-unstable, and controllable-uncontrollable. Attributions are important because they affect achievement beliefs, emotions, and behaviors. Attributional change programs attempt to alter students' dysfunctional attributions for failure, such as from low ability to insufficient effort. Attributional feedback for prior successes improves self-efficacy, motivation, and skill acquisition.

Social cognitive theory views motivation as resulting from goals and expectations. People set goals and act in ways they believe will help them attain their goals. By comparing present performance to the goal and noting progress, people experience a sense of efficacy for improvement. Motivation depends on believing that one will achieve desired outcomes from given behaviors (positive outcome expectations) and that one is capable of performing or learning to perform those behaviors (high self-efficacy). Social comparisons with others are important sources of information to form outcome and efficacy expectations. The theory integrates the concepts of motivation and learning.

Goal theory postulates important links between people's goals, expectations, attributions, conceptions of ability, motivational orientations, social and self comparisons, and achievement behaviors. In achievement contexts, learners may possess learning (mastery) or performance (ability-focused) goals. The theory predicts that learning goals focus attention better on skills and competencies needed for learning and that as students perceive progress, their self-efficacy and motivation are enhanced. In contrast, performance goals may not lead to the same focus on progress but rather result in social comparisons, which may not raise motivation. Goal orientations seem intimately linked with conceptions of ability that reflect an entity or incremental perspective.

Many cognitive theories stress people's desire to exert control over important aspects of their lives. Control beliefs have especially powerful effects in achievement settings. When people perceive independence between responses and outcomes, learned helplessness manifests itself in motivational, learning, and emotional deficits. Learned helplessness is applicable to many students with learning problems who display negative attributional patterns and low self-efficacy in their learning capabilities.

Theory and research on self-concept are relevant to motivation. Research suggests that self-concept (one's collective self-perception of oneself) is hierarchically organized and multifaceted. It develops from a concrete to a more abstract self-view. Self-concept and learning appear to influence one another in reciprocal fashion.

Intrinsic motivation is interest in engaging in an activity for its own sake. Intrinsically interesting activities are ends in themselves, in contrast to extrinsically motivated actions, which are means to some end. White and Harter hypothesized that young children have intrinsic motivation to understand and control their environments, which becomes more specialized with development and progression in school. Harter's theory highlights the role of socializing agents and perceived competence. Other theorists hypothesize that intrinsic motivation depends on the needs for optimal levels of psychological or physiological incongruity, on attempts to engage in self-determination, and on a flow-type involvement with activities. Much research has addressed the effect of rewards on intrinsic motivation. Offering rewards for task engagement decreases intrinsic motivation when rewards are seen as controlling behavior. Rewards given contingent on one's level of performance are informative of capabilities and foster students' self-efficacy, interest, and skill acquisition.

Although self-regulation and motivation are not synonymous, they are related. Such processes as goal setting, self-efficacy, and outcome expectations are important motivational variables that affect self-regulation. Researchers increasingly are examining the role of volition in achievement settings and especially as it relates to self-regulation. Other motivational factors that are important for self-regulation include values, goal orientations, self-schemas, and help seeking. Collectively, these factors may help to determine how achievement behavior is instigated and sustained as learners engage in choices regarding the content, location, timing, and outcomes of their learning.

CHAPTER

9

Content-Area Learning

The preceding chapters discussed learning processes generically as applicable to diverse content in varied settings. For example, processes such as modeling, encoding, and metacognition apply to many types of learning; they are not unique to certain learners or a few content areas.

This chapter examines learning in the content areas of language comprehension, reading, writing, mathematics, science, and social studies. Although generic learning processes apply to these areas, research has shown that content-area learning has unique features. Thus, although mathematics and reading comprehension are aided by goal setting, rehearsal, and problem solving, skill learning in these areas also depends on processes specific to each area. This chapter discusses these domain-specific processes, as well as how general processes operate in different domains. Initially, this chapter discusses the process of skill acquisition, after which it addresses the content areas.

This chapter does not cover content areas comprehensively, which is beyond the purpose of this book; indeed, each area could be a separate chapter or book. Rather, it offers a representative sample of learning research in each area. Extensive reviews can be found in other sources (e.g., Bruning et al., 1999; Byrnes, 1996; Farnham-Diggory, 1992; Gagné et al., 1993; Mayer, 1992, 1999). In addition, the *Handbook of Research on Teaching* (Richardson, 2001; Wittrock, 1986) and the *Handbook of Educational Psychology* (Berliner & Calfee,

1996) review learning in other areas not covered in this chapter (e.g., second-language learning, moral and values education, arts and aesthetics, and vocational and occupational education).

Unlike much of the earlier research on learning, contemporary work is heavily oriented toward investigating learning with content in actual settings where it occurs. Much content-area learning has addressed novice-expert differences, and researchers also are exploring the strategies that learners use and how these change as skills develop. It remains a challenge to integrate content-area learning with theories of instruction and learning so that a more comprehensive picture can be developed.

When you finish studying this chapter, you should be able to do the following:

- Distinguish between general and specific skills and discuss how they work together in the acquisition of competence.
- Describe the novice-to-expert research methodology.
- Explain the major components of language comprehension.
- Define *speech act* and discuss its components.
- Summarize the major principles of reading as demonstrated by research.
- Discuss top-down and bottom-up processing in reading decoding.
- Explain the main processes involved in reading comprehension.

- Sketch a process model of writing and explain the operation of its elements.
- Explain children's computational strategies and how computational skill becomes automatized.
- Discuss the steps involved in mathematical problem solving and some ways that experts and novices differ.

- Describe expert-novice differences in science proficiency and some ways that teachers can foster students' reasoning and conceptual change.
- Explain the skills necessary to develop competence in history and geography.

SKILL ACQUISITION

General and Specific Skills

Skills may be differentiated according to degree of specificity. *General skills* apply to a wide variety of disciplines; *specific skills* are useful only in certain domains. Setting goals and monitoring goal progress, for example, are general skills because they are useful in acquiring a range of cognitive, motor, and social skills. Factoring polynomials and solving square-root problems involve specific skills because they have limited mathematical applications.

Acquisition of general skills facilitates learning in many ways. Bruner (1985) noted that tasks such as "learning how to play chess, learning how to play the flute, learning mathematics, and learning to read the sprung rhymes in the verse of Gerard Manley Hopkins" (pp. 5–6) are similar in that they involve attention, memory, and persistence.

At the same time, each type of skill learning has unique features. Bruner (1985) contends that views of learning are not unambiguously right or wrong; rather, they can be evaluated only in light of conditions such as the nature of the task to be learned, the type of learning to be accomplished, and the characteristics learners bring to the situation. The many differences between tasks such as learning to balance equations in chemistry and learning to balance on a beam in gymnastics require different processes to explain learning.

Domain specificity is defined in various ways. Ceci (1989) used the term to refer to discrete declarative knowledge structures. Other researchers include procedural knowledge and view specificity as pertaining to the usefulness of knowledge (Perkins & Salomon, 1989). The issue really is not one of proving or disproving one position because we know that both general and specific intellectual skills are involved in learning (Voss, Wiley, & Carretero, 1995). Rather, the issue is one of specifying the extent to which each form of learning involves general and specific skills, what those skills are, and what course their acquisition follows.

Thinking of skill specificity ranging along a continuum is preferable, as Perkins & Salomon (1989) explain:

> General knowledge includes widely applicable strategies for problem solving, inventive thinking, decision making, learning, and good mental management, sometimes called

autocontrol, autoregulation, or metacognition. In chess, for example, very specific knowledge (often called local knowledge) includes the rules of the game as well as lore about how to handle innumerable specific situations, such as different openings and ways of achieving checkmate. Of intermediate generality are strategic concepts, like control of the center, that are somewhat specific to chess but that also invite far-reaching application by analogy. (p. 17)

We then can ask: What counts most for ensuring success in learning? Of course, some local knowledge is needed—one cannot become skilled at fractions without learning the rules governing fraction operations (e.g., adding, subtracting). As Perkins and Salomon (1989) noted, however, the more important questions are: Where are the bottlenecks in developing mastery? Can one become an expert with only domain-specific knowledge? If not, at what point do general competencies become important?

Ohlsson (1993) advanced a model of skill acquisition through practice that comprises three subfunctions: generate task-relevant behaviors, identify errors, correct errors. This model includes both general and task-specific processes. As learners practice, they monitor their progress by comparing their current state to their prior knowledge. This is a general strategy, but as learning occurs, it becomes increasingly adapted to specific task conditions. Errors often are caused by applying general procedures inappropriately (Ohlsson, 1996), but prior domain-specific knowledge helps learners detect errors and identify the conditions that caused them. With practice and learning, therefore, general methods become more specialized.

Problem solving (discussed in Chapter 5) is useful in much domain-specific learning; however, task conditions often require specific skills for the development of expertise. In many cases a merging of the two types of skills is needed. Research shows that expert problem solvers often use general strategies when they encounter unfamiliar problems and that asking general metacognitive questions (e.g., "What am I doing now?", "Is it getting me anywhere?") facilitates problem solving (Perkins & Salomon, 1989). Despite these positive results, general principles often do not transfer (Pressley et al., 1990; Schunk & Rice, 1993). Transfer requires combining general strategies with factors such as instruction on self-monitoring and practice in specific contexts.

In short, competence in a domain requires a rich knowledge base that includes the facts, concepts, and principles of the domain coupled with learning strategies that can be applied to different domains and that may have to be tailored to each domain. One would not expect strategies such as seeking help and monitoring goal progress to operate in the same fashion in disparate domains (e.g., calculus and pole vaulting). At the same time, Perkins and Salomon (1989) point out that general strategies are useful for coping with atypical problems in different domains regardless of one's overall level of competence in the domain. These findings imply that students need to be well grounded in basic content-area knowledge (Ohlsson, 1993), as well as in general problem-solving and self-regulatory strategies. Application 9.1 provides suggestions for integrating the teaching of general and specific skills.

APPLICATION 9.1
Integrating the Teaching of General and Specific Skills

As teachers work with students, they can effectively teach general skills to increase success in various domains, but they also must be aware of the specific skills that are needed for successful learning within a specific domain.

For example, Kathy Stone might work with her third-grade students on using goal setting to complete assignments. In reading, she might help students determine how to complete two chapters in a reading book by the end of the week. The students might establish a goal to read a certain number of pages or a subsection each day of the week. Because the goal comprises more than just reading the words on the pages, Mrs. Stone also must teach specific comprehension skills, such as locating main ideas and reading for details. Goal setting can be applied in mathematics by having students decide how many problems or activities to do each day to complete a particular unit by the end of the week. Specific skills that come into play in this context are determining what the problem is asking for, representing the problem, and knowing how to perform the computations; Mrs. Stone must ensure student learning in these areas.

In physical education students may use goal setting to master skills, such as working toward running a mile in 6 minutes. The students might begin by running the mile in 10 minutes and then work to decrease the running time every week. Motor skills must be developed to successfully meet the goal. Such skills are most likely to be specific to the context of running a short distance in a good time.

Novice-to-Expert Research Methodology

The emphasis on learning in content areas has heightened research interest in skill acquisition. This emphasis contrasts with that found in older research on comparisons of methods used to teach reading, writing, arithmetic, and so forth. This historical stress on methods is in part a reflection of the popularity of the reinforcement theory explanation of learning as changes in responses due to differential reinforcement (Chapter 2). With the growth of cognitive and constructivist views of learning, researchers have become more interested in students' beliefs and thought processes, and the research focus has shifted accordingly.

To investigate academic tasks, many researchers have used a *novice-to-expert model* with the following steps:

- Identify the skill to be learned.
- Find an expert (i.e., one who performs the skill well) and a novice (one who knows something about the task but performs it poorly).
- Determine how the novice can be moved to the expert level as efficiently as possible.

The last step often involves computer simulation to identify substeps leading to skill attainment. Intertask similarities occur in the simulations.

This research model is intuitively plausible. The basic idea is that if you want to understand how to become more skillful in an area, closely study someone who performs that skill well. In so doing you can learn what knowledge he or she possesses, what procedures and strategies are useful, how to handle difficult situations, and how to correct mistakes. The model has many real-world counterparts and is reflected in apprenticeships, on-the-job training, and mentoring. Using this model when learners pass through intermediate steps in developing competence is also helpful.

Much of the knowledge on how more- and less-competent persons differ in a domain comes from research based in part on assumptions of the novice-to-expert model (VanLehn, 1996). For this reason we know a lot about the stages of skill acquisition. Conducting such research is very labor-intensive and time-consuming because it requires studying learners over time, but it typically yields rich results.

At the same time, this model is descriptive rather than explanatory: It describes what learners do rather than explaining why they do it. The model also tacitly assumes that a fixed constellation of skills exists that constitutes expertise in a given domain, but this is not always the case. With respect to teaching, Sternberg and Horvath (1995) argue that no one standard exists; rather, expert teachers resemble one another in prototypical fashion. This makes sense given our experiences with master teachers who typically differ in several ways.

Finally, the model does not automatically suggest teaching methods. As such, it may have limited usefulness for classroom teaching and learning. Explanations for learning and corresponding teaching suggestions should be firmly grounded in theories and identify important personal and environmental factors. These factors are emphasized in this and other chapters in this book.

LANGUAGE COMPREHENSION

We begin our discussion of content domains with *language comprehension*, which is a central element for understanding the mind. Although humans and animals have similarities, they differ in many ways and a primary difference is in the acquisition and use of language. The gap between human language and animal communication systems is tremendous. Language is the principal means people use to teach, establish rules, and transmit cultural practices. Language allows us to study human cognition (Carpenter, Miyake, & Just, 1995), perhaps better than any other brain function. This section addresses the components of language comprehension, the role of parsing in comprehension, and the utilization of language.

Components of Comprehension

The research community has not accepted Skinner's (1957) explanation of language in terms of reinforcement contingencies (see Chapter 2). Chomsky (1959) criticized this approach as unsuitable to explain the richness and diversity of natural languages. Most investigators view language as reflecting cognitive processes, and language research significantly advanced the cognitive revolution in psychology (Carpenter et al., 1995). Much current research explores language processes in schools to include methods of language instruction (Fillmore & Valadez, 1986).

Language comprises both spoken and written communication. Although reading is crucially important in school, children understand spoken language before they learn to read:

> "By the age of three or four, virtually every child has learned a language." You immediately and properly understand the reference to spoken language. The child's linguistic performance matures through adolescence and beyond, but the essential characteristics of adult language appear in the preschooler's speech and comprehension, including a well-developed phonological system, a substantial store of morphemes and rules for adding to that store, a syntax that allows the child to parse and produce the strings of morphemes that relate ideas, and an understanding of the conventions for carrying on a conversation. (Calfee & Drum, 1986, p. 806)

Spoken and written comprehension share certain processes. Speech comprehension is the more basic phenomenon; reading comprehension incorporates additional processes. Anderson (1990) contends that efforts to comprehend spoken and written language represent a problem-solving process involving domain-specific declarative and procedural knowledge (production systems).

Comprehension has three major components: perception, parsing, and utilization (Anderson, 1990). *Perception* involves attending to and recognizing an input; in language comprehension, sound patterns are translated into words in working memory (WM). *Parsing* means mentally dividing the sound patterns into units of meaning. *Utilization* refers to the disposition of the parsed mental representation: storing it in long-term memory (LTM) if it is a learning task, giving an answer if it is a question, asking a question if it is not comprehended, and so forth. This section addresses parsing and utilization; Chapter 4 discussed perception (Application 9.2).

Parsing

Linguistic research shows that people understand the grammatical rules of their language, even though they usually cannot verbalize them (Clark & Clark, 1977). Beginning with the work of Chomsky (1957), researchers have investigated the role of deep structures containing prototypical representations of language structure. The English language contains a deep structure for the pattern "noun 1–verb–noun 2," which allows us to recognize these patterns in speech and interpret them as "noun 1 did verb to noun 2." Deep structures may be represented in LTM as productions (if-then statements). Chomsky postulated that the capacity for acquiring deep structures is innately human, although which structures are acquired depends on the language of one's culture.

Parsing includes more than just fitting language into production systems. When people are exposed to language, they construct a mental representation of the situation. They recall from LTM propositional knowledge about the context, into which they integrate new knowledge. A central point is that *all communication is incomplete*. Speakers do not provide all information relevant to the topic being discussed. Rather, they omit the information listeners are most likely to know (Clark & Clark,

APPLICATION 9.2
Language Comprehension

Students presented with confusing or vague information may misconstrue it or relate it to the wrong context. Teachers need to present clear and concise information and ensure that students have adequate background information to build networks and schemata.

Assume that Kathy Stone plans to present a social studies unit comparing city life with life in the country, but that most of her students have never seen a farm; thus, they will have difficulty comprehending the unit. They may never have heard words such as *silo, milking, sow,* and *livestock.* Mrs. Stone can produce better student understanding by providing farm-related experiences: take a field trip to a farm; hatch chicken eggs in the classroom; show films about farm life; or bring in small farm equipment, seeds, plants, small animals, and photographs. As students become familiar with farms, they will be better able to comprehend spoken and written communication about farms.

Very young children may have great difficulty following directions when they first attend preschool or kindergarten. Their limited use and understanding of language may cause them to interpret certain words or phrases differently than intended. For instance, if a teacher said to a small group of children playing in a "dress-up" center, "Let's get things tied up so we can work on our next activity," the teacher might return to find children tying clothes together instead of cleaning up. Or a teacher might say, "Make sure you color this whole page," to children working with crayons. Later the teacher may discover that some children took a single crayon and colored the entire page from top to bottom instead of using various colors to color the items on the page. Teachers must be careful to explain, demonstrate, and model what they want children to do. Then they can ask the children to repeat in their own words what they think they are supposed to do.

1977). For example, suppose Sam meets Kira and Kira remarks, "You won't believe what happened to me at the concert!" Sam is most likely to activate propositional knowledge in LTM about concerts. Then Kira says, "As I was locating my seat . . ." To comprehend this statement, Sam must know that one purchases a ticket with an assigned seat. Kira did not tell Sam these things because she assumed he knew them.

Effective language parsing requires knowledge and inferences (Resnick, 1985). When exposed to verbal communication, individuals access information from LTM about the described situation. This information exists in LTM as propositional networks hierarchically organized as *schemata* (prototypical versions of situations). Networks allow people to understand incomplete communications. Consider the following sentence: "I went to the grocery store and wrote a check for $25 over the amount." Knowledge that people buy merchandise in grocery stores and that they may write checks to pay for it enables listeners to comprehend this sentence. The missing information is filled in with knowledge in memory.

People often misconstrue communications because they fill in missing information with the wrong context. When given a vague passage about four friends getting together for an evening, music students interpreted it as a description of playing music, whereas physical education students described it as an evening of playing cards (Anderson, Reynolds, Schallert, & Goetz, 1977). The interpretative schemata salient in people's minds are used to comprehend problematic passages. As with many other linguistic skills, interpretations of communications become more reliable with development as children realize the intent of a message as well as its content (literal meaning; Beal & Belgrad, 1990).

That spoken language is incomplete can be shown by decomposing communications into propositions and identifying how propositions are linked. Consider the following example (Kintsch, 1979):

> The Swazi tribe was at war with a neighboring tribe because of a dispute over some cattle. Among the warriors were two unmarried men named Kakra and his younger brother Gum. Kakra was killed in battle.

Although this passage seems straightforward, analysis reveals the following 11 distinct propositions:

1. The Swazi tribe was at war.
2. The war was with a neighboring tribe.
3. The war had a cause.
4. The cause was a dispute over some cattle.
5. Warriors were involved.
6. The warriors were two men.
7. The men were unmarried.
8. The men were named Kakra and Gum.
9. Gum was the younger brother of Kakra.
10. Kakra was killed.
11. The killing occurred during battle.

Even this propositional analysis is incomplete. Propositions 1 through 4 link together, as do Propositions 5 through 11, but a gap occurs between 4 and 5. To supply the missing link, one might have to change Proposition 5 to "The dispute involved warriors."

Kintsch and van Dijk (1978) showed that features of communication influence comprehension. Comprehension becomes more difficult when more links are missing and when propositions are further apart (in the sense of requiring inferences to fill in the gaps). When much material has to be inferred, WM easily becomes overloaded and comprehension suffers.

Just and Carpenter (1992) formulated a *capacity theory of language comprehension*, which postulates that comprehension depends on WM capacity and individuals differ in this capacity. Elements of language (e.g., words, phrases) become activated in WM and can be operated on by other processes. If the total amount of activation available to the system is less than the amount required to perform a comprehension task, then some of the activation maintaining older elements will be dissipated (Carpenter et al., 1995); for example, elements comprehended at the start of a lengthy sentence may be lost by the end. Production-system rules presumably govern activation and the linking of elements in WM.

We see the application of this model in parsing of ambiguous sentences or phrases (e.g., "The soldiers warned about the dangers . . ."; MacDonald, Just, & Carpenter, 1992). Although alternative interpretations of such constructions initially may be activated, the duration of maintaining them depends on WM capacity. Persons with large WM capacities maintain the interpretations for quite a while, whereas those with smaller capacities typically maintain only the most likely (although not necessarily correct) interpretation. With increased exposure in the linguistic context, comprehenders can decide which interpretation is correct, and such identification is more reliable for persons with large WM capacities who still have the alternative interpretations in WM (Carpenter et al., 1995; King & Just, 1991).

In building representations, people include important information and omit details (Resnick, 1985). These *gist representations* include propositions most germane to comprehension. Listeners' ability to make sense of a text depends on what they know about the topic (Chiesi et al., 1979; Spilich et al., 1979). When the appropriate network or schema exists in listeners' memories, they employ a production that extracts the most central information to fill the slots in the schema. Comprehension proceeds slowly when a network must be constructed because it does not exist in LTM.

Stories exemplify how schemata are employed. Stories have a prototypical schema that includes setting, initiating events, internal responses of characters, goals, attempts to attain goals, outcomes, and reactions (Black, 1984; Rumelhart, 1975, 1977; Stein & Trabasso, 1982). When hearing a story, people construct a mental model of the situation by recalling the story schema and gradually fitting information into it (Bower & Morrow, 1990). Some categories (e.g., initiating events, goal attempts, consequences) are nearly always included, but others (internal responses of characters) may be omitted (Mandler, 1978; Stein & Glenn, 1979). Comprehension proceeds quicker when schemata are easily activated. People recall stories better when events are presented in the expected order rather than in a nonstandard order. When a schema is well established, people rapidly integrate information into it. Research shows that early home literacy experiences that include exposure to books relate positively to the development of listening comprehension (Sénéchal & LeFevre, 2002).

Utilization

Utilization refers to what people do with the language communications they receive. For example, if the communication asks a question, listeners retrieve information from LTM to answer it. In a classroom, students link the communication with related information in LTM.

To utilize sentences as speakers intend properly, listeners must encode three pieces of information: speech act, propositional content, and thematic content. A *speech act* is the speaker's purpose in uttering the communication, or what the speaker is trying to accomplish with the utterance (Austin, 1962; Searle, 1969). Speakers may be conveying information to listeners, commanding them to do something, requesting information from them, promising them something, and so on. *Propositional content* is information that can be judged true or false (see Chapter 4). *Thematic content* refers to the context in which the utterance is made. Speakers make assumptions about what listeners know. On hearing an utterance, listeners infer information not explicitly stated but germane to how it is utilized. The speech act and propositional and thematic contents are most likely encoded with productions.

Clark and Clark (1977) summarized utilization as follows:

1. On hearing an utterance, listeners identify the speech act, propositional content, and thematic content.
2. They next search memory for information that matches the given information.
3. Depending on the speech act, they deal with the new information:
   a. If the utterance is an assertion, they add the new information to memory.
   b. If the utterance is a yes/no question, they compare the new information with what is in memory and, depending on the match, answer yes or no.
   c. If the utterance is a WH-question, they retrieve the wanted information from memory and compose an answer conveying that information.
   d. If the utterance is a request, they carry out the action necessary to make the new information true. (p. 90)

As an example of this process, assume that Jim Marshall (see Chapter 1) is giving a history lesson and is questioning students about text material. Mr. Marshall asks, "What was Churchill's position during World War II?" The speech act is a request and is signaled by the sentence beginning with a WH word (e.g., who, which, where, when, and why). The propositional content refers to Churchill's position during World War II; it might be represented in memory as follows: Churchill–Prime Minister–Great Britain–World War II.

The thematic content refers to what the teacher left unsaid; the teacher assumes students have heard of Churchill and World War II. Thematic content also includes the classroom question-and-answer format. The students understand that Mr. Marshall will be asking questions for them to answer.

Of special importance for school learning is how students encode assertions. When teachers utter an assertion, they are conveying to students they believe the stated proposition is true. If Mr. Marshall says, "Churchill was the Prime Minister of Great Britain during World War II," he is conveying the belief that this assertion is true. Students record the assertion with related information in LTM.

Speakers facilitate the process whereby people relate new assertions with information in LTM by employing the *given-new contract* (Clark & Haviland, 1977), the terms of which are as follows:

The speaker agrees (a) to use given information to refer to information she thinks the listener can uniquely identify from what he already knows and (b) to use new information to refer to information she believes to be true but is not already known to the listener. (Clark & Clark, 1977, p. 92)

The given-new contract says that given information should be readily identifiable and new information should be unknown to the listener. We might think of the given-new contract as a production. In integrating information into memory, listeners identify given information, access it in LTM, and relate new information to it (i.e., store it in the appropriate "slot" in the network). For the given-new contract to enhance utilization, given information must be readily identified by listeners. When given information is not readily available because it is not in listeners' memories or has not been accessed in a long time, using the given-new production is difficult.

Although language comprehension is often overlooked in school in favor of reading and writing, it is a central component of literacy. Educators lament the poor listening and speaking skills of students, and these are valued attributes of leaders. Habit 5 of Covey's (1989) *Seven Habits of Highly Effective People* is "Seek first to understand, then to be understood," which emphasizes listening first and then speaking. Listening is intimately linked with high achievement. A student who is a good listener is rarely a poor reader. Among college students, measures of listening comprehension may be indistinguishable from those of reading comprehension (Miller, 1988). Reading—a second critical component of literacy and one in which volumes of research have been conducted—is considered next.

READING

As with language comprehension, *reading* involves perception, parsing, and utilization. The perceptual part of reading (recognizing words) is referred to as *lexical access* or *decoding. Comprehension*, or the attachment of meaning to printed information, involves parsing and utilization.

There is a vast amount of reading research (Barr, 2001). This research has substantiated the validity of four major principles (Hall, 1989). First, skilled reading is a complex task that involves perceptual, cognitive, and linguistic processes (Hiebert & Raphael, 1996). Second, reading is interactive in the sense that readers derive information from many levels (e.g., phonemic, morphemic, semantic, syntactic, pragmatic, and interpretative) rather than proceeding sequentially from basic decoding to comprehension. Third, the human information processing system limits our capacity for processing text (e.g., attention, perception, WM, and LTM). When lower-level processes (decoding) function automatically, this frees up more space for higher-level functions. Fourth, reading is strategic. Good readers set goals, select strategies, monitor progress; in short, they are metacognitively active (Byrnes, 1996). Most children with learning disabilities display reading problems, and these stem largely from shortcomings in strategic processing and metacognition (Gersten, Fuchs, Williams, & Baker, 2001). We now turn to a discussion of component processes.

Decoding

Decoding means deciphering printed symbols or making letter-sound correspondences by using a whole-word (matching/pattern recognition) or a phonetic (sound-out/recoding) approach (Gagné et al., 1993). In the *whole-word approach*, the printed word is matched to a similar pattern in LTM, which activates the word's meaning for comprehension. This approach relies on pattern recognition procedures; the patterns are in one's sight vocabulary. In the *phonetic approach*, one sounds out a word by dividing it into syllables and generating corresponding sound patterns. The phonetic patterns activate the word's meaning in memory. Regardless of approach, word recognition is a critical aspect of beginning reading instruction (Biemiller, 1994; Mayer, 1999).

The phonetic and whole-word techniques employ bottom-up and top-down processing, respectively (Just & Carpenter, 1980; Resnick, 1985). In *bottom-up* (or *data-driven*) *processing* (Bruning et al., 1999), people recognize features of letters, combine letters into syllables, and combine syllables into words. Word recognition precedes meaning. Reading is controlled by the printed input. Less-skilled readers often employ bottom-up processing, and it is used by good readers when they encounter unfamiliar words.

In *top-down* (or *conceptually driven*) *processing* (Bruning et al., 1999), readers create a context based on prior knowledge and current information. Reading is controlled by higher-level processes such as forming expectations about what will occur and drawing inferences. The context is made up of propositional networks and schemata with empty slots. Readers fill in the required information and confirm or disconfirm hypotheses about what will occur (Frederiksen, 1979). They employ production systems to extract the expected information from text. With efficient top-down processing, readers do not encode separate words but rather propositions or larger units.

Figure 9.1 shows examples of top-down and bottom-up processing. Assume that a student has been reading a passage about a tall boy. The reader encounters the sentence, "Martin was outside playing _____." Using top-down processing, the reader might expect to find the word *basketball*. With bottom-up processing, the reader would construct the word from individual syllables.

In skilled reading, much information is processed automatically. *Automaticity* of word recognition, rather than actual recognition, distinguishes good from poor readers. Automatic processing is important because the WM has a limited capacity (Calfee & Drum, 1986). Readers can rapidly transfer information in WM to LTM and move to new material (Resnick, 1985).

Gough (1972) developed an eye-tracking model of reading comprehension. In studies of eye fixations during reading, good readers spend significantly less time on both unfamiliar and familiar words (Just & Carpenter, 1980). The former also sound out unfamiliar words faster than the latter. Good readers tend to parse passages at the end of phrases and sentences; they pause longer there than in the middle. They integrate information at natural break points (units of thought), which helps them draw inferences and construct meaning. Children with poor phonological skills adopt less-than-optimal reading strategies, which then result in low performance (Tunmer & Chapman, 1996).

Although speed in reading does not guarantee total comprehension, a moderately positive relation exists between decoding speed and comprehension skill (Curtis, 1980). Rapid decoding seems to activate learners' comprehension processes sooner so that they comprehend more information in less time. Slow decoding takes more time to activate comprehension processes; in the meantime, some information previously decoded is lost from WM and is inaccessible for comprehension. de Jong

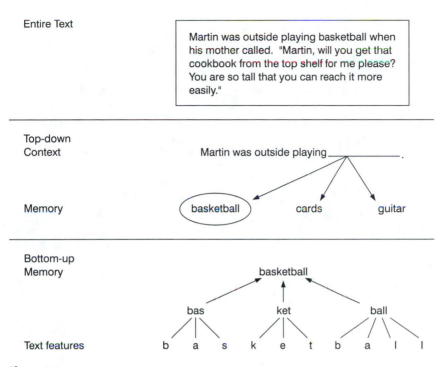

Entire Text

Martin was outside playing basketball when his mother called. "Martin, will you get that cookbook from the top shelf for me please? You are so tall that you can reach it more easily."

Top-down Context

Martin was outside playing _____.

Memory

basketball   cards   guitar

Bottom-up Memory

basketball

bas   ket   ball

Text features

b   a   s   k   e   t   b   a   l   l

Figure 9.1
Examples of top-down and bottom-up processing.

(1998) concluded that children with reading disabilities have great difficulty concurrently processing and storing information.

Correlational data do not imply causality, but the evidence suggests that children who have decoding problems also have difficulty learning to comprehend. Educational researchers and practitioners advocate that children be able to decode largely automatically (Adams, 1990). Readers who spend time and mental effort decoding do not have the proper mental resources to comprehend what they read. This suggestion does not commit one to a particular method of reading instruction (e.g., phonics, whole language; Gagné et al., 1993). There are proponents for each. Developing decoding skills requires practice and feedback, which helps to build reading self-efficacy (Tunmer & Chapman, 2002). Application 9.3 gives suggestions for teaching decoding.

Comprehension

Basic Processes. *Comprehension* involves attaching meaning to printed information and using the information for a particular purpose. Successful comprehension requires conceptual understanding, automated basic skills, and effective use of strategies (Byrnes, 1996; Gagné et al., 1993; Mayer, 1999). Different levels of comprehension exist (Perfetti, 1985). At a basic level, readers access a word's meaning as a

APPLICATION 9.3
Teaching Decoding

Teachers must work with young readers in helping them develop various decoding skills. A first-grade teacher might help young children learn to read new material by asking key questions that students can use as they develop the techniques. When children have trouble with a specific word, the teacher might encourage top-down processing by asking:

- What word might make sense in the sentence? Read the sentence again and see if you can think of one.
- What was being talked about in the sentence? What might you expect to happen?
- Close your eyes and imagine what is happening. Now what might you expect to see next?

Alternatively, the teacher might encourage bottom-up processing with these questions:

- Do you see any little words you know inside this word?
- Does this word look like any other word you know?
- Can you sound out the letters in this word to make the whole word?

Jim Marshall is working with small groups in his American history class as they develop a skit depicting a scene that might have occurred during the Great Depression. As he works with the students, he encourages them to close their eyes and visualize a scene that could have been a great concern to a family during that time. They might try visualizing and thinking about these questions:

- What areas of life (e.g., jobs, schooling) were affected by the Great Depression?
- What hardships were caused by the Great Depression?
- What compromises did families have to make to adjust to the hardships created by the Great Depression?
- How did the Great Depression affect relationships within the family?
- How did the Great Depression affect friendships?

consequence of decoding. At a higher level, readers move beyond the literal meaning of printed words and engage in mental activities, such as drawing inferences, deciding on main ideas, inferring the writer's purpose or bias, and anticipating how events will unfold in text.

Once a word is decoded, readers access the meaning stored with the letter-sound correspondence in LTM. Understanding word meanings depends on one's store of declarative knowledge. Proficient readers have rich vocabularies and fast access to word meanings, which relate positively to reading comprehension (Goldberg, Schwartz, & Stewart, 1977).

Comprehension is influenced by the reading context (Hiebert & Raphael, 1996). Good readers employ top-down processing more than poor readers and are faster in part because they usually rely on context to identify words. Skilled readers also take advantage of word context to parse sentences into natural units, even when punctuation marks are absent. Readers derive contextual cues that signal where units are to be parsed, such as word order, word endings, and punctuation. In the sentence, "The plodols went home," readers will not know the meaning of "plodols" (there is no such word) but will surmise that it is a plural noun because it follows *the* in the first position of the sentence and because it ends in *s*.

Goodman (1982) felt that readers use text as a means of confirming or not confirming predictions about what the text is going to say (a top-down model). Four cycles occur interactively: optical (receiving the visual input), perceptual (identifying letters and words), syntactic (identifying structure of the text), and meaning (constructing meaning for the input). Once reading begins, readers construct an initial meaning for the text, which serves as the basis for predictions of future input. Reading continues as predictions are confirmed, but the reader slows down or rereads to get a better meaning if the initial prediction is incorrect. Errors (miscues), therefore, are fairly common and actually can facilitate comprehension.

Literal comprehension is important for reading texts such as a restaurant menu or directions for assembling a bookcase. People often find that they must go beyond literal meaning to understand better what they are reading. *Inferential comprehension* is involved in activities such as identifying main ideas, getting the gist, summarizing and integrating information, and drawing conclusions. Inferential comprehension requires mentally linking different ideas in text. Consider the following sentences:

- The Senate failed to ratify the treaty.
- Senator Milhoudy was livid.

These sentences are linked in the sense that both refer to the Senate, but their meanings are not linked. A reader might infer that the reason Senator Milhoudy was livid was because the senator wanted the treaty ratified and voted to ratify it but the vote failed in the Senate.

Compared with poor readers, skilled readers integrate ideas better within and between sentences (Perfetti & Roth, 1981). For example, skilled readers are quicker to determine a pronoun's referent, whereas poor readers benefit when noun phrases are repeated.

Another inferential comprehension process is *summarization*, or grouping important points into a coherent structure by drawing inferences and using words and phrases that signal main ideas (e.g., "in summary"; Kintsch & van Dijk, 1978). Good readers are more proficient at summarizing than poor readers (Meyer, Brandt, & Bluth, 1980). The ability to identify and use structure improves with development.

Skilled readers are more knowledgeable about how texts are organized and are better equipped with strategies for acquiring information to complement the organization than are poor readers. Poor readers also do not utilize strategies effectively

(Cataldo & Cornoldi, 1998). Skilled readers have mental schemata representing prototypical organizations of texts (Meyer, 1984). A text may compare and contrast, discuss cause and effect, show how ideas are related, state an idea or principle with examples, or present a problem with solutions. When reading, skilled readers identify the text pattern, access the schema from LTM, and integrate information from text into the appropriate schema slots.

Inferential comprehension also involves *elaboration*, or adding to new knowledge by using prior knowledge. Following are some ways to elaborate new knowledge:

- Think of examples of the ideas or principles described.
- Anticipate what will happen in the story.
- Fill in missing details in text.
- Draw an analogy between new material and what is known.
- Think about implications of what is stated.
- Relate details to main ideas.
- Compare ideas to your beliefs.

Elaborations help link new information to organizational structures already in memory. Skilled readers are more facile at employing elaborations than are poor readers.

Metacognition.   *Metacognition* (see Chapter 5) is relevant to reading because it is involved in understanding and monitoring of reading purposes and strategies (Paris, Wixson, & Palincsar, 1986). Beginning readers often do not understand the conventions of printed material: In the English language, one reads words from left to right and top to bottom. Beginning and poorer readers typically do not monitor their comprehension or adjust their strategies accordingly (Baker & Brown, 1984). Older and skilled readers are better at comprehension monitoring than are younger and less-skilled readers, respectively (Alexander, Carr, & Schwanenflugel, 1995; Paris et al., 1986).

Metacognition is involved when learners set goals, evaluate goal progress, and make necessary corrections (McNeil, 1987). Skilled readers do not approach all reading tasks identically. They determine their goal: find main ideas, read for details, skim, get the gist, and so on. They then use a strategy they believe will accomplish the goal. When reading skills are highly developed, these processes may occur automatically.

While reading, skilled readers check their progress. If their goal is to locate important ideas, and if after reading a few pages, they have not located any important ideas, they are apt to reread those pages. If they encounter a word they do not understand, they try to determine its meaning from context or consult a dictionary rather than continue reading.

Developmental evidence indicates a trend toward greater recognition and correction of comprehension deficiencies (Alexander et al., 1995; Byrnes, 1996; Garner & Reis, 1981). Younger children recognize comprehension failures less often than do older children. Younger children who are good comprehenders may recognize a problem but may not employ a strategy to solve it (e.g., rereading). Older children who are good comprehenders recognize problems and employ correction strategies.

Children develop metacognitive abilities through interactions with parents and teachers (Langer & Applebee, 1986). Adults help children solve problems by guiding them through solution steps, reminding them of their goal, and helping them plan how to reach their goal. An effective teaching procedure includes informing children of the goal, making them aware of information relevant to the task, arranging a situation conducive to problem solving, and reminding them of their goal progress.

Because many children do not use effective strategies, researchers have recommended teaching strategies. *Strategy instruction* programs generally have been successful in helping students learn strategies and maintain their use over time. Brown and her colleagues advocate strategy training incorporating practice in use of skills, instruction in how to monitor outcomes of one's efforts, and feedback on when and where a strategy may be useful (Brown, 1980; Brown, Palincsar, & Armbruster, 1984).

Palincsar and Brown (1984) identified seventh graders with poor comprehension skills. They trained students in self-directed summarizing (review), questioning, clarifying, and predicting. Summarizing included stating what had happened in the text and also served as a self-test on the content. Questioning addressed determining what main idea question a teacher or test might ask about that material. Clarifying was used when portions of the text were unclear and students could not adequately summarize. Predicting was used when text cues signaled forthcoming information.

Researchers taught these activities as part of an interactive dialogue between teacher and student known as *reciprocal teaching*. During the lessons, an adult teacher met with two students. Initially the teacher modeled the activities. The teacher and students silently read a passage, after which the teacher asked a question that a teacher or test might ask, summarized the content, clarified troublesome points, and predicted future content. Following the teacher's modeled demonstration, the teacher and students took turns being the teacher. At first, students had difficulty assuming the role of teacher; the teacher often had to construct paraphrases and questions for students. Eventually students became more capable of following the procedure and implementing the four activities.

Compared with a condition in which students received instruction on locating information in text, reciprocal teaching led to greater comprehension gains, better maintenance over time, and better generalization to classroom comprehension tests. Students exposed to reciprocal teaching also showed greater improvements in quality of summaries and questions asked. The maintenance and generalization results are important because changes brought about by strategy training programs often do not maintain themselves or generalize to other tasks (Phye, 2001).

The dialogue about the following text occurred between teacher (T) and student (S) early in the training program (Palincsar & Brown, 1984).

> The snake's skeleton and parts of its body are very flexible—something like a rubber hose with bones. A snake's backbone can have as many as 300 vertebrae, almost 10 times as many as a human's. These vertebrae are connected by loose and rubbery tissues that allow easy movement. Because of this bendable, twistable spinal construction, a snake can turn its body in almost any direction at almost any point.
>
> S: Like, if a snake is turning around, he wouldn't break any bones because he is flexible.
>
> T: And the reason he is so flexible is . . .
>
> S: If someone stepped on his tail, he wouldn't be able to move unless he was flexible.

T: O.K. That explains why it would be helpful to be so flexible, but what makes the snake so flexible? I think that is an important part of the summary.

S: So he can move faster?

T: That is another reason for being flexible. Let me do a summary for you. Sara [the student] is right. The most important thing we have learned is that snake[s are] very flexible. The reason they can bend so easily is that they have so many little bones in their backbones and each of them can move separately, making the snake very flexible. Does that make sense? (p. 142)

The last statement by the teacher is a modeled demonstration of summarization.

The *Informed Strategies for Learning* (*ISL*) program by Paris and his colleagues (Paris et al., 1984; Paris & Oka, 1986) also includes strategy training incorporating metacognitive elements. ISL is based on the premise that reading requires declarative, procedural, and conditional knowledge. The program also attempts to enhance students' self-efficacy for effectively applying strategies. Children exposed to this program typically show gains in awareness of comprehension strategies and monitoring skills, which in turn bear a positive relationship to reading achievement. The program benefits students with high, average, and low reading abilities, which enhances its potential for classroom use.

Motivation plays a critical role in reading comprehension (Schunk, 1995). Guthrie, Wigfield, and VonSecker (2000) integrated reading strategy instruction with science content and found significant benefits on students' motivation compared with traditional instruction emphasizing coverage of material. Student interest presumably was heightened with the real-world use of effective reading strategies. Other research shows that task-mastery goals predict students' use of learning strategies in reading instruction (Meece & Miller, 2001). After reviewing a large number of studies, Blok, Oostdam, Otter, and Overmaat (2002) concluded that computer-assisted instruction was effective in beginning reading instruction. It is possible that the motivational benefits of computers may aid in the development of early reading skill, but the issue requires additional investigation.

WRITING

Another important component of literacy is writing. *Writing* refers to translating ideas into linguistic symbols in print. Reading and writing utilize many of the same cognitive processes, although reading is somewhat easier than writing (Fitzgerald & Shanahan, 2000). Relative to reading, less research has been conducted on writing. In part, historical reluctance to investigate writing may have stemmed from the erroneous beliefs that good writers are born rather than made and that, because good writing is creative and inspirational, words should flow with little effort. Contemporary research has debunked these myths by showing that excellence in writing, as with excellence in other domains, can be developed and that effective instruction is critical (Flower, 1981; Flower & Hayes, 1980; Scardamalia & Bereiter, 1986; Sperling & Freedman, 2001).

Early models subdivided writing into stages such as prewriting, writing, and rewriting (Rohman, 1965). One benefit of these stage models is that they call attention to the phases of writing. Good writers do not simply spew forth words; they spend much time thinking and organizing their thoughts and rewriting what they have written. At the same time, writing does not seem to be a straightforward, linear process, as conceptualized by stage models. As we write words, we also mentally plan, organize, and revise (Sommers, 1980).

Writers use four types of knowledge: topical, audiences, genres, and language (Byrnes, 1996). *Topical knowledge* is needed to generate and organize ideas. *Knowledge of audiences* includes what the writer thinks readers know and want to hear. *Genres* are types of writing (e.g., essays, narrative stories, or poems). *Language* includes vocabulary, grammar, and pragmatics (e.g., how to convey tone or emotion). With development, children become more knowledgeable of each of these types, but equally important, they develop the capability to reflect on and effectively use each type of knowledge while writing.

Contemporary writing models examine writers' mental processes as they engage in different aspects of writing (deBeaugrande, 1984; Byrnes, 1996; Mayer, 1999; McCutchen, 2000). A general research goal is to define expertise. By comparing expert writers with novice writers, researchers identify how their mental processes diverge (Bereiter & Scardamalia, 1986). One useful strategy is having writers think aloud (say aloud everything they think about) while writing (Hayes & Flower, 1980). Think-aloud protocols are recorded, transcribed, and analyzed to determine which mental processes are associated with indicators of writing expertise (e.g., writing prizes, high grades in writing courses, or extent of professional writing).

This section discusses composition processes that translate initial ideas into print and reviewing processes that alter learners' original thoughts and writings. These components are not mutually exclusive; writing involves interacting with the environment rather than proceeding through absolute stages. Application 9.4 provides classroom exercises in writing.

Composition Processes

Flower and Hayes (1980, 1981a; Hayes & Flower, 1980) formulated a model that conceptualizes writing as a set of thinking processes that writers organize while composing. Writing is goal-directed behavior; writers generate superordinate and subordinate goals incorporating their purposes and alter their goals based on what they learn while writing. Rather than focus on products of writing, Flower and Hayes emphasize the processes that writers employ throughout writing. The Flower and Hayes model reflects the general problem-solving framework developed by Newell and Simon (1972; see Chapter 5). Writers define a problem space and perform operations on their mental representation of the problem to attain their goals (Figure 9.2).

The *rhetorical problem* includes the writer's topic, intended audience, and goals. In classrooms, the rhetorical problem often is well defined; teachers assign a term paper topic, the audience is the teacher, and the goal (e.g., to inform, to persuade) is provided; however, the rhetorical problem is never defined completely by someone other than the writer. Writers interpret problems in their own ways.

APPLICATION 9.4
Writing

Teachers can incorporate planning, transcribing, and revising activities into lessons. If Kathy Stone wanted her third-grade students to write a paragraph describing their summer vacations, she might have students share what they did during the summer. Following this large-group activity, Mrs. Stone and the children might jointly develop and edit a paragraph about the teacher's summer vacation. This exercise would emphasize the important elements of a good paragraph and components of the writing process.

Students then could be paired and share orally with each other some things done during the summer. Sharing helps students generate ideas to use in transcribing. Following this activity, children can write their summer activities. For the transcribing, students will use their lists to formulate sentences of a paragraph and share their written products with their partners. Partners will provide feedback about clarity and grammar, after which students revise their paragraphs.

The faculty sponsor of the high school newspaper can incorporate planning, transcribing, and revising activities into producing the paper each week. When the sponsor meets with the newspaper staff each Monday, the sponsor and the students generate topics to be covered for the next issue and plan the layout (e.g., front page stories, types of human interest articles, sports events to cover during the week, or editorial focus), as well as who will be responsible for each piece. Then the students work with partners throughout the week as they transcribe and revise their articles with input from the sponsor.

Gina Brown works with members of her undergraduate educational psychology class as they write their first research paper. She has each student select a topic, develop a basic outline, and compile a list of possible sources, after which she meets with students individually. Then she has students begin the first draft of the paper, giving more attention to the introduction and conclusion. She meets again with students individually to discuss their first drafts and progress and guides them toward what should be done to complete the finished product.

The writer's LTM plays a crucial role. Writers differ in their knowledge of the topic, audience, and mechanics of writing (organization, grammar, spelling, punctuation). Writers knowledgeable about their topics include fewer irrelevant statements in their compositions but more auxiliary statements (designed to elaborate upon main points) compared with less knowledgeable writers (Voss, Vesonder, & Spilich, 1980). Differences in declarative knowledge affect the quality of writing.

Figure 9.2
Process model of writing.
Source: Adapted from "A Cognitive Process Theory of Writing," by L. Flower and J. R. Hayes, 1981, *College Composition and Communication, 32*, p. 370. Copyright 1981 by the National Council of Teachers of English. Reprinted with permission.

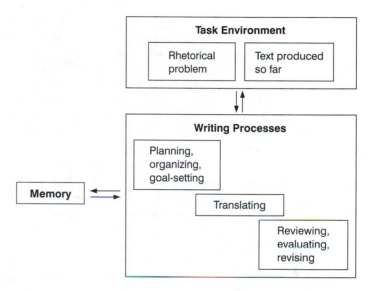

Planning involves forming an internal representation of knowledge to be used in composing. The internal representation generally is more abstract than the actual writing. Planning includes several subprocesses, such as generating ideas by retrieving relevant information from memory or other sources. These ideas may be well formed or fragmentary. Organizing helps give ideas better meaning by grouping them into superordinate and subordinate roles. Organizing also includes deciding on the flow of the text—what to present first, next, and so on.

A major subprocess is *goal setting*. Goals are substantive (what the writer wants to communicate) and procedural (how to communicate or how points should be expressed). Good writers often alter their goals based on what they have already produced. Writers have goals in mind prior to writing, but as they proceed, they may realize that a certain goal is not relevant to the composition. New goals are suggested by actual writing.

There are wide individual differences in writers' planning skills. The Flower and Hayes model may not be entirely appropriate for children, whose writing typically resembles "knowledge telling" (McCutchen, 1995; Scardamalia & Bereiter, 1982). Children often follow a "retrieve and write" strategy; they access LTM with a cue from the topic or the genre and write down what they know. Relative to the Flower and Hayes model, children do little planning and reviewing and much translating. Whereas older writers also retrieve content from LTM, they do it as part of planning, after which they evaluate its appropriateness prior to translating. With children, the retrieval and translation are integrated in seamless fashion (Scardamalia & Bereiter, 1986).

Young children produce fewer ideas than older ones (Scardamalia & Bereiter, 1986). Among older students, higher scores on the verbal portion of the Scholastic Assessment Test (SAT) are associated with greater idea generation (Glynn, Britton, Muth, & Dogan, 1982). Idea generation depends on students' cues to produce more ideas. Younger children benefit from prompting by others (e.g., "Can you write some more?"). Englert, Raphael, Anderson, Anthony, and Stevens (1991) showed that fourth and fifth graders' writing improved when they were exposed to teachers who modeled metacognitive components of the writing process (e.g., which strategies were useful, when and why they were useful) and when they were taught to generate questions during text planning. Older and better writers make greater use of internal prompts. They search relevant topics in LTM and assess knowledge before they begin composing. Teachers can foster idea generation by cueing students to think of ideas and by having them read and save articles on topics to serve as sources of ideas (Bruning et al., 1999).

Organization is conveyed through *cohesion* among sentence parts and coherence across sentences. Cohesive devices tie ideas together with pronouns, definite articles, conjunctions, and word meanings. For example, in the following sentences, the referent of *he* is unclear: "Joe and Jim sat together during the game. He left to get some food." Cohesion is obtained as follows: "Joe and Jim sat together during the game. Joe left to get some food." Young children have more difficulty with cohesion, but unskilled writers of any age use cohesion less well. Developmental differences also are found in coherence. Young writers have difficulty linking sentences with one another and with the topic sentence (McCutchen & Perfetti, 1982). Good writers have better coherence than poor writers.

Goals of good and poor writers differ. The primary goal of skilled writers is to communicate meaning. Similar to many children, poor writers often practice *associative writing* (Bereiter, 1980); they put onto paper the contents of LTM relevant to the topic. They may believe the goal of writing is to regurgitate everything they know about the topic; order is less important than inclusiveness. Another goal of less-skilled writers is to avoid making errors. When asked to critique their own writing, good writers focus on how well they communicated their intentions, whereas poor writers cite surface considerations (spelling, punctuation) more often.

Translation (see Figure 9.2) refers to putting one's ideas into print. For children and inexperienced writers, translating often overburdens WM. They must keep in mind their goal, the ideas they wish to express, and the necessary organization and mechanics. Good writers concern themselves less with surface features during translation; they focus more on meaning and apparently think that they can correct surface problems later. Poor writers concentrate more on surface features and write more slowly than good writers. Better writers take stylistic and surface considerations into account when they pause during writing. Poorer writers benefit when they read what they have written as they prepare to compose.

A common problem in translation is *writer's block*, or difficulty in beginning to compose. Block may be caused by inadequate knowledge of the topic or by lack of interest. Rose (1980) found that adopting rigid rules for writing can cause block. For example, writers who believe they must begin with a quote or make three important points may get stuck when they find that they cannot follow these rules.

The Flower and Hayes model has proven to be remarkably durable and has served as the conceptual framework for much research. Recently, investigators have expanded the model to provide greater clarity (Hayes, 1996; McCutchen, 2000). One key modification postulates a type of long-term working memory (LT-WM), which contains elements activated in short-term (working) memory (STM, WM; see Chapter 4) and retrieval structures that link items in STM to related elements in long-term memory (LTM). In this view, writing expertise develops as writers more effectively use LT-WM to coordinate elements in LTM and employ them in writing. Novice writers show limitations in both WM and LT-WM, whereas skilled writers not only possess better LTM knowledge but also coordinate its use better during writing (McCutchen, 2000).

Reviewing Processes

Reviewing consists of *evaluating* and *revising.* Reviewing occurs when writers read what they have written as a precursor to further translation or systematic evaluation and revision (Flower & Hayes, 1981a; Hayes & Flower, 1980). During reviewing, writers evaluate and modify plans and alter subsequent writing.

These processes are important because writers may spend as much as 70% of their writing time *pausing* (Flower & Hayes, 1981b), much of which is spent on sentence-level planning. Writers reread what they have written and decide what to say next. These *bottom-up processes* construct a composition a section at a time. When such building up is accomplished with the overall plan in mind, the composition continues to reflect the writers' goals.

Poor writers typically depend on bottom-up writing. While pausing, good writers engage in rhetorical planning not directly linked to what they have produced. This type of planning reflects a *top-down view* of writing as a problem-solving process; writers keep an overall goal in mind and plan how to attain it or decide that they need to alter it. Abstract planning may include information about content (deciding what topic to discuss) and style (deciding to alter the style by inserting an anecdote). This abstract or whole-text planning subsumes sentence-level planning and is characteristic of mature writers (Bereiter & Scardamalia, 1986).

Elementary school children often recognize when their writing contains problems but do little revising without teacher or peer support (Fitzgerald, 1987). Students benefit from instruction designed to improve the quality of their writing. Fitzgerald and Markham (1987) gave average sixth-grade writers instruction on types of revisions: additions, deletions, substitutions, and rearrangements. The teacher explained and modeled each revision strategy, after which students worked in pairs (*peer conferences*). Instruction improved students' knowledge of revision processes and their actual revisions. Beal, Garrod, and Bonitatibus (1990) found that third- and sixth-grade children who were trained to apply a self-questioning strategy (e.g., "What is happening in the story?") located and revised significantly more target text than did nontrained students.

Evaluation skills develop earlier than revision skills. Even when fourth graders recognize writing problems, they may not successfully correct them as often as 70% of the time (Scardamalia & Bereiter, 1983). When children correct problems, differences between good and poor writers become evident. Among fourth- and seventh-grade students, poor writers revise errors in spelling and punctuation, whereas better writers revise for stylistic reasons (Birnbaum, 1982).

Older students also sometimes fail to recognize problems in writing. Among high school students, good writers revise more than average writers (Stallard, 1974), and a greater proportion of good writers' revisions involve problems in word choice (meaning). Stallard found these two groups did not differ in spelling, punctuation, or other syntactic revisions.

Given the complexity of writing, the course of skill acquisition is better characterized as the development of *fluency* rather than automaticity that is seen in other domains (e.g., reading; McCutchen, 1995). Automatic processes become routinized and require few attentional or WM resources, whereas fluent processes—although rapid and resource efficient—are thoughtful and can be altered "online." Thus, good writers follow plans but revise them as they write. Were this process automatic, writers' plans—once adopted—would be followed without interruption. Although component skills of writing (i.e., spelling, vocabulary) often become automatic, the overall process does not.

Motivation and Self-Regulation

Like other forms of learning, the development of writing skill is affected by motivation and self-regulation. Bruning and Horn (2000) characterized this development as "a highly fluid process of problem solving requiring constant monitoring of progress toward task goals" (p. 25). Goal setting and self-monitoring of goal progress are key motivational processes (Schunk, 1995). Although more research is needed on the effects of instructional procedures on motivation to write, writing motivation can be enhanced by using authentic writing tasks and by creating a supportive context for writing (e.g., the task appears doable with requisite effort).

Klassen (2002) reviewed the literature on self-efficacy for writing. Most studies found that self-efficacy was a significant predictor of writing achievement. Some studies yielded gender differences in self-efficacy with boys' judgments higher than those of girls, although there were no performance differences. Establishing a classroom environment that builds self-efficacy is conducive to improving writing.

Self-regulation also has been identified as a key variable influencing writing. Writing is demanding and requires attention control, self-monitoring, and volitional control. Graham and Harris (2000) noted that self-regulation affects writing in two ways. For one, self-regulatory processes (e.g., planning, monitoring, and evaluating) provide building blocks that are assembled to complete a writing task. For another, these processes can lead to strategic adjustments in writing and longer-term effects. Thus, successful planning will increase its likelihood of future use and build self-efficacy for writing, which in turn positively impacts motivation and future writing. Teaching students self-regulatory skills in the context of writing assignments results in higher achievement (Graham & Harris, 2000).

MATHEMATICS

Let us now turn to the content area of *mathematics*, which has been an especially fertile area of cognitive and constructivist research (Ball, Lubienski, & Mewborn, 2001; Voss et al., 1995). Topics that have been explored include how learners construct mathematical knowledge, how experts and novices differ, and which methods of instruction are most effective (Byrnes, 1996; Mayer, 1999).

A distinction is typically made between mathematical *computation* (use of rules, procedures, and algorithms) and *concepts* (problem solving and use of strategies). Computational and conceptual problems require students to implement productions involving rules and algorithms. The difference between these two categories lies in how explicitly the problem tells students which operations to perform. The following are computational problems.

- 26 + 42 = ?
- $5x + 3y = 19$
  $7x - y = 11$
  Solve for x and y.
- What is the length of the hypotenuse of a right triangle with sides equal to 3 and 4 inches?

Although students are not explicitly told what to do in problems 2 and 3, recognition of the problem format and knowledge of procedures lead them to perform the correct operations.

Now contrast those problems with the following:

- Alex has 20 coins composed of dimes and quarters. If the quarters were dimes and the dimes were quarters, he would have 90 cents more than he has now. How much money does Alex have?
- If a passenger train takes twice as long to pass a freight train after it first overtakes the freight train as it takes the two trains to pass when going in opposite directions, how many times faster than the freight train is the passenger train?
- When she hikes, Shana can average 2 mph going uphill and 6 mph going downhill. If she goes uphill and downhill and spends no time at the summit, what will be her average speed for an entire trip?

These word problems use mathematical computations no more difficult than those required by the problems in the first set; however, the latter problems do not explicitly tell students what to do. They must decide how to solve the problems, which involves recognizing their problem formats, generating appropriate productions, and performing the computations.

This is not to suggest that conceptual expertise is better than computational proficiency, although Rittle-Johnson and Alibali (1999) found that conceptual understanding had a greater influence on procedural knowledge than did the reverse. Deficiencies in either area cause problems. Understanding how to solve a problem but not being able to perform the computations results in incorrect answers, as does being computationally proficient but not being able to conceptualize problems. Mathematical proficiency requires learning computation and problem solving together.

Computation Skills

The earliest computational skill children use is *counting* (Byrnes, 1996; Resnick, 1985). Children count objects on their fingers and in their heads using a strategy (Groen & Parkman, 1972). The *sum model* involves setting a hypothetical counter at zero, counting in the first addend in increments of one, and then counting in the second addend to arrive at the answer. For the problem "2 + 4 = ?" children might count from 0 to 2 and then count out 4 more. A somewhat more efficient strategy is to set the counter at the first addend (2) and then count in the second addend (4) in increments of one. Still more efficient is the *min model*: Set the counter at the larger of the two addends (4) and then count in the smaller addend (2) in increments of one (Romberg & Carpenter, 1986). Children as young as $4\frac{1}{2}$ years have been observed to use the min model, even though they never have been instructed in its use (Groen & Resnick, 1977).

This type of invented procedure is efficient and successful. Children and adults often construct procedures to solve mathematical problems. Errors generally are not random but rather reflect *buggy algorithms*, or systematic mistakes in thinking and reasoning (Brown & Burton, 1978). Buggy algorithms reflect the constructivist assumption that students form procedures based on their interpretation of experiences (see Chapter 7). A common mistake in subtraction is to subtract the smaller number from the larger number in each column, regardless of direction, as follows:

$$
\begin{array}{r}
53 \\
-27 \\
\hline
34
\end{array}
\qquad
\begin{array}{r}
602 \\
-274 \\
\hline
472
\end{array}
$$

Mathematical bugs probably develop when students encounter new problems and incorrectly generalize productions. In subtraction without regrouping, for example, students subtract the smaller number from the larger one column by column; seeing how they could generalize this procedure to problems requiring regrouping is easy. Rather than ceasing to work problems when they do not know what to do, students modify their rules to fit new problems. Buggy algorithms are durable and can instill in students a false sense of self-efficacy (Chapter 3), perhaps because their computations produce answers.

Another source of computational difficulties is poor declarative knowledge of number facts. Many children do not have basic addition, subtraction, multiplication, and division facts involving simple numbers well established in their memories. The problem "8 × 7 = ?" is a cue to retrieve this fact from LTM. Until facts become established through practice, children count or compute answers. Speed of mathematical fact retrieval from memory relates directly to overall mathematical achievement in students from elementary school through college (Royer, Tronsky, Chan, Jackson, & Marchant, 1999).

Many difficulties in computation result from using overly complex but technically correct productions to solve problems. Such procedures produce correct answers, but because they are complex, the risk of computational errors is high. The problem 256 divided by 5 can be solved by the division algorithm or by successively subtracting 5 from 256 and counting the number of subtractions. The latter procedure is technically correct but inefficient and has a high probability of error. One of the goals of computation instruction is for students to become skilled in using efficient procedures.

The development of skill acquisition as discussed in Chapter 4 is relevant to computational skills (Anderson, 1990). Learners initially represent the skill as declarative knowledge in a propositional network. Facts concerning the different steps (e.g., in the algorithm) are committed to memory through mental rehearsal and overt practice. The production that guides performance at this stage is general; for example:

If the goal is to solve this division problem, *then* apply the method the teacher taught us.

Learners insert the steps they have memorized into this general heuristic. With added practice, the declarative representation changes into a domain-specific procedural representation and eventually becomes automated. Early counting strategies are replaced with more-efficient rule-based strategies (Hopkins & Lawson, 2002). At the automatic stage, learners quickly recognize the problem pattern (e.g., division problem, square root problem) and implement the procedure without much conscious deliberation. As a skill develops, learners are able to execute it rapidly and achieve greater accuracy in their answers.

Problem-Solving Skills

Successful mathematical problem solving depends on students possessing knowledge and problem-solving skills. According to Mayer (1989), the most basic type of knowledge involves *resources*, or knowledge of basic facts and procedures. A second type of knowledge is of *heuristics*, or general strategies for solving problems (see Chapter 5). Problem solvers especially need strategies for problem representation and solution planning. Another type of knowledge is *metacognitive* (or *control for monitoring*); it concerns how to manage the problem-solving process. Control is involved in monitoring one's execution of a solution to include discovering errors in computation.

Mathematical problem solving requires that students first accurately represent the problem to include the given information and the goal and then select and apply a problem-solving production (Mayer, 1985, 1999). Translating a problem from its linguistic representation to a mental representation is often difficult.

Formats commonly found in problems given to children include *change problems* (start with a set that increases or decreases due to some action; e.g., Joe has 3 marbles, Tom gave him 5 more, how many marbles does Joe have now?); *combine problems* (two sets that do not change but are combined; e.g., Joe has 3 marbles, Tom has 5 marbles, how many marbles do they have together?); *compare problems* (two sets that do not change but the difference between them is determined; e.g., Joe has 5 marbles, Tom has 3 more marbles than Joe, how many marbles does Tom have?; Mayer, 1992). Research shows that children often fail to represent problems correctly and that they are more likely to perform correct computations on incorrect representations. Thus, children may transform one problem type into another (e.g., in the preceding compare example, transform "Tom has more marbles than Joe" into "Joe has more marbles than Tom"). When that happens, an incorrect solution results.

The language used can make even easy word problems difficult (Bruning et al., 1999). The more abstract the language, the more difficult the text comprehension and the lower the likelihood of solution (Cummins, Kintsch, Reusser, & Weimer, 1988). Students who have difficulty comprehending show poorer recall of information and lower performance. This is especially true for younger children, who have difficulty translating abstract linguistic representations.

Translation also requires good declarative and procedural knowledge. Solving the earlier problem about Alex with 20 coins requires knowledge that dimes and quarters are coins, that a dime is one-tenth ($0.10) of $1, and that a quarter is one-fourth ($0.25) of $1. This declarative knowledge needs to be coupled with procedural understanding that dimes and quarters are variables such that the number of dimes plus the number of quarters equals 20.

One reason experts translate problems better is that their knowledge is better organized in LTM; the organization reflects the underlying structure of the subject matter (Romberg & Carpenter, 1986). Experts overlook surface features of a problem and analyze it in terms of the operations required for solution. Novices are swayed more by surface features.

Silver (1981) asked students to sort mathematical word problems into categories by type and tested their problem-solving skills. Students were classified as good, average, or poor problem solvers. Good problem solvers organized problems according to the process required for solution; poor problem solvers were more likely to group problems with similar content (e.g., money, trains). For example (Mayer, 1982):

> On a ferry trip, the fare for each adult was 50 cents and for each child was 25 cents. The number of passengers was 30 and the total paid was $12.25. How many adults and children were there? (p. 203)

This problem involves two equations with two unknowns. If x = number of adults and y = number of children, then:

$$x + y = 30$$
$$.5x + .25y = 12.25$$

Multiplying the first equation by .5 and subtracting the second equation leaves .25y = 2.75, or y = 11. Substituting the value of y into the first equation yields x = 19. Compared with novices, experts are more likely to classify this problem according to solution process (two equations with two unknowns) rather than surface features (money).

In addition to problem translation and classification, experts and novices differ in productions (Greeno, 1980). Novices often adopt a *working backward strategy*, beginning with the goal and working their way back to the givens. Successful use of this strategy requires that problem solvers understand the problem domain sufficiently to realize what knowledge is required to attain each subgoal. Working backward is a good general heuristic useful in the early stages of learning when learners have acquired some domain knowledge but are not competent enough to recognize problem formats quickly. As domain-specific knowledge is learned, more powerful problem-solving productions become available (Anderson, 1990).

In contrast to novices, experts often adopt a *working forward strategy*. They identify the problem type and select the appropriate production to solve the problem. Hegarty, Mayer, and Monk (1995) showed that more and less successful problem solvers used different general approaches for understanding word problems. Successful problem solvers used a problem model approach, translating the problem into a mental model in which the numbers in the problem statement were tied to their variable names. In contrast, less successful solvers were more likely to employ a direct translation approach, combining the numbers in the problem with the arithmetic operations primed by the key words (e.g., addition is the operation linked with the key word "more"). The latter strategy is superficial and based on surface features, whereas the former strategy is linked better with meanings.

Experts develop sophisticated procedural knowledge for classifying mathematical problems according to type. High school algebra problems fall into roughly 20 general categories such as motion, current, coins, and interest/investment (Mayer, 1992). These categories can be aggregated into six major groups. For example, the amount-per-time group includes motion, current, and work problems. These problems are solvable with the general formula: amount = rate × time. The development of mathematical problem-solving expertise depends on being able to classify a problem into the correct group.

As with other skills, classification is developed through teaching and solving different types of problems. Students initially may apply a working backward approach, but with experience they develop accurate classification procedures. How this novice-to-expert progression occurs is not well understood. Research addressing this progression will have important implications for teaching students to become better problem solvers. Application 9.5 gives some classroom examples of teaching problem solving.

Constructivism

Many theorists contend that constructivism (Chapter 7) represents a viable model for explaining how mathematics is learned (Cobb, 1994; Lampert, 1990; Resnick, 1989). As with other forms of knowledge, mathematical knowledge is not passively absorbed from the environment but rather is constructed by individuals as a consequence of their interactions. This construction process also includes children's inventing of procedures that incorporate implicit rules.

The following unusual example illustrates this rule-based procedural invention:

Some time ago I was working with a teacher to identify children in her class who might benefit from additional instruction in long division. She named several students

---

APPLICATION 9.5
Mathematical Problem Solving

Teachers use various ways to help students improve problem-solving skills. As students solve mathematical word problems, they can state each problem in their own words, draw a sketch, decide what information is relevant, and state the ways they might solve the problem. Kathy Stone could use these and other similar questions to help focus her third-grade students' attention on important task aspects and guide their thinking:

- What information is important?
- What information is missing?
- Which formulas are necessary?
- What is the first thing to do?

and said that Tim also might qualify but she was not sure. Some days he worked his problems correctly, whereas other days his work was incorrect and made no sense. I gave him problems to solve and asked him to verbalize aloud while working because I was interested in what children thought about while they solved problems. This is how Tim began the first problem:

The problem is 17 divided into 436. I start on the side of the problem closest to the door . . .

I then knew why on some days his work was accurate and on other days it was not. It depended on which side of his body was closest to the door!

As noted in Chapter 7, the process of constructing knowledge begins in the preschool years (Resnick, 1989). Geary (1995) distinguished *biologically primary* (biologically based) from *biologically secondary* (culturally taught) *abilities*. Biologically primary abilities are grounded in neurobiological systems that have evolved in particular ecological and social niches and that serve functions related to survival or reproduction. In humans, these neurocognitive systems can be co-opted for tasks unrelated to their original evolution-based function. Thus, people have evolved neurocognitive systems that are sensitive to features of the three-dimensional physical universe (Shepard, 1994). Consequently, we have developed the capacity to create art in three dimensions. Another example of co-opting may be seen in Euclidean geometry, where the co-optation is of knowledge inherent in understanding of habitat navigation. Map-like environmental representations are used by many species, and the underlying neurocognitive systems seem responsive to Euclidean features of the (three-dimensional) physical universe (Geary, 1995).

Biologically primary abilities should be seen cross-culturally, whereas biologically secondary abilities show greater cultural specificity (e.g., as a function of schooling). Furthermore, many of the former should be seen in very young children. Geary (1995) contends that mathematics-related play may help to develop primary abilities. Play is found across cultures, and preschoolers often engage in play that involves numerical activities such as counting. Indeed, counting is a natural activity that is seen in preschoolers without direct teaching (Gelman & Gallistel, 1978; Resnick, 1985). Even infants may be sensitive to different properties of numbers (Geary, 1995). Preschoolers show increasing numerical competence involving the concepts of part-whole additivity and changes as increases/decreases in quantities.

Conceptual change proceeds quickly during the elementary school years (Resnick, 1989). That children construct mathematical procedures is seen in invented algorithms. Not surprisingly, children have differing amounts of difficulty comprehending story problems. Those easiest to comprehend are those that match their emerging capabilities. "Change" stories are relatively easy, especially when the quantity being asked for is the result of the increase/decrease. The problem is much harder when the unknown is the starting amount (Resnick, 1989), which indicates that children understand part-whole relations. Teaching children to use schematic diagrams to represent story problems facilitates problem solving (Fuson & Willis, 1989).

In addition to biological tendencies and knowledge construction, mathematical competence also depends on sociocultural influence (Cobb, 1994). As discussed in Chapter 7, Vygotsky (1978) stressed the role of competent other persons in the *zone of proximal development* (*ZPD*). In contrast to the constructivist emphasis on cognitive reorganizations among individual students, sociocultural theorists advocate cultural practices—especially social interactions (Cobb, 1994). The sociocultural influence is incorporated through using activities such as peer teaching, instructional scaffolding, and apprenticeships. Results of a meta-analysis of the literature by Springer, Stanne, and Donovan (1999) showed that small-group learning (2–10 student collaborative/cooperative groups) significantly raised college students' achievement in mathematics and science. Coordination of the constructivist and sociocultural perspectives is possible; for example, students develop knowledge through social interactions but then idiosyncratically construct uses of that knowledge.

Individual Differences

Much has been written in recent years on gender and ethnic differences in mathematical achievement (Byrnes, 1996; Meece, 2002). Some evidence shows that boys tend to outperform girls and that Asian Americans and White Americans do better than African Americans and Hispanic Americans; however, the literature is complex, often contradictory, and not subject to easy interpretation.

With respect to gender, male students outperform female students on the mathematics portion of the Scholastic Assessment Test (SAT) by roughly 40 points (Royer et al., 1999); a similar result is obtained on the American College Test (ACT). Boys seem to perform better on problem solving if the students either are older than age 14 or gifted, whereas girls perform better on computations when the students are younger than age 15 and when the test requires knowing whether the students have sufficient information to solve the problems and the students are gifted (Becker, 1990; Byrnes, 1996). Royer et al. (1999) found that among higher-performing students boys displayed faster mathematical fact retrieval than did girls. Nonetheless, girls typically earn better mathematics grades than boys (Meece, 2002).

Ethnic differences in mathematical achievement are more consistent and pronounced. Based on several research studies, experts draw the following conclusions (Byrnes, 1996):

- White American students perform better than African American and Hispanic American students.
- Asian American students perform better than White Americans.
- Researchers find no significant difference in mathematical achievement between African American and Hispanic American students.

A few caveats are in order. A confounding factor is socioeconomic status (SES); Stevenson, Chen, and Uttal (1990) found that differences between White American, African American, and Hispanic American students disappeared when SES was taken into account. Regardless of ethnicity, mathematics achievement bears a significant and positive relation to SES. Second, differences are most pronounced for formal (curriculum-based) mathematics achievement (Byrnes, 1996). Researchers find little evidence for ethnic differences in children's informal (constructed) knowledge. These findings are consistent with Geary's (1995) contention that biologically primary abilities should be evident across cultures whereas biologically secondary abilities are more susceptible to cultural influence.

Other variables that have been shown to influence mathematical achievement are school transitions and motivation. Anderman (1998) studied adolescents with learning disabilities and found higher achievement among those who did not make a transition until the ninth grade compared with students who made an earlier transition. School transitions can lead to declines in motivation and achievement (see Chapter 10), and they seem especially problematic for students with learning problems.

Motivational variables (Chapter 8) have been implicated as causes of mathematical performance (Meece, 2002; Schutz, Drogosz, White, & DiStefano, 1998). Among sixth graders, Vermeer, Boekaerts, and Seegers (2000) found that girls reported lower perceived competence (i.e., self-efficacy) than boys on applied problem solving and were more likely to attribute poor performance to low ability and high task difficulty (attributions to uncontrollable variables). Goal setting (McNeil & Alibali, 2000) and self-efficacy enhancing interventions (Schunk & Ertmer, 2000) are effective for promoting motivation in mathematics.

SCIENCE

We now turn to the fourth content domain: science. Much current research in scientific domains compares novices with experts to identify the components of expertise. Researchers also are investigating implicit theories and reasoning processes that students use during activities involving problem solving and learning (Voss et al., 1995; C. Zimmerman, 2000). Let us begin by discussing expert-novice differences in knowledge and strategies.

Expert-Novice Differences

Experts in scientific domains differ from novices in quantity and organization of knowledge. Experts possess more domain-specific knowledge and are more likely to organize it in hierarchies, whereas novices often demonstrate little overlap between scientific concepts.

In the Chi et al. (1981) study, novices classified physics problems based on superficial features (e.g., apparatus); experts classified the problems based on the principle needed to solve the problem. Experts and novices also differed in declarative knowledge memory networks. "Inclined plane," for example, was related in novices' memories with descriptive terms such as "mass," "friction," and "length." Experts had these descriptors in their memories, but in addition had stored principles of mechanics (e.g., conservation of energy, Newton's force laws). The experts' greater knowledge (in terms of principles) was organized with descriptors subordinate to principles.

Novices often use principles erroneously to solve problems. McCloskey and Kaiser (1984) posed the following question to college students:

> A train is speeding over a bridge that spans a valley. As the train rolls along, a passenger leans out of a window and drops a rock. Where will it land?

Figure 9.3
Possible answers to falling rock problem.

About one-third of the students said the rock would fall straight down (Figure 9.3). They believed that an object pushed or thrown acquires a force but that an object being carried by a moving vehicle does not acquire a force, so it drops straight down. The analogy the students made was with a person standing still who drops an object, which falls straight down. The path of descent of the rock from the moving train is, however, parabolic. The idea that objects acquire force is erroneous because objects move in the same direction and at the same speed as their moving carriers. When the rock is dropped, it continues to move forward with the train until the force of gravity pulls it down. Novices overgeneralized their basic knowledge and arrived at an erroneous solution.

Another difference between novices and experts concerns the use of *problem-solving strategies* (Larkin, 1980; Larkin, McDermott, Simon, & Simon, 1980; White & Tisher, 1986). When confronted with scientific problems, novices often use a means-ends analysis, determining the goal of the problem and deciding which formulas might be useful to reach that goal. They work backward and recall formulas containing quantities in the target formula. If they become uncertain how to proceed, they may abandon the problem or attempt to solve it based on their current knowledge.

As is the case in mathematics, experts quickly recognize the problem format, work forward toward intermediate subgoals, and use that information to reach the ultimate goal. Experience in working scientific problems builds knowledge of problem types. Experts often automatically recognize familiar problem features and carry out necessary productions. Even when they are less certain how to solve a problem, experts begin with some information given in the problem and work forward to the solution. Notice that the last step experts take is often novices' first step. Klahr and Simon (1999) contended that the process of scientific discovery is a form of problem solving and that the general heuristic approach is much the same across domains.

Reasoning

Reasoning refers to the mental processes involved in generating and evaluating logical arguments (Anderson, 1990). Reasoning yields a conclusion from thoughts, percepts, and assertions (Johnson-Laird, 1999), and involves working through problems to explain why something happened or what will happen (Hunt, 1989). Reasoning skills include clarification, basis, inference, and evaluation (Ennis, 1987; Quellmalz, 1987; Table 9.1 and Application 9.6).

Clarification. *Clarification* requires identifying and formulating questions, analyzing elements, and defining terms. These skills involve determining which elements in a situation are important, what they mean, and how they are related. At times, scientific questions are posed, but at other times students must develop questions such as "What is the problem, hypothesis, or thesis?" Clarification corresponds to the representation phase of problem solving; students define the problem to obtain a clear mental representation. Little productive reasoning occurs without a clear problem statement.

Table 9.1
Reasoning skills.

Skill	Definition	Sample Questions
Clarification	Identifying and formulating questions, analyzing elements, defining terms	"What do I know?" "What do I need to figure out?"
Basis	Determining source(s) of support for conclusions about a problem	"Is this a fact or opinion?" "What is the source of this information?"
Inference	Reasoning inductively from specific cases to general principles or deductively from general principles to specific cases	"What do these diverse examples have in common?" (Induction) "How can I apply these general rules to this example?" (Deduction)
Evaluation	Using criteria to judge adequacy of a problem solution	"Do I need more information?" "Is my conclusion reasonable?"

APPLICATION 9.6
Reasoning

Teachers can teach students how to ask questions to produce an accurate mental representation of a problem. A teacher might give primary students objects to classify according to shape. To help students identify and clarify the problem the teacher could ask questions such as:

- What have you been asked to do?
- What items do you have?
- What are some of the shapes you know?
- Does it matter if the items are different colors?
- Does it matter if some of the items are little and some are big?
- Does it matter if some of the items are soft and some are hard?
- What do you think you will do with the items you have?

Students verbalize what information they need to use and what they are supposed to do with that information. Each time the teacher works with students in solving a problem, the teacher can help them generate questions to determine what information is important for solving the problem.

A medical researcher working with a group of interns gives them an "unknown" virus to identify. To assist the students in the identification process, the instructor might generate a list of questions similar to the following:

- What effect does the virus have on blood cells?
- What effect does the virus have on human tissue?
- How quickly does the virus appear to grow, and under what conditions does it grow?
- What does the virus do when exposed to warmth?
- What does the virus do when exposed to cold?
- What does the virus do when exposed to moisture?
- What does the virus do in an airtight environment?
- What reaction does the virus have when exposed to various drugs?

Basis. People's conclusions about a problem are supported by information from personal observations, statements by others, and previous inferences. Judging the credibility of a source is important. In so doing, one must distinguish between fact, opinion, and reasoned judgment. Assume that a suspect armed with a gun is apprehended near the scene of a murder. That the suspect had a gun when arrested is a fact. Laboratory tests on the gun, the bullets, and the victim lead to the reasoned judgment that the gun was used in the crime. Someone investigating the case might be of the opinion that the suspect is the murderer.

Inference.   Scientific reasoning proceeds inductively or deductively. *Induction* is the process whereby general rules, principles, and concepts are developed from observation and knowledge of specific examples (Pellegrino, 1985). It requires determination of a model and its associated rules of inference (Hunt, 1989). People reason inductively when they extract similarities and differences among specific objects and events and arrive at generalizations, which are tested by applying them to new experiences. Individuals retain their generalizations as long as they are effective, and they modify them when they experience conflicting evidence.

Some of the more common types of tasks used to assess inductive reasoning are *classification, concept,* and *analogy problems.* Consider the following analogy (Pellegrino, 1985):

sugar : sweet :: lemon : _____
yellow sour fruit squeeze tea

The appropriate mental operations represent a type of production system. Initially, the learner mentally represents critical attributes of each term in the analogy. She activates networks in LTM involving each term, which contain critical attributes of the terms to include subordinate and superordinate concepts. Next, she compares the features of the first pair to determine the link. "Sweet" is a property of sugar that involves taste. She then searches the "lemon" network to determine which of the five features listed corresponds in meaning to "lemon" as "sweet" does to "sugar." Although all five terms are most likely stored in her "lemon" network, only "sour" directly involves taste.

Children begin to display basic inductive reasoning ability around age 8. With development, children can reason faster and with more complex material. This occurs because their LTM networks become more complex and better linked, which in turn reduces the burden on the WM. To help foster inductive thinking, teachers might use a guided discovery approach, in which children learn different examples and try to formulate a general rule. For example, children may collect leaves and formulate some general principles involving stems, veins, sizes, and shapes of leaves from different trees. *Discovery learning* (Bruner, 1960; see Chapter 6) can enhance inductive thinking. To use this method, the teacher might pose a problem for students, such as "Why does metal sink in water but metal ships float?" Rather than tell students how to solve the problem, the teacher might provide materials and encourage them to formulate and test hypotheses as they work on the task. (See Phye, 1997, for a discussion of effective teaching methods and programs that have been used to teach inductive reasoning to students.)

Deduction is the process of applying inference rules to a formal model of a problem to decide whether specific instances logically follow. When individuals reason deductively, they proceed from general concepts (premises) to specific instances (conclusions) to determine whether the latter follow from the former. A deduction is valid if the premises are true and if the conclusion follows logically from the premises (Johnson-Laird, 1985, 1999).

Linguistic and deductive reasoning processes are intimately linked (Falmagne & Gonsalves, 1995; Polk & Newell, 1995). One type of deduction problem is the *three-term series* (Johnson-Laird, 1972). For example,

If Karen is taller than Tina, and
If Mary Beth is not as tall as Tina, then
Who is the tallest?

The problem-solving processes employed with this problem are similar to those discussed previously. Initially one forms a mental representation of the problem, such as K > T, MB < T. One then works forward by combining the propositions (K > T > MB) to solve the problem. Developmental factors limit children's proficiency in solving such problems. Children may have difficulty keeping relevant problem information in WM and may not understand the language used to express the relationships.

Another type of deductive reasoning problem is the *syllogism*. Syllogisms are characterized by premises and a conclusion containing the words *all, no,* and *some.* The following are sample premises:

All university professors are lazy.
Some graduate students are not lazy.
No undergraduate student is lazy.

A sample syllogism is as follows:

All the students in Ken's class are good in math.
All students who are good in math will attend college.
(Therefore) All the students in Ken's class will attend college.

Researchers debate what mental processes people use to solve syllogisms, including whether people represent the information as Venn (circle) diagrams or as strings of propositions (Johnson-Laird, 1985). A production system analysis of syllogisms gives a basic rule: A syllogism is true only if there is no way to interpret the premises to imply the opposite of the conclusion; that is, a syllogism is true unless an exception to the conclusion can be found. Research needs to examine the types of rules people apply to test whether the premises of a syllogism allow an exception.

Research also is needed on the mechanisms of the deductive reasoning process. Three major views have been proposed (Johnson-Laird, Byrne, & Tabossi, 1989). One view holds that reasoning proceeds on the basis of formal rules of inference. People learn the rules (e.g., the *modus ponens* rule governs "if p then q" statements) and then match instances to the rules. A second, related view postulates content-specific rules. They may be expressed as productions such that specific instances trigger the production rules. Thus, a production may involve all cars, and may be triggered when a specific car ("my brand X") is encountered.

A third view holds that reasoning depends on semantic procedures that search for interpretations of the premises that are counterexamples to conclusions. According to this view, people construct one or more mental models for the assertions they encounter (interpretations of the premises); the models differ in structure and are used to test the logic of the situation. Students may repeatedly re-encode the problem based on information; thus, deduction largely is a form of verbal reasoning (Polk & Newell, 1995). Johnson-Laird and colleagues (Johnson-Laird, 1999; Johnson-Laird, Byrne, & Schaeken, 1992; Johnson-Laird et al., 1989) have extended this semantic analysis to various classes of inferences (e.g., those involving *if, or, and, not,* and multiple quantifiers). Further research also will help determine instructional implications of these theoretical analyses.

Evaluation.   *Evaluation* involves using criteria to judge the adequacy of a problem solution. In evaluating, students address questions such as, "Are the data sufficient to solve the problem?", "Do I need more information?", and "Are my conclusions based on facts, opinions, or reasoned judgments?" Evaluation also involves deciding what ought to happen next—that is, formulating hypotheses about future events, assuming that one's problem solving is correct so far.

Metacognitive processes enter into all aspects of scientific reasoning. Learners monitor their efforts to ensure that questions are properly posed, that data from adequate sources are available and used to draw inferences, and that relevant criteria are employed in evaluation. Teaching reasoning requires instruction in skills and in metacognitive strategies.

Deductive reasoning also can be affected by content apart from the logic. Wason (1966) put four cards (A B 2 3) in front of participants. They were told that each card contained a letter on one side and a number on the other, and they were given a conditional rule: "If a card has A on one side, then it has 2 on the other." Their task was to select the cards that needed to be turned over to determine whether the rule was true. Although most participants picked the A card and many also chose the 2, few picked the 3; however, it must be turned over because if there is an A on the other side, then the rule is false. When the content was changed to an everyday generalization (e.g., letter = hair color, number = eye color, A = blond hair, 2 = blue eyes), most people made the correct selections (Wason & Johnson-Laird, 1972). These results speak to the importance of not assuming generalization in reasoning but rather giving students experience working on different types of content.

Constructivism and Scientific Beliefs

The core concept of constructivism—that knowledge is built by learners rather than simply transmitted among persons—is shared by many researchers and science educators (Driver et al., 1994). One tradition concerns personal theories and the conceptions of phenomena that students develop during environmental interactions. An interesting issue is how students develop scientific misconceptions. From an instructional perspective, an important task is to help students reorganize their theories by challenging and correcting misconceptions (Sandoval, 1995). A second constructivist tradition focuses on the role of mentors and apprenticeships in the development of scientific knowledge. Other traditions examine how knowledge evolves from the interaction of students' beliefs with classroom instructional practices and from the process of enculturating students into scientific discourse and practices. Finally, many educators are concerned with *scientific literacy*, which, depending on how it is defined, could involve: (a) understanding the foundations, current status, and many problems in the life and physical sciences, or (b) understanding (and possibly reciting) technical definitions of phenomena (Shamos, 1988).

Recall the earlier discussion of learning as a mental process that involves conceptual change (Chapter 5). Piaget (see Chapter 10) postulated that change originates from disequilibrium and modifications of knowledge. From a constructivist perspective, teaching to encourage cognitive conflict (and thereby promote learning) involves providing students with experiences that produce conflict and help them resolve it (Sandoval, 1995; Williams & Tolmie, 2000). Much science instruction focuses on helping students confront and change misconceptions (Mayer, 1999). This might entail having students engage in hands-on activities and work with others (e.g., in discussions) to interpret their experiences through selective questioning (e.g., "Why do you think that?", "How did you figure that?"). This approach fits well with the Vygotskian emphasis on social influences on knowledge construction (Chapter 7).

According to Driver et al. (1994):

> Learning science is not a matter of simply extending young people's knowledge of phenomena—a practice perhaps more appropriately called nature study—nor of developing and organizing young people's commonsense reasoning. It requires more than challenging learners' prior ideas through discrepant events. Learning science involves young people entering into a different way of thinking about and explaining the natural world; becoming socialized to a greater or lesser extent into the practices of the scientific community with its particular purposes, ways of seeing, and ways of supporting its knowledge claims. (p. 8)

Before they can become socialized into the discourse practices of the scientific community, students must engage in personal construction and meaning making. The socialization does not require them to abandon commonsense reasoning. They still will have available these ideas, which often are effective because many scientific phenomena reflect commonsense reasoning. Rather than switch from one theory to another, developing scientific literacy involves knowing what theories are and how they become articulated. This process becomes more refined with development (Byrnes, 1996; Williams & Affleck, 1999).

Nussbaum and Novick (1982) proposed a three-stage model for changing student beliefs:

- Reveal and understand student preconceptions.
- Create conceptual conflict with those conceptions.
- Facilitate the development of new or revised schemata about the phenomena under consideration.

Application 9.7 offers some suggestions for addressing scientific beliefs in the classroom.

Finally, the role of *motivation* is important in science learning as in other content areas. Although science has many themes that ought to be interesting, studying science holds little interest for many students. Teachers are wise to use hands-on instruction and link it to aspects of students' lives. For example, motion can be linked to the path of soccer balls, electricity to CD players, and ecology to natural environments in the community. Enhancing interest in topics also can improve the quality of student learning (Sandoval, 1995). Thus, using illustrations helps students to

APPLICATION 9.7
Changing Scientific Misconceptions

From prior learning students come to new situations with general and specific knowledge that can interfere with new learning. Particularly in the area of science other learning may impede progress. Teachers can help students by designing activities that will reveal students' preconceptions, create conceptual conflict with those preconceptions, and facilitate the development of new learning.

As middle school students begin working for the first time with unknown chemicals, they may become very confused. The science teacher might hold up a beaker that contains a blue-colored liquid and a beaker with a yellow-colored liquid and begin to combine these liquids into a larger container. Due to prior learning as it relates to color combinations, the students assume the liquid will change to green, but instead the combined liquid turns bright pink. The students are perplexed, and the teacher begins the first lesson on properties of various chemicals and their reactions to being combined with other chemicals.

understand scientific concepts (Hannus & Hyönä, 1999), although effects are most pronounced for high-ability children. Students may need to be taught how to study illustrations as part of text learning.

SOCIAL STUDIES

The final content domain we examine is social studies, which Byrnes (1996) defines as follows:

> The social studies consist of an interrelated set of topics related to the history, environment, economics, lifestyles, and governments of peoples who live in this and other regions of the world. (p. 206)

The social studies typically are viewed as comprising history, geography, civics, and political science; economics, psychology, and sociology also may be included. The boundaries for social studies are rather porous, and in school curricula social studies typically encompass education for citizenship (Seixas, 2001).

Relative to the other content domains discussed in this chapter, less research has been conducted in social studies; however, that situation is changing as researchers increasingly are conducting studies related to teaching and learning. Given the breadth of the field, no attempt is made here to discuss learning in all disciplines. Interested readers should consult other sources (Armento, 1986; Byrnes, 1996; Wineburg, 1996). This section discusses history and geography, which are central to the K–12 curriculum.

History

Although many people think of history as learning facts, much more than that is included in its study. Educators want students to know not only what happened but also why it happened, why it was significant, and how it fits into a larger chronology of events. These types of learning require that students be able to (Byrnes, 1996):

- Order events in time.
- Understand causal relations among events.
- Realize that historians do not simply report events but rather interpret them.

Let us consider these in turn.

Learning Processes.   The ability to *order events in time* shows a developmental progression. Beginning at approximately age 2, children understand the difference between the past and present; however, children's conception of the past is much different from ours (Friedman, 1990). Given children's brief histories, their pasts are not well differentiated. The distinction between the immediate past and the distant past may be clouded.

By age 6 or 7 children can correctly order seasons and holidays, days of the week, and months of the year (Friedman, 1990). This capability improves with development; thus, attempts to teach history as a timeline to young children may be unsuccessful. Schools typically take this into account by focusing early social studies instruction on understanding of neighborhoods and communities. Systematic history instruction generally does not begin until the fifth grade (Byrnes, 1996).

Children's history learning is aided by hands-on activities such as visits to museums and historic venues. Role playing also is encouraged. For example, Kathy Stone may teach a unit on Abraham Lincoln by having the children read a book and watch a video. After this, children might be assigned parts and put on a class play (in period costumes) about some aspect of Lincoln's life.

Understanding causality is difficult for most students. A common problem is that they tend to simplify causes and attribute outcomes to personal motives and preceding actions, when in fact the causes of most significant historical events are complex. When historical causes are not provided in texts, children often simplify them to simple associations between events.

Chapter 8 discussed *attributions*, or perceived causes of actions. Attribution research shows that children's causal thinking prior to approximately age 7 or 8 is very basic and that they do not distinguish inner qualities well. Thus, children may believe that someone who is smarter may perform better but may equate "smartness" with "effort" (i.e., the one who works hard also is smart). Differentiation of attributions begins in the later elementary years and continues through adolescence (Nicholls, 1978, 1979).

Understanding that *historians select and interpret events* also is difficult for children because they tend to believe that one reality exists and that when two persons observe the same event they will report it in the same way (Byrnes, 1996). Full understanding of multiple interpretations may not become evident until college age or later.

To help foster the understanding of different perspectives, teachers might have students write their observations of an event and then read these aloud. Children will see how students reported the same event differently. Byrnes (1996) suggests that children act as judges for a display and their ratings then be compared, which will show how children's ratings of the same display do not agree.

Conceptual Change. As with other domains, students often bring misconceptions to history learning. These misconceptions serve as a core through which new information is filtered. For example, Sinatra, Beck, and McKeown (1992) interviewed fifth graders to determine what they understood about history. Even after a year of instruction, students demonstrated poor understanding of significant events. The majority of students did not link the American Revolution with Great Britain. Students' historical knowledge often was intertwined with other significant events (e.g., the Declaration of Independence linked with the freeing of slaves).

Conceptual change also requires that students be taught to use effective problem-solving strategies. Wineburg (1996) reports that historians use three strategies to evaluate historical documents:

- *Corroboration*: Comparing details of a document to others
- *Contextualization*: Situating events in the document in concrete contexts
- *Sourcing*: Evaluating the authors of a document for their fairness and accuracy prior to analyzing the document

These strategies are used infrequently by high school students. Rather, even older students view documents as a form of conveying information that should be added to their current knowledge. In short, students' trust of historical documents results in their integrating new information with their existing knowledge.

This type of expert-novice research is illuminating and suggests that teachers can work with students to teach skills of historical analysis. Researchers found some evidence that having students critically question historical material can foster conceptual change (Armento, 1986; Wineburg, 1996). Application 9.8 offers some applications of history and geography learning in classrooms.

Geography

Geography can cover many types of skills, including map reading and interpretation, identifying major landforms and bodies of water, and locating major cultural regions, political groups, and natural resources (Farrell & Cirrincione, 1989). Teachers—especially at the elementary level—consider map skills and locations to be the most important, and these are emphasized in the curriculum. These are addressed in turn.

Map Skills. Proficiency in map reading requires competence in several subskills including (Byrnes, 1996):

- Recognizing and differentiating among symbols used in maps.
- Understanding that these symbols have three-dimensional counterparts in real life.

APPLICATION 9.8
History and Geography

A way to assist students with analyzing historical information is to have them compare various sources. Jim Marshall might have his ninth-grade American history students take a famous speech given by a president or member of Congress and relate it to the actual events taking place at that time. The students have an opportunity then to analyze the contents of the speech and determine whether the facts were accurate. This helps students in evaluating the document.

Geography skills are often learned best if teachers go beyond just locating specific items on maps to relating map skills to another subject area or to a meaningful task. Kathy Stone asks each student in her third-grade class to pick a state (other than the one they live in) that they believe could attract new residents because of the geographic attributes of that state. Then she asks students to create a poster depicting the most important attributes of that state. Somewhere on the poster students will put a map of the state they selected.

■ Projecting the spatial arrangements of map symbols onto the physical world.
■ Using maps even when they are not aligned with the user's perspective.

By the time children enter kindergarten they possess some basic map reading skills. For example, if given a map of a room with the location of an object shown on it, most children are able to locate the object in the room. They have greater difficulty if they are shown the object in the room and asked to indicate its location on the map. Maps rotated away from children's perspective also cause difficulty in interpretation. These skills develop during the elementary years (Byrnes, 1996).

In part this skill acquisition is aided by the development of children's spatial abilities (Liben & Downs, 1993). Children's early experience with map reading can assist skill learning. Using realistic symbols on maps (e.g., a square representing a building rather than a dot) is helpful, along with giving children practice in mentally rotating maps. Verdi and Kulhavy (2002) summarized research showing that map features along the edge or on interior lines are learned better than those elsewhere in the interior and that viewing a map prior to reading a text leads to better learning than the reverse order. Proper map construction and sequencing of instruction can play critical roles in geography learning.

Identifying Locations.   Much has been written about the poor geography identification knowledge of school children, despite the fact that teachers consider such knowledge important. Youngsters in the United States have fared badly on tests assessing knowledge of locations of countries (U.S. Department of Education, 1990). Although location knowledge improves with schooling, even college students are remarkably uninformed about locations.

Using imagery is an effective means of assisting location skills (see Chapter 4). For example, teachers can link countries with particular shapes and ask children to imagine those shapes (e.g., Italy in the shape of a boot). The section in Chapter 5 on self-regulation discusses memory strategies, and many of these are helpful. Acronyms and initialisms can be used; the west-to-east configuration of Norway-Sweden-Finland can be remembered with the initialism "NSF," which also stands for "National Science Foundation."

Another way to improve learning of locations is to integrate geography with other content areas, especially history. Thus, Switzerland's location between the major powers of World War II is easy to remember when this knowledge is linked with information about its neutrality in that war. Similarly, Panama's location can be remembered when students understand that this is the narrowest land mass between the Atlantic and Pacific Oceans.

SUMMARY

Developing competence within an academic domain requires a strong knowledge of the facts, principles, and concepts of that domain, coupled with generic learning strategies that can be applied across domains and that may need to be modified for each domain. Research reveals many differences between experts and novices. Experts possess more domain-specific knowledge organized to reflect the underlying structure of the content. Experts form a more accurate problem representation and usually work forward from the givens to reach the goal. Novices often adopt a working backward strategy. Experts and novices do not seem to differ in their knowledge of problem-solving strategies.

Language comprehension requires perception, parsing, and utilization. People parse language in ways that reflect their deep mental structures. They construct a context and fill in the elements as they comprehend them. Experts have more fully developed mental representations of situations. Utilization requires listeners to determine the function of the communication: to inform, to request, to command, and so forth. Speakers and listeners may operate according to a given-new contract.

Reading involves decoding and comprehension. Decoding proceeds in top-down and bottom-up fashion. Novices use much bottom-up processing, but as skill develops, learners construct a mental representation of the context and develop expectations about what will appear in print. Experts rely on top-down processing, much of which occurs automatically. Text is comprehended when it activates meanings in LTM. Inferential comprehension is aided when schemata are activated and learners implement productions to fill in slots with information acquired from text. Metacognitive processes assist students' comprehension. Strategy instruction helps students learn to monitor their text understanding.

Writing requires composition and reviewing. Expert writers plan text around a goal of communicating meaning. They generate more ideas and link them better than novices. Experts also keep their goal in mind during reviewing. Novices write by putting down what they can recall about a topic. They focus on what to write next rather than keeping their goal in mind. Although components of writing may become automatic, writing proficiency requires thoughtful consideration of goals, translation, and revising.

Children display early mathematical competence with counting. Computational skills require algorithms and declarative knowledge; deficient procedural or declarative knowledge leads to computational difficulties. Students often overgeneralize procedures, which results in buggy algorithms. In problem solving, students acquire knowledge of problem types through task experience. Experts readily recognize the problem type and apply the appropriate production to solve the problem. They work forward through the solution. Novices work backward by applying formulas that include quantities given in the problem. The sciences involve similar strategies. In mathematics and science, learners seem to construct a great deal of their knowledge based on their environmental interactions. A key skill in reasoning is drawing inferences. Expertise in induction and deduction reflects the application of rule-based productions.

The social studies are composed of a diverse set of content areas, including history, geography, civics, political science, economics, psychology, and sociology. History learning requires developing knowledge about what happened, why it happened, and why it was significant. History subskills include ordering events in time, understanding causality, and realizing that historians interpret events as they report them. Development is important, and effective teaching incorporates role playing and hands-on activities. Geography includes map reading and knowledge of locations. Students must be able to recognize symbols, understand that these correspond to physical reality, and realign themselves with a map's perspective. Spatial ability is critical, but teachers can aid learning by having students use imagery and strategies and by integrating geography across the curriculum.

10

Development and Learning

This chapter discusses human development and its relation to learning. *Development* refers to changes over time that follow an orderly pattern and enhance survival (Meece, 2002). These changes are progressive (rather than sudden) and occur over the course of the life span (rather than at only one point in time).

Development is an important educational topic, although it often is taken for granted. In earlier chapters several learning principles were explained; however, these do not exist in a vacuum. Each principle of learning could be prefaced with, "Assuming proper level of development . . ." For example, in discussing the formation of memory networks, we noted that students link information in memory. The capability to do this improves with development. Older students have more extensive memory networks and can make connections that younger students cannot.

Development is intimately linked with learning. In Chapter 1, learning was defined as relatively permanent changes in an individual due to experiences, and we contrasted these changes with those arising from maturation. Both learning and maturation may be thought of as components of development. At any given time, developmental level places constraints on learning possibilities: the what, where, when, why, and how of learning. This chapter focuses on cognitive development because this is most relevant to learning; however, other types of development (e.g., physical, social, emotional, and moral) can affect learning.

Many developmental theories postulate that cognitive development involves *construction* of knowledge as a function of the individual's experiences (see Chapter 7). This contrasts with the view that knowledge is received passively from the environment and processed without substantially altering its form. Constructivist principles also are inherent in principles of content-area learning (Chapter 9).

This chapter begins with material on the historical and philosophical foundations of the scientific study of development to include the important contributions of the Child Study Movement. Various theoretical perspectives on development are explained with an emphasis on cognitive and constructivist perspectives. The theories of Piaget and Bruner are covered, along with contemporary developmental research on cognitive processes. The related topics of developmentally appropriate instruction and transitions in schooling are addressed. Separate sections are included on familial influences, brain development, motivation, and development and instruction.

When you finish studying this chapter, you should be able to do the following:

■ Describe the major influences leading to the scientific study of human development.

■ State some of the major contributions and shortcomings of the Child Study Movement.

■ Explain developmental issues relevant to learning and major perspectives on human development.

- Compare and contrast structural and functional accounts of development.

- Summarize the major processes in Piaget's theory that are involved in learning and some implications for instruction.

- Describe the types of knowledge representation proposed by Bruner and what is meant by the "spiral curriculum."

- Discuss some major changes in cognitive information processing that occur during development.

- Explain what is meant by developmentally appropriate instruction and why transitions in schooling affect learning and teaching.

- Discuss the relation of socioeconomic status, home environment, and parental involvement to development and learning.

- Summarize major developmental changes in brain structures and their links to cognitive learning.

- Describe developmental changes in motivation and their implications for learning.

- Explain Case's developmental instruction model and the role of teacher-student interactions in learning.

BEGINNINGS OF THE SCIENTIFIC STUDY OF DEVELOPMENT

The beginnings of the scientific study of human development are deeply rooted in history and philosophy. Let us examine these in turn.

Historical Foundations

Educators acknowledge the influence of development on teaching and learning, but this has not always been the case. During the 1800s, life in the United States and the role of children in society were very different than they are today (Mondale & Patton, 2001). Despite the guarantees of the U.S. Constitution, education was not universal but rather pursued mostly by children of middle- and upper-class families. Many children—especially those from rural and working-class backgrounds—worked to earn money or otherwise helped to support their families. These children attended school sporadically and many quit at young ages. At the elementary level, the major goal was to teach reading; the "3 Rs" had not yet become standard. Secondary schools were largely preparatory schools for the universities, which were oriented toward the humanities and religion.

The period between the Civil War and World War I, known as the Industrial Revolution, is widely hailed for significant progress, but life was harsh. Economic conditions created an underclass, despite many people working long hours 6 days per week. Inadequate sanitary conditions gave rise to the spread of diseases in large cities.

School masters were strict and lessons often were long and boring. Children were expected to study and learn; if they failed to learn, they (and not society, parents, or teachers) were held responsible. Individualized instruction was nonexistent; all students worked on the same lesson at the same time. School masters lectured and held recitations. They were trained in school subjects, not pedagogy.

Into this picture entered scores of immigrants to the United States, especially between 1880 and 1920. This vast influx necessitated major increases in numbers of schools and teachers. Normal schools and universities were not equipped to produce large numbers of high-quality teachers. Normal schools were the major source of teacher preparation, but increasingly they were perceived as inadequate, especially for the preparation of secondary teachers (Davidson & Benjamin, 1987). In the latter half of the nineteenth century, schools of education were established in greater numbers at major colleges and universities. The challenge was to train teachers to deal with large numbers of students from diverse backgrounds.

Philosophical Foundations

The writings of educational philosophers and critics also helped to establish the scientific study of development and improvement of education. A number of European philosophers, including Rousseau, Pestalozzi, and Froebel, wrote extensively about the nature of children. As their writings became better known in the United States, educators and others increasingly questioned whether U.S. education was appropriate for students.

Rousseau (1712–1778) believed that children were basically good and that the purpose of education was to help develop this propensity. Teachers should establish one-to-one relationships with students (i.e., tutor/tutee) and consider their individual needs and talents in arranging learning activities. Above all, learning should be satisfying and self-directed; children should learn from hands-on experience and not be forced to learn.

Pestalozzi (1746–1827) emphasized that education should be for everyone and that learning should be self-directed rather than rote, which was the dominant style of learning at the time in U.S. schools. Pestalozzi stressed the emotional development of students, which could be enhanced through close relationships between teachers and learners.

Froebel (1782–1852) believed that children were basically good and needed to be nurtured starting at an early age. He founded the *kindergarten* ("garden for children"), which reflected his belief that children—like young plants—needed to be nurtured.

Recall the Chapter 1 discussion of how psychology underwent a transformation beginning at the end of the nineteenth century from a branch of philosophy to a science of its own. A similar transformation occurred in education. The emergence of psychology, writings on the goodness of children and the need for their nurturing, and pressure for the education of all children triggered by large numbers of immigrants— along with other influences (e.g., social Darwinism, compulsory attendance laws)— led to a call for the scientific study of children. By the end of the nineteenth century:

> Immigration and industrialization heightened the need for schooling, the increasing enrollment of students sparked a demand from parents and teachers for information about how to teach children; the social Darwinists and individual difference psychologists wanted to know about how adult differences started, and the child welfare workers wanted help in planning programs to help children. The Child Study Movement attempted to meet these diverse needs. (Davidson & Benjamin, 1987, p. 46)

We now turn to a discussion of the Child Study Movement.

The Child Study Movement

Hall's Work.   The generally acknowledged founder of the Child Study Movement is G. (Granville) Stanley Hall (1844–1924). After receiving his doctorate from Harvard University, Hall studied in Germany for 2 years and became enamored with the German educational system and its view of the child's nature (Davidson & Benjamin, 1987). In 1882 he spoke before the National Education Association and called for child study as the core of the study of pedagogy. Subsequently he conducted a large-scale study of Boston children entering school. He administered a lengthy questionnaire designed to determine what they knew about various subjects (e.g., animals, mathematics). The results showed that children were ignorant of many features of U.S. life (e.g., 93% were unaware that leather came from animals).

As a professor of psychology at Johns Hopkins University, Hall was in prime position to establish child study as a scientific discipline. Hall (1894) stated that the new science of psychology had a natural application to education. Unfortunately, Hall did not remain active in the movement because he moved to Clark University as its president; however, he continued to speak publicly on its importance and publish extensively (Hall, 1894, 1896, 1900, 1903). Others became proponents of child study, and active centers were established in universities and normal schools.

From the outset, the Child Study Movement was broad and somewhat ill defined:

> It is a nondescript and . . . unparalleled movement—partly psychology, partly anthropology, partly medico-hygiene. It is closely related at every step to the study of instinct in animals, and to the rites and beliefs of primitive people; and it has a distinct ethico-philosophical aspect . . . with a spice of folk-lore and of religious evolution, sometimes with an alloy of gossip and nursery tradition, but possessing a broad, practical side in the pedagogy of all stages. It has all the advantages and the less grave disadvantages of its many-sidedness. (Hall, 1900, p. 689)

Despite Hall's glowing description, the broad scope of the Child Study Movement eventually contributed to its undoing.

Goals and Methods.   The need for child study was felt by teachers, parents, and others who believed that teaching and child raising would improve through proper understanding of children. A major goal of child study was to assist education (Davidson & Benjamin, 1987). Prior to the Child Study Movement, the predominant belief was that knowledge of children could be acquired by teaching. Child study advocates believed that such knowledge should be acquired prior to teaching so that education would be more successful and satisfying. "From this standpoint it is plain that the teacher must know two things: (1) the subject matter to be taught; and (2) the nature and capacity of the minds in which it is to be rooted" (Hall, 1900, p. 699). The Child Study Movement helped to establish schools of education in universities with strong ties to public schools.

Another goal was to discover knowledge that would help parenting (Davidson & Benjamin, 1987). By understanding child development, parents would be in a better position to ensure that children developed to their full potential.

Given its close link with psychology, the Child Study Movement also had a research agenda. Primarily this was to understand children better through testing. Hall developed an extensive questionnaire, and others followed suit. Other research methods used were naturalistic observations, aptitude and ability testing, and psychophysical studies of vision and perception.

Contributions.   The Child Study Movement contributed in several ways to psychology and education. One contribution was the *baby biography*, which consisted of a series of observations on a single child over a lengthy period. Baby biographies provided detailed accounts of children's actions, responses, and verbalizations, and highlighted changes in processes with development. This type of longitudinal research using naturalistic observations is common today, especially by researchers interested in infants and toddlers.

A second contribution was the use of children as research participants. The experimental methods of the new science of psychology were increasingly applied to children. The Child Study Movement helped to create the belief that children could be legitimate participants in research. As research results accumulated, they required outlets for publication and presentation; thus, new journals and professional associations were begun.

The Child Study Movement also affected teacher training. Normal schools and schools of education in universities were charged with providing high-quality preservice training so that graduates could assume teaching duties. As with other professions, teaching benefited from teacher education programs that were firmly rooted in educational theory and research.

Finally, the Child Study Movement filled an important public void. People wanted information about children and child study advocates obliged (Davidson & Benjamin, 1987). Child-care professionals, such as teachers and social workers, felt the need for more information to help them perform their jobs better. The growth in journals led to articles published on ways to teach specific school subjects. With respect to teaching methods, some of the emphasis on drills and recitations lessened as children were increasingly allowed free expression and exploration of interests (including through play). In short, the Child Study Movement had a humanizing effect on educational practice.

Critique.   Some psychologists and educators criticized the Child Study Movement because they questioned the soundness of the discipline. Although purportedly research based, many studies of children had suspect validity due to weaknesses in methods and assessment instruments. Parents and teachers often collected data. Such participatory research is common today, but in Hall's time it was opposed by many professionals because they believed that only trained experts should collect data.

Perhaps the major problem with the Child Study Movement was the same one that plagued functionalism (Chapter 1): Its focus was simply too broad to hold it together. The Child Study Movement was an amalgamation of individuals with diverse interests and agendas—researchers, practitioners, parents, child-care providers, and administrators. Because it tried to accomplish too much, it accomplished little very well. Hall's self-imposed dissociation from child study, coupled with his writings on controversial topics (e.g., corporal punishment, role of women in education), created a leadership void. The rise of behaviorism in psychology (Chapters 1 and 2) further contributed to its demise.

Nonetheless, the legacy of child study lives on in several venues, including psychology (educational, developmental, school, experimental child, and mental testing), education (early education, teacher training, physical education, and special education), and counseling (social work, vocational) (Davidson & Benjamin, 1987). As child study became more scientific, new child development centers flourished at universities.

The Child Study Movement touched many individuals who became influential in their own right. John Dewey (Chapter 1) studied with Hall at Johns Hopkins and worked with other child study advocates. Arnold Gesell (discussed later in this chapter) capitalized on child study's emphasis on normative data to produce age-related norms. Edward L. Thorndike (Chapter 1) provided a much-needed methodological sophistication to educational research and attempted to make sense out of findings of child study research studies. Thorndike continued the emphasis on the integration of learning and development (Davidson & Benjamin, 1987).

By the 1920s the Child Study Movement was no longer viable and effectively had been replaced in psychology by behaviorism. We now consider types of developmental theories that have emerged since then.

PERSPECTIVES ON HUMAN DEVELOPMENT

Many perspectives on human development exist. This section examines those that have the greatest relevance to learning. First let us consider some issues that are controversial and bear directly on learning.

Issues Relevant to Learning

Although most investigators could agree with the definition of development presented earlier, theories of development differ in many ways. Table 10.1 shows some issues that theorists disagree about and which have implications for learning (Meece, 2002; Zimmerman & Whitehurst, 1979).

Nature Versus Nurture.   This is one of the oldest controversies in behavioral science. Theories differ in the weights they assign to heredity, environment, and their combination (interaction) as contributors to development. Psychoanalytic theories stress the role of heredity. As we saw in the preceding section, child study proponents placed a fair amount of emphasis on the child's emerging nature (heredity); however, because they also emphasized good teaching, the implication was that environmental and hereditary influences interacted to produce development.

Conversely, behaviorists take an extreme environmental view. The right conditions produce learning; heredity is important only for providing the necessary physical and mental prerequisites needed to respond to stimuli in the environment.

Table 10.1
Developmental issues relevant to learning.

- Nature Versus Nurture: Does development depend more on heredity, environment, or a combination?

- Stability Versus Change: Are developmental periods flexible, or do certain critical times exist in which developmental changes must occur for development to proceed normally?

- Continuity Versus Discontinuity: Does development occur continuously via small changes, or do sudden, abrupt changes occur?

- Passivity Versus Activity: Do changes occur regardless of children's actions, or do children play an active role in their development?

- Structure Versus Function: Does development consist of a series of changes in cognitive structures or processes?

The implications for learning are clear. If we assume that development primarily is hereditary, then learning will proceed pretty much at its own rate and others cannot do much about it. If we assume that the environment makes a difference, then we can structure it to foster development.

Stability Versus Change.   Theories differ in whether they predict that developmental periods are relatively fixed or have more flexibility. Readiness—what children are capable of doing or learning at various points in development—relates directly to this issue. A strict view holds that because developmental periods are relatively fixed, only certain types of learning are possible at a given time. Most school curricula reflect this idea to some degree because they specify content to be taught at particular grade levels.

Other theories contend that because developmental periods have a lot of leeway, children should have more latitude to learn at their own pace. Thus, most children will develop the prerequisite abilities to learn to read in the first grade, but some will not, and forcing these children to read will create problems. A key issue, therefore, is how to assess readiness.

Continuity Versus Discontinuity.   Whether development proceeds in continuous or discontinuous fashion is a subject of debate. Behavioral theories posit continuous development. As behaviors develop, they form the basis for acquiring new ones. Conversely, Piaget's theory describes a process of discontinuity. Changes from one mode of thinking to another may occur abruptly, and children will differ in how long they remain at a particular stage.

Educationally speaking, discontinuity is more difficult to plan for because activities that are effective now need to be changed as students' thinking develops. Continuous views allow for a better-ordered sequence of curriculum. Although many school curricula are established assuming continuous development, educators readily admit that the process rarely proceeds smoothly.

Passivity Versus Activity.   This issue refers to whether development proceeds in natural fashion or whether more and varied experiences can promote it. This has important implications for teaching because it speaks to the issue of how active students should be. If activity is important, then lessons need to incorporate hands-on activities. Whether learning can be accelerated through modeling and practice has been the focus of much research with positive results (Rosenthal & Zimmerman, 1978).

Throughout this text we have discussed *self-regulation*, or self-generated thoughts and actions directed toward learning. Theories that stress learner activity are compatible with the suggestion by educators that students be taught self-regulatory skills and encouraged to engage in independent learning.

Structure Versus Function.   *Structural theories* of human development assume that development consists of changes in structures (or schemas). Development proceeds in a fixed, invariant fashion because each structural change follows preceding ones. A common assumption of structural theories is that human learning reflects one's general organization of knowledge (Zimmerman & Whitehurst, 1979). Behavior is given relatively less emphasis because it is assumed that behavior is an incomplete reflection of one's structures. Structural theories often (but not necessarily) label the different periods of development as "stages." Readers should note that the label "stage" is not an explanation of learning but rather a shorthand way of referring to a constellation of activities that tend to occur together.

In contrast, *functional theories* do not employ stages but rather talk in terms of the types of functions or processes that a child is able to do at a particular time. Behavior is given more weight because behavior reflects functions. Although most children end up with the same basic competencies, the order and rate of development of functions can vary. Most contemporary views of development are functional. Some combination of these two approaches is possible; for example, a structural theory might include some functional elements.

Types of Developmental Theories

Meece (2002) identified five primary classes of theories: biological, psychoanalytical, behavioral, cognitive, and contextual (Table 10.2). These are considered in turn.

Biological Theories.   Biological theories cast human development as an *unfolding* process. Children proceed through a set sequence of invariant stages of development in roughly the same time. The environment provides opportunities for growth but exerts no direct influence; rather, development is overwhelmingly determined by genetics.

A primary proponent was Arnold Gesell, who, together with his colleagues, published age-based norms for growth and behavioral changes (Gesell & Ilg, 1946; Gesell, Ilg, & Ames, 1956). The Gesell norms provide general expectations and may be useful for identifying children who do not fit the age-based expectations (e.g., a child who displays excessive "baby" behavior in the third grade). At the same time, the wide variation in developmental changes between children means that the norms have limited usefulness. When any norms are misused as readiness criteria, they can retard educational progress. A school administrator related that in her school system one criterion for determining whether a child should pass from kindergarten to first grade was that the child had lost at least one baby tooth. Parents were known to take

Table 10.2
Types of developmental theories.

Type	Key Developmental Processes
Biological	Individuals proceed through an invariant sequence of stages; stage progression is largely determined by genetics.
Psychoanalytic	Development represents a series of changes in personality brought about by need satisfaction. Stages are qualitatively distinct.
Behavioral	Development represents changes in behaviors produced by conditioning; changes are continuous and quantitative.
Cognitive	Development represents changes in mental structures or processes that occur as individuals take in information and mentally construct understandings.
Contextual	Social and cultural factors affect development; changes in persons or situations interact with and influence other changes.

their children to dentists to have baby teeth pulled so that the children would not have to repeat kindergarten!

Current biological work focuses on the extent that cognitive, behavioral, and personality characteristics have genetic predispositions (see the section later in this chapter on brain research). Thus, the tendency for children to understand counting may be largely inherited (Geary, 1995; see Chapter 9), and the capacity for language acquisition seems biologically predisposed (Chomsky, 1957; see Chapter 2 and later in this chapter). A long-standing debate concerns the extent that intelligence is inherited. Researchers are exploring how genetics and environmental factors interact to influence development (Plomin, 1990).

Psychoanalytic Theories. Psychoanalytic theories emphasize the fulfillment of *needs*, which differ as a function of developmental level (Meece, 2002). Development is viewed as progressive changes in personality, which emerges as children seek to satisfy their needs. Children pass through a series of stages (discussed later in this chapter), each of which is qualitatively different from preceding ones. Children interact with their environments to fulfill needs, and their successes in resolving conflicts associated with need fulfillment influence personality.

Two well-known psychoanalytic theorists were Sigmund Freud and Erik Erikson. Freud (1966) believed that the basic structure of a child's personality was established during the first 5 years of life. Erikson (1963), on the other hand, felt that development was a lifelong process and thus postulated developmental stages into old age. Psychoanalytic theories emphasize the role of innate factors in development. Needs are innate, and how they are resolved affects development. The role of learning in development is downplayed in favor of need resolution.

Psychoanalytic theories have their share of problems. As with other stage theories, stage progression from child to child often is so uneven that using theories to explain development is difficult. Although the needs and conflicts described by psychoanalytic theories are well known to parents, caregivers, and teachers, how they can be successfully resolved is left open. Consequently, how significant others in children's lives can best foster development is unclear. For example, should adults provide for all of children's needs or teach children self-regulation skills so they can begin to satisfy their own needs? Theories that offer clearer predictions about development and especially the role of learning have greater applicability to education.

Behavioral Theories.   In contrast to biological and psychoanalytical theories that stress innate factors, behavioral theories—while acknowledging developmental capabilities—postulate that development can be explained by the same principles that explain other behaviors. The major developmental changes occur as a result of *conditioning* (see Chapters 1 and 2). Behavioral theories represent a continuity position: Small changes occur over time. Developmental changes are best viewed in quantitative terms: Children learn to do more in less time. The primary mechanism of learning is shaping of new behaviors through differential reinforcement of successive approximations to the target behaviors (Chapter 2).

Behavioral theories do not specify critical periods in development. The capacity for learning continues throughout the life span. They also emphasize that the major changes in behavior emanate from the environment, which provides the stimuli to which children respond and the consequences of their actions (e.g., reinforcement, punishment). Behavioral theories downplay the role of personal factors associated with learners (e.g., thoughts, emotions) and the interaction between learners and their environments. Behavioral theories also have little to say about self-regulation; for the most part, the topic has been treated as the establishment of self-reinforcement contingencies. As noted in Chapter 2, behavioral methods often are useful in teaching and learning but behavioral explanations for learning and development are incomplete because they negate the role of personal influences.

Cognitive Theories.   Beginning with the work of Piaget in the early 1960s, cognitive theories have gained ascendance in the field of human development. Cognitive theories focus on how children construct their understandings of themselves and of the world about them (Meece, 2002). Cognitive theories are constructivist (Chapter 7) in that they postulate that understanding is not automatic. Others do not convey information that children simply process rotely; rather, children take in information and formulate their own knowledge. They are active seekers and processors of information. Cognitive theories are interactional because they explain development in terms of interactions between personal, behavioral, and environmental factors. Prominent cognitive theories are Piaget's, Bruner's, Vygotsky's, information processing, and social cognitive theory.

This chapter discusses Piaget's theory, Bruner's theory, and contemporary information processing theory. Vygotsky's theory is covered in Chapter 7. Bandura's (1986, 1997) social cognitive theory is described in Chapters 3 and 8. With respect to development, the major points of Bandura's theory are that personal functioning represents a process of *triadic reciprocality* in which personal factors, behaviors, and environmental influences interact with and affect each other. Social cognitive theory also stresses that much learning occurs vicariously through observation of others. Research in the social cognitive tradition highlights the importance of modeling and guided practice as facilitators of developmental changes and acquisition of cognitive skills (Rosenthal & Zimmerman, 1978).

Some cognitive theories (e.g., Piaget's and information processing but not Vygotsky's or social cognitive theory) have been criticized because they tend to emphasize the role of the learner and downplay the influence of the social environment. Constructivist theories are criticized for their vagueness in explaining how knowledge construction occurs.

Contextual Theories.   These theories highlight the roles played by social and cultural factors. Evidence supporting this perspective comes from cross-cultural comparisons showing wide variability in developmental patterns as well as from studies demonstrating that even within societies there is considerable variation in development (Meece, 2002). Societal practices clearly play a major role in development.

A well-known contextual model was formulated by Bronfenbrenner (1979), who postulated that the child's social world can be conceptualized as a set of concentric circles with the child at the common point of three intersecting circles: school, peers, and family. Outside of these is a larger circle containing neighborhood, extended family, community, church, workplace, and mass media. The outermost circle contains such influences as laws, cultural values, political and economic systems, and social customs. The model assumes that changes in one level can affect other levels. Thus, physical changes in children can alter their social groups, which in turn are affected by cultural values. The model is highly interactional and is useful for understanding the complexity of influences on human development and its effects.

Cognitive and contextual theories stress that children are active constructors of knowledge and that development is a continuous process across the life span. Contextual theories emphasize the altered nature of social patterns and how these lead children into different interactions with peers and adults. Cognitive development occurs largely as a consequence of these interactions. In turn, children's behaviors alter environments. Thus, children may develop new interests that change the peer groups with which they closely associate. Some cognitive theories (e.g., Vygotsky's and social cognitive) also are contextual in nature.

Contextual theories often are vague in their predictions of how changes in some aspects may affect development and vice versa. They also can be very complex, with a host of variables postulated to affect one another. This situation makes it difficult to conduct research. Despite these limitations, contextual theories call our attention to the need to study the many factors that are involved in human development.

Structural Theories

Remember that an issue confronting the study of human development is whether development represents changes in cognitive structures or functions. Most contemporary views posit changes in functions, but structural theories have figured prominently in the discipline.

Structural theories postulate that development involves changes in cognitive structures, or *schemata*. Information that is learned (i.e., enters the structure) can help to alter the structure. These theories do not equate "structure" with a physical location in the brain; rather, structures are construed as constellations of capabilities or characteristic means of processing information.

Two structural theories with relevance to learning are described in this section: Chomsky's (1957) psycholinguistic theory and classic information processing theory (Atkinson & Shiffrin, 1968). Piaget's theory—another prominent structural theory— is discussed later.

Psycholinguistic Theory.   Chomsky (1957, 1959) formulated a theory of language acquisition based on a system of *transformational grammar*. According to Chomsky, language can be differentiated into two levels: an overt *surface structure* that involves speech and syntax and a covert *deep structure* that includes meaning. A single deep structure can be represented by multiple surface structures. To illustrate this distinction, assume that Rhonda is playing basketball with Steve. The meaning as it might be represented as propositions in memory is:

Rhonda—playing basketball (with)—Steve

This meaning could be translated in various surface structures (utterances and sentences), such as:

- Rhonda is playing basketball with Steve.
- Steve is playing basketball with Rhonda.
- Rhonda? Playing basketball with Steve.
- Basketball is being played by Rhonda and Steve.

Chomsky's transformational grammar contains a number of rules that people presumably use to transform varying surface structures into the same meaning (deep structure). The deep structures are assumed to be part of the individual's genetic makeup. Language development, then, involves the progressive capability of mapping surface structures onto their corresponding deep structures.

Importantly, the rules do not allow for all transformations. Thus, "Basketball Steve Rhonda playing," maps onto no deep structure, nor could any deep structure generate such a surface structure. Chomsky (1957) postulated the existence of a *language acquisition device* (*LAD*), which has the capability of forming and verifying transformational rules to account for overt language (spoken, written). Presumably the LAD is innate; children were endowed with deep structures and a LAD that could alter the nature of the deep structures but only in fixed ways.

Chomsky's theory accounts for language development in terms of structures that change in predictable ways. Empirical support for the LAD is mixed (Moerk, 1989). Moerk argued that the LAD was not necessary to explain linguistic development. Moerk summarized research showing that significant others in the child's environment (parents, siblings, caregivers) fulfilled the LAD's functions by assisting language development. Rather than the LAD being the mediating device between instances of language and development of a formalized grammar, Moerk found evidence that modeling (primarily maternal) related to the speed of language acquisition. Mothers verbalize simple utterances ("This is a dog") to their children, often in abbreviated form (mother points to the dog and says "dog"). This language, known as *motherese*, breaks down complex ideas into simple utterances and builds up simple utterances into complex sentences.

Furthermore, mothers tend to repeat utterances, and such repetition creates invariant structures in their children's minds. Mothers not only model utterances, they also perform much information processing on children's behalf by maintaining the accessibility of language through repetition and by rephrasing children's utterances into complete sentences (e.g., child says "milk," to which mother replies, "Do you want milk?").

Moerk concluded that mothers (or more generally primary caregivers) performed all of the functions ascribed to the LAD. Consequently, a special language structure was not necessary to explain language learning. Moerk's account is functional because it accounts for language acquisition in terms of the functions played by significant others in the environment. This is one example in the developmental literature of structural and functional accounts being applied to explain the same phenomenon.

Classical Information Processing Theory. Classical information processing theory provides another structural account of development. The model presented in Chapter 4 is based largely on the pioneering work of Atkinson and Shiffrin (1968, 1971). This model assumes that the computer is a useful metaphor for the operation of the human mind. The computer (with corresponding information processing) components are: input (sensory registers), desktop processing (short-term memory), storage (long-term memory), output (response), and programming (executive, control processes).

The analogy between the structures of the mind and the computer is useful. Although the mind's structures do not necessarily correspond to physical locations (i.e., the operations performed may occur in multiple locations), structures are constrained in terms of what they do. Once information enters the system, it is processed in linear fashion (i.e., it follows a set path determined by its content) and little room exists for environmental impact (Zimmerman & Whitehurst, 1979). The operation of the structures is largely preprogrammed.

Developmental change occurs in the capacity and efficiency of processing. Through the use of strategies such as rehearsal and organization, older learners—compared with younger ones—are able to hold more information in working memory (WM), relate it better to information in long-term memory (LTM), and have more extensive memory networks. With development, information processing of routinized activities becomes largely automatic. Teaching can help to improve processing, as we saw in Chapter 9 (differences between experts and novices in content areas).

Chapter 4 addressed the concerns of the classical model. The model assumes that information is processed in linear, serial fashion; yet experience shows that people are able to process multiple inputs simultaneously (e.g., talk on the phone and read at the same time). The notion of "control processes" is vague. Perhaps the most serious concern involves how processing develops. Maturation and learning are important, but the theory does not address adequately many of the critical issues presented earlier in this chapter. A contemporary information processing perspective on development (discussed later) is better positioned to address these issues.

We now will review two constructivist theoretical accounts of human development—the theories of Piaget and Bruner. These perspectives are constructivist because they posit that people form or construct much of what they learn and understand.

PIAGET'S THEORY OF COGNITIVE DEVELOPMENT

Piaget's theory was little noticed when it first appeared, but gradually it ascended to a leading position in the field of human development. Piaget's theory covers many types of development and is complex; a complete summary is beyond the scope of this text. Interested readers should consult other sources (Brainerd, 2003; Furth, 1970; Ginsburg & Opper, 1988; Meece, 2002; Phillips, 1969; Piaget, 1952, 1970; Piaget & Inhelder, 1969; Wadsworth, 1996). What follows is a concise overview of the major points relevant to cognitive development and learning.

Developmental Processes

Equilibration.   According to Piaget, cognitive development depends on four factors: biological maturation, experience with the physical environment, experience with the social environment, and equilibration. The first three are self-explanatory, but their effects depend on the fourth. *Equilibration* refers to a biological drive to produce an optimal state of equilibrium (or *adaptation*) between cognitive structures and the environment (Duncan, 1995). Equilibration is the central factor and the motivating force behind cognitive development. It coordinates the actions of the other three factors and makes internal mental structures and external environmental reality consistent with each other.

To illustrate the role of equilibration, consider 6-year-old Allison riding in a car with her father. They are going 65 mph, and about 100 yards in front of them is a car. They have been following this car for some time, and the distance between them stays the same. Her dad points to the car and asks Allison, "Who's going faster, us or them, or are we going the same speed?" Allison replies that the other car is going faster. When her dad asks why, she replies, "Because it's in front of us." If her dad then said, "We're actually going the same speed," this would create a conflict for Allison. She believes the other car is going faster, but she has received conflicting environmental input.

To resolve this conflict, Allison can use one of the two component processes of equilibration: assimilation and accommodation. *Assimilation* refers to fitting external reality to the existing cognitive structure. When we interpret, construe, and frame, we alter the nature of reality to make it fit our cognitive structure. *Accommodation* refers to changing internal structures to provide consistency with external reality. We accommodate when we adjust our ideas to make sense of reality.

To assimilate the information, Allison might alter reality by believing that her dad is teasing her or perhaps at that moment the two cars were going the same speed but that the other car had been going faster beforehand. To accommodate her belief system (structures) to the new information, she might believe her dad without understanding why or she might change her belief system to include the idea that all cars in front of them are going the same speed as they are. Assimilation and accommodation are complementary processes: As reality is assimilated, structures are accommodated.

Stages.   Piaget noted from his research that children's cognitive development passed through a fixed sequence. The pattern of operations that children can perform may be thought of as a level or *stage*. Each level or stage is defined by how children view the world. Piaget's and other stage theories make certain assumptions:

- Stages are discrete, qualitatively different, and separate. Progression from one stage to another is not a matter of gradual blending or continuous merging.
- The development of cognitive structures is dependent on preceding development.
- Although the order of structure development is invariant, the age at which one may be in a particular stage will vary from person to person. Stages should not be equated with ages.

Table 10.3 shows how Piaget characterized his stage progression. Much has been written on these stages and an extensive research literature exists on each. The stages are only briefly described here; interested readers should consult other sources (Brainerd, 2003; Byrnes, 1996; Meece, 2002; Wadsworth, 1996).

In the *sensorimotor* stage, children's actions are spontaneous and represent an attempt to understand the world. Understanding is rooted in present action; for example, a ball is for throwing and a bottle for sucking. The period is characterized by rapid change; a 2-year-old is cognitively far different from an infant. The equilibration process is operational as children actively construct knowledge, albeit at a primitive level. Schemata are constructed and altered, and the motivation to do this is internal. The notion of *effectance motivation* (Chapter 8) is relevant to sensorimotor children. By the end of the sensorimotor period, children have attained sufficient cognitive development to progress to increased conceptual-symbolic thinking characteristic of the preoperational stage (Wadsworth, 1996).

Preoperational children are able to imagine the future and reflect on the past, although they remain heavily perceptually oriented in the present. They are apt to believe that 10 coins spread out in a row are more than 10 coins in a pile. They also are

Table 10.3
Piaget's stages of cognitive development.

Stage	Approximate Age Range (Years)
Sensorimotor	Birth to 2
Preoperational	2 to 7
Concrete operational	7 to 11
Formal operational	11 to adult

unable to think in more than one dimension at a time; thus, if they focus on length, they are apt to think a longer object (a yardstick) is bigger than a shorter one (a brick) even though the shorter one is wider and deeper. Preoperational children demonstrate *irreversibility*; that is, once things are done, they cannot be changed (e.g., the box flattened cannot be remade into a box). They have difficulty distinguishing fantasy from reality. Cartoon characters appear as real as people. The period is one of rapid language development. Another characteristic is that children become less *egocentric*: They realize that others may think and feel differently than they do.

The *concrete operational* stage is characterized by remarkable cognitive growth and is a formative one in schooling, because it is when children's language and basic skills acquisition accelerate dramatically. Children begin to show some abstract thinking, although it typically is defined by properties or actions (e.g., honesty is returning money to the person who lost it). Concrete operational children display less egocentric thought, and language increasingly becomes social. *Reversibility* in thinking is acquired along with classification and seriation—concepts essential for the acquisition of mathematical skills. Concrete operational thinking no longer is dominated by perception; children draw on their experiences and are not always swayed by what they perceive.

The *formal operational* stage extends concrete operational thought. No longer is thought focused exclusively on tangibles; children are able to think about hypothetical situations. Reasoning capabilities improve, and children can think about multiple dimensions and abstract properties. Egocentrism emerges in adolescents' comparing reality to the ideal; thus, they often show idealistic thinking.

Piaget's stages have been criticized on many grounds (Byrnes, 1996). One problem is that children often grasp ideas and are able to perform operations earlier than Piaget found. Another problem is that cognitive development across domains typically is uneven; rarely does a child think in stage-typical ways across all topics (e.g., mathematics, science, or history). This also is true for adults; the same topic may be understood quite differently. For example, some adults may think of baseball in preoperational terms ("Hit the ball and run"), others might think of it concrete operationally ("What do I do in different situations?"), and some can reason using formal operational thought (e.g., "Explain why a curve ball curves"). As a general framework, however, the stages describe the thought patterns that tend to co-occur, which is useful knowledge for educators, parents, and others who work with children.

Mechanisms of Learning.   Equilibration is an internal, organismic property (Duncan, 1995). As such, cognitive development can occur only when *disequilibrium* or *cognitive conflict* exists. Thus, an event occurs that produces a disturbance in the child's internal structures (schemata) so that the child's beliefs do not match the observed reality. Equilibration seeks to resolve the conflict through assimilation and accommodation.

Piaget felt that development would proceed naturally through regular interactions with the physical and social environments. The impetus for developmental change is internal. Environmental factors are extrinsic; they can influence development but not direct it. This point has profound implications for education because it seems to suggest that teaching may have little impact on development. Teachers can arrange the environment to cause conflict, but how any particular child resolves the conflict is not predictable.

Learning occurs, then, when children experience cognitive conflict and engage in assimilation or accommodation to construct or alter internal structures. Importantly, however, the conflict should not be too great because this will not trigger equilibration. Learning will be optimal when the conflict is small and especially when children are in transition between stages. Information must be partially understood (assimilated) before it can promote structural change (accommodation). Environmental stimulation to facilitate change should have negligible effect unless the critical stage transitions have begun so that the conflict can be successfully resolved via equilibration. Thus, learning is limited by developmental constraints (Brainerd, 2003).

The research evidence on cognitive conflict is not overwhelmingly supportive of Piaget's position (Zimmerman & Blom, 1983a, 1983b; Zimmerman & Whitehurst, 1979). Rosenthal and Zimmerman (1978) summarized data from several research studies showing that preoperational children can master concrete operational tasks through teaching involving verbal explanations and modeled demonstrations. According to the theory, this should not happen unless the children are in stage transition, at which time cognitive conflict would be at a reasonable level.

The stage-like changes in children's thinking seem to be linked to more gradual changes in attention and cognitive processing (Meece, 2002). Thus, children may not demonstrate Piagetian stage understanding for various reasons, including not attending to the relevant stimuli, improperly encoding information, not relating information to prior knowledge, or using ineffective means to retrieve information (Siegler, 1991). When children are taught to use cognitive processes more effectively, they often can perform tasks at higher cognitive levels.

Piaget's theory is constructivist because it assumes that children impose their concepts on the world to make sense of it (Byrnes, 1996). These concepts are not inborn; rather, children acquire them through their normal experiences. Information from the environment (including people) is not automatically received but rather is processed according to the child's prevailing mental structures. Children make sense of their environments and construct reality based on their capabilities at the present time. In turn, these basic concepts develop into more sophisticated views with increasing experience.

Implications for Instruction

Piaget contended that cognitive development could not be taught, although research evidence shows that it can be accelerated (Zimmerman & Whitehurst, 1979). The theory and research suggest some implications for instruction (Table 10.4).

Table 10.4
Implications of Piaget's theory for education.

- Understand cognitive development.
- Keep students active.
- Create incongruity.
- Provide social interaction.

Understand Cognitive Development.   Teachers will benefit when they understand at what levels their students are functioning. All students in a class should not be expected to be operating at the same level. Many Piagetian tasks are easy to administer (Wadsworth, 1996). Teachers should try to ascertain levels and gear their teaching accordingly. Students who seem to be in stage transition may benefit from teaching at the next higher level, because the conflict will not be too great for them.

Keep Students Active.   Piaget decried teachers actively teaching while learners remained passive. Children need rich environments that allow for active exploration and hands-on activities. This arrangement facilitates active construction of knowledge.

Create Incongruity.   Development occurs only when environmental inputs do not match students' schemata. Ideally material should not be readily assimilated but not too difficult to preclude accommodation. Incongruity also can be created by allowing students to solve problems and arrive at wrong answers. Nothing in Piaget's theory says that children always have to succeed; teacher feedback indicating incorrect answers can promote disequilibrium.

Provide Social Interaction.   Although Piaget's theory contends that development can proceed without social interaction, the social environment is nonetheless a key source for cognitive development. Teachers must design some activities that provide social interactions. Learning that others have different points of view can help make children less egocentric. Application 10.1 offers some ways that teachers can help to foster cognitive development.

BRUNER'S THEORY OF COGNITIVE GROWTH

Jerome Bruner, a developmental psychologist, formulated a theory of cognitive growth. Rather than link changes in development to cognitive structures as Piaget did, Bruner highlighted the various ways that children represent knowledge. Bruner's views represent a functional account of human development and have important implications for teaching and learning.

Cognitive Growth and Knowledge Representation

According to Bruner (1964), "The development of human intellectual functioning from infancy to such perfection as it may reach is shaped by a series of technological advances in the use of mind" (p. 1). These technological advances depend on increasing language facility and exposure to systematic instruction (Bruner, 1966). As children develop, their actions are constrained less by immediate stimuli. Cognitive processes (thoughts, beliefs) mediate the relationship between stimulus and response so that learners can maintain the same response in a changing environment or perform different responses in the same environment, depending on what they consider adaptive.

People represent knowledge in three ways, which emerge in a developmental sequence: enactive, iconic, and symbolic (Bruner, 1964; Bruner, Olver, & Greenfield,

> **APPLICATION 10.1**
> *Piaget and Education*
> ___
>
> At all grades teachers should evaluate the developmental levels of their students prior to planning lessons. Teachers need to know how their students are thinking so they can introduce cognitive conflict at a reasonable level, where students can resolve it through assimilation and accommodation. Kathy Stone, for example, is apt to have students who are operating at both the preoperational and concrete operational levels, which means that one lesson will not suffice for any particular unit. Furthermore, because some children will grasp operations more quickly than others, she needs to build enrichment activities into her lessons.
>
> In developing units for his history classes, Jim Marshall includes components that require basic understanding and also those that necessitate abstract reasoning. Thus, when he plans units, he always includes activities that require exact, factual answers, as well as activities that have no right or wrong answers but that require students to think abstractly and develop their own ideas through reasoned judgments based on data. For students who are not fully operating at the formal operational level, the components requiring abstract reasoning may produce desired cognitive conflict and enhance a higher level of thinking. For students who already are operating at a formal operational level, the reasoning activities will continue to challenge them.

1966). These modes are not structures but rather involve different forms of cognitive processing (i.e., functions; Table 10.5).

Enactive representation involves motor responses, or ways to manipulate the environment. Actions such as riding a bicycle and tying a knot are represented largely in muscular actions. Stimuli are defined by the actions that prompt them. Among toddlers, a ball (stimulus) is represented as something to throw and bounce (actions).

Iconic representation refers to action-free mental images. Children acquire the capability to think about objects that are not physically present. They mentally transform objects and think about their properties separately from what actions can be performed with the objects. Iconic representation allows one to recognize objects.

Symbolic representation uses symbol systems (e.g., language, mathematical notation) to encode knowledge. Such systems allow one to understand abstract concepts (e.g., the x variable in $3x - 5 = 10$) and to alter symbolic information as a result of verbal instruction. Symbolic systems represent knowledge with remote and arbitrary features. The word *Philadelphia* looks no more like the city than a nonsense syllable (Bruner, 1964).

The symbolic mode is the last to develop and quickly becomes the preferred mode, although people maintain the capability to represent knowledge in the enactive and iconic modes. One might experience the "feel" of a tennis ball, form a mental picture

Table 10.5
Bruner's modes of knowledge representation.

Mode	Type of Representation
Enactive	Motor responses; ways to manipulate objects and aspects of the environment
Iconic	Action-free mental images; visual properties of objects and events that can be altered
Symbolic	Symbol systems (e.g., language, mathematical notation); remote and arbitrary

of it, and describe it in words. The primary advantage of the symbolic mode is that it allows learners to represent and transform knowledge with greater flexibility and power than is possible with the other modes (Bruner, 1964).

Spiral Curriculum

That knowledge can be represented in different ways suggests that teachers ought to vary instructional presentations depending on learners' developmental levels. Before children can comprehend abstract mathematical notation, they are exposed to mathematical concepts and operations represented enactively (with blocks) and iconically (in pictures). Bruner emphasized teaching as a means of prompting cognitive development. To say that a particular concept cannot be taught because students will not understand it (i.e., they lack readiness) really is saying that students will not understand the concept the way teachers plan to teach it. Instruction needs to be matched to children's cognitive capabilities.

Bruner (1960) is well known for his controversial proposition that any content can be taught in meaningful fashion to learners of any age:

> Experience over the past decade points to the fact that our schools may be wasting precious years by postponing the teaching of many important subjects on the ground that they are too difficult. . . . The foundations of any subject may be taught to anybody at any age in some form. . . . The basic ideas that lie at the heart of all science and mathematics and the basic themes that give form to life and literature are as simple as they are powerful. To be in command of these basic ideas, to use them effectively, requires a continual deepening of one's understanding of them that comes from learning to use them in progressively more complex forms. It is only when such basic ideas are put in formalized terms as equations or elaborated verbal concepts that they are out of reach of the young child, if he has not first understood them intuitively and had a chance to try them out on his own. (pp. 12–13)

Bruner's adage has been misinterpreted to mean that learners at any age can be taught anything; that simply is not true. Bruner recommended that content be revisited: Concepts initially should be taught in a simple fashion (so children can understand them) and presented in a more complex fashion as they grow older. In literature, children may be able to understand intuitively the concepts of "comedy" and "tragedy" even though they cannot verbally describe them in literary terms (e.g., "Comedies are funny and tragedies are sad"). With development, students will read, analyze, and write papers on comedies and tragedies. Students should address topics at increasing levels of complexity as they move through the curriculum, rather than encountering a topic only once.

Bruner's theory is constructivist because it assumes that at any age learners assign meaning to stimuli and events based on their cognitive capabilities and experiences with the social and physical environments. Bruner's modes of representation bear some similarity to the operations that students engage in during Piaget's stages (i.e., sensorimotor—enactive, concrete operational—iconic, formal operational—symbolic), although Bruner's is not a stage theory. Bruner's theory also allows for concepts to be mentally represented in multiple modes simultaneously: An adolescent knows how to throw a basketball, can visualize its appearance, and can compute its circumference with the formula $c = \pi d$. Application 10.2 gives some examples of Bruner's ideas applied to teaching and learning.

APPLICATION 10.2
Modes of Knowledge Representation

Bruner's theory elaborates ways that students can represent knowledge and recommends revisiting learning through a spiral curriculum. A good application is in the field of mathematics. Before students can comprehend an abstract mathematical notation, teachers must ensure that students understand the concepts enactively and iconically. Kathy Stone works with both the second- and fourth-grade teachers as she prepares her math units for the year. She wants to ensure that students understand previous concepts before tackling new ones, and she introduces ideas that will be further developed during the next year. When introducing multiplication, Mrs. Stone first reviews with her third graders addition and counting by multipliers (e.g., 2, 4, 6, 8; 4, 8, 12, 16). Then she has the students work with manipulatives (enactive representation), and she provides visual (iconic) representation of multiplication. Eventually she presents problems in symbolic mode (e.g., $4 \times 2 = ?$).

Jim Marshall examines curriculum guides and checks with middle school teachers to determine what American history material has been covered prior to the ninth grade. As he develops units, he starts the first lesson with a review of the material that students studied previously and asks students to share what they can recall. Once he evaluates the mastery level of the students, he is able to build on the unit and add new material. He typically employs all modes of knowledge representation in his teaching: enactive—role playing, dramatization; iconic—pictures, videos; symbolic—print materials, websites.

CONTEMPORARY THEMES IN DEVELOPMENT AND LEARNING

In recent years, cognitive information processing has gained priority in the psychological study of human development (Siegler, 1991). Cognitive information processing focuses on functions rather than on structures. This section summarizes the developmental changes that occur in the functions of attention, encoding and retrieval, and metacognition. Other contemporary themes that are discussed in this section are developmentally appropriate instruction and transitions in schooling.

Developmental Changes

Attention.   Sustained attention is difficult for young children, as is attending to relevant rather than irrelevant information. Children also have difficulty switching attention rapidly from one activity to another. It behooves teachers to forewarn students of the attentional demands required to learn. Outlines and study guides can serve as advance organizers and cue learners about the types of information that will be important. While students are working, teachers can use prompts, questions, and feedback to help students remain focused on important task aspects (Meece, 2002).

Encoding and Retrieval.   A simple way to assess children's information processing is with a *digit-span task*. In this task, a researcher reads a series of digits (e.g., 5—3—8—10—2—9) to a child at a rate of one per second, and when the researcher finishes, the child attempts to repeat the same sequence. An average 5-year-old can repeat four digits; this increases to six or seven by age 12 (Meece, 2002).

Underlying this developmental improvement are information processing capacities and actual cognitive processes. In all likelihood these interact: As information processing capacity expands, better cognitive processes can be applied. For example, as children's capacities for attention, encoding, and storage increase, those who employ better strategies for attending, rehearsing, organizing, and retrieving demonstrate enhanced cognitive development.

Most of a child's basic cognitive processes are well in place by early childhood. From this point onward, developmental changes primarily involve learning how to make better and more efficient use of existing perceptual and attentional processes. Some of the more important changes include the ability to make fine discriminations between stimulus objects, the development of automaticity and selective attention, and the ability to exert control over attentional processes. (Meece, 2002)

Automaticity is an important function (see also Chapters 4, 5, and 9). Automatic attention means that children gradually eliminate attention as an active cognitive process. When attention becomes automatic, less cognitive effort is needed in the early stages of information processing, and thus children can put forth effort where it is needed. For example, as decoding becomes automatic (see Chapter 9), more cognitive processing can be shifted to comprehension. Poor readers, for whom decoding is not automatic, expend much effort to decode, with the result that comprehension suffers.

Much developmental research has focused on the strategies that children use in encoding, retention, and retrieval. Chapter 4 discussed the usefulness of having mental representations of often-repeated events, or *scripts* (Wellman, 1988), which create predictability in a child's world and also organize information for quicker processing. With experience, children acquire a larger repertoire of scripts (Flavell, 1985).

Children also improve in their knowledge and use of encoding strategies. *Rehearsal* appears early and improves as children become older (Flavell, Beach, & Chinsky, 1966). In other areas such as organization and elaboration (Chapter 4), children's use of strategies improves with age. These strategies can be taught and enhance children's memory and understanding (Meece, 2002).

With respect to retrieval, older children use better strategies than younger ones (Flavell, 1985). For example, older children are more likely to conduct an exhaustive memory search and not quit when the needed information does not come to mind immediately. Older children also have learned different ways to access information, such as by thinking about different situations where that information may be useful.

Metacognition.   Much of children's understanding about cognition, or *metacognition*, is acquired between the ages of 5 and 10 (Siegler, 1991). Metacognitive improvements are a hallmark of development as children acquire methods for monitoring their level of understanding, asking themselves questions about what they have read, and summarizing information. They learn what strategies to use for different tasks, and with development they are more likely to believe that strategy use leads to better performance (Paris et al., 1983).

Children's metacognitive awareness develops gradually. Alexander et al. (1995) found that steady developmental improvements occurred in declarative metacognitive knowledge, as well as in the metacognitive skills of cognitive monitoring and self-regulation of strategy use. Zimmerman et al. (1996) recommended the use of *self-monitoring*, or deliberately attending to aspects of one's performance. Self-monitoring is aided with *self-recording*, such as with checklists. The list can contain essential aspects of the task to be completed. For example, if students are engaged in reading comprehension, the checklist can contain steps such as reading the passage, determining who are the main characters, deciding on the main action, and so forth.

Developmentally Appropriate Instruction

Another theme of contemporary cognitive views of human development involves the idea of developmentally appropriate instruction. Instruction that is *developmentally appropriate* is matched (compatible) with children's developmental levels. That idea sounds basic, but unfortunately instructional activities and developmental levels often are mismatched. Teaching may involve nothing more than presenting information to students, who receive and process it. Not only might the information be presented in such a way that students have difficulty processing it; they also might process it in ways that produce learning quite different from what the teacher desires.

Developmentally appropriate instruction relies upon several assumptions, which follow from the material discussed in this chapter. First, students construct knowledge based on their prior experiences and present schemata. Knowledge never is transmitted automatically; the construction of knowledge and integration with current mental structures are the means whereby learning proceeds. Thus, instruction must be designed to foster such knowledge construction. Piaget recommended active exploration, a notion that is compatible with instructional methods such as discovery learning and small-group projects.

Second, the social environment is important. This notion is seen clearly in Vygotsky's theory. When interacting with others, children receive ideas and opinions that conflict with their own; this sets the equilibration process into motion (Meece, 2002). The cognitive conflict that ensues is considered the impetus behind learning in many developmental theories.

Third, conflict is created when the material to be learned is just beyond students' present understandings. This creates the ZPD, within which learning can occur through cognitive conflict, reflection, and conceptual reorganization (Meece, 2002). Little conflict exists when material is too far advanced beyond current understandings; conflict similarly is minimized when learning is at children's current levels.

Finally, developmentally appropriate instruction incorporates active exploration and hands-on activities. Bruner's theory clearly indicates that enactive learning occurs first, followed by iconic and symbolic. Although children's learning is based largely on what they do, hands-on learning is beneficial at all developmental levels. Adults who are learning computer skills benefit from observing teachers demonstrate them (iconic) and explain them (symbolic), as well as by performing the skills themselves (enactive).

What would a developmentally appropriate classroom look like? Meece (2002) suggested several appropriate practices that are summarized in Table 10.6. Some classroom applications of developmentally appropriate instruction are provided in Application 10.3.

Transitions in Schooling

There has been much research activity exploring developmental issues involved during transitions in schooling. In the U.S. educational system natural transition times occur that typically involve changing schools and major shifts in curricula and activities. These are preschool to elementary, elementary to middle/junior high, middle/junior high to senior high, and senior high to college.

Table 10.6
Developmentally appropriate instructional practices.

- Teachers structure the learning environment to include adults, other children, materials, and opportunities for children to engage in active exploration and interaction.

- Children select many of their own activities from a variety.

- Children stay active as they engage in much self-directed learning.

- Children work most of the time in small groups or individually.

- Children work with concrete, hands-on activities.

- Teachers actively monitor children's work to ensure continued involvement.

- Teachers focus on the process children use to arrive at answers and not insist always on one right answer.

APPLICATION 10.3
Developmentally Appropriate Instruction

Students learn best in a classroom where instruction is developmentally appropriate. Even in a primary class, developmental levels will vary. Beginning in preschool and kindergarten, teachers should ensure that students have the opportunity to learn in different ways to address the learning mode that is most appropriate for each child's developmental level.

Betty Thompson is a kindergarten teacher. For a unit on magnets, she designs a learning station where students individually use magnets of different sizes and shapes. On one particular day Mrs. Thompson divides the students into small groups and has them work cooperatively to discover the differences between items that can and cannot be picked up by magnets. She works with each small group to complete a chart looking at the differences between items attracted by magnets. For story time that day, Mrs. Thompson reads a book about the uses of magnets; while she reads, each student has a magnet and items to test. For homework, she asks students to bring two items to class the next day, one of which can be picked up by a magnet and one that cannot. The next day in small groups students test their items and then discuss why some items were and others were not attracted; Mrs. Thompson moves around the room and interacts with each group.

Transitions are important, because as with any major change they can produce disruptions in routines and ways of thinking but also because of students' developmental levels at the times they occur (Eccles & Midgley, 1989). Thus, the transition from elementary school to middle school/junior high would be disruptive for anyone, but it becomes especially so for students at that age given the bodily changes they are undergoing and their typical insecurities about their sense of self and appearance. Transitional variables and development most likely interact in reciprocal fashion. Developmental variables can make a transition smooth or rough, but in turn factors associated with the transition might affect students' personal, social, and cognitive development.

The transition to middle school/junior high school is especially problematic (Eccles & Midgley, 1989). This transition occurs at a significant period of physical change in young adolescents with its attendant personal and social changes. Furthermore, numerous changes occur in school and class structures and subject areas. In elementary school, children typically are with the same teacher and peers for most of the school day. The teacher often has a warm and nurturing relationship with the children. Instruction frequently is individualized, and teachers track and report individual progress in content areas. Ability-level differences within a class may be wide, with students ranging from learning disabled to gifted.

In contrast, in middle and junior high schools students typically change classes for each subject, which results in different teachers and peers. Teachers develop close relationships with few, if any, students. Instruction is provided to the entire class and rarely individualized. Grades—whether based on absolute or normative standards—do not reflect individual progress, nor is that generally reported. Ability-level within-class differences may be minimal if students are "tracked." In general, then, middle school and junior high classes are more formal, impersonal, evaluative, and competitive (Meece, 2002). Eccles and her colleagues (Eccles & Midgley, 1989; Eccles, Midgley, & Adler, 1984) contended that these structural and curricular changes produce changes in students' achievement-related beliefs and motivation.

Later in this chapter motivation and human development are discussed (see also Chapter 8). For now, the point is that school transitions need not be so difficult. In theory, anyway, middle schools should help to ease the transition. Although some middle schools resemble junior high schools except for a different grade organization (typically grades 6 to 8 in middle schools and grades 7 to 9 in junior high schools), many middle schools attempt to ease the transition by keeping students together for much of the day and using interdisciplinary teams of teachers (e.g., four teachers, one each for language arts, social studies, mathematics, and science). These teachers work to ensure an integrated curriculum. They rotate in and out of the classroom such that although the teachers change, the peers do not. Alternatively, children may change classes but they have some of the same peers in two or more classes. Greater efforts also may be made to report individual progress. Less emphasis on evaluative comparisons among peers helps to lighten young adolescents' self-concerns so typical at this time. Application 10.4 gives some additional suggestions for ways to ease transitions in schooling.

FAMILIAL INFLUENCES

Although common sense tells us that families have profound influences on children's development and learning, some critics contend that the family's role has been overstated (Harris, 1998). Research is, however, increasingly showing that families do make a difference and often a great one (Collins, Maccoby, Steinberg, Hetherington, & Bornstein, 2000). Some of the key familial influences on development and learning are socioeconomic status, home environment, and parental involvement.

Socioeconomic Status

Definition. *Socioeconomic status* (*SES*) has been defined in various ways, with definitions typically comprising social status (position, rank) and economic indicators (wealth, education). Recent investigators stress the idea of *capital* (resources, assets) (Bradley & Corwyn, 2002). Capital includes such indices as financial or material resources (e.g., income and assets), human or nonmaterial resources (e.g., education), and social resources (e.g., those obtained through social networks and connections) (Putnam, 2000). Each of these seems intuitively to impact children's development and learning.

However SES is defined, it is important to remember that it is a descriptive variable, not an explanatory one (Pintrich & Schunk, 2002). To say that children lag in

APPLICATION 10.4
Transitions in Schooling

Making the transition from one school level to another is difficult for many students. Ability and socioemotional levels vary widely, and students differ in their ability to cope with the numerous organizational changes that occur. The transition from elementary to middle school/junior high level is especially troublesome.

Kay Appleton is a sixth-grade social studies teacher at a middle school. She understands that students become accustomed to having one teacher for most content areas. She works with fifth-grade teachers to suggest activities that they might incorporate, such as using assignment notebooks, that will help students when they are faced with changing classes and being responsible for remembering and completing assignments for each class. She also spends time at the start of the school year helping her students to set up their assignment books and organize their materials. She makes herself available during lunch and after school to give students assistance they might need about transition issues.

Jim Marshall asks eighth-grade social studies teachers about their policies for assigning classwork and homework, giving tests, requiring projects, receiving late work, allowing students to make up missed work, and so forth. He tries to incorporate some of the same approaches in his ninth-grade history classes so that these class procedures will be familiar and will reduce student concerns that could impede learning.

development because they are from poor families does not explain why they lag in development. Rather, the factors that typically accompany poor families may be responsible for the development difficulties. Conversely, not all children from poor families lag in development. There are countless stories of successful adults who were raised in impoverished conditions. Thus, it is more meaningful to speak of a relation between SES and development and then look for the responsible factors.

SES and Development.   There is much correlational evidence showing that poverty and low parental education relate to poorer development and learning (Bradley & Corwyn, 2002). What is less clear is which aspects of SES are responsible for this relation.

Undoubtedly family resources are critical. Families with less education, money, and social connections cannot provide many resources that help to stimulate cognitive development. Compared with wealthier families, they cannot provide their children with computers, books, games, travel, and cultural experiences. Regardless of their perspective, developmental theorists agree that the richness of experiences is central to cognitive development. On this count, then, it is little wonder that SES relates to cognitive development.

Another key factor is socialization. Schools and classrooms have a middle-class orientation, and there are accepted rules and procedures that children must follow to succeed (e.g., pay attention, do your work, study, and work cooperatively with others). Socialization influences in lower-SES homes may not match or prepare students for these conditions (Pintrich & Schunk, 2002). To the extent that this occurs, lower-SES children may have more discipline and behavior problems in school and, thereby, not learn as well.

SES also appears to affect school attendance and years of schooling (Bradley & Corwyn, 2002). SES is, unfortunately, one of the best predictors of school dropout. Lower SES children may not understand the benefits of schooling (Meece, 2002); they may not realize that more education leads to better jobs, more income, and a better lifestyle than they have experienced. They may be drawn by immediate short-term benefits of leaving school (e.g., money from working full-time) and not be swayed by potential long-term assets. In their home environments they may not have positive role models displaying the benefits of schooling or parental encouragement to continue.

The relation of SES to cognitive development seems complex, with some factors contributing directly and others serving a moderating influence (Bradley & Corwyn, 2002). While the effects of material, human, and social capital seem clear, the influence of other factors may be indirect. For example, large families are not inherently beneficial or harmful to cognitive development. But in deprived conditions they may be harmful as already scarce resources are spread among more children.

The literature suggests that early educational interventions for children from low-SES families (e.g., Head Start) are critical to ensuring that they are prepared for schooling. Unfortunately the effects of such early interventions do not always persist over time as children progress in school, but there are promising results. Campbell, Pungello, Miller-Johnson, Burchinal, and Ramey (2001) evaluated the Abecedarian Project, a full-time educational child-care project for children from low-income families. These researchers found that the benefits of the intervention persisted through the last evaluation when many of the children had attained age 21. Given the longitudinal nature of this project (it began when the participants were infants), it is difficult to determine when and how it better prepared them to work in school environments. SES is an active area of developmental research, and we are sure to learn more as researchers attempt to unravel these complexities.

Home Environment

There is much variability in the richness of home environments, and this is not always isomorphic with SES. Some homes provide rich experiences replete with economic capital (computers, games, and books), human capital (parents help children with homework, projects, and studying), and social capital (through social contacts parents get children involved in activities and teams). Other homes lack in one or more of these respects.

The effects of the home environment on cognitive development seem most pronounced in infancy and early childhood (Meece, 2002). Children's social networks expand as they grow older, especially as a consequence of schooling and participation in activities. Thus, peer influence becomes increasingly important with development.

There is much evidence that the quality of children's early home learning relates positively to the development of intelligence (Pintrich & Schunk, 2002). Important home factors include mother's responsiveness, discipline style, and child involvement; organization present in the home; availability of stimulating materials; opportunities for interaction. Parents who provide a warm and responsive home environment tend to encourage children's explorations and stimulate their curiosity and play, which accelerate intellectual development (Meece, 2002).

The increasing role of peer influence was found in longitudinal research by Steinberg, Brown, and Dornbusch (1996). Over a 10-year period these researchers surveyed more than 20,000 adolescents from high schools in different states and interviewed many teachers and parents. These authors found that peer influence rose during childhood and peaked around grades 8 and 9, after which it declined somewhat in high school. A key period of influence is roughly between the ages of 12 and 16. It is noteworthy that this is the period during which parental involvement in children's activities declines. Thus, with parental involvement declining and peer involvement rising, early adolescents are especially vulnerable to peer pressures.

These authors also tracked students over a 3-year period, from when they entered high school until their senior year. Not surprisingly, students who were part of more academically oriented crowds achieved better in school compared with those in less academically oriented crowds. Those who started high school in the former crowd but moved away from it also showed lower achievement.

Although parents do not have total control over the crowds with which their children associate, they can exert indirect influence by steering them in appropriate directions. For example, parents who urge their children to participate in activities in which the children of other like-minded parents participate steer them toward appropriate peer influence regardless of whom they select as friends. Parents who offer their home as a place where friends are welcome further steer their children in positive directions.

Parental Involvement

Harris (1998) downplayed the influence of parents on children past infancy and concluded that peers exert a much greater effect; however, there is substantial evidence that parental influence continues to be strong well past infancy (Vandell, 2000). This section considers the role of parental involvement in children's activities, which is a key factor influencing cognitive development (Meece, 2002). Such involvement occurs in and away from the home, such as in school and activities.

There is evidence that parental involvement in schools has a positive impact on children, teachers, and the school itself (Pintrich & Schunk, 2002). One effect of parent involvement, as noted above, is that parents can be influential in "launching" their children onto particular trajectories by involving them in groups and activities (Steinberg et al., 1996). Thus, parents who want their children to be academically focused are likely to involve them in activities that stress academics.

Fan and Chen (2001) conducted a meta-analysis of research on the relation of parental involvement to children's academic attainments. The results showed that parents' expectations for their children's academic successes bore a positive relation to their actual cognitive achievements. The relation was strongest when academic attainment was assessed globally (e.g., GPA) than by subject-specific indicators (e.g., grade in a particular class). There also is evidence that parent involvement effects on children's achievement are greatest when there is a high level of parent involvement in the neighborhood (Collins et al., 2000).

Parental involvement is a critical factor influencing children's self-regulation, which is central to the development of cognitive functioning. Research by Stright, Neitzel, Sears, and Hoke-Sinex (2001) found that the type of instruction parents provide and how they provide it relate to children's subsequent self-regulation in school. Children of parents who provided understandable metacognitive information displayed greater classroom monitoring, participation, and metacognitive talk. Children's seeking and attending to classroom instruction also were related to whether parents' instruction was given in an understandable manner. These authors suggested that parental instruction helps to create the proper conditions for their children to develop self-regulatory competence. Some suggestions for parents working with their children are given in Application 10.5.

Positive effects of parental involvement have been obtained in research with ethnic minority children and those from impoverished environments (Masten & Coatsworth, 1998). Some forms of parent involvement that make a difference are contacting the school about their children, attending school functions, communicating strong educational values to their children, conveying the value of effort, expecting children to perform well in school, and monitoring or helping children with homework and projects. Miliotis, Sesma, and Masten (1999) found that after families left homeless shelters, high parent involvement in children's education was one of the best predictors of children's school success.

One of the strongest advocates of community and parental involvement in education is James Comer. Comer and his colleagues began the *School Development Program* in two schools 35 years ago, and it has now spread to more than 500 schools.

The SDP (or Comer Program) is based on the principles shown in Table 10.7 (Comer, 2001; Emmons, Comer, & Haynes, 1996). Children need positive interactions with adults because these help to form their behaviors. Planning for child development should be a collaborative effort between professionals and community members.

Three guiding principles of SDP are consensus, collaboration, and no-fault (Pintrich & Schunk, 2002). Decisions are arrived at by consensus to discourage taking sides for critical votes. Collaboration means working as part of a team. No-fault implies that everyone is responsible for change.

School staff and community members are grouped into teams. The School Planning and Management Team includes the building principal, teachers, parents, and support staff. This team plans and coordinates activities. The Parent Team involves parents in all school activities. The Student and Staff Support Team is responsible for school-wide prevention issues and individual student cases.

APPLICATION 10.5
Parental Involvement

Kathy Stone understands the importance of parental involvement for children's learning and self-regulation. Early in the academic year, the school holds an open house for parents. When Kathy meets with her parents, she explains the many ways that parents can become involved. She asks for volunteers for three groups: school learning, out-of-school learning, and planning. School-learning parents volunteer a half-day per week to work in class, assisting with small-group and individual work. Out-of-school-learning parents accompany the class on field trips and organize and work with children on community projects (e.g., a walk through the neighborhood to identify types of trees). Planning-group parents periodically meet as a group with Kathy, where she explains upcoming units and asks parents to help design activities. Kathy's goal is 100% involvement of at least one parent or guardian per child, which she usually is able to attain because of the options available.

Jim Marshall knows what a valuable resource parents are in American history because they have lived through some of the events his students learn about. Jim contacts parents at the start of the year and provides them with a list of events in the past 40 years that students will study in class (e.g., Vietnam War, Cold War, Kennedy assassination, or the fall of the Berlin wall). Jim seeks the assistance of every family on at least one event, such as by the parent coming to class to discuss it (i.e., what they remember about it, why it was important, how it affected their lives). When several parents volunteer for the same event, he forms them into a panel to discuss the event. If there are living grandparents in the area, Jim asks them to share their experiences about such events as the Great Depression, World War II, and the Eisenhower presidency. Jim's students set up a website containing information about key events and excerpts from parents and grandparents about them.

At the core of the SDP is a comprehensive school plan with such components as curriculum, instruction, assessment, social and academic climate, and information sharing. This plan provides structured activities addressing academics, social climate, staff development, and public relations. The School Planning and Management Team establishes priorities and coordinates school improvement.

Comer and his colleagues report impressive effects on children's cognitive achievement due to implementation of the SDP (Haynes, Emmons, Gebreyesus, & Ben-Avie, 1996). Comer schools often show gains in student achievement and out-perform school district averages in reading, mathematical, and language skills. Cook, Murphy, and Hunt (2000) evaluated the Comer SDP in 10 inner-city Chicago schools over 4 years. Using students in grades 5 through 8, these authors found that by the

Table 10.7
Principles of the school development program.

- Children's behaviors are determined by their interactions with the physical, social, and psychological environments.

- Children need positive interactions with adults to develop adequately.

- Child-centered planning and collaboration among adults facilitate positive interactions.

- Planning for child development should be done collaboratively by professional and community members.

Source: From "Translating Theory into Practice: Comer's Theory of School Reform," by C. L. Emmons, J. P. Comer, and N. M. Haynes, 1996, in *Rallying the Whole Village: The Comer Process for Reforming Education* (pp. 27–41) by J. P. Comer, N. M. Haynes, E. T. Joyner, and M. Ben-Avie (Eds.), New York: Teachers College Press.

last years Comer program students showed greater gains in reading and mathematics compared with control students. Regardless of whether schools adopt the Comer program, it contains many points that should aid in children's cognitive development.

THE BRAIN AND DEVELOPMENT

Recent years have witnessed a great deal of interest in neurophysiological research on brain development and functions. Many educators view brain research with interest, because they believe that it might suggest ways to make educational materials and instruction compatible with how children process information and learn.

This section reviews some brain research relevant to human development and learning. The first part covers basic brain development, after which locations of brain functions are explained. The section concludes with a discussion of the educational implications of this research.

Brain Development

Composition.   The brain is made up of billions of cells or *neurons* that send and receive information across muscles and organs (Trawick-Smith, 2003). Each neuron has a body, around which are *dendrites* (elongated tissues that receive messages). Each neuron also has an *axon*—a long thread of tissue that sends messages. A message from a cell being sent to another cell results from *neurotransmitters*, or chemical secretions traveling along the axon to dendrites of the next cell. Where axon and dendrites meet is called a *synapse. Myelin sheath* surrounds the axon and facilitates the travel of signals.

The brain is organized into regions that are responsible for specific functions. Important regions are sensory (send and receive sense organ information), motor (regulate movement), and association (regulate thinking). The frontal cortex is associated with the expression and regulation of emotions.

The brain also is *lateralized*, which means that the left and right sides control different functions. The left hemisphere governs analytical thinking and language and the right hemisphere governs spatial and auditory perception (Trawick-Smith, 2003). The right hemisphere controls the left visual field and vice versa.

There is much debate among cognitive neuroscientists about the extent of lateralization. Some argue that specific cognitive functions are localized in specific areas of the brain, whereas others believe that different regions have the ability to perform various tasks (Byrnes & Fox, 1998). In fact, there is research evidence to support both positions. Different parts of the brain have different functions, but functions are rarely, if ever, completely localized in one section of the brain. This is especially true for complex mental operations, which depend on several more basic ones whose functions may be spread out in several areas. As Byrnes and Fox (1998) contend, "Nearly any task requires the participation of both hemispheres, but the hemispheres seem to process certain types of information more efficiently than others" (p. 310). Educationally speaking, therefore, the practice of teaching to different sides of the brain (right brain, left brain) is not supported by empirical research.

Early Brain Development.   Brain development occurs rapidly in infants. By the age of 2 years, a child will have as many synapses as an adult, and by the age of 3 years the child will have billions more. Young children's brains are referred to as *super dense* because they have so many complex neural connections and more than at any other time in life (Trawick-Smith, 2003).

In fact, young children have too many synapses. With development, children and adolescents actually lose far more brain synapses than they gain. By the time adolescents turn 18 they have lost about half of their infant synapses. Brain connections that are not used or needed simply disappear. This "use it or lose it" strategy means that connections that are used will be reinforced whereas those not used will be permanently lost.

Brain development, then, seems to reflect the interaction between heredity and environment discussed in Chapter 1. The cultural experiences of infants will determine to a large extent which brain synapses they retain. If the culture stresses motor functions, then these should be strengthened, whereas if it stresses cognitive processes, then these will ascend.

The implication for facilitating early brain development is to provide rich experiences for infants and young children stressing perceptual, motor, and language functions. This is especially critical in the first 3 years of life. These experiences should enhance the formation of dendrites and increase the number of synapses. There also is evidence that babies who have suffered *in utero* (e.g., from mothers' drug or alcohol abuse) as well as those with developmental disabilities (e.g., retardation, autism) benefit from early intervention in the first 3 years (Shore, 1997).

Another critical factor is that infants bond emotionally with parents or caregivers (Trawick-Smith, 2003), because this bonding protects the brain from trauma. When babies experience stress, the level of the hormone *cortisol* becomes elevated in their bodies. Cortisol retards brain development because it reduces the number of synapses and leaves neurons vulnerable to damage. This process produces poor brain development. In contrast, when babies form attachments and maintain them later on, cortisol levels do not become elevated (Gunnar, 1996). When attachments are secure, cortisol levels do not rise to dangerous levels even under stressful conditions. Thus, it is critical that young children believe that their parents or caregivers love them and are reliable.

Language Acquisition and Use

It is beyond the scope of this text to discuss brain research on different mental abilities. In this section a brief overview is given of what brain research has shown in the area of language acquisition and use. This is a key aspect of cognitive development and one that has profound implications for learning.

Unfortunately most brain research on language has been conducted on persons who have suffered brain injury and experienced some degree of language loss. Such research is informative of what functions are affected by injury to particular brain areas, but it does not address language acquisition and use in children's developing brains.

What brain trauma studies have shown conclusively is that the left side of the brain's cerebral cortex is central to reading and that the posterior cortical association areas of the left hemisphere are critical for understanding and using language and for normal reading (Vellutino & Denckla, 1996). Reading dysfunctions often are symptoms of left posterior cortical lesions. Autopsies of brains of adolescents and young adults with a history of reading difficulties have shown structural abnormalities in the left hemispheres. Reading dysfunctions also are sometimes associated with brain lesions in the anterior (frontal) lobes—the area that controls speech—although the evidence is much stronger with posterior abnormalities. Since these results come from studies of persons who knew how to read (to varying degrees) and then lost some or all of the ability, what we can conclude is that the primarily left-sided areas of the brain associated with language and speech are central to the maintenance of reading.

Brain studies of developing children, while less common, have offered interesting insights into the development of language functions. Studies often have compared normally developing children with those who have difficulties learning in school. In place of surgical techniques used on brain-injured or deceased patients, these studies often employ *event-related potentials*, or changes in brain waves measured while children are engaged in various tasks.

One finding from these studies is that children who are normally developing show extensive bilateral and anterior activation and accentuated left-sided activations in language and speech areas. Thus, in contrast to reading maintenance, it appears that reading development also depends on anterior activation, perhaps on both sides of the brain (Vellutino & Denckla, 1996). Other research shows that among developing children those who experience left-sided dysfunction apparently compensate somewhat by learning to read using the right hemisphere. Thus, the right hemisphere may be able to support and sustain an adequate level of reading, but it seems critical that this function occurs prior to the development of language competence. Such assumption of language functions by the right hemisphere may not occur among adults who have sustained left-hemisphere damage.

In summary, it appears that both sides of the brain participate in language development in normally developing children, although left-hemisphere contributions seem more prominent than right-hemisphere ones and that over time the functions are heavily subsumed by the left hemisphere. In particular, reading skill seems to require left-hemisphere control. Much more research is needed before we fully understand the relationships between brain functions and developing language and reading competencies.

Educational Implications

The history of behavioral science reflects a disconnect between brain research and learning theories. Research on the brain and behavior is not new; Hebb (1949), for example, formulated a neuropsychological theory of behavior. Learning theorists in various traditions, while acknowledging the importance of brain research, have tended to formulate and test theories independently of brain research findings.

That situation clearly has begun to change. Educational researchers increasingly believe that understanding brain processes provides additional insights into the nature of learning and development (Byrnes & Fox, 1998). Indeed, some cognitive explanations for learning (e.g., activation of information in memory, transfer of information from short- to long-term memory) undoubtedly have biological referents, and brain psychology may be able to identify how such activation and transfer occur. In fact, brain research actually supports many findings from learning research studies.

It is unfortunate that some educators have overgeneralized results of brain research to make unwarranted instructional recommendations. Remember that while brain functions are to some extent localized, there is much evidence that tasks require activity of both hemispheres and that their differences are more relative than absolute (Byrnes & Fox, 1998). The identification of "right-brained" and "left-brained" students often is based on informal observations rather than on scientifically valid and reliable measures and instruments. The result is that some educational methods are being used with students not because of proven effects on learning but rather because they presumably utilize students' brain preferences.

Brain research does offer some valid educational implications, which are substantiated by research. One certainly involves developmental changes. The fact that children's brains are super-dense implies that more is not necessarily better. In fact, there likely is an optimal state of functioning in which brains have the "right" number of neurons and synapses, not too many or too few. Development, then, may progress as the brain approaches its optimal state. Atypical development—resulting in developmental disabilities—may occur because this paring-down process does not proceed normally.

This suggests the importance of early childhood education. Infancy and preschool periods seem critically important for the development of school competencies (Byrnes & Fox, 1998). Many states are stressing preschool education programs, and brain research justifies this emphasis.

A second implication is that instruction and learning experiences must be planned to take into account the complexities of cognitive processes such as attention and memory. Thus, cognitive neuroscience research has shown that attention is not a unitary process but rather includes as many as seven components (e.g., alerting to a change in the current state, localizing the source of the change). Memory is similarly differentiated into as many as five types. The implication is that educators cannot assume that a particular instructional technique "commands students' attention" or "helps them remember"; rather, effects of instruction must be stated as specific effects.

Third, brain research suggests that the key to correcting deficiencies in a specific subject is to determine with which aspects of the subject the learner is having difficulty. Mathematics includes many subcomponents, such as comprehension of written numbers and symbols, fact retrieval, and inability to write numbers. Reading, for example, comprises orthographic, phonological, semantic, and syntactic processes. To say that one is a poor reader does not diagnose where the difficulty lies. Only fine-tuned assessment will make that identification. Once it is known, then a corrective procedure can be implemented that will address the specific deficiency. A general reading program that addresses all aspects of reading (e.g., word identification, word meanings) is analogous to a general antibiotic given to one who is sick; it may not be the best therapy. It seems educationally advantageous to offer corrective instruction in those areas that require correction most.

Finally, brain research has shown that multifaceted theories of learning seem to capture the actual state of affairs better than do parsimonious models. There is much redundancy in brain functions, which accounts for the common finding that when an area of the brain known to be associated with a given function is traumatized, the function may not completely disappear (another reason why the "right-brain" and "left-brain" distinctions do not hold much credibility). Over the years theories of learning have become more complex; compare the simpler explanations of Thorndike and Skinner with those of Bandura, cognitive psychologists, and constructivists. In fact, the latter better reflect brain reality. Thus, educators are advised to accept the complexity of school learning environments and investigate ways that their many aspects can work together to improve student learning.

MOTIVATION AND DEVELOPMENT

Motivation (Chapter 8) is not a static process but changes with development. Motivational influences on children may not have much effect on adolescents, and what motivates adolescents may be ineffective with adults. Within any developmental period not everyone is motivated in the same way.

Developmental researchers have identified ways that motivation changes with development (Table 10.8). These are discussed in turn.

Developmental Changes

We have seen in Chapter 8 that children's understanding of motivational processes changes with development (Wigfield & Eccles, 2002). For example, young children tend to equate ability with outcome and believe that children who perform better are more able. With development, the concepts of ability and effort are disentangled and children understand that both can affect outcomes. We also have seen how

Table 10.8
Developmental changes in
motivation.

With Development:
■ Children's understanding of motivational processes changes.
■ Motivation becomes more differentiated and complex.
■ Levels of motivation change.
■ Beliefs, values, and goals correspond better with choices and performances.
■ Long-term motivation is sustained better.

understanding of social comparison changes, from a focus more on physical characteristics to underlying qualities.

A related change is that motivation becomes more differentiated and complex (Wigfield & Eccles, 2002). Young children have a global sense of what they can do. As they develop and progress in school, they begin to focus their interests and develop separate conceptions of their abilities in different domains.

Third, the levels of children's motivation change with development (Wigfield & Eccles, 2002). We have noted how young children often are highly confident about what they can do but that these perceptions decline with development. Many factors have been implicated as producing this decrease, including school transitions, norm-referenced achievement feedback, social comparisons, and grading practices. It should be noted that this change is not always problematic. Focusing one's efforts on what one feels confident about learning or doing well can result in successes and a strong sense of self-efficacy. Similarly, avoiding what one feels one cannot do well can prevent failures. Still, in some children the decline becomes generalized to all academic areas, with resulting low performance, grades, and continuing motivation.

Fourth, with development children's beliefs, values, and goals correspond better with their performances and choices (Wigfield & Eccles, 2002). As children develop specific interests and feel competent about them, these are the activities in which they engage. Thus, motivation and behavior bear a closer resemblance to one another. It is not that one causes the other; they undoubtedly are related reciprocally. Whatever children feel competent to do, they work at and develop skills, and their perceptions of better performance increase self-efficacy (Bandura, 1997).

Finally, children become better able to sustain long-term motivation. Motivation among youngsters is short-term, as elementary teachers well know. With development students are able to represent long-term goals in thought, subdivide tasks into short-term subgoals, and assess progress. Self-monitoring of progress and changing strategies when they do not work well are hallmarks of higher-performing students in school.

Implications

The preceding points suggest how motivation strategies should be modified depending on students' developmental levels. With respect to goal setting, the suggestion is that short-term (proximal) and specific goals be used with young children. Given their immediate time frames of reference, a goal beyond the immediate context is apt to have little or no motivational effect.

It is important to work with students on goal setting and help them break long-term goals into subgoals with timelines. When teachers assign projects, they can help students understand the component tasks and formulate completion schedules. Students then can check their progress against the plan to determine whether they are on track to finish on time. Goal setting and self-monitoring of progress are key motivational processes contributing to self-regulation (B. Zimmerman, 2000).

That most young children generally are optimistic about what they can do seems desirable for motivation. The down side, however, is that they may attempt many tasks beyond their means and experience failures. Since most work in elementary grades involves basic skills, teachers present tasks to students that they should be able to master. As tasks become tougher, teachers may want to warn students about the added difficulty. Trying hard and not succeeding on a difficult task does not have the negative effects on perceived ability that can result when students perceive a task as easy.

As the capacity to socially compare increases to include internal qualities (e.g., abilities), it behooves teachers to try to focus students' comparisons on their own progress rather than on how their performances compare with those of their peers. Earlier in this text (Chapters 3 and 8) it was noted that self-evaluations of progress exert important effects on self-efficacy. Even when children know that their performances lag behind those of others, if they believe they have made progress, they also may believe that they can continue to do so and eventually they will be at the higher levels.

Many schools have mottos such as "All children can learn." This type of motto implies that teachers and administrators do not accept excuses for failure. Even if there is a decline in children's perceived capabilities as they grow older, it should not lead to failure so long as the decline is not great and there is an attitude in the school that students need not fail. If the decline results in more-accurate correspondence with actual performance, then students are in good position to assess their strengths and weaknesses and help identify areas where they need additional instruction. Keeping capability self-perceptions tied to progress is critical for motivation. Applications based on developmental changes in motivation are given in Application 10.6.

DEVELOPMENT AND INSTRUCTION

Developmental theories and principles suggest many ways to tailor instruction to take developmental differences into account. Earlier in this chapter we examined developmentally appropriate instruction and the instructional implications of Piaget's and Bruner's theories. This section covers Case's instructional model and teacher-student interactions.

Case's Model of Instruction

Case (1978a, 1978b, 1981) described cognitive development as the acquisition of efficient strategies for processing information. Development produces an increase in the size of working memory (WM). As strategies become more efficient (automatic), they consume less WM space, which frees space for acquiring new strategies.

Motivation and Development

Research offers several insights into how teachers can appeal to motivational processes at different points in development. Young children are motivated by teacher praise and positive consequences of their actions. Kathy Stone sets the tone for her class by always reminding them that they can learn. She praises students for their learning progress (e.g., "That's great—you really are learning how to do this"). Students earn free time by completing their work and following classroom rules. She also praises desirable behavior (e.g., "I like the way you are working so hard today"), and uses social comparative information to change undesirable behavior (e.g., "Tisha, see how well Brianna is working—I know that you can do just as well").

Jim Marshall knows that not all of his students are intrinsically interested in history. He also knows that his students are concerned about perceptions of ability and do not want to be seen as incapable of learning. In class he attempts to minimize activities that highlight ability differences, such as history bees and quick answers to questions. Rather, he has students work on group projects in which each student is responsible for certain tasks contributing to the final product. Group members also share the responsibility for class presentations and dramatizations of historical events. Although Jim gives grades for tests and assignments, in the public arena he provides a context in which all students can succeed and be perceived positively by others.

Gina Brown capitalizes on her knowledge that as students become older they can evaluate their capabilities more realistically. In preparation for unit tests she has students evaluate their capabilities to perform different tasks, such as, "Define key terms in Piaget's theory," and, "Explain how peer models might be used in a classroom to teach skills and build observers' self-efficacy." She provides study materials on appropriate topics for students who evaluate themselves low in a particular area. She reviews with the class those topics in which self-evaluations are generally low. In conjunction with students' field placements in schools, she asks them to evaluate their skills for such tasks as "Tutor a child in reading," and "Assist the teacher in designing a lesson on fractions." Working with teachers in the schools, Dr. Brown holds tutorials on topics in which students' self-evaluations indicate low perceived capabilities. Allowing students to provide self-evaluations helps them take more responsibility for their learning and inculcates the type of self-reflection on teaching that their academic programs are attempting to foster.

Case emphasized providing instruction to help students process information more automatically. One first identifies the learning goal and the steps through which learners must proceed to reach the goal. Instructional designers follow a *novice-to-expert approach* by comparing the performances and reported thoughts of experts with those of novices (see Chapter 9). Instruction is designed to include exercises demonstrating to students inadequacies of their less-efficient task approaches. During instruction, demands on WM are reduced by not presenting too much new material at once and by breaking each complex step into simpler steps.

This process can be illustrated with missing addend problems of the form 4 + __ = 7 (Case, 1978b). The required steps are as follows:

- Read symbols from left to right.
- Note that quantity to be found is one of the two addends.
- Decide that the known addend must be subtracted from the known total.
- Note and store value of the given addend.
- Note and store value of the total.
- Perform the subtraction. (p. 214)

Children commonly make two types of strategy errors in solving the above problem: (a) They give either 4 or 7 as the answer, seemingly by first looking at the symbols and reading one of them, then copying this symbol as the answer; and (b) they add the two given numbers to get 11 by performing the following strategy:

- Look at and store the first symbol.
- Count out that many (on fingers).
- Look at and store the second symbol.
- Count out that many.
- Count out the total number.
- Write this number as the answer.

To show children that their strategies are incorrect, a teacher might use faces. A full face is placed on one side of an equal sign and a half face on the other. Children see that these faces are not the same. Then a full face is portrayed on one side of the equal sign and two half faces on the other side, where one half face has markings on it and the other is blank. Children fill in the markings on the blank half to make it the same as the full face. Eventually numerical symbols are introduced to replace the faces.

Case's model, like Gagné's conditions of learning (Chapter 6), assesses learners' initial states of knowledge and specifies learning goals and a sequence of steps to move learners from lower to higher levels of proficiency. The models differ in the organization of steps. Gagné specifies component intellectual skills learners must master before acquiring the target skill; Case emphasizes the strategies learners employ. Case also places greater importance on minimizing WM demands and designing instruction to show learners the problems with their current approaches.

Case (1978a) cited evidence showing that the previous method is more effective than either structured practice or traditional instruction. Case's theory has been applied to the design of instruction and other areas such as assessment and early childhood education (Case, 1993). One drawback of the theory is the time required to diagnose, analyze, and plan. Case recommends its use with students with mental handicaps and those requiring remedial assistance because they tend to use inefficient strategies and have WM limitations. It seems, however, that the model may be appropriate for use with any learner, especially with difficult tasks and where objectives and solution strategies can be clearly specified.

Teacher-Student Interactions

Classrooms are active places. Teachers ask questions, provide feedback, administer rewards and punishments, praise and criticize, and respond to students' questions and requests for assistance. These interactions affect student learning. This section covers feedback and classroom climate from a developmental perspective.

Feedback. Teachers need to provide performance feedback (e.g., "Correct," "Good") and maintain lesson momentum when students make mistakes by giving corrective feedback but not completely reexplaining the process (Rosenshine & Stevens, 1986). Reteaching is called for when many students do not understand the material. When leading lessons, teachers should keep interactions with younger students brief (30 or fewer seconds) when such interactions are geared to leading them toward the correct answer with hints or simple questions. Longer contacts lose other students' attention.

Reteaching and leading students to correct answers are effective ways to promote learning (Rosenshine & Stevens, 1986). Asking simpler questions and giving hints are useful when contacts can be kept short (Anderson, Evertson, & Brophy, 1979). Reteaching is helpful when many students make errors during a lesson (Good & Grouws, 1979). Feedback informing students that answers are correct motivates because it indicates the students are becoming more competent and are capable of further learning (Schunk, 1989). Feedback indicating an error also can build efficacy if followed by corrective information on how to perform better. Younger students benefit from frequent feedback.

Similarly, other interactions involving rewards, goals, contracts, and so forth must be linked with student progress. For example, rewards linked to progress build self-efficacy (Schunk, 1983e). With children, progress is best indicated with short-term tasks. Rewards given merely for participation regardless of level of performance actually may convey negative efficacy information. Students may wonder whether they are capable of performing better.

Classroom Climate. Teachers help to establish a *classroom climate* that affects interactions. A classic study by Lewin, Lippitt, and White (1939) showed that a *democratic (collaborative) leadership style* is effective. The teacher works cooperatively with students, motivating them to work on tasks, posing questions, and having them share their ideas. Although an *authoritarian style* can produce high achievement, high anxiety levels characterize such classrooms and productivity drops off when the teacher is absent. A *laissez-faire style* with the teacher providing little classroom direction results in wasted time and aimless activities. Democratic leadership encourages independence and initiative in students, who continue to work productively in the teacher's absence.

Teacher-student interactions often include praise and criticism. An extensive literature exists on the effects of these variables on student behavior.

Praise goes beyond simple feedback on accuracy of work or appropriateness of behavior because it conveys positive teacher affect and provides information about the worth of students' behaviors (Brophy, 1981). Thus, a teacher who says, "Correct, your work is so good," is providing both performance feedback ("Correct") and praise ("Your work is so good").

Brophy (1981) reviewed research on teacher praise and found that it does not always reinforce desirable behavior (Chapter 2) because teachers often do not give it based on student responses. Rather, it may be infrequent, noncontingent, general, and highly dependent on teachers' perceptions of students' need for praise (Wittrock, 1986). Many studies also show that praise is not strongly related to student achievement (Dunkin & Biddle, 1974). The effects of praise seem to depend on developmental level, socioeconomic status (SES), and ability. In the early elementary grades, praise correlates weakly but positively with achievement among low SES and low-ability students but weakly and negatively or not at all with achievement among high SES and high-ability students (Brophy, 1981).

After the first few grades in school, praise is a weak reinforcer. Up to approximately age 8, children want to please adults, which makes praise effects powerful, but this desire to please weakens with development. Praise also can have unintended effects. Because it conveys information about teachers' beliefs, teachers who praise students for success convey that they do not expect students to learn much. Students believe the teacher thinks they have low ability, and this negatively affects motivation and learning (Weiner et al., 1983).

When linked to progress in learning, praise substantiates students' beliefs that they are becoming more competent and raises self-efficacy and motivation for learning. Praise used indiscriminantly carries no information about capabilities and has little effect on behavior (Pintrich & Schunk, 2002).

Criticism provides information about undesirability of student behaviors. Criticism ("I'm disappointed in you") is distinguished from performance feedback ("That's wrong"). Interestingly, research shows criticism is not necessarily bad (Dunkin & Biddle, 1974). We might expect that criticism's effect on achievement will depend on the extent to which it conveys that students are competent and can perform better with more effort or better use of strategies. Thus, a statement such as, "I'm disappointed in you. I know you can do better if you work harder" might motivate students to learn because it contains positive self-efficacy information. As with praise, other variables temper the effects of criticism. Some research shows that criticism is given more often to boys, African American students, students for whom teachers hold low expectations, and students of lower SES status (Brophy & Good, 1974).

As a motivational technique to aid learning, criticism probably is not a good choice because it can have variable effects. Younger children may misinterpret academic criticism to mean that the teacher does not like them or is mean. Some students respond well to criticism. In general, however, teachers are better advised to

APPLICATION 10.7
Using Praise and Criticism

The praise and criticism teachers use as they interact with their students can impact student performance. Teachers must be careful to use both appropriately and remember that criticism generally is not a good choice because it can have variable effects.

Praise is most effective when it is simple and direct and is linked with accomplishment of specific actions. For example, a teacher who is complimenting a student for sitting quietly, concentrating, and completing his or her work accurately that day should not say, "You really have been good today" (too general). Instead, the teacher might say something such as, "I really like the way you worked hard at your seat and finished all of your math work today. It paid off because you got all of the division problems correct. Great job!"

When a student answers a question in American history class during a discussion about a chapter, it is desirable that Jim Marshall let him or her know why the answer was a good one. Instead of replying, "Good answer," Mr. Marshall adds, "You outlined very well the three points in that chapter."

If criticism is used, it should convey that students are competent and can perform better, which may motivate performance. For example, assume that a capable student submitted a very poor educational psychology project that did not fulfill the assignment. Gina Brown says to her student, "John, I am very disappointed in you. You are one of the best students in our class. You always share a great deal in class and perform well on all the tests. I know you are capable of completing an outstanding project. Let's work some more on this assignment and try harder as you redo this project."

provide positive feedback about ways to improve performance than to criticize present performance. Application 10.7 offers ways to use praise and criticism in learning settings.

SUMMARY

Development refers to changes over time that follow an orderly pattern and enhance survival. These changes are progressive and occur during the life span. Development is intimately linked with learning because at any time developmental level places constraints on learning.

The scientific study of human development began in the late 1800s. Major societal changes occurred through technological advances and vast influxes of immigrants. Society needed teachers and schools to educate many students from diverse backgrounds. Drawing from psychology and philosophy, many educators banded together under the loosely organized Child Study Movement. Early efforts at child study generated research and provided implications of development for teachers and parents, but the broad agenda of the Child Study Movement eventually was replaced by behaviorism and other theories.

Researchers have many perspectives on development: biological, psychoanalytic, behavioral, cognitive, and contextual. Regardless of perspective, certain issues exist that developmental theories address, including the role of heredity, the stability of developmental periods, the continuity of processes, the role of learner activity, and the locus of developmental changes (structures or functions).

Structural theories include Chomsky's psycholinguistic theory, classical information processing theory, and Piaget's theory. These theories postulate that development involves changes in cognitive structures. Information that is learned can help to alter the structures. Piaget's theory is well known. It postulates that children pass through a series of qualitatively different stages: sensorimotor, preoperational, concrete operational, and formal operational. The chief developmental mechanism is equilibration, which helps to resolve cognitive conflicts by changing the nature of reality to fit existing structures (assimilation) or changing structures to incorporate reality (accommodation). Piaget's, Vygotsky's, and many other theories of development reflect a constructivist perspective because they postulate that knowledge is not acquired automatically but rather that learners construct their own understandings.

Bruner's theory of cognitive growth discusses the ways that learners represent knowledge: enactively, iconically, and symbolically. He also advocated the spiral curriculum, in which subject matter is periodically revisited with increasing cognitive development and student understanding.

Many developmental researchers study how cognitive information processes change as a function of experiences and schooling. Developmental changes are seen especially in the functions of attention, encoding, retrieval, metacognition, and self-regulation. Cognitive developmental theory and research have important implications for designing developmentally appropriate instruction and for helping to ease transitions in schooling.

Familial influences on development include socioeconomic status (SES), home environment, and parental involvement. SES relates to school socialization, attendance, and years of schooling. Higher SES families have greater capital and provide more and richer opportunities for children. Early interventions for low-SES families help prepare children for school. Home environment effects on cognitive development are most pronounced in infancy and early childhood. With development, social networks expand and peers become more important. Parents can launch children onto trajectories by involving them in groups and activities. Parents' expectations for children relate positively to their achievement. Comer's School Development Program involves parents and community members in school planning.

The brain develops rapidly in infants; young children have complex neural connections. As children lose brain synapses, those they retain depend partly on the activities they engage in. Early brain development benefits from rich experiences and emotional bonding with parents and caregivers. Brain functions become lateralized with the left hemisphere governing language and analytical thinking and the right hemisphere responsible for spatial and auditory perception, although research shows that most tasks require activity by both hemispheres and that lateralization differences are more relative than absolute. Brain research suggests that early education is critical, instruction should take children's cognitive complexities into account, and assessment of specific problems is necessary to plan proper interventions.

With development motivation becomes more differentiated and complex; children's understanding of motivational processes (e.g., goals, social comparisons) and levels of motivation change; there is better correspondence between children's values, beliefs, and goals and their choices and performances; and long-term motivation becomes important. Children are motivated by short-term, specific goals and comparisons of progress in performance. With development, breaking tasks into subgoals and self-evaluations of progress become more motivating.

Developmental theories suggest that instruction be tailored to take differences into account. Case's model emphasizes helping students process information more automatically. After learners' initial knowledge is assessed, learning goals and task sequences are specified to move learners to greater proficiency. Teacher-student interactions should reflect developmental changes. Teachers who structure feedback and provide a positive classroom climate—which includes effectively using praise and criticism—help motivate students and improve their learning.

Glossary

Accommodation The process of changing internal structures to provide consistency with external reality.

Accretion Encoding new information in terms of existing schemata.

Achievement Motivation The striving to be competent in effortful activities.

Act A class of movements that produces an outcome.

Action Control Potentially modifiable self-regulatory volitional skills and strategies.

Activation Level Extent that information in memory is being processed or is capable of being processed quickly; information in an active state is quickly accessible.

Actualizing Tendency Innate motive that is a precursor to other motives and is oriented toward personal growth, autonomy, and freedom from external control.

Adaptation See *Equilibration*.

Adapting Instruction Tailoring instructional conditions at the system, course, or individual class level to match important individual differences to ensure equal learning opportunities for all students.

Advance Organizer Device that helps connect new material with prior learning, usually with a broad statement presented at the outset of a lesson.

Affective Learning Technique Specific procedure included in a learning strategy to create a favorable psychological climate for learning by helping the learner cope with anxiety, develop positive beliefs, set work goals, establish a place and time for working, or minimize distractions.

All-or-None Learning View that a response is learned by proceeding from zero or low strength to full strength rapidly (e.g., during one trial).

Analogical Reasoning Problem-solving strategy in which one draws an analogy between the problem situation and a situation with which one is familiar, works through the problem in the familiar domain, and relates the solution to the problem situation.

Apprenticeship Situation in which novice works with expert in joint work-related activities.

Aptitude-Treatment Interaction Differential response to variations in instruction depending on learner characteristics.

Archival Record Permanent record that exists independently of other assessments.

Artificial Intelligence Programming computers to engage in human activities such as thinking, using language, and solving problems.

Assimilation The process of fitting external reality to existing cognitive structures.

Assistive Technology Equipment adapted for use by students with disabilities.

Associative Shifting Process of changing behavior whereby responses made to a particular stimulus eventually are made to a different stimulus as a consequence of altering the stimulus slightly on repeated trials.

Associative Strength Strength of association between a stimulus and a response.

Associative Structure Means of representing information in long-term memory; bits of information that occur close together in time or that otherwise are associated and stored together so that when one is remembered, the other also is remembered.

Associative Writing Writing that reflects one's knowledge of a topic without regard for elements of style.

Asynchronous Learning Nonreal-time interactions.

Attention The process of selecting some environmental inputs for further information processing.

Attribution Perceived cause of an outcome.

Attribution Retraining Intervention strategy aimed at altering students' attributional beliefs, usually from dysfunctional attributions (e.g., failure attributed to low ability) to those conducive to motivation and learning (failure attributed to low effort).

Autoclitic Behaviors Class of verbal responses that depend on or express a relation to other responses.

Automaticity Cognitive processing with little or no conscious awareness.

Axon Long thread of brain tissue in a neuron that sends messages.

Baby Biography A report on a single child based on a series of observations over a lengthy period.

Balance Theory Theory postulating the tendency for people to balance relations between persons, situations, and events.

Behavior Modification (Therapy) Systematic application of behavioral learning principles to facilitate adaptive behaviors.

Behavior Rating An estimate of how often a behavior occurs in a given time.

Behavioral Objective Statement describing the behaviors a student will perform as a result of instruction, the conditions under which behaviors will be performed, and the criteria for assessing behaviors to determine whether the objective has been accomplished.

Behavioral Theory Theory that views learning as a change in the form or frequency of behavior as a consequence of environmental events.

Behavioral Trace See *Archival Record*.

Biologically Primary Ability An ability that is largely biologically based.

Biologically Secondary Ability An ability that is largely culturally taught.

Blended Model Instruction that combines face-to-face instruction with E-learning.

Bottom-Up Processing Pattern recognition of visual stimuli that proceeds from analysis of features to building a meaningful representation.

Brainstorming Problem-solving strategy that comprises defining the problem, generating possible solutions, deciding on criteria to use in judging solutions, and applying criteria to select the best solution.

Branching Program Type of programmed instruction in which students complete different sequences depending on how well they perform.

Buggy Algorithm An incorrect rule for solving a mathematical problem.

Capital Socioeconomic indicator that includes one's financial, material, human, and social resources.

Categorical Clustering Recalling items in groups based on similar meaning or membership in the same category.

Categorization Style   Cognitive style referring to the criteria used to perceive objects as similar to one another.

Chaining   The linking of three-term contingencies so that each response alters the environment and that altered condition serves as a stimulus for the next response.

Chameleon Effect   Nonconscious mimicking of behaviors and mannerisms of persons in one's social environment.

Chunking   Combining information in a meaningful fashion.

Classical Conditioning   Descriptive term for Pavlov's theory in which a neutral stimulus becomes conditioned to elicit a response through repeated pairing with an unconditioned stimulus.

Closed-Loop Theory   Theory of motor skill learning postulating that people develop perceptual traces of motor movements through practice and feedback.

Cognitive Behavior Modification   Behavior modification techniques that incorporate learners' thoughts (overt and covert) as discriminative and reinforcing stimuli.

Cognitive Consistency   Idea that people have a need to make behaviors and cognitions consistent.

Cognitive Dissonance   Mental tension that is produced by conflicting cognitions and that has drive-like properties leading to reduction.

Cognitive Map   Internal plan comprising expectancies of which actions are required to attain one's goal.

Cognitive Modeling   Modeled explanation and demonstration incorporating verbalizations of the model's thoughts and reasons for performing given actions.

Cognitive Style   Stable variation among learners in ways of perceiving, organizing, processing, and remembering information.

Cognitive (Response) Tempo   Cognitive style referring to the willingness to pause and reflect on the accuracy of information in a situation of response uncertainty.

Cognitive Theory   Theory that views learning as the acquisition of knowledge and cognitive structures due to information processing.

Collective Teacher Efficacy   Perceptions of teachers in a school that their efforts as a whole will positively affect students.

Comer Program   See *School Development Program*.

Comparative Organizer   Type of advance organizer that introduces new material by drawing an analogy with familiar material.

Comprehension   Attaching meaning to verbal (printed or spoken) information and using it for a particular purpose.

Comprehension Monitoring   Cognitive activity directed toward determining whether one is properly applying knowledge to material to be learned, evaluating whether one understands the material, deciding that the strategy is effective or that a better strategy is needed, and knowing why strategy use improves learning. Monitoring procedures include self-questioning, rereading, paraphrasing, and checking consistencies.

Computer-Based (-Assisted) Instruction   Interactive instruction in which a computer system provides information and feedback to students and receives student input.

Computer Learning   Learning that occurs with the aid of a computer.

Computer Literacy   The minimum knowledge of computers and capabilities to operate them that people need to function well in society.

Computer-Mediated Communication   Technological applications that allow users to communicate with one another (e.g., distance education, computer conferencing).

Concept   Labeled set of objects, symbols, or events sharing common characteristics (critical attributes).

Concept Learning   Identifying attributes, generalizing them to new examples, and discriminating examples from non-examples.

Conception of Ability   One's belief/theory about the nature of intelligence (ability) and how it changes over time.

Concrete Operational Stage   Third of Piaget's stages of cognitive development, encompassing roughly ages 7 to 11.

Conditional Knowledge   Knowledge of when to employ forms of declarative and procedural knowledge and why doing so is important.

Conditional Regard   Regard that is contingent on certain actions.

Conditioned Response (CR)   The response elicited by a conditioned stimulus.

Conditioned Stimulus (CS)   A stimulus that, when repeatedly paired with an unconditioned stimulus, elicits a conditioned response similar to the unconditioned response.

Conditions of Learning   Circumstances that prevail when learning occurs and that include internal conditions (prerequisite skills and cognitive processing requirements of the learner) and external conditions (environmental stimuli that support the learner's cognitive processes).

Connectionism   Descriptive term for Thorndike's theory postulating learning as the forming of connections between sensory experiences (perceptions of stimuli or events) and neural impulses that manifest themselves behaviorally.

Connectionist Model   Computer simulation of learning processes in which learning is linked with neural system processing where impulses fire across synapses to form connections.

Constructivism   Doctrine stating that learning takes place in contexts and that learners form or construct much of what they learn and understand as a function of their experiences in situations.

Contiguity (Contiguous Conditioning)   The basic principle of Guthrie's theory, which refers to learning that results from a pairing close in time of a response with a stimulus or situation.

Contingency Contract   Written or oral agreement between teacher and student specifying what work the student must accomplish to earn a particular reinforcer.

Continuous Reinforcement   Reinforcement for every response.

Control (Executive) Processes   Cognitive activities that regulate the flow of information through the processing system.

Cooperative Learning   Situation in which a group of students work on a task that is too great for any one student to complete and in which an objective is to develop in students the ability to work collaboratively.

Coping Model   Model who initially demonstrates the typical fears and deficiencies of observers but gradually demonstrates improved performance and self-confidence in his or her capabilities.

Correlational Research   A study in which an investigator explores naturally existing relations among variables.

Cortisol   Bodily hormone that when elevated in babies can retard their brain development.

Declarative Knowledge   Knowledge that something is the case; knowledge of facts, beliefs, organized passages, and events of a story.

Decoding   Deciphering printed symbols or making letter-sound correspondences.

Deductive Reasoning   Process of deriving specific points from general principles.

Deep Structure   The meaning of the speech and syntax of a language.

Dendrite   Elongated brain tissue surrounding a neuron that receives messages.

Descriptive Research   See *Qualitative Research*.

Determining Tendency   Process that allows a goal to be translated into action.

Development   Changes in people over time that follow an orderly pattern and enhance survival.

Developmental Status   What an individual is capable of doing given his or her present level of development.

Developmentally Appropriate Instruction   Instruction matched to students' developmental levels.

Dialectical Constructivism   Constructivist perspective stating that knowledge derives from interactions between persons and their environments.

Dialogue   Conversation between two or more persons while engaged in a learning task.

Dichotic Listening   Hearing two verbal inputs simultaneously.

Differentiated Task Structure   Class situation in which all students work on different tasks and materials or methods are tailored to students' needs.

Digit-Span Task   Information processing task in which participants hear a series of digits and then attempt to recall them in the same order.

Direct Observations   Instances of behavior that are observed.

Discovery Learning   A type of inductive reasoning in which one obtains knowledge by formulating and testing hypotheses through hands-on experiences.

Discrimination   Responding differently, depending on the stimulus.

Discriminative Stimulus   The stimulus to which one responds in the operant model of conditioning.

Disinhibition   See *Inhibition/Disinhibition*.

Distance Learning (Education)   Instruction that originates at one site and is transmitted to students at one or more remote sites; it may include two-way interactive capabilities.

Domain Specificity   Discrete declarative and procedural knowledge structures.

Drive   Internal force that energizes and propels one into action.

Dual-Code Theory   The view that long-term memory represents knowledge with a verbal system that includes knowledge expressed in language and an imaginal system that stores visual and spatial information.

Dual-Memory Model of Information Processing   See *Two-Store (Dual-Memory) Model of Information Processing*.

Duration Measure   Amount of time a behavior occurs during a given period.

Echo   Sensory memory for auditory sounds.

Echoic   Type of verbal response that imitates or is associated with another response.

Effectance Motivation (Mastery Motivation)   Motivation to interact effectively with one's environment and control critical aspects.

Efficacy Expectations   See *Self-Efficacy*.

Ego Involvement   Motivational state characterized by self-preoccupation, a desire to avoid looking incompetent, and viewing learning as a means to the end of avoiding appearing to lack ability.

Egocentrism   Cognitive inability to take the perspective of another person.

Eidetic Imagery   Photographic memory in which an image appears and disappears in segments.

Elaboration   The process of expanding upon new information by adding to it or linking it to what one already knows.

Elaboration Theory of Instruction   Means of presenting instruction in which one begins with a general view of the content, moves to specific details, and returns later to the general view with review and practice.

E-Learning   Learning through electronic means.

Electronic Bulletin Board (Conference)   Electronic means for posting messages and participating in a discussion (chat group).

Empiricism   The doctrine that experience is the only source of knowledge.

Enactive Learning   Learning through actual performance.

Enactive Representation   Representing knowledge through motor responses.

Encoding   The process of putting new, incoming information into the information processing system and preparing it for storage in long-term memory.

Encoding Specificity   The idea that retrieval of information from long-term memory is maximized when retrieval cues match those present during encoding.

Endogenous Constructivism   Constructivist perspective stating that people construct mental structures out of preexisting structures and not directly from environmental information.

Entity Theory   The belief that abilities represent fixed traits over which one has little control.

Episodic Memory   Memory of particular times, places, persons, and events, which is personal and autobiographical.

Epistemology   Study of the origin, nature, limits, and methods of knowledge.

Equilibration   A biological drive to produce an optimal state of equilibrium; it includes the complementary processes of assimilation and accommodation.

Event-Related Potentials   Changes in brain waves measured while individuals are engaged in various tasks.

Executive Processes   See *Control (Executive) Processes*.

Exogenous Constructivism Constructivist perspective stating that the acquisition of knowledge represents a reconstruction of structures that exist in the external world.

Expectancy-Value Theory Psychological theory postulating that behavior is a function of how much one values a particular outcome and one's expectation of obtaining that outcome as a result of performing that behavior.

Experimental Research A study in which an investigator systematically varies conditions (independent variables) and observes changes in outcomes (dependent variables).

Expert A person who has attained a high level of competence in a domain.

Expert System Computer system that is programmed with a large knowledge base and that behaves intelligently by solving problems and providing instruction.

Expository Organizer Type of advance organizer that introduces new material with concept definitions and generalizations.

Expository Teaching Deductive teaching strategy in which material is presented in an organized and meaningful fashion with general ideas followed by specific points.

Extinction Decrease in intensity and disappearance of a conditioned response due to repeated presentations of the conditioned stimulus without the unconditioned stimulus.

Extrinsic Motivation Engaging in a task as a means to the end of attaining an outcome (reward).

Facilitator One who arranges resources and shares feelings and thoughts with students in order to promote learning.

Fatigue Method of Behavioral Change Altering behavior by transforming the cue for engaging in the behavior into a cue for avoiding it through repeated presentation.

Fear of Failure The tendency to avoid an achievement goal that derives from one's belief concerning the anticipated negative consequences of failing.

Fear of Success The tendency to avoid succeeding at an achievement task that derives from anxiety and the anticipated negative consequences of succeeding (e.g., social rejection).

Feature Analysis Theory of perception postulating that people learn the critical features of stimuli, which are stored in long-term memory as images or verbal codes and compared with environmental inputs.

Field Dependence and Independence Cognitive style referring to the extent that one is dependent on or distracted by the context in which a stimulus or event occurs. Also called Global and Analytical Functioning.

Field Expectancy Perceived relation between two stimuli or between a stimulus, response, and stimulus.

Field Research Study conducted where participants live, work, or go to school.

Filter Theory Theory of attention contending that information not perceived is not processed beyond the sensory register.

First Signal System See *Primary Signals*.

Flow Total involvement in an activity.

Forgetting Loss of information from memory or inability to recall information due to interference or improper retrieval cues.

Formal Operational Stage Fourth of Piaget's stages of cognitive development, encompassing roughly ages 11 to adult.

Free Recall Recalling stimuli in any order.

Frequency Count Frequency of a behavior in a given time period.

Functional Analysis of Behavior Process of determining the external variables of which behavior is a function.

Functional Fixedness Failure to perceive different uses for objects or new configurations of elements in a situation.

Functional Theories of Development Theories postulating the types of functions or processes that a child is able to perform at a particular time.

Functionalism Doctrine postulating that mental processes and behaviors of living organisms help them adapt to their environments.

Game Activity that creates an enjoyable learning context by linking material to sport, adventure, or fantasy.

General Skill Skill applying to many domains (e.g., goal setting).

Generalization Occurrence of a response to a new stimulus or in a situation other than that present during original learning. See also *Transfer*.

Generalized Reinforcer A secondary reinforcer that becomes paired with more than one primary or secondary reinforcer.

Generate-and-Test Strategy Problem-solving strategy in which one generates (thinks of) a possible problem solution and tests its effectiveness.

Gestalt Principles *Figure-ground relationship*: A perceptual field is composed of a figure against a background. *Proximity*: Elements in a perceptual field are viewed as belonging together according to their closeness in space or time. *Similarity*: Perceptual field elements similar in such respects as size or color are viewed as belonging together. *Common direction*: Elements of a perceptual field appearing to constitute a pattern or flow in the same direction are perceived as a figure. *Simplicity*: People organize perceptual fields in simple, regular features. *Closure*: People fill in incomplete patterns or experiences.

Gestalt Psychology Psychological theory of perception and learning stressing the organization of sensory experiences.

Given-New Contract Implicit agreement between speaker and listener in which speaker mentally identifies information that is known (given) and unknown (new) to the listener and communicates new information by referring when necessary to given information.

Global and Analytical Functioning See *Field Dependence and Independence*.

Goal The behavior (outcome) that one is consciously trying to perform (attain).

Goal Orientations Reasons for engaging in academic tasks.

Goal Setting Process of establishing a standard or objective to serve as the aim of one's actions.

Grammar The underlying abstract set of rules governing a language.

Grouping Structure Instructional method for linking attainment of students' goals. *Cooperative*—positive; *competitive*—negative; *individualistic*—no link.

Habit Behavior established to many cues.

Hedonism Philosophical position that humans seek pleasure and avoid pain.

Heuristic A method for solving problems in which one employs principles (rules of thumb) that usually lead to a solution.

Higher-Order Conditioning Use of a conditioned stimulus to condition a new, neutral stimulus by pairing the two stimuli.

Hill Climbing See *Working Forward*.

Holism Idea that we must study people's behaviors, thoughts, and feelings together and not in isolation.

Homeostasis Optimal levels of physiological states.

Hope for Success The tendency to approach an achievement goal that derives from one's subjective estimate of the likelihood of succeeding.

Humanistic Theory Theory emphasizing people's capabilities to make choices and seek control over their lives.

Hypothesis Assumption that can be empirically tested.

Icon Sensory memory for visual inputs.

Iconic Representation Representing knowledge with mental images.

Identical Elements View of transfer postulating that application of a response in a situation other than the one in which it was learned depends on the number of features (stimuli) common to the two situations.

Imitation Copying the observed behaviors and verbalizations of others.

Implicit Theories Students' beliefs about themselves, others, and their environments.

Inclusion Process of integrating students with disabilities into regular classroom instruction.

Incompatible Response Method of Behavioral Change Altering behavior by pairing the cue for the undesired behavior with a response incompatible with (i.e., that cannot be performed at the same time as) the undesired response.

Incremental Learning View that learning becomes established gradually through repeated performances (exemplified by Thorndike's theory).

Incremental Theory The belief that abilities are skills that can improve through learning.

Inductive Reasoning Process of formulating general principles based on specific examples.

Information Processing Sequence and execution of cognitive events.

Inhibition In Pavlov's theory, a type of neural excitation that works antagonistically to an excitation producing conditioning and that diminishes the conditioned response in intensity or extinguishes it.

Inhibition/Disinhibition Strengthening/weakening of inhibitions over behaviors previously learned, which results from observing consequences of the behaviors performed by models.

Inquiry Teaching Socratic teaching method in which learners formulate and test hypotheses, differentiate

necessary from sufficient conditions, make predictions, and decide when more information is needed.

Insight A sudden perception, awareness of a solution, or transformation from an unlearned to a learned state.

Instinct A natural behavior or capacity.

Instructional Quality The degree to which instruction is effective, efficient, appealing, and economical in promoting student performance and attitude toward learning.

Instructional Scaffolding See *Scaffolding*.

Instructional Self-Efficacy Personal beliefs about one's capabilities to help students learn.

Interference Blockage of the spread of activation across memory networks.

Intermittent Reinforcement Reinforcement for some but not all responses.

Internalization Transforming information acquired from the social environment into mechanisms of self-regulating control.

Internet International collection of computer networks.

Interval Schedule Reinforcement is contingent on the first response being made after a specific time period.

Interview Situation in which interviewer presents questions or points to discuss and respondent answers orally.

Intrinsic Motivation Engaging in a task for no obvious reward except for the activity itself (the activity is the means and the end).

Introspection Type of self-analysis in which individuals verbally report their immediate perceptions following exposure to objects or events.

Irreversibility The cognitive belief that once something is done it cannot be changed.

Keller Plan (Personalized System of Instruction) Instructional program incorporating student self-pacing, mastery learning, and self-study of materials.

Keyword Method Mnemonic technique in which one generates an image of a word sounding like the item to be learned and links that image with the meaning of the item to be learned.

Laboratory Research Study conducted in a controlled setting.

Language Acquisition Device Mental structure that forms and verifies transformational rules to account for overt language.

Latent Learning Learning that occurs from environmental interactions in the absence of a goal or reinforcement.

Lateralization Control of specific functions by different sides of the brain.

Law of Disuse That part of the Law of Exercise postulating that the strength of a connection between a situation and response is decreased when the connection is not made over a period of time.

Law of Effect The strength of a connection is influenced by the consequences of performing the response in the situation: Satisfying consequences strengthen a connection; annoying consequences weaken a connection. Eventually modified by Thorndike to state that annoying consequences do not weaken connections.

Law of Exercise Learning (unlearning) occurs through repetition (nonrepetition) of a response. Eventually discarded by Thorndike.

Law of Readiness   When an organism is prepared to act, to do so is satisfying and not to do so is annoying. When an organism is not prepared to act, forcing it to act is annoying.

Law of Use   That part of the Law of Exercise postulating that the strength of a connection between a situation and response is increased when the connection is made.

Learned Helplessness   Psychological state involving a disturbance in motivation, cognition, and emotions due to previously experienced uncontrollability (lack of contingency between action and outcome).

Learning   An enduring change in behavior or in the capacity to behave in a given fashion resulting from practice or other forms of experience.

Learning Goal   A goal of acquiring knowledge, behaviors, skills, or strategies.

Learning Hierarchy   Organized set of intellectual skills.

Learning Method   Specific procedure or technique included in a learning strategy and used to attain a learning goal.

Learning Strategy   Systematic plan oriented toward regulating academic work and producing successful task performance.

Learning Style   See *Cognitive Style.*

Levels of Processing   Conceptualization of memory according to the type of processing that information receives rather than the processing's location.

Lexical Access   See *Decoding.*

Linear Program   Programmed instructional materials that all students complete in the same sequence.

Locus of Control   Motivational concept referring to generalized control over outcomes; individuals may believe that outcomes occur independently of how they act (external control) or are highly contingent on their actions (internal control).

Long-Term Memory   Stage of information processing corresponding to the permanent repository of knowledge.

Mand   Verbal response under the control of conditions associated with deprivation or aversive stimulation and reinforced when fulfilled by a listener.

Mapping   Learning technique in which one identifies important ideas and specifies how they are related.

Mastery Learning   A systematic instructional plan that has as its objective students demonstrating high achievement and that includes the components of defining mastery, planning for mastery, teaching for mastery, and grading for mastery.

Mastery Model   Model who demonstrates faultless performance and high self-confidence throughout the modeled sequence.

Mastery Motivation   See *Effectance Motivation.*

Matched-Dependent Behavior   Behavior matched to (the same as) that of the model and dependent on (elicited by) the model's action.

Meaningful Reception Learning   Learning of ideas, concepts, and principles when material is presented in final form and related to students' prior knowledge.

Means-Ends Analysis   Problem-solving strategy in which one compares the current situation with the goal to identify the differences between them, sets a subgoal to reduce one of the differences, performs operations to reach the subgoal, and repeats the process until the goal is attained.

Mediation   Mechanism that bridges the link between external reality and mental processes and affects the development of the latter.

Mental Discipline   The doctrine that learning certain subjects in school enhances mental functioning better than does studying other subjects.

Mental Imagery   Mental representation of spatial knowledge that includes physical properties of the object or event represented.

Metacognition   Deliberate conscious control of one's cognitive activities.

Method of Loci   Mnemonic technique in which information to be remembered is paired with locations in a familiar setting.

Mimesis   See *Imitation.*

Min Model   Counting method in which one begins with the larger addend and counts in the smaller one.

Mnemonic   A type of learning method that makes to-be-learned material meaningful by relating it to information that one already knows.

Modeling   Behavioral, cognitive, and affective changes deriving from observing one or more models.

Molar Behavior   A large sequence of behavior that is goal directed.

Motherese   Speaking to children in simple utterances, often in abbreviated form.

Motivated Learning   Motivation to acquire new knowledge, skills, and strategies, rather than merely to complete activities.

Motivation   The process of instigating and sustaining goal-directed activities.

Movement   Discrete behavior that results from muscle contractions.

Multidimensional Classroom   Classroom having many activities and allowing for diversity in student abilities.

Multimedia   Technology that combines the capabilities of computers with other media such as film, video, sound, music, and text.

Myelin Sheath   Brain tissue surrounding an axon and facilitating travel of signals.

Naïve Analysis of Action   The way that common people interpret events.

Narration   Written account of behavior and the context in which it occurs.

Negative Reinforcer   A stimulus that, when removed by a response, increases the future likelihood of the response occurring in that situation.

Negative Transfer   Prior learning makes subsequent learning more difficult.

Network   A set of interrelated propositions in long-term memory.

Networking   Computers in various locations connected to one another and to central peripheral devices.

Neuron   Brain cell that sends and receives information across muscles and organs.

Neurotransmitter   Chemical secretions that travel along a brain axon to dendrites of the next cell.

Nonsense Syllable   Three-letter (consonant-vowel-consonant) combination that makes a nonword.

Novice   A person who has some familiarity with a domain but performs poorly.

Novice-to-Expert Approach to Learning   Means of analyzing learning by comparing behaviors and reported thoughts of skilled individuals (experts) with those of less-skilled persons (novices) and deciding on an efficient means of moving novices to the expert level.

Observational Learning   Display of a new pattern of behavior by one who observes a model; prior to the modeling, the behavior has a zero probability of occurrence by the observer even with motivational inducements in effect.

Operant Behavior   Behavior that produces an effect on the environment.

Operant Conditioning   Presenting reinforcement contingent on a response emitted in the presence of a stimulus to increase the rate or likelihood of occurrence of the response.

Operational Definition   Definition of a phenomenon in terms of the operations or procedures used to measure it.

Oral Responses   Verbalized questions or answers to questions.

Outcome Expectation   Belief concerning the anticipated outcome of actions.

Overjustification   Decrease in intrinsic interest (motivation) in an activity subsequent to engaging in it under conditions that make task engagement salient as a means to some end (e.g., reward).

Paired-Associate Recall   Recalling the response of a stimulus-response item when presented with the stimulus.

Paradigm   Model for research.

Parsing   Mentally dividing perceived sound patterns into units of meaning.

Participant Modeling   Therapeutic treatment (used by Bandura) comprising modeled demonstrations, joint performance between client and therapist, gradual withdrawal of performance aids, and individual mastery performance by the client.

Pattern Recognition   See *Perception*.

Peer Collaboration   Learning that occurs when students work together and their social interactions serve an instructional function.

Peer Tutoring   Situation in which a student who has learned a skill teaches it to one who has not.

Pegword Method   Mnemonic technique in which the learner memorizes a set of objects rhyming with integer names (e.g., one is a bun, two is a shoe, etc.), generates an image of each item to be learned, and links it with the corresponding object image. During recall, the learner recalls the rhyming scheme with its associated links.

Perceived Control   Belief that one can influence task engagement and outcomes.

Perception   Process of recognizing and assigning meaning to a sensory input.

Performance Goal   A goal of completing a task.

Phi Phenomenon   Perceptual phenomenon of apparent motion caused by lights flashing on and off at short intervals.

Phonetic Approach   Reading method based on sounding out words by dividing them into syllables and generating corresponding sound patterns.

Positive Regard   Feelings such as respect, liking, warmth, sympathy, and acceptance.

Positive Reinforcer   A stimulus that, when presented following a response, increases the future likelihood of the response occurring in that situation.

Positive Self-Regard   Positive regard that derives from self-experiences.

Positive Transfer   Prior learning facilitates subsequent learning.

Postdecisional Processes   Cognitive activities engaged in subsequent to goal setting.

Predecisional Processes   Cognitive activities involved in making decisions and setting goals.

Premack Principle   The opportunity to engage in a more-valued activity reinforces engaging in a less-valued activity.

Preoperational Stage   Second of Piaget's stages of cognitive development, encompassing roughly ages 2 to 7.

Primacy Effect   Tendency to recall the initial items in a list.

Primary Qualities   Characteristics of objects (e.g., size, shape) that exist in the external world as part of the objects.

Primary Reinforcement   Behavioral consequence that satisfies a biological need.

Primary Signals   Environmental events that can become conditioned stimuli and produce conditioned responses.

Private Events   Thoughts or feelings accessible only to the individual.

Private Speech   The set of speech phenomena that has a self-regulatory function but is not socially communicative.

Proactive Interference   Old learning makes new learning more difficult.

Problem   A situation in which one is trying to reach a goal and must find a means of attaining it.

Problem Solving   One's efforts to achieve a goal for which one does not have an automatic solution.

Problem Space   The problem-solving context that comprises a beginning state, a goal state, and possible solution paths leading through subgoals and requiring application of operations.

Procedural Knowledge   Knowledge of how to do something: employ algorithms and rules, identify concepts, solve problems.

Process-Product Research   Study that relates changes in teaching processes to student products or outcomes.

Production   Translating visual and symbolic conceptions of events into behaviors.

Production Deficiency   The failure to generate task-relevant verbalizations when they could improve performance.

Production System (Production)   Memory network of condition-action sequences (rules), where the condition is the set of circumstances that activates the system and the action is the set of activities that occurs.

Productive Thinking   See *Problem Solving*.

Programmed Instruction (PI)   Instructional materials developed in accordance with behavioral learning principles.

Proposition   The smallest unit of information that can be judged true or false.

Prototype   Abstract form stored in memory that contains the basic ingredients of a stimulus and is compared with an environmental input during perception.

Punishment   Withdrawal of a positive reinforcer or presentation of a negative reinforcer contingent on a response, which decreases the future likelihood of the response being made in the presence of the stimulus.

Purposive Behaviorism   Descriptive term for Tolman's theory emphasizing the study of large sequences of (molar) goal-directed behaviors.

Qualitative Research   Study characterized by depth and quality of analysis and interpretation of data through the use of methods such as classroom observations, use of existing records, interviews, and think-aloud protocols.

Questionnaire   Situation in which respondents are presented with items or questions asking about their thoughts and actions.

Ratings by Others   Evaluations of students on quality or quantity of performance.

Ratio Schedule   Reinforcement is contingent on the number of responses.

Rationalism   The doctrine that knowledge derives from reason without the aid of the senses.

Readiness   What children are capable of doing or learning at various points in development.

Reasoning   Mental processes involved in generating and evaluating logical arguments.

Recency Effect   Tendency to recall the last items in a list.

Reciprocal Teaching   Interactive dialogue between teacher and students in which teacher initially models activities, after which teacher and students take turns being the teacher.

Reflective Teaching   Thoughtful teacher decision making that takes into account knowledge about students, the context, psychological processes, learning and motivation, and self-knowledge.

Rehearsal   Repeating information to oneself aloud or subvocally.

Reinforcement   Any stimulus or event that leads to response strengthening.

Reinforcement History   Extent that an individual has been reinforced previously for performing the same or similar behavior.

Reinforcing Stimulus   The stimulus in the operant model of conditioning that is presented contingent on a response being emitted and increases the probability of the response being emitted in the future in the presence of the discriminative stimulus.

Relativism   The doctrine that all forms of knowledge are justifiable because they are constructed by learners, especially if they reflect social consensus.

Research   Systematic investigation designed to develop or contribute to generalizable knowledge.

Resource Allocation   Learning model specifying that attention is a limited resource and is allocated to activities as a function of motivation and self-regulation.

Respondent Behavior   Response made to an eliciting stimulus.

Response Facilitation   Previously learned behaviors of observers are prompted by the actions of models.

Response Tempo   See *Cognitive (Response) Tempo*.

Restructuring   Process of forming new schemata.

Retention   Storage of information in memory.

Retroactive Interference   New learning makes recall of old knowledge and skills more difficult.

Reversibility   Cognitive ability to sequence operations in opposite order.

Rhetorical Problem   The problem space in writing, which includes the writer's topic, intended audience, and goals.

Robotics   Programming machines to perform manual tasks.

Satiation   Fulfillment of reinforcement that results in decreased responding.

Savings Score   Time or trials necessary for relearning as a percentage of time or trials required for original learning.

Scaffolding   Process of controlling task elements that are beyond the learner's capabilities so that the learner can focus on and master those task features that he or she can grasp quickly.

Schedule of Reinforcement   When reinforcement is applied.

Schema   A cognitive structure that organizes large amounts of information into a meaningful system.

Schema Theory   Theory explaining how people develop schemas (organized memory structures composed of related information).

School Development Program   System of community and parental involvement in schools stressing consensus, collaboration, and no-fault.

Scientific Literacy   Understanding the meanings, foundations, current status, and problems of scientific phenomena.

Script   A mental representation of an often-repeated event.

Second Signal System   Words and other features of language that are used by humans to communicate and that can become conditioned stimuli.

Secondary Qualities   Characteristics of objects (e.g., color, sound) that depend on individuals' senses and cognitions.

Secondary Reinforcement   Process whereby a behavioral consequence (e.g., money) becomes reinforcing by being paired with a primary reinforcer (e.g., food).

Self-Actualization   The desire for self-fulfillment or for becoming everything one is capable of becoming; the highest level in Maslow's hierarchy of needs.

Self-Concept   One's collective self-perceptions that are formed through experiences with, and interpretations of, the environment, and that are heavily influenced by reinforcements and evaluations by significant other persons.

Self-Confidence   The extent that one believes one can produce results, accomplish goals, or perform tasks competently (analogous to Self-Efficacy).

Self-Determination   Motive aimed at developing competence, which begins as undifferentiated but eventually differentiates into specific areas.

Self-Efficacy (Efficacy Expectations)   Personal beliefs concerning one's capabilities to organize and implement actions necessary to learn or perform behaviors at designated levels.

Self-Esteem   One's perceived sense of self-worth; whether one accepts and respects oneself.

Self-Evaluation   Process involving self-judgments of current performance by comparing it to one's goal and self-reactions to these judgments by deeming performance noteworthy, unacceptable, and so forth.

Self-Instruction   In a learning setting, discriminative stimuli that are produced by the individual and that set the occasion for responses leading to reinforcement.

Self-Instructional Training   Instructional procedure that comprises cognitive modeling, overt guidance, overt self-guidance, faded overt self-guidance, and covert self-instruction.

Self-Judgment   Comparing one's current performance level with one's goal.

Self-Modeling   Changes in behaviors, thoughts, and affects that derive from observing one's own performances.

Self-Monitoring (-Observation, -Recording)   Deliberate attention to some aspect of one's behavior, often accompanied by recording its frequency or intensity.

Self-Reaction   Changes in one's beliefs and behaviors after judging performance against a goal.

Self-Regulation (Self-Regulated Learning)   The process whereby students personally activate and sustain behaviors, cognitions, and affects, which are systematically oriented toward the attainment of learning goals.

Self-Reinforcement   The process whereby individuals, after performing a response, arrange to receive reinforcement that increases the likelihood of future responding.

Self-Reports   People's judgments and statements about themselves.

Self-Schema   Manifestation of enduring goals, aspirations, motives, and fears, which includes cognitive and affective evaluations of ability, volition, and personal agency.

Self-Worth   Perceptions of one's value, grounded largely in beliefs about ability.

Semantic Memory   Memory of general information and concepts available in the environment and not tied to a particular individual or context.

Sensorimotor Stage   First of Piaget's stages of cognitive development, encompassing birth to roughly age 2.

Sensory Register   State of information processing concerned with receiving inputs, holding them briefly in sensory form, and transferring them to working memory.

Serial Recall   Recalling stimuli in the order in which they are presented.

Shaping   Differential reinforcement of successive approximations to the desired rate or form of behavior.

Short-Term (Working) Memory   Information processing stage corresponding to awareness, or what one is conscious of at a given moment.

Simulation   Real or imaginary situation that cannot be brought into a learning setting.

Situated Cognition (Learning)   Idea that thinking is situated (located) in physical and social contexts.

Social Comparison   Process of comparing one's beliefs and behaviors with those of others.

Social Constructivism   Constructivist perspective emphasizing the importance of the individual's social interactions in the acquisition of skills and knowledge.

Socially Mediated Learning   Learning influenced by aspects of the socio-cultural environment.

Socioeconomic Status (SES)   Descriptive term denoting one's capital (resources, assets)

Specific Skill   Skill applying only to certain domains (e.g., regrouping in subtraction).

Speech Act   The speaker's purpose in uttering a communication, or what a speaker is trying to accomplish with the utterance.

Spiral Curriculum   Building on prior knowledge by presenting the same topics at increasing levels of complexity as students move through schooling.

Spontaneous Recovery   Sudden recurrence of the conditioned response following presentation of the conditioned stimulus after a time lapse in which the conditioned stimulus is not presented.

Spreading Activation   Activation in long-term memory of propositions that are associatively linked with material currently in one's working memory.

SQ3R Method   Method of studying text that stands for Survey-Question-Read-Recite-Review; modified to SQ4R with addition of Reflection.

Stimulated Recall   Research procedure in which people work on a task and afterward recall their thoughts at various points; the procedure may include videotaping.

Stimulus-Response (S-R) Theory   Learning theory emphasizing associations between stimuli and responses.

Strategy Value Information   Information linking strategy use with improved performance.

Structural Theories of Development   Theories positing that development consists of changes in mental structures.

Structuralism   Doctrine postulating that the mind is composed of associations of ideas and that studying the complexities of the mind requires breaking associations into single ideas.

Successive Approximations   See *Shaping*.

Sum Model   Counting method in which one counts in the first addend and then the second one.

Surface Structure   The speech and syntax of a language.

Syllogism   Deductive reasoning problem that includes premises and a conclusion containing *all, no,* or *some.*

Symbolic Representation   Representing knowledge with symbol systems (e.g., language, mathematical notation).

Synapse   Point where axon and dendrites meet in the brain.

Synchronous Learning   Real-time interactions.

Systematic Desensitization   Therapeutic procedure used to extinguish fears by pairing threatening stimuli with cues for relaxation.

Tabula Rasa   Native state of a learner (blank tablet).

Tact   Verbal response under the discriminative control of an object or event and reinforced by a listener when it correctly names the object or event.

TARGET   Classroom motivation variables: task, authority, recognition, grouping, evaluation, time.

Task Involvement   Motivational state characterized by viewing learning as a goal and focusing on task demands rather than on oneself.

Technology   The designs and environments that engage learners.

Template Matching   Theory of perception postulating that people store templates (miniature copies of stimuli) in memory and compare these templates with environmental stimuli during perception.

Textual Behaviors   Verbal responses under the control of visual stimuli.

Theory   Scientifically acceptable set of principles offered to explain a phenomenon.

Think-Aloud   Research procedure in which participants verbalize aloud their thoughts, actions, and feelings while performing a task.

Three-Term Contingency   The basic operant model of conditioning: A discriminative stimulus sets the occasion for a response to be emitted, which is followed by a reinforcing stimulus.

Threshold Method of Behavioral Change   Altering behavior by introducing the cue for the undesired response at a low level and gradually increasing its magnitude until it is presented at full strength.

Time Needed for Learning   Amount of academically engaged time required by a student to learn a task.

Time Out (From Reinforcement)   Removal of an individual from a situation where reinforcement can be obtained.

Time-Sampling Measure   Measure of how often a behavior occurs during an interval of a longer period.

Time Spent in Learning   Amount of academically engaged time expended to learn.

Tools   The objects, language, and social institutions of a culture.

Top-Down Processing   Pattern recognition of stimuli that occurs by forming a meaningful representation of the context, developing expectations of what will occur, and comparing features of stimuli to expectations to confirm or disconfirm one's expectations.

Trace Decay   Loss of a stimulus from the sensory register over time.

Transfer (Generalization)   Application of skills or knowledge in new ways or situations.

Transformational Grammar   System of rules that individuals presumably use to change varying linguistic surface structures into the same deep structure (meaning).

Translation   Aspect of writing involving putting one's ideas into print.

Triadic Reciprocality   Reciprocal interactions (causal relations) among behaviors, environmental variables, and cognitions and other personal factors.

Trial and Error   Learning by performing a response and experiencing the consequences.

Tuning   Modification and refinement of schemata as they are used in various contexts.

Two-Store (Dual-Memory) Model of Information Processing   Conceptualization of memory as involving stages of processing and having two primary areas for storing information (short- and long-term memory).

Type R Behavior   See *Operant Behavior*.

Type S Behavior   See *Respondent Behavior*.

Unconditional Positive Regard   Attitudes of worthiness and acceptance with no conditions attached.

Unconditioned Response (UCR)   The response elicited by an unconditioned stimulus.

Unconditioned Stimulus (UCS)   A stimulus that when presented elicits a natural response from the organism.

Undifferentiated Task Structure   Class situation in which all students work on the same or similar tasks and instruction uses a small number of materials or methods.

Unidimensional Classroom   Classroom having few activities that address a limited range of student abilities.

Unitary Theory   Theory postulating that all information is represented in long-term memory in verbal codes.

Unlearning   See *Forgetting*.

Utilization   The use made of parsed sound patterns (e.g., store in memory, respond if a question, or seek additional information).

Utilization Deficiency   Failure to use a strategy of which one is cognitively aware.

Value   The perceived importance or usefulness of learning.

Verbal Behavior   Vocal responses shaped and maintained by the actions of other persons.

Vicarious Learning   Learning that occurs without overt performance, such as by observing live or symbolic models.

Virtual Reality   Computer-based technology that incorporates input and output devices and that allows students to experience and interact with an artificial environment as if it were the real world.

Volition   The act of using the will; the process of dealing with the implementation of actions to attain goals.

Volitional Style   Stable individual differences in volition.

Whole-Word Approach   Reading method based on pattern recognition of printed words, which are comprehended by being matched to long-term memory meanings.

Will   That part of the mind that reflects one's desire, want, or purpose.

Worked Example   Step-by-step problem solution that may include diagrams.

Working Backward   Problem-solving strategy in which one starts with the goal and asks which subgoals are necessary to accomplish it, what is necessary to accomplish these subgoals, and so forth until the beginning state is reached.

Working Forward   Problem-solving strategy in which one starts with the beginning problem state and decides how to alter it to progress toward the goal.

Working Memory   See *Short-Term Memory*.

Working Self-Concept   Those self-schemas that are mentally active at any time; currently accessible self-knowledge.

Writer's Block   Difficulty in beginning to compose.

Written Responses   Performances on tests, quizzes, homework, term papers, reports, and computer documents.

Zero Transfer   One type of learning has no obvious effect on subsequent learning.

Zone of Proximal Development   The amount of learning possible by a student given the proper instructional conditions.

References

Abramson, L. Y., Seligman, M. E. P., & Teasdale, J. D. (1978). Learned helplessness in humans: Critique and reformulation. *Journal of Abnormal Psychology, 87*, 49–74.

Ach, N. (1910). *Über den Willensakt und das Temperament.* [On the will and the temperament]. Leipzig, Germany: Quelle & Meyer.

Adams, J. A. (1971). A closed-loop theory of motor learning. *Journal of Motor Behavior, 3*, 111–150.

Adams, M. J. (1990). *Beginning to read: Thinking and learning about print.* Cambridge, MA: MIT Press.

Akamatsu, T. J., & Thelen, M. H. (1974). A review of the literature on observer characteristics and imitation. *Developmental Psychology, 10*, 38–47.

Alderman, M. K. (1985). Achievement motivation and the preservice teacher. In M. K. Alderman & M. W. Cohen (Eds.), *Motivation theory and practice for preservice teachers* (pp. 37–51). Washington, DC: ERIC Clearinghouse on Teacher Education.

Alderman, M. K. (1999). *Motivation for achievement: Possibilities for teaching and learning.* Mahwah, NJ: Erlbaum.

Alexander, J. E., Carr, M., & Schwanenflugel, P. J. (1995). Development of metacognition in gifted children: Directions for future research. *Developmental Review, 15*, 1–37.

Alexander, P. A., & Murphy, P. K. (1998). Profiling the differences in students' knowledge, interest, and strategic planning. *Journal of Educational Psychology, 90*, 435–447.

American Psychological Association (1992). Special issue: Reflections on B. F. Skinner and psychology. *American Psychologist, 47*, 1269–1533.

American Psychological Association Work Group of the Board of Educational Affairs (1997). *Learner-centered psychological principles.* Washington, DC: Author.

Ames, C. (1981). Competitive versus cooperative reward structures: The influence of individual and group performance factors on achievement attributions and affect. *American Educational Research Journal, 18*, 273–287.

Ames, C. (1984). Competitive, cooperative, and individualistic goal structures: A cognitive-motivational analysis. In R. Ames & C. Ames (Eds.), *Research on motivation in education* (Vol. 1, pp. 177–208). New York: Academic Press.

Ames, C. (1985). Attributions and cognitions in motivation theory. In M. K. Alderman & M. W. Cohen (Eds.), *Motivation theory and practice for preservice teachers* (pp. 16–21). Washington, DC: ERIC Clearinghouse on Teacher Education.

Ames, C. (1987). The enhancement of student motivation. In M. L. Maehr & D. A. Kleiber (Eds.), Advances in motivation and achievement (Vol. 5, pp. 123–148). Greenwich, CT: JAI Press.

Ames, C. (1992a). Achievement goals and the classroom motivational climate. In D. H. Schunk & J. L. Meece (Eds.), *Student perceptions in the classroom* (pp. 327–348). Hillsdale, NJ: Erlbaum.

Ames, C. (1992b). Classrooms: Goals, structures, and student motivation. *Journal of Educational Psychology, 84*, 261–271.

Ames, C., & Archer, J. (1987). Mothers' beliefs about the role of ability and effort in school learning. *Journal of Educational Psychology, 79*, 409–414.

Ames, C., & Archer, J. (1988). Achievement goals in the classroom: Student learning strategies and motivation processes. *Journal of Educational Psychology, 80*, 260–267.

Ames, C., & Felker, D. (1979). An examination of children's attributions and achievement-related evaluations in competitive, cooperative, and individualistic reward structures. *Journal of Educational Psychology, 71*, 413–420.

Anand, P. G., & Ross, S. M. (1987). Using computer-assisted instruction to personalize arithmetic materials for elementary school children. *Journal of Educational Psychology, 79*, 72–78.

Anderman, E. M. (1998). The middle school experience: Effects on the math and science achievement of adolescents with LD. *Journal of Learning Disabilities, 31*, 128–138.

Anderman, E. M., Austin, C. C., & Johnson, D. M. (2002). The development of goal orientation. In A. Wigfield & J. S. Eccles (Eds.), *Development of achievement motivation* (pp. 197–220). San Diego: Academic Press.

Anderman, E. M., & Maehr, M. L. (1994). Motivation and schooling in the middle grades. *Review of Educational Research, 64*, 287–309.

Anderson, J. R. (1976). *Language, memory and thought.* Hillsdale, NJ: Erlbaum.

Anderson, J. R. (1980). Concepts, propositions, and schemata: What are the cognitive units? In J. H. Flowers (Ed.), *Nebraska Symposium on Motivation, 1980* (Vol. 28, pp. 121–162). Lincoln, NE: University of Nebraska Press.

Anderson, J. R. (1982). Acquisition of cognitive skill. *Psychological Review, 89*, 369–406.

Anderson, J. R. (1983). A spreading activation theory of memory. *Journal of Verbal Learning and Verbal Behavior, 22*, 261–295.

Anderson, J. R. (1984). Spreading activation. In J. R. Anderson & S. M. Kosslyn (Eds.), *Tutorials in learning and memory: Essays in honor of Gordon Bower* (pp. 61–90). San Francisco: Freeman.

Anderson, J. R. (1990). *Cognitive psychology and its implications* (3rd ed.). New York: Freeman.

Anderson, J. R. (1993). Problem solving and learning. *American Psychologist, 48*, 35–44.

Anderson, J. R. (1996). ACT: A simple theory of complex cognition. *American Psychologist, 51*, 355–365.

Anderson, J. R., Fincham, J. M., & Douglass, S. (1997). The role of examples and rules in the acquisition of a cognitive skill. *Journal of Experimental Psychology: Learning, Memory, and Cognition, 23*, 932–945.

Anderson, J. R., Reder, L. M., & Lebiere, C. (1996). Working memory: Activation limitations on retrieval. *Cognitive Psychology, 30*, 221–256.

Anderson, J. R., Reder, L. M., & Simon, H. A. (1996). Situated learning and education. *Educational Researcher, 25*(4), 5–11.

Anderson, L. M., Evertson, C. M., & Brophy, J. E. (1979). An experimental study of effective teaching in first-grade reading groups. *Elementary School Journal, 79*, 193–222.

Anderson, L. W. (1976). An empirical investigation of individual differences in time to learn. *Journal of Educational Psychology, 68*, 226–233.

Anderson, L. W. (2003). Benjamin S. Bloom: His life, his works, and his legacy. In B. J. Zimmerman & D. H. Schunk (Eds.), *Educational psychology: A century of contributions* (pp. 367–389). Mahwah, NJ: Erlbaum.

Anderson, R. C. (1982). Allocation of attention during reading. In A. Flammer & W. Kintsch (Eds.), *Discourse processing* (pp. 292–305). Amsterdam: North Holland Publishing Company.

Anderson, R. C., & Pichert, J. W. (1978). Recall of previously unrecallable information following a shift in perspective. *Journal of Verbal Learning and Verbal Behavior, 17*, 1–12.

Anderson, R. C., Reynolds, R. E., Schallert, D. L., & Goetz, T. E. (1977). Frameworks for comprehending discourse. *American Educational Research Journal, 14*, 367–381.

Andre, T. (1986). Problem solving and education. In G. D. Phye & T. Andre (Eds.), *Cognitive classroom learning:*

Understanding, thinking, and problem solving (pp. 169–204). Orlando: Academic Press.

Andrews, G. R., & Debus, R. L. (1978). Persistence and the causal perception of failure: Modifying cognitive attributions. *Journal of Educational Psychology, 70,* 154–166.

Angell, J. R. (1907). The province of functional psychology. *Psychological Review, 14,* 61–91.

Armento, B. (1986). Research on teaching social studies. In M. C. Wittrock (Ed.), *Handbook of research on teaching* (pp. 942–951). New York: Macmillan.

Armstrong, D. G., & Savage, T. V. (2002). *Teaching in the secondary school: An introduction* (5th ed.). Upper Saddle River, NJ: Merrill/Prentice Hall.

Aronson, E. (1966). The psychology of insufficient justification: An analysis of some conflicting data. In S. Feldman (Ed.), *Cognitive consistency: Motivational antecedents and behavioral consequences* (pp. 109–133). New York: Academic Press.

Asarnow, J. R., & Meichenbaum, D. (1979). Verbal rehearsal and serial recall: The mediational training of kindergarten children. *Child Development, 50,* 1173–1177.

Ashton, P. T. (1985). Motivation and the teacher's sense of efficacy. In C. Ames & R. Ames (Eds.), *Research on motivation in education. Vol. 2: The classroom milieu* (pp. 141–171). Orlando: Academic Press.

Ashton, P. T., & Webb, R. B. (1986). *Making a difference: Teachers' sense of efficacy and student achievement.* New York: Longman.

Assor, A., & Connell, J. P. (1992). The validity of students' self-reports as measures of performance affecting self-appraisals. In D. H. Schunk & J. L. Meece (Eds.), *Student perceptions in the classroom* (pp. 25–47). Hillsdale, NJ: Erlbaum.

Atkinson, J. W. (1957). Motivational determinants of risk-taking behavior. *Psychological Review, 64,* 359–372.

Atkinson, J. W., & Birch, D. (1978). *Introduction to motivation* (2nd ed.). New York: D. Van Nostrand.

Atkinson, J. W., & Feather, N. T. (1966). *A theory of achievement motivation.* New York: Wiley.

Atkinson, J. W., & Raynor, J. O. (1974). *Motivation and achievement.* Washington, DC: Hemisphere.

Atkinson, J. W., & Raynor, J. O. (1978). *Personality, motivation, and achievement.* Washington, DC: Hemisphere.

Atkinson, R. C. (1975). Mnemotechnics in second-language learning. *American Psychologist, 30,* 828–921.

Atkinson, R. C., & Raugh, M. R. (1975). An application of the mnemonic keyword method to the acquisition of a Russian vocabulary. *Journal of Experimental Psychology: Human Learning and Memory, 104,* 126–133.

Atkinson, R. C., & Shiffrin, R. M. (1968). Human memory: A proposed system and its control processes. In K. W. Spence & J. T. Spence (Eds.), *The psychology of learning and motivation: Advances in research and theory* (Vol. 2, pp. 89–195). New York: Academic Press.

Atkinson, R. C., & Shiffrin, R. M. (1971). The control of short-term memory. *Scientific American, 225,* 82–90.

Atkinson, R. K., Derry, S. J., Renkl, A., & Wortham, D. (2000). Learning from examples: Instructional principles from the worked examples research. *Review of Educational Research, 70,* 181–214.

Austin, J. L. (1962). *How to do things with words.* Oxford, England: Oxford University Press.

Ausubel, D. P. (1963). *The psychology of meaningful verbal learning: An introduction to school learning.* New York: Grune & Stratton.

Ausubel, D. P. (1968). *Educational psychology: A cognitive view.* New York: Holt, Rinehart & Winston.

Ausubel, D. P. (1977). The facilitation of meaningful verbal learning in the classroom. *Educational Psychologist, 12,* 162–178.

Ausubel, D. P. (1978). In defense of advance organizers: A reply to the critics. *Review of Educational Research, 48,* 251–257.

Ausubel, D. P., & Robinson, F. G. (1969). *School learning: An introduction to educational psychology.* New York: Holt, Rinehart & Winston.

Ayllon, T., & Azrin, N. (1968). *The token economy: A motivational system for therapy and rehabilitation.* New York: Appleton-Century-Crofts.

Baddeley, A. D. (1978). The trouble with levels: A reexamination of Craik and Lockhart's framework for memory research. *Psychological Review, 85,* 139–152.

Baddeley, A. D. (1992). Working memory. *Science, 255,* 556–559.

Baddeley, A. D. (1998). *Human memory: Theory and practice* (Rev. ed.). Boston: Allyn and Bacon.

Baddeley, A. D. (2001). Is working memory still working? *American Psychologist, 56,* 851–864.

Bailey, T. (1993). Can youth apprenticeship thrive in the United States? *Educational Researcher, 22*(3), 4–10.

Baker, L. (1989). Metacognition, comprehension monitoring, and the adult reader. *Educational Psychology Review, 1,* 3–38.

Baker, L., & Brown, A. L. (1984). Metacognitive skills and reading. In P. D. Pearson (Ed.), *Handbook of reading research* (pp. 353–394). New York: Longman.

Ball, D. L., Lubienski, S. T., & Mewborn, D. S. (2001). Mathematics. In V. Richardson (Ed.), *Handbook of research on teaching* (4th ed., pp. 433–456). Washington, DC: American Educational Research Association.

Bandura, A. (1969). *Principles of behavior modification.* New York: Holt, Rinehart & Winston.

Bandura, A. (1973). *Aggression: A social learning analysis.* Englewood Cliffs, NJ: Prentice Hall.

Bandura, A. (1977a). Self-efficacy: Toward a unifying theory of behavioral change. *Psychological Review, 84,* 191–215.

Bandura, A. (1977b). *Social learning theory.* Englewood Cliffs, NJ: Prentice Hall.

Bandura, A. (1981). Self-referent thought: A developmental analysis of self-efficacy. In J. H. Flavell & L. Ross (Eds.), *Social cognitive development: Frontiers and possible futures* (pp. 200–239). Cambridge, England: Cambridge University Press.

Bandura, A. (1982a). The self and mechanisms of agency. In J. Suls (Ed.), *Psychological perspectives on the self* (Vol. 1, pp. 3–39). Hillsdale, NJ: Erlbaum.

Bandura, A. (1982b). Self-efficacy mechanism in human agency. *American Psychologist, 37,* 122–147.

Bandura, A. (1986). *Social foundations of thought and action: A social cognitive theory.* Englewood Cliffs, NJ: Prentice Hall.

Bandura, A. (1988). Self-regulation of motivation and action through goal systems. In V. Hamilton, G. H. Bower, & N. H. Frijda (Eds.), *Cognitive perspectives on emotion and motivation* (pp. 37–61). Dordrecht, The Netherlands: Kluwer Academic Publishers.

Bandura, A. (1991). Self-regulation of motivation through anticipatory and self-reactive mechanisms. In R. A. Dienstbier (Ed.), *Nebraska Symposium on Motivation, 1990* (Vol. 38, 69–164). Lincoln, NE: University of Nebraska Press.

Bandura, A. (1993). Perceived self-efficacy in cognitive development and functioning. *Educational Psychologist, 28,* 117–148.

Bandura, A. (1994). Social cognitive theory and the exercise of control over HIV infection. In R. DiClemente & J. Peterson (Eds.), *Preventing AIDS: Theories and methods of behavioral interventions* (pp. 25–59). New York: Plenum.

Bandura, A. (1997). *Self-efficacy: The exercise of control.* New York: Freeman.

Bandura, A. (2001). Social cognitive theory: An agentic perspective. *Annual Review of Psychology, 52,* 1–26.

Bandura, A., & Adams, N. E. (1977). Analysis of self-efficacy theory of behavioral change. *Cognitive Therapy and Research, 1,* 287–308.

Bandura, A., Adams, N. E., & Beyer, J. (1977). Cognitive processes mediating behavioral change. *Journal of Personality and Social Psychology, 35,* 125–139.

Bandura, A., Barbaranelli, C., Caprara, G. V., & Pastorelli, C. (1996). Multifaceted impact of self-efficacy beliefs on academic functioning. *Child Development, 67,* 1206–1222.

Bandura, A., Barbaranelli, C., Caprara, G. V., & Pastorelli, C. (2001). Self-efficacy beliefs as shapers of children's aspirations and career trajectories. *Child Development, 72,* 187–206.

Bandura, A., & Cervone, D. (1983). Self-evaluative and self-efficacy mechanisms governing the motivational effects of goal systems. *Journal of Personality and Social Psychology, 45,* 1017–1028.

Bandura, A., & Cervone, D. (1986). Differential engagement of self-reactive influences in cognitive motivation. *Organizational Behavior and Human Decision Processes, 38,* 92–113.

Bandura, A., & Harris, M. B. (1966). Modification of syntactic style. *Journal of Experimental Child Psychology, 4,* 341–352.

Bandura, A., & Jeffery, R. W. (1973). Role of symbolic coding and rehearsal processes in observational learning. *Journal of Personality and Social Psychology, 26,* 122–130.

Bandura, A., & Kupers, C. J. (1964). Transmission of patterns of self-reinforcement through modeling. *Journal of Abnormal and Social Psychology, 69,* 1–9.

Bandura, A., Ross, D., & Ross, S. A. (1963). Imitation of film-mediated aggressive models. *Journal of Abnormal and Social Psychology, 66,* 3–11.

Bandura, A., & Schunk, D. H. (1981). Cultivating competence, self-efficacy, and intrinsic interest through proximal self-motivation. *Journal of Personality and Social Psychology, 41,* 586–598.

Bandura, A., & Walters, R. H. (1963). *Social learning and personality development.* New York: Holt, Rinehart & Winston.

Bangert, R. L., Kulik, J. A., & Kulik, C. C. (1983). Individualized systems of instruction in secondary schools. *Review of Educational Research, 53,* 143–158.

Bargh, J. A., & Ferguson, M. J. (2000). Beyond behaviorism: On the automaticity of higher mental processes. *Psychological Bulletin, 126,* 925–945.

Barnes, B. R., & Clawson, E. U. (1975). Do advance organizers facilitate learning? Recommendations for further research based on an analysis of 32 studies. *Review of Educational Research, 45,* 637–659.

Barr, R. (2001). Research on the teaching of reading. In V. Richardson (Ed.), *Handbook of research on teaching* (4th ed., pp. 390–415). Washington, DC: American Educational Research Association.

Bartlett, F. C. (1932). *Remembering: A study in experimental and social psychology.* Cambridge, England: Cambridge University Press.

Basden, B. H., Basden, D. R., Devecchio, E., & Anders, J. A. (1991). A developmental comparison of the effectiveness of encoding tasks. *Genetic, Social, and General Psychology Monographs, 117,* 419–436.

Beal, C. R., & Belgrad, S. L. (1990). The development of message evaluation skills in young children. *Child Development, 61,* 705–712.

Beal, C. R., Garrod, A. C., & Bonitatibus, G. J. (1990). Fostering children's revision skills through training in comprehension monitoring. *Journal of Educational Psychology, 82,* 275–280.

Becker, B. J. (1990). Item characteristics and gender differences on the SAT-M for mathematically able youths. *American Educational Research Journal, 27,* 65–87.

Becker, W. C. (1971). *Parents are teachers: A child management program.* Champaign, IL: Research Press.

Beery, R. (1975). Fear of failure in the student experience. *Personnel and Guidance Journal, 54,* 190–203.

Belfiore, P. J., & Hornyak, R. S. (1998). Operant theory and application to self-monitoring in adolescents. In D. H. Schunk & B. J. Zimmerman (Eds.), *Self-regulated learning: From teaching to self-reflective practice* (pp. 184–202). New York: Guilford Press.

Bell, D. R., & Low, R. M. (1977). *Observing and recording children's behavior.* Richland, WA: Performance Associates.

Belmont, J. M. (1989). Cognitive strategies and strategic learning: The socio-instructional approach. *American Psychologist, 44,* 142–148.

Bempechat, J., London, P., & Dweck, C. S. (1991). Children's conceptions of ability in major domains: An interview and experimental study. *Child Study Journal, 21,* 11–36.

Benjamin, L. T., Jr. (1988). A history of teaching machines. *American Psychologist, 43,* 703–712.

Benjamin, L. T., Jr. (2000). The psychological laboratory at the turn of the 20th century. *American Psychologist, 55,* 318–321.

Benjamin, L. T., Jr., Durkin, M., Link, M., Vestal, M., & Acord, J. (1992). Wundt's American doctoral students. *American Psychologist, 47,* 123–131.

Bereiter, C. (1980). Development in writing. In L. W. Gregg & E. R. Steinberg (Eds.), *Cognitive processes in writing* (pp. 73–93). Hillsdale, NJ: Erlbaum.

Bereiter, C. (1994). Constructivism, socioculturalism, and Popper's World 3. *Educational Researcher, 23*(7), 21–23.

Bereiter, C., & Scardamalia, M. (1986). Levels of inquiry into the nature of expertise in writing. In E. Z. Rothkopf (Ed.), *Review of research in education* (Vol. 13, pp. 259–282). Washington, DC: American Educational Research Association.

Berger, S. M. (1977). Social comparison, modeling, and perseverance. In J. M. Suls & R. L. Miller (Eds.), *Social comparison processes: Theoretical and empirical perspectives* (pp. 209–234). Washington, DC: Hemisphere.

Berk, L. E. (1986). Relationship of elementary school children's private speech to behavioral accompaniment to task, attention, and task performance. *Developmental Psychology, 22,* 671–680.

Berliner, D. C., & Calfee, R. C. (Eds.) (1996). *Handbook of educational psychology.* New York: Macmillan.

Berlyne, D. E. (1960). *Conflict, arousal, and curiosity.* New York: McGraw-Hill.

Berlyne, D. E. (1963). Motivational problems raised by exploratory and epistemic behavior. In S. Koch (Ed.), *Psychology: A study of a science* (Vol. 5, pp. 284–364). New York: McGraw-Hill.

Bernier, M., & Avard, J. (1986). Self-efficacy, outcome, and attrition in a weight-reduction program. *Cognitive Therapy and Research, 10,* 319–338.

Biemiller, A. (1994). Some observations on beginning reading instruction. *Educational Psychologist, 29,* 203–209.

Bilodeau, E. A. (1966). *Acquisition of skill.* New York: Academic Press.

Birnbaum, J. C. (1982). The reading and composing behaviors of selected fourth- and seventh-grade students. *Research in the Teaching of English, 16,* 241–260.

Black, J. B. (1984). Understanding and remembering stories. In J. R. Anderson & S. M. Kosslyn (Eds.), *Tutorials in learning and memory: Essays in honor of Gordon Bower* (pp. 235–255). San Francisco: Freeman.

Block, J. H., & Burns, R. B. (1977). Mastery learning. In L. S. Shulman (Ed.), *Review of research in education* (Vol. 4, pp. 3–49). Itasca, IL: Peacock.

Blok, H., Oostdam, R., Otter, M. E., & Overmaat, M. (2002). Computer-assisted instruction in support of beginning reading instruction: A review. *Review of Educational Research, 72*, 101–130.

Bloom, B. S. (1976). *Human characteristics and school learning.* New York: McGraw-Hill.

Bloom, B. S., Hastings, J. T., & Madaus, G. F. (1971). *Handbook on formative and summative evaluation of student learning.* New York: McGraw-Hill.

Blumenfeld, P. C. (1992). Classroom learning and motivation: Clarifying and expanding goal theory. *Journal of Educational Psychology, 84*, 272–281.

Bobrow, D. G., & Norman, D. A. (1975). Some principles of memory schemata. In D. G. Bobrow & A. Collins (Eds.), *Representation and understanding* (pp. 131–150). New York: Academic Press.

Boersma, F. J., & Chapman, J. W. (1981). Academic self-concept, achievement expectations, and locus of control in elementary learning-disabled children. *Canadian Journal of Behavioural Science, 13*, 349–358.

Bong, M., & Clark, R. (1999). Comparisons between self-concept and self-efficacy in academic motivation research. *Educational Psychologist, 34*, 139–154.

Bonk, C. J., & King, K. S. (Eds.) (1998). *Electronic collaborators: Learner-centered technologies for literacy, apprenticeship, and discourse.* Mahwah, NJ: Erlbaum.

Bork, A. (1985). *Personal computers for education.* New York: Harper & Row.

Borkowski, J. G. (1985). Signs of intelligence: Strategy generalization and metacognition. In S. Yussen (Ed.), *The growth of reflection in children* (pp. 105–144). New York: Academic Press.

Borkowski, J. G., & Cavanaugh, J. C. (1979). Maintenance and generalization of skills and strategies by the retarded. In N. R. Ellis (Ed.), *Handbook of mental deficiency, psychological theory and research* (2nd ed., pp. 569–617). Hillsdale, NJ: Erlbaum.

Borkowski, J. G., Johnston, M. B., & Reid, M. K. (1987). Metacognition, motivation, and controlled performance. In S. J. Ceci (Ed.), *Handbook of cognitive, social, and neuropsychological aspects of learning disabilities* (Vol. 2, pp. 147–173). Hillsdale, NJ: Erlbaum.

Bouffard-Bouchard, T., Parent, S., & Larivee, S. (1991). Influence of self-efficacy on self-regulation and performance among junior and senior high-school age students. *International Journal of Behavioral Development, 14*, 153–164.

Bourne, L. E., Jr. (1992). Cognitive psychology: A brief overview. *Psychological Science Agenda, 5*(5), 5, 20.

Bousfield, W. A. (1953). The occurrence of clustering in the recall of randomly arranged associates. *Journal of General Psychology, 49*, 229–240.

Bousfield, W. A., & Cohen, B. H. (1953). The effects of reinforcement on the occurrence of clustering in the recall of randomly arranged associates. *Journal of Psychology, 36*, 67–81.

Bouton, M. E., Nelson, J. B., & Rosas, J. M. (1999). Stimulus generalization, context change, and forgetting. *Psychological Bulletin, 125*, 171–186.

Bower, G. H. (1970). Organizational factors in memory. *Cognitive Psychology, 1*, 18–46.

Bower, G. H., & Hilgard, E. R. (1981). *Theories of learning* (5th ed.). Englewood Cliffs, NJ: Prentice Hall.

Bower, G. H., & Morrow, D. G. (1990). Mental models in narrative comprehension. *Science, 247*, 44–48.

Braaksma, M. A. H., Rijlaarsdam, G., & van den Bergh, H. (2002). Observational learning and the effects of model-observer similarity. *Journal of Educational Psychology, 94*, 405–415.

Bradley, R. H., & Corwyn, R. F. (2002). Socioeconomic status and child development. *Annual Review of Psychology, 53*, 371–399.

Brainerd, C. J. (2003). Jean Piaget, learning research, and American education. In B. J. Zimmerman & D. H. Schunk (Eds.), *Educational psychology: A century of contributions* (pp. 251–287). Mahwah, NJ: Erlbaum.

Bransford, J. D., & Johnson, M. K. (1972). Contextual prerequisites for understanding: Some investigations of comprehension and recall. *Journal of Verbal Learning and Verbal Behavior, 11*, 717–726.

Bransford, J. D., & Stein, B. S. (1984). *The IDEAL problem solver: A guide for improving thinking, learning, and creativity.* New York: Freeman.

Bransford, J. D., Stein, B. S., Vye, N. J., Franks, J. J., Auble, P. M., Mezynski, K. J., & Perfetto, G. A. (1982). Differences in approaches to learning: An overview. *Journal of Experimental Psychology: General, 111*, 390–398.

Braun, C. (1976). Teacher expectation: Sociopsychological dynamics. *Review of Educational Research, 46*, 185–213.

Breedlove, C. J., & Cicirelli, V. G. (1974). Women's fear of success in relation to personal characteristics and type of occupation. *Journal of Psychology, 86*, 181–190.

Brewer, W. F. (1974). There is no convincing evidence for operant or classical conditioning in adult humans. In W. B. Weimer & D. S. Palermo (Eds.), *Cognition and the symbolic processes* (pp. 1–42). Hillsdale, NJ: Erlbaum.

Brewer, W. F., & Treyens, J. C. (1981). Role of schemata in memory for places. *Cognitive Psychology, 13*, 207–230.

Brigham, T. A. (1982). Self-management: A radical behavioral perspective. In P. Karoly & F. H. Kanfer (Eds.), *Self-management and behavior change: From theory to practice* (pp. 32–59). New York: Pergamon.

Britton, B. K., & Tesser, A. (1991). Effects of time-management practices on college grades. *Journal of Educational Psychology, 83*, 405–410.

Broadbent, D. E. (1958). *Perception and communication.* London: Pergamon.

Broadhurst, P. L. (1957). Emotionality and the Yerkes-Dodson Law. *Journal of Experimental Psychology, 54*, 345–352.

Brody, G. H., & Stoneman, Z. (1985). Peer imitation: An examination of status and competence hypotheses. *Journal of Genetic Psychology, 146*, 161–170.

Brodzinsky, D. M. (1982). Relationship between cognitive style and cognitive development: A 2-year longitudinal study. *Developmental Psychology, 18*, 617–626.

Bronfenbrenner, U. (1979). *The ecology of human development: Experiments by nature and design.* Cambridge, MA: Harvard University Press.

Brooks, J. G., & Brooks, M. G. (1999). *In search of understanding: The case for constructivist classrooms.* Alexandria, VA: Association for Supervision and Curriculum Development.

Brophy, J. E. (1981). Teacher praise: A functional analysis. *Review of Educational Research, 51*, 5–32.

Brophy, J. E. (1985). Teacher-student interaction. In J. B. Dusek (Ed.), *Teacher expectancies* (pp. 303–328). Hillsdale, NJ: Erlbaum.

Brophy, J. E., & Good, T. L. (1974). *Teacher-student relationships: Causes and consequences.* New York: Holt, Rinehart & Winston.

Brophy, J. E., & Good, T. L. (1986). Teacher behavior and student achievement. In M. C. Wittrock (Ed.), *Handbook of research on teaching* (3rd ed., pp. 328–375). New York: Macmillan.

Brown, A. L. (1980). Metacognitive development and reading. In R. J. Spiro, B. C. Bruce, & W. F. Brewer (Eds.), *Theoretical issues in reading comprehension* (pp. 453–481). Hillsdale, NJ: Erlbaum.

Brown, A. L., Palincsar, A. S., & Armbruster, B. B. (1984). Instructing comprehension-fostering activities in interactive learning situations. In H. Mandl, N. L. Stein, & T. Trabasso (Eds.), *Learning and comprehension of text* (pp. 255–286). Hillsdale, NJ: Erlbaum.

Brown, I., Jr., & Inouye, D. K. (1978). Learned helplessness through modeling: The role of perceived similarity in competence. *Journal of Personality and Social Psychology, 36,* 900–908.

Brown, J. (1968). Reciprocal facilitation and impairment of free recall. *Psychonomic Science, 10,* 41–42.

Brown, J. S., & Burton, R. R. (1978). Diagnostic models for procedural bugs in basic mathematical skills. *Cognitive Science, 2,* 155–192.

Bruner, J. S. (1960). *The process of education.* New York: Vintage.

Bruner, J. S. (1961). The act of discovery. *Harvard Educational Review, 31,* 21–32.

Bruner, J. S. (1964). The course of cognitive growth. *American Psychologist, 19,* 1–15.

Bruner, J. S. (1966). *Toward a theory of instruction.* New York: Norton.

Bruner, J. S. (1984). Vygotsky's zone of proximal development: The hidden agenda. In B. Rogoff & J. V. Wertsch (Eds.), *Children's learning in the "zone of proximal development"* (pp. 93–97). San Francisco: Jossey-Bass.

Bruner, J. S. (1985). Models of the learner. *Educational Researcher, 14*(6), 5–8.

Bruner, J. S., Goodnow, J., & Austin, G. A. (1956). *A study of thinking.* New York: Wiley.

Bruner, J. S., Olver, R. R., & Greenfield, P. M. (1966). *Studies in cognitive growth.* New York: Wiley.

Bruning, R. H., & Horn, C. (2000). Developing motivation to write. *Educational Psychologist, 35,* 25–37.

Bruning, R. H., Schraw, G. J., & Ronning, R. R. (1999). *Cognitive psychology and instruction* (3rd ed.). Upper Saddle River, NJ: Merrill/Prentice Hall.

Bryan, J. H., & Bryan, T. H. (1983). The social life of the learning disabled youngster. In J. D. McKinney & L. Feagans (Eds.), *Current topics in learning disabilities* (Vol. 1, pp. 57–85). Norwood, NJ: Ablex.

Bryan, J. H., & Walbek, N. H. (1970). Preaching and practicing generosity: Children's actions and reactions. *Child Development, 41,* 329–353.

Bryan, T., Cosden, M., & Pearl, R. (1982). The effects of cooperative goal structures and cooperative models on LD and NLD students. *Learning Disability Quarterly, 5,* 415–421.

Butkowsky, I. S., & Willows, D. M. (1980). Cognitive-motivational characteristics of children varying in reading ability: Evidence for learned helplessness in poor readers. *Journal of Educational Psychology, 72,* 408–422.

Butler, D. L. (1998a). The strategic content learning approach to promoting self-regulated learning: A report of three studies. *Journal of Educational Psychology, 90,* 682–697.

Butler, D. L. (1998b). A strategic content learning approach to promoting self-regulated learning by students with learning disabilities. In D. H. Schunk & B. J. Zimmerman (Eds.), *Self-regulated learning: From teaching to self-reflective practice* (pp. 160–183). New York: Guilford Press.

Butler, R. (1992). What young people want to know when: Effects of mastery and ability goals on interest in different kinds of social comparisons. *Journal of Personality and Social Psychology, 62,* 934–943.

Butler, R. (1998). Age trends in the use of social and temporal comparison for self-evaluation: Examination of a novel developmental hypothesis. *Child Development, 69,* 1054–1073.

Byrnes, J. P. (1996). *Cognitive development and learning in instructional contexts.* Boston: Allyn and Bacon.

Byrnes, J. P., & Fox, N. A. (1998). The educational relevance of research in cognitive neuroscience. *Educational Psychology Review, 10,* 297–342.

Calfee, R. (1981). Cognitive psychology and educational practice. In D. C. Berliner (Ed.), *Review of research in education* (Vol. 9, pp. 3–73). Washington, DC: American Educational Research Association.

Calfee, R., & Drum, P. (1986). Research on teaching reading. In M. C. Wittrock (Ed.), *Handbook of research on teaching* (3rd ed., pp. 804–849). New York: Macmillan.

Callahan, C., & Smith, R. M. (1990). Keller's Personalized System of Instruction in a junior high gifted program. *Roeper Review, 13,* 39–44.

Cameron, J., & Pierce, W. D. (1994). Reinforcement, reward, and intrinsic motivation: A meta-analysis. *Review of Educational Research, 64,* 363–423.

Campbell, F. A., Pungello, E. P., Miller-Johnson, S., Burchinal, M., & Ramey, C. T. (2001). The development of cognitive and academic abilities: Growth curves from an early childhood educational experiment. *Developmental Psychology, 37,* 231–242.

Campione, J. C., Brown, A. L., Ferrara, R. A., & Bryant, N. R. (1984). The zone of proximal development: Implications for individual differences and learning. In B. Rogoff & J. V. Wertsch (Eds.), *Children's learning in the "zone of proximal development"* (pp. 77–91). San Francisco: Jossey-Bass.

Cantor, N., & Kihlstrom, J. F. (1987). *Personality and social intelligence.* Englewood Cliffs, NJ: Prentice Hall.

Carney, R. N., & Levin, J. R. (2002). Pictorial illustrations *still* improve students' learning from text. *Educational Psychology Review, 14,* 5–26.

Carpenter, P. A., Miyake, A., & Just, M. A. (1995). Language comprehension: Sentence and discourse processing. *Annual Review of Psychology, 46,* 91–120.

Carroll, J. B. (1963). A model of school learning. *Teachers College Record, 64,* 723–733.

Carroll, J. B. (1965). School learning over the long haul. In J. D. Krumboltz (Ed.), *Learning and the educational process* (pp. 249–269). Chicago: Rand McNally.

Carroll, J. B. (1989). The Carroll model: A 25-year retrospective and prospective view. *Educational Researcher, 18*(1), 26–31.

Carroll, W. R., & Bandura, A. (1982). The role of visual monitoring in observational learning of action patterns: Making the unobservable observable. *Journal of Motor Behavior, 14,* 153–167.

Carver, C. S., & Scheier, M. F. (1982). An information processing perspective on self-management. In P. Karoly & F. H.

Kanfer (Eds.), *Self-management and behavior change: From theory to practice* (pp. 93–128). New York: Pergamon.

Carver, C. S., & Scheier, M. F. (1990). Origins and functions of positive and negative affect: A control-process view. *Psychological Review, 97,* 19–35.

Carver, C. S., & Scheier, M. F. (1998). *On the self-regulation of behavior.* New York: Cambridge University Press.

Carver, C. S., & Scheier, M. F. (2000). On the structure of behavioral self-regulation. In M. Boekaerts, P. R. Pintrich, & M. Zeidner (Eds.), *Handbook of self-regulation* (pp. 41–84). San Diego: Academic Press.

Case, R. (1978a). A developmentally based theory and technology of instruction. *Review of Educational Research, 48,* 439–463.

Case, R. (1978b). Piaget and beyond: Toward a developmentally based theory and technology of instruction. In R. Glaser (Ed.), *Advances in instructional psychology* (Vol. 1, pp. 167–228). Hillsdale, NJ: Erlbaum.

Case, R. (1981). Intellectual development: A systematic reinterpretation. In F. H. Farley & N. J. Gordon (Eds.), *Psychology and education: The state of the union* (pp. 142–177). Berkeley, CA: McCutchan.

Case, R. (1993). Theories of learning and theories of development. *Educational Psychologist, 28,* 219–233.

Cataldo, M. G., & Cornoldi, C. (1998). Self-monitoring in poor and good reading comprehenders and their use of strategy. *British Journal of Developmental Psychology, 16,* 155–165.

Ceci, S. J. (1989). On domain specificity . . . More or less general and specific constraints on cognitive development. *Merrill-Palmer Quarterly, 35,* 131–142.

Cervone, D., Jiwani, N., & Wood, R. (1991). Goal setting and the differential influence of self-regulatory processes on complex decision-making performance. *Journal of Personality and Social Psychology, 61,* 257–266.

Chapin, M., & Dyck, D. G. (1976). Persistence in children's reading behavior as a function of *N* length and attribution retraining. *Journal of Abnormal Psychology, 85,* 511–515.

Chapman, J. W. (1988). Learning disabled children's self-concepts. *Review of Educational Research, 58,* 347–371.

Chapman, J. W., & Tunmer, W. E. (1995). Development of young children's reading self-concepts: An examination of emerging subcomponents and their relationship with reading achievement. *Journal of Educational Psychology, 87,* 154–167.

Chartrand, T. L., & Bargh, J. A. (1999). The Chameleon Effect: The perception-behavior link and social interaction. *Journal of Personality and Social Psychology, 76,* 893–910.

Chen, Z. (1999). Schema induction in children's analogical problem solving. *Journal of Educational Psychology, 91,* 703–715.

Cherry, E. C. (1953). Some experiments on the recognition of speech with one and two ears. *Journal of the Acoustical Society of America, 25,* 975–979.

Chi, M. T. H., Bassok, M., Lewis, M. W., Reimann, P., & Glaser, R. (1989). Self-explanations: How students study and use examples in learning to solve problems. *Cognitive Science, 13,* 145–182.

Chi, M. T. H., Feltovich, P. J., & Glaser, R. (1981). Categorization and representation of physics problems by experts and novices. *Cognitive Science, 5,* 121–152.

Chi, M. T. H., & Glaser, R. (1985). Problem-solving ability. In R. J. Sternberg (Ed.), *Human abilities: An information-processing approach* (pp. 227–250). New York: Freeman.

Chi, M. T. H., Glaser, R., & Farr, M. J. (Eds.). (1988). *The nature of expertise.* Hillsdale, NJ: Erlbaum.

Chi, M. T. H., Glaser, R., & Rees, E. (1982). Expertise in problem solving. In R. J. Sternberg (Ed.), *Advances in the psychology of human intelligence* (Vol. 1, pp. 7–75). Hillsdale, NJ: Erlbaum.

Chiesi, H. L., Spilich, G. J., & Voss, J. R. (1979). Acquisition of domain-related information in relation to high and low domain knowledge. *Journal of Verbal Learning and Verbal Behavior, 18,* 257–274.

Childs, C. P., & Greenfield, P. M. (1981). Informal modes of learning and teaching: The case of Zincanteco weaving. In N. Warren (Ed.), *Studies in cross-cultural psychology* (Vol. 2, pp. 269–319). London: Academic Press.

Chomsky, N. (1957). *Syntactic structures.* The Hague: Mouton.

Chomsky, N. (1959). Review of *Verbal Behavior* by B. F. Skinner. *Language, 35,* 26–58.

Clark, C. M., & Peterson, P. L. (1986). Teachers' thought processes. In M. C. Wittrock (Ed.), *Handbook of research on teaching* (3rd ed., pp. 255–296). New York: Macmillan.

Clark, C. M., & Yinger, R. J. (1979). Teachers' thinking. In P. L. Peterson & H. J. Walberg (Eds.), *Research on teaching: Concepts, findings, and implications* (pp. 231–263). Berkeley, CA: McCutchan.

Clark, H. H., & Clark, E. V. (1977). *Psychology and language: An introduction to psycholinguistics.* New York: Harcourt Brace Jovanovich.

Clark, H. H., & Haviland, S. E. (1977). Psychological processes as linguistic explanation. In R. O. Freedle (Ed.), *Discourse production and comprehension* (pp. 1–40). Norwood, NJ: Ablex.

Clark, J. M., & Paivio, A. (1991). Dual coding theory and education. *Educational Psychology Review, 3,* 149–210.

Clark, R. E., & Salomon, G. (1986). Media in teaching. In M. C. Wittrock (Ed.), *Handbook of research on teaching* (3rd ed., pp. 464–478). New York: Macmillan.

Clements, D. H. (1986). Effects of Logo and CAI environments on cognition and creativity. *Journal of Educational Psychology, 78,* 309–318.

Clements, D. H. (1991). Enhancement of creativity in computer environments. *American Educational Research Journal, 28,* 173–187.

Clements, D. H. (1995). Teaching creativity with computers. *Educational Psychology Review, 7,* 141–161.

Clements, D. H., & Gullo, D. F. (1984). Effects of computer programming on young children's cognition. *Journal of Educational Psychology, 76,* 1051–1058.

Clements, D. H., & Nastasi, B. K. (1988). Social and cognitive interactions in educational computer environments. *American Educational Research Journal, 25,* 87–106.

Coates, B., & Hartup, W. W. (1969). Age and verbalization in observational learning. *Developmental Psychology, 1,* 556–562.

Cobb, P. (1994). Where is the mind? Constructivist and sociocultural perspectives on mathematical development. *Educational Researcher, 23*(7), 13–20.

Cofer, C. N., Bruce, D. R., & Reicher, G. M. (1966). Clustering in free recall as a function of certain methodological variations. *Journal of Experimental Psychology, 71,* 858–866.

Cognition and Technology Group at Vanderbilt. (1996). Looking at technology in context: A framework for understanding technology and education research. In D. C. Berliner & R. C. Calfee (Eds.), *Handbook of educational psychology* (pp. 807–840). New York: Macmillan.

Cohen, E. G. (1994). Restructuring the classroom: Conditions for productive small groups. *Review of Educational Research, 64,* 1–35.

Collins, A. (1977). Processes in acquiring knowledge. In R. C. Anderson, R. J. Spiro, & W. E. Montague (Eds.), *Schooling and the acquisition of knowledge* (pp. 339–363). Hillsdale, NJ: Erlbaum.

Collins, A., & Loftus, E. F. (1975). A spreading-activation theory of semantic processing. *Psychological Review, 82*, 407–428.

Collins, A., & Quillian, M. R. (1969). Retrieval time from semantic memory. *Journal of Verbal Learning and Verbal Behavior, 8*, 240–247.

Collins, A., & Stevens, A. L. (1983). A cognitive theory of inquiry teaching. In C. M. Reigeluth (Ed.), *Instructional-design theories and models: An overview of their current status* (pp. 247–278). Hillsdale, NJ: Erlbaum.

Collins, J. L. (1982, March). *Self-efficacy and ability in achievement behavior*. Paper presented at the annual meeting of the American Educational Research Association, New York.

Collins, W. A., Maccoby, E. E., Steinberg, L., Hetherington, E. M., & Bornstein, M. H. (2000). Contemporary research on parenting: The case for nature and nurture. *American Psychologist, 55*, 218–232.

Comer, J. P. (2001, April 23). Schools that develop children. *The American Prospect*, 30–35.

Cook, T. D., Murphy, R. F., & Hunt, H. D. (2000). Comer's School Development Program in Chicago: A theory-based evaluation. *American Educational Research Journal, 37*, 535–597.

Cooper, A. J. R., & Monk, A. (1976). Learning for recall and learning for recognition. In J. Brown (Ed.), *Recall and recognition* (pp. 131–156). London: Wiley.

Cooper, H. M., & Good, T. L. (1983). *Pygmalion grows up: Studies in the expectation communication process*. New York: Longman.

Cooper, H. M., & Tom, D. Y. H. (1984). Teacher expectation research: A review with implications for classroom instruction. *Elementary School Journal, 85*, 77–89.

Cooper, L. A., & Shepard, R. N. (1973). Chronometric studies of the rotation of mental images. In W. G. Chase (Ed.), *Visual information processing* (pp. 95–176). New York: Academic Press.

Cooper, W. H. (1983). An achievement motivation nomological network. *Journal of Personality and Social Psychology, 44*, 841–861.

Corno, L. (1989). Self-regulated learning: A volitional analysis. In B. J. Zimmerman & D. H. Schunk (Eds.), *Self-regulated learning and academic achievement: Theory, research, and practice* (pp. 111–142). New York: Springer-Verlag.

Corno, L. (1993). The best-laid plans: Modern conceptions of volition and educational research. *Educational Researcher, 22*(2), 14–22.

Corno, L. (1994). Student volition and education: Outcomes, influences, and practices. In D. H. Schunk & B. J. Zimmerman (Eds.), *Self-regulation of learning and performance: Issues and educational applications* (pp. 229–251). Hillsdale, NJ: Erlbaum.

Corno, L., & Kanfer, R. (1993). The role of volition in learning and performance. In L. Darling-Hammond (Ed.), *Review of research in education* (Vol. 19, pp. 301–341). Washington, DC: American Educational Research Association.

Corno, L., & Snow, R. E. (1986). Adapting teaching to individual differences among learners. In M. C. Wittrock (Ed.), *Handbook of research on teaching* (3rd ed., pp. 605–629). New York: Macmillan.

Covey, S. R. (1989). *The seven habits of highly effective people: Restoring the character ethic*. New York: Simon and Schuster.

Covington, M. V. (1983). Motivated cognitions. In S. G. Paris, G. M. Olson, & H. W. Stevenson (Eds.), *Learning and motivation in the classroom* (pp. 139–164). Hillsdale, NJ: Erlbaum.

Covington, M. V. (1984). The self-worth theory of achievement motivation: Findings and implications. *Elementary School Journal, 85*, 5–20.

Covington, M. V. (1992). *Making the grade: A self-worth perspective on motivation and school reform*. Cambridge, England: Cambridge University Press.

Covington, M. V., & Beery, R. G. (1976). *Self-worth and school learning*. New York: Holt, Rinehart & Winston.

Covington, M. V., & Dray, E. (2002). The developmental course of achievement motivation: A need-based approach. In A. Wigfield & J. S. Eccles (Eds.), *Development of achievement motivation* (pp. 33–56). San Diego: Academic Press.

Covington, M. V., & Omelich, C. L. (1979). Effort: The double-edged sword in school achievement. *Journal of Educational Psychology, 71*, 688–700.

Cox, B. D. (1997). The rediscovery of the active learner in adaptive contexts: A developmental-historical analysis of transfer of training. *Educational Psychologist, 32*, 41–55.

Craik, F. I. M. (1979). Human memory. *Annual Review of Psychology, 30*, 63–102.

Craik, F. I. M., & Lockhart, R. S. (1972). Levels of processing: A framework for memory research. *Journal of Verbal Learning and Verbal Behavior, 11*, 671–684.

Craik, F. I. M., & Tulving, E. (1975). Depth of processing and the retention of words in episodic memory. *Journal of Experimental Psychology: General, 104*, 268–294.

Crisafi, M. A., & Brown, A. L. (1986). Analogical transfer in very young children: Combining two separately learned solutions to reach a goal. *Child Development, 57*, 953–968.

Cronbach, L. J., & Snow, R. E. (1977). *Aptitudes and instructional methods*. New York: Irvington/Naiburg.

Crouse, J. H. (1971). Retroactive interference in reading prose materials. *Journal of Educational Psychology, 52*, 39–44.

Crowley, K., & Siegler, R. S. (1999). Explanation and generalization in young children's strategy learning. *Child Development, 70*, 304–316.

Csikszentmihalyi, M. (1975). *Beyond boredom and anxiety*. San Francisco: Jossey-Bass.

Csikszentmihalyi, M., & Rathunde, K. (1993). The measurement of flow in everyday life: Toward a theory of emergent motivation. In J. E. Jacobs (Ed.), *Nebraska symposium on motivation 1992* (Vol. 40, pp. 57–97). Lincoln, NE: University of Nebraska Press.

Cummins, D. D., Kintsch, W., Reusser, K., & Weimer, R. (1988). The role of understanding in solving word problems. *Cognitive Psychology, 20*, 405–438.

Cuny, H. (1965). *Pavlov: The man and his theories* (P. Evans, Trans.). New York: Paul S. Eriksson.

Curtis, M. E. (1980). Development of components of reading skill. *Journal of Educational Psychology, 72*, 656–669.

Dansereau, D. F. (1978). The development of a learning strategies curriculum. In H. F. O'Neil, Jr. (Ed.), *Learning strategies* (pp. 1–29). New York: Academic Press.

Dansereau, D. F. (1988). Cooperative learning strategies. In C. E. Weinstein, E. T. Goetz, & P. A. Alexander (Eds.), *Learning and study strategies: Issues in assessment, instruction, and evaluation* (pp. 103–120). San Diego: Academic Press.

Dansereau, D. F., McDonald, B. A., Collins, K. W., Garland, J., Holley, C. D., Diekhoff, G. M., & Evans, S. H. (1979). Evaluation of a learning strategy system. In H. F. O'Neil, Jr., & C. D. Spielberger (Eds.), *Cognitive and affective learning strategies* (pp. 3–43). New York: Academic Press.

Darwin, C. J., Turvey, M. T., & Crowder, R. G. (1972). An auditory analogue of the Sperling partial report procedure: Evidence for brief auditory storage. *Cognitive Psychology, 3*, 255–267.

Davidson, E. S., & Benjamin, L. T., Jr. (1987). A history of the child study movement in America. In J. A. Glover & R. R. Ronning (Eds.), *Historical foundations of educational psychology* (pp. 41–60). New York: Plenum.

Davidson, E. S., & Smith, W. P. (1982). Imitation, social comparison, and self-reward. *Child Development, 53*, 928–932.

Day, J. D. (1983). The zone of proximal development. In M. Pressley & J. R. Levin (Eds.), *Cognitive strategy instruction: Psychological foundations* (pp. 155–175). New York: Springer-Verlag.

de Beaugrande, R. (1984). *Text production: Toward a science of composition.* Norwood, NJ: Ablex.

de Charms, R. (1968). *Personal causation: The internal affective determinants of behavior.* New York: Academic Press.

de Charms, R. (1976). *Enhancing motivation: Change in the classroom.* New York: Irvington.

de Charms, R. (1984). Motivation enhancement in educational settings. In R. Ames & C. Ames (Eds.), *Research on motivation in education* (Vol. 1, pp. 275–310). Orlando: Academic Press.

Deci, E. L. (1975). *Intrinsic motivation.* New York: Plenum.

Deci, E. L. (1980). *The psychology of self-determination.* Lexington, MA: D. C. Heath.

Deci, E. L., & Porac, J. (1978). Cognitive evaluation theory and the study of human motivation. In M. R. Lepper & D. Greene (Eds.), *The hidden costs of reward: New perspectives on the psychology of human motivation* (pp. 149–176). Hillsdale, NJ: Erlbaum.

Deci, E. L., & Ryan, R. M. (1991). A motivational approach to self: Integration in personality. In R. A. Dienstbier (Ed.), *Nebraska symposium on motivation 1990* (Vol. 38, pp. 237–288). Lincoln, NE: University of Nebraska Press.

Dede, C. J. (1992). The future of multimedia: Bridging to virtual worlds. *Educational Technology, 32*(5), 54–60.

DeGrandpre, R. J. (2000). A science of meaning: Can behaviorism bring meaning to psychological science? *American Psychologist, 55*, 721–739.

de Jong, P. F. (1998). Working memory deficits of reading disabled children. *Journal of Experimental Child Psychology, 70*, 75–96.

de Jong, T., & van Joolingen, W. R. (1998). Scientific discovery learning with computer simulations of conceptual domains. *Review of Educational Research, 68*, 179–201.

Denney, D. R. (1975). The effects of exemplary and cognitive models and self-rehearsal on children's interrogative strategies. *Journal of Experimental Child Psychology, 19*, 476–488.

Denney, N. W., & Turner, M. C. (1979). Facilitating cognitive performance in children: A comparison of strategy modeling and strategy modeling with overt self-verbalization. *Journal of Experimental Child Psychology, 28*, 119–131.

Derry, S. J. (1996). Cognitive schema theory in the constructivist debate. *Educational Psychologist, 31*, 163–174.

Deutsch, M. (1949). A theory of cooperation and competition. *Human Relations, 2*, 129–152.

Dewey, J. (1896). The reflex arc concept in psychology. *Psychological Review, 3*, 357–370.

Dewey, J. (1900). Psychology and social practice. *Psychological Review, 7*, 105–124.

Dewsbury, D. A. (2000). Introduction: Snapshots of psychology circa 1900. *American Psychologist, 55*, 255–259.

Dick, W., & Carey, L. (1985). *The systematic design of instruction* (2nd ed.). Glenview, IL: Scott, Foresman.

DiClemente, C. C. (1981). Self-efficacy and smoking cessation maintenance: A preliminary report. *Cognitive Therapy and Research, 5*, 175–187.

DiClemente, C. C. (1986). Self-efficacy and the addictive behaviors. *Journal of Social and Clinical Psychology, 4*, 302–315.

DiClemente, C. C., Prochaska, J. O., & Gilbertini, M. (1985). Self-efficacy and the stages of self-change in smoking. *Cognitive Therapy and Research, 9*, 181–200.

Diener, C. I., & Dweck, C. S. (1978). An analysis of learned helplessness: Continuous changes in performance, strategy, and achievement cognitions following failure. *Journal of Personality and Social Psychology, 36*, 451–462.

Diener, C. I., & Dweck, C. S. (1980). An analysis of learned helplessness: II. The processing of success. *Journal of Personality and Social Psychology, 39*, 940–952.

Dillon, A., & Gabbard, R. (1998). Hypermedia as an educational technology: A review of the quantitative research literature on learner comprehension, control, and style. *Review of Educational Research, 68*, 322–349.

DiPardo, A., & Freedman, S. W. (1988). Peer response groups in the writing classroom: Theoretic foundations and new directions. *Review of Educational Research, 58*, 119–149.

Dowrick, P. W. (1983). Self-modelling. In P. W. Dowrick & S. J. Biggs (Eds.), *Using video: Psychological and social applications* (pp. 105–124). Chichester, England: Wiley.

Dragoi, V., & Staddon, J. E. R. (1999). The dynamics of operant conditioning. *Psychological Review, 106*, 20–61.

Driver, R., Asoko, H., Leach, J., Mortimer, E., & Scott, P. (1994). Constructing scientific knowledge in the classroom. *Educational Researcher, 23*(7), 5–12.

Duchastel, P. (1979). Learning objectives and the organization of prose. *Journal of Educational Psychology, 71*, 100–106.

Duchastel, P., & Brown, B. R. (1974). Incidental and relevant learning with instructional objectives. *Journal of Educational Psychology, 66*, 481–485.

Duda, J. L., & Nicholls, J. G. (1992). Dimensions of achievement motivation in schoolwork and sport. *Journal of Educational Psychology, 84*, 290–299.

Duell, O. K. (1986). Metacognitive skills. In G. D. Phye & T. Andre (Eds.), *Cognitive classroom learning: Understanding, thinking, and problem solving* (pp. 205–242). Orlando: Academic Press.

Duncan, R. M. (1995). Piaget and Vygotsky revisited: Dialogue or assimilation? *Developmental Review, 15*, 458–472.

Duncker, K. (1945). On problem-solving (L. S. Lees, Trans.). *Psychological Monographs, 58*(5, Whole No. 270).

Dunham, P. (1977). The nature of reinforcing stimuli. In W. K. Honig & J. E. R. Staddon (Eds.), *Handbook of operant behavior* (pp. 98–124). Englewood Cliffs, NJ: Prentice Hall.

Dunkin, M. J., & Biddle, B. J. (1974). *The study of teaching.* New York: Holt, Rinehart and Winston.

Dusek, J. B. (Ed.) (1985). *Teacher expectancies.* Hillsdale, NJ: Erlbaum.

Dweck, C. S. (1975). The role of expectations and attributions in the alleviation of learned helplessness. *Journal of Personality and Social Psychology, 31*, 674–685.

Dweck, C. S. (1986). Motivational processes affecting learning. *American Psychologist, 41*, 1040–1048.

Dweck, C. S. (1991). Self-theories and goals: Their role in motivation, personality, and development. In R. A. Dienstbier (Ed.), *Nebraska Symposium on Motivation, 1990* (Vol. 38, pp. 199–235). Lincoln, NE: University of Nebraska Press.

Dweck, C. S. (1999). *Self-theories: Their role in motivation, personality, and development.* Philadelphia: Taylor & Francis.

Dweck, C. S. (2002). The development of ability conceptions. In A. Wigfield & J. S. Eccles (Eds.), *Development of achievement motivation* (pp. 57–88). San Diego: Academic Press.

Dweck, C. S., & Bempechat, J. (1983). Children's theories of intelligence: Consequences for learning. In S. G. Paris, G. M. Olson, & H. W. Stevenson (Eds.), *Learning and motivation in the classroom* (pp. 239–256). Hillsdale, NJ: Erlbaum.

Dweck, C. S., Davidson, W., Nelson, S., & Enna, B. (1978). Sex differences in learned helplessness: II. The contingencies of evaluative feedback in the classroom and III. An experimental analysis. *Developmental Psychology, 14*, 268–276.

Dweck, C. S., & Leggett, E. L. (1988). A social-cognitive approach to motivation and personality. *Psychological Review, 95*, 256–273.

Dweck, C. S., & Repucci, N. D. (1973). Learned helplessness and reinforcement responsibility in children. *Journal of Personality and Social Psychology, 25*, 109–116.

Ebbinghaus, H. (1964). *Memory: A contribution to experimental psychology* (H. A. Ruger & C. E. Bussenius, Trans.). New York: Dover. (Original work published 1885).

Eccles, J. S. (1983). Expectancies, values, and academic behaviors. In J. T. Spence (Ed.), *Achievement and achievement motivation* (pp. 75–146). San Francisco: Freeman.

Eccles, J. S., & Midgley, C. (1989). Stage-environment fit: Developmentally appropriate classrooms for young adolescents. In C. Ames & R. Ames (Eds.), *Research on motivation in education* (Vol. 3, pp. 139–186). San Diego: Academic Press.

Eccles, J. S., Midgley, C., & Adler, T. F. (1984). Grade-related changes in the school environment: Effects on achievement motivation. In J. Nicholls (Ed.), *Advances in motivation and achievement* (Vol. 3, pp. 283–311). Greenwich, CT: JAI Press.

Eccles, J. S., & Wigfield, A. (1985). Teacher expectations and student motivation. In J. B. Dusek (Ed.), *Teacher expectancies* (pp. 185–226). Hillsdale, NJ: Erlbaum.

Egger, M. D., & Miller, N. E. (1963). When is a reward reinforcing? An experimental study of the information hypothesis. *Journal of Comparative and Physiological Psychology, 56*, 132–137.

Ehri, L. C. (1996). Development of the ability to read words. In R. Barr, M. L. Kamil, P. B. Mosenthal, & P. D. Pearson (Eds.), *Handbook of reading research* (Vol. 2, pp. 382–417). Mahwah, NJ: Erlbaum.

Elashoff, J. D., & Snow, R. E. (1971). *Pygmalion reconsidered*. Worthington, OH: Jones.

Elliot, A. J., & Church, M. A. (1997). A hierarchical model of approach and avoidance achievement motivation. *Journal of Personality and Social Psychology, 72*, 218–232.

Elliot, A. J., & Harackiewicz, J. M. (1996). Approach and avoidance achievement goals and intrinsic motivation: A mediational analysis. *Journal of Personality and Social Psychology, 70*, 461–475.

Elliott, E. S., & Dweck, C. S. (1988). Goals: An approach to motivation and achievement. *Journal of Personality and Social Psychology, 54*, 5–12.

Ellis, S., & Rogoff, B. (1982). The strategies and efficacy of child versus adult teachers. *Child Development, 53*, 730–735.

Elstein, A. S., Shulman, L. S., & Sprafka, S. A. (1978). *Medical problem solving*. Cambridge, MA: Harvard University Press.

Emmons, C. L., Comer, J. P., & Haynes, N. M. (1996). Translating theory into practice: Comer's theory of school reform. In J. P. Comer, N. M. Haynes, E. T. Joyner, & M. Ben-Avie (Eds.), *Rallying the whole village: The Comer process for reforming education* (pp. 27–41). New York: Teachers College Press.

Engberg, L. A., Hansen, G., Welker, R. L., & Thomas, D. (1972). Acquisition of keypecking via autoshaping as a function of prior experience: Learned laziness? *Science, 178*, 1002–1004.

Englert, C. S., Raphael, T. E., Anderson, L. M., Anthony, H. M., & Stevens, D. D. (1991). Making strategies and self-talk visible: Writing instruction in regular and special education classrooms. *American Educational Research Journal, 28*, 337–372.

Ennis, R. H. (1987). A taxonomy of critical thinking dispositions and abilities. In J. B. Baron & R. J. Sternberg (Eds.), *Teaching thinking skills: Theory and practice* (pp. 9–26). New York: Freeman.

Epstein, J. L. (1989). Family structures and student motivation: A developmental perspective. In C. Ames & R. Ames (Eds.), *Research on motivation in education* (Vol. 3, pp. 259–295). San Diego: Academic Press.

Erickson, F. (1986). Qualitative methods in research on teaching. In M. C. Wittrock (Ed.), *Handbook of research on teaching* (3rd ed., pp. 119–161). New York: Macmillan.

Ericsson, K. A., & Charness, N. (1994). Expert performance: Its structure and acquisition. *American Psychologist, 49*, 725–747.

Ericsson, K. A., Krampe, R. T., & Tesch-Römer, C. (1993). The role of deliberate practice in the acquisition of expert performance. *Psychological Review, 100*, 363–406.

Erikson, E. (1963). *Childhood and society* (2nd ed.). New York: Norton.

Ertmer, P. A. (1999). Addressing first-and second-order barriers to change: Strategies for technology integration. *Educational Technology Research & Development, 47*, 47–61.

Ertmer, P. A., Driscoll, M. P., & Wager, W. W. (2003). The legacy of Robert Mills Gagné. In B. J. Zimmerman & D. H. Schunk (Eds.), *Educational psychology: A century of contributions* (pp. 303–330). Mahwah, NJ: Erlbaum.

Ertmer, P. A., & Newby, T. J. (1993). Behaviorism, cognitivism, constructivism: Comparing critical features from an instructional design perspective. *Performance Improvement Quarterly, 6*(4), 50–72.

Estes, W. K. (1970). *Learning theory and mental development*. New York: Academic Press.

Estes, W. K. (1997). Processes of memory loss, recovery, and distortion. *Psychological Review, 104*, 148–169.

Evans, R. B. (2000). Psychological instruments at the turn of the century. *American Psychologist, 55*, 322–325.

Fabos, B., & Young, M. D. (1999). Telecommunication in the classroom: Rhetoric versus reality. *Review of Educational Research, 69*, 217–259.

Falmagne, R. J., & Gonsalves, J. (1995). Deductive inference. *Annual Review of Psychology, 46*, 525–559.

Fan, X., & Chen, M. (2001). Parental involvement and students' academic achievement: A meta-analysis. *Educational Psychology Review, 13*, 1–22.

Farnham-Diggory, S. (1992). *Cognitive processes in education* (2nd ed.). New York: HarperCollins.

Farrell, R. T., & Cirrincione, J. M. (1989). The content of the geography curriculum—teachers' perspective. *Social Education, 53*, 105–108.

Faw, H. W., & Waller, T. G. (1976). Mathemagenic behaviours and efficiency in learning from prose materials: Review, critique and recommendations. *Review of Educational Research, 46*, 691–720.

Feld, S. (1967). Longitudinal study of the origins of achievement strivings. *Journal of Personality and Social Psychology, 7*, 408–414.

Ferster, C. S., & Skinner, B. F. (1957). *Schedules of reinforcement*. New York: Appleton-Century-Crofts.

Festinger, L. (1954). A theory of social comparison processes. *Human Relations, 7*, 117–140.

Festinger, L. (1957). *A theory of cognitive dissonance.* Stanford, CA: Stanford University Press.

Fillmore, L. W., & Valadez, C. (1986). Teaching bilingual learners. In M. W. Wittrock (Ed.), *Handbook of research on teaching* (3rd ed., pp. 648–685). New York: Macmillan.

Fincham, F. D., & Cain, K. M. (1986). Learned helplessness in humans: A developmental analysis. *Developmental Review, 6*, 301–333.

Fischler, M. A., & Firschein, O. (1987). *Intelligence: The eye, the brain, and the computer.* Reading, MA: Addison-Wesley.

Fish, M. C., & Pervan, R. (1985). Self-instruction training: A potential tool for school psychologists. *Psychology in the Schools, 22*, 83–92.

Fisher, C., Dwyer, D. C., & Yocam, K. (Eds.) (1996). *Education and technology: Reflections on computing in classrooms.* San Francisco: Jossey-Bass.

Fitts, P. M., & Posner, M. I. (1967). *Human performance.* Belmont, CA: Brooks/Cole.

Fitzgerald, J. (1987). Research on revision in writing. *Review of Educational Research, 57*, 481–506.

Fitzgerald, J., & Markham, L. (1987). Teaching children about revision in writing. *Cognition and Instruction, 4*, 3–24.

Fitzgerald, J., & Shanahan, T. (2000). Reading and writing relations and their development. *Educational Psychologist, 35*, 39–50.

Flavell, J. H. (1985). *Cognitive development* (2nd ed.). Englewood Cliffs, NJ: Prentice Hall.

Flavell, J. H., Beach, D. R., & Chinsky, J. M. (1966). Spontaneous verbal rehearsal in a memory task as a function of age. *Child Development, 37*, 283–299.

Flavell, J. H., Friedrichs, A. G., & Hoyt, J. D. (1970). Developmental changes in memorization processes. *Cognitive Psychology, 1*, 324–340.

Flavell, J. H., Green, F. L., & Flavell, E. R. (1995). Young children's knowledge about thinking. *Monographs of the Society for Research in Child Development, 60*(1) (Serial No. 243).

Flavell, J. H., & Wellman, H. M. (1977). Metamemory. In R. B. Kail, Jr., & J. W. Hagen (Eds.), *Perspectives on the development of memory and cognition* (pp. 3–33). Hillsdale, NJ: Erlbaum.

Flower, L. (1981). *Problem-solving strategies for writing.* New York: Harcourt Brace Jovanovich.

Flower, L., & Hayes, J. R. (1980). The dynamics of composing: Making plans and juggling constraints. In L. W. Gregg & E. R. Steinberg (Eds.), *Cognitive processes in writing* (pp. 31–50). Hillsdale, NJ: Erlbaum.

Flower, L., & Hayes, J. R. (1981a). A cognitive process theory of writing. *College Composition and Communication, 32*, 365–387.

Flower, L., & Hayes, J. R. (1981b). The pregnant pause: An inquiry into the nature of planning. *Research in the Teaching of English, 15*, 229–243.

Franks, J. J., & Bransford, J. D. (1971). Abstraction of visual patterns. *Journal of Experimental Psychology, 90*, 65–74.

Frauenglass, M. H., & Diaz, R. M. (1985). Self-regulatory functions of children's private speech: A critical analysis of recent challenges to Vygotsky's theory. *Developmental Psychology, 21*, 357–364.

Frederiksen, C. H. (1979). Discourse comprehension and early reading. In L. B. Resnick & P. A. Weaver (Eds.), *Theory and practice of early reading* (Vol. 1, pp. 155–186). Hillsdale, NJ: Erlbaum.

Freud, S. (1966). *The complete introductory lectures on psychoanalysis* (J. Strachey, Trans.). New York: Norton.

Friedman, D. E., & Medway, F. J. (1987). Effects of varying performance sets and outcome on the expectations, attributions, and persistence of boys with learning disabilities. *Journal of Learning Disabilities, 20*, 312–316.

Friedman, W. (1990). *About time: Inventing the fourth dimension.* Cambridge, MA: MIT Press.

Friend, R., & Neale, J. (1972). Children's perceptions of success and failure: An attributional analysis of the effects of race and social class. *Developmental Psychology, 7*, 124–128.

Frieze, I. H. (1980). Beliefs about success and failure in the classroom. In J. H. McMillan (Ed.), *The social psychology of school learning* (pp. 39–78). New York: Academic Press.

Frieze, I. H., Francis, W. D., & Hanusa, B. H. (1983). Defining success in classroom settings. In J. M. Levine & M. C. Wang (Eds.), *Teacher and student perceptions: Implications for learning* (pp. 3–28). Hillsdale, NJ: Erlbaum.

Frolov, Y. P. (1937). *Pavlov and his school* (C. P. Dutt, Trans.). New York: Oxford University Press.

Fuchs, D., Fuchs, L. S., Mathes, P. G., & Simmons, D. C. (1997). Peer-assisted learning strategies: Making classrooms more responsive to diversity. *American Educational Research Journal, 34*, 174–206.

Fuhrer, M. J., & Baer, P. E. (1965). Differential classical conditioning: Verbalization of stimulus contingencies. *Science, 150*, 1479–1481.

Furth, H. G. (1970). *Piaget for teachers.* Englewood Cliffs, NJ: Prentice Hall.

Fuson, K. C. (1979). The development of self-regulating aspects of speech: A review. In G. Zivin (Ed.), *The development of self-regulation through private speech* (pp. 135–217). New York: Wiley.

Fuson, K. C., & Willis, G. B. (1989). Second graders' use of schematic drawings in solving addition and subtraction word problems. *Journal of Educational Psychology, 81*, 514–520.

Gaa, J. P. (1973). Effects of individual goal-setting conferences on achievement, attitudes, and goal-setting behavior. *Journal of Experimental Education, 42*, 22–28.

Gaa, J. P. (1979). The effects of individual goal-setting conferences on academic achievement and modification of locus of control orientation. *Psychology in the Schools, 16*, 591–597.

Gage, N. L. (1978). *The scientific basis of the art of teaching.* New York: Teachers College Press.

Gagné, E. D., Yekovich, C. W., & Yekovich, F. R. (1993). *The cognitive psychology of school learning* (2nd ed.). New York: HarperCollins.

Gagné, R. M. (1984). Learning outcomes and their effects: Useful categories of human performance. *American Psychologist, 39*, 377–385.

Gagné, R. M. (1985). *The conditions of learning* (4th ed.). New York: Holt, Rinehart & Winston.

Gagné, R. M., & Briggs, L. J. (1979). *Principles of instructional design* (2nd ed.). New York: Holt, Rinehart & Winston.

Gagné, R. M., & Dick, W. (1983). Instructional psychology. *Annual Review of Psychology, 34*, 261–295.

Gagné, R. M., & Glaser, R. (1987). Foundations in learning research. In R. M. Gagné (Ed.), *Instructional technology: Foundations* (pp. 49–83). Hillsdale, NJ: Erlbaum.

Galbreath, J. (1992). The educational buzzword of the 1990's: Multimedia, or is it hypermedia, or interactive multimedia, or . . . ? *Educational Technology, 32*(4), 15–19.

Garcia, J., & Garcia y Robertson, R. (1985). Evolution of learning mechanisms. In B. L. Hammonds (Ed.), *Psychology and learning: Master lecture series* (Vol. 4, pp. 191–243). Washington, DC: American Psychological Association.

Garcia, J., & Koelling, R. A. (1966). Relation of cue to consequence in avoidance learning. *Psychonomic Science, 4,* 123–124.

Garcia, T., & Pintrich, P. R. (1994). Regulating motivation and cognition in the classroom: The role of self-schemas and self-regulatory strategies. In D. H. Schunk & B. J. Zimmerman (Eds.), *Self-regulation of learning and performance: Issues and educational applications* (pp. 127–153). Hillsdale, NJ: Erlbaum.

Garner, R., & Reis, R. (1981). Monitoring and resolving comprehension obstacles: An investigation of spontaneous text lookbacks among upper-grade good and poor comprehenders. *Reading Research Quarterly, 16,* 569–582.

Geary, D. C. (1995). Reflections of evolution and culture in children's cognition: Implications for mathematical development and instruction. *American Psychologist, 50,* 24–37.

Gelman, R., & Gallistel, C. R. (1978). *The child's understanding of number.* Cambridge, MA: Harvard University Press.

George, T. R., Feltz, D. L., & Chase, M. A. (1992). Effects of model similarity on self-efficacy and muscular endurance: A second look. *Journal of Sport and Exercise Psychology, 14,* 237–248.

Gersten, R., Fuchs, L. S., Williams, J. P., & Baker, S. (2001). Teaching reading comprehension strategies to students with learning disabilities: A review of research. *Review of Educational Research, 71,* 279–320.

Gesell, A., & Ilg, F. (1946). *The child from five to ten.* New York: Harper Brothers.

Gesell, A., Ilg, F., & Ames, L. (1956). *Youth: The years from ten to sixteen.* New York: Harper Brothers.

Gibson, S., & Dembo, M. H. (1984). Teacher efficacy: A construct validation. *Journal of Educational Psychology, 76,* 569–582.

Gick, M. L., & Holyoak, K. J. (1980). Analogical problem solving. *Cognitive Psychology, 12,* 306–355.

Gick, M. L., & Holyoak, K. J. (1983). Schema induction and analogical transfer. *Cognitive Psychology, 15,* 1–38.

Ginsburg, H., & Opper, S. (1988). *Piaget's theory of intellectual development* (2nd ed.). Englewood Cliffs, NJ: Prentice Hall.

Gitomer, D. H., & Glaser, R. (1987). If you don't know it work on it: Knowledge, self-regulation and instruction. In R. E. Snow & M. J. Farr (Eds.), *Aptitude, learning, and instruction* (Vol. 3, pp. 301–325). Hillsdale, NJ: Erlbaum.

Glaser, R. (1990). The reemergence of learning theory within instructional research. *American Psychologist, 45,* 29–39.

Glaser, R., & Bassok, M. (1989). Learning theory and the study of instruction. *Annual Review of Psychology, 40,* 631–666.

Glass, D. C., & Singer, J. E. (1972). *Urban stress: Experiments on noise and social stressors.* New York: Academic Press.

Glover, J. A., Plake, B. S., Roberts, B., Zimmer, J. W., & Palmere, M. (1981). Distinctiveness of encoding: The effects of paraphrasing and drawing inferences on memory from prose. *Journal of Educational Psychology, 73,* 736–744.

Glover, J. A., Ronning, R. R., & Bruning, R. H. (1990). *Cognitive psychology for teachers.* New York: Macmillan.

Glynn, S. M., Britton, B. K., Muth, K. D., & Dogan, N. (1982). Writing and revising persuasive documents. *Journal of Educational Psychology, 74,* 557–567.

Goble, F. G. (1970). *The third force: The psychology of Abraham Maslow.* New York: Grossman.

Goddard, R. D., Hoy, W. K., & Hoy, A. W. (2000). Collective teacher efficacy: Its meaning, measure, and impact on student achievement. *American Educational Research Journal, 37,* 479–507.

Godden, D. R., & Baddeley, A. D. (1975). Context-dependent memory in two natural environments: On land and underwater. *British Journal of Psychology, 66,* 325–332.

Godding, P. R., & Glasgow, R. E. (1985). Self-efficacy and outcome expectations as predictors of controlled smoking status. *Cognitive Therapy and Research, 9,* 583–590.

Goldberg, R. A., Schwartz, S., & Stewart, M. (1977). Individual differences in cognitive processes. *Journal of Educational Psychology, 69,* 9–14.

Goldin-Meadow, S., Alibali, M. W., & Church, R. B. (1993). Transitions in concept acquisition: Using the hand to read the mind. *Psychological Review, 100,* 279–297.

Gollub, L. (1977). Conditioned reinforcement: Schedule effects. In W. K. Honig & J. E. R. Staddon (Eds.), *Handbook of operant behavior* (pp. 288–312). Englewood Cliffs, NJ: Prentice Hall.

Good, T. L., & Brophy, J. E. (1984). *Looking in classrooms* (3rd ed.). New York: Harper & Row.

Good, T. L., & Grouws, D. A. (1979). The Missouri mathematics effectiveness project. *Journal of Educational Psychology, 71,* 355–362.

Goodman, K. S. (1982). Reading: A psycholinguistic guessing game. In E. V. Gollasch (Ed.), *Language and literacy* (Vol. 1, pp. 19–31). Boston: Routledge & Kegan Paul.

Gottfried, A. E. (1985). Academic intrinsic motivation in elementary and junior high school students. *Journal of Educational Psychology, 77,* 631–645.

Gottfried, A. E. (1990). Academic intrinsic motivation in young elementary school children. *Journal of Educational Psychology, 82,* 525–538.

Gottfried, A. E., Fleming, J. S., & Gottfried, A. W. (1998). Role of cognitively stimulating home environment in children's academic intrinsic motivation: A longitudinal study. *Child Development, 69,* 1448–1460.

Gough, P. B. (1972). One second of reading. In E. Kavanagh & I. G. Mattingly (Eds.), *Language by ear and by eye* (pp. 331–358). Cambridge, MA: MIT Press.

Gould, D., & Weiss, M. (1981). The effects of model similarity and model talk on self-efficacy and muscular endurance. *Journal of Sport Psychology, 3,* 17–29.

Grabe, M. (1986). Attentional processes in education. In G. D. Phye & T. Andre (Eds.), *Cognitive classroom learning: Understanding, thinking, and problem solving* (pp. 49–82). Orlando: Academic Press.

Grabe, M., & Grabe, C. (1998a). *Integrating technology for meaningful learning* (2nd ed.). Boston: Houghton Mifflin.

Grabe, M., & Grabe, C. (1998b). *Learning with Internet tools: A primer.* Boston: Houghton Mifflin.

Graham, S. (1991). A review of attribution theory in achievement contexts. *Educational Psychology Review, 3,* 5–39.

Graham, S. (1994). Motivation in African Americans. *Review of Educational Research, 64,* 55–117.

Graham, S., & Golan, S. (1991). Motivational influences on cognition: Task involvement, ego involvement, and depth of information processing. *Journal of Educational Psychology, 83,* 187–194.

Graham, S., & Harris, K. R. (2000). The role of self-regulation and transcription skills in writing and writing development. *Educational Psychologist, 35,* 3–12.

Graham, S., & Long, A. (1986). Race, class, and the attributional process. *Journal of Educational Psychology, 78*, 4–13.

Graham, S., & Taylor, A. Z. (2002). Ethnicity, gender, and the development of achievement values. In A. Wigfield & J. S. Eccles (Eds.), *Development of achievement motivation* (pp. 121–146). San Diego: Academic Press.

Gray, C. R., & Gummerman, K. (1975). The enigmatic eidetic image: A critical examination of methods, data, and theories. *Psychological Bulletin, 82*, 383–407.

Greeno, J. G. (1980). Trends in the theory of knowledge for problem solving. In D. Tuma & F. Reif (Eds.), *Problem solving and education: Issues in teaching and research* (pp. 9–23). Hillsdale, NJ: Erlbaum.

Greeno, J. G. (1989). A perspective on thinking. *American Psychologist, 44*, 134–141.

Greeno, J. G., & the Middle School Mathematics Through Applications Project Group (1998). The situativity of knowing, learning, and research. *American Psychologist, 53*, 5–26.

Griffin, M. M. (1995). You can't get there from here: Situated learning, transfer, and map skills. *Contemporary Educational Psychology, 20*, 65–87.

Groen, G., & Parkman, J. M. (1972). A chronometric analysis of simple addition. *Psychological Review, 79*, 329–343.

Groen, G., & Resnick, L. B. (1977). Can preschool children invent additional algorithms? *Journal of Educational Psychology, 69*, 645–652.

Grolnick, W. S., Gurland, S. T., Jacob, K. F., & Decourcey, W. (2002). The development of self-determination in middle childhood and adolescence. In A. Wigfield & J. S. Eccles (Eds.), *Development of achievement motivation* (pp. 147–171). San Diego: Academic Press.

Grossen, B. (1991). The fundamental skills of higher order thinking. *Journal of Learning Disabilities, 24*, 343–353.

Gunnar, M. R. (1996). *Quality of care and buffering of stress physiology: Its potential for protecting the developing human brain.* Minneapolis: University of Minnesota Institute of Child Development.

Gupta, P., & Cohen, N. J. (2002). Theoretical and computational analysis of skill learning, repetition priming, and procedural memory. *Psychological Review, 109*, 401–448.

Guskey, T. R., & Passaro, P. D. (1994). Teacher efficacy: A study of construct dimensions. *American Educational Research Journal, 31*, 627–643.

Guthrie, E. R. (1930). Conditioning as a principle of learning. *Psychological Review, 37*, 412–428.

Guthrie, E. R. (1938). *The psychology of human conflict.* New York: Harper & Brothers.

Guthrie, E. R. (1940). Association and the law of effect. *Psychological Review, 47*, 127–148.

Guthrie, E. R. (1942). Conditioning: A theory of learning in terms of stimulus, response, and association. In N. B. Henry (Ed.), *The psychology of learning: The forty-first yearbook of the National Society for the Study of Education* (Part II, pp. 17–60). Chicago: University of Chicago Press.

Guthrie, E. R. (1952). *The psychology of learning* (Rev. ed.). New York: Harper & Brothers.

Guthrie, E. R. (1959). Association by contiguity. In S. Koch (Ed.), *Psychology: A study of a science* (Vol. 2, pp. 158–195). New York: McGraw-Hill.

Guthrie, E. R., & Horton, G. P. (1946). *Cats in a puzzle box.* New York: Rinehart & Company.

Guthrie, J. T., Wigfield, A., & VonSecker, C. (2000). Effects of integrated instruction on motivation and strategy use in reading. *Journal of Educational Psychology, 92*, 331–341.

Hall, G. S. (1894). The new psychology as a basis of education. *The Forum, 17*, 710–720.

Hall, G. S. (1896). The case of the public schools. *Atlantic Monthly, 77*, 402–413.

Hall, G. S. (1900). Child study and its relation to education. *The Forum, 29*, 688–702.

Hall, G. S. (1903). Child study at Clark University. *American Journal of Psychology, 14*, 96–106.

Hall, V., Howe, A., Merkel, S., & Lederman, N. (1986). Behavior, motivation, and achievement in desegregated junior high school science classes. *Journal of Educational Psychology, 78*, 108–115.

Hall, W. S. (1989). Reading comprehension. *American Psychologist, 44*, 157–161.

Hallahan, D. P., Kneedler, R. D., & Lloyd, J. W. (1983). Cognitive behavior modification techniques for learning disabled children: Self-instruction and self-monitoring. In J. D. McKinney & L. Feagans (Eds.), *Current topics in learning disabilities* (Vol. 1, pp. 207–244). Norwood, NJ: Ablex.

Halpern, D. F., Hansen, C., & Riefer, D. (1990). Analogies as an aid to understanding and memory. *Journal of Educational Psychology, 82*, 298–305.

Hamilton, R. J. (1985). A framework for the evaluation of the effectiveness of adjunct questions and objectives. *Review of Educational Research, 55*, 47–85.

Hannafin, M. J., & Peck, K. L. (1988). *The design, development, and evaluation of instructional software.* New York: Macmillan.

Hannus, M., & Hyönä, J. (1999). Utilization of illustrations during learning of science textbook passages among low- and high-ability children. *Contemporary Educational Psychology, 24*, 95–123.

Harari, O., & Covington, M. V. (1981). Reactions to achievement behavior from a teacher and student perspective: A developmental analysis. *American Educational Research Journal, 18*, 15–28.

Hardiman, P. T., Dufresne, R., & Mestre, J. P. (1989). The relation between problem categorization and problem solving among experts and novices. *Memory & Cognition, 17*, 627–638.

Harris, B. (1979). Whatever happened to Little Albert? *American Psychologist, 34*, 151–160.

Harris, J. R. (1998). *The nurture assumption: Why children turn out the way they do.* New York: Free Press.

Harris, K. R. (1982). Cognitive-behavior modification: Application with exceptional students. *Focus on Exceptional Children, 15*, 1–16.

Harris, K. R., & Pressley, M. (1991). The nature of cognitive strategy instruction: Interactive strategy construction. *Exceptional Children, 57*, 392–404.

Harter, S. (1978). Effectance motivation reconsidered: Toward a developmental model. *Human Development, 21*, 34–64.

Harter, S. (1981). A model of mastery motivation in children: Individual differences and developmental change. In W. A. Collins (Ed.), *Aspects on the development of competence: The Minnesota symposia on child psychology* (Vol. 14, pp. 215–255). Hillsdale, NJ: Erlbaum.

Harter, S., & Connell, J. P. (1984). A comparison of children's achievement and related self-perceptions of competence, control, and motivational orientation. In J. G. Nicholls (Ed.), *Advances in motivation and achievement* (Vol. 3, pp. 219–250). Greenwich, CT: JAI Press.

Hattie, J. (1992). *Self-concept.* Hillsdale, NJ: Erlbaum.

Hattie, J., Biggs, J., & Purdie, N. (1996). Effects of learning skills interventions on student learning: A meta-analysis. *Review of Educational Research, 66*, 99–136.

Haviland, S. E., & Clark, H. H. (1974). What's new? Acquiring new information as a process in comprehension. *Journal of Verbal Learning and Verbal Behavior, 13*, 512–521.

Hayes, J. R. (1996). A new framework for understanding cognition and affect in writing. In C. M. Levy & S. Ransdell (Eds.), *The science of writing: Theories, methods, individual differences, and applications* (pp. 1–27). Mahwah, NJ: Erlbaum.

Hayes, J. R., & Flower, L. (1980). Identifying the organization of writing processes. In L. W. Gregg & E. R. Steinberg (Eds.), *Cognitive processes in writing* (pp. 3–30). Hillsdale, NJ: Erlbaum.

Hayes-Roth, B., & Thorndyke, P. W. (1979). Integration of knowledge from text. *Journal of Verbal Learning and Verbal Behavior, 18*, 91–108.

Haynes, N. M., Emmons, C. L., Gebreyesus, S., & Ben-Avie, M. (1996). The School Development Program evaluation process. In J. P. Comer, N. M. Haynes, E. T. Joyner, & M. Ben-Avie (Eds.), *Rallying the whole village: The Comer process for reforming education* (pp. 123–146). New York: Teachers College Press.

Hebb, D. O. (1949). *The organization of behavior: A neuropsychological theory.* New York: Wiley.

Heckhausen, H. (1991). *Motivation and action.* Berlin: Springer-Verlag.

Hegarty, M., Mayer, R. E., & Monk, C. A. (1995). Comprehension of arithmetic word problems: A comparison of successful and unsuccessful problem solvers. *Journal of Educational Psychology, 87*, 18–32.

Heidbreder, E. (1933). *Seven psychologies.* New York: Appleton-Century-Crofts.

Heider, F. (1946). Attitudes and cognitive organization. *Journal of Psychology, 21*, 107–112.

Heider, F. (1958). *The psychology of interpersonal relations.* New York: Wiley.

Henderson, J. G. (1996). *Reflective teaching: The study of your constructivist practices* (2nd ed.). Englewood Cliffs, NJ: Merrill/Prentice Hall.

Henderson, R. W., & Cunningham, L. (1994). Creating interactive sociocultural environments for self-regulated learning. In D. H. Schunk & B. J. Zimmerman (Eds.), *Self-regulation of learning and performance: Issues and educational applications* (pp. 255–281). Hillsdale, NJ: Erlbaum.

Hidi, S. E. (1995). A reexamination of the role of attention in learning from text. *Educational Psychology Review, 7*, 323–350.

Hiebert, E. H., & Raphael, T. E. (1996). Psychological perspectives on literacy and extensions to educational practice. In D. C. Berliner & R. C. Calfee (Eds.), *Handbook of educational psychology* (pp. 550–602). New York: Macmillan.

Higgins, E. T. (1981). Role taking and social judgment: Alternative developmental perspectives and processes. In J. H. Flavell & L. Ross (Eds.), *Social cognitive development: Frontiers and possible futures* (pp. 119–153). Cambridge, England: Cambridge University Press.

Highet, G. (1950). *The art of teaching.* New York: Vintage.

Hilgard, E. R. (1996). Perspectives on educational psychology. *Educational Psychology Review, 8*, 419–431.

Hirsch, E. D., Jr. (1987). *Cultural literacy: What every American needs to know.* New York: Houghton Mifflin.

Hirschbuhl, J. J. (1992). Multimedia: Why invest? *Interactive Learning International, 8*, 321–323.

Hirt, E. R., Erickson, G. A., & McDonald, H. E. (1993). Role of expectancy timing and outcome consistency in expectancy-guided retrieval. *Journal of Personality and Social Psychology, 65*, 640–656.

Hofer, B. K., Yu, S. L., & Pintrich, P. R. (1998). Teaching college students to be self-regulated learners. In D. H. Schunk & B. J. Zimmerman (Eds.), *Self-regulated learning: From teaching to self-reflective practice* (pp. 57–85). New York: Guilford Press.

Hoffman, L. W. (1974). Fear of success in males and females: 1965 and 1971. *Journal of Consulting and Clinical Psychology, 42*, 353–358.

Hogan, D. M., & Tudge, J. R. H. (1999). Implications of Vygotsky's theory for peer learning. In A. M. O'Donnell & A. King (Eds.), *Cognitive perspectives on peer learning* (pp. 39–65). Mahwah, NJ: Erlbaum.

Holland, J. G. (1992). Obituary: B. F. Skinner (1904–1990). *American Psychologist, 47*, 665–667.

Holland, J. G., & Skinner, B. F. (1961). *The analysis of behavior.* New York: McGraw-Hill.

Holley, C. D., Dansereau, D. F., McDonald, B. A., Garland, J. C., & Collins, K. W. (1979). Evaluation of a hierarchical mapping technique as an aid to prose processing. *Contemporary Educational Psychology, 4*, 227–237.

Hollis, K. L. (1997). Contemporary research on Pavlovian conditioning: A "new" functional analysis. *American Psychologist, 52*, 956–965.

Holyoak, K. J. (1984). Mental models in problem solving. In J. R. Anderson & S. M. Kosslyn (Eds.), *Tutorials in learning and memory: Essays in honor of Gordon Bower* (pp. 193–218). San Francisco: Freeman.

Holyoak, K. J., & Thagard, P. (1997). The analogical mind. *American Psychologist, 52*, 35–44.

Hom, H. L., Jr., & Murphy, M. D. (1985). Low need achievers' performance: The positive impact of a self-determined goal. *Personality and Social Psychology Bulletin, 11*, 275–285.

Homme, L., Csanyi, A. P., Gonzales, M. A., & Rechs, J. R. (1970). *How to use contingency contracting in the classroom.* Champaign, IL: Research Press.

Hooper, S., & Hannafin, M. J. (1991). Psychological perspectives on emerging instructional technologies: A critical analysis. *Educational Psychologist, 26*, 69–95.

Hopkins, S. L., & Lawson, M. J. (2002). Explaining the acquisition of a complex skill: Methodological and theoretical considerations uncovered in the study of simple addition and the moving-on process. *Educational Psychology Review, 14*, 121–154.

Horner, M. S. (1972). Toward an understanding of achievement-related conflicts in women. *Journal of Social Issues, 28*, 157–175.

Horner, M. S. (1978). The measurement and behavioral implications of fear of success in women. In J. W. Atkinson & J. O. Raynor (Eds.), *Personality, motivation, and achievement* (pp. 41–70). Washington, DC: Hemisphere.

Horowitz, F. D. (1992). John B. Watson's legacy: Learning and environment. *Developmental Psychology, 28*, 360–367.

Hosford, R. E. (1981). Self-as-a-model: A cognitive social learning technique. *The Counseling Psychologist, 9* (1), 45–62.

Howard, R. W. (1987). *Concepts and schemata: An introduction.* Philadelphia: Taylor and Francis.

Hull, C. L. (1943). *Principles of behavior: An introduction to behavior theory.* New York: Appleton-Century-Crofts.

Humphrey, G. (1921). Imitation and the conditioned reflex. *Pedagogical Seminary, 28*, 1–21.

Hunt, E. (1989). Cognitive science: Definition, status, and questions. *Annual Review of Psychology, 40,* 603–629.

Hunt, J. McV. (1963). Motivation inherent in information processing and action. In O. J. Harvey (Ed.), *Motivation and social interaction* (pp. 35–94). New York: Ronald.

Hunt, M. (1993). *The story of psychology.* New York: Doubleday.

Hunter, M. (1982). *Mastery teaching.* El Segundo, CA: TIP Publications.

Jacoby, L. L., Bartz, W. H., & Evans, J. D. (1978). A functional approach to levels of processing. *Journal of Experimental Psychology: Human Learning and Memory, 4,* 331–346.

Jagacinski, C. M., & Nicholls, J. G. (1984). Conceptions of ability and related affects in task involvement and ego involvement. *Journal of Educational Psychology, 76,* 909–919.

Jagacinski, C. M., & Nicholls, J. G. (1987). Competence and affect in task involvement and ego involvement: The impact of social comparison information. *Journal of Educational Psychology, 79,* 107–114.

James, W. (1890). *The principles of psychology* (Vols. I & II). New York: Henry Holt.

James, W. (1892). *Psychology: Briefer course.* New York: Henry Holt.

Jensen, A. (1969). How much can we boost IQ and achievement? *Harvard Educational Review, 39,* 1–123.

Johnson, D. S. (1981). Naturally acquired learned helplessness: The relationship of school failure to achievement behavior, attributions, and self-concept. *Journal of Educational Psychology, 73,* 174–180.

Johnson, D. W., & Johnson, R. T. (1974). Instructional goal structure: Cooperative, competitive, or individualistic. *Review of Educational Research, 44,* 213–240.

Johnson-Laird, P. N. (1972). The three-term series problem. *Cognition, 1,* 57–82.

Johnson-Laird, P. N. (1985). Deductive reasoning ability. In R. J. Sternberg (Ed.), *Human abilities: An information-processing approach* (pp. 173–194). New York: Freeman.

Johnson-Laird, P. N. (1999). Deductive reasoning. *Annual Review of Psychology, 50,* 109–135.

Johnson-Laird, P. N., Byrne, R. M. J., & Schaeken, W. (1992). Propositional reasoning by model. *Psychological Review, 99,* 418–439.

Johnson-Laird, P. N., Byrne, R. M. J., & Tabossi, P. (1989). Reasoning by model: The case of multiple quantification. *Psychological Review, 96,* 658–673.

Jonassen, D. H. (1989). *Hypertext/hypermedia.* Englewood Cliffs, NJ: Educational Technology Publications.

Jonassen, D. H. (1996). *Computers in the classroom: Mind tools for critical thinking.* Englewood Cliffs, NJ: Merrill/Prentice Hall.

Jonassen, D. H., Peck, K. L., & Wilson, B. G. (1999). *Learning with technology: A constructivist perspective.* Upper Saddle River, NJ: Merrill/Prentice Hall.

Jourden, F. J., Bandura, A., & Banfield, J. T. (1991). The impact of conceptions of ability on self-regulatory factors and motor skill acquisition. *Journal of Sport and Exercise Psychology, 8,* 213–226.

Juel, C. (1996). Beginning reading. In R. Barr, M. L. Kamil, P. B. Mosenthal, & P. D. Pearson (Eds.), *Handbook of reading research* (Vol. 2, pp. 759–788). Mahwah, NJ: Erlbaum.

Just, M. A., & Carpenter, P. A. (1980). A theory of reading: From eye fixations to comprehension. *Psychological Review, 87,* 329–354.

Just, M. A., & Carpenter, P. A. (1992). A capacity theory of comprehension: Individual differences in working memory. *Psychological Review, 99,* 122–149.

Justice, E. M., Baker-Ward, L., Gupta, S., & Jannings, L. R. (1997). Means to the goal of remembering: Developmental changes in awareness of strategy use-performance relations. *Journal of Experimental Child Psychology, 65,* 293–314.

Kagan, J. (1966). Reflection-impulsivity: The generality and dynamics of conceptual tempo. *Journal of Abnormal Psychology, 71,* 17–24.

Kagan, J., Moss, H. A., & Sigel, I. E. (1960). Conceptual style and the use of affect labels. *Merrill-Palmer Quarterly, 6,* 261–278.

Kagan, J., Pearson, L., & Welch, L. (1966). Modifiability of an impulsive tempo. *Journal of Educational Psychology, 57,* 359–365.

Kail, R. B., Jr., & Hagen, J. W. (1982). Memory in childhood. In B. B. Wolman (Ed.), *Handbook of developmental psychology* (pp. 350–366). Englewood Cliffs, NJ: Prentice Hall.

Kanfer, F. H., & Gaelick, L. (1986). Self-management methods. In F. H. Kanfer & A. P. Goldstein (Eds.), *Helping people change: A textbook of methods* (3rd ed., pp. 283–345). New York: Pergamon.

Kanfer, R., & Ackerman, P. L. (1989). Motivation and cognitive abilities: An integrative/aptitude-treatment interaction approach to skill acquisition. *Journal of Applied Psychology, 74,* 657–690.

Kanfer, R., & Kanfer, F. H. (1991). Goals and self-regulation: Applications of theory to work settings. In M. L. Maehr & P. R. Pintrich (Eds.), *Advances in motivation and achievement* (Vol. 7, pp. 287–326). Greenwich, CT: JAI Press.

Kardash, C. A. M., Royer, J. M., & Greene, B. A. (1988). Effects of schemata on both encoding and retrieval of information from prose. *Journal of Educational Psychology, 80,* 324–329.

Karoly, P., & Harris, A. (1986). Operant methods. In F. H. Kanfer & A. P. Goldstein (Eds.), *Helping people change: A textbook of methods* (3rd ed., pp. 111–144). New York: Pergamon.

Karpov, Y. V., & Haywood, H. C. (1998). Two ways to elaborate Vygotsky's concept of mediation: Implications for instruction. *American Psychologist, 53,* 27–36.

Katona, G. (1940). *Organizing and memorizing.* New York: Columbia University Press.

Keeney, T. J., Cannizzo, S. R., & Flavell, J. H. (1967). Spontaneous and induced verbal rehearsal in a recall task. *Child Development, 38,* 953–966.

Keller, F. S. (1966). A personal course in psychology. In R. Ulrich, T. Stachnik, & J. Mabry (Eds.), *Control of human behavior* (pp. 91–93). Glenview, IL: Scott, Foresman.

Keller, F. S. (1968). Good-bye, teacher. . . . *Journal of Applied Behavior Analysis, 1,* 79–89.

Keller, F. S. (1977). *Summers and sabbaticals: Selected papers on psychology and education.* Champaign, IL: Research Press.

Keller, F. S., & Ribes-Inesta, E. (1974). *Behavior modification: Applications to education.* New York: Academic Press.

Keller, F. S., & Schoenfeld, W. N. (1950). *Principles of psychology: A systematic text in the science of behavior.* New York: Appleton-Century-Crofts.

Keller, F. S., & Sherman, J. G. (1974). *The Keller Plan handbook.* Menlo Park, CA: W. A. Benjamin.

Kerst, S. M., & Howard, J. H., Jr. (1977). Mental comparisons for ordered information on abstract and concrete dimensions. *Memory & Cognition, 5,* 227–234.

Kiewra, K. A., & Dubois, N. F. (1998). *Learning to learn: Making the transition from student to life-long learner.* Boston: Allyn & Bacon.

King, J., & Just, M. A. (1991). Individual differences in syntactic processing: The role of working memory. *Journal of Memory and Language, 30,* 580–602.

Kintsch, W. (1974). *The representation of meaning in memory.* Hillsdale, NJ: Erlbaum.

Kintsch, W. (1979). On modeling comprehension. *Educational Psychologist, 14,* 3–14.

Kintsch, W., & van Dijk, T. A. (1978). Toward a model of text comprehension and production. *Psychological Review, 85,* 363–394.

Kirkland, K., & Hollandsworth, J. G. (1980). Effective test taking: Skills-acquisition versus anxiety-reduction techniques. *Journal of Consulting and Clinical Psychology, 48,* 431–439.

Kitsantas, A., & Zimmerman, B. J. (1998). Self-regulation of motoric learning: A strategic cycle view. *Journal of Applied Sport Psychology, 10,* 220–239.

Klahr, D., & Simon, H. A. (1999). Studies of scientific discovery: Complementary approaches and convergent findings. *Psychological Bulletin, 125,* 524–543.

Klassen, R. (2002). Writing in early adolescence: A review of the role of self-efficacy beliefs. *Educational Psychology Review, 14,* 173–203.

Klatzky, R. L. (1980). *Human memory: Structures and processes* (2nd ed.). New York: Freeman.

Klausmeier, H. J. (1990). Conceptualizing. In B. F. Jones & L. Idol (Eds.), *Dimensions of thinking and cognitive instruction* (pp. 93–138). Hillsdale, NJ: Erlbaum.

Klausmeier, H. J. (1992). Concept learning and concept teaching. *Educational Psychologist, 27,* 267–286.

Koffka, K. (1922). Perception: An introduction to the Gestalt-theorie. *Psychological Bulletin, 19,* 531–585.

Koffka, K. (1924). *The growth of the mind* (R. M. Ogden, Trans.). London: Kegan Paul, Trench, Trubner.

Koffka, K. (1926). Mental development. In C. Murchison (Ed.), *Psychologies of 1925* (pp. 129–143). Worcester, MA: Clark University Press.

Köhler, W. (1925). *The mentality of apes* (E. Winter, Trans.). New York: Harcourt, Brace & World.

Köhler, W. (1926). An aspect of Gestalt psychology. In C. Murchinson (Ed.), *Psychologies of 1925* (pp. 163–195). Worcester, MA: Clark University Press.

Köhler, W. (1947). *Gestalt psychology: An introduction to new concepts in modern psychology.* New York: Liveright. (Reprinted 1959, New American Library, New York)

Kolodner, J. L. (1997). Educational implications of analogy: A view from case-based reasoning. *American Psychologist, 52,* 57–66.

Kopp, C. B. (1982). Antecedents of self-regulation: A developmental perspective. *Developmental Psychology, 18,* 199–214.

Kosiewicz, M. M., Hallahan, D. P., Lloyd, J., & Graves, A. W. (1982). Effects of self-instruction and self-correction procedures on handwriting performance. *Learning Disability Quarterly, 5,* 71–78.

Kosslyn, S. M. (1980). *Image and mind.* Cambridge, MA: Harvard University Press.

Kosslyn, S. M. (1984). Mental representation. In J. R. Anderson & S. M. Kosslyn (Eds.), *Tutorials in learning and memory: Essays in honor of Gordon Bower* (pp. 91–117). San Francisco: Freeman.

Kosslyn, S. M. (1988). Aspects of a cognitive neuroscience of mental imagery. *Science, 240,* 1621–1626.

Kosslyn, S. M., & Pomerantz, J. P. (1977). Imagery, propositions, and the form of internal representations. *Cognitive Psychology, 9,* 52–76.

Kozma, R. B. (1991). Learning with media. *Review of Educational Research, 61,* 179–211.

Kozulin, A. (1986). The concept of activity in Soviet psychology: Vygotsky, his disciples and critics. *American Psychologist, 41,* 264–274.

Kuhl, J. (1984). Volitional aspects of achievement motivation and learned helplessness: Toward a comprehensive theory of action control. In B. A. Maher (Ed.), *Progress in experimental personality research* (Vol. 13, pp. 99–171). New York: Academic Press.

Kuhl, J. (1985). Volitional mediators of cognition-behavior consistency: Self-regulatory processes and action versus state orientation. In J. Kuhl & J. Beckmann (Eds.), *Action control: From cognition to behavior* (pp. 101–128). New York: Springer-Verlag.

Kuhl, J., & Blankenship, V. (1979a). Behavioral change in a constant environment: Shift to more difficult tasks with constant probability of success. *Journal of Personality and Social Psychology, 37,* 549–561.

Kuhl, J., & Blankenship, V. (1979b). The dynamic theory of achievement motivation: From episodic to dynamic thinking. *Psychological Review, 86,* 141–151.

Kulik, C. C., Kulik, J. A., & Bangert-Drowns, R. L. (1990). Effectiveness of mastery learning programs: A meta-analysis. *Review of Educational Research, 60,* 265–299.

Kulik, J. A., Kulik, C. C., & Cohen, P. A. (1979). A meta-analysis of outcome studies of Keller's Personalized System of Instruction. *American Psychologist, 34,* 307–318.

Kulik, J. A., Kulik, C. C., & Cohen, P. A. (1980). Effectiveness of computer-based college teaching: A meta-analysis of findings. *Review of Educational Research, 50,* 525–544.

Kyllonen, P. C., & Stephens, D. L. (1990). Cognitive abilities as determinants of success in acquiring logic skill. *Learning and Individual Differences, 2,* 129–160.

Lampert, M. (1990). When the problem is not the question and the solution is not the answer: Mathematical knowing and teaching. *American Educational Research Journal, 27,* 29–63.

Lan, W. Y. (1998). Teaching self-monitoring skills in statistics. In D. H. Schunk & B. J. Zimmerman (Eds.), *Self-regulated learning: From teaching to self-reflective practice* (pp. 86–105). New York: Guilford Press.

Lange, P. C. (1972). What's the score on: Programmed instruction? *Today's Education, 61,* 59.

Langer, J. A., & Applebee, A. N. (1986). Reading and writing instruction: Toward a theory of teaching and learning. In E. Z. Rothkopf (Ed.), *Review of research in education* (Vol. 13, pp. 171–194). Washington, DC: American Educational Research Association.

Lanier, J. (1992). Virtual reality: The promise of the future. *Interactive Learning International, 8,* 275–279.

Larkin, J. H. (1980). Teaching problem solving in physics: The psychological laboratory and the practical classroom. In D. Tuma & F. Reif (Eds.), *Problem solving and education: Issues in teaching and research* (pp. 111–125). Hillsdale, NJ: Erlbaum.

Larkin, J. H., McDermott, J., Simon, D. P., & Simon, H. A. (1980). Models of competence in solving physics problems. *Cognitive Science, 4,* 317–345.

Lattal, K. A. (1992). B. F. Skinner and psychology: Introduction to the special issue. *American Psychologist, 47,* 1269–1272.

Leask, J., Haber, R. N., & Haber, R. B. (1969). Eidetic imagery in children: II. Longitudinal and experimental results. *Psychonomic Monograph Supplement, 3* (3, Whole No. 35).

Lee, C. (1988). The relationship between goal setting, self-ef-ficacy, and female field hockey team performance. *International Journal of Sport Psychology, 20*, 147–161.

Lee, F. J., & Anderson, J. R. (2001). Does learning a complex task have to be complex? A study in learning decomposition. *Cognitive Psychology, 42*, 267–316.

Leeper, R. (1935). A study of a neglected portion of the field of learning—The development of sensory organization. *Pedagogical Seminary and Journal of Genetic Psychology, 46*, 41–75.

Lefcourt, H. M. (1976). *Locus of control: Current trends in theory and research*. Hillsdale, NJ: Erlbaum.

Lenneberg, E. H. (1967). *The biological foundations of language*. New York: Wiley.

Lent, R. W., Brown, S. D., & Hackett, G. (2000). Contextual supports and barriers to career choice: A social cognitive analysis. *Journal of Counseling Psychology, 47*, 36–49.

Lepper, M. R. (1983). Extrinsic reward and intrinsic motivation: Implications for the classroom. In J. M. Levine & M. C. Wang (Eds.), *Teacher and student perceptions: Implications for learning* (pp. 281–317). Hillsdale, NJ: Erlbaum.

Lepper, M. R. (1985). Microcomputers in education: Motivational and social issues. *American Psychologist, 40*, 1–18.

Lepper, M. R., & Greene, D. (1978). Overjustification research and beyond: Toward a means-ends analysis of intrinsic and extrinsic motivation. In M. R. Lepper & D. Greene (Eds.), *The hidden costs of reward: New perspectives on the psychology of human motivation* (pp. 109–148). Hillsdale, NJ: Erlbaum.

Lepper, M. R., Greene, D., & Nisbett, R. E. (1973). Undermining children's intrinsic interest with extrinsic rewards: A test of the "overjustification" hypothesis. *Journal of Personality and Social Psychology, 28*, 129–137.

Lepper, M. R., & Gurtner, J. (1989). Children and computers: Approaching the twenty-first century. *American Psychologist, 44*, 170–178.

Lepper, M. R., & Hodell, M. (1989). Intrinsic motivation in the classroom. In C. Ames & R. Ames (Eds.), *Research on motivation in education* (Vol. 3, pp. 73–105). San Diego: Academic Press.

Lepper, M. R., & Malone, T. W. (1987). Intrinsic motivation and instructional effectiveness in computer-based education. In R. E. Snow & M. J. Farr (Eds.), *Aptitude, learning, and instruction: Cognitive and affective process analysis* (Vol. 3, pp. 255–286). Hillsdale, NJ: Erlbaum.

Lepper, M. R., Sethi, S., Dialdin, D., & Drake, M. (1997). Intrinsic and extrinsic motivation: A developmental perspective. In S. S. Luthar, J. A. Burack, D. Cicchetti, & J. R. Weisz (Eds.), *Developmental psychopathology: Perspectives on adjustment, risk, and disorder* (pp. 23–50). New York: Cambridge University Press.

Lesgold, A. M. (1984). Acquiring expertise. In J. R. Anderson & S. M. Kosslyn (Eds.), *Tutorials in learning and memory: Essays in honor of Gordon Bower* (pp. 31–60). San Francisco: Freeman.

Lewin, K., Lippitt, R., & White, R. K. (1939). Patterns of aggressive behavior in experimentally created "social climates." *Journal of Social Psychology, 10*, 271–299.

Liben, L. S., & Downs, A. M. (1993). Understanding person-space-map relations: Cartographic and developmental perspectives. *Developmental Psychology, 29*, 739–752.

Licht, B. G., & Kistner, J. A. (1986). Motivational problems of learning-disabled children: Individual differences and their implications for treatment. In J. K. Torgesen & B. W. L. Wong (Eds.), *Psychological and educational perspectives on learning disabilities* (pp. 225–255). Orlando: Academic Press.

Lindsay, P. H., & Norman, D. A. (1977). *Human information processing* (2nd ed.). New York: Academic Press.

Linnenbrink, E. A., & Pintrich, P. R. (2002). Achievement goal theory and affect: An asymmetrical bi-directional model. *Educational Psychologist, 37*, 69–78.

Lirgg, C. D., & Feltz, D. L. (1991). Teacher versus peer models revisited: Effects on motor performance and self-efficacy. *Research Quarterly for Exercise and Sport, 62*, 217–224.

Littleton, K., Light, P., Joiner, R., Messer, D., & Barnes, P. (1998). Gender, task scenarios and children's computer-based problem solving. *Educational Psychology, 18*, 327–338.

Locke, E. A., Frederick, E., Lee, C., & Bobko, P. (1984). Effect of self-efficacy, goals, and task strategies on task performance. *Journal of Applied Psychology, 69*, 241–251.

Locke, E. A., & Latham, G. P. (1990). *A theory of goal setting and task performance*. Englewood Cliffs, NJ: Prentice Hall.

Locke, E. A., Shaw, K. N., Saari, L. M., & Latham, G. P. (1981). Goal setting and task performance: 1969–1980. *Psychological Bulletin, 90*, 125–152.

Lockhart, R. S., Craik, F. I. M., & Jacoby, L. (1976). Depth of processing, recognition and recall. In J. Brown (Ed.), *Recall and recognition* (pp. 75–102). London: Wiley.

Logan, G. D. (2002). An instance theory of attention and memory. *Psychological Review, 109*, 376–400.

Lohman, D. F. (1989). Human intelligence: An introduction to advances in theory and research. *Review of Educational Research, 59*, 333–373.

Lovaas, O. I. (1977). *The autistic child: Language development through behavior modification*. New York: Irvington.

Love, S. Q. (1983). *Prediction of bulimic behaviors: A social learning analysis*. Unpublished doctoral dissertation, Virginia Polytechnic Institute and State University.

Luchins, A. S. (1942). Mechanization in problem solving: The effect of Einstellung. *Psychological Monographs, 54*(6, Whole No. 248).

Luiten, J., Ames, W., & Ackerson, G. (1980). A meta-analysis of the effects of advance organizers on learning and retention. *American Educational Research Journal, 17*, 211–218.

Luria, A. R. (1961). *The role of speech in the regulation of normal and abnormal behavior* (J. Tizard, Trans.). New York: Liveright.

Maag, J. W. (2001). Rewarded by punishment: Reflections on the disuse of positive reinforcement in schools. *Exceptional Children, 67*, 173–186.

Maccoby, E. E., & Jacklin, C. N. (1974). *The psychology of sex differences*. Stanford, CA: Stanford University Press.

MacCorquodale, K. (1970). On Chomsky's review of Skinner's *Verbal Behavior. Journal of the Experimental Analysis of Behavior, 13*, 83–99.

MacDonald, M. C., Just, M. A., & Carpenter, P. A. (1992). Working memory constraints on the processing of syntactic ambiguity. *Cognitive Psychology, 24*, 56–98.

Mace, F. C., Belfiore, P. J., & Hutchinson, J. M. (2001). Operant theory and research on self-regulation. In B. J. Zimmerman & D. H. Schunk (Eds.), *Self-regulated learning and academic achievement: Theoretical perspectives* (2nd ed., pp. 39–65). Mahwah, NJ: Erlbaum.

Mace, F. C., Belfiore, P. J., & Shea, M. C. (1989). Operant theory and research on self-regulation. In B. J. Zimmerman & D. H. Schunk (Eds.), *Self-regulated learning and academic achievement: Theory, research, and practice* (pp. 27–50). New York: Springer-Verlag.

Mace, F. C., & Kratochwill, T. R. (1988). Self-monitoring: Applications and issues. In J. Witt, S. Elliott, & F. Gresham

(Eds.), *Handbook of behavior therapy in education* (pp. 489–502). New York: Pergamon.

Mace, F. C., & West, B. J. (1986). Unresolved theoretical issues in self-management: Implications for research and practice. *Professional School Psychology, 1*, 149–163.

Maddux, J. E. (1993). Social cognitive models of health and exercise behavior: An introduction and review of conceptual issues. *Journal of Applied Sport Psychology, 5*, 116–140.

Maes, S., & Gebhardt, W. (2000). Self-regulation and health behavior: The health behavior goal model. In M. Boekaerts, P. R. Pintrich, & M. Zeidner (Eds.), *Handbook of self-regulation* (pp. 343–368). San Diego: Academic Press.

Mager, R. (1962). *Preparing instructional objectives.* Palo Alto, CA: Fearon.

Maier, S. F., & Seligman, M. E. P. (1976). Learned helplessness: Theory and evidence. *Journal of Experimental Psychology, 105*, 3–46.

Manderlink, G., & Harackiewicz, J. M. (1984). Proximal versus distal goal setting and intrinsic motivation. *Journal of Personality and Social Psychology, 47*, 918–928.

Mandler, J. M. (1978). A code in the node: The use of a story schema in retrieval. *Discourse Processes, 1*, 14–35.

Mandler, J. M., & Johnson, N. S. (1976). Some of the thousand words a picture is worth. *Journal of Experimental Psychology: Human Learning and Memory, 2*, 529–540.

Mandler, J. M., & Ritchey, G. H. (1977). Long-term memory for pictures. *Journal of Experimental Psychology: Human Learning and Memory, 3*, 386–396.

Markus, H., & Nurius, P. (1986). Possible selves. *American Psychologist, 41*, 954–969.

Markus, H., & Wurf, E. (1987). The dynamic self-concept: A social psychological perspective. *Annual Review of Psychology, 38*, 299–337.

Marsh, H. W., & Shavelson, R. (1985). Self-concept: Its multifaceted, hierarchical structure. *Educational Psychologist, 20*, 107–123.

Marshall, H. H., & Weinstein, R. S. (1984). Classroom factors affecting students' self-evaluations: An interactional model. *Review of Educational Research, 54*, 301–325.

Martin, J. (1980). External versus self-reinforcement: A review of methodological and theoretical issues. *Canadian Journal of Behavioural Science, 12*, 111–125.

Maslow, A. H. (1968). *Toward a psychology of being* (2nd ed.). New York: Van Nostrand Reinhold.

Maslow, A. H. (1970). *Motivation and personality* (2nd ed.). New York: Harper & Row.

Masten, A. S., & Coatsworth, J. D. (1998). The development of competence in favorable and unfavorable environments: Lessons from research on successful children. *American Psychologist, 53*, 205–220.

Mautone, P. D., & Mayer, R. E. (2001). Signaling as a cognitive guide in multimedia learning. *Journal of Educational Psychology, 93*, 377–389.

Mayer, R. E. (1979). Can advance organizers influence meaningful learning? *Review of Educational Research, 49*, 371–383.

Mayer, R. E. (1982). Memory for algebra story problems. *Journal of Educational Psychology, 74*, 199–216.

Mayer, R. E. (1984). Aids to text comprehension. *Educational Psychologist, 19*, 30–42.

Mayer, R. E. (1985). Mathematical ability. In R. J. Sternberg (Ed.), *Human abilities: An information-processing approach* (pp. 127–150). New York: Freeman.

Mayer, R. E. (1989). Introduction to the special section: Cognition and instruction in mathematics. *Journal of Educational Psychology, 81*, 452–456.

Mayer, R. E. (1992). *Thinking, problem solving, cognition* (2nd ed.). New York: Freeman.

Mayer, R. E. (1996). Learners as information processors: Legacies and limitations of educational psychology's second metaphor. *Educational Psychologist, 31*, 151–161.

Mayer, R. E. (1997). Multimedia learning: Are we asking the right questions? *Educational Psychologist, 32*, 1–19.

Mayer, R. E. (1999). *The promise of educational psychology: Learning in the content areas.* Upper Saddle River, NJ: Merrill/Prentice Hall.

Mayer, R. E., & Chandler, P. (2001). When learning is just a click away: Does simple user interaction foster deeper understanding of multimedia messages? *Journal of Educational Psychology, 93*, 390–397.

Mayer, R. E., & Moreno, R. (2002). Animation as an aid to multimedia learning. *Educational Psychology Review, 14*, 87–99.

Mayer, R. E., Moreno, R., Boire, M., & Vagge, S. (1999). Maximizing constructivist learning from multimedia communications by minimizing cognitive load. *Journal of Educational Psychology, 91*, 638–643.

McClelland, D. C., Atkinson, J. W., Clark, R. A., & Lowell, E. L. (1953). *The achievement motive.* New York: Appleton-Century-Crofts.

McCloskey, M., & Kaiser, M. (1984). The impetus impulse: A medieval theory of motion lives on in the minds of children. *The Sciences, 24*(6), 40–45.

McCullagh, P. (1993). Modeling: Learning, developmental, and social psychological considerations. In R. N. Singer, M. Murphey, & L. K. Tennant (Eds.), *Handbook of research on sport psychology* (pp. 106–126). New York: Macmillan.

McCutchen, D. (1995). Cognitive processes in children's writing: Developmental and individual differences. *Issues in Education: Contributions from Educational Psychology, 1*, 123–160.

McCutchen, D. (2000). Knowledge, processing, and working memory: Implications for a theory of writing. *Educational Psychologist, 35*, 13–23.

McCutchen, D., & Perfetti, C. A. (1982). Coherence and connectedness in the development of discourse production. *Text, 2*, 113–139.

McDougall, W. (1926). *An introduction to social psychology* (Rev. ed.). Boston: John W. Luce.

McGregor, G., & Vogelsberg, R. T. (1998). *Inclusive schooling practices: Pedagogical and research foundations.* Baltimore: Paul H. Brookes.

McKeachie, W. J. (1990). Learning, thinking, and Thorndike. *Educational Psychologist, 25*, 127–141.

McNeil, J. D. (1987). *Reading comprehension: New directions for classroom practice* (2nd ed.). Glenview, IL: Scott, Foresman.

McNeil, N. M., & Alibali, M. W. (2000). Learning mathematics from procedural instruction: Externally imposed goals influence what is learned. *Journal of Educational Psychology, 92*, 734–744.

Medin, D. L., Lynch, E. B., & Solomon, K. O. (2000). Are there kinds of concepts? *Annual Review of Psychology, 51*, 121–147.

Meece, J. L. (1991). The classroom context and students' motivational goals. In M. L. Maehr & P. R. Pintrich (Eds.), *Advances in motivation and achievement* (Vol. 7, pp. 261–285). Greenwich, CT: JAI Press.

Meece, J. L. (1994). The role of motivation in self-regulated learning. In D. H. Schunk & B. J. Zimmerman (Eds.), *Self-regulation of learning and performance: Issues and educational applications* (pp. 25–44). Hillsdale, NJ: Erlbaum.

Meece, J. L. (2002). *Child and adolescent development for educators* (2nd ed.). New York: McGraw-Hill.

Meece, J. L., Blumenfeld, P. C., & Hoyle, R. H. (1988). Students' goal orientations and cognitive engagement in classroom activities. *Journal of Educational Psychology, 80,* 514–523.

Meece, J. L., & Courtney, D. P. (1992). Gender differences in students' perceptions: Consequences for achievement-related choices. In D. H. Schunk & J. L. Meece (Eds.), *Student perceptions in the classroom* (pp. 209–228). Hillsdale, NJ: Erlbaum.

Meece, J. L., & Miller, S. D. (2001). A longitudinal analysis of elementary school students' achievement goals in literacy activities. *Contemporary Educational Psychology, 26,* 454–480.

Meece, J. L., Parsons, J. E., Kaczala, C. M., Goff, S. B., & Futterman, R. (1982). Sex differences in math achievement: Towards a model of academic choice. *Psychological Bulletin, 91,* 324–348.

Meichenbaum, D. (1977). *Cognitive behavior modification: An integrative approach.* New York: Plenum.

Meichenbaum, D. (1986). Cognitive behavior modification. In F. H. Kanfer & A. P. Goldstein (Eds.), *Helping people change: A textbook of methods* (3rd ed., pp. 346–380). New York: Pergamon.

Meichenbaum, D., & Asarnow, J. (1979). Cognitive-behavior modification and metacognitive development: Implications for the classroom. In P. C. Kendall & S. D. Hollon (Eds.), *Cognitive behavioral interventions: Theory, research, and procedures* (pp. 11–35). New York: Academic Press.

Meichenbaum, D., & Goodman, J. (1971). Training impulsive children to talk to themselves: A means of developing self-control. *Journal of Abnormal Psychology, 77,* 115–126.

Merrill, M. D., Reigeluth, C. M., & Faust, G. W. (1979). The Instructional Quality Profile: A curriculum evaluation and design tool. In H. F. O'Neil, Jr. (Ed.), *Procedures for instructional systems development* (pp. 165–204). New York: Academic Press.

Merrill, M. D., Richards, R. E., Schmidt, R. V., & Wood, N. D. (1977). *The instructional strategy diagnostic profile: Training manual.* San Diego: Courseware, Inc.

Merrill, P. F. (1987). Job and task analysis. In R. M. Gagné (Ed.), *Instructional technology: Foundations* (pp. 141–173). Hillsdale, NJ: Erlbaum.

Messer, S. (1970). Reflection-impulsivity: Stability and school failure. *Journal of Educational Psychology, 61,* 487–490.

Messick, S. (1984). The nature of cognitive styles: Problems and promise in educational practice. *Educational Psychologist, 19,* 59–74.

Messick, S. (1994). The matter of style: Manifestations of personality in cognition, learning, and teaching. *Educational Psychologist, 29,* 121–136.

Meyer, B. J. F. (1984). Text dimensions and cognitive processing. In H. Mandl, N. L. Stein, & T. Trabasso (Eds.), *Learning and comprehension of text* (pp. 3–47). Hillsdale, NJ: Erlbaum.

Meyer, B. J. F., Brandt, D. M., & Bluth, G. J. (1980). Use of the top-level structure in text: Key for reading comprehension of ninth-grade students. *Reading Research Quarterly, 16,* 72–103.

Meyer, D. E., & Schvaneveldt, R. W. (1971). Facilitation in recognizing pairs of words: Evidence of a dependence between retrieval operations. *Journal of Experimental Psychology, 90,* 227–234.

Meyer, D. K., & Turner, J. C. (2002). Discovering emotion in classroom motivation research. *Educational Psychologist, 37,* 107–114.

Middleton, T. (1992). Applications of virtual reality to learning. *Interactive Learning International, 8,* 253–257.

Miliotis, D., Sesma, A., Jr., & Masten, A. S. (1999). Parenting as a protective process for school success in children from homeless families. *Early Education & Development, 10,* 111–133.

Miller, A. (1987). Cognitive styles: An integrated model. *Educational Psychology, 7,* 251–268.

Miller, G. A. (1956). The magical number seven, plus or minus two: Some limits on our capacity for processing information. *Psychological Review, 63,* 81–97.

Miller, G. A. (1988). The challenge of universal literacy. *Science, 241,* 1293–1299.

Miller, G. A., Galanter, E., & Pribham, K. H. (1960). *Plans and the structure of behavior.* New York: Holt, Rinehart & Winston.

Miller, N. E., & Dollard, J. (1941). *Social learning and imitation.* New Haven, CT: Yale University Press.

Miller, P. H. (1994). Individual differences in children's strategic behaviors: Utilization deficiencies. *Learning and Individual Differences, 6,* 285–307.

Moerk, E. L. (1989). The LAD was a lady and the tasks were ill-defined. *Developmental Review, 9,* 21–57.

Mondale, S., & Patton, S. B. (Eds.) (2001). *School: The story of American public education.* Boston: Beacon Press.

Montemayor, R., & Eisen, M. (1977). The development of self-conceptions from childhood to adolescence. *Developmental Psychology, 13,* 314–319.

Monty, R. A., & Perlmuter, L. C. (1987). Choice, control, and motivation in the young and aged. In M. L. Maehr & D. A. Kleiber (Eds.), *Advances in motivation and achievement* (Vol. 5, pp. 99–122). Greenwich, CT: JAI Press.

Moore, M. T. (1990). Problem finding and teacher experience. *Journal of Creative Behavior, 24,* 39–58.

Moray, N., Bates, A., & Barnett, T. (1965). Experiments on the four-eared man. *Journal of the Acoustical Society of America, 38,* 196–201.

Moreno, R., & Mayer, R. E. (2000). Engaging students in active learning: The case for personalized multimedia messages. *Journal of Educational Psychology, 92,* 724–733.

Morris, C. D., Bransford, J. D., & Franks, J. J. (1977). Levels of processing versus transfer-appropriate processing. *Journal of Verbal Learning and Verbal Behavior, 16,* 519–533.

Morse, W. H., & Kelleher, R. T. (1977). Determinants of reinforcement and punishment. In W. K. Honig & J. E. R. Staddon (Eds.), *Handbook of operant behavior* (pp. 174–200). Englewood Cliffs, NJ: Prentice Hall.

Mosatche, H. S., & Bragonier, P. (1981). An observational study of social comparison in preschoolers. *Child Development, 52,* 376–378.

Moscovitch, M., & Craik, F. I. M. (1976). Depth of processing, retrieval cues, and uniqueness of encoding as factors in recall. *Journal of Verbal Learning and Verbal Behavior, 15,* 447–458.

Moshman, D. (1982). Exogenous, endogenous, and dialectical constructivism. *Developmental Review, 2,* 371–384.

Mueller, C. G. (1979). Some origins of psychology as science. *Annual Review of Psychology, 30,* 9–29.

Muller, U., Sokol, B., & Overton, W. F. (1998). Reframing a constructivist model of the development of mental representation: The role of higher-order operations. *Developmental Review, 18,* 155–201.

Murray, D. J., Kilgour, A. R., & Wasylkiw, L. (2000). Conflicts and missed signals in psychoanalysis, behaviorism, and Gestalt psychology. *American Psychologist, 55,* 422–426.

Murray, H. A. (1936). Techniques for a systematic investigation of fantasy. *Journal of Psychology, 3,* 115–143.

Murray, H. A. (1938). *Explorations in personality.* New York: Oxford University Press.

Muth, K. D., Glynn, S. M., Britton, B. K., & Graves, M. F. (1988). Thinking out loud while studying text: Rehearsing key ideas. *Journal of Educational Psychology, 80,* 315–318.

Myers, M., II, & Paris, S. G. (1978). Children's metacognitive knowledge about reading. *Journal of Educational Psychology, 70,* 680–690.

National Council of Teachers of Mathematics. (1991). *Professional standards for teaching mathematics.* Reston, VA: Author.

Neisser, U. (1967). *Cognitive psychology.* Englewood Cliffs, NJ: Prentice Hall.

Nelson, R. O., & Hayes, S. C. (1981). Theoretical explanations for reactivity in self-monitoring. *Behavior Modification, 5,* 3–14.

Nelson, T. O. (1977). Repetition and depth of processing. *Journal of Verbal Learning and Verbal Behavior, 16,* 151–171.

Newell, A., & Simon, H. A. (1972). *Human problem solving.* Englewood Cliffs, NJ: Prentice Hall.

Newman, R. S. (1994). Adaptive help seeking: A strategy of self-regulated learning. In D. H. Schunk & B. J. Zimmerman (Eds.), *Self-regulation of learning and performance: Issues and educational applications* (pp. 283–301). Hillsdale, NJ: Erlbaum.

Newman, R. S. (2002). What do I need to do to succeed . . . when I don't understand what I'm doing!?: Developmental influences on students' adaptive help seeking. In A. Wigfield & J. S. Eccles (Eds.), *Development of achievement motivation* (pp. 285–306). San Diego: Academic Press.

Newman, R. S., & Schwager, M. T. (1992). Student perceptions and academic help-seeking. In D. H. Schunk & J. L. Meece (Eds.), *Student perceptions in the classroom* (pp. 123–146). Hillsdale, NJ: Erlbaum.

Nicholls, J. G. (1978). The development of the concepts of effort and ability, perception of academic attainment, and the understanding that difficult tasks require more ability. *Child Development, 49,* 800–814.

Nicholls, J. G. (1979). Development of perception of own attainment and causal attribution for success and failure in reading. *Journal of Educational Psychology, 71,* 94–99.

Nicholls, J. G. (1983). Conceptions of ability and achievement motivation: A theory and its implications for education. In S. G. Paris, G. M. Olson, & H. W. Stevenson (Eds.), *Learning and motivation in the classroom* (pp. 211–237). Hillsdale, NJ: Erlbaum.

Nicholls, J. G. (1984). Achievement motivation: Conceptions of ability, subjective experience, task choice, and performance. *Psychological Review, 91,* 328–346.

Nicholls, J. G., Cobb, P., Wood, T., Yackel, E., & Patashnick, M. (1990). Assessing students' theories of success in mathematics: Individual and classroom differences. *Journal for Research in Mathematics Education, 21,* 109–122.

Nicholls, J. G., & Miller, A. T. (1984). Reasoning about the ability of self and others: A developmental study. *Child Development, 55,* 1990–1999.

Nicholls, J. G., Patashnick, M., & Nolen, S. B. (1985). Adolescents' theories of education. *Journal of Educational Psychology, 77,* 683–692.

Nicholls, J. G., & Thorkildsen, T. A. (1989). Intellectual conventions versus matters of substance: Elementary school students as curriculum theorists. *American Educational Research Journal, 26,* 533–544.

Nolen, S. B. (1988). Reasons for studying: Motivational orientations and study strategies. *Cognition and Instruction, 5,* 269–287.

Nolen, S. B. (1996). Why study? How reasons for learning influence strategy selection. *Educational Psychology Review, 8,* 335–355.

Nolen-Hoeksema, S., Girgus, J. S., & Seligman, M. E. P. (1986). Learned helplessness in children: A longitudinal study of depression, achievement, and explanatory style. *Journal of Personality and Social Psychology, 51,* 435–442.

Norman, D. A. (1976). *Memory and attention: An introduction to human information processing* (2nd ed.). New York: Wiley.

Norman, D. A., & Rumelhart, D. E. (1975). *Explorations in cognition.* San Francisco: Freeman.

Nussbaum, J., & Novick, N. (1982). Alternative frameworks, conceptual conflict, and accommodation: Toward a principled teaching strategy. *Instructional Science, 11,* 183–200.

O'Day, E. F., Kulhavy, R. W., Anderson, W., & Malczynski, R. J. (1971). *Programmed instruction: Techniques and trends.* New York: Appleton-Century-Crofts.

O'Donnell, A. M., Dansereau, D. F., & Hall, R. H. (2002). Knowledge maps as scaffolds for cognitive processing. *Educational Psychology Review, 14,* 71–86.

Ohlsson, S. (1993). The interaction between knowledge and practice in the acquisition of cognitive skills. In S. Chipman & A. L. Meyrowitz (Eds.), *Foundations of knowledge acquisition: Cognitive models of complex learning* (pp. 147–208). Boston: Kluwer.

Ohlsson, S. (1996). Learning from performance errors. *Psychological Review, 103,* 241–262.

O'Leary, K. D., & Drabman, R. (1971). Token reinforcement programs in the classroom: A review. *Psychological Bulletin, 75,* 379–398.

O'Leary, S. G., & Dubey, D. R. (1979). Applications of self-control procedures by children: A review. *Journal of Applied Behavior Analysis, 12,* 449–466.

Ollendick, T. H., & Hersen, M. (1984). *Child behavioral assessment: Principles and procedures.* New York: Pergamon.

Oppenheimer, T. (1997, July). The computer delusion. *The Atlantic Monthly, 285,* 45–48, 50–56, 61–62.

Osborn, A. F. (1963). *Applied imagination.* New York: Scribner's.

Oser, F. K., & Baeriswyl, F. J. (2001). Choreographies of teaching: Bridging instruction to learning. In V. Richardson (Ed.), *Handbook of research on teaching* (4th ed., pp. 1031–1065). Washington, DC: American Educational Research Association.

Paivio, A. (1970). On the functional significance of imagery. *Psychological Bulletin, 73,* 385–392.

Paivio, A. (1971). *Imagery and verbal processes.* New York: Holt, Rinehart & Winston.

Paivio, A. (1978). Mental comparisons involving abstract attributes. *Memory & Cognition, 6,* 199–208.

Paivio, A. (1986). *Mental representations: A dual-coding approach.* New York: Oxford University Press.

Pajares, F. (1996). Self-efficacy beliefs in achievement settings. *Review of Educational Research, 66,* 543–578.

Pajares, F. (1997). Current directions in self-efficacy research. In M. Maehr & P. R. Pintrich (Eds.), *Advances in motivation and achievement* (Vol. 10, pp. 1–49). Greenwich, CT: JAI Press.

Pajares, F., & Miller, M. D. (1994). The role of self-efficacy and self-concept beliefs in mathematical problem-solving: A path analysis. *Journal of Educational Psychology, 86,* 193–203.

Pajares, F., & Miller, M. D. (1995). Mathematics self-efficacy and mathematics performances: The need for specificity of assessment. *Journal of Counseling Psychology, 42,* 190–198.

Pajares, F., & Schunk, D. H. (2001). Self-beliefs and school success: Self-efficacy, self-concept, and school achievement. In R. J. Riding & S. G. Rayner (Eds.), *Self-perception* (pp. 239–265). Westport, CT: Ablex.

Pajares, F., & Schunk, D. H. (2002). Self and self-belief in psychology and education: A historical perspective. In J. Aronson (Ed.), *Improving academic achievement: Impact of psychological factors on education* (pp. 3–21). San Diego, CA: Academic Press.

Palincsar, A. S., & Brown, A. L. (1984). Reciprocal teaching of comprehension-fostering and comprehension-monitoring activities. *Cognition and Instruction, 1,* 117–175.

Palmer, D. J., Drummond, F., Tollison, P., & Zinkgraff, S. (1982). An attributional investigation of performance outcomes for learning-disabled and normal-achieving pupils. *Journal of Special Education, 16,* 207–219.

Palumbo, D. B. (1990). Programming language/problem-solving research: A review of relevant issues. *Review of Educational Research, 60,* 65–89.

Papert, S. (1980). *Mindstorms: Children, computers, and powerful ideas.* New York: Basic Books.

Papini, M. R., & Bitterman, M. E. (1990). The role of contingency in classical conditioning. *Psychological Review, 97,* 396–403.

Paris, S. G., & Byrnes, J. P. (1989). The constructivist approach to self-regulation and learning in the classroom. In B. J. Zimmerman & D. H. Schunk (Eds.), *Self-regulated learning and academic achievement: Theory, research, and practice,* (pp. 169–200). New York: Springer-Verlag.

Paris, S. G., Byrnes, J. P., & Paris, A. H. (2001). Constructing theories, identities, and actions of self-regulated learners. In B. J. Zimmerman & D. H. Schunk (Eds.), *Self-regulated learning and academic achievement: Theoretical perspectives* (2nd ed., pp. 253–287). Mahwah, NJ: Erlbaum.

Paris, S. G., Cross, D. R., & Lipson, M. Y. (1984). Informed strategies for learning: A program to improve children's reading awareness and comprehension. *Journal of Educational Psychology, 76,* 1239–1252.

Paris, S. G., Lipson, M. Y., & Wixson, K. K. (1983). Becoming a strategic reader. *Contemporary Educational Psychology, 8,* 293–316.

Paris, S. G., & Oka, E. R. (1986). Children's reading strategies, metacognition, and motivation. *Developmental Review, 6,* 25–56.

Paris, S. G., Wixson, K. K., & Palincsar, A. S. (1986). Instructional approaches to reading comprehension. In E. Z. Rothkopf (Ed.), *Review of research in education* (Vol. 13, pp. 91–128). Washington, DC: American Educational Research Association.

Park, O., Perez, R. S., & Seidel, R. J. (1987). Intelligent CAI: Old wine in new bottles, or a new vintage? In G. Kearsley (Ed.), *Artificial intelligence and instruction: Applications and methods* (pp. 11–45). Reading, MA: Addison-Wesley.

Pavlov, I. P. (1927). *Conditioned reflexes* (G. V. Anrep, Trans.). London: Oxford University Press.

Pavlov, I. P. (1928). *Lectures on conditioned reflexes* (W. H. Gantt, Trans.). New York: International Publishers.

Pavlov, I. P. (1932a). Neuroses in man and animals. *Journal of the American Medical Association, 99,* 1012–1013.

Pavlov, I. P. (1932b). The reply of a physiologist to psychologists. *Psychological Review, 39,* 91–127.

Pavlov, I. P. (1934). An attempt at a physiological interpretation of obsessional neurosis and paranoia. *Journal of Mental Science, 80,* 187–197.

Pearl, R. A., Bryan, T., & Donahue, M. (1980). Learning disabled children's attributions for success and failure. *Learning Disability Quarterly, 3,* 3–9.

Pellegrino, J. W. (1985). Inductive reasoning ability. In R. J. Sternberg (Ed.), *Human abilities: An information-processing approach* (pp. 195–225). New York: Freeman.

Perfetti, C. A. (1985). Reading ability. In R. J. Sternberg (Ed.), *Human abilities: An information-processing approach* (pp. 59–81). New York: Freeman.

Perfetti, C. A., & Lesgold, A. M. (1979). Coding and comprehension in skilled reading and implications for reading instruction. In L. B. Resnick & P. A. Weaver (Eds.), *Theory and practice of early reading* (pp. 57–84). Hillsdale, NJ: Erlbaum.

Perfetti, C. A., & Roth, S. (1981). Some of the interactive processes in reading and their role in reading skill. In A. M. Lesgold & C. A. Perfetti (Eds.), *Interactive processes in reading* (pp. 269–297). Hillsdale, NJ: Erlbaum.

Perkins, D. N., & Salomon, G. (1989). Are cognitive skills context-bound? *Educational Researcher, 18*(1), 16–25.

Perry, D. G., & Bussey, K. (1979). The social learning theory of sex differences: Imitation is alive and well. *Journal of Personality and Social Psychology, 37,* 1699–1712.

Perry, N. E. (1998). Young children's self-regulated learning and contexts that support it. *Journal of Educational Psychology, 90,* 715–729.

Peterson, L. R., & Peterson, M. J. (1959). Short-term retention of individual verbal items. *Journal of Experimental Psychology, 58,* 193–198.

Petri, H. L. (1986). *Motivation: Theory and research* (2nd ed.). Belmont, CA: Wadsworth.

Phares, E. J. (1976). *Locus of control in personality.* Morristown, NJ: General Learning Press.

Phillips, D. C. (1995). The good, the bad, and the ugly: The many faces of constructivism. *Educational Researcher, 24*(7), 5–12.

Phillips, J. L., Jr. (1969). *The origins of intellect: Piaget's theory.* San Francisco: Freeman.

Phye, G. D. (1989). Schemata training and transfer of an intellectual skill. *Journal of Educational Psychology, 81,* 347–352.

Phye, G. D. (1990). Inductive problem solving: Schema inducement and memory-based transfer. *Journal of Educational Psychology, 82,* 826–831.

Phye, G. D. (1992). Strategic transfer: A tool for academic problem solving. *Educational Psychology Review, 4,* 393–421.

Phye, G. D. (1997). Inductive reasoning and problem solving: The early grades. In G. D. Phye (Ed.), *Handbook of academic learning: The construction of knowledge* (pp. 451–471). San Diego: Academic Press.

Phye, G. D. (2001). Problem-solving instruction and problem-solving transfer: The correspondence issue. *Journal of Educational Psychology, 93,* 571–578.

Phye, G. D., & Sanders, C. E. (1992). Accessing strategic knowledge: Individual differences in procedural and strategy transfer. *Contemporary Educational Psychology, 17,* 211–223.

Phye, G. D., & Sanders, C. E. (1994). Advice and feedback: Elements of practice for problem solving. *Contemporary Educational Psychology, 19,* 286–301.

Piaget, J. (1952). *The origins of intelligence in children.* New York: International Universities Press.

Piaget, J. (1962). *Play, dreams and imitation.* New York: Norton.

Piaget, J. (1970). Piaget's theory. In P. Mussen (Ed.), *Carmichael's manual of child psychology* (3rd ed., Vol. 1, pp. 703–732). New York: Wiley.

Piaget, J., & Inhelder, B. (1969). *The psychology of the child.* New York: Basic Books.

Pintrich, P. R. (2000a). Multiple goals, multiple pathways: The role of goal orientation in learning and achievement. *Journal of Educational Psychology, 92,* 544–555.

Pintrich, P. R. (2000b). The role of goal orientation in self-regulated learning. In M. Boekaerts, P. R. Pintrich, & M. Zeidner (Eds.), *Handbook of self-regulation* (pp. 451–502). San Diego: Academic Press.

Pintrich, P. R., Cross, D. R., Kozma, R. B., & McKeachie, W. J. (1986). Instructional psychology. *Annual Review of Psychology, 37,* 611–651.

Pintrich, P. R., & De Groot, E. V. (1990). Motivational and self-regulated learning components of classroom academic performance. *Journal of Educational Psychology, 82,* 33–40.

Pintrich, P. R., & Garcia, T. (1991). Student goal orientation and self-regulation in the college classroom. In M. L. Maehr & P. R. Pintrich (Eds.), *Advances in motivation and achievement* (Vol. 7, pp. 371–402). Greenwich, CT: JAI Press.

Pintrich, P. R., Marx, R. W., & Boyle, R. A. (1993). Beyond cold conceptual change: The role of motivational beliefs and classroom contextual factors in the process of conceptual change. *Review of Educational Research, 63,* 167–199.

Pintrich, P. R., & Schrauben, B. (1992). Students' motivational beliefs and their cognitive engagement in classroom academic tasks. In D. H. Schunk & J. L. Meece (Eds.), *Student perceptions in the classroom* (pp. 149–183). Hillsdale, NJ: Erlbaum.

Pintrich, P. R., & Schunk, D. H. (2002). *Motivation in education: Theory, research, and applications* (2nd ed.). Upper Saddle River, NJ: Merrill/Prentice Hall.

Pintrich, P. R., & Zusho, A. (2002). The development of academic self-regulation: The role of cognitive and motivational factors. In A. Wigfield & J. S. Eccles (Eds.), *Development of achievement motivation* (pp. 249–284). San Diego: Academic Press.

Plato. (1965). *Plato's Meno: Text and Criticism* (A. Sesonske & N. Fleming, eds.). Belmont, CA: Wadsworth.

Plomin, R. (1990). *Nature and nurture.* Pacific Grove, CA: Brooks/Cole.

Poag-DuCharme, K. A., & Brawley, L. R. (1993). Self-efficacy theory: Use in the prediction of exercise behavior in the community setting. *Journal of Applied Sport Psychology, 5,* 178–194.

Pokay, P., & Blumenfeld, P. C. (1990). Predicting achievement early and late in the semester: The role of motivation and use of learning strategies. *Journal of Educational Psychology, 82,* 41–50.

Polk, T. A., & Newell, A. (1995). Deduction as verbal reasoning. *Psychological Review, 102,* 533–566.

Polya, G. (1945). *How to solve it.* Princeton, NJ: Princeton University Press. (Reprinted 1957, Doubleday, Garden City, NY)

Posner, M. I., & Keele, S. W. (1968). On the genesis of abstract ideas. *Journal of Experimental Psychology, 77,* 353–363.

Postman, L. (1961). The present status of interference theory. In C. N. Cofer (Ed.), *Verbal learning and verbal behavior* (pp. 152–179). New York: McGraw-Hill.

Postman, L., & Stark, K. (1969). Role of response availability in transfer and interference. *Journal of Experimental Psychology, 79,* 168–177.

Premack, D. (1962). Reversibility of the reinforcement relation. *Science, 136,* 255–257.

Premack, D. (1971). Catching up with common sense or two sides of a generalization: Reinforcement and punishment.

In R. Glaser (Ed.), *The nature of reinforcement* (pp. 121–150). New York: Academic Press.

Pressley, M., Harris, K. R., & Marks, M. B. (1992). But good strategy instructors are constructivists! *Educational Psychology Review, 4,* 3–31.

Pressley, M., Levin, J. R., & Delaney, H. D. (1982). The mnemonic keyword method. *Review of Educational Research, 52,* 61–91.

Pressley, M., & McCormick, C. B. (1995). *Advanced educational psychology for educators, researchers, and policymakers.* New York: HarperCollins.

Pressley, M., Woloshyn, V., Lysynchuk, L. M., Martin, V., Wood, E., & Willoughby, T. (1990). A primer of research on cognitive strategy instruction: The important issues and how to address them. *Educational Psychology Review, 2,* 1–58.

Purdie, N., Hattie, J., & Douglas, G. (1996). Student conceptions of learning and their use of self-regulated learning strategies: A cross-cultural comparison. *Journal of Educational Psychology, 88,* 87–100.

Putnam, R. D. (2000). *Bowling alone: The collapse and revival of American community.* New York: Simon & Schuster.

Pylyshyn, Z. W. (1973). What the mind's eye tells the mind's brain: A critique of mental imagery. *Psychological Bulletin, 80,* 1–24.

Quellmalz, E. S. (1987). Developing reasoning skills. In J. B. Baron & R. J. Sternberg (Eds.), *Teaching thinking skills: Theory and practice* (pp. 86–105). New York: Freeman.

Quillian, M. R. (1969). The teachable language comprehender: A simulation program and theory of language. *Communications of the Association for Computing Machinery, 12,* 459–476.

Rachlin, H. (1974). Self-control. *Behaviorism, 2,* 94–107.

Rachlin, H. (1991). *Introduction to modern behaviorism* (3rd ed.). New York: Freeman.

Radziszewska, B., & Rogoff, B. (1991). Children's guided participation in planning imaginary errands with skilled adult or peer partners. *Developmental Psychology, 27,* 381–389.

Ramsel, D., & Grabe, M. (1983). Attentional allocation and performance in goal-directed reading: Age differences in reading flexibility. *Journal of Reading Behavior, 15,* 55–65.

Ray, J. J. (1982). Achievement motivation and preferred probability of success. *Journal of Social Psychology, 116,* 255–261.

Reder, L. M. (1979). The role of elaborations in memory for prose. *Cognitive Psychology, 11,* 221–234.

Reder, L. M. (1982). Plausibility judgment versus fact retrieval: Alternative strategies for sentence verification. *Psychological Review, 89,* 250–280.

Reigeluth, C. M. (1979). In search of a better way to organize instruction: The elaboration theory. *Journal of Instructional Development, 2*(3), 8–15.

Reigeluth, C. M., & Curtis, R. V. (1987). Learning situations and instructional models. In R. M. Gagné (Ed.), *Instructional technology: Foundations* (pp. 175–206). Hillsdale, NJ: Erlbaum.

Reigeluth, C. M., Merrill, M. D., & Bunderson, C. V. (1978). The structure of subject-matter content and its instructional design implications. *Instructional Science, 7,* 107–126.

Relich, J. D., Debus, R. L., & Walker, R. (1986). The mediating role of attribution and self-efficacy variables for treatment effects on achievement outcomes. *Contemporary Educational Psychology, 11,* 195–216.

Rescorla, R. A. (1972). Informational variables in conditioning. In G. H. Bower (Ed.), *The psychology of learning and motivation* (Vol. 6, pp. 1–46). New York: Academic Press.

Rescorla, R. A. (1976). Pavlovian excitatory and inhibitory conditioning. In W. K. Estes (Ed.), *Handbook of learning and cognitive processes* (Vol. 2, pp. 7–35). Hillsdale, NJ: Erlbaum.

Rescorla, R. A. (1987). A Pavlovian analysis of goal-directed behavior. *American Psychologist, 42*, 119–129.

Resnick, L. B. (1981). Instructional psychology. *Annual Review of Psychology, 32*, 659–704.

Resnick, L. B. (1985). Cognition and instruction: Recent theories of human competence. In B. L. Hammonds (Ed.), *Psychology and learning: The master lecture series* (Vol. 4, pp. 127–186). Washington, DC: American Psychological Association.

Resnick, L. B. (1989). Developing mathematical knowledge. *American Psychologist, 44*, 162–169.

Reynolds, R., & Anderson, R. (1982). Influence of questions on the allocation of attention during reading. *Journal of Educational Psychology, 74*, 623–632.

Riccio, D. C., Rabinowitz, V. C., & Axelrod, S. (1994). Memory: When less is more. *American Psychologist, 49*, 917–926.

Richardson, V. (Ed.) (2001). *Handbook of research on teaching* (4th ed.). Washington, DC: American Educational Research Association.

Richter, C. P. (1927). Animal behavior and internal drives. *Quarterly Review of Biology, 2*, 307–343.

Rilling, M. (1977). Stimulus control and inhibitory processes. In W. K. Honig & J. E. R. Staddon (Eds.), *Handbook of operant behavior* (pp. 432–480). Englewood Cliffs, NJ: Prentice Hall.

Rips, L. J., Shoben, E. J., & Smith, E. E. (1973). Semantic distance and the verification of semantic relations. *Journal of Verbal Learning and Verbal Behavior, 12*, 1–20.

Rittle-Johnson, B., & Alibali, M. W. (1999). Conceptual and procedural knowledge of mathematics: Does one lead to the other? *Journal of Educational Psychology, 91*, 175–189.

Robin, A. L. (1976). Behavioral instruction in the college classroom. *Review of Educational Research, 46*, 313–354.

Robinson, F. P. (1946). *Effective study.* New York: Harper.

Robinson, T. R., Smith, S. W., Miller, M. D., & Brownell, M. T. (1999). Cognitive behavior modification of hyperactivity-impulsivity and aggression: A meta-analysis of school-based studies. *Journal of Educational Psychology, 91*, 195–203.

Rogers, C. R. (1959). A theory of therapy, personality, and interpersonal relationships, as developed in the client-centered framework. In S. Koch (Ed.), *Psychology: A study of a science* (Vol. 3, pp. 184–256). New York: McGraw-Hill.

Rogers, C. R. (1963). The actualizing tendency in relation to "motives" and to consciousness. In M. R. Jones (Ed.), *Nebraska symposium on motivation* (Vol. 11, pp. 1–24). Lincoln, NE: University of Nebraska Press.

Rogers, C. R. (1969). *Freedom to learn.* Columbus, OH: Merrill.

Rogoff, B. (1986). Adult assistance of children's learning. In T. E. Raphael (Ed.), *The contexts of school-based literacy* (pp. 27–40). New York: Random House.

Rogoff, B. (1990). *Apprenticeship in thinking: Cognitive development in the social context.* New York: Oxford University Press.

Rohman, D. G. (1965). Pre-writing: The stages of discovery in the writing process. *College Composition and Communication, 16*, 106–112.

Rohrkemper, M. M. (1989). Self-regulated learning and academic achievement: A Vygotskian view. In B. J. Zimmerman & D. H. Schunk (Eds.), *Self-regulated learning and academic achievement: Theory, research, and practice* (pp. 143–167). New York: Springer-Verlag.

Romberg, T. A., & Carpenter, T. P. (1986). Research on teaching and learning mathematics: Two disciplines of scientific

inquiry. In M. C. Wittrock (Ed.), *Handbook of research on teaching* (3rd ed., pp. 850–873). New York: Macmillan.

Root-Bernstein, R. S. (1988). Setting the stage for discovery. *The Sciences, 28*(3), 26–34.

Rosch, E. (1973). Natural categories. *Cognitive Psychology, 4*, 328–350.

Rosch, E. (1975). Cognitive representations of semantic categories. *Journal of Experimental Psychology: General, 104*, 192–233.

Rosch, E. (1978). Principles of categorization. In E. Rosch & B. Lloyd (Eds.), *Cognition and categorization* (pp. 9–31). Hillsdale, NJ: Erlbaum.

Rose, M. (1980). Rigid rules, inflexible plans, and the stifling of language: A cognitivist analysis of writer's block. *College Composition and Communication, 31*, 389–401.

Rosen, B., & D'Andrade, R. C. (1959). The psychosocial origins of achievement motivation. *Sociometry, 22*, 185–218.

Rosenberg, M., & Kaplan, H. B. (1982). *Social psychology of the self-concept.* Arlington Heights, IL: Harlan Davidson.

Rosenholtz, S. J., & Rosenholtz, S. H. (1981). Classroom organization and the perception of ability. *Sociology of Education, 54*, 132–140.

Rosenholtz, S. J., & Simpson, C. (1984). The formation of ability conceptions: Developmental trend or social construction? *Review of Educational Research, 54*, 31–63.

Rosenshine, B., & Stevens, R. (1986). Teaching functions. In M. C. Wittrock (Ed.), *Handbook of research on teaching* (3rd ed., pp. 376–391). New York: Macmillan.

Rosenstock, I. M. (1974). The health belief model and preventive health behavior. *Health Education Monographs, 2*, 354–386.

Rosenthal, R. (1974). *On the social psychology of the self-fulfilling prophecy: Further evidence for Pygmalion effects and their mediating mechanisms.* New York: MSS Modular Publications.

Rosenthal, R., & Jacobson, L. (1968). *Pygmalion in the classroom.* New York: Holt, Rinehart & Winston.

Rosenthal, T. L., & Bandura, A. (1978). Psychological modeling: Theory and practice. In S. L. Garfield & A. E. Bergin (Eds.), *Handbook of psychotherapy and behavior change: An empirical analysis* (2nd ed., pp. 621–658). New York: Wiley.

Rosenthal, T. L., Moore, W. B., Dorfman, H., & Nelson, B. (1971). Vicarious acquisition of a simple concept with experimenter as model. *Behavior Research and Therapy, 9*, 217–227.

Rosenthal, T. L., & Zimmerman, B. J. (1978). *Social learning and cognition.* New York: Academic Press.

Ross, S. M., McCormick, D., Krisak, N., & Anand, P. (1985). Personalizing context in teaching mathematical concepts: Teacher-managed and computer-assisted models. *Educational Communication and Technology Journal, 33*, 169–178.

Rotter, J. B. (1966). Generalized expectancies for internal versus external control of reinforcement. *Psychological Monographs, 80*(1, Whole No. 609).

Royer, J. M. (1986). Designing instruction to produce understanding: An approach based on cognitive theory. In G. D. Phye & T. Andre (Eds.), *Cognitive classroom learning: Understanding, thinking, and problem solving* (pp. 83–113). Orlando: Academic Press.

Royer, J. M., Tronsky, L. N., Chan, Y., Jackson, S. J., & Marchant, H., III. (1999). Math-fact retrieval as the cognitive mechanism underlying gender differences in math test performance. *Contemporary Educational Psychology, 24*, 181–266.

Ruble, D. N. (1983). The development of social-comparison processes and their role in achievement-related self-socialization. In E. T. Higgins, D. N. Ruble, & W. Hartup (Eds.), *Social cognition and social development* (pp. 134–157). New York: Cambridge University Press.

Ruble, D. N., Boggiano, A. K., Feldman, N. S., & Loebl, J. H. (1980). Developmental analysis of the role of social comparison in self-evaluation. *Developmental Psychology, 16*, 105–115.

Ruble, D. N., Feldman, N. S., & Boggiano, A. K. (1976). Social comparison between young children in achievement situations. *Developmental Psychology, 12*, 191–197.

Rumelhart, D. E. (1975). Notes on a schema for stories. In D. G. Bobrow & A. M. Collins (Eds.), *Representation and understanding: Studies in cognitive science* (pp. 211–236). New York: Academic Press.

Rumelhart, D. E. (1977). Understanding and summarizing brief stories. In D. Laberge & S. J. Samuels (Eds.), *Basic processes in reading* (pp. 265–303). Hillsdale, NJ: Erlbaum.

Rumelhart, D. E., & McClelland, J. L. (1986). *Parallel distributed processing: Explorations in the microstructure of cognition.* Cambridge, MA: MIT Press.

Rumelhart, D. E., & Norman, D. A. (1978). Accretion, tuning, and restructuring: Three modes of learning. In J. W. Cotton & R. L. Klatzky (Eds.), *Semantic factors in cognition* (pp. 37–53). Hillsdale, NJ: Erlbaum.

Rumelhart, D. E., & Ortony, A. (1977). The representation of knowledge in memory. In R. C. Anderson, R. J. Spiro, & W. E. Montague (Eds.), *Schooling and the acquisition of knowledge* (pp. 99–135). Hillsdale, NJ: Erlbaum.

Rundus, D. (1971). Analysis of rehearsal processes in free recall. *Journal of Experimental Psychology, 89*, 63–77.

Rundus, D., & Atkinson, R. C. (1970). Rehearsal processes in free recall: A procedure for direct observation. *Journal of Verbal Learning and Verbal Behavior, 9*, 99–105.

Ryan, A. M., Gheen, M. H., & Midgley, C. (1998). Why do some students avoid asking for help? An examination of the interplay among students' academic efficacy, teachers' social-emotional role, and the classroom goal structure. *Journal of Educational Psychology, 90*, 528–535.

Ryan, B. A. (1974). *Keller's Personalized System of Instruction: An appraisal.* Washington, DC: American Psychological Association.

Ryan, R. M., Connell, J. P., & Deci, E. L. (1985). A motivational analysis of self-determination and self-regulation in education. In C. Ames & R. Ames (Eds.), *Research on motivation in education* (Vol. 2, pp. 13–51). Orlando: Academic Press.

Sagotsky, G., Patterson, C. J., & Lepper, M. R. (1978). Training children's self-control: A field experiment in self-monitoring and goal-setting in the classroom. *Journal of Experimental Child Psychology, 25*, 242–253.

Sakitt, B. (1976). Iconic memory. *Psychological Review, 83*, 257–276.

Sakitt, B., & Long, G. M. (1979). Spare the rod and spoil the icon. *Journal of Experimental Psychology: Human Perception and Performance, 5*, 19–30.

Salatas, H., & Flavell, J. H. (1976). Retrieval of recently learned information: Development of strategies and control skills. *Child Development, 47*, 941–948.

Salomon, G., & Perkins, D. N. (1989). Rocky roads to transfer: Rethinking mechanisms of a neglected phenomenon. *Educational Psychologist, 24*, 113–142.

Sandoval, J. (1995). Teaching in subject matter areas: Science. *Annual Review of Psychology, 46*, 355–374.

Scardamalia, M., & Bereiter, C. (1982). Assimilative processes in composition planning. *Educational Psychologist, 17*, 165–171.

Scardamalia, M., & Bereiter, C. (1983). The development of evaluative, diagnostic, and remedial capabilities in children's composing. In M. Martlew (Ed.), *The psychology of written language: A developmental approach* (pp. 67–95). London: Wiley.

Scardamalia, M., & Bereiter, C. (1986). Research on written composition. In M. C. Wittrock (Ed.), *Handbook of research on teaching* (3rd ed., pp. 778–803). New York: Macmillan.

Schaffer, L. C., & Hannafin, M. J. (1986). The effects of progressive interactivity on learning from interactive video. *Educational Communication and Technology Journal, 34*, 89–96.

Schiefele, U. (1996). Topic interest, text representation, and quality of experience. *Contemporary Educational Psychology, 21*, 3–18.

Schmidt, R. A. (1975). A schema theory of discrete motor skill learning. *Psychological Review, 82*, 225–260.

Schraw, G., & Moshman, D. (1995). Metacognitive theories. *Educational Psychology Review, 7*, 351–371.

Schunk, D. H. (1981). Modeling and attributional effects on children's achievement: A self-efficacy analysis. *Journal of Educational Psychology, 73*, 93–105.

Schunk, D. H. (1982a). Effects of effort attributional feedback on children's perceived self-efficacy and achievement. *Journal of Educational Psychology, 74*, 548–556.

Schunk, D. H. (1982b). Verbal self-regulation as a facilitator of children's achievement and self-efficacy. *Human Learning, 1*, 265–277.

Schunk, D. H. (1983a). Ability versus effort attributional feedback: Differential effects on self-efficacy and achievement. *Journal of Educational Psychology, 75*, 848–856.

Schunk, D. H. (1983b). Developing children's self-efficacy and skills: The roles of social comparative information and goal setting. *Contemporary Educational Psychology, 8*, 76–86.

Schunk, D. H. (1983c). Goal difficulty and attainment information: Effects on children's achievement behaviors. *Human Learning, 2*, 107–117.

Schunk, D. H. (1983d). Progress self-monitoring: Effects on children's self-efficacy and achievement. *Journal of Experimental Education, 51*, 89–93.

Schunk, D. H. (1983e). Reward contingencies and the development of children's skills and self-efficacy. *Journal of Educational Psychology, 75*, 511–518.

Schunk, D. H. (1984a). Enhancing self-efficacy and achievement through rewards and goals: Motivational and informational effects. *Journal of Educational Research, 78*, 29–34.

Schunk, D. H. (1984b). Sequential attributional feedback and children's achievement behaviors. *Journal of Educational Psychology, 76*, 1159–1169.

Schunk, D. H. (1985). Participation in goal setting: Effects on self-efficacy and skills of learning disabled children. *Journal of Special Education, 19*, 307–317.

Schunk, D. H. (1986). Verbalization and children's self-regulated learning. *Contemporary Educational Psychology, 11*, 347–369.

Schunk, D. H. (1987). Peer models and children's behavioral change. *Review of Educational Research, 57*, 149–174.

Schunk, D. H. (1989). Self-efficacy and cognitive skill learning. In C. Ames & R. Ames (Eds.), *Research on motivation in education. Vol. 3: Goals and cognitions* (pp. 13–44). San Diego: Academic Press.

Schunk, D. H. (1990). Goal setting and self-efficacy during self-regulated learning. *Educational Psychologist, 25*, 71–86.

Schunk, D. H. (1991). Self-efficacy and academic motivation. *Educational Psychologist, 26,* 207–231.

Schunk, D. H. (1994). Self-regulation of self-efficacy and attributions in academic settings. In D. H. Schunk & B. J. Zimmerman (Eds.), *Self-regulation of learning and performance: Issues and educational applications* (pp. 75–99). Hillsdale, NJ: Erlbaum.

Schunk, D. H. (1995). Self-efficacy and education and instruction. In J. E. Maddux (Ed.), *Self-efficacy, adaptation, and adjustment: Theory, research, and applications* (pp. 281–303). New York: Plenum.

Schunk, D. H. (1996). Goal and self-evaluative influences during children's cognitive skill learning. *American Educational Research Journal, 33,* 359–382.

Schunk, D. H. (1998). Teaching elementary students to self-regulate practice of mathematical skills with modeling. In D. H. Schunk & B. J. Zimmerman (Eds.), *Self-regulated learning: From teaching to self-reflective practice* (pp. 137–159). New York: Guilford Press.

Schunk, D. H. (1999). Social-self interaction and achievement behavior. *Educational Psychologist, 34,* 219–227.

Schunk, D. H. (2001). Social cognitive theory and self-regulated learning. In B. J. Zimmerman & D. H. Schunk (Eds.), *Self-regulated learning and academic achievement: Theoretical perspectives* (2nd ed., pp. 125–151). Mahwah, NJ: Erlbaum.

Schunk, D. H., & Cox, P. D. (1986). Strategy training and attributional feedback with learning disabled students. *Journal of Educational Psychology, 78,* 201–209.

Schunk, D. H., & Ertmer, P. A. (1999). Self-regulatory processes during computer skill acquisition: Goal and self-evaluative influences. *Journal of Educational Psychology, 91,* 251–260.

Schunk, D. H., & Ertmer, P. A. (2000). Self-regulation and academic learning: Self-efficacy enhancing interventions. In M. Boekaerts, P. R. Pintrich, & M. Zeidner (Eds.), *Handbook of self-regulation* (pp. 631–649). San Diego: Academic Press.

Schunk, D. H., & Gunn, T. P. (1986). Self-efficacy and skill development: Influence of task strategies and attributions. *Journal of Educational Research, 79,* 238–244.

Schunk, D. H., & Hanson, A. R. (1985). Peer models: Influence on children's self-efficacy and achievement. *Journal of Educational Psychology, 77,* 313–322.

Schunk, D. H., & Hanson, A. R. (1989a). Influence of peer-model attributes on children's beliefs and learning. *Journal of Educational Psychology, 81,* 431–434.

Schunk, D. H., & Hanson, A. R. (1989b). Self-modeling and children's cognitive skill learning. *Journal of Educational Psychology, 81,* 155–163.

Schunk, D. H., Hanson, A. R., & Cox, P. D. (1987). Peer-model attributes and children's achievement behaviors. *Journal of Educational Psychology, 79,* 54–61.

Schunk, D. H., & Rice, J. M. (1986). Extended attributional feedback: Sequence effects during remedial reading instruction. *Journal of Early Adolescence, 6,* 55–66.

Schunk, D. H., & Rice, J. M. (1987). Enhancing comprehension skill and self-efficacy with strategy value information. *Journal of Reading Behavior, 19,* 285–302.

Schunk, D. H., & Rice, J. M. (1989). Learning goals and children's reading comprehension. *Journal of Reading Behavior, 21,* 279–293.

Schunk, D. H., & Rice, J. M. (1991). Learning goals and progress feedback during reading comprehension instruction. *Journal of Reading Behavior, 23,* 351–364.

Schunk, D. H., & Rice, J. M. (1993). Strategy fading and progress feedback: Effects on self-efficacy and comprehension among students receiving remedial reading services. *Journal of Special Education, 27,* 257–276.

Schunk, D. H., & Swartz, C. W. (1993a). Goals and progress feedback: Effects on self-efficacy and writing achievement. *Contemporary Educational Psychology, 18,* 337–354.

Schunk, D. H., & Swartz, C. W. (1993b). Writing strategy instruction with gifted students: Effects of goals and feedback on self-efficacy and skills. *Roeper Review, 15,* 225–230.

Schunk, D. H., & Zimmerman, B. J. (Eds.) (1994). *Self-regulation of learning and performance: Issues and educational applications.* Hillsdale, NJ: Erlbaum.

Schunk, D. H., & Zimmerman, B. J. (1996). Modeling and self-efficacy influences on children's development of self-regulation. In J. Juvonen & K. R. Wentzel (Eds.), *Social motivation: Understanding children's school adjustment* (pp. 154–180). Cambridge, England: Cambridge University Press.

Schunk, D. H., & Zimmerman, B. J. (1997). Social origins of self-regulatory competence. *Educational Psychologist, 32,* 195–208.

Schunk, D. H., & Zimmerman, B. J. (Eds.) (1998). *Self-regulated learning: From teaching to self-reflective practice.* New York: Guilford Press.

Schutz, P. A., Drogosz, L. M., White, V. E., & DiStefano, C. (1999). Prior knowledge, attitude, and strategy use in an introduction to statistics course. *Learning and Individual Differences, 10,* 291–308.

Searle, J. R. (1969). *Speech acts.* Cambridge, England: Cambridge University Press.

Segal, E. (1977). Toward a coherent psychology of language. In W. K. Honig & J. E. R. Staddon (Eds.), *Handbook of operant behavior* (pp. 628–653). Englewood Cliffs, NJ: Prentice Hall.

Seidel, R. J., Anderson, R. E., & Hunter, B. (1982). *Computer literacy: Issues and directions for 1985.* New York: Academic Press.

Seixas, P. (2001). Review of research on social studies. In V. Richardson (Ed.), *Handbook of research on teaching* (4th ed., pp. 545–565). Washington, DC: American Educational Research Association.

Self, J. (1988). *Artificial intelligence and human learning: Intelligent computer-aided instruction.* London: Chapman and Hall.

Seligman, M. E. P. (1975). *Helplessness: On depression, development, and death.* San Francisco: Freeman.

Sénéchal, M., & LeFevre, J. (2002). Parental involvement in the development of children's reading skill: A five-year longitudinal study. *Child Development, 73,* 445–460.

Shallis, M. (1984). *The silicon idol: The micro revolution and its social implications.* New York: Schocken Books.

Shamos, M. (1988). The lesson every child need not learn: Scientific literacy for all is an empty goal. *The Sciences, 28*(4), 14–20.

Shapiro, E. S. (1987). *Behavioral assessment in school psychology.* Hillsdale, NJ: Erlbaum.

Shavelson, R. J., & Bolus, R. (1982). Self-concept: The interplay of theory and methods. *Journal of Educational Psychology, 74,* 3–17.

Shell, D. F., Murphy, C. C., & Bruning, R. H. (1989). Self-efficacy and outcome expectancy mechanisms in reading and writing achievement. *Journal of Educational Psychology, 81,* 91–100.

Shepard, R. N. (1978). The mental image. *American Psychologist, 33,* 125–137.

Shepard, R. N. (1994). Perceptual-cognitive universals as reflections of the world. *Psychonomic Bulletin & Review, 1,* 2–28.

Shepard, R. N., & Cooper, L. A. (1983). *Mental images and their transformations.* Cambridge, MA: MIT Press.

Shipman, S., & Shipman, V. C. (1985). Cognitive styles: Some conceptual, methodological, and applied issues. In E. W. Gordon (Ed.), *Review of research in education* (Vol. 12, pp. 229–291). Washington, DC: American Educational Research Association.

Shore, N. (1997). *Rethinking the brain: New insights into early development.* New York: Families and Work Institute.

Short, E. J., Friebert, S. E., & Andrist, C. G. (1990). Individual differences in attentional processes as a function of age and skill level. *Learning and Individual Differences, 2,* 389–403.

Shuell, T. J. (1986). Cognitive conceptions of learning. *Review of Educational Research, 56,* 411–436.

Shuell, T. J. (1988). The role of the student in learning from instruction. *Contemporary Educational Psychology, 13,* 276–295.

Shuell, T. J. (1990). Phases of meaningful learning. *Review of Educational Research, 60,* 531–547.

Shuell, T. J. (1996). Teaching and learning in a classroom context. In D. C. Berliner & R. C. Calfee (Eds.), *Handbook of educational psychology* (pp. 726–764). New York: Macmillan.

Shultz, T. R., & Lepper, M. R. (1996). Cognitive dissonance reduction as constraint satisfaction. *Psychological Review, 103,* 219–240.

Siegler, R. S. (1989). Mechanisms of cognitive development. *Annual Review of Psychology, 40,* 353–379.

Siegler, R. S. (1991). *Children's thinking* (2nd ed.). Englewood Cliffs, NJ: Prentice Hall.

Sigel, I. E., & Brodzinsky, D. M. (1977). Individual differences: A perspective for understanding intellectual development. In H. Hom & P. Robinson (Eds.), *Psychological processes in early education* (pp. 295–329). New York: Academic Press.

Silberman, H. F., Melaragno, R. J., Coulson, J. E., & Estavan, D. (1961). Fixed sequence versus branching autoinstructional methods. *Journal of Educational Psychology, 52,* 166–172.

Silver, E. A. (1981). Recall of mathematical problem information: Solving related problems. *Journal for Research in Mathematics Education, 12,* 54–64.

Simon, H. A. (1974). How big is a chunk? *Science, 183,* 482–488.

Simon, H. A. (1979). Information processing models of cognition. *Annual Review of Psychology, 30,* 363–396.

Simpson, T. L. (2002). Dare I oppose constructivist theory? *The Educational Forum, 66,* 347–354.

Sinatra, G. M., Beck, I. L., & McKeown, M. G. (1992). A longitudinal characterization of young students' knowledge of their country's government. *American Educational Research Journal, 29,* 633–662.

Sivan, E. (1986). Motivation in social constructivist theory. *Educational Psychologist, 21,* 209–233.

Skinner, B. F. (1938). *The behavior of organisms.* New York: Appleton-Century-Crofts.

Skinner, B. F. (1948). *Walden two.* New York: Macmillan. (Paperback version published in 1976).

Skinner, B. F. (1953). *Science and human behavior.* New York: Free Press.

Skinner, B. F. (1954). The science of learning and the art of teaching. *Harvard Educational Review, 24,* 86–97.

Skinner, B. F. (1957). *Verbal behavior.* New York: Appleton-Century-Crofts.

Skinner, B. F. (1958). Teaching machines. *Science, 128,* 969–977.

Skinner, B. F. (1961). Why we need teaching machines. *Harvard Educational Review, 31,* 377–398.

Skinner, B. F. (1968). *The technology of teaching.* New York: Appleton-Century-Crofts.

Skinner, B. F. (1970). B. F. Skinner . . . An autobiography. In P. B. Dews (Ed.), *Festschrift for B. F. Skinner* (pp. 1–21). New York: Appleton-Century-Crofts.

Skinner, B. F. (1971). *Beyond freedom and dignity.* New York: Knopf.

Skinner, B. F. (1974). *About behaviorism.* New York: Knopf.

Skinner, B. F. (1978). *Reflections on behaviorism and society.* Englewood Cliffs, NJ: Prentice Hall.

Skinner, B. F. (1984). The shame of American education. *American Psychologist, 39,* 947–954.

Skinner, B. F. (1987). Whatever happened to psychology as the science of behavior? *American Psychologist, 42,* 780–786.

Skinner, B. F. (1990). Can psychology be a science of mind? *American Psychologist, 45,* 1206–1210.

Skinner, E. A., Wellborn, J. G., & Connell, J. P. (1990). What it takes to do well in school and whether I've got it: A process model of perceived control and children's engagement and achievement in school. *Journal of Educational Psychology, 82,* 22–32.

Slavin, R. E. (1983). *Cooperative learning.* New York: Longman.

Slavin, R. E. (1994). *Using team learning* (4th ed.). Baltimore: Johns Hopkins University, Center for Research on Elementary Schools.

Smith, E. E., & Medin, D. L. (1981). *Categories and concepts.* Cambridge, MA: Harvard University Press.

Smith, E. R. (1996). What do connectionism and social psychology offer each other? *Journal of Personality and Social Psychology, 70,* 893–912.

Smith, R. E. (1989). Effects of coping skills training on generalized self-efficacy and locus of control. *Journal of Personality and Social Psychology, 56,* 228–233.

Snow, R. E. (1989). Toward assessment of cognitive and conative structures in learning. *Educational Researcher, 18*(9), 8–14.

Snow, R. E., Corno, L., & Jackson, D., III. (1996). Individual differences in affective and conative functions. In D. C. Berliner & R. C. Calfee (Eds.), *Handbook of educational psychology* (pp. 243–310). New York: Macmillan.

Snowman, J. (1986). Learning tactics and strategies. In G. D. Phye & T. Andre (Eds.), *Cognitive classroom learning: Understanding, thinking, and problem solving* (pp. 243–275). Orlando: Academic Press.

Sommers, N. (1980). Revision strategies of student writers and experienced adult writers. *College Composition and Communication, 31,* 378–388.

Spence, J. T. (1984). Gender identity and its implications for the concepts of masculinity and femininity. In T. B. Sonderegger (Ed.), *Nebraska Symposium on Motivation, 1984* (Vol. 32, pp. 59–95). Lincoln, NE: University of Nebraska Press.

Spence, K. W. (1936). The nature of discrimination learning in animals. *Psychological Review, 43,* 427–449.

Spence, K. W. (1937). The differential response in animals to stimuli varying within a single dimension. *Psychological Review, 44,* 430–444.

Sperling, G. (1960). The information available in brief visual presentations. *Psychological Monographs, 74*(Whole No. 498).

Sperling, M., & Freedman, S. W. (2001). Research on writing. In V. Richardson (Ed.), *Handbook of research on teaching*

(4th ed., pp. 379–389). Washington, DC: American Educational Research Association.

Spilich, G. J., Vesonder, G. T., Chiesi, H. L., & Voss, J. F. (1979). Text-processing of domain-related information for individuals with high and low domain knowledge. *Journal of Verbal Learning and Verbal Behavior, 18,* 275–290.

Springer, L., Stanne, M. E., & Donovan, S. S. (1999). Effects of small-group learning on undergraduates in science, mathematics, engineering, and technology: A meta-analysis. *Review of Educational Research, 69,* 21–51.

Stallard, C. K. (1974). An analysis of the writing behavior of good student writers. *Research in the Teaching of English, 8,* 206–218.

Stanovich, K. E. (1996). Word recognition: Changing perspectives. In R. Barr, M. L. Kamil, P. B. Mosenthal, & P. D. Pearson (Eds.), *Handbook of reading research* (Vol. 2, pp. 418–452). Mahwah, NJ: Erlbaum.

Stein, B. S., Littlefield, J., Bransford, J. D., & Persampieri, M. (1984). Elaboration and knowledge acquisition. *Memory & Cognition, 12,* 522–529.

Stein, N. L., & Glenn, C. G. (1979). An analysis of story comprehension in elementary school children. In R. O. Freedle (Ed.), *New directions in discourse processing* (pp. 53–120). Norwood, NJ: Ablex.

Stein, N. L., & Trabasso, T. (1982). What's in a story: An approach to comprehension and instruction. In R. Glaser (Ed.), *Advances in instructional psychology* (Vol. 2, pp. 213–267). Hillsdale, NJ: Erlbaum.

Steinberg, L., Brown, B. B., & Dornbusch, S. M. (1996). *Beyond the classroom: Why school reform has failed and what parents need to do.* New York: Simon & Schuster.

Sternberg, R. J. (1986). Cognition and instruction: Why the marriage sometimes ends in divorce. In R. F. Dillon & R. J. Sternberg (Eds.), *Cognition and instruction* (pp. 375–382). Orlando: Academic Press.

Sternberg, R. J., & Grigorenko, E. L. (1997). Are cognitive styles still in style? *American Psychologist, 52,* 700–712.

Sternberg, R. J., & Horvath, J. A. (1995). A prototype view of expert teaching. *Educational Researcher, 24*(6), 9–17.

Sternberg, S. (1969). Memory-scanning: Mental processes revealed by reaction-time experiments. *American Scientist, 57,* 421–457.

Stevenson, H. W., Chen, C., & Uttal, D. H. (1990). Beliefs and achievement: A study of black, white, and Hispanic children. *Child Development, 61,* 508–523.

Stipek, D. J. (1996). Motivation and instruction. In D. C. Berliner & R. C. Calfee (Eds.), *Handbook of educational psychology* (pp. 85–113). New York: Macmillan.

Stipek, D. J. (1998). *Motivation to learn: From theory to practice* (3rd ed.). Boston: Allyn & Bacon.

Stipek, D. J. (2002). Good instruction is motivating. In A. Wigfield & J. S. Eccles (Eds.), *Development of achievement motivation* (pp. 309–332). San Diego: Academic Press.

Stipek, D. J., & Kowalski, P. S. (1989). Learned helplessness in task-orienting versus performance-orienting testing conditions. *Journal of Educational Psychology, 81,* 384–391.

Stipek, D. J., & Ryan, R. H. (1997). Economically disadvantaged preschoolers: Ready to learn but further to go. *Developmental Psychology, 33,* 711–723.

Strain, P. S., Kerr, M. M., & Ragland, E. U. (1981). The use of peer social initiations in the treatment of social withdrawal. In P. S. Strain (Ed.), *The utilization of classroom peers as behavior change agents* (pp. 101–128). New York: Plenum.

Strecher, V. J., DeVellis, B. M., Becker, M. H., & Rosenstock, I. M. (1986). The role of self-efficacy in achieving health behavior change. *Health Education Quarterly, 13*(1), 73–91.

Stright, A. D., Neitzel, C., Sears, K. G., & Hoke-Sinex, L. (2001). Instruction begins in the home: Relations between parental instruction and children's self-regulation in the classroom. *Journal of Educational Psychology, 93,* 456–466.

Sunshine, P. M., & DiVesta, F. J. (1976). Effects of density and format on letter discrimination by beginning readers with different learning styles. *Journal of Educational Psychology, 68,* 15–19.

Suppes, P. (1974). The place of theory in educational research. *Educational Researcher, 3*(6), 3–10.

Tait, K., Hartley, J. R., & Anderson, R. C. (1973). Feedback procedures in computer-assisted arithmetic instruction. *British Journal of Educational Psychology, 13,* 161–171.

Tarde, G. (1903). *The laws of imitation.* New York: Henry Holt.

Taylor, A. M., Josberger, M., & Whitely, S. E. (1973). Elaboration instruction and verbalization as factors facilitating retarded children's recall. *Journal of Educational Psychology, 64,* 341–346.

Taylor, R. P. (1980). *The computer in the school: Tutor, tool, tutee.* New York: Teachers College Press.

Tennyson, R. D. (1980). Instructional control strategies and content structure as design variables in concept acquisition using computer-based instruction. *Journal of Educational Psychology, 72,* 525–532.

Tennyson, R. D. (1981). Use of adaptive information for advisement in learning concepts and rules using computer-assisted instruction. *American Educational Research Journal, 18,* 425–438.

Tennyson, R. D., & Park, O. (1980). The teaching of concepts: A review of instructional design research literature. *Review of Educational Research, 50,* 55–70.

Tennyson, R. D., Steve, M. W., & Boutwell, R. C. (1975). Instance sequence and analysis of instance attribute representation in concept acquisition. *Journal of Educational Psychology, 67,* 821–827.

Terrace, H. S. (1963). Discrimination learning with and without "errors." *Journal of the Experimental Analysis of Behavior, 6,* 1–27.

Tharp, R. G. (1989). Psychocultural variables and constants: Effects on teaching and learning in schools. *American Psychologist, 44,* 349–359.

Tharp, R. G., & Gallimore, R. (1988). *Rousing minds to life: Teaching, learning, and schooling in social context.* New York: Cambridge University Press.

Thelen, M. H., Fry, R. A., Fehrenbach, P. A., & Frautschi, N. M. (1979). Therapeutic videotape and film modeling: A review. *Psychological Bulletin, 86,* 701–720.

Thomson, D. M., & Tulving, E. (1970). Associative encoding and retrieval: Weak and strong cues. *Journal of Experimental Psychology, 86,* 255–262.

Thorndike, E. L. (1906). *The principles of teaching: Based on psychology.* New York: A. G. Seiler.

Thorndike, E. L. (1911). *Animal intelligence: Experimental studies.* New York: Macmillan.

Thorndike, E. L. (1912). *Education: A first book.* New York: Macmillan.

Thorndike, E. L. (1913a). *Educational psychology: Vol. 1. The original nature of man.* New York: Teachers College Press.

Thorndike, E. L. (1913b). *Educational psychology: Vol. 2. The psychology of learning.* New York: Teachers College Press.

Thorndike, E. L. (1914). *Educational psychology: Vol. 3. Mental work and fatigue and individual differences and their causes.* New York: Teachers College Press.

Thorndike, E. L. (1924). Mental discipline in high school studies. *Journal of Educational Psychology, 15,* 1–22, 83–98.

Thorndike, E. L. (1927). The law of effect. *American Journal of Psychology, 39,* 212–222.

Thorndike, E. L. (1932). *The fundamentals of learning.* New York: Teachers College Press.

Thorndike, E. L., & Gates, A. I. (1929). *Elementary principles of education.* New York: Macmillan.

Thorndike, E. L., & Woodworth, R. S. (1901). The influence of improvement in one mental function upon the efficiency of other functions. *Psychological Review, 8,* 247–261, 384–395, 553–564.

Thorndyke, P. W., & Hayes-Roth, B. (1979). The use of schemata in the acquisition and transfer of knowledge. *Cognitive Psychology, 11,* 82–106.

Tiedemann, J. (1989). Measures of cognitive styles: A critical review. *Educational Psychologist, 24,* 261–275.

Timberlake, W., & Farmer-Dougan, V. A. (1991). Reinforcement in applied settings: Figuring out ahead of time what will work. *Psychological Bulletin, 110,* 379–391.

Titchener, E. B. (1909). *Lectures on the experimental psychology of the thought processes.* New York: Macmillan.

Tobias, C. U. (1994). *The way they learn: How to discover and teach to your child's strengths.* Colorado Springs: Focus on the Family Publishing.

Tobias, S. (1989). Another look at research on the adaptation of instruction to student characteristics. *Educational Psychologist, 24,* 213–227.

Tollefson, N., Tracy, D. B., Johnsen, E. P., Farmer, A. W., & Buenning, M. (1984). Goal setting and personal responsibility training for LD adolescents. *Psychology in the Schools, 21,* 224–233.

Tolman, E. C. (1932). *Purposive behavior in animals and men.* New York: Appleton-Century-Crofts. (Reprinted 1949, 1951, University of California Press, Berkeley, CA)

Tolman, E. C. (1942). *Drives toward war.* New York: Appleton-Century-Crofts.

Tolman, E. C. (1949). There is more than one kind of learning. *Psychological Review, 56,* 144–155.

Tolman, E. C. (1951). *Collected papers in psychology.* Berkeley, CA: University of California Press.

Tolman, E. C. (1959). Principles of purposive behavior. In S. Koch (Ed.), *Psychology: A study of a science* (Vol. 2, pp. 92–157). New York: McGraw-Hill.

Tolman, E. C., & Honzik, C. H. (1930). Introduction and removal of reward, and maze performance in rats. *University of California Publications in Psychology, 4,* 257–275.

Tolman, E. C., Ritchie, B. F., & Kalish, D. (1946a). Studies in spatial learning. I. Orientation and the short-cut. *Journal of Experimental Psychology, 36,* 13–24.

Tolman, E. C., Ritchie, B. F., & Kalish, D. (1946b). Studies in spatial learning. II. Place learning versus response learning. *Journal of Experimental Psychology, 36,* 221–229.

Tracey, T. J. G. (2002). Development of interests and competency beliefs: A 1-year longitudinal study of fifth- to eighth-grade students using the ICA-R and structural equation modeling. *Journal of Counseling Psychology, 49,* 148–163.

Trappl, R. (1985). Artificial intelligence: A one-hour course. In R. Trappl (Ed.), *Impacts of artificial intelligence: Scientific, technological, military, economic, societal, cultural, and political* (pp. 5–30). Amsterdam: Elsevier Science Publishers.

Trawick-Smith, J. (2003). *Early childhood development: A multicultural perspective* (3rd ed.). Upper Saddle River, NJ: Merrill/Prentice Hall.

Treffinger, D. J. (1985). Review of the Torrance Tests of Creative Thinking. In J. Mitchell (Ed.), *Ninth Mental Measurements Yearbook* (pp. 1633–1634). Lincoln, NE: Buros Institute of Mental Measurement.

Treffinger, D. J. (1995). Creative problem solving: Overview and educational implications. *Educational Psychology Review, 7,* 301–312.

Treisman, A. M. (1960). Contextual cues in selective listening. *Quarterly Journal of Experimental Psychology, 12,* 242–248.

Treisman, A. M. (1964). Verbal cues, language, and meaning in selective attention. *American Journal of Psychology, 77,* 206–219.

Treisman, A. M. (1992). Perceiving and re-perceiving objects. *American Psychologist, 47,* 862–875.

Tschannen-Moran, M., Hoy, A. W., & Hoy, W. K. (1998). Teacher efficacy: Its meaning and measure. *Review of Educational Research, 68,* 202–248.

Tudge, J. R. H., & Scrimsher, S. (2003). Lev S. Vygotsky on education: A cultural-historical, interpersonal, and individual approach to development. In B. J. Zimmerman & D. H. Schunk (Eds.), *Educational psychology: A century of contributions* (pp. 207–228). Mahwah, NJ: Erlbaum.

Tudge, J. R. H., & Winterhoff, P. A. (1993). Vygotsky, Piaget, and Bandura: Perspectives on the relations between the social world and cognitive development. *Human Development, 36,* 61–81.

Tulving, E. (1972). Episodic and semantic memory. In E. Tulving & W. Donaldson (Eds.), *Organization of memory* (pp. 381–403). New York: Academic Press.

Tulving, E. (1974). Cue-dependent forgetting. *American Scientist, 62,* 74–82.

Tulving, E. (1983). *Elements of episodic memory.* Oxford, England: Clarendon Press.

Tunmer, W. E., & Chapman, J. W. (1996). A developmental model of dyslexia: Can the construct be saved? *Dyslexia, 2,* 179–189.

Tunmer, W. E., & Chapman, J. W. (2002). The relation of beginning readers' reported word identification strategies to reading achievement, reading-related skills, and academic self-perceptions. *Reading and Writing: An Interdisciplinary Journal, 15,* 341–358.

Tuovinen, J. E., & Sweller, J. (1999). A comparison of cognitive load associated with discovery learning and worked examples. *Journal of Educational Psychology, 91,* 334–341.

Tweney, R. D., & Budzynski, C. A. (2000). The scientific status of American psychology in 1900. *American Psychologist, 55,* 1014–1017.

Ullmann, L. P., & Krasner, L. (1965). *Case studies in behavior modification.* New York: Holt, Rinehart & Winston.

Ulrich, R., Stachnik, T., & Mabry, J. (1966). *Control of human behavior.* Glenview, IL: Scott, Foresman.

Underwood, B. J. (1957). Interference and forgetting. *Psychological Review, 64,* 49–60.

Underwood, B. J. (1961). Ten years of massed practice on distributed practice. *Psychological Review, 68,* 229–247.

Underwood, B. J. (1983). *Attributes of memory.* Glenview, IL: Scott, Foresman.

U.S. Department of Education. (1990). *Digest of educational statistics.* Washington, DC: Author.

Valentine, C. W. (1930a). The innate base of fear. *Journal of Genetic Psychology, 37,* 394–419.

Valentine, C. W. (1930b). The psychology of imitation with special reference to early childhood. *British Journal of Psychology, 21,* 105–132.

Vandell, D. L. (2000). Parents, peer groups, and other socializing influences. *Developmental Psychology, 36,* 699–710.

VanLehn, K. (1996). Cognitive skill acquisition. *Annual Review of Psychology, 47,* 513–539.

Vellutino, F. R., & Denckla, M. B. (1996). Cognitive and neuropsychological foundations of word identification in poor and normally developing readers. In R. Barr, M. L. Kamil, P. B. Mosenthal, & P. D. Pearson (Eds.), *Handbook of reading research* (Vol. 2, pp. 571–608). Mahwah, NJ: Erlbaum.

Verdi, M. P., & Kulhavy, R. W. (2002). Learning with maps and texts: An overview. *Educational Psychology Review, 14,* 27–46.

Vermeer, H. J., Boekaerts, M., & Seegers, G. (2000). Motivational and gender differences: Sixth-grade students' mathematical problem-solving behavior. *Journal of Educational Psychology, 92,* 308–315.

Veroff, J. (1969). Social comparison and the development of achievement motivation. In C. P. Smith (Ed.), *Achievement-related motives in children* (pp. 46–101). New York: Russell Sage Foundation.

Vispoel, W. P. (1995). Self-concept in artistic domains: An extension of the Shavelson, Hubner, and Stanton (1976) model. *Journal of Educational Psychology, 87,* 134–153.

Voss, J. F., Vesonder, G. T., & Spilich, G. J. (1980). Text generation and recall by high-knowledge and low-knowledge individuals. *Journal of Verbal Learning and Verbal Behavior, 19,* 651–657.

Voss, J. F., Wiley, J., & Carretero, M. (1995). Acquiring intellectual skills. *Annual Review of Psychology, 46,* 155–181.

Vygotsky, L. (1962). *Thought and language.* Cambridge, MA: MIT Press.

Vygotsky, L. (1978). *Mind in society: The development of higher psychological processes.* Cambridge, MA: Harvard University Press.

Vygotsky, L. (1987). *The collected works of L. S. Vygotsky: Vol. 1. Problems of general psychology* (R. W. Rieber & A. S. Carton, Vol. Eds.; N. Minick, Trans.). New York: Plenum.

Wadsworth, B. J. (1996). *Piaget's theory of cognitive and affective development* (5th ed.). White Plains, NY: Longman.

Wallas, G. (1921). *The art of thought.* New York: Harcourt, Brace, & World.

Wang, M. C. (1980). Adaptive instruction: Building on diversity. *Theory into Practice, 19,* 122–128.

Wang, M. C. (1983). Development and consequences of students' sense of personal control. In J. M. Levine & M. C. Wang (Eds.), *Teacher and student perceptions: Implications for learning* (pp. 213–247). Hillsdale, NJ: Erlbaum.

Wason, P. C. (1960). On the failure to eliminate hypotheses in a conceptual task. *Quarterly Journal of Experimental Psychology, 12,* 129–140.

Wason, P. C. (1966). Reasoning. In B. M. Foss (Ed.), *New horizons in psychology* (pp. 135–151). Harmondsworth, England: Penguin.

Wason, P. C., & Johnson-Laird, P. N. (1972). *The psychology of deduction: Structure and content.* Cambridge, MA: Harvard University Press.

Watson, J. B. (1914). *Behavior: An introduction to comparative psychology.* New York: Henry Holt.

Watson, J. B. (1916). The place of the conditioned-reflex in psychology. *Psychological Review, 23,* 89–116.

Watson, J. B. (1919). *Psychology from the standpoint of a behaviorist.* Philadelphia: Lippincott.

Watson, J. B. (1924). *Behaviorism.* New York: Norton.

Watson, J. B. (1926a). Experimental studies on the growth of the emotions. In C. Murchison (Ed.), *Psychologies of 1925* (pp. 37–57). Worcester, MA: Clark University Press.

Watson, J. B. (1926b). What the nursery has to say about instincts. In C. Murchison (Ed.), *Psychologies of 1925* (pp. 1–35). Worcester, MA: Clark University Press.

Watson, J. B., & MacDougall, W. (1929). *The battle of behaviorism.* New York: Norton.

Watson, J. B., & Rayner, R. (1920). Conditioned emotional reactions. *Journal of Experimental Psychology, 3,* 1–14.

Weiner, B. (1974). An attributional interpretation of expectancy-value theory. In B. Weiner (Ed.), *Cognitive views of human motivation* (pp. 51–69). New York: Academic Press.

Weiner, B. (1979). A theory of motivation for some classroom experiences. *Journal of Educational Psychology, 71,* 3–25.

Weiner, B. (1985). An attributional theory of achievement motivation and emotion. *Psychological Review, 92,* 548–573.

Weiner, B. (1990). History of motivational research in education. *Journal of Educational Psychology, 82,* 616–622.

Weiner, B. (1992). *Human motivation: Metaphors, theories, and research.* Newbury Park, CA: SAGE Publications.

Weiner, B., Frieze, I. H., Kukla, A., Reed, L., Rest, S., & Rosenbaum, R. M. (1971). *Perceiving the causes of success and failure.* Morristown, NJ: General Learning Press.

Weiner, B., Graham, S., Taylor, S. E., & Meyer, W. (1983). Social cognition in the classroom. *Educational Psychologist, 18,* 109–124.

Weiner, B., & Kukla, A. (1970). An attributional analysis of achievement motivation. *Journal of Personality and Social Psychology, 15,* 1–20.

Weiner, B., & Peter, N. (1973). A cognitive-developmental analysis of achievement and moral judgments. *Developmental Psychology, 9,* 290–309.

Weinstein, C. E. (1978). Elaboration skills as a learning strategy. In H. F. O'Neil, Jr. (Ed.), *Learning strategies* (pp. 31–55). New York: Academic Press.

Weinstein, C. E., & Hume, L. M. (1998). *Study strategies for lifelong learning.* Washington, DC: American Psychological Association.

Weinstein, C. E., & Mayer, R. E. (1986). The teaching of learning strategies. In M. C. Wittrock (Ed.), *Handbook of research on teaching* (3rd ed., pp. 315–327). New York: Macmillan.

Weinstein, C. E., & Palmer, D. R. (1990). *LASSI-HS: Learning and Study Strategies Inventory—High School Version.* Clearwater, FL: H & H Publishing Company.

Weinstein, C. E., Palmer, D. R., & Schulte, A. C. (1987). *LASSI: Learning and Study Strategies Inventory.* Clearwater, FL: H & H Publishing Company.

Weiss, M. R. (1983). Modeling and motor performance: A developmental perspective. *Research Quarterly for Exercise and Sport, 54,* 190–197.

Weiss, M. R., Ebbeck, V., & Wiese-Bjornstal, D. M. (1993). Developmental and psychological factors related to children's observational learning of physical skills. *Pediatric Exercise Science, 5,* 301–317.

Weiss, M. R., & Klint, K. A. (1987). "Show and tell" in the gymnasium: An investigation of developmental differences in modeling and verbal rehearsal of motor skills. *Research Quarterly for Exercise and Sport, 58,* 234–241.

Wellman, H. M. (1977). Tip of the tongue and feeling of knowing experiences: A developmental study of memory monitoring. *Child Development, 48*, 13–21.

Wellman, H. M. (1988). The early development of memory strategies. In F. Weinert & M. Perlmutter (Eds.), *Memory development: Universal changes and individual differences* (pp. 3–29). Hillsdale, NJ: Erlbaum.

Wellman, H. M. (1990). *The child's theory of mind.* Cambridge, MA: MIT Press.

Wentzel, K. R. (1992). Motivation and achievement in adolescence: A multiple goals perspective. In D. H. Schunk & J. L. Meece (Eds.), *Student perceptions in the classroom* (pp. 287–306). Hillsdale, NJ: Erlbaum.

Wentzel, K. R. (1996). Social goals and social relationships as motivators of school adjustment. In J. Juvonen & K. R. Wentzel (Eds.), *Social motivation: Understanding children's school adjustment* (pp. 226–247). Cambridge, England: Cambridge University Press.

Wertheimer, M. (1945). *Productive thinking.* New York: Harper & Row.

Wertsch, J. V. (1979). From social interaction to higher psychological processes: A clarification and application of Vygotsky's theory. *Human Development, 22*, 1–22.

Wertsch, J. V. (1984). The zone of proximal development: Some conceptual issues. In B. Rogoff & J. V. Wertsch (Eds.), *Children's learning in the "zone of proximal development"* (pp. 7–18). San Francisco: Jossey-Bass.

Wertsch, J. V. (1985). *Culture, communication, and cognition: Vygotskian perspectives.* New York: Cambridge University Press.

White, P. H., Kjelgaard, M. M., & Harkins, S. G. (1995). Testing the contribution of self-evaluation to goal-setting effects. *Journal of Personality and Social Psychology, 69*, 69–79.

White, R. T., & Tisher, R. P. (1986). Research on natural sciences. In M. C. Wittrock (Ed.), *Handbook of research on teaching* (3rd ed., pp. 874–905). New York: Macmillan.

White, R. W. (1959). Motivation reconsidered: The concept of competence. *Psychological Review, 66*, 297–333.

Whitely, S. E., & Taylor, A. M. (1973). Overt verbalization and the continued production of effective elaborations by EMR children. *American Journal of Mental Deficiency, 78*, 193–198.

Wickelgren, W. A. (1979). *Cognitive psychology.* Englewood Cliffs, NJ: Prentice Hall.

Wigfield, A. (1994). The role of children's achievement values in the self-regulation of their learning outcomes. In D. H. Schunk & B. J. Zimmerman (Eds.), *Self-regulation of learning and performance: Issues and educational applications* (pp. 101–124). Hillsdale, NJ: Erlbaum.

Wigfield, A., & Eccles, J. S. (1992). The development of achievement task values: A theoretical analysis. *Developmental Review, 12*, 265–310.

Wigfield, A., & Eccles, J. S. (2000). Expectancy-value theory of motivation. *Contemporary Educational Psychology, 25*, 68–81.

Wigfield, A., & Eccles, J. S. (2002). Introduction. In A. Wigfield & J. S. Eccles (Eds.), *Development of achievement motivation* (pp. 1–11). San Diego: Academic Press.

Williams, J. M., & Affleck, G. (1999). The effects of an age-appropriate intervention on young children's understanding of inheritance. *Educational Psychology, 19*, 259–275.

Williams, J. M., & Tolmie, A. (2000). Conceptual change in biology: Group interaction and the understanding of inheritance. *British Journal of Developmental Psychology, 18*, 625–649.

Windholz, G. (1997). Ivan P. Pavlov: An overview of his life and psychological work. *American Psychologist, 52*, 941–946.

Wineburg, S. S. (1996). The psychology of learning and teaching history. In D. C. Berliner & R. C. Calfee (Eds.), *Handbook of educational psychology* (pp. 423–437). New York: Macmillan.

Winett, R. A., & Winkler, R. C. (1972). Current behavior modification in the classroom: Be still, be quiet, be docile. *Journal of Applied Behavior Analysis, 5*, 499–504.

Winn, W. (1990). Some implications of cognitive theory for instructional design. *Instructional Science, 19*, 53–69.

Winne, P. H. (2001). Self-regulated learning viewed from models of information processing. In B. J. Zimmerman & D. H. Schunk (Eds.), *Self-regulated learning and academic achievement: Theoretical perspectives* (2nd ed., pp. 153–189). Mahwah, NJ: Erlbaum.

Witkin, H. A. (1969). Social influences in the development of cognitive style. In D. A. Goslin (Ed.), *Handbook of socialization theory and research* (pp. 687–706). Chicago: Rand McNally.

Witkin, H. A., Moore, C. A., Goodenough, D. R., & Cox, P. W. (1977). Field-dependent and field-independent cognitive styles and their educational implications. *Review of Educational Research, 47*, 1–64.

Wittrock, M. C. (Ed.). (1986). *Handbook of research on teaching* (3rd ed.). New York: Macmillan.

Wolleat, P. L., Pedro, J. D., Becker, A. D., & Fennema, E. (1980). Sex differences in high school students' causal attributions of performance in mathematics. *Journal for Research in Mathematics Education, 11*, 356–366.

Wolpe, J. (1958). *Psychotherapy by reciprocal inhibition.* Stanford, CA: Stanford University Press.

Wolters, C. A. (1998). Self-regulated learning and college students' regulation of motivation. *Journal of Educational Psychology, 90*, 224–235.

Wolters, C. A. (1999). The relation between high school students' motivational regulation and their use of learning strategies, effort, and classroom performance. *Learning and Individual Differences, 3*, 281–299.

Wolters, C. A., Yu, S. L., & Pintrich, P. R. (1996). The relation between goal orientation and students' motivational beliefs and self-regulated learning. *Learning and Individual Differences, 8*, 211–238.

Wood, D. A., Rosenberg, M. S., & Carran, D. T. (1993). The effects of tape-recorded self-instruction cues on the mathematics performance of students with learning disabilities. *Journal of Learning Disabilities, 26*, 250–258, 269.

Wood, D. J., Bruner, J. S., & Ross, G. (1976). The role of tutoring in problem solving. *Journal of Child Psychology and Psychiatry, 17*, 89–100.

Wood, G., & Underwood, B. J. (1967). Implicit responses and conceptual similarity. *Journal of Verbal Learning and Verbal Behavior, 6*, 1–10.

Wood, R., & Bandura, A. (1989). Impact of conceptions of ability on self-regulatory mechanisms and complex decision-making. *Journal of Personality and Social Psychology, 56*, 407–415.

Woodward, J., Carnine, D., & Gersten, R. (1988). Teaching problem solving through computer simulations. *American Educational Research Journal, 25*, 72–86.

Woodworth, R. S. (1918). *Dynamic psychology.* New York: Columbia University Press.

Woodworth, R. S., & Schlosberg, H. (1954). *Experimental psychology* (Rev. ed.). New York: Holt, Rinehart & Winston.

Woolfolk, A. E., & Hoy, W. K. (1990). Prospective teachers' sense of efficacy and beliefs about control. *Journal of Educational Psychology, 82*, 81–91.

Wurtele, S. K. (1986). Self-efficacy and athletic performance: A review. *Journal of Social and Clinical Psychology, 4*, 290–301.

Wylie, R. C. (1979). *The self-concept* (Vol. 2). Lincoln, NE: University of Nebraska Press.

Yerkes, R. M., & Dodson, J. D. (1908). The relation of strength of stimulus to rapidity of habit-formation. *Journal of Comparative Neurology and Psychology, 18*, 459–482.

Zeiler, M. (1977). Schedules of reinforcement: The controlling variables. In W. K. Honig & J. E. R. Staddon (Eds.), *Handbook of operant behavior* (pp. 201–232). Englewood Cliffs, NJ: Prentice Hall.

Zimmerman, B. J. (1977). Modeling. In H. Hom & P. Robinson (Eds.), *Psychological processes in children's early education* (pp. 37–70). New York: Academic Press.

Zimmerman, B. J. (1986). Becoming a self-regulated learner: Which are the key subprocesses? *Contemporary Educational Psychology, 11*, 307–313.

Zimmerman, B. J. (1989). Models of self-regulated learning and academic achievement. In B. J. Zimmerman & D. H. Schunk (Eds.), *Self-regulated learning and academic achievement: Theory, research, and practice* (pp. 1–25). New York: Springer-Verlag.

Zimmerman, B. J. (1990). Self-regulating academic learning and achievement: The emergence of a social cognitive perspective. *Educational Psychology Review, 2*, 173–201.

Zimmerman, B. J. (1994). Dimensions of academic self-regulation: A conceptual framework for education. In D. H. Schunk & B. J. Zimmerman (Eds.), *Self-regulation of learning and performance: Issues and educational applications* (pp. 3–21). Hillsdale, NJ: Erlbaum.

Zimmerman, B. J. (1998). Developing self-fulfilling cycles of academic regulation: An analysis of exemplary instructional models. In D. H. Schunk & B. J. Zimmerman (Eds.), *Self-regulated learning: From teaching to self-reflective practice* (pp. 1–19). New York: Guilford Press.

Zimmerman, B. J. (2000). Attaining self-regulation: A social cognitive perspective. In M. Boekaerts, P. R. Pintrich, & M. Zeidner (Eds.), *Handbook of self-regulation* (pp. 13–39). San Diego: Academic Press.

Zimmerman, B. J. (2001). Theories of self-regulated learning and academic achievement: An overview and analysis. In B. J. Zimmerman & D. H. Schunk (Eds.), *Self-regulated learning and academic achievement: Theoretical perspectives* (2nd ed., pp. 1–38). Mahwah, NJ: Erlbaum.

Zimmerman, B. J., & Bandura, A. (1994). Impact of self-regulatory influences on writing course achievement. *American Educational Research Journal, 31*, 845–862.

Zimmerman, B. J., Bandura, A., & Martinez-Pons, M. (1992). Self-motivation for academic attainment: The role of self-efficacy beliefs and personal goal setting. *American Educational Research Journal, 29*, 663–676.

Zimmerman, B. J., & Blom, D. E. (1983a). On resolving conflicting views of cognitive conflict. *Developmental Review, 3*, 62–72.

Zimmerman, B. J., & Blom, D. E. (1983b). Toward an empirical test of the role of cognitive conflict in learning. *Developmental Review, 3*, 18–38.

Zimmerman, B. J., Bonner, S., & Kovach, R. (1996). *Developing self-regulated learners: Beyond achievement to self-efficacy.* Washington, DC: American Psychological Association.

Zimmerman, B. J., Greenberg, D., & Weinstein, C. E. (1994). Self-regulating academic study time: A strategy approach. In D. H. Schunk & B. J. Zimmerman (Eds.), *Self-regulation of learning and performance: Issues and educational applications* (pp. 181–199). Hillsdale, NJ: Erlbaum.

Zimmerman, B. J., & Kitsantas, A. (1996). Self-regulated learning of a motoric skill: The role of goal setting and self-monitoring. *Journal of Applied Sport Psychology, 8*, 60–75.

Zimmerman, B. J., & Kitsantas, A. (1997). Developmental phases in self-regulation: Shifting from process goals to outcome goals. *Journal of Educational Psychology, 89*, 29–36.

Zimmerman, B. J., & Koussa, R. (1975). Sex factors in children's observational learning of value judgments of toys. *Sex Roles, 1*, 121–132.

Zimmerman, B. J., & Martinez-Pons, M. (1990). Student differences in self-regulated learning: Relating grade, sex, and giftedness to self-efficacy and strategy use. *Journal of Educational Psychology, 82*, 51–59.

Zimmerman, B. J., & Martinez-Pons, M. (1992). Perceptions of efficacy and strategy use in the self-regulation of learning. In D. H. Schunk & J. L. Meece (Eds.), *Student perceptions in the classroom* (pp. 185–207). Hillsdale, NJ: Erlbaum.

Zimmerman, B. J., & Ringle, J. (1981). Effects of model persistence and statements of confidence on children's self-efficacy and problem solving. *Journal of Educational Psychology, 73*, 485–493.

Zimmerman, B. J., & Rosenthal, T. L. (1974). Observational learning of rule-governed behavior by children. *Psychological Bulletin, 81*, 29–42.

Zimmerman, B. J., & Schunk, D. H. (Eds.) (2001). *Self-regulated learning and academic achievement: Theoretical perspectives* (2nd ed.). Mahwah, NJ: Erlbaum.

Zimmerman, B. J., & Whitehurst, G. J. (1979). Structure and function: A comparison of two views of the development of language and cognition. In G. J. Whitehurst & B. J. Zimmerman (Eds.), *The functions of language and cognition* (pp. 1–22). New York: Academic Press.

Zimmerman, C. (2000). The development of scientific reasoning skills. *Developmental Review, 20*, 99–149.

Zuckerman, M., & Wheeler, L. (1975). To dispel fantasies about the fantasy-based measure of fear of success. *Psychological Bulletin, 82*, 932–946.

Author Index

Subject Index